HEINRICH SCHÜTZ: HIS LIFE AND WORK

Heinrich Schütz in his eighty-fifth year. Original – discovered by Professor Schüneman –
in the *Öffentliche Wissenschaftliche Bibliothek* in Berlin

Heinrich Schütz

HIS LIFE AND WORK

by

HANS JOACHIM MOSER

Translated from the Second Revised Edition

by

CARL F. PFATTEICHER

CONCORDIA PUBLISHING HOUSE, SAINT LOUIS

Printed in
West Germany

Contents

Part One: The Life

Part Two: The Works

A. Early Master Years

49058

B. The Middle Period

C. Creations of Old Age

Illustrations

Grouped at end of book

Foreword

Carl F. Pfatteicher died before he could put the final touches to his translation of Hans Joachim Moser's exhaustive biography of Heinrich Schütz. He passed away on September 29, 1957. A few galleys were sent to him shortly before his death. His wife took them to his bedside and tried to show him that the work to which he had devoted so much time, effort, and care was now beginning to appear in print. But Dr. Pfatteicher had lost consciousness. The joy of seeing the fruition of his labor of love was denied him.

While preparing the manuscript for publication, I was in frequent communication with Dr. Pfatteicher, just as he himself had often consulted outstanding scholars while he was engaged in the taxing and exacting work of translating Moser's book. It was his concern to reproduce clearly and accurately the thoughts and the conclusions of the author, who must be numbered among the most erudite musicographers of our time.

It was a pleasure to work with Dr. Pfatteicher. He invariably focused the light of profound and penetrating scholarship on the matters we discussed. His wide-reaching knowledge of music and his extensive ability as a linguist stood him in good stead. He did not strive to embellish or polish Moser's way of writing; it was his purpose to say in English what the learned author says in German — even to the extent of giving translations that are sometimes tangibly literal. He was keenly aware of the fact that Moser's pithy style — the style of an exceedingly painstaking savant rather than that of an adept in the field of belles-lettres — is by no means easy to translate into another language.

By making Moser's comprehensive and authoritative work on Schütz available in English, Dr. Pfatteicher has rendered the world of music an immeasurable service. Even though many students of the tonal art have heard and read that Schütz was a great master, the majority of them do not know why or in what respects he was great. It is not at all wide of the mark to say that to countless devotees of music in the United States and in many other parts of the world Schütz and his music are unknown quantities.

Schütz was a sincere Christian, a man of profound learning, and a great composer. He foreshadowed many subsequent developments in the art of composition. He was a past master of artistically expressed realism; he was a remarkably resourceful painter in tone — both vocal and instrumental.

It was Dr. Pfatteicher's desire to enable many others to share with him the realization of the abiding greatness of Schütz. Now he is gone. But his translation of Moser's book will be a monument to his zeal for an important cause. The world of music is in his debt.

Moser was born in Berlin on May 25, 1889. He is the son of Andreas Moser (1859-1925), who wrote a biography of Joseph Joachim, under whom he studied the violin; *Johannes Brahms im Briefwechsel mit Joseph Joachim; Violinschule; Geschichte des Violinspiels;* and other works. The author of *Heinrich Schütz: His Life and Work* pursued the study of music under his father and other famous German scholars. For a time he was a concert singer. Throughout his career as artist, teacher, and writer he has devoted himself to intensive study of many aspects of the tonal art. He is a doctor of philology and a doctor of theology. He had an important part in the preparation of the thirty-fifth volume of the Weimar edition of the works of Martin Luther. Among the numerous writings that have brought him to fame and influence are *Die mehrstimmige Vertonung des Evangeliums, Die Melodien der Lutherlieder, Lehrbuch der Musikgeschichte,* and an invaluable *Musiklexikon.*

Dr. Pfatteicher, the son of a German Lutheran clergyman, was born in Easton, Pa., in 1882. After his graduation from Lafayette College he spent three years at Lutheran Theological Seminary, Mt. Airy, Philadelphia. He did further graduate work at Harvard and at the universities of Heidelberg, Tübingen, and Freiburg im Breisgau. From Harvard he received the degree of doctor of theology, and the University of Freiburg conferred on him the degree of doctor of philosophy. For thirty-five years he was director of music at Phillips Academy, Andover, Mass., where he had a superb organ at his disposal. Every year he undertook to play in public all the organ works of Johann Sebastian Bach. No less an authority than Pablo Casals, world-renowned master of the violoncello and one of the great Bach exponents of our time, commended his Bach-playing in the warmest terms.

About ten years ago Dr. Pfatteicher retired from Phillips Academy. Since that time he lectured at Trinity University, San Antonio, Tex.; at Franklin and Marshall

College, Lancaster, Pa.; and at the University of Pennsylvania. His *The Oxford American Hymnal for Schools and Colleges* (Oxford University Press, 1930) has been called "the finest hymnal published in America, if not indeed in the English language." It won high praise from the late Sir Walford Davies, Musician to the King. His English edition of Karl Nef's *History of Music* (Columbia University Press) is now in its eighth printing. Albert Schweitzer has referred to his *Church Organist's Golden Treasury*, edited in conjunction with Archibald T. Davison, of Harvard, as "three magnificent volumes" *(drei prachtvolle Bände).* In addition, Dr. Pfatteicher edited *The Christian Church Year in Chorales; The Office Hymns of the Church in Their Plainsong Settings, with Latin and English Texts;* and *The Organ Works of John Redford,* organist of St. Paul's Cathedral in the days of King Henry VIII. In recent years Dr. Pfatteicher had been devoting as much time as he could to a comprehensive work for which he had chosen the title *The Chorale: Its Root, Its Stem, and Its Flower.* This work will be completed by one of his close friends.

Since I knew that Dr. Pfatteicher had devoted special care to the translations he chose for the titles of Schütz's compositions and for quotations from the texts of the master's works, I have considered it both inappropriate and unwise to make or suggest changes. After all, he was an authority in this field. It is possible that he might have asked for alterations here and there in the body of the book had his death not deprived him of the opportunity to read the galleys. My own deepfelt respect for his judgment and his learning prevented me from attempting to emend anything without consulting him.

CONCORDIA PUBLISHING HOUSE
St. Louis, Missouri
January 20, 1958

Walter A. Hansen

Preface to the English Edition

The late Alfred Einstein called Heinrich Schütz the most spiritual musician the world has ever seen. Johannes Brahms and Franz Liszt, who differed radically from each other in the type of music they composed, set great store by the sweep and the power of Schütz's genius. In fact, one need not hesitate to speak of Sagittarius — a name which Schütz himself frequently used — as the greatest German composer before Johann Sebastian Bach.

Schütz was born in 1585, one hundred years before Bach and George Frideric Handel, who are often referred to as the Dioscuri in music. He died in 1672 at the ripe age of eighty-seven. For fifty-seven years he was Kapellmeister at the Electoral Saxon Court in Dresden, though three times the vicissitudes of the Thirty Years' War compelled him to leave his native land for Denmark. Like Handel, his great countryman, he, too, drank at the music fountains of Italy. For approximately four years he sat at the feet of the famous Giovanni Gabrieli (1557-1612) in Venice. Later he visited Italy again to observe at first hand the development of music in that country, especially under Claudio Monteverdi (1567-1643).

Thus Schütz became a great eclectic cosmopolite, as his compositions so thoroughly illustrate. His madrigals show that he could vie with his Italian exemplars in this field. His Latin *Cantiones sacrae* reveal him as a master who was aware of the ecumenical character of the Christian Church and whose music often reflects a mystical bent. The *Becker Psalter* shows him as a writer of simple hymn tunes and at the same time as a composer thoroughly conversant with the church modes. His *Psalms of 1619* make it clear that he was the greatest composer of psalm settings in the history of music. His *Absolom, My Son,* from the *Symphoniae sacrae I,* is probably the outstanding *lamento* in the entire domain of composition; and his *Saul, Saul, Why Persecutest Thou Me?* from the *Symphoniae sacrae III,* introduced to Vienna by Brahms, has been called "the most convulsive dream of terror in the older music."

The *Kleine geistliche Konzerte*, a collection of compositions meagerly scored because of the exigencies of the Thirty Years' War but by no means meager in the artistry they exemplify, show Schütz as a master of the monodic style and of madrigalistic word painting. The *Geistliche Chormusik* reveals him, the devout Lutheran, as thoroughly versed in the classical polyphony of his forbears.

For the church year we have the ever-fresh *Christmas Oratorio;* the passions according to St. Matthew, St. Luke, and St. John, wonderful works from the pen of Schütz the octogenarian — not archaic precursors of the great dramatic passions of Bach but the greatest representatives of the liturgical passion, with a neo-Gregorianism developed by the master himself; for Good Friday, the *Seven Last Words on the Cross.* Is there in the whole literature of music a more dramatic outcry than Schütz's treatment of the words "My God, my God, why hast Thou forsaken Me?" For Easter we have the wonderfully mystical *Resurrection History.* For funerals we have the *Musikalische Exequien,* and for the Sundays of the church year there are the many Gospel settings, such as *The Sower and the Seed, The Pharisee and the Publican, The Draught of Fishes, Dives and Lazarus,* to mention but a few. Surely a royal banquet!

No one who listens carefully to this great word painter, this man who knew all the secrets of rhythm and syncopation, this "modern" chromaticist and harmonist, this master of the linear Gothic polyphony, of Venetian polychoral writing, of Florentine monody, of the Italian madrigal, of the old German lied — not to mention the many effects of the baroque period which he helped to usher in — will fail to realize that he is in the presence of one of music's mighty prophets. Schütz was no mere volcano thrust up to imposing heights in the seventeenth century; he was and is a primal mountain range. Furthermore, Sagittarius was a man who walked humbly with his God.

It remains for me to express my sincerest thanks to two men who rendered invaluable assistance in the preparation of this translation: Dr. Henry S. Drinker, who spent endless hours deleting and rectifying many vestiges of the hand of the translator, and Dr. Otto Kinkeldey, who devoted many hours to a discussion of problems of interpretation.

Philadelphia, March 1, 1957

Carl F. Pfatteicher

Preface to the German Edition

This book reflects fifteen years of study devoted to Heinrich Schütz. The second volume of my *Geschichte der deutschen Musik*[1] and my portrayal of Schütz in the *Zeitschrift für Musikwissenschaft*[2] in 1922 were stages along this path. So were the course of lectures on Schütz which I gave at the University of Berlin in the winter semester of 1929-30 and the preparation for the Berlin Schütz Festival of the Academy for Church and School Music,[3] together with my article *Schütz und das evangelische Kirchenlied*[4] in volume three of the academy's annual and my Schütz essays in *Musik und Kirche*.[5] With my books *Die mehrstimmige Vertonung des Evangeliums*[6] and *Corydon, das ist, Geschichte des mehrstimmigen Generalbassliedes im deutschen Barok*[7] I came to ever closer grips with the subject. By no means, however, do I claim any finality for my present conclusions. While I have attempted to present an encyclopedic account of everything substantial that has resulted from the research carried on during the past hundred years, it has become doubly clear to me during the final formulation of the results of this investigation how unsettled many things still are in this field, and always will be. And this is due, not only to the changing points of view of the different investigators and to the new problems encountered by them but also to the material itself. As one of the fruits of the studies here presented there has been an increase in the available number of Schütz works and documents.[8] Unfortunately, during the twenty-five

---

[1] *History of German Music.*
[2] "Journal for the Study of Music."
[3] Held in 1935.
[4] "Schütz and the Evangelical Chorale."
[5] "Music and the Church."
[6] *The Polyphonic Settings of the Gospels*, Vol. I, 1930.
[7] *Corydon, or The History of Polyphonic Song with Thorough Bass in the German Baroque,* two vols. 1933.
[8] See the new motets, recently published by me through Peters; the dialog *Ach Herr du Sohn Davids* (B & H); the *Motet à 6: Ich weiss, dass mein Erlöser lebt* (Bärenreiter Edition).

years that have elapsed since the issue of the *Denkmäler Editions* there has been a loss of manuscripts as a result of the careless guarding of the libraries of small *Kantoreien*,[9] a situation that evokes the wish for sharper vigilance and more careful custody.

In 1935, the year of Schütz's 350th birthday, his picture appeared on the German postage stamps. This was a significant sign of the welcome resurgence of the Schütz movement, which urgently demanded an effort to describe the life and works of the great man as fully as possible.

A brief review of the research to date will clarify the conditions that led to the development of the present Schütz cult.

The situation in the musical world in 1672, when Schütz died at the age of eighty-seven, is presented in the final chapter of this book. The numerous manuscripts he left in Dresden, Copenhagen, and Gera were destroyed by fire during the eighteenth century, and the valuable musical documents in Kassel, Breslau, and Königsberg, as well as other documents in the libraries of the Saxon *Kantoreien*, lay unnoticed. Practically all that was known were the catalog of his publications and the outline of his biography in the necrology of M. Geyer,[10] flowing as a little stream through the lexica of J. G. Walther[11] and E. L. Gerber. In addition, a few authentic facts or anecdotes, mostly from the pupils of Schütz, had been picked up by Mattheson and Werkmeister. But since about 1736 Schütz's art had been almost completely moribund,[12] and the radiance of his mighty personality had been in eclipse.[13] This continued for a full hundred years, until the appearance, in 1834 in Berlin, of the three-volume work of C. von Winterfeld, *Johannes Gabrieli und sein Zeitalter*.[14] Here we find in Volume 1, 50 f. and in Volume 2, 168-212, on some forty-six large quarto pages, a characterization of Schütz which

---

[9] The term *Kantorei* refers to many types of singing organizations, especially church choirs.

[10] The essential part of it, namely *Kurtze Beschreibung des (Tit.) Herrn Heinrich Schützens / Chur-Fürstl. Sächs. ältern Capellmeisters / geführten müheseeligen Lebenslauff*, which forms the point of departure of the real Schütz literature, recently appeared in attractive facsimile in the *Bärenreiter-Verlag* in Kassel.

[11] His essay has been reprinted in the treatise by Alfred Einstein (Bärenreiter edition).

[12] Even the *Zeitz Castle Hymn Book*, edited in 1736 by Schemelli, with the co-operation of J. S. Bach, did not contain Schütz's melodies to Cornelius Becker's *Psalm Hymns*.

[13] That Schütz's art was not completely forgotten after 1736 is revealed by Peter Mortimer, the Englishman among the Moravians in Herrnhut, in his book titled *Der Choralgesang zur Zeit der Reformation (Chorale Singing at the Time of the Reformation)*, Berlin, 1821, p. 12. He tells us that Schütz's melodies to the *Becker Psalter* "up to the most recent times" (at least then up to about 1800) were sung "at the midweek services in the (Lutheran) Court Church in Dresden." The court organist Joh. Gottfried Kirsten is said to have made a special study of their modal settings. Mortimer frequently cites this work of Schütz (p. 29, 110, etc.) and, therefore, deserves honorable mention as a white raven in the period of Schütz's eclipse.

[14] *Giovanni Gabrieli and His Times.*

amounts to a rediscovery. When we consider that the author had very limited bibliographical material at his disposal, that he knew neither the Italian nor the German madrigals, nor the *Psalms of David* of 1619, nor the *Exequien*, and that Schütz's German musical environment was still for the most part *terra incognita*, we are filled with admiration for Winterfeld's accomplishment. He discusses (for the most part from the point of view of a critical investigation of style) excellently chosen examples, of which he presents, in Volume III, three large specimens in score: *Absalom, My Son*[15] (1629); *Why Troublest Thou Thyself?*[16] (1639); *Saul, Saul, Why Persecutest Thou Me?*[17] (1650); and excerpts from the *Cantiones sacrae* and from the *Symphoniae sacrae* I and III as well as from the *Kleine geistliche Konzerte*.[18] He attempts to portray Schütz's personel development, and he points out the master's dependence both on Gabrieli's earlier and on his later style. He even recognizes to a certain extent the evolution of a new individual style which continued for half a generation. Despite his old-fashioned prolixity, Winterfeld thus produced a portrait of Schütz to which for half a century German romanticism could look up in reverence, until the brothers Spitta ushered in a new age of Schütz investigation. As a significant example, Winterfeld's portrayal of the vocal *Konzert*[19] presenting the conversion of St. Paul will be given in its entirety further on.

In the meantime researches into archives unearthed further source material. In 1849 Moritz Fürstenau, as Dresden chamber musician, published his *Beiträge zur Geschichte der kgl. sächsischen musikalischen Kapelle*,[20] followed in 1861 by his book *Zur Geschichte der Musik und des Theaters am Hofe zu Dresden*.[21] Between these stands the important compilation of letters and official documents, edited in part by Fürstenau and published by Wilhelm Schäfer in his *Sachsenchronik I*,[22]

----

[15] *Fili mi Absalom.*
[16] *Was betrübst du dich?*
[17] *Saul, Saul, was verfolgst du mich?*
[18] *Small Sacred Concerti.*
[19] It has been suggested that the word *Konzert* comes from the Latin *concertare* (to contend with), *consortium* (fellowship), or *conserere* (to join or twine together). The word *concerto* or *concertare* was used at the end of the sixteenth and in the seventeenth century for any mingling in performance of human voices and instruments. In the first half of the seventeenth century it became associated with a particular style as exhibited in the works of Monteverdi and other Italians and of such Germans as Schütz and Hammerschmidt. Only later did it acquire a connotation of rivalry between a small group and a larger body, as in the *concerto grosso*, and later still between a solo instrument and orchestra. As used repeatedly in this book, the term *Konzert*, or *concerto*, means simply a sacred composition for one or more voices with one or more instruments.
[20] *Contribution to the History of the Music at the Royal Saxon Chapel.*
[21] *On the History of Music and the Theater at the Court of Dresden.*
[22] *Saxon Chronicle.*

500 ff. (1854). In her *Musikerbriefe*[23] La Mara presented some of the principal selections to a wider public. There followed the study by Fr. Chrysander in his *Jahrbuch für musikalische Wissenschaft*[24] (I, 1863) under the title *Geschichte der Braunschweigisch-Wolfenbüttelschen Capelle und Oper vom 16. bis 18. Jahrhundert*,[25] which gives the exchange of letters between Schütz and Duke August and Duchess Sophia Elisabeth.[26] In 1864 the young Johannes Brahms startled the Viennese by presenting at one of his first concerts with the *Singakademie* Schütz's *Saul, Saul* after compositions by Gabrieli and Eccard.

In 1870 a modest Schütz renaissance actually began when the Leipzig choral conductor Carl Riedel patched together a kind of *Gospel Harmony* from the four passions which had become known under Schütz's name. The work was published by E. W. Fritzsch and was known as *Die Schützsche Passion*. Despite the objections of Moritz Hauptmann, it persisted for numerous performances. However, it at once reveals a lack of real understanding on the part of the editor in that the greater number of its choruses are taken from the *St. Mark Passion*, which is now known not to be by Schütz. Riedel acted somewhat more conservatively in the case of the *Seven Last Words*. How much more praiseworthy was the procedure of Franz Wüllner in his editing of three of the *Psalms of 1619!*

The jubilee year 1885 markedly advanced the incipient Schütz movement through the Bonn (then Strassburg) circle of friends, Friedrich Spitta, Julius Smend,[27] and Arnold Mendelssohn, whose leadership was then assumed by Friedrich's brother, Philipp Spitta, as musual historian. The latter, in his great Bach biography (1873-79), had opened new avenues of approach to Schütz's historical background, and had excellently co-ordinated the evolution of Schütz's works. The two brothers now heartily espoused the cause of Sagittarius.[28] Friedrich Spitta, as a distinguished theologian and hymnologist, recognized the great significance of Schütz in the development of evangelical church music, and, in his writing *Die*

---

[23] *Letters by Musicians.*

[24] *Year Book for the Study of Music.*

[25] *History of the Choir and Opera at Brunswick-Wolfenbüttel from the Sixteenth to the Eighteenth Century.*

[26] Whether Wagner, as Dresden *Kapellmeister*, found at hand a living Schütz tradition, as E. Kurth, *Die romantische Harmonik und ihre Krise in Wagners Tristan* (1920), believes (p. 417), seems very questionable to me. At best it could have been a Schütz renaissance, due to the influence of Winterfeld. But this is scarcely likely at the Catholic Court Church. Schütz is never mentioned in Wagner's writings.

[27] Cf. his essay *Das Bibelwort bei H. Schütz* (ZfMW V) and, in his *Vorträge und Aufsätze* (1925), *H. Schütz und die evangelische Gemeinde*. Twelve essays by him on Schütz in *Monatshefte für Gottesdienst und kirchliche Kunst*. Annuals 3, 5, 8, 15, 16, 19, 20, 27 (1898-1922).

[28] Schütz often designated himself with this Latin version of "Schütz".

Passionen von Heinrich Schütz nach den vier Evangelien,[29] demanded the return to
Schütz's original form for their performance. In addition, he wrote *Heinrich Schütz,
Gedächtnisrede*[30] (1886) and *Heinrich Schütz ein Meister der Musica Sacra*[31]
(Neue Cristoterpe, 1925). In 1885 Ph. Spitta presented the masterly Essay *Händel,
Bach und Schütz.*[32] Though at the time he had to confess: "The great majority of
educated Germans doubtless scarcely even know the name of Schütz," he nevertheless concluded with the prophetic statement: "In another hundred years, Heinrich Schütz, as one of the noblest sons of Germany, will have received his due from
the hand of history" — words that for a long time were cited as depicting the well-
intentioned Utopia of a visionary. In 1893 Spitta presented a very thoughtful and
just comparison of a phase of the work of Bach and Schütz in an essay titled *Die
Passionsmusiken von Bach und Schütz.* In R. von Liliencron's *Allgemeine deutsche
Biographie*[33] he also provided the first fundamental biography of the master,
which again appeared in 1894 in his *Musikgeschichtliche Aufsätze.*[34] Above all,
however, Ph. Spitta (in part on the basis of the many volumes of scores of Friedrich Chrysander) laid the philological foundation for all future study of Schütz's
music in the sixteen-volume edition of his works, published by Breitkopf & Hartel,
a task which occupied the final decade of the honored scholar's life (1885-94).

On this foundation the cult of Schütz could now expand. Spitta's voice edition
of the *Cantiones sacrae* (Breitkopf) remained almost unnoticed. Arnold Mendelssohn, however, edited the *Passions* in practical editions, which Fr. Spitta himself
sang with his choir in Strassburg. To be sure, both still believed that the recitatives
required organ accompaniment, but it is gratifying that A. Mendelssohn had already
designated the *a cappella* rendition as the true ideal for the future. He deserves
great credit for having brought it about that the *Passions*, without any forced
editorial usurpations — although with a very well conceived interpretation of the
harmonic progressions — made a deep impression wherever they were heard.
However, as thus presented they were listened to as concerts rather than experienced as a liturgical service. But in Kretzschmar's *Führer durch den Konzertsaal*[35]
(which was also effective in spreading the knowledge of Schütz) we are told that
the *Passions* were sung in their original form in the *Lutherkirche* in Leipzig as
early as 1890. In our day the *a cappella* performances of A. Sittard in Hamburg,

[29] *The Passions of Schütz According to the Four Gospels.*
[30] *Commemorative Address on Heinrich Schütz.*
[31] *Heinrich Schütz, a Master of Sacred Music.*
[32] Reprinted in his book *Zur Musik* (1892).
[33] *General German Biography.*
[34] *Essays on the History of Music.*
[35] *Guide Through the Concert Hall.*

W. Reimann in Berlin, and F. Schmidt in Celle have further paved the way for the original form of presentation. Today no one should employ the superfluous assistance[36] of the added thorough bass for the solos. The possible strengthening of the chorus by the organ (as found in the manuscript of the *St. Luke Passion* belonging to Chr. Schultze, 1653) would raise the question as to a possible practice of the time, which, to be sure, does not affect the music as a work of art.

In 1894 Felix Woyrsch did splendid service for the re-introduction of Schütz's choruses into the evangelical liturgy with his practical selection in three brochures, published by Fritzsch. And when, in 1896, Fr. Spitta and J. Smend founded the *Monatsschrift für Gottesdienst und kirchliche Kunst*,[37] this publication remained for a long time the chief protagonist for the return of Schütz to the church, his original home.

A more quiescent period followed, during which, however, the movement received a powerful stimulus from the basic works of Max Seiffert, the faithful pupil of Chrysander and of Ph. Spitta. Seiffert, through *Denkmäler* volumes and treatises, depicted the environment of Schütz's later period (Weckmann, Bernhard, etc.).[38] We must also draw attention to the local investigation by A. Werner in Weissenfels and Zeitz; to the works of A. Hammerich, C. Elling, and C. Thrane concerning the Danish court music under Christian IV; and to the works of E. Zulauf and W. Nagel concerning the Kassel court chapel until 1630. Th. Goldschmidt's selection from the *Becker Psalms* (B & H, 1902) was a greeting from Switzerland indicating the cultivation of Schütz in the churches there. In 1908 A. Schering discovered in Upsala the almost complete Schütz *Christmas Oratorio*, which, as Vol. XVII, now supplements the complete edition. In 1913 there appeared the most useful biography since Spitta's sketch — Andre Pirro's *Schütz* (Alcan, Paris, 1924). Approaching the subject from his *Buxtehude*, the French scholar, with exemplary care, developed further details and also portrayed the works with remarkable sympathy — although essentially from the artistic point of view. The present book owes much to Pirro's suggestions.[39]

While the chorus of St. Thomas Church at Leipzig, under G. Schreck and Karl Straube, naturally promoted the use of the *Geistliche Chormusik*, which had been dedicated to it, the monumental works received special attention only after World War I. S. Ochs in Berlin, Max Schneider in Breslau, and Fritz Sporn in Zuelenroda

---

[36] *Pons asinorum.*
[37] "Monthly Periodical for the Church Service and Ecclesiastical Art."
[38] Also his practical editions of German and Italian madrigals by Schütz, and of *Vater Abraham* in his collection *Organum* must be commended.
[39] Cf. also A. Schweitzer's *Bach*, ch. 6.

are to be mentioned as prime movers in this field. They also embodied the results
of their experience in practical editions (B & H). The duets and choruses edited
by Johs. Dittberner served both church and domestic music. Erich H. Müller
founded the *Heinrich Schütz Gesellschaft*. On the occasion of the first Schütz
Festival in Dresden, in honor of the 250th anniversary of Schütz's death (1922),
Müller edited a work, in tabular form: *Heinrich Schütz: Leben und Werke* (Rar-
Verlag). He followed this with a brief biography (B & H, 1925) — and this, in
turn, with the collection *Heinrich Schütz, gesammelte Briefe und Schriften*[40] (Bosse,
1931). After the dissolution of the first *Schütz Gesellschaft* the *Neue Schütz Gesellschaft* was organized in 1929, in connection with the Celle Schütz Festival,
with myself and Prof. Otto Richter as the principal officers and with K. Vötterle
of the Bärenreiter-Verlag in Kassel as business executive. Since its foundation in
1929 this society has been under the protectorship of His Royal Highness, Prince
Philipp of Hesse, whose ancestor, Landgrave Moritz the Learned, was Schütz's
patron. Under the auspices of this society Schütz festivals have been held in Berlin,
Flensburg (Johs. Roeder), Barmen (Gottfr. Grote), Dresden (R. Mauersberger), and,
in co-operation with the society, in Stuttgart (Martin Hahn, 1931 and 1935). The
society supported the cause of the master with a series of practical editions for its
members, with essays,[41] and with the exchange of loan material. It was also instrumental in obtaining the naming of streets after him in Dresden and Kassel. It has
become the center of the German Schütz cult. This movement has been particularly
dependent on the enthusiastic and tireless work of student singing groups. Mention
should especially be made of a Marburg circle under Rudolf Holle (cf. his edition of
the *Deutsche Messe*); of the *Heinrich Schütz-Kreis* (W. Kamlah), which organized
entire Schütz song weeks; the Berlin Schütz Circle (G. Arndt). The *Arbeitskreis für
Hausmusik*, with its Kassel Music Days, Hugo Holle's Madrigal Choir in Stuttgart,
and the Hamburg Circle under Hans Hoffmann[42] all devoted themselves to the
master's work. Robert Unger in Homburg successfully drew upon the church
trombone choirs for his Schütz performances. Many other circles might be mentioned. The interest in Schütz on the part of the participants in the German folk-
singing movement resulted in numerous new editions, published by the Bären-

---

[40] *Heinrich Schütz: Collected Letters and Writings.* To certain statements in the text of this
book I must take exception, but in order to avoid unnecessary repetition, I nevertheless assume
the book to be in the reader's possession.

[41] In *Musik und Kirche* Blume, Gerber, Birtner, Hoffmann, Moser; in *Musik und Volk* Fritz
Dietrich; in *Lied und Volk* H. Birtner; in the *Zeitschrift für Hausmusik,* IV, 2 and 4, W. Blankenburg.

[42] See his essays in *Musikpflege,* as well as his new editions in the Bärenreiter-Verlag: *Ich
werde nicht sterben* and *Es ging ein Sämann.*

reiter-Verlag of Kassel. In accordance with the musicological findings, the simple original text was used in these editions, and the previous little beautifying addenda[43] were discarded. As examples there may be mentioned three selections from the *Symphoniae sacrae* (H. Birtner); the first practical edition of the *Geistliche Chormusik* by W. Kamlah; the editions of the *St. Matthew Passion*, for the first time in its original form, by Schmidt; the *St. Luke* and *St. John Passion*, by Kamlah; the *Resurrection History*, by Huber; the *100th and 116th Psalms*, by R. Holle; the complete edition of the *Becker Psalms*, by W. Blankenburg; also the important student scores by Fritz Stein (Eulenburg). The *Flensburger Schützjahr* of 1934, under Pastor Kähler and Johs. Roeder, merits special mention as the most comprehensive attempt up to that time to place the church music of an entire town and of an entire year wholly under the constellation of Sagittarius. This accomplishment will be reflected further in the publishing of new editions.

The progress of the musicological literature runs parallel to this steeply ascending curve of the practical cultivation of Schütz. Valuable works emanated from the Göttingen student circle about Fr. Ludwig. In 1924 Heinrich Spitta, the son of Friedrich, took his doctorate there with a dissertation on *Schütz's Orchestra and Unpublished Works*.[44] From this, with the use of the Seiffert treatise *Anecdota Schütziana* (Sbd. IMG I, 1899), came the supplementary Vol. XVIII of the complete edition, together with a series of practical editions, especially through Peters. To the contents of the coming Vol. XIX will belong Heinrich Spitta's first edition of the double-chorus *Magnificat* of 1671 (B & H). J. M. Müller-Blattau is also to be counted in Ludwig's circle. He deserves credit for having published in 1926 the theoretical treatises of Chr. Bernhard under the title — doubtless rather pretentious — *Heinrich Schütz's Theory of Composition*.[45] Hermann Abert inspired his pupil Fr. Blume to work on Schütz in preparation for a broadly projected work on Bach, which resulted in his *Monodisches Prinzip in der evangelischen Kirchenmusik* (1925).[46] Also to be mentioned with appreciation are Blume's brochure "Music at the Court of Landgrave Maurice of Hesse"[47] (Bärenreiter), the Schütz chapter in his *Evangelische Kirchenmusik*,[48] and his selection of *Kleine geistliche Konzerte* (Kallmeyer). Blume's pupil, A. A. Abert, in Kiel, recently entered the scene with a study on the *Cantiones sacrae*. Rud. Gerber also belongs to Abert's circle. Among other things, Gerber wrote a careful inaugural dissertation for the

---

[43] Literally, "beauty plasters."
[44] *Schützens Orchester und unveröffentlichte Werke.*
[45] *Die Kompositionslehre H. Schützens.*
[46] *The Monodic Principle in Evangelical Church Music.*
[47] *Musik am Hofe des Landgrafen Moritz von Hessen.*
[48] *Evangelical Church Music.*

University of Giessen on *Schütz's Passion Recitative* (1929). Bern must be mentioned as a third focal point of the study of Schütz at the universities. Here in 1920 Ernst Kurth referred frequently to Schütz in his *Krise der romantischen Harmonik*.[49] In 1927 his pupil, W. Schuh, investigated the *Problems of Form in Heinrich Schütz*[50] on the basis of the concepts derived by Alfred Lorenz from his study of the works of Wagner. W. Kreidler[51] discussed the relation of Schütz to Monteverdi's *stile concitato*. The complete editions of Lasso (Haberl and Sandberger), H. L. Hassler,[52] of J. H. Schein (A. Prüfer, all B & H), of Scheidt (Ugrino-Bär.), and of M. Praetorius (Fr. Blume, Kallmeyer), all made possible a clearer delineation of Schütz's stature; and Blume's *Chorwerk* (Kallmeyer) planned a whole series of issues titled *Composers Contemporary with the Young Schütz*,[53] beginning impressively with Lasso's final work, *The Penitential Tears of St. Peter*.[54] In view of the service of H. Riemann in his *Handbuch der Musikgeschichte* II, 3 (1913), of H. Leichtentritt in his *Geschichte der Motette*,[55] and of A. Einstein in his *Schütz-Essai* (Ganymed, and Bär., 1928) in characterizing the master, especially from the point of view of the Italian influence, Schütz's function in music history has doubtless been determined with sufficient clarity for present purposes. While he formerly stood in the shadow — first merely as "the pupil of Gabrieli" and then as the supposed "preliminary step to Bach and Handel" — Fr. Spitta, in 1886, undertook to explain this hitherto stepmotherly treatment by his position between the Dioscuri (Bach and Handel) of 1685, on the one side, and the "old classical" *a cappella* masters of the sixteenth century, on the other. This point of view has long been exploded, in no small measure through the clarifying work of Herm. Kretzschmar.

Unquestionably, the time had come to evaluate the life and work of Schütz from the point of view of his spiritual background and growth. The authors just mentioned viewed him somewhat as an isolated phenomenon and as a purely artistic manifestation. Einstein indeed, approaching his subject manifestly from the madrigal, sought to discount the Protestant in him in favor of the artist. It was essential for the vital liturgical movement of our day to emphasize[56] that in his total ac-

---

[49] *Crisis Brought About by the Harmonies of the Romantic Movement.*
[50] *Formprobleme bei Heinrich Schütz.*
[51] Bern Dissertation, 1933, Bärenreiter.
[52] *Denkmäler deutscher Tonkunst* and *Denkmäler der Tonkunst in Bayern.*
[53] *Um den jungen Schütz.*
[54] *Die Busstränen des heiligen Petrus.*
[55] *History of the Motet.*
[56] For the utilization according to the church year see my article *Heinrich Schütz im Kirchenjahr* in *Musik und Kirche*, 1934. Cf. the comprehensive Schütz essay by Willibald Gurlitt in the *Petersjahrbuch* of 1936.

complishment, which went back to the foundations of the Protestant Reformation, Schütz, of all the masters of Protestant church music, is the most powerful preacher of the Word in tones. Through a mysterious synthesis he may be called both the most intellectually spiritual *(geistreichste)*, the most personal, and yet the most folklike and generally comprehensible expounder of the Bible; as the heir of Lassus, he was a man of almost unfettered personal, religious inspiration; and at the same time, as the great-grandchild of the Luther art as expounded by Joh. Walter, he was, in accordance with tradition, cantor of the church year. To be sure, we must guard against confining Schütz's universality too much within the bounds of confessionalism and Teutonism. In my *History of German Music* (1922) I have sketched, in broad outline, the great developmental curve which transmuted the young high Renaissance artist and the Italian enthusiast into the German baroque church cantor of 1648 who finally grew into the supertemporal and otherworldly Faust of the works of 1665 and thereabouts. Fr. Blume deepened and clarified the picture in his essay "Schütz in the Religious Currents of his Period."[57] In this connection, H. Birtner's discussion, "The Schütz Movement,"[58] must also be accorded honorable mention. W. Gurlitt's Barmen festival address (unfortunately, never published) opened valuable vistas based on the history of religion. To set in sharp profile these almost dramatic changes in Schütz's life and creative activity and thus to delineate his relationship to different artistic tendencies, posed one of the most fascinating problems for the following pages. Every attempt to picture the entire Schütz from but one of these perspectives would necessarily lead to a grave distortion of the manifold furrows of his countenance. That a generation ago Wilhelm Dilthey gave fertile attention to the phenomenon under consideration is shown by the fine chapter in his posthumous collection of 1932, *Von deutscher Dichtung und Musik*,[59] while Ricarda Huch, in her three-volume novel *Der große Krieg* (1912), splendidly portrayed Schütz, not only with poetic insight but also with fidelity to the sources. Acknowledgment should also be made here to the charming memorial to Schütz by Otto Michaelis (1935, Schloessmann). Although treating the works themselves in but a cursory manner, Michaelis pursues the family history even beyond the findings which Dr. Uhle set forth in the *Reports of the Historical Society of Chemnitz*[60] (1930), based on the archives.

Schütz's status among his contemporaries is given an entirely different aspect by the new interpretation of the baroque, as represented in the field of art by such

---

[57] *Heinrich Schütz in den geistigen Strömungen seiner Zeit, Musik und Kirche*, II, 6, 1930.
[58] *Zur Schützbewegung*, loc. cit. 1932.
[59] *On German Poetry and Music.*

names as Cornelius Gurlitt, Heinrich Wölfflin, Max Dvorak, Wilhelm Pinder, W. Weissbach; and in the field of literature by those of O. Walzel, H. Cyssarz, Günter Müller, W. Stammler, etc. According to this interpretation, the art of the Thirty Years' War period, when viewed from the sole perfectionism of the Renaissance, is no longer a tasteless, overgrown excrescence, a culture run wild, but appears it its exuberant development of power as a thoroughly self-justified epoch, in which a powerful Gothic-Nordic fantasy ever and again breaks through the smooth shell of the older art. While the unquestionable greatness of baroque music had hitherto appeared almost as a paradox in the course of the history of art, on account of which one rather spared it the epithet "baroque," it now shows itself as the great leader in this parade of the seventeenth-century arts; and Schütz does not become smaller but becames larger when he stands as the most illustrious molder of most of these progressive movements. Robert Haas, in his volume *Die Musik des Barock (Bückens Handbuch)*, has impressively presented these multifarious elements. To set them forth anew in the towering individual case of Schütz was one of the chief tasks of the present work. Obvious limitations guarded me against the enticing temptation to stray too far afield into the general history of culture. Another primary task seemed to me to consist in the presentation of a detailed description of the works, which would stimulate the uninitiated to recreative participation; would discuss with the initiated the formal, aesthetic, and historical problems, as well as those connected with practical performance; and which, in addition, would attempt to evaluate positively the life accomplishment of Schütz. To keep the solution of this task from becoming wearisome and boundless, limitations had to be imposed here too.[61] In the following pages every work of Schütz has been discussed to the extent that most of these analyses could be used as introductory program notes for Schütz performances. It was not, however, feasible to proceed with all the discussions according to all the points of view mentioned. If, in consequence, now the one, now the other consideration predominates, this is not because of any lack of principles of interpretation. On the one hand, it is the result of the special nature and adaptability of the composition in question, and, on the other hand, it is because of my desire to make the entire work readable by means of reasonable variety in presentation. It was not my intention to produce a lexicon of all the subjects of importance in Schütz, but a book, an organic presentation. Neither was I interested in torturing forth a one-sided, doctrinaire

---

[61] My treatise *Unbekannte Werke von H. Schütz* in the Z. f. MW, August 1933, and the essay in *Acta musicologica*, VII, 4, will help to justify omissions in the present book.

"Schütz-aesthetic"; it was my purpose to show how the mighty and many-sided phenomenon of the master stands the test of almost every method of consideration, every manner of research.

This work could not have been concluded so soon had I not received assistance from many quarters, for which I here express my heartfelt gratitude. Prof. Max Seiffert opened to me unreservedly the general catalog of the *Denkmäler deutscher Tonkunst;*[62] Dr. Fritz Piersig (Bremen) compiled the tables of contents; Prof. Arno Werner (Bitterfeld) compiled notes based on his investigations of various localities; Dr. R. Engländer (Dresden) reviewed anew the Schütz records in the chief Saxon Archive; Prof. W. Gurlitt (Freiburg i/Br.) offered valuable suggestions; Prof. A. Pirro (Paris) very willingly gave information; Prof. W. Vetter (Breslau) unselfishly put in score for me a number of compositions; Prof. G. Schünemann (Berlin) and Frl. Eva Petersen-Claudius (Copenhagen) contributed pictures.

For information and material I am indebted to the state archives in Marburg, Magdeburg, Greiz, Dresden; the state archive in Copenhagen; the municipal archives in Kassel, Weissenfels, Gera, Dresden, Hildesheim, Freiberg (Saxony), Naumburg, Mühlhausen (Thuringia); the court archives in Schleitz; the state and provincial libraries in Kassel (as well as the *Landgrafenmuseum* there), Berlin, Dresden, Wolfenbüttel, Danzig, Gotha, Copenhagen, Weimar; the municipal libraries of Breslau and Zwickau; the university library of Halle; the court library in Stolberg; the library of the Berlin *Singakademie;* the school libraries of Saalfeld, Freiberg, and Halle (the Francke Foundations); the Germanic museum in Nürnberg; the *Gesellschaft der Musikfreunde* in Vienna; and many other persons and authorities, especially in the circle of the Saxon *Kantoreien.*[63] The publishing houses of Peters, Kahnt, Schott, Kistner, and Siegel presented me with their new editions; the firm of Breitkopf & Härtel allowed me to examine theirs. Above all, however, the Bärenreiter-Verlag, Karl Vötterle, in an exemplary and magnanimous manner, carried out all my wishes with regard to the format of the book.

May this work go forth, then, both as an acknowledgment and as a challenge on the 350th birthday of a favored German; one who had to live through and experience endless tragedy and yet from his sorrow harvested for himself piety and devotion to God, while he sowed anew for his people blessing and happiness. May his immortal spirit lead us mortal ones on!

Berlin-Charlottenburg, August 15, 1935

D. Dr. Hans Joachim Moser

---

[62] *Monuments of German Tonal Art.*
[63] See note 9 on page XV.

To the New Edition of 1953

After the second half of the first edition had been destroyed by fire at the book-binder's during the bombardment of Kassel on March 8 and 9, 1945, and after I had lost, in July of the same year, my personal copy, filled with notes, because of the requisitioning of my house in Babelsberg in connection with the Potsdam Conference, the present work had to remain out of print for nine years before the publisher and the author could again undertake to make it available. Besides the elimination of slight oversights, numerous supplements were added. These were made in the body of the text where no extensive adjustments were involved; otherwise they were added in the Appendix.

I owe especial thanks to Dr. Konrad Ameln (Lüdenscheid) and to Pastor W. Engelhardt, who kindly placed at my disposal both their lists of *errata* and their *addenda*.

D. Dr. Hans Joachim Moser

Berlin-Charlottenburg, November 6, 1953
(on the 281st anniversary of Schütz's death)

Part One: The Life

The German World at the Time
of Schütz's Birth

"The true heaven, which is also the particular heaven of humanity, whither the soul fares when it parts from the body, has hitherto remained for the most part obscure to the children of men, who have entertained various ideas about it. People have ever believed that heaven is many hundreds and thousands of miles above our earth and that God dwells only in this heaven. Some physicists have indeed undertaken to measure its height and have brought forth strange things. I myself believed, before my enlightenment and revelation, that the only true heaven was that which, altogether blue, circumscribes the stars, in a circle. I thought that God has His special Being only there and that He rules in this world solely through the power of His Holy Spirit ... The true heaven, however, is everywhere, including the very spot on the earth in which each of us is standing and walking ... When the spirit penetrates beyond the earthly significance of God and grasps the essence of divinity, it has then found heaven ... For we must understand that this world is a part of the heaven above us and that there is only one heart, one being, one will, one God, all in all."

Jakob Böhme in *Aurora oder die Morgenröte im Aufgang*[1] (1612).

Heinrich Schütz was born in the same year as Richelieu. He was twenty-one years younger than Shakespeare and twenty-one years older than Rembrandt. The chart between pages 4 and 5 illustrates the life span of Schütz and of certain of his greatest contemporaries. (His life of eighty-seven years was the longest of any of them.)

When we survey this series of historical personalities, we are struck by certain common fundamental traits which clearly set them apart, both from the preceding and from the following period. The oldest of this group, Cervantes and Greco, in contrast with the somewhat laborious realism of the Renaissance, and still more when measured by the insipidity of the Period of the Enlightenment[2], show what we have in mind. They are characterized by imagination and fantasy — an excursion into regions where dreams are the only reality. Since collision with the world of reality must always bring with it disappointment to poets, whether of words, colors,

---

[1] *Aurora or Day in the Dawning.*
[2] The period of rationalism in the 18th century.

or tones, the tragedy of this situation includes the figures of the tragedian Shakespeare with his poems of humanity; of the court astrologer Kepler with his laws of heaven; or of Jacob Böhme, the Görlitz cobbler, with his far-flung visions. The reversion from realism in the latest Michelangelo and the late style of Tintoretto, whose influence on Greco was so unhappily called "mannerism,"[3] appear again and again in that generation in different forms: in the whipped-up color intoxication of Rubens and in the melancholy secrets of Rembrandt's twilight; in the laughing irony of Franz Hals and in the suffering skepticism of Velasquez; in the political Utopia of Wallenstein, in the merciless willfulness of Richelieu, and in the self-deification of Louis XIV. This power of peering into the world of dreams enables Descartes, Pascal, and Leibnitz to create their new spherical mathematics; it becomes creative in the feeling-tinged legal constructions of Grotius and Puffendorff. Before the eyes of a Calderon, a Grimmelshausen, a Gryphius, and a Murillo it transforms the world into inexhaustibly variegated and, at the same time, instructive legends; it makes of Opitz and Flemming restless searchers and collectors of the literatures of Holland, Italy, and France; it turns the Brandenburg Frederick William I into the "great elector," who prophetically sees in a starved and bleeding country the central state of a future German greatness. This is the spiritual Areopagus, gently pervaded by music, in which Heinrich Schütz appears as the great master, struggling for the realization of his visions.

Between his thirty-third and sixty-third years Schütz experienced the Thirty Years' War. He thus stands, as does scarcely another artist, in the midst of the storms of this catastrophe — a turning point for culture.

We know comparatively little about Schütz's personal life before 1619, the year of the Prague "defenestration" (Fenstersturz)[4]. Since, however, he, perhaps more than any other musician, stood in the closest cultural relation with the entire spiritual development of his time, it is not merely a "fashion of the history of culture" but a very real desire for biographical clarification that prompts the attempt to picture the cultural atmosphere into which Schütz was born and which was to accompany him to the threshold of his brief but happy married life (1619-25).

The political situation in Germany after the Augsburg religious peace of 1555, which gave to the Lutherans (although not to the Reformed) the cujus regio ejus

---

[3] Max Dvorak, Kunstgeschichte als Geistesgeschichte (History of Art as History of the Intellect), p. 268.

[4] The famous "defenestration of Prague" lit the flames of the Thirty Years' War. In answer to a royal decree forbidding Protestants to hold assemblies, the Bohemian nobles, at a violent interview in the Hradshin, the fortress palace in Prague, cast two Catholic ministers and a private secretary from a window into the castle ditch. (See H. A. L. Fisher, A History of Europe, II, 627; Houghton Mifflin Co., 1935.)

religio[5], showed externally the brilliant upswing of a long-lasting period of peace. As a matter of fact, however, this merely obscured to the superficial view the growing germs of decay. Lutheranism was split internally by the tension between the Jena Old Lutherans, under Flacius Illyricus, and the Wittenberg Melanchthonians with their crypto-Calvinism. In their timidity the Lutherans barred themselves against the Reformed with their Formula of Concord, made official in Saxony in 1577. The spirit of persecution in which these conflicts were fought out is seen in the miserable fate of Pastor Schulthess,[6] who was to become the father of Michael Praetorius. How worm-eaten must the confessional formulae have appeared to Schütz, who came to Dresden from the court of Landgrave Moritz, the man who had completed the Calvinistic *Lobwasser Psalter!* For in Dresden Schütz heard his patron, the court preacher Hoe von Hoenegg, prove, in stormy volume after volume, that these Reformed had more in common with the Turks and the atheists than with Christ — von Hoenegg, who all the while was pocketing the bribes of the Jesuits! In the face of such theological dissension Protestantism paid but little attention to the growing forces of Catholicism which, since the Council of Trent, were developing in secret—particularly the "storm troops" of the Counter Reformation under Ignatius Loyola. But the real thirst for God on the part of the Christians themselves was left unquenched in the flood of word-splitting semantics and quarreling by those who made the Bible their pope. Hence it sought religious substitutes in more or less dark and nebulous mysticism. Such mysticism, however, which ran in part straight across the boundaries of confessionalism, resulted in fruitful unions by means of the artist's vision and the poet's word. Thus in 1612 the Görlitz cobbler Jakob Böhme, wrestling laboriously with his visions, wrote in his *Aurora oder Morgenröte im Aufgang:* "O that I with my human pencil could record the Spirit of Knowledge! But I must falter over the great mystery like a child learning to walk. The earthly tongue cannot experience what the Spirit grasps and understands." His was but one of the many voices at that time. What in the case of the Erfurt revivalist Esajas Stiefel threatened to flare up as dangerous Anabaptism, discharged itself in Böhme in seraphic bliss:

> "That which is quiet in itself and without individual essence or substance *(Wesen)*, that has no darkness in itself, but is merely a quiet, clear bliss, without individual essence — and that is Eternity, without anything further, and is called the essential Godhead. For there is no evil therein, and it is without individual essence or substance . . . Thus God is within Himself but without name; He is in Himself the light, bright, and clear eternity without individual essence or substance."

---

[5] Religion follows the ruler.
[6] Gurlitt's dissertation on *M. Praetorius* (Leipzig, 1915).

Does one not feel in all this, beyond the stammering words, an urge and a thirst for music? When complaints of fanaticism were raised against the cobbler, and he was about to defend himself in Dresden — under the very eyes, as it were, of Schütz; and when the court preacher Polycarp Leyser sent the willing martyr home as a harmless fool, to the cobbler's unspeakable disappointment, we have a feeling that he would much rather have found peace and understanding for that which his spirit "grasped and understood" in the choir room of Sagittarius, with the "divine tongue" of the *Cantiones sacrae*. And when the cobbler died in 1624, the blue flame of his theosophy leapt over upon a Silesian born in the same year, the "cherubic pilgrim"[7] Johann Scheffler, who as *Angelus Silesius* fanned to the extreme the fervor of his communion with God to produce the perennial paradox:

> What man has said of God is not enough for me;
> The Super-Godhead is my Life and Light.
> I know that without me God cannot live a wink.
> Become I naught, He in distress must die.[8]

Schütz would doubtless have repudiated this theologically as madness, or he would have resolved it into its elements — into musical ecstasy and Biblically correct Christianity — in order greatly to enhance both, in orthodox manner, by his genius.

What one hears above all from these voices is a gasping distress, the terror of death and judgment, a fear of existence, which the evangelical princes of this time liked to drown in gluttony, drunkenness, and hunting, while the Catholics writhed in contrition in their confessionals. In the Hradshin in Prague the learned Jesuit pupil Emperor Rudolf II called on his astronomers Tycho de Brahe and Johannes Kepler, the Dane and the Swabian, to interpret the threatening constellations and comets in terms of coming events. Intemperance and vanity were widespread, so that a citizen, apprehensive on account of the revelry of this generation, prophetically wrote to the Council of Brunswick at the end of the sixteenth century: "O Germany, Germany, I fear that a great punishment will overwhelm Germany!"[9]

Besides astrology, alchemy appeared in the eyes of many as the possible savior. By extracting the essence of metals it was hoped to create elixirs more effective in healing the world than mere glittering gold. Paracelsus had already written: "Not

---

[7] *Cherubinischer Wandersmann.*
[8] *Was man von Gott gesagt, das genüget mir noch nicht;*
die Über-Gottheit ist mein Leben und mein Licht.
Ich weiß, daß ohne mich Gott nicht ein Nu kann leben.
Werd' ich zunicht, er muß vor Not den Geist aufgeben.
[9] *O Dudeslant, Dudeslant, ik fruchte, dat Dudeslant eyne grote strafe overgan wart.* Steinhausen, *Geschichte des deutschen Briefes,* II, 1.

like those who say, 'Alchemy, make gold, make silver,' here the attempt is to distil secret essences and to direct them against sickness."[10] Monteverdi, who was so highly revered by Schütz, was incidentally an enthusiastic maker of gold.

At the very time when Schütz returned from Italy to Germany, there appeared in Calvinistic Kassel (1614) an anonymous book that aroused tremendous attention and was characteristic of the general tenor of the time: "The *Fama fraternitatis,* or the Discovery of the Brotherhood of the Honorable Order of the Rosicrucians, to the Heads, Orders, and Scholars of Europe."[11] A year later, likewise in Kassel, appeared the *Confessio* belonging to the same work. Joh. Valentin Andreae, of Stuttgart, the young author of the *Chymische Hochzeit,* was the sponsor. With the fairy tale of Christian Rosenkreuz he wanted to bring about the "great Reformation" — first theosophic, then Christian — of a world which was terrorizing itself into the Thirty Years' War. Finally the whole movement evaporated, partly in professional swindling, partly in cabalistic or alchemistic abracadabra.[12]

"The center of the pansophic movement at that time seems to have been Hessia. Andreae's *Revelation of Divine Majesty*[13] was dedicated to Moritz of Hessia. In 1609 the landgrave established in Marburg a professorship of chemistry. Eglinus, supposedly the author of *The Declaration of the Brotherhood of Rosecrucians;* Croll, an enthusiastic alchemist, who wrote the *Basilica Chymica;* Michael Maier (the Rosicrucian), one of the most widely known Paracelsians; and Nollius were all at his court. In both Hessias the Rosecrucians gained ground. On this account extensive investigations were conducted at Marburg, at the University of Hessen-Kassel, at the end of the year 1619. Two teachers, Philipp Homagius and Georg Zimmermann, had disseminated pansophic thoughts for some time, had infected the pupils, and possessed heretical books ... And not only this. On December 18, 1619, they suddenly declared the *Disciplina paedagogica* to be devilish and anti-Christian, asserting that the children were offered to Moloch inasmuch as they were allowed to read the heathen authors..."

The three successive chief court preachers at Dresden must have had considerable influence on the spiritual comfort or discomfort of Schütz in his personal life. While the Protestant clergymen did not hold auricular confession, with absolution, they were confessors to the extent that they endeavored, as private advisers, to keep every Christian in proper spiritual discipline. After Polycarp Leyser's tenure (1594-1613) there followed, as a most highly problematical figure, the Australian nobleman Mathias Hoe von Hoenegg. Further on we shall speak of his notorious role in foreign politics. But the theologian in him, too, is most unedifying. Immeasurably vain, he considered his mission in life to be battling the Calvinists. In eight Assemblies (1621-29) he firmly knit together the electoral Saxon clergy who viewed themselves as a kind of supreme court in matters Lutheran. They sought

[10] Franz Strunz, *Th. Paracelsus* (1903), p. 22.
[11] *Die Fama Fraternitatis oder Entdeckung der Brüderschaft des Hochlöblichen Ordens der R(osen)C(reutzer): An die Häupter, Stände und Gelehrten Europae.*
[12] Will-Erich Peuckert, *Die Rosenkreutzer* (Jena, 1928), pp. 171 ff.
[13] *Offenbarung göttlicher Majestät.*

later to confirm their authority by means of the elector's leadership of the Protestants. To the very able syncretist of Helmstedt, Georg Calixt — whom these Saxon conservatives hated as they hated sin — they sent a threatening *Admonitio* and then a host of polemical writings. [14] In view of the difficulties surrounding the Leipzig Princes' Day of 1631 (for which Schütz had written music) Hoe von Hoenegg made slight concessions to the Reformed and also — though inwardly cold — delivered a moving memorial at the bier of Gustavus Adolphus. But in 1634 he was again most narrow-mindedly hostile to every non-Saxon variety of Lutheranism, and he remained the chief representative of the brand of theologians who, with Bible in hand, found there the formula to justify even the boldest transactions of state. [15]

O. Michaelis *(Schütz,* p. 32) paints the picture of this "truly demonic figure" in still greater detail. At twenty-two years of age Hoe was third court preacher in Dresden. At thirty-two he was first, and caused a sensation by his eloquence in the pulpit. He declared "that the Calvinistic doctrine was riddled with terrible blasphemies and both in fundamentals and other articles ran diametrically counter to the Word of God." Despite the fact that the electress saw through him, as father confessor he so dominated the elector that when the latter ventured to face Hoe of the flexible conscience, he did so only with bared head. The court preacher, originally endowed with no earthly means, piled riches upon riches, acquiring for himself three manors, while at the same time one of his colleagues at court waited in vain for the payment of a part of his salary, experienced only contempt and derision in the face of his urgent appeals that he "knew not how he could purchase for himself a pound of meat," "had no penny in his purse and was forced to carry on his difficult office with nothing but tears and sighs." [16] Hoe was curator of the electoral chapel. He officiated at Schütz's wedding and at the funeral of his wife Magdalene.

After Hoe's death (1645) the worthy Jakob Weller (of Molsdorf) succeeded him. Weller heartily supported the efforts of his contemporaries to attain a vital faith beyond the narrow orthodoxy of the old Lutherans. This is confirmed by his friendly relationship to a leader of this reform movement, the Nürnberg Saubert. Weller

---

[14] J. A. Dorner, *Gesch. der protest. Theologie* (Munich, 1867), pp. 609 and 618.

[15] Karl Holl, *Die Bedeutung des großen Krieges für das religiöse und kirchliche Leben innerhalb des deutschen Protestantismus,* 1917 *(The Significance of the Great War for the Religious and Church Life Within German Protestantism).* In his *Gesammelte Aufsätze zur Kirchengeschichte (Collected Essays on Church History),* III (1928), 312 ff.

[16] More favorable is the presentation by G. L. Zeissler, *Gesch. der sächs. Oberhofprediger* (Leipzig, 1856), pp. 50 ff. Doubtless, however, he is writing for the most part to ingratiate himself with the powers *(in usum Delphini).*

also successfully opposed the renewed wish of certain zealots who wanted to see Jakob Böhme damned as a heretic even after his death.

A commendatory introduction by Weller to Schütz's *Becker Psalter* indicates his good relations with the master. "As Weller had had a large following in Wittenberg before moving to Dresden, he now exerted a strong attraction as a popular preacher. When he preached about the 'restless clitter-clatter mill of the conscience,' his listeners were all attention. He also took seriously his pastoral duties at court and had the courage, to the horror of the court sycophants, to 'read the Levites' to Johann Georg II for his alcoholic excesses, the tendency to which he had inherited from his father[17] (O. Michaelis, loc. cit., p. 34). "Spener in his *Pia desideria* referred to the complaint made by Weller to his friends during a Regensburg Reichstag that the scholastic theology which Luther had driven out of the church had again made its entrance . . . .

"Weller's successor, the Leipzig professor, Martin Geier, stood in friendly relation with Spener . . . Geier is the author of a large number of devotional writings, which betray the influence of Joh. Arndt . . . The ethics he recommends is of an ascetic nature . . . In a sermon he preached in Meissen in the year 1666 at a meeting of the diet, he complained that disorders had entered the land on every side: every rank was trying to exalt itself above the other and to surpass it in ostentation. Geier's ideal was the reign of Theodosius the Younger, of whom it was said that his palace resembled a monastery, his capital a church."[18]

"When Weller died in 1664, the Leipzig bishop and professor, Martin Geier, accepted — although hesitatingly and unwillingly — the call to be court preacher. Geier was a peace-loving theologian who had chosen as his life motto the verse 'Blessed are the meek.' The Minister von Seckendorff bestowed high praise on him: 'In my limited experience, I can recall no preacher who at the proper occasion introduced a story or apolog in so fine a manner, with such restraint and such edification, as the splendid and very deserving Dr. Martin Geier. He knew how to appeal to his audience at court at the proper time, briefly, and, as was his custom, with simple, unaffected but meaningful and emphatic words.' When it was stated later, on his tombstone, that he had given an unusually shining example for others in his zeal, diligence, and piety, such a statement was no exaggeration. From the warmhearted appreciation which Geier bestowed on Schütz in his funeral sermon we may assume that the impressive and respected personality of the vener-

---

[17] This story in detail in Zeissler, pp. 67 ff.
[18] H. Leube, *Die Reformideen in der deutschen lutherischen Kirche zur Zeit der Orthodoxie* (Leipzig, 1924), pp. 61 ff.

able master had made a strong impression on him too. Geier's conscience was so
acute that he declined the elector's offer of a small garden, with a considerable
sum for its upkeep. He feared lest his official duties might be supplemented by
domestic ones. Geier also wrote hymns in which the language of devout piety
prevails." (O. Michaelis, p. 35.)

So Schütz's long life leads, at least when seen from without, from the happy
bloom of the high Renaissance to the transitory and sepulchral atmosphere of the
middle baroque. Germany, too, experienced to a certain measure what Britain
went through in the time between Shakespeare and Milton: the transition from
"Merrie old England" to Quakerism and Puritanism. For Schütz, too, the transition was to become a kind of *via purgatoria*, a way of purification and of self-
collection, a transition from self-glorifying artistry to voluntary devotion toward
the community. One can in no wise fathom this musical phenomenon, consisting
of such dissimilar elements and characterized much more by dynamic change than
by static conditions, by means of such simple equations as those so recently
popular: "Schütz = Old Netherlands singableness = community = we," in which
virtually every equality sign conceals a logically fallacious conclusion.

Did Schütz step into a Renaissance world? Here a preliminary problem confronts us. By straining a point one could perhaps speak of a Renaissance "world"
in Italy, where the romantic imagination of a rebirth of antiquity could be conceived in many respects as a popular eruption of the south against the ultra-
montane Gothicism of a fading German overlordship. In Germany, however, the
situation with regard to the Renaissance was almost the very opposite. For here,
to a wide extent, the Renaissance became merely the culture of the upper class,
artificially superimposed on the persisting Gothic-Nordic sentiment of the nation
as a whole. This superimposed Renaissance could maintain itself with some degree of purity only for a few generations — indeed, strictly speaking, through
barely six decades (1550 to 1610). For immediately after the turn of the century
this patrician humanism became amalgamated with, or, more accurately, was led
back to, the northern feeling for form and structure, and thus was created the style
of the German baroque. Perhaps nothing shows so clearly this half-foreign Renaissance — revealed from the point of view of architecture — as the Torgau
castle Hartenfels in which in 1627, with Schütz's *Dafne*, the first North German
opera was produced. In these pine forests, not far distant from where, a short time
before, the nailed-up money chest of the indulgence preacher Tetzel was filched,
Konrad Krebs, 1533-37, built the fantastic Wendelstein, which, despite the con-
ciliatory influence of Dessau and Meissen, gives the general impression that those

who planned it aimed to make of the "Town of the Heavy Beer" a second Ferrara!
And yet, just as almost every historical event has its inner compulsion and, on further
view, its justification, in its salutary effects, so ultimately in this case also. For even
if the foreign influence had become all too great at the time, nevertheless a certain
absorption and participation gave rise to a beneficial polishing of domestic crudity
and to a curtailment of excesses. The finely chiseled intimacy of a Hassler Italian-
German *canzonetta,* such as *Mein g'müt ist mir verwirret,* of 1601, placed beside
a corresponding small, German, ornamented building of those years, reveals a
delicacy and intimacy on the part of the German citizenry, of which the little
tavern songs and other popular ballads *(Bergreyen)* of the sixteenth century as yet
knew little. And it is no mere coincidence that in the very year, 1624, when Scheidt's
Tabulatura nova appeared, there was also published Opitz' *Buch von der teutschen
Poeterey.* To be sure, one may say that this book, by crowding out the doggerel
verse and by raising the banner of the Alexandrine verse, also opened the way for
the stuffy, artificial poetry of the seventeenth century. But, on the other hand, it
will become evident when we discuss Opitz' madrigals as texts for Schütz's compositions, that Opitz' work, like Scheidt's organ book with its Italian tendencies,
also ushered in very positive artistic values. Moreover, as justification for Opitz'
historical necessity, the "Bober Swan"[19] had both predecessors and contemporaries.
Their works were collected by J. W. Zincgref in 1624 with the programmatic and
patriotic foreword of one of the contributors:[20]

> Now, German Muse, step forth
> And boldly let thy tongue resound;
> For wherefore shouldst thou be afraid
> To sing in thine own mother tongue?
> Thinks one Germania has no wit?
> Should, then, the glory of the Greeks
> Or weighty might of Rome
> Alone the poet's treasure win?

So the end of the Middle Ages seemed to have been definitely announced. And
yet, despite such "moderns," the witch trials, the rack, the survivals from knight-
hood in the opera-related tournament ballets, and many other old customs continued
for a long time. It is enough to recall that dwarfs, fools, and harlequins, as favorites
of the electoral family, still fluttered about the Dresden court Kapellmeister Schütz[21]
and that his appointments with royalty were interspersed with bloody animal
hunts. It was a time of the most diverse transitions, with all their contradictions,

---

[19] Opitz.
[20] Wolfg. Stammler, *Von der Mystik zum Barock* (1927), p. 455.
[21] M. Fürstenau, *Zur Geschichte der Musik und des Theaters,* I, 67.

disorganizations, and birth pangs. The times also explain the contradictory elements in Schütz's tonal language: Gregorianism and psalmody-fauxbourdon side by side with polyphonic counterpoint, chordal harmony with Florentine monody and old German lied style — but all forced into a common spiritual mold by his robust personality.

While for the ordinary man of the late Gothic period (to which, in many respects, Luther's days must still be reckoned) the joyfully humble submission to church and community was a self-evident fact and one which directed the closely knit mass toward God, it must not be assumed that the Renaissance man of the German nation is a Borgia type. He is much more like Dürer's "Jerome in the Shrine," [22] a comfortable, passionless humanist browsing over his books, or a playful aesthete enjoying the new and rich ornamentation of patrician life. This peaceful lover of antiquity was doubtless a Greek or Roman *(Heide)* only to a modest degree. He was first, like Erasmus, devoted to the old church; then, like Melanchthon, he became a Protestant, even though he was fond of prating about Jupiter and Apollo. But with the advancing seventeenth century those "little gods" declined, and the classical witers became markedly more ecclesiastical. This Christianization of Greek and Roman authors at the time of the transition from Renaissance to baroque is clearly evinced in the title of M. Praetorius' *Musae Sioniae.* He himself elucidates it in the foreword to the seventh part of this work: "In order, however, that the author may not be viewed by devout hearts as having profaned and misused in heathen poems these spiritual things which belong to the honor of God and the service of his church, he desired to name his Muses and Graces, not according to Pindus and Parnassus but according to the holy and glorious Mount Zion on which the eternal, great, and highest God is praised and honored in many ways with fresh and joyful spirit by his dear angels, who then are the true, rightful, and wisest Muses and Graces." [23]

The baroque man is, therefore, again surcharged with dynamic resolution but is now under the pressure and compulsion which bring the individual man to worth and expressiveness. [24] "One seeks not common endeavor with the community but to use the latter as a sounding board for one's own activities." [25] For Schütz

---

[22] *Hieronymus im Gehäus.*
[23] W. Gurlitt, *M. Praetorius* (1920), unpublished portion.
[24] Fr. Blume, *Das monodische Prinzip in der protestantischen Kirchenmusik* (Leipzig, 1925); by the same author, *Heinrich Schütz in den geistigen Strömungen seiner Zeit (Musik u. Kirche,* II, 6).
[25] *Nicht das gemeinschaftliche Streben sucht man, sondern die Resonanz.* Willi Flemming, *Die Auffassung des Menschen im 17. Jahrhundert (Deutsche Vierteljahresschrift f. Literaturwissenschaft u. Geistesgeschichte,* VI, 1928), pp. 403 ff.

this transition from the world of the Renaissance to that of the baroque did not result, to be sure, in a break in his personality; but it did create a constant inner tension. This, however, made of him, not a plaintive survivor of the aristocracy of the "good old times" but, on the contrary, one of the greatest instigators of this strong, new, and restless art life. After a period of static expectancy Schütz became its most dynamic and vehement conqueror — who would create, as the result of this irrepressible inner urge to proclaim (Predigerdrang), his own peculiar forms of expression. It was fortunate that Schütz, aroused to a conciousness of his ego, did not have to expend himself, Narcissuslike, in feverish soliloquy. On the contrary, he found everywhere in the steadily and conservatively developing "folk" of his community a powerful echoing chorus. To be sure, they are no longer the glorious people of the battle days of Worms and of Augsburg, resembling a mighty host of Dürer apostles. They are now a more uniform group, greatly weakened individually, but one in which the few real leaders stand out all the more vividly.

Thus in his middle period Schütz blends, as later only Bach did, individual with group feeling in the most unusual and yet the most inevitable manner, until his old age once more led him into introspective Faustian solitude. This, however, was a solitude very different from, and deeper than, that which produced the new tonal articulation of the storm-and-stress period between 1605 and 1615 which he had passed through surrounded by a patricianism that practiced the cult of the embellishments of antiquity. We must return to this later on.

The desire for these decorative embellishments which, about in 1600, the brief episode of the pleasant Renaissance brought into German patrician life before the fury of the war led to an early blossoming of student music. This music is represented by such collections as Johs. Jeep's *Studentengärtlein* (I, 1607; II, 1613), H. Dedekind's *Studentenlust* (1613), Paul Rivander's *Studentenfreud* (1621), Erasmus Widmann's *Studentenmut* (1622), J. H. Schein's *Studentenschmaus* (1626), H. Dedekind's *Studentenleben* (Erfurt, 1627), and Daniel Friderici's *Hilarodicon* (1632). Through the musicianship of the cantors and the young theologians the general practice of music was greatly enhanced by means of the church choirs — so much so that Schütz's friend, J. H. Schein, recently appointed cantor at St. Thomas, proudly ventured to say in the preface to his *Banchetto Musicale* (1617): "By the grace of God and the reflective and diligent cultivation of distinguished masters, both foreign and domestic, the noble art of music has risen today to such excellence and height that one must doubt whether it can advance still further."

Let us also hear M. Praetorius in the preface to his *Polyhymnia caduceatrix et panegyrica* (1619), which contains the festival compositions he had conducted a short time before in Dresden, with Schütz as assistant Kapellmeister or organist:

> "God's special goodness is greatly to be thanked in that against the mighty lack and dis-
> paragement of art which the powerful devil of court and church, as a haughty prophet of
> gloom and moroseness and an enemy of joy, has aroused in these later days there have never-
> theless been raised up, through the stronger spirit of our Prince and Ruler of life, Christ,
> valiant heroes and potentates, kindly disposed and inclined to music with special affection,
> sound understanding, and high judgment. This has been manifested not only in their own
> persons. They have had their youth instructed and educated in music on instruments as
> thoroughly as if they were to devote their whole lives to music, seeking to become musicians
> of the first rank, who would support themselves solely by means of this profession. Thus in
> recent times a praiseworthy, Christian, high and mighty potentate ... remarked that he was
> of the opinion that no ruler could govern his people and his country well or that anyone could
> fruitfully gain and accomplish anything without musical understanding."

From the time of Luther's joyous church and domestic music through that of the
enmity against cantors and cantatas in the period of enlightenment there has
existed an ignoble hostilily toward music which indeed makes the history of evangelical church music during this time appear as a single protracted period of liturgical decadence. Despite Eccard, Schütz, and Bach such hostility often raised its
insolent head and even before the Thirty Years' War had to be roughly laid low —
so much so that the organist Elias Herlitz from Stralsund, an admirer and imitator
of the dramas of Duke Heinrich Julius of Brunswick (1564-1613) felt compelled
to write a satirical comedy in the year 1606, *Musicomastix*, on the subject of the
despiser of music.[26] Perhaps the twenty-one-year-old Schütz, who often saw the
English comedians in the Kassel Ottoneum, heard vague reports about this comedy.
Nevertheless, florid counterpoint flourished so generally that Michael Altenburg
could say in the year 1620: "Let one only consider how music is thriving everywhere. There is scarcely a little village, especially in Thüringia, in which both
vocal and instrumental music does not flourish and prosper. If there is no organ,
then vocal music is ornamented and adorned with at least five or six strings, something hardly known before this even in the cities."

Four war years, however, sufficed to demolish this picture almost completely
and to make exceptional in Germany the support and patronage of music by
municipalities and princes. The difficult life of the German musicians during the
thirty bloody years I have already pictured in my *Geschichte der deutschen Musik*.[27]
Other witnesses will testify to it further on in these pages. Burckhart Grossmann, of Jena, has presented the situation vividly in the preface to his collection
of the settings of the 116th Psalm (1623), to which Schütz made a significant contribution. Here he shows very clearly that the sudden callousness to the blessings

---

[26] Contents in the unpublished part of W. Gurlitt's *Michael Praetorius*.
[27] *History of German Music*, Vol. 2, ch. 1.

of music, which, of course, became almost catastrophic for Schütz in Dresden, was really the result of a long creeping dissoluteness of the spirit and a sluggishness of the heart, and that this constantly added new fuel to the thirty-year holocaust.

"There is scarcely a state, social or professional rank, community, or circle (Collegium) where one can still find genuine love, confidence, and unity. The disturber of the peace, the devil, turns all love to hatred . . . . In these recent times the wicked enemy strives for nothing so much as to extirpate completely the love between God and man, to supplant the beautiful harmony of the Holy Roman Empire with discord, and to burst the bonds of all fidelity, love, and unity. Candor and affection on the part of one toward another are despised and ridiculed among the politicians. Ostentation, dissimulation, and bombast now supplant genuine love, uprightness, and sincerity. It all reminds one of the relation of gilded to genuine coin. Noble music and its cultivators are equally scarce and despised. The devil is as hostile to them as he is to love. For although music as an art at all times won for itself gratitude, praise, and adherents, who learned the art and composed spiritual songs, this beautiful art also had its Midases and asses' heads. But I shall not do them the honor to name them lest such mention should increase their reputation with those of their kind. Indeed, noble music is particularly hated today, and that, too, among such as should especially cultivate it and preserve it to the glory of God. Many of these esteem it so little that they derive more pleasure, eloquence, and usefulness from the yelping of dogs, the bellowing of bulls, and the braying of asses than from the most beautiful Orphic strains, or from the well-ordered heavenly choir of our late blessed Michael Praetorius. Aforetime one attributed such contempt and insolence toward this art to ignorance, according to the saying: 'None hate art but the ignorant,'[28] and, as Frosch-meusseler's nightingale complains:

> Art suffers its greatest disgrace
> When it serves him who is unworthy of it.

But now the hellish nightowl with its ululations has brought it about, to the disgrace of God and His heavenly gift, that the learned as well as the unlearned, and indeed frequently the very ones who were raised from the dust by and for the sake of music and placed beside princes, either supress and persecute it or at least are ashamed of it. And in this connection I cannot forget Saul's spear which he, when the devil possessed and troubled him, hurled at David with such violence that it remained stuck in the wall while David was endeavoring to banish the devil with lovely music on his harp.

"For although Saul intended the spear for the body of David, Satan intended with this spear the destruction of the beautiful work of God through music. And even to the present day he has not allowed this spear to rust but uses it to pierce the art of music, to ruin with it all the choirs or chapels; and he has equipped countless numbers with it in order to have his bloody war trumpets advance to the glory of Mars.

"For, first of all, we find Saul's spear at court and especially in the chamber of the ex-chequer, barring the way to music, singers, and musicians when they approach, or driving them away, so that they must flee as David fled; or, possibly, as for the time being one must tolerate a few on account of the good favor of the nobility, until they take their departure before the hurling of the spear, one cuts their bread with Saul's spear into such small bits that they almost starve to death, so that of many a one it can be said, as I often heard from the lips of an old singer: 'Music benefits well, but nourishes badly.' Or its best compensation is and remains words, hopes, vain promises. Thus, according to Plutarch, Dionysius, King of Sicily, treated a very gifted lutenist. After long, diligent service the king rewarded the lutenist upon his demand for compensation with the words: 'You have already received your reward from me. I have given you pleasure in return for pleasure, for I have not delighted you less with hope than you have delighted me with your music.'

"Who would imagine that Saul's spear is also to be found in church and the house of God — indeed, as frequently there as elsewhere? I pass by the fact that in some towns and

---

[28] Ars non habet osorem nisi ignorantem.

places where music formerly flourished and one praised God on Sundays and festival days with sixteen and more voices in two, three, or more choirs, one can now only engage an old unaccompanied quartet; that cantors and organists, for whom the keys stick and the bellows freeze, complain and say: 'What else is the cause but that the trustees of the church property or the church fathers flourish and bear Saul's spear of ignorance and contempt, and hate music as they hate poison?' Indeed, at times they even seize on the spear of Judas with the other hand and pocket or apply elsewhere that which should be devoted to the choir, the instruction of little boys, the support of poor pupils, or the purchase of music books and instruments, appropriating even that which of old God-fearing Christian people, who before and after a good sermon had liked to hear good music and had experienced genuine pleasure and reverence in this way, had bequeathed. And these harpies not only use Saul's spear assiduously and diligently in the manner indicated in their contempt for, and their complete spearing of, noble music; they even use it when seeming to dispense with it a little.

"For, thirdly, they concede it to those schools, to those preceptors and cantors who rather swallow *(Schlingen)* or gulp than sing *(Singen)*, who stand before the keg *(Vass)* rather than before the bass *(Bass)*. And here this spear effects, not contempt but scarcity of music *(raritatem Musicae)*, and indeed wishes to cut the throat of music, so that in future no boy will learn to sing. Thus on all sides we hear the complaint that there is a lack of sopranos, for which, however, there is no other reason than that the cantors use the spear of Saul instead of the baton. For if the poor village sacristans did as is done today in Thuringia, where the peasant servants and youth on Sundays and festival days take their places at the choir desks after following the plow during the entire week, and both sing and play and far surpass many a quill hound in skill even if not in pronunciation; and if the diligent schoolmasters in the villages instruct their boys and from time to time send certain ones to the town schools, then the distinguished cantors in the town would have to sing choral (Gregorian chant) or settings for equal voices *(ad aequales)*.

"Fourthly, Saul's spear is also extensively found in printing establishments in order that noble music may not gain strength, or that one or another musical composition to the praise and glory of God may not see the light of day, since no one will devote himself to notes, rests, lines, and other characters necessary hereto, and among ten printer's journeymen scarcely one can be found who has learned how to set or print such things or has a desire to learn this. Such persons commonly excuse themselves on the basis of scarcity *(ex hoc capite raritatis)*, that is, that musical works are seldom called for.

"Fifthly, no peasant familiar with the Thuringian practice mentioned above will believe me that in distinguished universities one is more ashamed of music than of Saul's spear, and that in numerous places it appears as though one wished to weed out music altogether from among its six sisters and no longer wished to acknowledge it as belonging to the liberal arts. This is indeed the actual state of affairs. Formerly honorable and art-loving students in our universities, and among them some from the aristocracy, conducted *collegia musica* at times and places of recreation. They not only practiced music and edified themselves thereby but on festal occasions also waited on distinguished rectors and preceptors with instrumental music and honored them with it. They also welcomed with such music distinguished visitors on their arrival, as a result of which such occasions and places became widely and honorably known. Now they are supplanted by bagpipe players and performers on the shalmey, or at best by three fiddlers who play three octaves apart and occasionally play a measure or two in 'horsefifths' *(Rossquinten)*. They play no better than they have learned in their trade or than is demanded by the musical capacity of those for whom they are playing. Moreover, aforetimes in various places the professors objected to advancing servants and teachers and to commending aristocratic students who were not skilled in, and devoted to, music. And many a distinguished doctor took joy and pleasure in adding his voice at intimate collegiate get-togethers, when they assisted in singing a fine motet to the glory of God. Indeed, many a famous prince did not consider himself superior to such participation. I well recall this in the case of my late blessed prince and lord, Johansen, Duke of Saxony, in whose chapel I sang as a choir boy. Landgrave Moritz of Hessia is known far and wide for his gracious and praiseworthy devotion to music, his skill, his theoretical knowledge, and his practical proficiency, as well as for the musical establishment and performances at his court. As a third example I would to God one might know throughout the entire Holy Roman Empire as little about hostile armies, weapons, spears, and guns as one can see Saul's spear associated with His Excellency, the noble lord, Heinrich the Younger, and now also the Elder, Lord Reuss of Geraw, Graitz, Schlaitz, and Lobenstein, etc., my very gracious lord. His Grace has such affection for, and devotion to, music that I can truthfully say from personal experience in his church, school, and at his court that, next to God's Word and His Grace's beloved wife and children, His Grace knows nothing in the world more pleasing than music. Indeed, with him is music's true asylum. The affection and guidance which the revered Herr Reuss has so graciously shown to music and musicians speaks for itself. And this when many a learned man who associated a bit freely with music and musicans might well have feared the shipwreck of his dignity and respect, or that he might become despised, as happened to David when Michal espied him through the window. All this Saul's spear can indeed bring to pass against noble music."

Similarly Michael Lohr, cantor at the Holy Cross Church in Dresden from 1625 to 1654, says in *Ander Teil Neuer teutscher und lateinischer Kirchengesänge Konzerten (Second Part of the New German and Latin Church Concerti)*, of 1637: "Today people are found in Christendom who not only dislike both vocal and instrumental music but despise it with all kinds of contemptuous words; indeed, there are even those who, especially in these warlike days, would rather hear the thunders of the cannon and the crack of muskets, and who cannot even endure music in connection with the church service."

Thus, though we see all the good fairies of artistic inspiration placing their rose garlands on Schütz's cradle, wicked enchantresses, who were able to summon the apocalyptic Furies, seemed to stand alongside. But as Dürer's knight advanced on his way, determined and unperturbed, between death and devil, so, too, the warrior Schütz marches on without wavering until the genii of peace finally again crown the head of the sage, but now with the laurel of austerity.

Family and Youth in Weissenfels

Recent researches among the archives have shown that what Martin Geier, the Dresden court preacher, said in his memorial to Schütz in 1672 about a Thuringian grandfather, "Albrecht" Schütz,[1] was erroneous.[2] As a matter of fact, the master is descended from Thuringian stock only on his mother's side. His paternal forebears were from Chemnitz in Saxony. These relationships and the whole abundantly ramified family history are extensively clarified in the records of the "Schütz legacy" found there.

In the year 1569 Ulrich (III) Schütz, born in Chemnitz in 1513, established, when he was imperial secretary at Saragossa, a foundation amounting (at that time) to 4,000 gulden, the annual interest on which — 200 gulden — was to be awarded, upon application, as a wedding gift to the female descendants of his father, Hieronymus, burgomaster of Chemnitz, or of the latter's brothers. The legacy was administered by the council of Chemnitz under the supervision of electoral "commissars." Heinrich Schütz would have been pleased if he could have obtained the foundation in 1625, in 1637, and especially in 1648 for the marriage of his daughter Euphrosyne to the assistant judge, Dr. jur. Christof Pincker, in Leipzig. But as a result of the devastation of the Thirty Years' War the finances of Chemnitz had become so greatly impaired that the money was not obtainable despite numerous applications on the part of the Court Kapellmeister to both the town council and the elector. Finally, in 1657, nothing remained for the magistracy to do at the insistence of the elector but, in place of the capital which had melted away, to pledge the "New Mill" to Schütz's son-in-law as trustee for his little daughter

---

[1] "The precious Work, / from Ps. 119, v. 54: / Thy statutes have been my songs in the house of my pilgrimage; / delivered by the Electoral Saxon First Court-Preacher / Martino Geiero, D. / / Dresden / on the occasion of the well-attended funeral of the noble, esteemed, learned / Herr Heinrich Schütz / Electoral Saxon senior Capellmeister, / who departed this life here in Dresden, at peace with his Redeemer / in his 88th year, on the 6th of November of this year, 1672, / and entered his resting-place on the 17th in the Lieb Frauen-Kirche. / Published by Andr. Löffler in Dresden . . . . /" Not paged; with the elegy it embraces 12 sheets. The biography occupies only six leaves. Copies in Stolberg and in Dresden; a free extract by Beyer in *MfM*, 1875, pp. 171 ff., is scarcely usable. Facsimile in the Bärenreiter-Verlag, Kassel.

[2] Dr. Uhle in *Mitteilungen des Vereins für Chemnitzer Geschichte*, XXVII (1929-30): *Zur Lebensgeschichte des Tonschöpfers Heinrich Schütz (The Life History of the Composer Heinrich Schütz)*. The letters of the master taken from here (without giving this source) are also in the appendix of the collection of E. H. Müller (Bosse).

Gertraud Euphrosyne. This mill Dr. Pincker sold in 1670 to a citizen of Chemnitz by the name of Crusius, the town not being able to redeem it.

We owe our detailed knowledge of the Schütz family in Chemnitz to the legal proceedings relating to the legacy. The complicated relationships may be presented here in the form of a genealogical tree stemming from the ancestor Ulrich (I) Schütz. From this we note the descent of the master from a Christof (II) the Younger — in Gera, Köstritz, and Weissenfels — who ca. 1578, as Gera town clerk, married Euphrosyne, the daughter of the later Gera burgomaster Bieger (Piegert, Berger) and his wife Dorothea, nee Schreiber, from Gera. Christof Schütz's name still adorns, with the date 1616, the bay of the Weissenfels inn *Zum Schützen,* which he rebuilt at the time. His father, Christof (I) the Elder, had been an official substitute administrator[3] in Marienberg. And his father, the great-grandfather of the composer, was Ulrich (II) Schütz the Younger, "from Erdmannsdorf," an uncle of the founder of the legacy in Saragossa. Ulrich (II) was a son of Ulrich (I) Schütz, the Chemnitz burgomaster and large-scale contractor.[4] Thus it was a patrician family, and many of the daughters married into property and court nobility. As the first names — taken in the next generation almost invariably from parents,

---

[3] *Amtsverwalter.*

[4] O. Michaelis gives the following account of the family (*H. Schütz,* 1935, p. 7): "The Schütz family comes from Franconia. As early as 1409 it belonged to the aristocracy of Nürnberg. . . . . In 1470 a certain Ulrich Schütz acquired citizenship in Chemnitz, while his brother Hans died in Nürnberg in 1507. A Balthasar Schütz had preceded him to Chemnitz. Ulrich Schütz advanced from success to success. After the death of his father-in-law, the Chemnitz councilor Nikel Tyle, who had played a prominent role in the economic life of the Saxon town, he managed the *Saiger-hütte* near Chemnitz with a brother-in-law. In 1484 he was a member of the town council. In 1486 and again in 1498 the council showed its confidence by appointing him chief burgomaster. The conditions of the time offered his enterprising spirit a rich field of activity. Great advances were made in opening up the mining industry of the Erzgebirge. Silver, copper, tin, and other metals were discovered in new places." His marriage to the daughter of Nikel Tyle also enhanced his prosperity, and at the death of his father-in-law he inherited considerable mining property. In 1477 he erected a new hammer factory and, in addition, acquired mills, dye plants, and other property. His share in the mining industry reached as far as the Harz. After the early death of his wife Ulrich Schütz married a second time, and again riches were added to riches. Magdalene von Erdmannsdorf brought him control of the family property of Erdmannsdorf near Chemnitz. As burgomaster he became specially interested in the building development of Chemnitz. A Franciscan monastery was erected chiefly through the means of the family Schütz. The Schützes were accounted "rich and apostolic men." The privilege of being buried in the monastic enclave, now considered the most aristocratic burial place, was given to them in writing. . . . The confirmation of the Schütz coat of arms in 1486 for the brothers Ulrich and Hans by the Emperor Frederic III, may have been associated with the monastic burial privilege. But doubtless the family used the coat of arms before this imperial confirmation. A collateral line of the family was elevated to the hereditary nobility in 1539 by Emperor Charles V. His family still exists. "The eldest of the now noble family, Hieronymus von Schütz, who died in 1552, had voluntarily surrendered his Chemnitz burgomastership in 1544. He was an opponent of the Reformation, but he bowed to the superior power of its adherents. With regard to him the story was current that he declared in the Chemnitz council: 'One should bar the door against the new idea, for it

uncles and aunts — there must have been much association with family and friends in the Schütz clan. From Schütz's relationship as cousin to Heinrich Albert, and from that to the Colanders in Weissenfels and to his Dresden court organist Christof Kittel, one might suppose that the Schützes were a musical family. These relationships, however, were all by marriage.

According to Uhle, our master received his first name Heinrich from the Saxon duke with that name who was lord of Freiberg and Wolkenstein. We should also note an almost exactly contemporaneous Weissenfels nephew, Heinrich Schütz, whose name has given rise to considerable confusion with regard to the composer. This nephew, Heinrich Schütz, was the son of Mathes Schütz, a half-brother of the composer. Mathes was the son of Christof II by his first marriage (1575) with Margarethe Weidemann from Gera. Mathes was tax collector in Sachsenburg, as was his older brother Johann. Heinrich, Mathes' son, died in Weissenfels in 1621.

Christof (II), the master's father, appears for the first time in a petition of his father, Christof (I), in 1576 to the Chemnitz council for a grant of assistance from the foundation established by Ulrich (I) Schütz. In this petition he relates that his son, Christof (II), was in Neudulpach, working with the Bautzen court judge and

---

would bring no good'." Counselor Dr. E. Reinhardt (Berlin) is preparing a work of several volumes on the Schütz family and their mercantile relations (1430-1600), as well as an exhaustive work on Schütz's youngest brother, Benjamin (1596-1666), and his position with regard to the Erfurt revolution of 1664-65.

According to new researches by Counselor (Justice) Dr. Reinhardt (Berlin), Christof (II) Schütz, on coming to Weissenfels, first lived in a house at the corner of the *Judengasse*. He sold this in 1613. At present it is not yet clear when he took over the inn which in 1605 was still called *Zur Sackpfeife* (The Bagpipe) and was first designated in the records of 1616 as "now called *zum Schützen*". According to an early record of 1616, he paid the widow of the preceding owner, Schaller — later Frau Crator — her last portion of the property remittance, the customary widow's quarter, namely, 500 gulden. Inasmuch as the landgrave had spent the night in *Zum Schützen* as early as 1596 and Christof already possessed the extensive *Uechtritz* real estate in this year, he doubtless owned the inn in the *Nicolaistrasse* at this time. The following is a list of the proprietors:

    1) About 1544 the unknown possessor of a coat of arms with birds.
    2) A certain Ziegenhorn. The coat of arms at the time was a donkey playing a bagpipe. The inn was called "The Golden Donkey".
    3) Schaller, to 1596(?): "The Bagpipe".
    4) Christof Schütz: 1616, *Zum Schützen*.
    5) Since 1630 the son of the former, Christof (III) Schütz.

Concerning the house of Heinrich Schütz and Justina Thörmer in the "Zeitz quarter" see the chapter "Late Period in Weissenfels and Dresden" (p. 176).

Albrecht Schütz, Christof's older brother, must have been very well to do. Through his first or second wife he owned the *Goldener Kranich* ("Golden Crane") in Köstritz; in addition, a farm *(Bauerngut)* in Weissenfels and two houses, one of them the inn *Zum goldenen Ring* ("The Golden Ring"), with which, hewever, Heinrich Schütz, contrary to local opinion, had nothing to do.

imperial counselor, Georg von Berbissdorff (incidentally a relative also entitled to claim the legacy), who wanted to assist Christof (II) to a position in the imperial chancellery. As apparently nothing came of this plan, Christof II sought his fortune in Gera, and then, after a second marriage, moved from there to Köstritz as manager and lessee of the inn "The Golden Crane". In 1591 he moved to Weissenfels, where he fell heir to the positions of his brother Albrecht. As the genealogical table indicates, there were born to him and his wife, Euphrosyne Bieger,[5] at least six sons, of whom Christof was the eldest. There followed Georg, Heinrich, Christian, Benjamin (the distinguished government officer at Erfurt),[6] and Valentin, who fell in a duel in early life. There were also three daughters. As burgomaster of Weissenfels, husbandman, and innkeeper, Christof II must have attained to considerable means. This is proved not only by his stately house with the beautiful Renaissance bay, which later, when Schütz, in Dresden, was approaching fifty, lodged Wallenstein and Gustav Adolf, but also by the inventory documents at Weissenfels.[7] The inn in the *Nikolaistrasse*, which is reached through the *Grosse Kalandstrasse* (a name itself suggestive of music), bears the date 1544 and was called, before the Schütz family took it over, the inn *Zur Sackpfeife* ("The Bagpipe"). Unless this was merely intended as a house designation, the inn may originally have been a musicians' tavern. Later we shall have occasion to speak about the home the master lived in when he was an old man.

Actually, the Albrecht Schütz, whom Geier thought to be Schütz's grandfather, lived in Weissenfels. In 1578 he was a highly respected member of the town council. He died in 1590. Therefore the migration of Christof II from Köstritz to Weissenfels in the following year is actually connected with his death. For Albrecht was the older brother of Christof II, who had leased "The Golden Crane" in Köstritz to the latter. Albrecht left the Köstritz inn to his son Andreas and his Weissenfels inn, *Zum goldenen Ring* (The Golden Ring"), to his son Christof III. Christof II became guardian of the children of his brother Albrecht.

---

[5] Her younger sister, Justina, married to the Lohenstein magistrate Johann Albert of Gera, was the mother of the composer Heinrich Albert. This strengthens the surmise that Schütz's musical talent was inherited from his mother, while the inclination toward law came from the father.

[6] He studied in Leipzig in 1610 and 1617; the eldest, Johann, there also, in 1591; the brother, Christof, in 1608 (a like-named Weissenfelser in 1591); Georg in 1599; Henr. *Leucopetraeus* in 1602 and 1617; Valerius in 1610. Schütz's brother, Christof III, took over the inn. It has not been determined when this inn passed out of the family.

[7] Arno Werner, *Städtische und fürstliche Musikpflege in Weissenfels bis zum Ende des 18.Jahrh.* (*The Cultivation of Music in Town and Court in Weissenfels to the End of the 18th Century),* (B & H, 1911), pp. 44 ff. and 149 f. Further, above all, E. Reinhardt.

Ph. Spitta has pointed out that the birthday of the composer is not entirely certain.[8] According to the biography appended to the funeral sermon, Schütz was born in Köstritz on October 8, 1585, at seven o'clock in the evening — the astrologers required such precision — and was baptized, according to the church record, on October 9. Schütz himself, however, in a memorandum of January 14, 1651, to Elector Johann George I, mentions the day of St. Burkhard as his birthday — which would be October 14. There is now a memorial plaque on the house where he was born.[9] For the five children he brought with him from Köstritz in 1591 Christof II engaged a tutor in Weissenfels, the Hofmeister Michael N. The tutor died in 1594 and surely must have had a successor, as Heinrich did not leave Weissenfels until 1599. In his funeral sermon of 1672 Martin Geier refers to the matter as follows:

"Much more to be praised, however, is the fact that the Kapellmeister's honored parents in their Christian conscientiousness, seeking, above all, for their newborn son the Kingdom of God and that he might become its undoubted heir, presented him to our sole Redeemer Jesus Christ in Holy Baptism on the following ninth of the same month, through which rite he was endowed through the power of the blood of Christ with the high merit of his Savior and was received into God's family with the name of Heinrich. This blessed beginning of the Christian life the honored parents faithfully furthered through God-fearing education and timely instruction in the knowledge of God. And they sought eagerly how with increasing strength he might walk in the fear of God, might grow up to be a good Christian, and might attain to the real gifts and blessings of a gracious and lovable man. Wherefore, then, after his grandfather, Herr Albrecht Schütze, esteemed council chamberlain in Weissenfels, had died in 1591, according to God's providence, and the Kapellmeister's father, as heir to the property left behind, had to move to Weissenfels, he had Heinrich as well as his other children diligently instructed there, not only according to the well-laid foundation in godliness, in pursuit of virtuous conduct, a quiet life, and honorable manners but also in the proper sciences and languages, and indeed in higher studies; and he did this not only through private instructors but also through the instruction of other thoroughly learned men."

A promissory note of 1603 (in A. Werner) tells of the growing prosperity of Christof II: "An honorable and wise council here had, after due deliberation,

---

[8] *Musikgeschichtliche Aufsätze*, 1894, p. 4 *(Essays in Musical History).* According to the convincing proof presented by Othmar Wessely: *Zur Frage nach dem Geburtstag von H. Schütz (On the Question as to the Birthday of H. Schütz), Österr. Akad. d. W. phil.-hist. Anzeiger,* 1953 So. II, No. 15, the master was born on Oct. 4, old style (Julian calendar), which is Oct. 14, new style (Gregorian calendar), the day of St. Burkhard.

[9] See Plate I.

allowed me to purchase some property of the Uichteritz feudal estate, for which, God be thanked, I paid forthwith, with the exception of 1,000 gulden which were allowed me for six years free of interest on account of feudal service, on condition that I would at all times be willing and prepared, when commanded, to fulfill my feudal service, as is fitting and required . . . ."

The feeling of self-satisfaction expressed in this document makes it clear why the parents were reluctant to allow their son Heinrich to go to Kassel and later on to allow him to interrupt his Marburg studies in favor of a musical career. It also explains how it was almost a matter of course for his father to permit his son to continue his studies in Venice at his expense when the allowance of the land-grave had been exhausted. The father also doubtless bore the greater part of the expense of publishing *Op. 1*, the *Italian Madrigals*.

Heinrich Schütz remained in contact with the townspeople of Weissenfels in later years. In 1616 the Weissenfelsers paid for the organ lessons which another of their native sons, Antonius Colander, had with Schütz in Dresden. In 1619 they sent the master as a marriage gift 316 groschen and a goblet for the *Psalms of David*, a copy of which he had sent them. When in 1621 the town fathers had to conduct a trial in Dresden, their representatives with their entourage lodged and boarded with the recently married *Hofkapellmeister* for a number of weeks after March 1, for which hospitality Schütz received a compensation of 266 gulden. His father and a chamberlain visited him during the same fall, for which he received another eighty-seven gulden. For the wedding of Schütz's daughter Euphrosyne, in 1648, the Weissenfels council sent eleven gulden, nine groschen. On the oc-casion of Euphrosyne's death in 1655 a number of Weissenfelsers, among them Rector Andreas Albinus and the superintendent Lehmann, sent obituary poems. To be sure, as the result of deaths, the relationships became fewer. It was not Schütz's sister Dorothea who, as A. Werner assumed, died in 1620. This must have been one of the other Schützes, since she, according to Schütz's report to the au-thorities in charge of the legacy in Chemnitz, had married Simon Erfurt in Weissenfels in 1633. On October 9, 1631, Schütz lost his father. In 1635 he lost his mother, and in 1637 his brother George, who had become chief legal counsel in Leipzig and was counted among the "famous" citizens of Weissenfels. It is not likely, as has been surmised, that the composer's own brother-in-law, when he wrote his panegyrics in 1673 on the famous citizens of Weissenfels, omitted the master because of a lack of understanding of his work. It is more likely that he considered him a citizen of Köstritz or of Dresden rather than one of the *Singu-laria Weissenfelsiana*. But despite the less frequent exchanges between Schütz and the Weissenfelsers, the older he became, the more he clung to the quiet town on the Saale as the scene of a happy childhood. To be sure, not until 1680, some eight years after Schütz's death, did the "quiet" town become a musically historical *Residenz* resounding with both cantata and opera. As early as Michaelmas 1645 we find Schütz asking, in a memorandum to the elector, to be allowed to reside in Weissenfels, and to ask him to come to Dresden only for particular occasions. There he intended to complete musical compositions he had already begun, to establish a household with his widowed sister Justina Thörner (who still lived there in 1672), and with her to look after their modest mutual property. As a matter of fact, Schütz resided in Weissenfels in 1632, 1646, 1657, 1659, 1663, and 1665. In his testament he willed the Weissenfels hospitalers fifty gulden.

We need not stop here to consider the music situation in Köstritz, Heinrich's birthplace, as he left there when he was but six years of age. His continued devotion to the little town is shown, however, in his poem for the *Musikalische Exequien* of 1636.

On the other hand, Weissenfels, where Schütz lived until his fourteenth year, was old, fertile music soil, thanks primarily to the cantor Georg Weber (d. 1597) and the organist Heinrich Colander from Schwabach, who received his Weissenfels church appointment in 1580 when he was but twenty-three years of age and seems to have been a musician of importance. Moreover, as a close friend of Christof Schütz he became burgomaster and, in 1597, retired from his position of organist. He married the widow of Mathes Schütz.

George Weber, from a well-to-do Weissenfels family, had studied in Leipzig in 1554 and was a distinguished composer, as is shown by three large musical works: [10]

1) *German Psalms of David,* for four to six voices, printed 1568-69, Library Königsberg;
2) *52 German Songs and Psalms* for eight voices (DC) printed 1588-96, Gymn. Library Saalfeld;
3) *Book of Odes and Songs, (Liber odarum et canticorum),* a collection of introits for the entire church year (lost).

In the second work Weber provided chorale settings appropriate for each of the fifty-two Sundays and the three major festivals of the church year. Most of these he set first for a four-voice choir and then for an eight-voice double choir. There are 102 settings in all. Thus, for example, for Christmas we have:

---

[10] Of two manuscripts in the Berlin State Library which A. Werner attributes to him one apparently belongs to his Königsberg cousin of the same name or to his son; but perhaps the Latin motet for six voices in the Munich State Library (*Organ Tablature No. 257*) may be attributed to him.

Vom Himmel hoch

ich bring euch viel der neu = en Mär (uff.)

her,   ich bring euch (uff.)

It is quite probable that this was the first contrapuntal church music in which the boy Schütz participated. These settings are a modest parallel to the Venetian double-gallery, antiphonal technique.[11] The collection of Weber furnishes a good example of the seasonal church song of the time.[12] The Weissenfels *Kantorei* was transformed in 1590 into a patrician *Collegium musicum*, which was confirmed by the town council two years later. It was both a funeral brotherhood with common casket cloth and a jovial social gathering to which the magistracy annually appropriated money for Torgau beer. In 1615 J. H. Schein and the law student H. Schütz were among the boon companies there. In their music library were works by M. Altenburg, Dulichius, V. Leisring, Vintzius, M. Vulpius, G. Otto, Pinello. Of all these there is preserved only a manuscript setting of the passion by Scandello.

Later the choral society suffered heavily from the war. It was resurrected in 1649, but it was inactive again from 1652 to 1658. It was, therefore, doubtless of little significance for the old master. The young Schütz may have had friendly contact with a Weissenfels musician who was but a little older than he: Heinrich Steuccius, whose secular songs *Amores et lepores*, for five to six voices, in the style

---

[11] For the beginnings of Protestant polychoral music in the case of Johs. Walter (1566) and L. Schröter (1571) cf. Fr. Blume, *Das monodische Princip*, p. 44.

[12] With regard to this see especially R. v. Liliencron, *Geschichte des evang. Gottesdienstes 1524 bis 1700* (Schleswig, 1892), pp. 61 ff.

of Hassler, appeared in three series in Wittenberg in 1602, together with some intradas. He is represented in Bodenschatz' *Florilegium portense* by two motets.

The funeral sermon by Martin Geier reports concerning the great turning point in the life of the boy Schütz:

"As inclinations manifest themselves in early life, so in his youth a special inclination toward noble music was discovered in the boy. Therefore in a short time he had learned to sing accurately and quite well, with a special charm. This was by no means an unimportant reason for his advancement. For when His Grace, Landgrave Moritz of Hessen, had spent the night *(pernoctiret)* in 1598 with the Kapellmeister's parents, and had heard the boy sing so pleasantly, His Grace was moved to suggest to the parents that they allow the boy to accompany him to his court, promising that he would be educated in all good arts and praiseworthy virtues. When, however, his parents had misgivings with regard to allowing him to depart in his tender youth, His Grace urged the matter in writing, until finally, when the parents observed that the boy showed pleasure at the thought of setting forth into the world, they consented. He was conducted by his dear father on August 20, 1599, and delivered to His Grace, the landgrave."

Schütz thus entered the *Maurizianum,* which the landgrave had established in 1595.[13] As he was then fourteen years of age and thus near the time when his voice would change, his service as a choir boy must have been brief.

It must, however, be regarded as a happy disposition of fate that Schütz, like so many of the other old masters down to Haydn and Schubert, spent decisive years in a school for court choir boys. This service in the choir in his boyhood "from the ground up" plunged him deep, at the very outset of his musical career, into the practice of vocal music and helped to bring it about that Schütz eventually became one of the ablest vocal composers of Germany.

When Schütz's thoughts reverted to his parental home, he may often have recalled the remarks of the Erfurt preacher, Michael Hertz, in the eulogy on Benjamin Schütz in 1666: "If his youngest brother, Valentine, had not died in the bloom of his youth and had lived but a few years more, his dear parents would surely, by the grace of God, have reared and seen before their eyes three doctors of law and a world-famous musician. On account of which they were often considered blessed by many honorable people and also rejoiced heartily, especially when the whole family was assembled."

---

[13] Ph. Spitta says erroneously 1599.

School Days in Kassel

Kassel, the capital of the Landgrave of Hessia, enjoyed an ancient and rather distinguished music tradition. From 1469 to 1471 Johann Steinwert of Soest, who later became court Kapellmeister at Heidelberg, was active there as singer; Jakob Butzbach was organist in 1483; his immediate successors were Johann Hessebruch in 1512, Christoffer Endel in 1526, and Wilhelm Endel in 1564. In 1513 a famous organ with distinctive registers was built for the *Martinsstift*.[1] Georg Kern was singing master from at least 1512 to 1525.[2] His successor was Hans Heugel,[3] the greatest Kassel musician of the sixteenth century. This important master of the Senfl epoch was born in Deggendorf on the Danube ca. 1500. It is probable that he was a pupil of Balthasar Artopius. His compositions cover the period from 1535 to 1567. It is likely that during his thirties he worked in Kassel as an architect, but in 1547 we find him at the head of the court chapel. He lived until 1585. His settings of the *Psalter of Burkhart Waldis* were as highly esteemed as his settings of songs.[4] At all events, he was sufficiently well known that Erasmus Widmann, in his *Musikalischer Studentenmut* (Rothenburg, 1621), set to music a long farce about him (Nos. XVII—XIX), relating how, with crude pedagogy, Heugel had flogged a troublesome urchin *(Rossbube)* out of the choir. A full investigation of his Kassel manuscripts would be a rewarding task.

Heugel's successor was Georg Otto, who became the leading musician the young Schütz met in Kassel.[5] Otto was born in Torgau in 1544 and experienced at first hand the tradition associated with the original evangelical cantor and friend of Luther, Johannes Walter. Thus we have a most important artistic genealogical line running from Walter through Otto to Schütz. In 1564 Otto became a pupil in Schulpforta, a school which had a long and distinguished career in the history of church music. In 1570 he became cantor in Salza and applied twice (in 1570 and

---

[1] Its description by Euricius Cordus in my *Paul Hofhaimer*, p. 104.

[2] E. Zulauf, *Beiträge zur Geschichte der landgräflichen hessischen Hofkapelle zu Kassel bis auf die Zeit Moritz des Gelehrten (Contributions to the History of the Court Chapel of the Landgrave of Hessia Until the Time of Moritz the Learned)*. Leipzig dissertation, Kassel, 1902.

[3] Willibald Nagel, in *Sammelbd. IMG*, VII.

[4] For example, in Egenolf's *Gassenhauer und Reutterliedlein (Street Songs and Soldier Songs)*.

[5] F. H. Grössel, *Georg Otto*, Leipzig dissertation, 1933. A. A. Albert, *Die Cantiones sacrae* (1935), pp. 62 ff. and 84 ff.

1580) for the position of cantor at the Dresden court. It was only the opposition
of the Italians that kept him from obtaining this position. In 1588 he became head
of the court choir in Kassel. At the time of his death, in January 1619, the landgrave endeavored in vain to regain the services of Schütz as Otto's successor.

A list of Otto's works indicates that he was a prolific composer: A set of introits
for the church year (manuscript 1574)

Cantiones sacrae à 5—6 (printed in 1583)
24 Settings of Church Hymns à 5—6 (printed in 1588)
Settings for Lobwasser's *Psalter* (manuscript 1591)
65 Numbers of Gospel Duets for the Church Year (manuscript 1601)
Individual Psalms à 8—10 (manuscript without year; all in the *Landesbibliothek,*
Kassel)
Opus musicum novum: A Series of Gospel Settings for the Church Year à 4—8,
his chief work (printed in 1604)

One has only to read through his recently published works to be convinced that
Otto was a very capable musician and that he rated creditably with the pupils of
Lassus: Lechner, Eccard, de Vento, Raselius, even though not equalling in vivid
picturesqueness the tonal magicians H. L. Hassler, J. Gallus, Ph. Dulichius, and
H. Praetorius.[6] With his vigorous, still essentially imitative linear style (not the Venetian "surface style")[7] he belongs among the middle German masters Joachim a
Burgk, Seth Calvisius, Jakob Meiland, Gallus Dressler, and Leonhart Schröter.
Closely woven intertwinings of figures, open chords, a tendency toward *cantus
firmus*-like, sustained inner voices, point back to the Netherlands late Gothic period,
while chromatic steps, brilliant double-chorus concentrations or tuttis, widely flung
running figures with energetic octave leaps on a foundation of surface harmonies,
give premonitions of the oncoming early baroque. But still there is more similarity
to Lassus than to Schütz — of course, without traces of the genius of either. He
stands in the midst of the short Renaissance period in Germany, when embellish-

---

[6] Examples from the six-voice Gospel motets in my book: *Die mehrstimmige Vertonung des
Evangeliums (The Polyphonic Setting of the Gospel)*, (B & H, 1930) I, 32: *Homo quidam des-
cendebat* and II: *Cum intrasset Jesus*. Three introits, four duets, and an eight-voice *Ave Maria*
in the brochure of Fr. Blume, *Geistl. Musik am Hofe des Landgrafen Moritz (Religious Music at
the Court of the Landgrave Moritz)*, (Bär., 1930). G. Heinrichs presented duets and church hymn
settings in *Bll. f. d. Musikunterr. zu Homburg Bez. Kassel* and in *Aus alten Hessischen Choral-
büchern (From Old Hessian Chorale Books)*, the author's own publication, ibid.

[7] By "Venetian surface style" is meant the form of composition practiced especially by Giovanni Gabrieli in his polychoral compositions in which intricate, polyphonic, linear interweavings
are replaced by broad harmonies superimposed upon a common harmonic foundation.

ment flourished — a period which is still represented so splendidly by the architecture of the Kassel royal stables built in 1610. The last measures of the first introit are characteristic of his work. As found in Blume:

In the "old" style, we find the predominance of harmonies related at the third; the arrangement of the text — note the discant cadence with an appendix, bars 40—42 (soprano I); the avoidance of the sixth in descending (soprano II, 40; both sopranos, 44); the great distance between the sopranos and the alto, 43—44. The dissonant entrance of the bass "f" in bar 42 against the parallel sixths of the middle voices is in the "new" style; also the brilliantly sounding interwinding of the two discants in their high registers (bars 43—44). Notably modern is the chromaticism in the *Ecce concipies* of the *Ave Maria* with the motive: [8]

the development of which is not without harsh cross relations. At the conclusion of this work we find an instance of a characteristic of both Lassus and Schütz, namely, that of allowing, in the case of chordal pillars composed of numerous voices, a single voice to sound before or after other voices; at the same time the "endless" repetition of *non erit finis* is certainly a pretty "madrigalism." [9] I resolve the *chiavette* by transposing from g to *e:*

---

[8] (Blume's collection, pp. 29/31, 33).
[9] The term "madrigalism" is used by musicologists to denote the portrayal in music of phenomena of nature, conditions of space and time, psychological states, certain relationships, or number symbolism.

Otto also published, by commission of the landgrave, the principal work which a young choir colleague, Valentin Geuck, left at his early death. Geuck was born about 1570, was a soprano, then a tenor in the Kassel court *Kantorei*, finally chamberlain and distinguished musician *(musicus eximius)*. He died in 1596. As Otto had been commissioned to compose the Gospels in their usual prose form, the landgrave suggested to Geuck that he set to music a parallel set of Gospels arranged in the form of Latin distichs. When Geuck died before completing the work, the landgrave himself finished it — about one third of the total — an example of a fine Renaissance relationship in art between the prince and his chamberlain! Thus Geuck's "new and distinguished opus"[10] appeared in Kassel in 1604. Blume's collection includes from Geuck a five-, a six-, and an eight-voice motet. Perhaps one may recognize in him the style of a younger generation in that the melody is smoother, more primitive, less melismatic, but also directed more toward declamation. One notes passages like the first example on the next page or the Eccardian leap in the second example.

What brilliance Geuck at times unfolds is shown in an eight-voice Christmas composition (see third example, pp. 33 and 34).

His work often flies with the wings of youthful fervor. A great talent seems to have been extinguished all too soon.

---

[10] *Novum et insigne opus.* It is also noteworthy that the landgrave had established his own music press.

But the central figure of Schütz's Kassel was, of course, the landgrave himself.

The young prince was born in 1572. He was the son of the excellent ruler William the Wise. When still in his cradle he was greeted with a musical felicitation[11] by Joachim a Burgk of Mühlhausen. He had unusual talent for art and

[11] *Carmen genethliacon.*

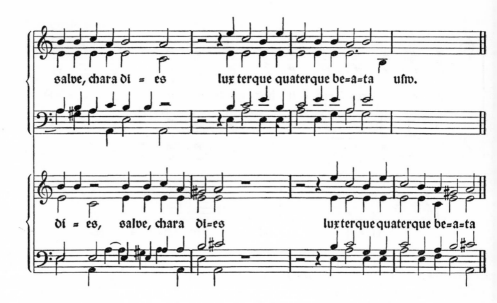

salve, chara di = es   lux terque quaterque be=a=ta   ufw.

di = es, salve, chara di=es   lux terque quaterque be=a=ta

learning, and he received a classical education, which must have made him an unusual phenomenon among the German princes, who were slipping from the heights of the Reformation into gluttony and intemperance. Duke Henry Julius of Brunswick and Henry Posthumus v. Reuss, the latter subsequently a friend of Schütz, should be mentioned as exemplary rulers like Landgrave Moritz. But apart from these, the Hessian prince stood almost alone when he began to reign in 1592 at the age of twenty. Quite properly he received the unique title "the Learned" *(der Gelehrte)*. He translated comedies and tragedies of classical antiquity, wrote much on the theory of poetry, on theology and classical philology, began a German rhetoric, and built in 1604-05 the so-called *Ottoneum* for his English comedians, the first permanent court theater in Germany. It stood beside "the old town wall, and had a stage that extended far into the orchestra, with four galleries for the spectators." For this, among other things, he wrote a rather good drama, *Die Belohnung der Gottesfurcht,*[12] which was rediscovered in 1931 by Joh. Bolte.[13] In 1623 he became a member of the *Fruchtbringende Gesellschaft* (Fruit-bearing Society). But his first marriage, with Agnes von Solms (d. 1602), he had four children; by his second marriage, with Juliane von Nassau, he had fourteen. The many

---

[12] *The Reward of Piety.*
[13] In the Phil. Hist. Class of the Prussian Academy of Sciences, Berlin (Report in the *DAZ* of 8-3-1931).

baptismal festivities themselves provided numerous musical tasks for the court ensemble (*Hofkapelle*). The young prince was determined to make his court in Kassel the most brilliant Renaissance court in Germany.[14] Among the famous musicians whom he distinguished as his guests in 1594-95 were Alessandro Orologio and the English lutenist John Dowland. In the latter's honor Moritz himself composed a pavan. In 1597 the prince vainly tried to induce Hans Leo Hassler to leave his position with Octavian Fugger at Augsburg to become his vice-Kapellmeister. After this unsuccessful attempt the position under Otto was given to Andr. Ostermaier from Torgau.[15] Since 1595 the court organist had been Joh. vom Ende (*de Fine*), who participated in the famous examination for approval of the organ in Gröningen. How highly Moritz was esteemed as a patron of music is shown by the list of music publications dedicated to him:

G. Otto, *Gesänge M. Lutheri à 5—6*, Torgau, 1588

Giov. Biffi, *First Book of Canzonettas à 6*, Nürnberg, 1596

H. L. Hassler, *Madrigals à 5—8*, Augsburg, 1596

Charles Tessier (lutenist in Poitiers, then Marburg), *Aires et villanelles*, Paris, 1604

H. Schütz, *Madrigals à 5*, Venice, 1611

M. Praetorius, *Konzertgesänge à 2—16*, Wolfenbüttel, 1617

Sessa d'Aranda, *First Book of Madrigals à 4*, Helmstädt, 1619.

There were dedications in manuscript by Hendr. Potamontius, Caspar Textor, B. Hoyoul, Joh. Polonus, Hundskopf, Matth. Märker, T. Mancinus, Schubhardt, etc.

Above all, however, Moritz — presumably as a pupil of G. Otto — was himself a very eminent composer. He began his completion of the *Lobwasser Psalter*, the hymnal of the Reformed Church, in 1607, by giving every psalm its own melody and setting. Hitherto a number of the psalms which had similar meters were sung

---

[14] The music inventory of the court chapel of 1613 contained church compositions by G. Otto, H. Praetorius, L. Päminger, Th. Riccio, J. Walter, Jak. Syring, Al. Utendal, G. Dressler, Lassus, Ingegneri, J. de Castro, M. Le Maistre, Jac. Wert, L. Lechner, Ivo de Vento, M. Praetorius, de Las Infantas, A. and G. Gabrieli, C. de Rore; motets by Palestrina; *Concertus* by Hassler; works by J. Nucius, de Kerle, J. Handl-Gallus, Casp. Hassler, Ph. de Monte, Giov. Croce, Cl. Stephani, M. Franck, A. Scandello, J. Meiland, Cl. Merulo; Sixt Dietrich's *Magnificats*; M. Vulpius, J. a Burgk, C. Demantius, Cr. Morales, N. Zangius; madrigals, etc., by Or. Vecchio, R. Giovanelli, Striggio, Flor. Maschera, Melch. Borchgrevingk, John Wilbye, M. da Gagliano, Th. Morley, L. Marenzio, V. Haussmann, Harnisch, Sartorius. There were instrumental works by Al. Orologio, W. Brade, Th. Simpson, M. Franck, Füllsack, Hildebrand, Giov. Valentini, etc. In the inventory of 1638 one finds the additional names of Greg. Lange, J. Eccard, Casp. Othmayr, J. Steurlein, B. Klingenstein, Greg. Aichinger, Ph. Dulichius, Sam. Scheidt, J. Rainer, A. Gumpelzhaimer, J. H. Schein, Farina, Grandi, D. Friederici, H. Schütz, and Cl. Monteverdi. (Even though both inventories are later than Schütz's student days at Kassel, they clearly illustrate the general atmosphere pervading the court chapel.)
[15] That he was the writer of the Schmalkald manuscript was shown by G. Kraft (*ZfMW*. XII, pp. 10 ff.).

to the same melody. For example, the Sixty-fourth Psalm had been sung to the
melody of the Fifth:

The landgrave composed a melody and setting of his own:

These pieces, the compulsory introduction of which into Hessia resulted in
tragicomic revolts by the peasants, concern us here not merely as obvious models
for the Cornelius Becker psalm settings by Schütz but particularly as striking con-
firmations of the basic classical point of view of the landgrave as composer. He

manifestly sympathizes with Glarean, who complained that melodies which he wrote to specific odes of Horace were used for other poems of the same meter and were published against his will. Glarean insisted that every poem demands its own musical ethos. Accordingly, the publisher Wessel says with regard to Moritz' *Psalter* that one should stress the enunciation of the text more than the tonal setting, St. Augustine having already emphasized that the rendition of the psalms in Alexandria was more a declamation of the words than actual singing. We can understand how this atmosphere must have paved the way for Schütz's relation to the Word!

Moritz also composed magnificats in each of the twelve modes. In 1612 he appended to the *Lobwasser Hymnal* of the Reformed the *Christl. Gesangbuch nach M. Luther* as Part Two, for four voices. He wrote twenty-four Villanellas *con parole di Petrarca* (manuscript, partly madrigals); nineteen very noteworthy instrumental fugues in four voices; nineteen motets and nine intradas in English style *à 6—8;* a *Canzon quinti toni à 8; Psalms 120* and *150, à 12,* with orchestra, anticipating the Schütz-Gabrieli style. These at least are what are left in Kassel. There is an eight-voice *Hosannah* in Bodenschatz.[16]

In alluding to the playing of his piano pupil Prince Louis Ferdinand, Beethoven said that he played "not at all like a prince." Similarly, concerning the compositions of Moritz it would be said that he composed "not at all like a landgrave" but as an expert craftsman. A slight weakness consists in the not infrequent and unintentional use of isorhythm, which introduces too many caesuras, as, for example, in the *Sinite pueros venire*[17] and the *Quam bona.*[18] Then, too, his chromaticism offends against the prevailing practice, the more so as no tone painting is suggested by the text:

To be sure, the sharp may possibly apply also to the preceding and the following note. The same may be true in the case of the example from Otto, cited above, p. 31.

---

[16] New prints in Tucher, Erk, Winterfeld *(Der ev. Kirchengesang und die Kunst des Tonsatzes);* in H. Riemann's *Alte Kammermusik;* in G. Heinrichs (loc. cit.) and in Blume's brochure. Cf. also the Marburg dissertation on Landgrave Moritz by W. Dane.
[17] *Suffer the Children to Come unto Me,* No. 12 in Blume's collection.
[18] *How Good,* No. 15 in Blume's collection.

But a piece like his six-voice *Saepe docens,* for school chorus (!) for equal voices *(ad voces aequales,* Blume, No. 14), with its trumpet imitation at the end, is well conceived dramatically.

From the viewpoint of the history of art the important thing, of course, is not so much the question how well the landgrave himself composed but the fact that through this gift and technique he was better able than any ruler of his time to recognize and promote musical talent. His chief claim to fame is that in the case of Schütz he did this in an exemplary manner.

Among the numerous journeys on which the court chapel generally accompanied the landgrave two trips to Dresden were of particular importance in the history of music: that in 1599, when, on his return trip, he invited Schütz to join the *Maurizianum* in Kassel; and that of 1613, which initiated Schütz's transfer to the Saxon court.

Let us hear what the master himself told his elector briefly in 1591:[19] ".... as early as my thirteenth year I had left the home of my blessed parents in Weissenfels, and since that time I lived away from home for the rest of my life. I served at first for some years as a choir boy in the court ensemble *(Hoffcapell)* of Landgrave Moritz in Kassel and attended school, besides my occupation with music — in order to learn Latin and other languages — until I lost my soprano voice." In Geier's *Köstlichste Arbeit (Most Precious Work)* we read in more detail: "Availing himself of such an opportunity, he remained there several years and attended a highly respected court school, or rather a preparatory school, together with dukes, aristrocrats of the nobility, and other talented students. Here he was inducted into all kinds of languages, arts, and other exercises. His diligence and pleasure in such studies were not in vain. He made astonishing progress in a short time in Latin, Greek, and French, and had soon shown progress equal to that of the others, so that his preceptors and professors, noticing his rapid advance, not only esteemed him highly but also wished and urged him to pursue his studies in the direction of each of their particular professions." In the Kassel school records a hitherto unnoticed school exercise of the young Schütz has been preserved — an oration on St. Mauritius, namely, a speech on the patron for whom the landgrave was named.[20]

Apparently we have before us here a rhetorical exercise delivered on the baptismal day of the landgrave, September 22. The subject matter deals with the legend

---

[19] This autobiographical *Memoriale* is first found in W. Schäfer (1854); then in La Mara, *Musikerbriefe aus vier Jahrhunderten,* E. H. Müller, No. 77.
[20] *Landesbibl.,* C II, N—Z, Bl. 165—68.

of Mauritius, the commander of the "Theban Legion," which latter suffered a martyr's death ca. 300 near St. Moritz in the canton of Wallis in Switzerland, because the legionnaires, themselves already Christians in secret, refused to assist at a persecution of Christians and hence mutinied.[21]

"The means rulers usually employ in order to reach the highest honor are many and varied. I believe, however, that no method is more acceptable to God and more praiseworthy among Christian men than the one which that bravest emperor Mauritius formerly used. He not only fought bravely for the true religion but also shed his blood for it up to the very hour of this death. Although many other emperors had made for themselves an immortal name by their outstanding abilities and stratagems, they do not seem to me to have reached the true purpose and end —without which no legitimate war can be waged—which this hero accomplished. We are, of course, placed in this world by the thrice-best and greatest God in order to make manifest His glory, to propagate the true religion, and for this to undergo all kinds of misfortune and hardships, even death itself. Since this emperor exposed himself and his life for the true religion, who could deny that he accomplished this purpose? Today we have come to a state of things where but few recognize this purpose of life, still fewer try to accomplish it, and only a very few actually attain it. Therefore this Mauritius certainly deserves that we renew his memory daily in order to make his deeds known to others for imitation, and that we explain them a little further.

"Although this would surely be sufficient to explain his fame (for nobody can merit higher praise than what he gains by accomplishing the highest purpose), still I cannot pass over in silence that high virtue through which he not only risked death himself for the true religion but also strengthened the faith of his army, delivered them from all fear of death, and, beyond any doubt, showed and opened to them the way to eternal life. What deed could be more outstanding? Could anything more laudable and more deserving of a Christian man ever be done than to snatch from the grip of the devil so many erring souls who are steeped in ignorance of the divine Word or see it only as through a mist, and to open to them the gate of eternal life? How great a joy do you believe the angels and all the chosen ones of God must have felt in this conversion? I am sure such joy has not entered our ears. Nor have our eyes seen it. Who, therefore, would not exalt with highest praises this emperor who enlightened so many blind hearts with the true faith? If we allowed this emperor's memory to vanish among us, we would be far more

---

[21] See, with regard to the historical events, G. Ulhorn in Herzog-Hauck, *Realenzyklopädie f. protest. Theologie und Kirche*, XII, 452 ff.

foolish than even those pagans who believed that fighting for their home and their altars deserved the highest praise and who without hesitation bestowed the greatest honors on those who refused to be lured away from the worship of their pagan gods by threats of punishment or by death. That wise philosopher Socrates could not be kept from the study of philosophy even though the lethal cup was offered him. After he had been condemned to death for his sincere devotion to philosophy, he turned to his judges, saying: 'I embrace you all with benevolence, yet I believe the immortal god must be obeyed rather than you.' Thus he clearly indicated that death had to be suffered rather than that something should be done against the command of the god. If, therefore, without the knowledge of the true God, those pagans deemed it praiseworthy to persevere in philosophy and not to give up such studies even under the threat of death, how much more should we, who, snatched out of the darkness of errors, walk in the light of the true knowledge of God, honor such perseverance in the true religion as that of the great Mauritius! Whenever we read the histories of pagans who suffered so many dangers for the sake of delivering their country, we also shall believe that great honor will come to us if we expose ourselves to all dangers and changes of fortune for the sake of the eternal fatherland. For we hope to find relief from all pains and for the peace prepared for us in that other life. Yet why should we say more? So great is the virtue of this emperor, so great his deeds, that even that light of eloquence, Cicero, could hardly express it sufficiently in words. So, lest with my weak speech I obscure, rather than elucidate, his praises, I shall say no more but shall break off the thread of my oration. But I should like to conclude with the eager admonition that all follow in the footsteps of this emperor and not refuse to suffer any hardships or dangers for the true religion. When one acts in such a manner, on him, as on that great Mauritius and all the chosen ones, God, the thrice best and the greatest, will certainly place the eternal and incorruptible crown of justice.

I have spoken.

Heinrich Schütz."

Light is thrown on Schütz's eagerness for knowledge by the statement about M. Weckmann in Mattheson's *Ehrenpforte*: "He was also advised by Kapellmeister Schütz to become conversant with the Hebrew language, not as though it were an actual necessity but because such familiarity would be useful in setting a text from the Old Testament."

Rich musical impressions must have encompassed the youth here in his most impressionable years. The preface to Mich. Praetorius' *Uranodia* indicates how well the court congregation in Kassel was versed in music. Praetorius (who had visited Kassel in 1605 and 1609) relates as a most unique experience: "I heard in the electoral Hessian court chapel some psalms sung in anthem form with the congregation participating *(per choros)*." On some occasions, as at the Baptism of a prince in the year 1600, music was performed by from eighty to a hundred executants — veritable monster performances for that day. The orchestra of the court ensemble *(Hofkapelle)* — for the most part in choirs of eight pieces each — consisted of instruments of the most varying lengths: bassoons, pommers or bomharts, schryari or old shawms, bassanelli, recorders, dwarf pipes *(Zwerchpfeiffen)*, soft cornets, cromornes, rankets, Italian gambas (including a *violino!*), English and German gambas, four *violini di brazzio*, lyre, trombones, fifteen "instruments," namely, regals, organs, positives, *Geigenwerke*, claviers, and *hölzerne Gelächter* ("wooden laughter"), that is, xylophones. We may imagine all these to have been tried out with the experimental enthusiasm of a Mich. Praetorius. Surely the young upperclassman must have handled them all himself, later drawing on his experience when he came to score his *Psalms of 1619* in such diverse ways. For just as the landgrave himself was a master of the organ as well as of other instruments — a fact which we shall find substantiated by a notation on a thorough-bass part of a Schütz composition — we may rest assured that the former choir boys did not themselves entirely relinquish these instruments to the town pipers and court players.[22] One of the latter, Christoff Cornett, subsequently the successor of G. Otto, became a friend of Schütz. It was perhaps Cornett who, having been sent to Venice in 1605 by the landgrave to continue his musical studies, gave the first personal account of Gabrieli to the young Heinrich. Cornett died in 1635 at the age of sixty-five. Shortly before his death Schütz composed for him as *sempre affettionatissimo per servirla*, the *Herr, nun lässest Du (Nunc dimittis)* for bass solo and two violins. One may interpret Schütz's inclusion of this number in the *Sinfoniae sacrae II*[23] of 1647 as an *in memoriam* to his friend.

The "Court School" at Kassel developed into the *Collegium Maurizianum* as the result of the landgrave's desire to provide companions for the princes in their higher education. Hence sons of court officials, pages, and choir boys received

----

[22] Thus it is stated in the collection of acts in the *Landesbibl.* Kassel, mss. hass. fol. 57, p. 25, with regard to the examination at Easter 1601 (and this surely applies also to Schütz) that as the voices of more than half of the *Symphoniaci* have changed, one should consider their dismissal and the substitution of newcomers; the two most advanced, however, when dismissed from the choir, should be trained in instrumental music.

[23] Unfortunately, none of Chr. Cornett's works seem to have been preserved. The Kassel ms. fol. 58, contains German songs *(Mein Freund komm; Komm Gott, Hymnen, gib gedeyen)*, by a certain Paul Cornetti. Was he a brother or a son? These songs immediately precede Schütz's (here anonymus) *Vier Hirtinnen gleich jung gleich schön*.

a training in the classics. Out of such court schools — one need only recall Pforta, Grimma, Meissen — later came the ablest clergymen, philologists, and function-aries. The pupils of the *Collegium* wore a black costume; only on visits to the town was an additional outer garb permitted. Among themselves they were required to speak nothing but Latin or French. The court physician was also the school physi-cian. He prescribed beer drinking for the preservation of the voices. According to the records, he was concerned as to whether even the smallest of the pupils were able to dress themselves and to maintain themselves in hygienic condition. There were paragraphs of school regulations dealing, respectively, with the head, the feet, the hands, and the clothes.

On account of the instruction in counterpoint, intended expressly for the older choir boys, the choir was placed under the immediate jurisdiction of the professor of mathematics — a survival of the old unity of these sciences in the *Quadrivium* of the Middle Ages. To learn proper etiquet, the choir boys, like the pages, had to wait on table. As Schütz was brought to the school from Weissenfels, so another, endowed with a voice, came from Dresden; a third came from Paris. One poor fellow was dishonorably dropped when it was discovered that one of his grand-parents had been a sow gelder.

The rudiments of Latin, a good voice, and good forebears were the conditions of acceptance to the school. Pupils were enrolled at twelve years of age. The land-grave laid the greatest stress on music instruction. The entire school had daily singing from twelve to one. Beside this, the choir rehearsed regularly with the Kapellmeister. In a travel order the landgrave impressed diligence on the students in their pursuit of music:

"Furthermore, beware lest all love and culture of music among you be lost. These exercises of vocal and instrumental music can always be used by you fairly well in Belgium and France, better in England, best of all in Italy." [24]

This reveals clearly what the musical situation was at that time. It was only mediocre in the Netherlands and in France, better in England, outstanding in Italy! So it is not surprising that on numerous occasions students before Schütz had applied for travel allowance to study with Gabrieli in Venice. When Schütz was composing at the Lido, three seniors presented a petition to the landgrave that they be excused from Vergil in order to devote all their time to music — a very un-Schützian request, indicative of a twilight glow in Renaissance humanism . . . At

---

[24] *Praeterea, ne Musices omnis amor et cultura inter vos abjecta sit, operam date, huius vero tum vocalis tum instrumentalis exercitia vobis esse poterunt perpetua, mediocra quidem in Belgia et Gallia, excellentiora in Anglia, in Italia vero excellentissima.*

the founding of the school eight scholarships were provided for choir boys. In July 1601 the number was raised to twelve, the landgrave having established free board and clothing for four instrumentalists. As these were undergoing change of voice (Schütz was sixteen years old!), they occupied a room above the court room near the rest of the students, and they were expected to learn, besides their other school studies, instrumental music to perfection *(usque ad unguem)*. He also provided them with an instructor in French and Italian.

The life of the school afforded much delightful variety by means of comedies and Renaissance pageants. Thus in the year 1600, on the occasion of the Baptism of a prince, the choir paraded through the streets of the capital dressed as gods, fauns, nymphs, wild men, and mythological ladies. But more important for Schütz was the participation of the choir in the church services four times a week, twice on Sunday and once each on Wednesday and Saturday.

The faculty was outstanding. The director, who was also tutor to the princes, was Hans von Bodenhausen, later the mathematician Nicolaus Krug. Georg Cruciger, from a distinguished Wittenberg family, taught Latin and Greek; Le Doux, whose *Tobie*, in French, was presented by the students in 1604, taught the modern languages.

A fact hitherto overlooked by Schütz research is that among Schütz's colleagues there was an unusually gifted student, Schütz's senior by only one year: Dietrich von dem Werder.[25] It is scarcely conceivable that the two should not have formed an intimate acquaintanceship or friendship. Born in 1584 in Werdershausen near Cöthen, of old Anhalt aristocracy, related to Hans von Bodenhausen, von dem Werder grew up as page in waiting of Moritz and received special inspiration at the *Maurizianum* from Rudolf Goclenius. Later he studied law and theology at Marburg, where Schütz doubtless met him again. He made the grand tour to France and Italy, and then in Kassel, after Schütz had returned from Italy, he became master of the horse and chamberlain, and later privy counselor. He shone equally in tournaments and as a traveling diplomat, as, for example, on the Mühlhausen princes' day of 1620. He became a member of the "Fruit-bearing Society" at the age of twenty, overseer *(Ephorus)* of the *Maurizianum*, and tutor to the children of the landgrave. In 1622 he fell into disfavor with Moritz and retired to his country estate, Rheinsdorf, near Cöthen. From here he conducted an important correspondence with his able prince, Ludwig von Anhalt, and also formed a friendship with Opitz. Here his true talents became apparent for the first time. He was the

---

[25] G. Witkowski in the *Allgemeine deutsche Biographie;* especially warmhearted is the evaluation by Jos. Nadler, *Dt. Lit. Gesch. nach Stämmen und Landschaften,* Vol. 2.

first to translate Tasso's *Jerusalem Redeemed* into German, 1624-26; likewise Ariosto's *Orlando Furioso,* and this indeed in so graceful manner as to reveal true sixteenth century charm. At the same time, as colonel in the pay of Anhalt, he led a Swedish cavalry regiment. Dietrich's own poetry is of varying quality.

The lament on the death of his wife (1625) is expressive of genuine feeling, while a collection of one hundred sonnets on the *Battle and Victory of Christ* (1631)[26] is devoid of good taste. Something that really might point to a relationship with Schütz is the fact that he came forward as poet-composer with twenty-four *Joyful Songs of Comfort,* which won the consideration of Kretzschmar.[27] As one is not likely to begin composing at sixty-nine, the origin of the melodies must be placed several decades earlier. Some of them, at least "in the early measures, reflect the atmosphere of the poem in quite appropriate and at times original turns." Von dem Werder died in 1657, a decrepit old man. The Nürnberg copy of his works contains only the first song; the Wolfenbüttel copy alone is complete.

We may also mention as characteristic of the whole atmosphere of the Hessian court that the landgrave's daughter, Princes Elizabeth, of about the same age as Schütz, translated a pastoral romance by Contarini into German, composed Italian sonnets, and translated Lobwasser psalms into Italian.

These Kassel years, their atmosphere saturated with Renaissance culture, inevitably shaped Schütz's inherent traits and tendencies. His broad education singles him out among all the masters of music. To be sure, it imposed doubts and restraints on his creative activity; but at the same time it purified and ennobled his creations, filling them with gold and precious jewels. The next stage of his life's journey rather encouraged than retarded this development. His way led him to the university of Philipp the Good, the University of Marburg, where he was surely no lighthearted playboy. But note how long his apprenticeship was! From his thirteenth to his twenty-second (!) year in the Kassel chapel, from his twenty-second to his twenty-fourth a student of law at Marburg, from his twenty-fourth to his twenty-eighth (!) a student of music in Venice. In the chapter titled "Early Individual Works" we shall have occasion to discuss a composition dating, as is supposed, from his early life, a significantly imperfect work in which he may be bidding farewell to an early affair.

---

[26] *Krieg und Sieg Christi.*
[27] *Gesch. des dt. Liedes* (1911), pp. 86 ff. One of the numbers is a poem on the last sigh of the Electress Sophie of Hessen.

Student in Marburg

First of all, let us hear the autobiography of the master, written when he was sixty-six years old.

"And as it was never the desire of my late parents that I should follow music as a profession, either at that time or later on, I complied with their wishes and betook myself to the University of Marburg after I had lost my soprano voice. I went there in the company of my brother Georg, who subsequently became a doctor of laws. He died a few years ago (1637) in Leipzig as a member of the supreme court and in the employ of Your Electoral Highness. In Marburg I intended to continue the studies I had pursued quite extensively apart from my music, to choose a definite profession, and to advance to an honorable degree of distinction therein. But such resolve on my part was soon altered, doubtless according to the plan of God. For when Landgrave Moritz, at whose court I had served as a choir boy, came to Marburg somewhat later, he seems again to have observed that I was endowed by nature with musical talent, and he made the following suggestions: that since there still lived at the time in Italy a very famous but at the same time quite aged musician and composer, I should not delay to visit him and learn something from him. His Grace the Prince also offered me a stipendium of two hundred thalers annually for this purpose. As a young man eager to see the world, I gratefully accepted this offer and departed for Venice in 1609, although against the wishes of my parents."

According to the records, here the aged master evidently had a conspicuous lapse of memory. The Marburg matriculation records show Schütz—according to whether he or his nephew of the same name was registered first—enrolled at the university as late as April 18 or even September 27, 1608, when he was twenty-two and a half or twenty-three years old. If we are not to assume that he sang falsetto for a long time after his voice had changed, and that he lost this ability as late as 1608, his remark "after I had lost my soprano voice" would have to be understood decidedly *cum grano salis*. As we know that Schütz was an outstanding pupil, his position as prefect would alone provide a reason for his remaining in the highest class until the end of his twenty-third year. It is, therefore, much more likely that, after being graduated from the Royal Academy, he assisted there for three or four years as male choir singer, instrumentalist, and organist of the *Kantorei* until a particular occasion took him to Marburg for the study of law. And indeed this particular occasion seems quite apparent. At that time Landgrave Moritz moved to Marburg with his entire court and remained there for more than half a year. At all events, the Kassel period was thus prolonged to nine years (as against Spitta's surmise of "1607"). Its significance for Schütz's development can hardly be over-emphasized.

But in this connection something seems to have been overlooked. In the memorandum of 1651 Schütz relates his intention "to continue studies begun and carried on quite extensively elsewhere." In addition, he tells us that when his study with Gabrieli had shown him clearly the difficulty of the study of composition, he almost regretted having given up the law. He says literally "that I turned away from the studies cultivated at the German universities, in which studies I had made considerable progress." This may imply that he had been a student at other German universities. It may be possible to unearth the name of Schütz in some other matriculation register. In this connection we must again return to Schütz's nephew of the same name. Certainly the Leipzig matriculation of 1599 applies to the nephew alone, though R. Wustmann in his *Musikgeschichte von Leipzig*, I, 218, still refers this to the composer. Our Schütz was only thirteen years old at the time. Since, on the other hand, under the announcement of the summer semester of 1602 regarding "Heinricus Schütz Leucopatraeus" we later find[1] "and in 1612, under the rectorship of Polycarp, he again presented his name and took the oath of matriculation among us," and since the Italian memorandum in the album of Friedrich Gleser (see below) proves that this time we are concerned with the composer, our hero had moved from Kassel to Leipzig when he was seventeen

---

[1] *Anno 1612 Rectore Polycarpo iterum nomen suum apud nos professus simul juravit.*
My surmise that Schütz also visited universities other than Marburg and Leipzig is confirmed by Weisse. Though the registers are silent with regard to this, Schütz was also in Frankfurt on the Oder and in Jena! The following passage also indicates that he considered himself endowed with better gifts for law than were his distinguished brothers:
> Your parents, to be sure, chose for you the work
> Into which have entered your two dear brothers (Dr. Benjamin, *juris candidatus* of Erfurt;
>   Dr. Georgius, *juris candidatus* of Leipzig).
> But yet in music were you to attain the highest praise.
> In all the learned arts your diligence was praised
> In ev'ry higher school* where you did choose to go;
> But yet in music were you to attain the highest praise."
> * Academy at Marburg, Frankfurt on the Oder, and Jena.

As it is clearly indicated both in the autobiography and in Geier's funeral sermon that Schütz went directly from Marburg to Venice, the sojourns at Frankfurt on the Oder and Jena could only have occurred between 1607 and 1609, or possibly in the time hitherto assumed for Leipzig, namely, 1613.

years old, provided that the Leipzig dean did not fall into the same error of confusing the two Schützes in 1612. But this all remains somewhat uncertain.

The University of Marburg had become Reformed in 1605. Its student register contains the following entries in the hand of the rector, Gregorius Schönfeldt, professor and doctor of theology:[2]

Henricus Schütz, Weissenfelsensis, *Misnicus,* 1608, 18. April

„   Schützius, *Misnicus,* 27. Sept.

Georg Schütz, Weissenfelsensis, *Misnicus,* 30 Dez.

Thus we also note that the three relatives did not enter the university at the same time but at the beginning of three different terms of a three-term scholastic year. From events in connection with the court we may assume that the earliest of these three dates applies to the composer. The great sensation of the rectorship of Schönfeldt, which began in January 1608, was the matriculation of two of the sons of the landgrave, Moritz and Wilhelm, together with their tutor, Crato Seiler. At the same time the landgrave gave the university six hundred gulden for the erection of new buildings. The university thus enjoyed an almost unequalled period of splendor. Students from many nations directed their steps thither. Besides Germans from all Protestant territories, there were Danes, Russians, Hungarians, Swiss, Poles, Bohemians, Scotch, Moravians, Lithuanians, Dutchmen, etc. Some came from patrician families, some from the nobility. The landgrave arrived with his court at the beginning of June 1608. When, on October 17, a princess was born to him, the event was celebrated with great festivities, in the music for which Schütz must surely have taken part. Many members of the student body were invited to a baptismal banquet. A painful incident was the filching of some table silver by one of the "sons of the Muses." Later the chief even escaped from the lockup. The incident was settled by the solemn apologies on the part of the student body, the senate, and the royal house. In 1609 Prince Moritz himself became rector of the university *honoris causa,* with Hermann Vultejus as acting rector. For the occasion the landgrave donated new academic caps and gowns. Prince Moritz' younger brother, Prince Wilhelm, became rector *honoris causa* in 1610. The interest of the *gran Maurizio* in the intellectual development of the rising generation is indicated by the fact that he himself dictated a German-Latin *extemporale* in the Marburg high school and had the results preserved in the archives.

Unfortunately, when Schütz set out on his journey south, the university's period of glory was at an end. Many people were carried away by the cholera epidemic;

---

[2] Julius Caesar: *Catalogus studiosorum scholae Marpurgensis,* Par. IV (1605-28), pp. 33 ff.; in connection with this. *Register of Persons and Places* by W. Falkenheiner (1904).

there were brawls and window smashings, expulsions and fatal duels, etc. The "international" student body also had its dark sides.[3] Nevertheless Sagittarius must have retained pleasant memories of his Alma Mater, for in 1615 his brother Benjamin also matriculated here. The most encyclopedic intellect on the faculty at the time was the polyhistorian, philosopher, and poet, Rud. Goclenius the Elder. The most famous jurist, whose lectures Schütz doubtless attended, was Herman Vultejus,[4] born in 1555 in Wetter in Hessia. Colleagues of Vultejus were the latter's son-in-law Christophorus Deichmann and Joh. Goddaeus. The lectures of Gottfried Antoni and Antonius Matthaeus were also well attended. It is not known who supervised Schütz's disputation *De legatis,* nor is the work now extant. We do know that Vultejus pioneered in influencing the form of such disputations along pedagogical lines. The funeral sermon summarizes this as follows:

"After he had submitted everything to the direction of God, he chose the study of law and cast about where to continue his studies. He found no difficulty in making his decision, as it happened that about the year 1607 his late parents sent his brother George and his cousin, Heinrich Schütz, to Marburg. On learning this, the composer obtained permission from His Princely Highness to accompany these to Marburg. Having obtained his wish, he applied himself with the greatest diligence to his legal studies. He devoted himself assiduously to the *Institutiones juris, Quaestiones Hoenonii,* and other distinguished authors, and after a short time demonstrated in a disputation *De legatis* that he had used his time to good advantage."

Apparently Marburg did not have a chair of music at that time. But the beautiful city on the Lahn had a fairly active musical life. Notably, it had long possessed several large organs.[5] Landgrave Ludwig VI had resided there with his own court

---

[3] See Georg Heer, *Marburger Studentenleben 1527-1927* (Marburg, 1927), pp. 34 ff. Note there, as a fine title page, the gay picture of a Marburg student with his lute, from 1578.

[4] Wilhelm Dilichius, *Urbs et Academia Marpurgensis* (ca. 1622); published by J. Caesar (Marburg, 1867), pp. 66 ff. — H. Hermelink and S. A. Kaehler, *Die Philipps Universität in Marburg, 1527-1927* (Marburg, 1927), pp. 199 ff.

[5] In my *Hofhaimer,* p. 90: The Cathedral of St. Elizabeth had had two organs since 1467. One of them was renovated by Johann von Allendorf in 1479, the smaller one by Master Niklas of Paderborn in 1492. In 1513 Master Arnold Rucker of Seligenstadt built the new large organ for which the Order of Teutonic Knights paid 383 pounds. Renovated in 1662 and 1776, the instrument remained in use until 1850 (!); part of the case is still preserved. In 1543 both organs stood in the choir of St. Elizabeth's. In 1513 the chaplain of the Order, Mathias Weidelbach, who had studied with Konrad Gobe in Mainz at the expense of the Order, was appointed organist. With the Reformation he entered the municipal service. In the "Parish Church" an organ was torn down in 1457 and was supplanted by an instrument built by a Master Konrad, who used thirty-three hundredweight (*Zentner*) of lead and tin. In 1473 he renovated "both" organs, as did Arnold Rucker in 1521-22. The Marburg castle also possessed an organ in 1478.

music. When he died in 1604, Landgrave Moritz took over his chamber musicians: Augustin Kramer, Georg Graumann, Balthasar Radau, and Nik. Hagenbruch. In Schütz's time[6] (1607-08) Bernhard von Ende *(de Fine)* is often mentioned in the accounts as university organist. Apparently he was a relative of the Kassel organ master. The cantor Joh. Brasch is also frequently mentioned. Perhaps he was a son of the Augsburg organist Abel Braschius (d. 1592), who was a friend of Jacob Paix.[7]

Some notices in the records will give an idea of the unpretentious musical life: "To Master Michael, the tower musician; Heinr. Diem (called from Würzburg in 1612); Hans Kölsch, Hans Hübner 'tower apprentices'; Marburg public fund *(Kastenrechnung)*: Bernhard de fine organista; Joh. Arnshausen, bookkeeper, pays 4 fl. for two *Lobwasser Psalters* in folio, one of which is used by the pupils for singing, the other by the organist. Likewise 1607: 1 fl., 16 albus for some *cantica virginis Mariae (= Magnificats)* composed by Melchior Vulpius; by order of the local superintendent 4 fl. paid to the four musicians from the castle who were employed for the music in the church, as honorarium." 1608 Marburg Council Protocol: "Hans Peter has requested that his two boys be allowed to go about and sing with the poor boys." There also: "Our gracious prince and lord decreed and granted to ten trumpeters two *Reichsthaler* for their meals, in view of their 'impetuous perseverance'." 1609: "11 Pfd. 1 schock, 1 fl., 16 alb. to a messenger from Brunswick who brought the songs *(cantica)* of Michael Praetorius hither on Jan. 31." In 1610 the student Joh. Eberh. Schmidt in Marburg writes to his father about the expense connected with his receiving his master's degree: "There are still further incidentals, such as compensating the cantor who conducted the music at the festivities, compensation for the cornet players, etc."[8]

The aristocratic law student Schütz, who looked forward to soon becoming an electoral court counselor or a municipal burgomaster, probably did not have much contact with these Marburg musicians. At most he may have employed them when he celebrated a festival banquet with his colleagues.

In Martin Geyer's biographical sketch, appended to the funeral sermon, we read: "It happened soon thereafter, in 1609, that His Esteemed High Princely Grace, Landgrave Moritz, came to Marburg. When Schütz, as was his duty, waited on

---

[6] According to the kind information of Counselor of the Archives Dr. Gutbier which Prof. Dr. H. Stephani graciously obtained.

[7] Upon order of the rector and the professors, 5 fl. to Master Johann Braschio, *cantori musico:* 20 alb. 6 groschen to Master Joh. Braschio, *praeceptori classico,* for the purchase of several *cantiones musicae* to the same 1 fl., 31 alb, 1¹/₂ gr. for the purchase of several *cantiones* (1609).

[8] *Zs. d. V. f. hess. Geschichte und Landeskunde (Periodical of the Society for Hessian History and Knowledge of the Country),* 33, p. 389.

the elector, the latter, I do not know by what fate, remarked to Schütz that he had learned of his turning principally to the study of law and added that he had observed in him a special inclination toward the profession of noble music. Accordingly, since the world-famous Johann Gabrieli of Venice was still alive, he would be inclined, in case Schütz looked upon the suggestion favorably, to give him the necessary funds and send him to Italy in order that he might seriously continue the study of music there. Since young people seldom decline such offers, he (Schütz), too, resolved to accept the proffered favor with most humble thanks, intending, however, immediately upon his return from Italy, again to take up his books and continue his studies."

The Venice of Giovanni Gabrieli

The Queen of the Adriatic was one of the richest cities of the world in musical culture. The German traveler Paul Heussner very properly referred to it in 1599 as the Paradise of Delights.[1] Venice maintained its reputation for several centuries. From 1337 to 1368 the organist Francesco da Pesaro had been a distinguished representative of the *ars nova* there. The exhilarating motet *Stirps Mocenigo* of Antonius Romanus, composed in 1413 for the elevation of the doge,[2] gives a glorious echo of the old Venetian state music. From 1445 to 1459 the German musician Bernhard Murer, an original genius, was the organist at St. Mark's, and from 1507 to 1516 Dionisio Memmo, a favorite pupil of Paul Hofhaimer,[3] had the same position. Albrecht Dürer reports in his diary that the strings at the cathedral played so beautifully that the players "could not hold back their tears." Among other distinguished early names are Francesco d'Ana, Don Michele Pesenti, and Tromboncino. Other composers of *frottole* whose works were published by Petrucci also adorn the ranks. Gardane and Scotto became the first great printers of madrigals. From the time of the appointment in 1527 of the Netherlander Adrian Willaert[4] as choirmaster of the cathedral, the City of Canals stood at the focal point of musical world history. Probably only St. Peter's in Rome and St. Thomas' in Leipzig can contribute names of musicians as brilliant as those who served at St. Mark's:[5]

1. Kapellmeister:	1. Organ:	2. Organ:
Willaert, appointed 1527	Jacques Buus, 1541	Fra Armonio, 1516
Cyprian de Rore, 1563	Girol. Parabosco, 1551	Annibale Padovano, 1552
Jos. Zarlino, 1565	Cl. Merulo, 1557	Andr. Gabrieli, 1556
Bald. Donati, 1590	Giov. Gabrieli, 1584	Vinc. Bell'aver, 1586

[1] Pirro, *Schütz*, p. 32.
[2] Given in Schering, *Gesch. d. Musik in Beispielen,* No. 30.
[3] Concerning both see my *Hofhaimer,* pp. 40 f. and 98.
[4] Died 1563.
[5] The old presentation by Caffi: *La Capella granducale di Venezia* (1850) has now been supplanted by the Introduction of Giac. Benvenuti to the 1st and 2nd vols. of the *Istituzioni e monumenti dell' arte musicale Italiana: Andr. e Giov. Gabrieli e la musica strumentale in San Marco* (Ricordi, Milan, 1931).

Giov. Croce, 1603   (later, Mass. Neri,   Fr. Guami, 1588
J. C. Martinengo, 1609   Lotti, etc.)   Fr. Cavalli, 1638
Cl. Monteverdi, 1613   P. A. Ziani, 1668
Giov. Rovetta, 1649
Fr. Cavalli, 1668
(later, among others:
Legrenzi, Lotti,
Galuppi, Bertoni)

In addition to these, there is an impressive list of assistant Kapellmeisters, among them Alessandro Grandi, who was appointed in 1620.

It is no wonder that with such talent, to which must be added distinguished singers and independent composers such as Verdelot, music flourished in the highest degree both in its practice and in composition. How musical the atmosphere of Venice was can be felt even from the paintings of the brothers Bellini, Carpaccio, Palma Vecchio, Titian, Paolo Veronese, and Tintoretto, whose gentle, soft shades were again strongly reflected in the local musical style of Venice. The use of opposing or supplementary tonal effects was encouraged by the fact that San Marco had two galleries, each with its own choir and organ. While, to be sure, the use of echo choirs (cori spezzati) was not invented in Venice,[6] it was most highly perfected there. In Venice the first specific orchestral literature was also developed, along with the church motet, under the two Gabrielis. In 1542 Cavazzoni had founded there a prolific school of organ composition.[7] The oriental, soft, fairy-tale atmosphere of the gold cupola city particularly stimulated chromaticism, which here emerged from the humanistic Renaissance experiment to enhance the expression of emotion[8] and became the essential element of the musical genius loci. Such chromaticism led Willaert to compose a little two-voice virtuoso piece, Quidnam ebrietas, which, with the "proper" use of accidentals, concludes in E double flat instead of in E. This Venetian tendency toward color will be definitely demonstrated in the evolution of the madrigal.

---

[6] L. Söhner, in Die Musik an der Münchener Frauenkirche (1934), p. 9, thought to discredit the exposition by me in my Hofhaimer, p. 99, of the art of performing simultaneously on two organs, as practiced in and around Venice prior to this period. Tinctoris, however, mentioned with regard to Naples (1470), as did Antonio de Beatis with regard to Angers (1518), the "good harmonizing" of two organs responding to each another. In addition to a Mass of the Dom of Speier (1488) cum duobus cantoribus in organis, further proof appears from Orleans, 1470 (M. Brenet, Les Concerts en France, p. 12), where two municipal musicians played together publicly deux personnes ayant chacune un orgue.
[7] See L. Torchi: L'arte musicale, Vol. 3.
[8] Note the enharmonic claviers of Nicola Vicentino and Zarlino about 1550.

Schütz arrived in Venice at the happy moment when the city, relieved of the long dangers of war, could again breathe freely. In 1605 the Venetian state had been placed under the ban by Pope Paul V because it had offered asylum to the Servite priest Paolo Sarpi, who had viewed the Council of Trent, so to speak, through Pfitzner eyes and had sharply questioned the infallibility of the pope, thus playing a role in a contest between church and state that flooded the whole of Europe with pamphlets and finally ended in 1607 with a genuine peace.

The old and close commercial relations between the South German cities and Venice are well known. The *Fondaco dei Tedeschi* was a kind of club house for all German visitors to the City of Canals.[9] The fact that more and more German musicians gathered there is explained primarily by the drawing power of one man, Giovanni Gabrieli, who himself had various ties with Germany and between 1575 and 1579, together with Zacconi, had been in the court chapel at Munich under Lassus. This fact doubtless explains the appearance of two of Lassus' madrigals in the second volume of Cos. Bottrigari (Venice, 1575), a work dedicated to the Bavarian Duke. In the very year that Giovanni Gabrieli took charge of the first organ at San Marco, a young Nürnberger, Hans Leo Hassler, came to Venice to study with Giovanni's equally famous uncle and teacher, Andrea Gabrieli. The two pupils of Andrea, the nephew Giovanni and the Nürnberger Hassler, became lifelong friends. In 1600 they jointly composed a wedding song for their common friend Georg Gruber in Nürnberg, and three years after the death of both Giovanni and Hassler (1612) Gruber published through Paul Kauffmann *Reliquiae sacrorum concentuum Giov. Gabrieli & Joh. Leonis Hassleri utriusque praestantissimi musici et aliquot aliorum excellentium aetatis nostrae artificum motectae 6—19 vocum.*[10]

---

[9] In the travel book *Paradisus deliciarum Italiae* (author: George Kranitz v. Wertheim), Cologne, 1616, p. 36, we read: "On passing from San Marco beneath the clock, you will come to the *Merceria*, on both sides of which are found extensive shops, especially those dealing in silks. These extend for quite a distance. Thereupon one immediately comes to the German House, in which none but German merchants live. They pay the duke weekly a hundred *Zeckin*, i. e., 200 *Gülden.*" And the Saxon court historiographer Hieronymus Megiserus says in his *Paradisus deliciarum*, or *Beschreibing der wunderbaren Stadt Venedig* (Leipzig, 1610), p. 127: "On the other side of this bridge (the Rialto) toward San Marco stands the German House, called the Fontigo. It covers 512 *schuch* and has on its exterior 22 shops from which much gold is derived annually. In this House there are 200 chambers and apartments *(Losamenter)*. The community derives a tremendous benefit and income from this House on account of the great trade conducted by the Germans. By reason of this, they receive high privileges from the authorities. But there are only South Germans and no Netherlanders there."

[10] *Some Sacred Songs by Giov. Gabrieli and Hans Leo Hassler, Both of Them Most Distinguished Musicians, and Some Motets of from Six to Nineteen Voices, by Some Other Excellent Masters of Our Time*, including works by Bell'aver, Bianciardi, Buel, Cantoni, Erbach, M. Franck, Jak. Hassler, C. v. d. Hoven, Marenzio, Massaino, Monteverdi, Naldo, Peccius, Spontone.

Giovanni Gabrieli was also a close friend of the Fuggers. He dedicated the *Concerti* of 1587, written by him and Andrea, to Jakob Fugger, commending especially the great commercial house for remaining Catholic.[11] In 1597 Giovanni was invited by Georg Fugger to his wedding in Augsburg but did not attend. In the same year he dedicated his *Sinfoniae sacrae* II to the four sons of Marcus Fugger.[12] Giovanni also occupies a leading place in seven German collections published before 1608, especially in those of the Nürnberg organist of St. Aegidius, Friedr. Lindner. After Gabrieli's death his pupil Aloisio Grani dedicated a portion of Giovanni's posthumous works to a friend of Giovanni, Johannes Merck of Mindelheim, the abbot of the Augsburg Imperial Foundation of St. Udalrich and Afra. In the dedication Grani thus expressed himself on the subject of the nature of posthumous fame:[13] "Though Giovanni Gabrieli, that destinguished musician, second to none of his age, has been relieved of earthly bonds and has laid aside his bodily and earthly frame, I may nevertheless consider him happy inasmuch as in this life through his ability and his knowledge he laid the foundation for eternal memory and imperishable praise. Even though he himself has become silent, his songs, the sweetness of which has captivated the world, will never cease to sing." Similarly, the Venetian Augustinian Padre Taddäus, in dedicating in 1615 the unpublished *Canzoni e sonate* of Gabrieli to Duke Albrecht of Bavaria, describes Giovanni as an Ornament of the Graces. In the preface to Grabbe's madrigals Gabrieli is referred to as *quel vivo sole della Musica*,[14] in Pedersön's dedication as *quel vero lume*.[15] Most important of all, however, hear Schütz himself in the dedication to the landgrave of his *Opus 1* — the *Italian Madrigals* of 1611 — when Gabrieli was still living: "It was you who gave me the impetus to go to Italy and to plunge myself into that flood which bears the whole of Italy along in its rushing euphony, resembling the harmony of heaven. I mean the very famous Gabrieli who made me a partner in the gold of his chests. *Si ricche in questa qualità di studii, che né al Tago né al Pattolo inuidiar certo ponno.* In other words, Gabrieli, through the excellence of his instruction, surpassed even the gold-bearing streams, the Tagus and the Pactolus. And when Schütz, in 1628, visited the Lido for the second time, *he* wrote in the Latin dedication of his *Sinfoniae sacrae I* to the Electoral Prince of Saxony: "Again I cast my anchor there, where in the days of my youth I spent the first years of instruction in my art under the great Gabrieli. Yes, Gabrieli —! What a man he was! Had the ancients, rich in

---

[11] Reprinted in *Istituzioni e Monumenti,* I, lxxxi.
[12] The affectionate preface may be found in C. v. Winterfeld, *Johs. Gabrieli,* I, 43.
[13] Winterfeld I, 51.
[14] "that living sun of music."
[15] "that true light."

words, known him, they would have preferred him to Amphion;[16] or had the Muses desired marriage, Melpomene would have taken no other husband than him, such a master of song was he. His undying reputation confirms this. I myself was abundantly a witness to his greatness, having worked under him for four whole years, certainly to my great advantage." Because it is without the pomp of ebullient rhetoric, Schütz's German testimony in the memorial of 1651 is the most convincing: "And thereupon in 1609, although against the wishes of my parents, I left for Venice. Upon my arrival, after I had been but a short time with my teacher, I found out how important and difficult was the study of composition which I had undertaken, and I realized that I still had a poor foundation in it. While I rejoiced that I had turned from the studies ordinarily presented at the German universities — in which studies I had made considerable progress — I had nonetheless to submit myself to patience and to subject myself to the one for whose instruction I had come. Hence from this time on I put away all my previous studies and began to devote myself with all possible diligence to the study of music alone, in order to see how I would succeed in this. In three years (a year before my return from Italy) I had progressed, with divine help, so far that I published in the Italian language my first little musical work, and I say without boasting that it won the praise of the most distinguished musicians then in Venice. I dedicated and sent this in humble gratitude to Landgrave Moritz. Upon the publication of this my humble work, I was advised and urged, not only by my preceptor, Giovanni Gabrieli, but also by the Kapellmeister and others among the most distinguished musicians there to keep on with the study of music, and I was also assured by them that I might look forward to genuine success in this field. After I had continued my sojourn in Venice for still another year, though at my parents' expense — in order to gain still further experience in this branch — it happened that my preceptor, mentioned above, died in Venice. I accompanied his body to its last resting place. On his deathbed, as an indication of special affection, he bequeathed to me one of his rings as a memento, which was presented to me by his father confessor, an Augustinian monk, from the monastery in which Dr. Luther had stayed.[17] The landgrave's loan offered at Marburg was based on

---

[16] Amphion, the son of Zeus and Antiope and the husband of Niobe. He built the walls of Thebes by charming each stone into position with a lyre given him by Hermes.

[17] Evidently the executor of the will, Father Taddeus, who is also mentioned "among musicians." That Luther, on his journey to Rome, traveled by way of Venice remains "altogether uncertain" (kind information imparted by Prof. D. O. Albrecht). According to Köstlin-Kawerau's *Biography*, I, 95 f. and note on p. 749, the tradition in question is only "legendary." At all events, it was doubtless a misunderstanding on the part of Ph. Spitta when he interpreted the text as meaning the father had come from the Augustinian monastery in Erfurt.

the surmise that he who wished to learn something from this very highly gifted man should not further delay.[18]

"When, then, in 1613, I returned to Germany from my first visit to Italy...."

On numerous occasions Gabrieli apparently had Schütz act as his substitute at the church services, and indeed Sagittarius almost became organist at St. Mark's:

> Venice knew thee already sixty-three years ago,
> And hadst thou so desired, thou might'st indeed have been
> The other Gabriel, who often did entrust
> To thee his duties at St. Mark's
> And on his deathbed gave to thee his finest ring
> In token of his love: for he regarded thee
> As equally endowed; but thou prefer'dst to choose
> A simple life at home rather than wealth abroad.
>
> *Venedig kennt dich schon vor drey und Sechzig Jahren /*
> *Und wenn du nur gewolt / so hättstu können seyn*
> *Der Andre Gabriel / der mit dir so verfahren /*
> *Das er an seine statt dich offt gesetzet ein.*
> *Er liess dir auch / schon todt / den besten Ring verehren /*
> *Zum Zeichen seiner Gunst / und dass er dich Ihm gleich*
> *Bey Lebens-Zeit geschätzt: Du woltest aber kehren*
> *Viel lieber arm zu Hauss / als dorte werden reich.*

At this point we must clarify the chronology. Giovanni Gabrieli died on August 12, 1612. If Schütz returned home in the spring of 1613, as he indicates, after studying in Venice for four years, he apparently arrived in Venice in the spring of 1609, the year indicated by him. During the last year he studied at the expense of his parents. Accordingly, the subsidy from the landgrave would have extended from the spring of 1609 to the spring of 1612. There results, however, one contradiction: Schütz says he had his *Italian Madrigals, Op. 1* printed after a three-year period of study in Italy and one year before his return. This would have been in the spring of 1612, which seems plausible as a *quid pro quo* for the landgrave's assistance. The preface to the madrigals, however, is dated May, 1611, and the title page bears the same year. How can this be explained? A double error in printing would scarcely seem likely. May we be confronted by a lapse of memory on the part of the aged master? Did he let the work lie a year before he forwarded it to the landgrave? Or are we confronted by a local date computation according to the Venetian style? In any event, it does not seem impossible that the madrigals first appeared in May 1612.

The Kapellmeister who had encouraged Schütz in his musicianship was apparently the Rev. Giulio Cesare Martinengo, born of aristocratic stock in Verona in 1585, the year of Schütz's birth. Despite his youth he was advanced in 1609 from the position of Church Kapellmeister in Udine to the highest position at San Marco, though, to be sure, he had to content himself with a salary of 200 ducats

---

[18] See the article by v. Schallenberg in *Musik und Kirche*, XIV, 1942, pp. 141 ff.

instead of the 300 received by his predecessor, Giov. Croce. On his death in July 1613, shortly before the departure of Schütz from Venice, he was succeeded by Monteverdi. An evil star ruled over the musical material which Martinengo left at his death. Only the alto and tenor parts of a *Popule meus* and a *Tantum ergo*, found in Giov. Croce's *Nove Lamentazioni* of 1610, have survived, in Bologna. However, the only complete surviving motet, found in Leonardo Simonetti's *Ghirlanda sacra*[19] must have fascinated Schütz as a monody in "modern" style — a little soprano solo cantata with organ continuo:

[19] Venice, 1625, 36, *Stadtbibl.* Breslau.

As an indication of the approaching revolution, one may call attention to the fact that the text *Tornate o cari bacci,* which Schütz set in 1611 as a madrigal quintet without thorough bass, was composed by someone else only six years later as a thorough-bass monody (Ambros IV, 335). The absence of a figured bass in the case of Schütz's *Op. 1* was not indicative of any immaturity on his part but was a pedagogical measure. This the master indicated again in the preface to his *Geistliche Chormusik,* where he expressly told the "rising composers" that the linear setting should be complete *(hieb- und stichfest),* without any dependence on supplementary chord fillings — the school of counterpoint in which the riders dispensed with stirrups.

The funeral sermon again reveals how well Schütz made use of his time in Italy, not only in learning music but also in acquiring wordly wisdom:

"In God's name he went to Italy in 1609, particularly to Venice, in order to attain the goal he had set for himself. In Venice he committed himself to the instruction of the far-famed Giovanni Gabrieli and remained there into the fourth year. During this sojourn he not only sought to make the proper use of his 'peregrination,' observing what one place or another possessed that was worthy of attention, diligently seeking out learned and wise men, corresponding with them, noting what was worthy of imitation and in general pondering the injunction of the apostle to think on 'whatsoever things are honest, whatsoever things are just, whatsoever things are pure, whatsoever things are lovely, whatsoever things are of good report: if there be any virtue and if there be any praise'; but he also, by the grace of God, surpassed the others of his circle in music and had a little work printed in Venice which won the honor, respect, and praise of everyone."

In regard to the musical practice which Schütz found in Venice, Pirro presents (loc. cit., p. 18) the reports of a French and of an English traveler. The Parisian lawyer J. B. du Val, in 1607, heard a vesper service in the church of San Salvatore about which he says: "A concert was presented by the best local vocal and instrumental musicians with six portable organs, in addition to the very good church organ and trombones, oboes, viols, lutes, cornets, recorders, piccolos . . . The musical harmony is very sonorous; they sing very well in their own style, to which, to be sure, one must first accustom oneself, as it is quite different from our own." After the Christmas Mass in St. Mark's, du Val again notes how sonorous the Venetian music sounds to him: with double organ and an orchestra of trombones, cornets, violins, interchanging with voices — "all this fills the church well and presents a great harmony." In April 1609 he admires in the Frari church the music as *fort bien concerté* and *bien remplie.* He admires especially a very outstanding *joueur de flageollet.* Thomas Coryate, in 1608, finds the music *si bonne, si délectable, si rare, si admirable, si superexcellente,* and feels himself transported into the third heaven when, on the occasion of the Festival of St. Roche, sixteen to twenty singers and sixteen instruments (ten trombones, four cornets, two bass gambas) perform together — now in ten parts (six trombones and four cornets), now in two (cornet and violin, doubtless with continuo). Among the violinists he admired three as especially skillful. "They sing and play simultaneously; two theorbos carried out the continuo delicately. The manner in which seven small organs and three or four wonderful voices combine results in such beauty as one finds nowhere else in all Christendom.

Therefore the teacher of the world who was primarily responsible for luring talented young composers to Venice was Giovanni Gabrieli. Seth Calvisius and Michael Praetorius repeatedly held him up to their contemporaries as a model who could not lead them astray. He and his renowned uncle Andrea were able to exert an influence on Schütz by their own works in at least two fields: church music for many voices and madrigals. Their most significant innovation, the development of an altogether independent church-orchestra style,[20] was to find in Schütz a vacuum still to be filled. Moreover, Gabrieli in all probability gave Schütz a decisive impetus through his fundamental technical innovations, such as the tonal answer in the fugue and the orchestral support of the choir by means of unison and octave doubling. The extent to which Gabrieli's motet art became Schütz's very flesh and blood is illustrated by the singular fact that Schütz, in the *Geistliche Chormusik* of 1648, published the seven-voice concert piece *(Konzert)* of Andrea Gabrieli (1587), *Angelus ad pastores ait,*[21] in German as his own work. Apparently Schütz had completely forgotten that, possibly some thirty-five years before, he had merely translated this Christmas antiphon into German. From the point of view of technical performance it is instructive to place the original by Gabrieli and the arrangement in the German translation by Schütz side by side (see pp. 62 and 63).

A. A. Abert[22] admirably sketches the steps by which Giovanni Gabrieli's style developed. She compares the *O Jesu mi dulcissime* of the *Symphoniae sacrae* of

---

[20] Gabrieli's instrumental works printed anew in Wasielewski, *Die Violine im 17. Jahrhundert;* in Riemann, *Alte Kammermusik* and his *Musikgeschichte in Beispielen,* Schering, *Beispiel* 148. Now, however, especially *Istituzioni e monumenti,* Vol. 2 (fourteen *Canzonas* for eight to sixteen voices).

[21] VIII, 171.

[22] *Die Cantiones sacrae von Schütz* (1935), pp. 178 ff. and 187 ff.

1597 with the setting in Part II of the *Symphoniae sacrae* of 1615: "In the relation of the composer to the textual content a fundamental change has taken place. While the earlier composition still moves completely in the uniform and super-personal solemnity of the old motet style, the later one is thoroughly saturated with manifold sentiments suggested by the text. Every word has its independent significance for this manner of composition. The later motets of G. Gabrieli were written probably during Schütz's sojourn in Venice, so that here he not only learned the motet ideal of the future but even witnessed its very beginning at its source. Here for the first time he comes in contact with the fully developed new textual interpretation . . . and its musical possibilities, and herein lies the great significance of his student years in Venice."

As technical imitations of Giovanni Gabrieli's vocal compositions for the church only Schütz's polychorus *Psalms of David* of 1619 and the individual companion pieces need be considered. As to these, so independent a composer as Schütz, even when intending to imitate, for the most part recreates. In *The History of the Resurrection*,[23] the *Cantiones sacrae*, and especially the *Sinfoniae sacrae I* he has consciously abandoned the basis of Gabrieli's art-technique, while in the *Geistliche Chormusik* of 1648 he reverts, not to the Gabrieli technique but to the roots of German choral music.

A fairly exhaustive evaluation of the work of G. Gabrieli would today demand more space than the three-volume work of Carl von Winterfeld, published over a hundred years ago. To be sure, von Winterfeld's work sifted a very extensive amount of material, as was fitting in the case of this master-musician (1557-1612), who was one of the greatest figures in all musical history. One is left with the image of a "singing tree," or a magical "stationary wave of sound," on hearing one of Gabrieli's characteristic vocal works well rendered. See, for example, the *Song of Homage* of 1587 to the Fuggers, for single chorus; *Sacri di Giove augei* (Torchi II, 159); or the motet *Angelus ad pastores* for six high and six low voices (loc. cit., 177); or the *Jubilate Deo* (1597) for eight voices (published by C. Hirsch, Forberg),[24] a text set a number of times by Schütz also; or the three motets edited by Besseler in Blume's *Chorwerk*, Brochure 10 (Kallmeyer, 1931); or the superb Christmas composition *Salvator noster* for three choruses of five voices.[25] On the broadest harmonic surfaces, which, however, can also decidedly transmute themselves through all kinds of chromatic coloring, the parts, originating chiefly from

---

[23] *Auferstehungshistorie.*
[24] Edited for four voices (TTBB) by A. T. Davison, E. C. Schirmer, Boston.
[25] In Winterfeld's manuscript collection, Prussian State Library, Berlin.

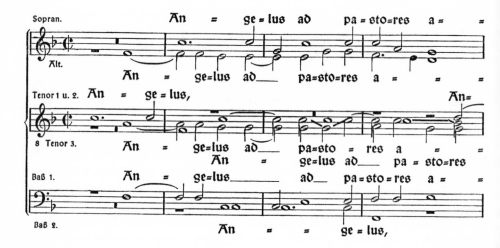

triadic themes, move along in wavelike motion, while at the same time they are subject to strict counterpoint. The rhythm is presented at times in gently rolling, rippling motions which mutually supplement one another; at times it is contracted into jubilant, dancelike three-part movement. Above all, however, the sense for tonal color predominates, which (as in the last-named piece) so graduates a genuine fifteen-voice composition that while each of the three choruses extends from the soprano to the bass, the upper chorus has three soprano parts, the lowest, three bass parts. We are confronted by monumental temples above the comparatively impersonal high-Renaissance pomp of which the rising baroque illumination pours its more variegated lights, particularly when one takes into consideration the improvisational embellishments of the time (Gorgiapraxis) in the upper voices and the supporting contrabasses below, which, after Gombert, were recognized as authentic. While a Lassus fascinates with the tense, exciting art of a born painter of history, and while a Palestrina forces one to one's knees by means of his more objective and awe-inspiring religious expression, Gabrieli presents the warm, golden glow of a a vesper atmosphere with its lyrical hymns. One should study thoroughly his twenty-seven compositions in the volume of musical examples in Winterfeld's Gabrieli. Here there is unfolded before us a treasure of the most vivid inspirations — at times downright word painting or madrigalisms — despite strict subservience to rules, impressing the musician above all as an expression of the living word. One should note Besseler's words that "from the expressive pathos of his text interpretation, the passionate vividness of his melody, there speaks the will to overpower the heart through the magic of sound and to draw it along to a vision of the unspeakable. Thus Netherlands music, at the end of its historical development, returns here, in a certain sense, to its origin. Some 150 years before it was the piety of Netherlands mysticism that had prepared the ground for its growth. As this music since then has formed one of the strongest symbols of unity in occidental life, transcending all boundaries of creed, so also the transformation it received in Venice was seized upon almost more intensely by Protestant Germany than by Rome and Spain. Gabrieli's spiritual successor . . . is his pupil Heinrich Schütz."

Strangely enough, even in the case of Sagittarius' madrigals of 1611, which grew under the very eyes of Gabrieli, the chasm between these and Gabrieli's own compositions in this category is extremely great. The story of the legacy of the ring shows that here no hostile tension could have existed as was present in the similar situation between the aged Haydn and the "great mogul" Beethoven with regard to the latter's Op. 1, 3. On the contrary, it speaks for the inner greatness of Gabrieli that Schütz's modernisms seemed to have confirmed for him the significance of the young German. A. Einstein[26] suggests: "Venice was the

---

[26] Heinrich Schütz (Bärenreiter, 1928), p. 18.

only Italian city in which the northern Protestant could feel at home and free from antagonism. Venice, moreover, at least at the time of Schütz's first journey, was in matters musical the conservative city which offered points of contact to the pupil from Germany and made it easier for him to take advantage of them. The great battles with regard to the new monodic style had long ago been fought in Florence, Mantua, yes, even in Rome. But Venice was in no haste to recognize the victory of the iconoclasts of counterpoint. What Schütz learned from Giov. Gabrieli was the old art of the sixteenth century. To be sure, on the solid foundation of polyphony there stands the wonderful new structure of the luxurious style, freely mingling polychoral and instrumental, solo and concerted, homophonic and polyphonic, elements. At the same time that he observed this mass movement (*Konzertieren*) of the voices and instruments Schütz must also have become acquainted with the concertizing of the individual voices above the *basso continuo*, even though, in his case, this acquaintance bore fruit only at a later time." Of these remarks the last is doubtless the most correct, as indicated by the above-cited pre-Monteverdi monodic example of Martinengo. In the same Venice, in 1611, the year of Schütz's *Op. 1*, there appeared unheard-of modernisms, such as the fifth madrigal book of Carlo Gesualdo, Prince of Venosa.[27] Here, in 1607 to 1608, the first five books of Monteverdi's madrigals had been republished.[28] In 1599 the ninth volume of Marenzio's madrigals, almost as bold, had appeared.[29] Venice was not merely the place of publication but surely also the outstanding place for the performance of such ventures. As the composer of his own madrigals, Schütz did not need a conservative city to which to attach himself; and indeed the Venice of 1609 to 1613 was not conservative. But he did need close contact with an authoritative genius as teacher, and Gabrieli was the greatest authority in the musical world of the time. Monteverdi was to be the other authority, and of him, too, Schütz made ample use. Gabrieli possessed a unique personality which doubtless influenced Schütz more decisively than any instruction in the "counterpoint of the sixteenth century" or in any other time-limited practice of the trade.

From those instances where Schütz and his fellow pupils composed the same text one can easily see how far Schütz surpassed them.

Gabrieli seems to have assigned to all these foreign pupils the same task for their journeyman's or student's piece — to write madrigals for five voices. We have such

---

[27] See from this the five-voiced madrigal *Dolcissima mia vita* in Schering, *Beispielsammlung*, No. 167.
[28] New edition by Malipiero (Universal-Edition).
[29] See from this the *Solo e pensoso* in Schering, *Beispielsammlung*, No. 165.

madrigals by the Dane Hans Nielsen, who called himself Giov. Fontejo, printed in 1606 (Paris, Nat'l. Library); by his countryman Mogens Pedersön *(Magno Petreo)*, printed in 1608 *(Landesbibl.,* Kassel), and by Johannes Grabbe (1609, loc. cit.) from Lippe-Detmold. Schütz met the last two in Venice. The Danes had been sent to Venice by their great king, Christian IV, in the company of his Court Kapellmeister Melchior Borchgrevink, who had studied with Gabrieli in 1599. His two-volume collection *Giardino novo bellissimo di varii fiori musicali scieltissimi* of 1605-1606[30] gives the most extensive view of the Venetian madrigal literature at the beginning of the sixteenth century. It is remarkable that the two Gabrielis are missing. Contributors are Monteverdi, Sal. Rossi, S. Molinaro, Bianciardi, B. Pallavicino, Fontejo, and lesser lights. With the exception of Giaches de Wert and Giov. Croce, they are for the most part representatives of the younger generation.

Another hitherto unnoticed fellow pupil of Schütz under Gabrieli can be identified: the German Christof Clemsee (Klemsee) who on April 18, 1613, as private tutor at Arnstadt, dedicated his madrigals, with a Latin preface, as first fruits to the Duke of Schwarzburg: *Il primo libro de madrigali a cinque voci* (published in Jena by Weidner). In the introduction[31] he says that the duke had given him a scholarship *(stipendium)* "in order to visit and to hear the 'apple of the eye' of all perfect music and the ornament of Italy, Giovanni Gabrieli." [32] He had been permitted "to drink with open mouth from the sacred breast of one the most limpid fountains of the art of music." [33] Unfortunately, of the five voice books, the three in Lancy are inaccessible, and one has disappeared. The alto, preserved in Wolfenbüttel, and the bass in the *Staatl. Akad. f. Kirchen- und Schulmusik* (Berlin), show among the eighteen compositions no textual counterpart of the madrigals of Schütz.

In Borchgrevink, too, as later in the case of Schütz, one finds the simultaneous double-motif technique to be the burning problem, as illustrated in a piece by Gabrieli Fattorini from Faenza: [34]

---

[30] Part I, dedicated to Christian IV, Part II to James I of England. *Landesbibl.* Kassel.
[31] E. Vogel, *Bibl. der weltl. Vokalmusik Italiens,* I, 174.
[32] *Ut perfectorum Musicorum omnium ejus aetatis Ocellum et Italiae gemmam Johannem Gabrielem adiret et audiret.*
[33] *Hujus sacro pectore hianti ore bibere limpidissimos artis Musicae fontes.*
[34] First printed in his own second book of madrigals, Venice, 1604.

Or one may observe in Pedersön-Petrejo this madrigal beginning, where contrasting themes are first presented in succession and are subsequently combined simultaneously:

In reality this is something that Italy had known a hundred years before in similar form in the "double songs" of Isaac and Josquin. Only now it seems plucked to pieces in quick, sudden changes and is enlivened in a charming manner.

Of course, when we place beside Schütz these, his Venetian working companions, we see mere mediocrity confronted by genius. Pirro has demonstrated this in the case of the somewhat trivial *Fuggi, fuggi* of Fontejo-Nielsen (loc. cit., p. 160). Similarly, we place the *Alma afflitta* of Joh. Grabbe alongside the Schütz madrigal beginning to show the same result, even though the Detmold musician is by no means to be despised (see pp. 70 and 71).

Schütz's greatness lies in the simplicity with which he always resolves, at the closest interval, suspensions of the second into primes, while Grabbe somewhat overloads his obviously intensive monodic effect.

Or, finally, let us compare Giov. Priuli's[35] *Feritevi* (in Borchgrevinck II, 14) with that of Schütz (see pp. 72 and 73).

A certain external similarity between the two passages can scarcely conceal the fact that while in Priuli everything is treated in a skillful musical manner, the individual voices have quite a mechanical turn; in Schütz, on the other hand, organically tense climaxes over the contrasting bass enliven every part. The greater closeness of texture at the word *Viperette* especially presents a definite serrated expression of deep emotion, while in Priuli we have merely metrical scansion at half-measure intervals.

When one examines the present Kassel stock of music, it becomes quite clear what music Schütz either sent to, or brought back for, the landgrave from Venice. As an indication of his taste and an evidence of his interest at that time we briefly mention the thirteen most important works. Other compositione may since have disappeared.

1—3. Giov. Priuli, *Il primo, secondo, terzo libro de Madrigali à 5*, Ven., 1604/07/12.

    4. Henrico Sagittario, Allemano, *Il primo libro Madrigali à 5*, Ven., 1611.

    5. Giov. Grabbe, Wesphalo, *Org. del. ill. et ecc. S. Conte di Lippe, Madrigali à 5*, Ven., 1609.

    6. Magno Petreo, Dano, *Il primo libro dei Madr. à 5*, Ven., 1608.

    7. Francesco Spongia detto Usper, *Madrigali à 5*, Ven., 1604.

---

[35] Priuli was Kapellmeister in Graz and Vienna (d. 1629).

8. M. Angelo Nantermi, *Madrigali à 5*, Ven., 1609.

9. Amante Franzoni, *Madrigali à 5*, Ven., 1608.

10. Giov. Ghizzolo, da Brescia, *Madrigali à 5*, Ven., 1608.

11. A. Banchieri, *Il terzo libro dei Madrigali à 5: Festino nella sera del Giovedi grasso avanti Cena*, Ven., 1608.

12. Cl. Monteverdi, *Il terzo libro de Madrigali à 5*, Ven., 1604.

13. Or. Vecchi, *Le veglie di Siena*, Ven., 1604.

Priuli III (1612) and Nantermi (1609) already have thorough-bass parts. Schütz himself has written out in Fol. 57, h, the greater part of the *Udite chiari Tritoni à 16* of G. Gabrieli.[36]

---

[36] C. Israel's *Catalogue of the Cassel Music Manuscripts*, pp. vi and 27 (according to Chrysander).

Interim

When Schütz returned to his fatherland, he apparently did not go at once to Kassel, or, if so, for only a short time.[1] He seems first to have gone to Weissenfels to see his parents. During this visit he decided to take up again the study of law which had been broken off in Marburg four years before. In the Memorial of 1651 he reports to the Elector Johann Georg I of Saxony: "When now, in 1613, I returned to Germany from my first visit to Italy, I made up my mind to wait and, as it were, keep to myself the good foundations I had thus laid in music until I had developed them somewhat further and was able to come out with a worthy work." Again we observe this strange, shy hesitancy to appear as a master of his art; his lofty seriousness; his consciousness of a special mission; and yet apparently also the plan for *The Psalms of David* of 1619, along the lines of Gabrieli. "I did not at the time lack advice from my parents and relatives, who urged me to do something useful, to seek advancement by means of my obviously modest qualities in other fields, and to follow music as an avocation. I was finally persuaded to accede to their incessant admonitions and again took up my books which for a time I had laid aside."

This decision was probably the more painful to him since just at this time he met in the Weissenfels *Collegium musicum* a musician of about his own age, Johann Hermann Schein, who, until his death, was to be a warm personal friend. From 1613 to 1615 Schein was tutor and music director in the home of the electoral Saxon counselor,[2] Gottfried von Wolffersdorff, who later recommended this highly talented young musician from the *Erzgebirge* for Court Kapellmeister in Weimar and then for cantor at St. Thomas' in Leipzig. Since Schütz later believed that his own call to Dresden probably owed its origin to von Wolffersdorff, he must surely have proved his artistic talent in this musical home. Perhaps Samuel Scheidt, who is known to have had connections with Weissenfels, also came over from Halle. In

---

[1] From the elegy by David Schirmer it is apparent that Schütz, evidently at the behest of Landgrave Moritz, brought distinguished Italian scholars to Germany on his return from Venice:
> Such scholars as ere this
> Gave fame to Italy, themselves immortalized,
> He brought when he returned unto his fatherland.

[2] *Hauptmann.* Today he would be called *Landrat.*

this event the three great S's would have met. Perhaps Schütz attended the Naumburg Princes' Day in the spring of 1614, where about ninety musicians gathered. Johann Georg of Saxony brought twenty-one; Johann Sigismund of Brandenburg arrived with thirty-three trumpeters, some Italians, and six English fiddlers; his brother came with fifteen trumpeters and a Kapellmeister; Duke Ernst of Sachsen-Eisenach and Landgrave Ludwig of Hesse each brought but three; the Administrator of Magdeburg, seven. Under the leadership of Michael Praetorius four choruses performed in the church of St.Wenceslaus in such impressive manner that the local cantor, Stifelius, was moved to tears. The Dresden choir boys sang from the choir of the church; one orchestra played from the organ loft, a second was stationed "near Herr Weiss's epitaph," while a third stood beside the baptismal font.[3]

First, however, Schütz was destined to unroll the pandects and the *corpus juris* a second time. As his father bore the expense, the son had a free choice and determined upon Leipzig, where the list of matriculated already bore the names of so many *Sagittarii Leucopetraei*. Even if the mention of Heinrich Schütz alone might be taken to refer to the cousin of the same name,the presence of our Heinrich Schütz ("the Venetian") is unequivocally established by an entry in the album of a Leipzig fellow student, Friedrich Gleser from Pegau, which says:[4]

Ama iddio, e non fallir,	*Viro antiquae Virtutis et Fidei*
Fa pur 'ten e lascia dir.	*Dno. Frederico Glesero in*
Sic hodie vivitur, Ut multi famam	*Testimonium sinceri ejus Animi*
pauci conscientiam vereant.	*et Nostrae Amicitiae opposuit*
Aliter Vir Sanctus, cui fixum in omni	*Heinrich Schutz*
vita a recta conscientia non latum	*Weissenfels Misnicus.*[5]
Unguem discedere.	

Except for the Mauritius address *(Oratiuncula de S. Mauritio)*, this is apparently the earliest preserved Schütz autograph. It is at the same time a fine testimonial to Schütz's high moral character. Even though the sojourn of the young law student at Leipzig does not seem to have lasted long, he, having now matured into a full-

---

[3] Friedr. Hoppe, *Die Pflege der Musik in Naumburg (The Cultivation of Music in Naumburg),* Naumburg, 1914, p. 13.

[4] According to Werner's translation into German: "Love God and do not fail, do only right, no matter what anyone says. People live today in fear of reputation rather than of conscience. Different is the holy man for whom it has become a firm principle of life not to deviate a fingerbreadth from his conscience. This is dedicated to the man of tried virtue and fidelity in testimony to his pure heart and to our friendship by Heinrich Schütz from Weissenfels, Saxony."

[5] P. 223, in the possession of Judge *(Amtsgerichtsrat)* Glaeser in Weissenfels; imparted by Prof. Arno Werner in *Neue Zeitschr. f. M. Annual 86* (1919), p. 181.

grown musician — altogether different from the Marburg days — must have been stimulated by the musical activity of a great German university city and commercial center.[6]

In the Leipzig bookshops one could obtain everything of interest in the way of music publications: lute books by Kargel, Neusiedler, Reimann, Rude; theoretical syllabi by Calvisius, Listenius, Dressler, Faber, Crusius, Lossius, Wilflingseder; German secular chorus songs by Harnisch, Brechtel, Hassler, Haussmann, Elsbeth, Jeep, Demantius; music for instruments by Brade and Füllsack; passions by Gesius and a Burck; motets by Lasso, Dulichius, Demantius; as well as the modern compositions by Italian composers, such as madrigals, ballets, canzonets. With the latter Schütz was, of course, better acquainted because of his sojourn in Venice. Even at that time Leipzig was famous as a center for the publication of music, with new appearances such as the *Magnificats* by Bodenschatz, V. Otto, and Pinello, Rühling's organ tabulature, Lüttichius' German songs, and pavans by V. Otto and Schein.

He heard the choir of St. Thomas under the aged, highly learned, and excellent composer Seth Calvisius, who, as a liberal and benevolent theoretician, spared his pupils from the ligatures of the sixteenth-century notation but otherwise still represented the old strict taste in church-music composition. It is significant for the state of religious music in Saxony that as late as 1628 a funeral sermon on the death of the organist Christian Graefenthal contains the words:[7]

> "On February 12, 1593, he went to Wittenberg, where the university and the council had unanimously chosen him as organist. He performed in a splendid, versatile manner, assiduously playing the devout old songs according to the electoral church order, which required the old, well-established compositions such as those by Josquin, Clemens non Papa, and the like to be performed, and not the new, untried ones."

Nevertheless, from every direction the moderns were knocking at the Leipzig church door.[8]

The organist at St. Thomas was Andreas Düben the Elder, the founder of the family of musicians that later attained brilliance in Sweden. At this very time he had sent his son Andreas, Jr. to study with Sweelinck in Amsterdam. The organist at St. Paul's was George Engelmann. The lutenist Matthaeus Reymann, from Thorn, also played a prominent part in the musical community. Schütz must have been

---

[6] See R. Wustmann, *Musikgeschichte v. Leipzig (Musical History of Leipzig)*, I, 170 ff.

[7] *Mhfte f. Mg.*, VII, 179.

[8] In the Torgau *Kantorei* statute of 1628 it is further suggested to the conservative cantor that he use in the choir "besides the beautiful old motets of Orlandus and others, also new pieces by present composers insofar as they are good." O. Taubert, *Die Pflege der Musik in Torgau (The Practice of Music in Torgau)*, 1868, p. 15.

particularly delighted to meet here again his old Weissenfels friend Anton Colander, who had been a law student since 1610 and probably organist at St. John's. When Colander died sometime before April 1622, he was court organist in Dresden.[9] Since he does not appear in the court budget of 1612 for Dresden, we may assume that Schütz brought him to the Saxon court in 1616. The fact that as late as 1643 *concerti* by Colander were still printed in Dresden indicates a long-enduring appreciation of him and strengthens our desire to become acquainted with his style of writing.[10] Among the twelve compositions which an anonymous music lover presented from the Seyffert press in Dresden in order that no "Aesopian crow" might adorn himself with these feathers, the seven German works give a most congenial picture of this early-deceased composer, who here, apparently earlier than Schütz, developed solo duets (also a terzet and a quartet) with thorough bass. Most of these consist of chorale melodies embellished with free and effective melismas. The fantasy and bold Schützlike harmony with which Colander wrote may be observed in his conclusion of *Da Jesus an dem Kreuze stund.* Here we find the kernel of the melody deflected from the E Phrygian of the melody proper into the sphere of A minor, in the same way that Schütz later, at the beginning of *The Seven Last Words,* transmuted the core of the melody into an almost new F Aeolian. A comparison with the setting in Schein's *Opella nova* of 1618[11] is suggested. Both have the same scoring, but Colander writes much more à la Schütz than à la Schein and proceeds much more freely than the St. Thomas cantor:

[9] *Musikgeschichte von Leipzig,* I, 195; A. Werner, in *Musikgeschichte von Weissenfels,* p. 41, on the other hand, reports that he was born on October 30, 1590, in Weissenfels, was a student at Schulpforta under Bodenschatz beginning in 1602, studied law in Leipzig "about 1606," and after this had devoted himself to music; that he lived for four years in Prague, where he was cofounder of the *Collegium Musicum,* and that he then studied with his cousin Schütz in Dresden, for which the town fathers of Weissenfels sent Schütz a honorarium (Werner, p. 46).
[10] Further references to compositions in A. Werner, p. 43.
[11] Prüfer, V, 18 ff.

wundt   so gar mit bit = term Schmertzen,

wundt so gar mit bit = te = rem Schmertzen,   so gar mit

so gar mit   bit = term Schmer = tzen; die sie=ben

bit = term Schmertzen, mit bit = term Schmertzen;   die

Wort,   die   Er da spracht,   die Er   da

sie=ben   Wort, die sie=ben   Wort, die Je = sus

spracht: be = tracht,   be = tracht,   be = tracht,   be =

spracht: be=tracht,   be=tracht,   be=tracht,

Because of the rarity of such early German solo *concerti* the quartet is also of unusual interest, especially as Schütz published (through Profe) a seven-voice setting of almost the same text in so ingenious a form.

Colander formulates the love play of the *Song of Songs* into an "echo" consisting of three *versus,* the first of which, despite the alto, is manifestly intended for three male solo voices. After nine solo measures by the tenor they have the *tutti* (see p. 81).

As echo, Sulamith (soprano solo) answers in the second *versus* with Caccinilike nightingale "sobs," in the rhythm of the later "Lombardian taste" (see pp. 81 and 82).

With a joyful quartet *(versus* three), first in three time *(Dreitakt),* then in soaring oratorical style *(Mein Freund ist mein, und ich bin sein),*[12] the fine little piece reaches its climax. With every detail of textual division its model is found in Schein, this time in the *Cymbalum Sionium.*[13] But again, in place of the more compact presentation in Schein (3 plus 3 voices), there appears in Colander a more monodic

[12] "My Friend Is Mine, and I Am His."
[13] 1615, XI. (Prüfer IV, 1, pp. 89 ff.)

Wo iſt dein Freund hin = gan=gen? Wo iſt dein Freund hingangen?
O du ſchönſte

O du ſchönſte un = ter den Wei=bern!
un=ter den Wei = bern!   Wo hat ſich denn dein

Mein Freund iſt hin = ab=ge=gan=gen in ſei=nen___ Gar = = =

ten, zu den Wurtz=gär = = = te = lein, daß er ſich wei=

de und Ro=ſen___ bre = = = = = =

che, daß er sich wei-de und Ro-sen bre = = = che.

and more embellished form, inclining toward Monteverdi and Schütz's coming *Sinfoniae sacrae I.* Colander is fond of these sobs in his chorale settings. Even more than Schein, he usually molds them into the most subjective, expressive form. Schütz must have greatly enjoyed this companion in law and music. Perhaps it was on the occasion of Colander's death that he sang the noble funeral song of 1621: "I Am the Resurrection and the Life." [14]

This student period at Leipzig — possibly the second — cannot have been long, for we soon meet Schütz again at the court of the landgrave in Kassel, where his patron Moritz created for him the post of second court organist. This was doubtless a formal appointment to insure the composer an income and to place him above the singers and instrumentalists without making him the equal of the much older Kapellmeisters Otto and Ostermayer. The funeral eulogy even places this appointment before the Weissenfels-Leipzig interlude:

"After his protector in Venice had died, he left there in 1612 and again turned to Germany to the honorable landgrave, who advanced him 200 gulden until he should receive a definite appointment. Since, however, it did not satisfy him to continue with music in these circumstances, he preferred to take his books in hand again to make up for what he had neglected in Italy and to use his music as an avocation for advancement along further lines."

Schütz doubtless played the continuo for the church and chamber music. Even at that time there were great concert organists, but Schütz evidently was not one of them. It could be a mere accident that not a single note of organ music by him has been preserved or even mentioned. Once, in Dresden encomiums, his "hand" is mentioned in addition to his "voice." [15] It is much more significant that later he never instructed any of his highly talented pupils at the keyboard but took his favorites to the Hamburg pupils of Sweelinck. In addition to his musical duties, the "learned one" (the landgrave) also employed Schütz as private secretary and as tutor for his children.

---

[14] *Ich bin die Auferstehung.* Vol. VI, Part II, No. 19, p. 135.

[15] According to Gerber's *Tonkünstlerlexikon*, p. 784, M. Weckmann learned from Schütz "to develop *(variieren)* a motet on two manuals from the mere thorough bass; apart from the lack of clarity of this notice, both as to content and as to source, it, too, would seem to point to a function of composition rather than to special manual technique on the part of Schütz."

That even at this time Schütz must have been very much in demand as a Kapell-meister is apparent from the Bückeburg records of Duke Ernst of Schaumburg-Lippe.[16] This young prince, orphaned at an early age, a free student at Helmstädt, was twice sent into foreign parts by his guardian, Duke Simon of Detmold. These two journeys went far to awaken his cultural interests. In Kassel, in 1597, he married the sister of Moritz the Learned, with whom he had had friendly relations at least since 1593. In Bückeburg, Ernst built the castle and the castle chapel and established there in 1606 both sacred and secular music, the former under Conrad Hagius[17] from Rinteln, the latter, for the time being, under Johann Grabbe, with six English musicians whom Moritz had dismissed from Kassel. There were very distinguished performers among these Englishmen, as, for example, the much-traveled William Brade; the excellent Thomas Simpson; the lutenist George Webs-ter, who was later advanced to the position of London court lutenist; and his son — ambassadors from Elizabethan England who were epoch-making for the string technique of the German suite. The necessary money for the expenses involved in all this was provided for the duke from the Holstein tariffs exacted by him at Pinneberg before the gates of Hamburg, and also by a wise economy which he practiced despite all his Maecenean lavishness. Rist, at a much later time, praised this little sovereign who rewarded his musicians like privy counselors and pre-sented their income to them in silk purses. For a time the road leading from Frank-furt and Kassel by way of Bückeburg and Pinneberg to Hamburg and Copenhagen was a veritable highway for virtuosi. Despite territorial friction Duke Ernst also carried on a most friendly interchange of artists with King Christian IV.

The most important musician of his circle was the Gabrieli pupil whom we have already met in Venice, Johann Grabbe (Crabbe), born in 1585. He was first em-ployed by Duke Simon as court organist. Since St. Michael's Day in 1614 he was Vice-Kapellmeister in Bückeburg and was buried there in 1655. In addition to his Italian madrigals, the library at Kassel possessed his *Cantiones aliquot sacrae*, now

---

[16] I owe the information concerning the sources to the kindness of Max Seiffert.

[17] Compositions by Hagius from 1588 (in the *Dodekatonon Triciniorum* of Henning Dede-kind). In Düsseldorf he published *Ulenberg Psalms* (1589); in 1594 he sent the Council of Dan-zig a musical felicitation from Thorn, made friends in Linz, was attached to the court of Det-mold; prefaced in 1604 in Heidelberg a collection of new German spiritual and secular terzets dedicated to Duke Ernst (with a portrait of Hagius); in 1606 he dedicated from Mainz his twelve *Magnificats* to the Fuggers (in part parodied on *Prototypos* (printed in Dillingen); finally, in 1615, from Rintelen he writes for the Bückeburg Duke a collection of six-voice *In-tradas* and recalls in connection therewith journeys through "Austria, Bohemia, Hungary, Po-land, Prussia, Lithuania." In addition to this, lost compositions are mentioned in the catalogs of the Leipzig fair and some individual movements. One work published by M. Seiffert in *Musik am Hof des Grafen Ernst*.

lost. Further pieces of his are two pavans in Hagius (1617), three pieces in Simpson (1621), and one in Brade (1617).

The alto (falsetto) singer Christoph Schubhardt, whose *Canzonettes* have been mentioned above (p. 35) is also worthy of comment as a composer belonging to the Schütz circle in Kassel from 1598 to 1606. Schubhardt, together with his son, took part in the music of Bückeburg from 1612 to 1614.

Michael Praetorius was associated in various ways with Duke Ernst. He dedicated the third part of his *Musae Sioniae* (1607) to the duke; put him in touch with Esajas Compenius, who built a famous organ for the Bückeburg town church;[18] conveyed, in 1612, a miniature picture of the duke to the Saxon Electress Hedwig; and transmitted to the duke letters from an alchemist imprisoned in Hildesheim.

Since Easter 1615 Schütz's name appears in the account books of Duke Ernst — first in the budget set for 1615-16. We find the following entry: "Payment for Sagittarius 1,000 florins for board. A velvet suit and free lodging." After this comes a reference concerning a noteworthy composer as cornetist. "Martin Caesar, 900 florins, and 100 florins traveling expenses, and to his wife, after his death, 200 florins."[19]

In the ledger there stands in place of this in thaler:

Sagittarius 1,000 fl.	832
Kleidung	80
Martin Caesar	750

We must compare with this the fact that the other musicians received only 100 to 300 thaler, though Crabbe, as gambist, received 380. The pensioned Hagius received only 100. Inasmuch as such allowances are not specified under the "Ordinary and Extraordinary Expenditures," perhaps they were merely entries. Likewise, the account "Support of the Music from Easter 1616" begins:

	Thaler
Sagittarius	833
clothing	80
lodging	10
Vice-Kapellmeister	300

---

[18] Cf. The Berlin dissertation (1934) of my pupil Thekla Schneider: *Die Orgelbauerfamilie Compenius.*

[19] Caesar was probably an Italian by birth. From 1610 until his death in 1667 he was employed in Munich as chamber cornet player. A whole series of printed works by him is referred to in Eitner, *Quellen-Lexikon.*

Inasmuch, however, as the actual account has merely the following:

	Thaler
Kapellmeister	300
Hagius	100

we must assume that Schütz's appointment did not materialize but that, instead, Tobias Hoffkuntz, who had been intended as his substitute, became the independent leader of the court music.[20] After Easter 1617-18 we have only the actual payments, and they state at the end

	Thaler
Sagittarius 500 florins	416, 24 gr.
Martin Caesar 450 florins	375

Both names are again crossed out as an indication of a change in plans.

Since only half of the salaries originally allotted were actually paid, the meaning becomes clear. Schütz and Caesar were compensated only for services in absentia (von Haus aus), that is, for occasional counsel, forwarding of compositions, etc., not for real services on the spot. In connection with the expenditures of 1618-19, both are mentioned as receiving full pay; but later they were stricken out. Therewith ends any mention of Schütz in the Bückeburg documents. We may interpret this as indicating that our master was so firmly bound to Dresden, and was so busy there, that Duke Ernst considered it to no purpose to claim him even in absentia; but the duke smoothed over the dismissal very generously by actually paying Schütz, for once, the full salary. Unfortunately, no correspondence with Schütz has been preserved, nor have any compositions connected with this relationship to Bückeburg come down to us. Shortly after Duke Ernst's death the military rabble of the Thirty Years' War made a clean sweep in Bückeburg.

This intermezzo has been spun out somewhat in order to show in this "promoter of the free arts" (as Matthias Merker calls Duke Ernst in the dedication of his Paduanas, Bückeburg, 1619) the rich and joyous picture of the German music world shortly before the great catastrophe.

Philipp Spitta, with some positiveness, identifies but one of Schütz's extant works as having been written for Kassel before he went to Dresden — the four-chorus Veni Sancte Spiritus.[21] On one of the violin parts is written M. Tiratore, meaning

---

[20] After 1642 Joh. Heinr. Hofkunze was the assistant Kapellmeister under Schütz, perhaps the son of the Bückeburger. He was certainly born in German Bohemia. For his decree of appointment see W. Schafer, Sachsenchronik, I (1854), 425.

[21] Complete edition, XIV, 16.

Schütz. This composition, which will be discussed with other early works, is to be assigned approximately to Whitsuntide 1614. On the parts of the fourth chorus, where the others have *Positieff, Im Chor, Frawen-Zimmer* (= virginal), there are the letters L.H.A. This has led Ph. Spitta to interpret the letters as *Landgravi Hassiae Altissimi (organum),* that is, "a portative from the chambers of Moritz." I think a simpler explanation is that the landgrave, an experienced composer and executant, himself conducted from the cembalo or the house organ this most important and unique chorus for six voices on the occasion of the Whitsuntide concert in his apartments.

Possibly *Christ ist erstanden* ("Christ Is Arisen") and the original form of Psalm 19, *Die Himmel rühmen* ("The Heavens Declare") also belong to this period. The fact that Schütz did not publish this psalm among the psalms of 1619 but only in final form in the *Geistliche Chormusik* of 1648, can readily be explained by the fact that, since it is a work for single chorus, it appeared to him too meagerly set for the 1619 collection.

The Dresden Court Kapellmeister
till 1628

Electoral Saxony, that is, since 1548 the Albertinian part of the lands of the
Wettins, was the most important Protestant territory in the century before the
blossoming-forth in 1648 of Brandenburg-Prussia. Among the obligatory court
duties resulting from this prestige one of the most important in a country desiring
to preserve Luther's heritage was the maintenance of an appropriate court choral
organization *(Kantorei)*. The list of the Dresden court Kapellmeisters is indeed one
to be proud of: Johann Walter, M. Le Maistre, Scandello, Pinello, G. Forster, Roger
Michael. But after Johann Georg I ascended the electoral throne of his fathers,[1] a
rejuvenation of the court ensemble *(Capelle)* seemed in order, as the result of an
investigation in the year 1612. This reorganization was called for both on account
of the reputation of the ensemble and because of the personal devotion to music
on the part of the prince, who was fond of the chase and of the cup. The court
composer and court organist, Hans Leo Hassler, had just died. Both the other
organists, August Nörmiger[2] and the Kapellmeister, Roger Michael, were burdened
by advancing years. Among the instrumentalists Greg. Hoyer and Zacharias Füllsack were highly esteemed. A *viola bastarda* player, Walter (Rowe?), was a valuable asset. With the exception of these, however, the singers and players were
apparently only mediocre. While a new leader was being found, Michael Praetorius of Wolfenbüttel took charge of the ensemble on festal occasions as visiting
conductor (Kapellmeister *in absentia*). When, in 1613, on the occasion of such a
festival, Landgrave Moritz journeyed to Dresden and took Schütz along, the latter,
as director of one of the choirs, apparently made such an impression that he was
engaged for the Saxon court for September and October 1614.[3]

---

[1] He reigned from 1611 to 1656.
[2] His organ tabulature of 1598 has been preserved in the Berlin *Staatsbibliothek* as Ms. 40089.
[3] See Moritz Fürstenau, *Beiträge zur Geschichte der Kgl. sächs. Musikalischen Kapelle* (Dresden, 1849), pp. 42 ff. Based on Müller, *Forschungen zur sächsischen Geschichte* (1838); and, in
still greater detail, Wilhelm Schäfer, in *Sachsenchronik* I (Dresden, 1854), 429 ff. and 500 ff.
Further, W. Dane: *ZfMW*, XVII.

On September 3, 1614, Landgrave Moritz wrote to Johann Georg from Nordenstadt:

> "We have received your gracious letter of August 27 just past and have gathered therefrom that you wish to have our organist, Heinrich Schütz, at Dresden on the occasion of the Baptism of your God-given infant son on the 18th of this month. We are eager to serve Your Highness in this as well as in other matters, and accordingly we have given the desired permission to Schütz and shall see that he appears at the proper place and time; and we assume that after the Baptism he will, with your sanction, duly return to us. . . ."

As a matter of fact, Schütz was actually sent back to Kassel after the Baptism of Duke August, as is indicated in a letter of Johann Georg of October 10:

> "Although we shall grievously miss Schütz among our musicians for such a long time, and, furthermore, although we cannot otherwise now fill his position, nevertheless, to show you our good fraternal disposition, we shall grant permission to our organist to return, in order that he may remain at your court for a number of years and be of humble service there."

However, the elector later wrote from Langensalza (April 25, 1615) to the landgrave:

> "We are fraternally grateful that you will allow your organist Heinrich Schütz to be with us for a while during the coming year. We should, of course, not impose further on your generosity. However, should Schütz's qualities please us greatly, and should he delight us with his art, we cannot refrain from asking you to show us your good will still further and graciously to permit said Schütz to return to us for a few years until certain musicians whom we have sent to Italy and elsewhere[4] to acquire this art may return to us."

Landgrave Moritz was certainly not pleased to surrender his best young talent, in which he had made so considerable an investment; but he could not readily antagonize his powerful neighbor. Accordingly, he acceded, and on April 27 he wrote his reluctant consent to the elector, sending Schütz from Kassel to Dresden on August 28 with a letter to the elector: "I have acceded to your request on the assumption that Your Electoral Highness will not detain him longer than the two years specified, and that you will then allow him to return to us. On these conditions we have given our consent."

The elector (Zörbig, May 2, 1615) thanked the landgrave heartily for his cooperation, and on the same day bade Privy Counselor Loss receive Schütz most cordially. On September 30 he also informed Kassel that the organist had duly arrived in Dresden. "In recognition of Schütz's diligence and deportment we shall grant him our gracious favor."

As early as December 1616 Moritz demanded the return of his protégé "inasmuch as we are resolved to use him for the education of our, thank God, now advancing young lordships." Moritz thus wished to employ Schütz again as tutor to the princes. With regard to this desire of the landgrave, the elector's privy

---

[4] This was the case with Joh. Nauwach and Joh. Klemme.

counselor, Christof von Loss, addressed the following memorandum to the elector, a document most complimentary both to Schütz's character and to his activities:

"Most gracious elector and lord. Enclosed I am humbly forwarding to Your Electoral Grace a letter from His Princely Grace, Landgrave Moritz of Hessen, Besides other things, you will learn therefrom what the respected Herr Landgrave kindly imparts to you concerning Heinrich Schütz. . . . To be sure, the wishes on the part of Your Electoral Grace in the matter are clear; moreover, it is not unknown to you that if the music at the church and at the table is to be conducted as before, a person who is practiced in composition, conversant with instruments, and familiar with the repertoire of church music cannot be dispensed with. In my humble opinion, I know of no one to be preferred to Schütz in these matters. He [Schütz] has also shown Your Electoral Grace with especial distinction what he is able to accomplish in these respects. I am concerned lest, if his services are lost, he cannot be replaced, since it would be impossible to find his counterpart. To be sure, Your Electoral Grace still also has Herr Praetorius in his employ; nevertheless, you graciously know that he serves only *in absentia* and that he cannot always obtain leave from the court ensemble (*Capell*) at Brunswick. Consequently, in his absence and without Schütz, it would be impossible to arrange concerted music in church. Furthermore, all rehearsals would be suspended. As a result, your music would suffer no small amount of harm. . . . At Your Electoral Grace's most gracious pleasure I have compiled the accompanying letter to the distinguished Herr Landgrave in your name . . . but await your command as to whether you wish to execute it thus or whether you have any changes to suggest. I have also suggested in my reply that the aforementioned Schütz be left altogether in the service of Your Electoral Grace in order that in the future you may not be in danger of such requisitioning. And inasmuch as Otto von Starscheddel [in Altenburg, then Kassel], with whom I discussed the matter relating to Schütz at the recent wedding in Borna, is still living here, and since he has offered to do everything in his power to the end that Schütz may remain completely in the service of Your Electoral Grace, he [von Loss] was willing to request Starschädel (sic) once more to intercede with the landgrave."

On December 13 the elector executed the draft presented to him by von Loss, and Schütz himself wrote to Moritz on December 16. But as early as December 24, 1616, the "learned one" answered:[5]

The only letter of importance among these is one, hitherto unknown, to the landgrave by Schütz himself. It has also been published by Herbert Birtner in the *Zeitschrift Hessenland*, forty-sixth year, brochure 7-8. It reads as follows:

Your Serene Highness, Right Honorable Prince, Gracious Lord, Your Princely Grace: In addition to my wishes for your temporal and eternal well-being, be ever assured of my altogether dutiful, subservient, and obedient services to the best my ability.

Right Honorable Prince, Gracious Lord, Your Princely Grace: I have humbly received the gracious command which you recently sent me. I have noted therein the gracious command and citation to betake my humble self to Kassel. . . . Though it would have given me personally great pleasure to have humbly and dutifully obeyed Your Princely Grace's command, His Electoral Grace of Saxony has indicated to me that I should not absent myself according to Your Princely Grace's plan. He was doubtless prompted by the fact that he could not well dispense with my humble services at the coming festivities, especially in view of the absence of Michael Praetorius, the nominal Kapellmeister *in absentia* here.

However, I have no doubt His Electoral Grace, after the conclusion of the festivities, will graciously be pleased to allow me humbly to comply with Your Princely Grace's command, whereupon I shall promptly appear at Kassel. I shall use the utmost diligence to bring about this consummation.

---

[5] Werner Dane published some further letters between Landgrave Moritz and Elector Johann Georg concerning Schütz in the *Zeitschrift für Musikwissenschaft* (XVII, 1935, pp. 343-355).

In the meanwhile, I trust Your Princely Grace will graciously accept this my delay and will not understand it otherwise than that I, apart from the power of God, would not for one moment have evaded your gracious command had I been able to comply with it with His Electoral Highness' permission.

I entertain, however, the comforting unswerving, humble confidence that Your Princely Grace will graciously be satisfied on this one occasion with my excuse and will continue to be disposed toward me with your hitherto customary grace... And indeed I am as eager as I am in duty bound, as all natural and divine laws remind me, to serve with all possible submission throughout my life both Your Princely Grace and your praiseworthy princely house.... I herewith call upon Almighty God in behalf of Your Princely Grace and your beloved young princely reigning wife that He, besides a blessed, happy New Year, may richly bestow on you a happy reign, complete health of body, together with all well-being of body and soul.

Dated Dresden December 16, 1616

> Your Princely Grace's
> subservient, dutiful,
> obedient servant
> Heinrich Schütz, Mpp.

(Address)

To His Serene Highness, Right Honorable Prince and Lord, Lord Moritz, Landgrave of Hessen, Duke of Katzenelnbogen, Diehtz, Ziegenhain and Nidda, etc.

> To my Gracious Prince and Lord

(Secretarial note:)

Heinrich Schütz, concerning his recall from Dresden.
Kassel, December 22, 1616.

"Your [E.L.] gracious reply in the matter of our alumnus and organist Heinrich Schütz was delivered to us in due time last evening. We note with pleasure that Schütz so conducted himself that Your Excellency has hitherto been graciously satisfied with him and his services. We would like nothing better than that we might surrender him to you completely in the manner desired. But we would not like to leave Your Grace misinformed that the matter concerns our music in a manner quite otherwise than may have been presented to you, inasmuch as, in the first place, the musicians mentioned by you are not available, and, furthermore, with regard to Schütz the situation is such that even if we could dispense with him with regard to our music, we could only with great difficulty do so in other respects. We have indicated such things to you in a recent writing. Such matters could not be achieved without his presence...." But in order that the elector may not doubt his good intentions, "we shall, as a brotherly favor, however inconvenient it may be, grant that the frequently mentioned Schütz may remain in your service somewhat longer in order to bring your music to the desired state of excellence"... Finally, the suggestion "whether it cannot be arranged that though we surrender Schütz completely to Your Grace, he may nevertheless remain in our employ and service that we may at times utilize his services as occasions arise. With regard to this suggestion Your Excellency is not unaware that this practice is variously indulged in, and indeed to the best of our knowledge you yourself employ Praetorius unter these conditions..."

But the Wettin was not satisfied with this compromise. On January 1, 1617, he referred to the fact that the annual payment for Praetorius served only for traveling expenses and board. He must have Schütz completely. Hereupon Moritz replied ruefully from Ziegenhain on January 16, 1617:

"With regard to the chief matter, concerning the ever-willing servant Schütz, I am not a little happy not only that my modest willingness to oblige you was agreeable to Your Excellency but also that his person and services were so acceptable that you again request these without limitation. I, of couse, recall that he is by descent one of your subjects[6] and thus is

---

[6] Not, as Ph. Spitta believed, because Reuss was still under Saxon feudal right but because the Schütz family came from Chemnitz.

under obligation to serve you above all other rulers. To be sure, I had hoped that Your Excellency might have been graciously content with the afore-suggested resolution of all difficulties. But I have resolved submissively to acquiesce in the further request of Your Excellency. And though I find it difficult to yield completely both him and the purpose for which I had him educated and advanced, it is and shall remain my greater pleasure to assure myself of your constant good favor and affection through my consent. For my part, I shall endeavor to reciprocate fully. I wish Your Excellency happiness and blessing from the Almighty in connection with the now completely surrendered servant, who in time can be of greater service to Your Excellency in his new position, and I most graciously pray that for my sake also you will let the aforementioned Heinrich Schütz be most graciously commended to you."

On February 17, 1617, Johann Georg gave Schütz, who again went to Kassel to adjust his affairs, a hearty letter of thanks to the landgrave. Seldom has there been such haggling and contention between two potentates for a musician. An affair of state almost resulted! But what a beautiful human touch it was that the "learned one" did not, on his part, withdraw his hand from the lost one but went out of his way to commend him again to the heart of his new master. Indeed, he did so a second time in a brief letter of March 20, 1617. Geier's memorial gives more details concerning the parting between Moritz and Schütz:

"The Almighty, however, who perhaps from his mother's womb had destined him for music, once again took the law books out of his hands. The deceased, contrary to all his previous plans, was summoned to Dresden in the year 1615 by the most honorable Elector of Saxony, Johann Georg I of blessed memory, to participate in the ceremonies at the Baptism of Prince Duke Augustus, at present administrator of the Archepiscopal Foundation at Magdeburg. Since he was in duty bound to obey the elector's gracious command, he journeyed to Dresden after receiving the necessary permission from the Herr Landgrave. Soon after the festivities he was offered the directorate of the electoral music. As he perceived in this the wonderful guidance of the Almighty, he did not decline the high call but accepted the opportunity humbly after being released by the landgrave. The latter indeed did not begrudge him his good fortune but, in reply to a letter from His Electoral Highness, dimissed him with a golden chain, a portrait, and appropriate words of leave-taking."

This chain was doubtless the one with the gold medal, the one shown on all three of the portraits of Schütz that have come down to us. The landgrave doubtless knew his Johann Georg and was aware of the fact that for the latter the victory in this struggle was at least as much a matter of pride and prestige as of art. The landgrave's last letters indicate a feeling of warm intimacy with the talent which he had reared with such special care. Even then he had not abandoned the hope to regain his Sagittarius. For when Georg Otto died as Kapellmeister at Kassel in 1619, the landgrave again offered the position to Schütz.[7] The elector replied negatively:[8]

"You will doubtless recall the reasons that heretofore prompted me to request from you the complete surrender of Schütz and the conclusion arrived at to our special satisfaction. Accordingly, we received him into our entourage, provided him with all kinds of conveniences, and

[7] Letter to Johann Georg of January 11, 1619.
[8] Dresden, January 25, 1619.

committed to him the direction of our entire chapel (*chori musici*). In connection with all this he has conducted himself in such a manner that we may graciously be well satisfied with him. Therefore we do not see — not having among our musical forces one who could take his place — how we could dispense with him without detriment to our music, especially, too, inasmuch as our former old Kapellmeister has reached such an age and such frailty that we can no longer avail ourselves of his services either in church or at table. Furthermore, at our own prompting Schütz has entered the estate of matrimony here and has promised his new relatives and friends that he will not leave this place or our service but will stay here. From all this Your Excellenc will sufficiently understand that we cannot dispense with Schütz, and also that he himself is strongly attached here. Therefore we beg of you in a most friendly manner to think no less well of us for not having acceded to your request. . . ."

So this plan also suffered shipwreck for the landgrave. He was compelled to fill the position of Court Kapellmeister with Schütz's old friend Christof Cornett. But even now the cordial relations between the landgrave and Schütz were not severed, as is evinced by the numerous manuscripts, for the most part autographs, which found their way to Kassel up to the death of the landgrave. According to the catalog of 1638,[9] the number of these was once far greater than those now in the possession of the Hessian court library, even though, as the result of the fires of Dresden, Gera, and Copenhagen, this library is still the richest in Schütz manuscripts.

Schütz himself either learned little about all these transactions back and forth between the princes, or the events became simplified and confused in his memory. For in the autobiography of 1651 he merely writes to the elector concerning the matter:

"Moreover, God Almighty, who doubtless had predestined me for the profession of music from my mother's womb, also ordained that in 1614 — I do not know whether perhaps through Herr Christoff von Loos, at the time privy counselor, or of chamber counselor Wolfersdorff, also commander at Weissenfels — I was summoned hither to Dresden in connection with the pending Baptism of Prince Duke August, at present administrator of the Archepiscopal Foundation at Magdeburg. When, after my arrival, I had given proof of my ability, I was graciously offered the directorate of your music. As a result, my parents, relatives, and I myself perceived the unchangeable will of God with regard to my person, and hereby a goal was set for my vacillating thoughts, and I was moved not to decline the honorable position offered me but to accept it with most submissive thanks and to fulfill my duties with the utmost zeal."

Although Schütz's position in Dresden was later on to become so unpleasant, it must nevertheless be conceded that at that time a good star guided him from Hessia to Saxony; for the fortunes of the Gran Maurizio had taken a very unfavorable turn at even a considerably earlier period. As a result of the war, his counselors, in 1620, advised him[10] to reduce the expenses of his chapel (*Kapellhaushalt*) from 4,000 gulden annually to half of that sum. Moritz replied in a manner

---

[9] In Zulauf, *Geschichte der Kasseler Hofkapelle bis auf Moritz den Gelehrten* (1902).
[10] Zulauf, pp. 73 ff.

as artistically noble as it was stubbornly unwise: "In my judgment the court chapel (Hofkappelstaat) should either be left as it is or should be given up altogether; for even if but two persons are dismissed, the whole organization will be ruined. This will neither enhance our reputation nor give us pleasure."

Friedrich Blume gives the following summary of the landgrave's later fortunes:[11]

"The political situation became ever more acute. Therefore Moritz began at an early period to cultivate relations with foreign countries — with France, with Elizabeth of England, and, in 1612, as the first German prince to do so, with Gustavus Adolfus. He was forced to this policy by the increasing quarrels with his neighbors. . . . To the external complications inner ones were added, in connection with which Moritz, as the result of his autocratic ideas of state, was, of course, not blameless. He had attempted to create for himself a stronger, more sovereign power over his vassals who, in turn, soon gained the support of the Catholic party in the empire. His subjects were further incensed at what was doubtless culturally and politically the most far-reaching act of his government: he officially joined the Reformed Church and attempted to impose this creed on his country. He acted with particular severity in Upper Hessia. Ruthlessly the Lutheran professors were ejected from the University of Marburg. . . . As a reaction, the University of Giessen was founded. . . . Thus the wisest ruler of his time had created for himself an untenable position. The net was drawn closer and closer around him. In the early years of the Thirty Years' War military defeats occurred, and in 1623 a catastrophe overtook him. Tilly occupied Hessia, and all the opponents of the landgrave seized their booty from the helpless corpse of the country. His boundaries shrank in an alarming manner, the emperor freed the feudal nobility from its duties toward Moritz, and in the deepest disgrace and impotence the landgrave, in 1627, had to abdicate in favor of his son Wilhelm (IV). The triumphant enemy inflicted their worst on the broken and embittered man when, in 1628, they executed his last faithful adviser and friend, his chancellor, Dr. Wolfgang Günther. Philosophical studies mitigated the loneliness of his voluntary exile in Eschwege, and there, in 1632, was ended the life of the prince which had begun with such brilliant prospects."

Schütz doubtless followed these tragic developments with the greatest sympathy. But at the same time the first important position in which he was

---

[11] *Geistliche Musik am Hofe des Landgr. Moritz, Einl.,* p. 9; *(Spiritual Music from the Court of the Landgrave Moritz,* Introduction, p. 9). This did not prevent a *Monumentum Sepulcrale* of several hundred pages, printed in 1638. However, musically this offers little that is new.

independent — at Dresden — demanded his entire attention. The reforms which he introduced in the Saxon court ensemble *(Hofkapelle)* can no longer be followed in detail. What new music he purchased or directed to be copied was later destroyed in the Seven Years' War. His personal appointments could be made but gradually, as vacancies occurred. Lists of musicians from 1612 down to practically 1627 are missing. In consequence, we learn only here and there from letters and dedications what persons he enlisted or at least recommended. Among these, doubtless at the very beginning, presumably as the successor of Nörminger, was Anton Colander, who, on his early death, was succeeded by G. Kretzschmar, then by Joh. Klemme,[12] and still later by M. Weckmann. Above all, from the very beginning Schütz devoted himself as father and teacher to his choir boys and had the development of new recruits ever at heart. The earliest letter of his that we have,[13] one addressed to privy counselor and master of the mint Ch. v. Loss in *(auf)* Schleinitz (September 23, 1616) is, from the viewpoint both of manly seriousness and vigor of speech, a fine tribute to his personality. About 1605 a Frenchman, Hans Bruno (Jean Bruneau?), had served as an instrumentalist in the Dresden ensemble *(Kapelle)*. Apparently the case which Schütz discusses in his letter has to do with Bruno's two sons. The older one, perhaps identical with a good-for-nothing organist named Bruno whom M. Praetorius in the same year (1616) took with him from Hamburg to Halle,[14] had run away from his father (now living elsewhere), had gone to Dresden, and there had not only stolen bed linen from the choir house but had persuaded his younger brother, Schütz's pupil, to accompany him.

"Meanwhile, up to the present time he has not been found, and we do not know whither he has gone. But, as a matter of fact, I see and feel that this apple comes from a bad stock, and I consider the whole tribe to be of little worth. The scamp has had a pleasant life, even though at times I upbraided him. I did this especially eight days ago when he went to confession and promised with tears in his eyes that he would behave properly; but the wolf changes his coat, not his disposition.[15] I can testify before God that I never struck him, that, accordingly, Your Excellency can be absolutely assured that he did **not** run away either from

---

[12] Klemme, born about 1593 in Oederan near Freiberg, Saxony; 1605 Dresden choir boy; 1612 instrumentalist; 1613-15 studied, with electoral stipend, under Christ. Erbach in Augsburg; then pupil of Schütz; 1625 second court organist; married 1626; died soon after 1651. M. Seiffert describes his printed clavierschool *(Tastenschule)*, *Partitura seu Tabulatura Italica*, Dresden 1631, in his *Geschichte der Klaviermusik*, pp. 100 ff. A six-voice motet is in the Zwickau Ms. 99.

[13] In E. H. Müller's Collection, No. 2, p. 38, according to W. Schäfer's *Sachsenchronik*, I, 1854, p. 519; the original now no longer extant.

[14] Two of his compositions are mentioned in Eitner's *Quellen-Lexikon*.

[15] *Sed lupus pilos mutat, animum non.*

fear or because of want. Therefore I blame his frivolous brother for enticing him and setting the whole thing in motion. . ." [16]

The letter concludes:

"I have recently been very much indisposed, as have also the boys entrusted to me. I am looking forward to better times. Caspar (Kittel) is almost well again, thank God, and is going out again. I expect to use him again next Sunday. Johannes (Vierdanck) is a fine fellow of good principles. He has laid a good foundation in composition. Therefore we may expect something from him in the near future. . . ."

Caspar Kittel was court singer from 1620 to 1624. In 1624-28 he was in Italy and later was "theorbo player and inspector of instruments" of the electoral ensemble *(Kapelle)*. Like Schütz, Kittel was eligible for the Schütz legacy at Chemnitz. He died after 1661 and was the composer of *German Arias and Cantatas* for from one to four voices (Dresden, 1638), which H. Kretzschmar so wrongfully disparaged. [17]

On Schütz's recommendation Johannes Vierdanck was educated by the imperial cornetist Sansoni in Vienna in 1641 and later gained distinction as organist at St. Mary's at Stralsund. His *Divertimenti and Spiritual Concerti* (1642-43) have recently found recognition. They have been published as monuments of Pomeranian music. [18]

Schütz soon found occasion to show the electoral ensemble *(Kapelle)* its new glory when, on July 15, 1617, a distinguished company, consisting of Emperor

---

[16] Georg Weisse expressed himself in a touching manner concerning Schütz as an educator of choir boys. One feels Weisse's personal devotion and thanks — as Asaph instructed the children of the Levites in song.

> Thus did you, worthy Schütz, induct some hundred boys
> To learn the art of song in royal chapel style,
> And brought to them renown; what these who live possess
> Is due to you alone and to the grace of God,
> As when a swarm of bees is guided in its search
> By one who leads them where the flowers grow.
> The honey that the little ones can gather thus
> They owe alone to him who charted out their course.
> I, too, was one of these who long ago
> Was taught by you and whom indeed you loved.
> And so when your distinguished son [*] in Dresden wrote
> To tell me of your death, I bitterly was grieved.
> And how else could it be? The father's death is sad
> To all his worthy sons; the pious pupil weeps,
> When his Gamaliel dies who loved him
> And ever meant so well with his devoted pupil.

[*] The son was *Magnificus Dn. D. Pinckerus, Sereniss, Sax. Elect. Consiliarius, Scabinus et Consul Lipsiensis senior Gener B(eati) Schüzzii.*

[17] *Geschichte des neuen deutschen Liedes*, pp. 52 ff. To the contrary see my *Corydon*, I, 12 ff. and II, 3 ff.; H. Riemann, *Hdb. d. MG*, II, 2, p. 348 ff.; Walter Vetter, *Das Frühdeutsche Lied*, I and II.

[18] Published by H. Engel in the Bärenreiter-Verlag.

Matthias with his wife, Anna; his cousin, Archduke Ferdinand (later Emperor Ferdinand II); and Archduke Maximilian, visited Dresden. In their entourage were Wallenstein, Cardinal Clesel, and Prince Eggenberg. On the occasion of their entrance into the palace "a beautiful music and one pleasing to hear"[19] was played on the forward balcony. In a specially printed document, *Panegyrici caesario-regio-archiducales,* the Hapsburg guests were welcomed by *aliquot territorij Elect. Saxon. celebribus poetis.* At the conclusion of the document were Latin and German poems "by Heinrich Schütz, musical director at the electoral Saxon court." In the opening number he shows in eleven grandiloquent and euphonious distichs[20] that as a master of classical culture he was qualified to mingle with the Muses, who greeted their lordships:

> *Et redimere chelyn, felices edere cantus*
> *Caepêre aptando voce tremente chelyn.*

> And they began to release the lyre, to bring forth happy songs,
> As they accompanied with trembling voice.

On the other hand, his German stanzas of welcome stumbled along somewhat in pre-Opitz manner. Perhaps they represent the prolog of *Fama* as "worthy servant" of the gods for a picturesque conversation between the nymphs of the Elbe *(nymphae Albiades)* and Neptune, who guided the imperial ship safely along the river to Dresden. This work, of which the music has, unfortunately, been lost, probably was arranged somewhat as follows:

1. Four-strophe chorus: *Die unsterblichen Götter all* ("All the immortal gods")
2. Chorus of nymphs: *Neptun, der dich, o Kaiser groß* ("Neptune, who thee, O mighty emperor")
3. Solo song of Neptune to the nymphs: *Ihr Wasser Göttin'n, auf zur Fahrt* ("Ye water gods, now set you sail")
4. Chorus of nymphs: *Wohlauff den Kaiser lobesan* ("All hail the noble emperor")

There follows the text of a genuine festival play which Schütz composed, but of which, unfortunately again, not a note has been preserved.[21]

> Astounding translocation
> Of the world-famous
> And splendid mountain of Parnassus
> And its nine goddesses / with their

---

[19] Anton Weck, *Beschreibung Dresden* (1680), pp. 389 ff.
[20] *Caesar, ave.*
[21] Anton Weck says: "On the 12th (of August) a ballet was presented at court in the evening."

Overlords and president Apollo /,
Who by the immortal gods
Were delegated to receive and to honor
His Imperial Royal Majesty,
Also His Archducal Serene Excellency,
In the well-guarded chief fortress Dresden.
Wherefore they themselves relate such
In the following manner.

The announcement of the title is followed by a presumably nine-voice ensemble of the Muses. It consists of nine (!) strophes, each with six lines with an a-a-b-c-c-b rhyme scheme[22]: "As recently we made music." Then follow — doubtless accompanied by changing, characteristic instrumental groups, as later in the case of the *intermedia* of the *Christmas Oratorio* — the solo songs of Apollo and the songs of the nine Muses. The Apollo songs consist of two similarly constructed stanzas with lines of unequal length, as in madrigals. The exact number of syllables can be reconstructed without difficulty. The dissimilarity of the structure of all the stanzas indicates that no simultaneous rendition of different texts is to be assumed.

The conclusion consists of a *Sonetto delle Muse nel Parnasso* in five strophes. Perhaps each of four voice parts was sung by two Muses, Apollo and one of the Muses taking a fifth, in which case the composition for five voices was probably accompanied by five instruments. The meter is the one made familar by Spee's and Brahms's *In stiller Nacht*. As this was one of the most popular meters of the sixteenth century, we may assume that the music was probably written in the Hassler *canzonetta* style, as for example, *Jungfrau, dein schöne g'stalt*. Actually, the ingenuous, unaffected nature of this German verse seems to bring us personally closer to Schütz than the pompous style of the Latin measures in the *Mauritianum;* for instance, when he has Urania sing heartily:

Himmel / Firmament /	Heaven and firmament,
Sonn / Mond / Element /	Sun, moon, and element,
Sich lustig soll erzeigen.	Now joyfully appear.
Ich jhr Regentin	I, their ruler
Und Praesidentin	And presiding officer,
Darzu mein gnad thue neigen.	Thereto bestow my grace.

---

[22] Accordingly, in E. H. Müller, No. 3, the last two lines of the eight-line third strophe are to be added to the four-line fourth strophe.

And in the words of Calliope which conclude the monodic middle portion of the festival play the master's voice sounds to us with especial folk-song intimacy:

Endlich daß diese Gsellschaft werth /	That this company's renown
Möcht unvergessen bleiben /	From oblivion be saved,
Will ich auf Adamanten hert /	I myself will write it down
Ihre Gedechtnüs schreiben /	With a diamond engraved.
Kein Zeit soll sie vertreiben /	No time shall efface it,
Kein Gwalt soll sie zerreiben /	No power shall erase it,
Kein Mißgunst sie beteuben /	No envy debase it,
Kein Wind sol sie zersteuben /	No tempest displace it;
Ewig sie soll bekleiben /	Er'er firm-rooted in its worth
So lang nur bleibt die Erd.	While endureth this our earth.

The 1617 centennial celebration of the Reformation offered Schütz one of the first great opportunities to make good in his new position as director and composer. Hoe von Hoenegg has left us the exact program[23] that was followed, principally in the Dresden court church. This church, which at the time was, of course, still evangelical, has nothing to do with the present Roman Catholic rococo edifice of Chiaveri (1739-51). How the interior of Schütz's chief center of activity looked is shown in the wide Renaissance structure pictured on the woodcut „Schütz in the Circle of His Musicians."[24]

To quote Hoe von Hoenegg:

"On October 30, at noon, the festival was rung in by the bells of all the churches in the city and the suburbs. Vespers were celebrated, and confessions were heard." "October 31, the first festival day, was ushered in with the joyful booming of guns at six o'clock in the morning. Other cannonading, as is customary here on high festival occasions, also took place. On the same day as well as on the first and second of November sermons were delivered both in the morning and in the afternoon, and with them glorious music was presented. And inasmuch as the music, especially in the court church, was very magnificent, delightful, and imposing, I must not neglect, for the sake of future information and as a lasting memorial, to relate here fully what kind of Masses, *concerti,* and psalms were performed, as well as the manner of their performance.

---

[23] Chr. Mahrenholz in *Musik und Kirche,* III, 149, according to Hoenegg's *Parasceve ad Solemnitatem Evangelicam,* i. e., Christian guidance derived from the Word of God, how the coming Evangelical Jubilee Festival is to be celebrated properly and usefully (1617). Also reprinted from this in the excellent *Buch vom deutschen Kantor, Spielleute Gottes,* ed. by Ad. Strube (Eckart Verlag, Berlin-Steglitz).

[24] H. Spitta's supplementary Vol. XVIII to the complete edition.

First Festival Day.

Introit: O sing unto the Lord a new song (Psalm 98), followed by the *Kyrie, Christe, Kyrie, Gloria in excelsis,* etc. *Et in terra Pax,* all in seven choirs, etc., with trumpets and kettledrums.

After the Epistle: *Allein zu dir, Herr Jesu Christ,* the choir alternating with the congregation.

After the Gospel: The *Credo,* the choir alternating with the congregation. In the pulpit, before the Lord's Prayer preceding the sermon, the portion from the *Te Deum laudamus:* Now help us, Lord, Thy servants, etc., to the conclusion; with choir and instruments but also with the congregation.

After the sermon: the usual German songs used at the Communion of His Electoral Grace, *Gott sei gelobet und gebenedeiet,* etc.; likewise *Jesus Christus unser Heiland.*

Afternoon Sermon

Intonation before the altar: *Deus adjutorium meum intende.*

Response: *Domine ad adjuvandum,* etc. *Gloria.*

Hereupon for the Introit: *Jubilant hodie omnes gentes,* with trumpets and Psalm 100, *Jubilate Deo,* as an *intermedium* between the trumpets in five choirs. "This is the day which the Lord hath made", etc., arranged for the festival choirs; likewise the Creed, the choir alternating with the congregation.

After the sermon: six-chorus *Magnificat* with kettledrums and trumpets; between every verse of the *Magnificat* a verse from Luther's hymn *Erhalt uns, Herr, bei deinem Wort;* in conclusion *Verleih uns Frieden gnädiglich,* etc., *Gib unserm Fürsten,* etc., everything *per choros, Benedicamus,* etc.

"This music was performed by the musicians of the Elector of Saxony, our most gracious Lord: eleven instrumentalists, eleven singers, three organists, four lutenists, one theorbist, three organ choir boys, five discantists with interchange of all kinds of magnificent instruments, with two organs, two regals, three clavicymbals, and, in addition, eighteen trumpeters and two kettledrums, all presented with due solemnity under the leadership of Heinrich Schütz from Weissenfels."

Thus we have an invaluable record which gives us an abundance of information concerning the works, the liturgical ritual, and the musical forces employed for the *Psalms of David.* Until there is evidence to the contrary, it is to be assumed that all these works were composed by Schütz during a long period of preparation, and we must inquire as to what has been preserved despite the Dresden conflagration of 1760. First of all, from the *Psalms of 1619, Psalm 98* and *Psalm 100.* As Schütz (except for the song-form *Missa Brevis,* written later) seems to have composed no *Missa Brevis,* we must conclude that here an older work by another hand was interpolated.[25] How the trumpets entered on such occasions with their intradas is shown by the score of *Psalm 136* (Complete Edition, III, 182 ff). "The Creed *figuraliter* with the congregation" is doubtless to be interpreted that Luther's hymn *Wir glauben all* was sung interchangeably, stanza by stanza: stanza one, congregation; stanza two, perhaps the *Kleines geistliches Konzert* (VI, 50), which follows very closely the church melody, this sung as solo quartet with organ bass; stanza three again by the congregation with the entire chorus.

Nun hilf uns, Herr, den Dienern dein[26] is the fourth section of Luther's German *Te Deum, Herr Gott, dich loben wir.* The nature of such a setting can be judged by the apocryphal piece which Heinrich Spitta (Vol. XVIII) has submitted (from Erfurt) according to the apparently hasty reworking by a pupil for the peace celebration of 1668.[27] *Jedoch mit der Gemeinde* points to an antiphonal interchange between the concertizing music by the choir and the singing of the congregation. The two Communion hymns were apparently performed merely as congregational hymns and not in figural settings.

At the afternoon Vespers, the Intonation and the Responsory were doubtless sung according to the Gregorian formulae. A figural *Jubilant hodie omnes gentes* is missing in the Complete Edition, as is *Dies ist der Tag, den der Herr gemacht.*[28] But we know from the Naumburg catalog that Schütz actually set this text for six voices.

Does the six-chorus *Magnificat* correspond to the five-chorus *Magnificat* from Upsala in Vol. XVIII? If one were to reckon the organ thorough bass or the trumpets and tympani as the sixth chorus, the apparent contradiction would be eliminated. Stylistically much reminds one of the *Psalms of 1619,* and the indication by Hoenegg, "Between each verse of the *Magnificat* a verse of *Erhalt uns Herr,*" would explain the special manner of setting concerning which Heinrich Spitta thinks that Schütz "has therewith intentionally removed the piece from the sphere of pure church music," whereas otherwise we have a responsive performance between altar and choir and organ.

In view of the fermatas before *quia fecit,* before *deposuit potentes,* and before *suscepit,* the arrangement here would be such that the congregation would have

---

[25] We shall consider later the fact that the two Masses on his *Psalm 150* are not original with him.

[26] "Now help us Lord, Thy servants."

[27] L. Plass *(Sammlung musikalischer Wahrzeichen deutscher Städte)* also possesses old Dresden trumpet parts of a *Herr Gott, dich loben wir,* which may well come from the time of Schütz.

[28] "This is the day the Lord hath made."

interpolated the three Luther strophes of *Erhalt uns Herr* at the places mentioned, where, in any event, general pauses occur. The *Verleih uns Frieden, per choros,* was, in view of this specification, doubtless neither the *Sinfonia sacra* (VII, 77) nor the five-voice motet (VIII, 20).

The year 1618 brought Schütz a distinguished commission that must have been fascinating both from the professional and from the personal point of view — the arrangement of the *Concertmusik* in the Magdeburg[29] Dom, in conjunction with Samuel Scheidt and Michael Praetorius. At this time the Wolfenbüttel master, Michael Praetorius, still received an honorary salary in Dresden of 200 gulden, while Schütz, as "organist and director of music," received 400.[30] Considerable talent was engaged in Magdeburg. Unfortunately, the conquest and the burning of the rich city in 1631 eliminated this fine cultural activity for more than one hundred years.[31]

Our Kapellmeister is now thirty-three, and wedding bells begin to chime. For the Dresden nuptials of his friend Dr. Joseph Avenarius[32] with Anna Dorothea Börlitz on April 21, 1618, he writes his polychorus concert *(Konzert)* with instruments:

---

[29] According to kind information by the State Archive of Magdeburg, no decrees pertaining to this have heretofore been found.

[30] State Archives, Dresden, Loc. 9921 (Gurlitt, loc. cit.).

[31] B. Engelke has sketched the *Geschichte der Musik im Magdeburger Dom (The History of Music in the Magdeburg Cathedral)* in the Magdeburg *Geschichtsblätter,* 1912-13. We meet with the first organ in 1173; two organs are mentioned during the course of the fifteenth century. The records mention a list of organists: 1417, Bartholomaeus; 1497, Johs. Grashof; 1516-20, Heinricus (= Wolf Heintz?); 1541, Michel; 1542-48, Elias Müllerstedt; until 1554, Moritz von der Heyden; 1566, Herm. Bernroder; then Jak. Rudolf; 1574, Ulrich Griesetopff (who was honored as senior at the test at Grönigen). In 1541, on the departure of Cardinal Albrecht from Halle, the Cathedral Chapter seized by law the large organ there and had it erected in the Magdeburg Cathedral. An important new organ was built in 1604 by Heinrich Compenius. Its specifications are given by M. Praetorius and by A. Werckmeister. With the reorganization of the figural music in 1619, Johs. Weinreich became Dom Kapellmeister, Henr. Telemonius (= Telemann?) organist and substitute Kapellmeister. The distinguished composer Heinrich Grimm, as cantor of the old town, was to fill in every four weeks. Further musicians were: Martin Streicher, discant violinist, with three helpers (cornets and bass viols); Jakob Fischer (string, i. e., fidel positiv, regal); Hier. Lösch (lute); Andr. Schön (tenor); Mich. Zimmerman (alto); Martin Tröger (soprano-falsetto). The music, which was not to extend beyond an hour, and which was rehearsed early on Saturday, included at the chief festivals: *Introitus choraliter, Kyrie figuraliter, Cantica post Epistolam choraliter, Symbolum Nicaenum figuraliter, Apostolicum choraliter, post concionem concertus figuraliter;* at Vespers: the versicles of the *Magnificat* interchangeably *choraliter* and *figuraliter,* followed by *concertus musicalis;* after the sermon: *Hymnus Germanicus* alternately *choraliter* and *figuraliter,* strophe by strophe. Only in 1644, with the appointment of Cantor Malachias Siebenhaar, a composer of the poems of Rist, does a first modest new tendency set in. *Choraliter* means a solo introduction by the minister or unison singing by the congregation; *figuraliter* means a polyphonic setting by the choir.

[32] As the Leipzig University matriculation list states, he came from Zeitz and was enrolled in the winter semester of 1596.

Wohl dem der ein tugendsam Weib hat;[33] for the Leipzig wedding of Michael Thoma[34] with Anna Schultze on June 15, 1618, a three-chorus wedding piece with orchestra: *Haus und Güter erbt man von den Eltern.*[35] His favorite brother, too, became engaged in the Athens on the Pleisse (Leipzig). The elector urged him likewise to establish a household of his own. No great wonder, then, that we find in Geier's *Köstlichste Arbeit:*

> Now after Herr Schütz had come to Dresden and on account of his good qualities and wide knowledge had won much favor and affection in the eyes of His Most Gracious Lordship and also God's blessing in his undertakings, and as he felt with grateful heart that everything in this place was progressing to his advantage through God's grace, he thought upon a proper marriage in order to better his condition here. Therefore he fervently called upon the faithful God for his fatherly direction in his Christian purpose. He further availed himself of the advice of his dear relatives, and, because he had experienced an unusual devotion to Jungfer Magdalene, most beloved daughter of the Electoral Saxon Land- and Beverage-Tax Bookkeeper, the honorable Herr Christian Wildeck, now deceased, in the name of the Allhighest, and with the good wishes and good will of his dearest relatives, he announced his devotion to Jungfer Wildeckin to her honorable parents with proper humility. After these, too, had called upon the Highest and had duly deliberated among themselves and with their relatives, they gave their dear daughter to the mentioned Herr Schütz in view of his God-fearing conduct, his gentle heart and spirit, his splendid erudition, and other especially commendable qualities, in the name of the Holy Trinity.[36] The honorable engagement was consummated in marriage by a clergyman on June 1, 1619. After this joyful and honorable light had arisen for him, the beneficent God increased it more and more and blessed his wife with two daughters, Anna Justina and Euphrosyne.

In the memorial to Schütz's chosen bride the court preacher, Mathias Hoe von Hoenegg, relates the most lovable traits of her childhood:

> She was born on February 20, 1601, and soon thereafter was brought to the Lord Jesus Christ by means of Holy Baptism and was incorporated into His kingdom. Her parents are known here everywhere as honorable, well-bred, devout Christians and God-loving people. The father is the honorable and highly esteemed Herr Christian Wildeck, respected Electoral Saxon bookkeeper who served faithfully under four electors and the present administration for a term of forty-four years. The mother is the honorable and virtuous Frau Anna, daughter of the late honorable and highly esteemed Herr Mathias Hanitzschen, Electoral Saxon land steward. The deceased Frau Magdalena was brought up from youth by her parents in the fear of God, obedience, domesticity, and other Christian virtues, while she, in turn, showed obedience to, and respect for, her parents as demanded by the Fourth Commandment as well as her duty. She committed to memory many psalms of David, many other beautiful, outstanding verses, many moving little prayers and songs. She attended church and God's Word diligently. The latter she often resorted to as a penitent sinner and thus served her God faithfully and from the heart.
>
> What a devout soul she was also in other respects, insofar as this is possible in human weakness; how she was ill-disposed toward no one; what a retiring, quiet life she led; how she was heartily opposed to all pride and luxury — all this is known here on all sides.

---

[33] "Happy is he who has a virtuous wife," Complete Ed. XIV, 109.

[34] According to the decrees of the Leipzig University, he was there as a student from the summer semester of 1599, and was a native of Weiden.

[35] "House and possessions are inherited from our elders," Complete Ed., XIV, 127.

[36] According to the letter from the elector to the landgrave of January 1619.

In her eighteenth year, with the approval of His Electoral Saxon Highness, she became engaged to her now sorrowing widower and was married to him on June 1, 1619. She lived in such wedlock six years and fourteen weeks less one day. She loved her husband intensely and from the bottom of her heart. He alone was the most valued in her eyes; daily she cared for him; when he returned from his duties, she rejoiced greatly over him; she went to meet him and accompanied him with joy. She loved with motherly affection and diligently tended the two little olive branches and daughters whom God had granted her in wedlock, the one of whom is not quite four years of age, the other only a year and three quarters.

In a most charming manner D. Schirmer recalls the days of Schütz's love:

> As when in darkening night the host of stars appear,
> And moon with silver light ascends the vault of heaven,
> They drive away the darkness from round about their path
> Until the glow of morn dawns with its rosy hue;
> Then wood and meadow smile, and spring bestirs herself
> And crowns with wreath of flowers herself who slept afore,
> And joy anew doth feel; e'en solitude itself
> Looks round to find the wished-for day.
> Not otherwise was it with Schütz, the world-renowned.
> The cares of night were gone, the light began to gleam;
> The more he sought the day, the more there entered in
> His lovely Wildeckin with her bright eyes aglow.
> Alas, so short a time! Who on the placid lake
> Does not foresee a storm can scarce pursue his course
> When, after sunlight's gold, a sudden tempest strikes.
> His dearest life companion soon closed her pilgrimage
> And said her last farewell. But whither now to turn?
> He yielded to God's will himself and his estate;
> Let, as a wise man does, the storm break round about
> While he stands like a rock until the very end.

There must have been a wonderful and lovely relationship between Schütz and his young wife, who was sixteen years his junior.

The father-in-law, Chr. Wildeck, also appears in the Chemnitz records.

On Easter 1618 he gave the council of this city, to which he must have stood in some relationship of old, "for the general good of the town" an advance of 400 gulden. Apparently he was a man of considerable means. The magistracy acknowledged its appreciation with a munificent wedding present to the daughter and son-in-law, as the municipal accounts dated June 27, 1619, relate.[37] "One shock, forty groschen, and six pfennigs to Caspar Besen; for a celebration at Leipzig, for one gilded cup (Peraligen), with which the bookkeeper at Dresden, Christian Wildeck, endowed his daughter on June 27, 1619." Schütz, in acknowledgment, sent to the council his Cantiones, i. e., the print of the polychorus Psalms, and received for them on December 30 of the same year 420 groschen in appreciation. Similar gifts, as already mentioned, came from Weissenfels and elsewhere. It was

---

[37] Chemnitzer Mitteilungen (Information Concerning Chemnitz), p. 16.

an ancient wedding custom, handed down from village times,[38] to invite guests who were to make a contribution *(Haussteuer)*. We shall come across such invitations on the part of Schütz in connection with the marriage of his daughter.[39]

Among the chief features in connection with the weddings in olden times were the wedding *carmina*, or poems — a feature still found in the case of Bach and Carl Loewe.

The Schütz bridal poem from the hand of Conrad Bayer (Bavarus) has been preserved in print in the Saxon *Landesbibliothek* in Dresden. There are both Latin and German versions, and they are virtually the same:

"For the hymeneal joys of the honorable, learned, world-famous musician, Herr Heinrich Schütz, Electoral Saxon Kapellmeister in Dresden, and the honorable, virtuous Fräulein Magdalene, daughter of Herr Christian Wildeck, Electoral Saxon bookkeeper (registrar). The festivities consummated in Dresden June 1, 1619. Marriage is a harmony. As they are joined by word of mouth, so pray that their two hearts be joined in one fidelity."[40]

1. Music, sweet harmony,
O'er all the elements
Rightly art thou exalted;
Nothing can be compared to thee.
To God's own praise and honor
Dost thou most rightly turn,
His fame to magnify.

2. The human voice and song
And sound of instrument
Are pleasing thus to God;
And in the whole wide world,
Nothing doth please man more,
Renew the heart and mind
And drive away all sadness.

3. The trees and all the beasts
Immediately set forth;
Straightway the voice did follow
Out of the wild, wild wood
When in entrancing song
Orpheus had begun
To sing.

4. Elector Johann Georg,
Who cares for all the land,
In honor holdeth music,
Holds it in high esteem.
Herr Schütz experienced this,
Enjoyed in youthful years
His patronage and grace.

5. The prince would give to him
A better gift than gold.
He spoke to Wildecken,
Who keeps the prince's books:
Look you on credit's page
What for our worthy Schütz
Would serve him best of all.

6. Herr Wildeck does not wait
To render his report
How things at present stand
Concerning worthy Schütz.
A Fräulein he would have,
Despising other gifts
On this occasion.

7. He has a daughter fair
Who would be to him
According to his pleasure and his mind.
Said he: I'll give him her.
He soon may train her well
To help him make a home
With her as mother.

8. May God give Schütz success
For his new masterwork.
Well has he now obtained
What none begrudged to him.
Things will still better sound,
When he will thereto add
Some young assistants.

---

[38] Cf. my *Tönende Volksaltertümer (Musical Antiquities)*, pp. 313 ff.
[39] Supra p. 185.
[40] *Conjugium harmonia est. Junguntur ut oribus ora: Una ita junguntur pectora bina fide.*

9. Many another maid,
Decked out so nice and fine,
Has had her eye on Schütz
Because he sang so well.
He is the one can make
· The heart to laugh within
With utter joy.

10. But he can have but one
Whom he can call his own;
He must indeed have peace
If he would gain success.
So do not trouble him,
Or he might write some fifths
Against all rules of art.

Of things related to poetry and music. F.C.B.

Schütz ingeniously combined the invitations to his wedding with the publication of his *Psalms*. The preface is dated the day of the wedding, June 1, 1619, although the actual printing had been completed some time before. In Weissenfels[41] the documents say: "Three Schock, 36 Gr. as a wedding honor to the Electoral Kapellmeister Herr Heinrich Schütz, and, inasmuch as he dedicated his *opus musicum* to the church, one beaker." The chapter of the Naumburg Cathedral on May 27 has in the minutes: "Heinrich Schütz, Electoral Saxon Kapellmeister in Dresden, sends to the gentlemen a copy of his published *Psalms of David* and invites them to his wedding on June 1. The gentlemen vote that five Rhenish gold gulden be sent him as a honorarium, which they have taken from the large iron chest." On May 27 the Leipzig council sent to Schütz's bride a "gilded silver beaker," forty-seven gulden, nineteen groschen and six pfennigs in value.[42] On May 9 the council of Zeitz had decided on four Rhenish gulden for the *Psalms* and the wedding.[43] The Magdeburg Cathedral chapter replied to the invitation by presenting a *Mauritius* (a gold medal) worth twenty-four taler.[44] The council of Dresden, however, was apparently the most liberal; for in its ledger, 1619-20, under the heading "expenses for *honoraria*" (p. 26 b), we read: "168 fl., 6 gr., for a barrel of R(hine) wine which the honorable council presented to the bookkeeper Christian Wildecken for his daughter's marriage to Heinrich Schütz, Electoral Saxon Kapellmeister. Paid, November 6, 1619.[45]"

One of these accompanying letters may be reprinted here,[46] as E. H. Müller has overlooked it in the compilation of his collection. It was addressed to the council of the city of Frankfurt on the Main and arrived there in the midst of the festivities connected with the crowning of Ferdinand II. It reads:

---

[41] A. Werner, *Weissenfels*, pp. 46 f. Ibid. further: "They possessed the work at the court at Rudolstadt and at Schulpforta. The *Psalms* were also sung in St. Michael's Church, in Erfurt, and in the grammar school in Saalfeld."

[42] R. Wustmann, I, 219.

[43] A. Werner, *Zeitz*, p. 60.

[44] Engelke, loc cit. Similar ones were also given to Scheidt and M. Praetorius.

[45] Information kindly given by the council archives in Dresden.

[46] For the first time in Caroline Valentin's *History of Music in Frankfurt on the Main*, 1906, pp. 123 ff.

"Noble, honorable, high and learned, highly esteemed and very kindly disposed sirs:

"I humbly impart to Your Excellencies that, in order to honor God, which is the duty of every man in his profession, I have set to music and now, at the instigation of many devout hearts, have brought out in print some of the psalms of the king and prophet David in the form in which he himself conceived them, and

"Since Your Excellencies have great renown for your affection toward music and indeed have shown this publicly by having all kinds of instrumental and vocal music cultivated and practiced at great expense in your well-appointed churches and schools,

"Therefore I entertain the unswerving assurance that Your Excellencies will show favor toward this my work, these spiritual *concerti*, and hence will allow me to forward to you the aforementioned work with the request that you accept it and allow me ever to commend myself to your favor. In return for which I shall ever be at your service.

Dresden, July 17, 1619.

Your Excellencies'
Obedient Servant,
Electoral Saxon Kapellmeister there,

Heinrich Schütz"

The fact that in 1619 Schütz issued a collection of free psalm *concerti* for many voices — containing only one single church-hymn setting — was certainly the result of the artistic urge in the young Gabrieli pupil, but perhaps also the result of a friendly rivalry with his close colleagues M. Praetorius and J. H. Schein. Praetorius' *Polyhymnia cadueatrix et panegyrica* of 1619 (for which Hoe von Hoenegg had written a rhymed preface and part of which was already familiar to Schütz as festival music at the Saxon court) contains, for convocations of princes, only settings of church hymns, with the exception of the *Psalm 133*, made popular for such occasions by Senfl's motet for the Diet of Augsburg in 1530. The Wolfenbüttel master molds the well-known melodies until quasi-Gabrieli *concerti* finally emerge — often indeed very effective and euphoniously beautiful settings. In the case of Schütz, however, one feels the much more lordly pleasure of keeping formatively aloof from the *cantus firmus* compulsion, with the single exception mentioned, which in itself proves him also master of this technique.

When Schütz, despite his devoted adherence to Gabrieli, here used without exception German psalm texts,[47] this was doubtless due, apart from the usage in the Dresden service, to a programmatic purpose to serve Luther's glorious German psalm translations. Indeed, Schütz's example served as a powerful stimulus to the polyphonic settings of the German psalms, which up to this time had lagged far behind the Latin, and indeed as a stimulus to the general German development of the verse motet.[48]

While Praetorius always writes out fully the diminution technique of the *gorgia* — the doctrine of the improvisation of the vocal embellishments in the sixteenth century — so that his scores of this time have many frills and embellishments, Schütz is much more restrained in these matters. One might suppose that he intentionally omitted such embellishments, leaving them for improvisation by the performer. But he also seems to have been more ascetic in his taste than was Praetorius — more captivated by the poetry than impelled by the technique. It is difficult to conceive in his case such tone-playfulness as the *Zim-Zim-Zim-Zim-Zimbeln schön* which is found in Praetorius' *Wachet auf concerto*. The Schein *concerti*, with Italian madrigal verses of welcome by Georg Schütz, although written in 1615, did not appear as *Opella nova* until 1618. Even if Wustmann's surmise that they were due to Heinrich Schütz's suggestion is correct, the Schein compositions present throughout almost their entire scoring the art of intimate chamber music, while Schütz's *Psalms,* having a much closer affinity to Praetorius, aim at being gigantic, mythically fantastic, and variegated; and they achieve this for the most part in a breath-taking manner.[49]

The dedicatory verses which precede the *Psalms*[50] familiarize us with Schütz's social enviroment. The electoral secretary and court poet Johs. Seussius (also anagrammatically Ivo ab Hus Senensis) praises Schütz for having transferred the chromaticism, hitherto limited to instrumental music, to the medieval modes of ecclesiastical vocal music. He states that the two Gabrielis of Venice were reborn in the one Schütz of Dresden; that one soul of Schütz dominates the voices, his other, the hand of the organist. Next, the Saxon court poet Elias Rudelius (Rüdel),

---

[47] Latin ones appear first in the *Cantiones sacrae* and *Psalm 24.*
[48] With regard to the question "Latin or German" in the evangelical church music of the time cf. Blume, *Das monodische Prinzip,* pp. 24—25.
[49] However, it is very fascinating to note how in most of the Saxon and Silesian manuscripts of the time the Schütz polychorus psalm *concerti,* with orchestra and figured bass, are almost throughout reduced to the old *Kantorei* practice of the *a cappella* motets for eight voices. Vice versa, it is quite possible that unaccompanied double-chorus pieces, preserved only in such sources, also were set by Schütz in a lost original form with orchestra and figured bass.
[50] In the preface to Vol. 2 of Ph. Spitta's complete edition.

who says beautifully in his distichs that Schütz, in the writing of his *Psalms*, does not resemble Orpheus, who moved the stones, as much as he resembles the archangel Raphael, who was allowed to sing into the ear of God. As a third tribute the familiar court organist Anton Colander imagines King David vainly searching Olympus for a true interpreter until he finds a congenial one in Schütz. A Weissenfels Henricus Luia is followed by the Leipzig attorney and friend of music Paul Froberger, who appears elsewhere as a bearer of musical dedications. Finally, the Dresden deacon and poet laureate, Samuel Rüling, known also as a composer,[51] offers a paean and good wishes.[52]

Shortly after his wedding Schütz made a journey to Bayreuth, where he joined the prince and friend of music Heinrich Posthumus von Reuss, and also Johann Staden of Nuremberg,[53] together with Scheidt and Michael Praetorius, the Magdeburg collaborators of the preceding year. Samuel Scheidt recalled the event in one of his prefaces.[54] A parish organ of thirty-five stops, which Margrave Christian of Brandenburg-Bayreuth had had built by the court organ builder Gottfried Fritsche, was solemnly dedicated. Even from distant Königsberg came the "leading musician." His name is not mentioned. Could it have been Stobäeus? In 1614 Fritsche had built the large organ in the Dresden court church under the supervision of Praetorius.[55]

Schütz's father apparently accompanied his distinguished son, and on this occasion he found in Heinrich Posthumus a gracious overlord of former times; for Spitta (loc. cit., p. 16) mentions the following notice from the records of the royal archives of Schleiz: "1 *fl.*, 16 *gr.*, in shiny new Reuss *Reichsthaler* for old Schütz von Weissenfels."

On August 9 Schütz attended the wedding of his favorite brother, George, in Leipzig. He presented to him, as an unusual wedding gift, a composition, not

---

[51] For example, in the Ms. Löbau 8.

[52] He became cantor at the *Kreuzschule* in Dresden in 1612, deacon of the Holy Cross Church in 1615, and died, about forty years of age, in 1626. Cf. K. Held, *Das Kreuzkantorat zu Dresden, Vjschr. f. MW*, X, 290 ff.

[53] A. Werner in *Sbd., IMG*, I, 422 f.

[54] In the *Pars prima concertuum sacrorum* (Hamburg, 1622) to Duke Friedrich Ulrich of Brunswick and Heinrich Posthumus v. Reuss: *Memini ut quam diutissime de vivo praedicare possim, Tu Deus amme, certe quam diu vivam, meminero, quanta animi voluptate beatam illam animam Michaelem Praetorium Henricum Schuzium et me tanquam Orpheos exilio desolatos inter bestias, sylvas et saxa canentes ... sed in Aula Illustri Biruthina, in consessu Principum et Magnum Dei summi laudes concinnentes audieris.* Note also Schütz's opinion, as a colleague, with regard to Scheidt's *Tabulatura nova*, I and II (the first part of which is dedicated to Elector Johann Georg), addressed to the electoral secretary of the chamber, Wilh. Ludwig Moser (30, 12, 1624; E. H. Müller, No. 14). He recommends as honorarium a beaker valued at 30—35 Taler.

[55] As to him see Schütz's letter to the secretary of the chamber, W. L. Moser (May 25, 1624; E. H. Müller, No. 13).

based on the tender Song of Songs, but on Psalm 133: "Behold, how good and
how pleasant it is for brethren to dwell together in unity!" a very personal and
affectionate thought which Schütz further underscored with a beautiful Latin
dedication in the heroic meter — a proud echo of the recently published major
work for church use:

> While late I sang so many melodious sweet psalms,
> Which as a gift accepts now the whole Teutonic world —
> To you alone this one is due, O brother of my heart,
> For double loyalty[56] has bound us two together.
> The same fidelity which bound us since our mother's arms
> Forever standeth firm and fast, this grant the gracious God.

This composition, which Schütz used again, although altered, in the third part
of the *Symphoniae sacrae* (1650), we shall discuss in the second half of the present
work.[57] At this time he received from Burkhart Grossmann of Jena a commission
to be one of the sixteen composers of Psalm 116. It, too, will be discussed in the
musical section.

Schütz was now thirty-five years old. When we stop to appraise him in the Saxon
court which he graced for more than half a century, we must concur with
Ph. Spitta's statement: "The spiritual level of the Dresden court stood incomparably lower than that to which he must have been accustomed in Kassel."[58] M. Fürstenau's fine tribute is correct:[59] "Schütz is one of those rare personalities whose
appearance always gives the impression of a purer, higher spirit from a better
world. The harmony to which he dedicated all his thought and purpose resounds
through his entire life. Wherever he appears, whether as artist or as man, we find
gentleness and strength combined, childlike humility and manly, fearless courage,
clarity, circumspection, and high enthusiasm. He was the grandest, most forth-
right, most outstanding and most lovable personality at the elector's court." And
as such Ricarda Huch portrayed him in several scenes of her work *The Great War
in Germany*[60] as the spiritual and radiant figure of the country of the Wettins.

---

[56] *Bina fides* probably with double meaning: first double "lyre" (?) — then "fidelity."
[57] See infra.
[58] *Musikgesch. Aufsätze* (Musical Essays), p. 13.
[59] *Beiträge zur Geschichte der Kgl. sächs. Musikal. Kapelle (Contributions to the History of the Music Chapel of the Saxon Court)*, p. 57.
[60] *Der große Krieg in Deutschland.*

In addition to his regular church and court duties, an endless sequence of
baptisms, weddings, funerals, and gatherings of princes[61] occupied the time of
the electoral Kappellmeister.

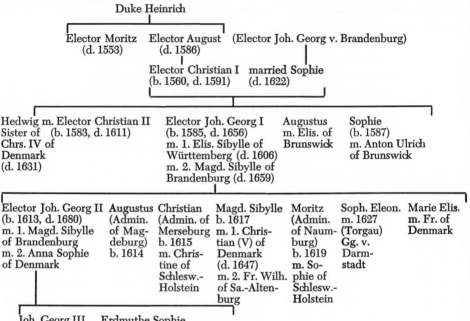

Everything depended on Johann Georg. He has been judged in the most varied
ways. Fürstenau (1849), who doubtless is inclined all too favorably, says of him
(loc. cit., p. 44): "Johann Georg never turned a deaf ear to the representations of
his Kapellmeister. He valued him highly on account of his integrity and his candor.
We must admire both: the lord and the servant." A modern reviewer (A. Einstein),
however, calls him "a crowned lout." Schütz himself would doubtless not have
been able to judge Johann Georg unequivocally; for in the elector, as in every
man, were mingled both the good and the bad. Today one is prone to refer to
Schütz's outburst of temper at the privy secretary Reichbrodt in 1651.[62] Schütz was
doubtless justified in saying that he would rather be cantor or organist in a small
town than continue longer as Kapellmeister at this court. One overlooks, however,

---

[61] As we shall meet a number of personalities of the Saxon royal house, a brief table is here
appended of such as may be of interest from the viewpoint of music history.
[62] E. H. Müller's collection, No. 81, p. 224.

the willing and devoted co-operation of the elector, frequently manifested and gratefully acknowledged by Schütz, not from mere servility. See, for example, the preface to the *Sinfoniae sacrae III* of 1650. Finally, one should properly evaluate the deep emotion with which Schütz in 1657 accompanied his benefactor and tormentor *(Gönner und Peiniger)* to his last resting place with his six-voice St. Simeon motets.[63] As a matter of fact, the elector (who was born the same year as Schütz) was by no means without musical training, as is evinced by the *Tabulatur Buch auff der Cythar. Johannes Georgius Hertzog zu Sachsen, 1592* (State Library, Dresden), which contains pageants, folk songs, galliards, and Christmas songs.[64] As bearing on the elector's personal interest in music Mattheson[65] tells of an incident when Froberger and Weckmann met at the Dresden court in 1653:

> "'My Mathies,' said the elector to Weckmann secretly, 'would you like to compete with Froberger on the clavier for a gold chain?' 'With all my heart,' answered Weckmann, 'but out of respect for His Imperial Majesty, Froberger should win the chain.' After he had played, Froberger immediately inquired about a man in the chapel called Weckmann. He remarked that he was very famous at the imperial court and that he would like to make his acquaintance. Weckmann stood close behind him. The elector struck him on the shoulder and said: 'Here stands my Matthies'..."

Ph. Hainhofer has this to say relative to a visit in 1629 to the chamber of instruments in Dresden: "A brass and a wooden zither-lute, on which His Electoral Highness played in his youth, as His Highness still enjoys hearing music; the older prince especially delights in it."[66]

The elector's musical standards and tastes are also indicated in the appointment of a first organist for the court. After using Johann Staden as a temporary substitute, the quasi-impresario at the time, von Loss (Georg's privy counselor), attempted, at the Regensburg Reichstag in the fall of 1613, to obtain the services of Alessandro Orologio.[67] A number of musical dedications to the elector seem likewise to confirm a musical interest on his part. At the same time the elector — altogether on his own initiative — won Michael Praetorius from his brother-in-law in Brunswick, at least as Kapellmeister *in absentia (von Haus aus).*[68]

---

[63] Complete edition, XII, 201.
[64] W. Gurlitt, *M. Praetorius* (unpublished part, 1920).
[65] *Ehrenpforte,* new edition, p. 396.
[66] O. Doering, *Ph.Hainhofers Reisen* (Vienna, 1901), p. 232.
[67] The letters concerned are in W. Schäfer's *Sachsenchronik,* I (1854).
[68] Praetorius signed the chief announcement of the *Syntagma* on June 24, 1614, and on February 5, 1615, the dedicatory letter to the *Syntagma* I, 2, from Dresden, and remained there till January 1616. As Schütz arrived in Dresden in September 1615, he was with Praetorius at that time almost five months. Inasmuch, however, as neither mentioned the other at any time, they apparently were not unduly fond of each other, doubtless because of too great a difference in their temperaments.

But let us hear what O. Michaelis has to say on the subject (pp. 25 f.): "The elector took pleasure in things altogether different from art: in the hunt and in the pleasures of the banquet board adorned with game, and particularly in the wine cup *(Trinktisch)*. Therefore the saying of the day: 'Drink, George, drink!'[69] applied to him also. But he failed in the domain of politics, just as he had in art. The Protestant prince, who was equally to blame for the fall of Magdeburg, later, when the consequences of his politics had materialized, brazenly complained that he, as a faithful, useful, and heroic elector, serving emperor and empire, did not merit the treatment accorded him. Truly this Johann Georg put feelings of loyalty on the part of his subjects to a hard test. . . . Schütz lived at a court where the librarian and the court poet were listed in the court record as common servants *(gemein Hofgesind)* along with the lionkeeper and the mousecatcher. Even if he knew about it, Johann Georg I surely took no umbrage. His wife, Electress Magdalene Sibylle, might rather have done so; for she had spiritual and intellectual interests, even though her domestic interests outweighed them. Far superior to her husband in intellect, soul, and character, she had developed the gracious gifts of a motherly regent and was at times her husband's warning conscience. She concerned herself with the Protestants expelled from Bohemia, admired Gustavus Adolphus, brought up her children carefully, morally, and religiously, and was anxious that the youths of the nobility who were educated with the princes should 'not grow up like dumb cattle.'"

The Dresden of the time was, to be sure, still a rather small town; but it was well-to-do and beautifully situated,[70] where one could visit, in addition to three palaces, the hunting lodge *(Jägerhof)*, the summer house *(Lusthaus)*, the Italian garden *(italienischer Garten)*, etc. The tendency to good living manifested itself ever and again, both before and after the war, despite strict regulations as to clothing and weddings and many exhortations on the part of the clergy.

The treasures of the vaulted Green Room *(grünes Gewölbe)*, with its wonderful rarities, ranging from a carved cherry pit to the seal caught in the upper Elbe, enticed strangers into the chief palace. Schütz, as a servant of the court, lived in the midst of many valuable treasures, such as paintings by Dürer and Cranach. Speaking of the electoral art chamber, Weck says: "There are in this room various regals, positives, organs and musical instruments, some of alabaster and marble, some

---

[69] *Sauf, Jörge, sauf!*
[70] Anton Weck, *Der Churfürstlichen Sächsischen weitberufenen Residentz- und Haupt-Vestung Dresden Beschreib- und Vorstellung* (Nürnberg, 1680). — M. B. Lindau, *Geschichte der Kgl. Haupt- und Residenzstadt* (Dresden, 1885).

entirely of glass, some of rare wood, artistically inlaid; one finds there a positive or organ made completely of stone, another of glass."

We have already mentioned the court church, newly decorated in 1614. The room in which Schütz's secular court music was heard on all festival occasions is thus described by Weck (p. 32):

"The great chamber (Riesen-Saal), which at the time of the enlargement of the palace Elector Moritz had constructed with a flat and low ceiling, Elector Joh. Georg I, of blessed memory . . . in 1627 demolished, together with the upper stories and supplanted it with a new raised or vaulted ceiling made altogether of cabinet work so that its height was now seventeen ells, its length one hundred ells, eight inches, and its width up to twenty-three ells. On the ceiling of the chamber the stars and constellations of the heavens, together with the fearful comet which appeared in November 1618, are so artistically pictured — all of metal and gilded over — that each star has its appropriate position and size according to the proportion of the room. From the ceiling hang seven beautiful, large chandeliers, each weighing many hundredweight. . . . In the upper part of the chamber on the wall could be seen the following memorial which Herr Augustus Buchner had composed at the time of the erection of this building and had dedicated to its founder. . . .
"On both sides of the hall, on the shafts of the columns and elsewhere, large giants are very artistically depicted on the stone or the plaster. . . . On the windows round about are pictured the nations from the four parts of the world, also the Saxon cities. In connection with the capital, Dresden, the artist Kilian Fabritius painted the pantheon of the Greek and Roman gods, while the poet Johann Seussius expressed his thoughts concerning this city and fortress as follows, using gilded Roman letters:

Juppiter aulam ornat, etc., or in translation:
Jupiter conducts the court, Pallas establishes buildings,
Mars enlarges the arsenal, Ceres gives the grain,
Bacchus provides the wine, Diana protects the beasts,
Flora plants the flowers, Pales nurtures fields,
Pomona tends the fruit, Napaea sets out trees,
Nais pours forth streams and therewith moistens all.

"At all events, as may be gathered from the facts just mentioned as well as from the observations of those who have visited foreign parts or have come hither from foreign parts, this splendid Electoral Saxon residence, if indeed it does not surpass, is at least the equal of, other residences of the nobility throughout the entire Roman Empire so far as size, art, decorations, luxurious interiors, and comforts are concerned."

Among the artistic impressions which Schütz received at the Dresden court, as well as previously in Kassel, we must reckon those made by the English comedians. In 1626 alone four Shakespeare dramas (Romeo and Juliet, Julius Caesar, Hamlet, and King Lear), Marlowe's Dr. Faustus, and many other plays were performed.

The chronicle of the external events during Schütz's brief married life is not very full, while the history of the war of the period consists of many volumes. From the fifth to the fourteenth of October 1621 Schütz was in the entourage of the prince on the journey to Breslau, where the elector was to receive the homage of the Silesian estates. We shall have occasion later to consider the "political music" composed by Schütz for this occasion.[71] The contact with Silesia may have been

---

[71] See infra.

important for Schütz's inner development. We do not know whether at this time he met the poet Opitz, who resided in Bunzlau; but the characteristically mystical piety of the *Cantiones sacrae* of 1625 has a typically Silesian coloring, and this mysticism may have impressed itself forcibly upon him at this time.

On Schütz's return in November, his wife presented him with his first daughter, Anna Justina.

Schütz's young cousin (their mothers were sisters), Heinrich Albert from Loben-stein, studied with him at this time, and there developed between them a friendship the influence of which is reflected artistically in Albert's arias. This friendship is also responsible for many a Schütz composition found in Königsberg copies. Again we note here the strange conservatism of the Schütz-Biegert-Albert families toward music:[72] "When Albert in the year 1622 left the high school at Gera, he did not go to a university town but to Dresden to his 'dear uncle' (according to the old usage of the term), the 'highly famous Kapellmeister Schütz.' The funeral sermon definitely testifies that he took this step with the approval of his parents. Nevertheless, a period of inner struggle for Albert began at this time. For though the members of his family were kindly disposed to music and desired his talent to be a lifelong companion, they did not want him to devote himself to art as a vocation. For this reason he was called away from his musical studies in 1623 and was sent to the University of Leipzig to study law and take up literature on the side." To be sure, here he probably elected J. H. Schein as mentor and doubtless had his attention directed to the German lied. When Albert went to Königsberg in 1626 with Simon Dach, Schütz sent him for the most part elaborate compositions in largest forms, doubtless in order that he should not narrow his horizon through small forms. In 1634 Schütz summoned this cousin as his assistant in Copenhagen.

On March 5, 1621, Schütz again appeared as poet-composer with the subject matter of Musagete (Apollo) and his companions of Parnassus. This work must be carefully distinguished from the one written for the imperial visit four years earlier. On this later occasion he was to grace the birthday of his elector. Again, unfortunately, only the text — not the music — has been preserved. However, this time at least the report of the scoring of the work, which probably employed several choruses, is extant. The twelve cornets undoubtedly included *grob* and "bass cornets." The title of the printed text, found only in the *Landesbibliothek* in Dresden *(Hist. Sax. C.,* 863), reads:[73]

---

[72] H. Kretzschmar in *DTD* XII, vii.
[73] Facsimile reprint by the old *Schütz Gesellschaft* for the Celle Schütz Festival (1929) in the Bärenreiter-Verlag; text reprint also in H. Müller, *Briefe,* No. 4.

Felicitation of Apollo
and the nine Muses,
Which on the
Birthday
Of His Excellency /
High-born prince and lord,
Herr Johann Georg
Duke in Saxony / Gülich / Cleve and Bergen / of the Holy
Roman Empire, Archmarshal and elector /, etc.
By His Electoral Grace's Collegium Musicum with twelve cornets and
as many living voices / beside trumpets and timpani, was humbly
presented in his honor on March 5.
Set to Music
by
Heinrich Schütz, Kapellmeister
Anno
1621
Printed in the Electoral Saxon mining (Bergk) town Freybergk /
by Georg Hofman.

The ten four-line strophes are in German, constructed with regular alternations
between iambic eight-and eleven- syllable lines but otherwise decked out with all
the mythological bric-a-brac. Apollo calls to the Muses to greet the prince "in a
new manner." While this first movement, "Welcome, O welcome, beautiful
Aurora," may have been performed *tutti*, the Muses themselves, who appear one
after the other in changing strophic forms, doubtless did homage to the new solo
song. Finally the god summons the nine goddesses:

> So let us all together now
> Conclude in full strong chorus
> And make resound with joyful strain
> Each hill and vale and river.

The concluding chorus presents as a refrain three times:

> Long live our mighty Saxon hero.
> His fame and honor now and ever grow,

between which two brief passages occur. To be sure, the wish expressed in the
second:

> May patriots adorn the land
> And justice ever rule.
> May Mars all time an exile be,
> Eternal peace e'er flourish.

represents, to a certain extent, wishful thinking, since this was but the third year of the Thirty Years' War.

Who knows how many more such works for special occasions may have been produced by Schütz during this period? Even if anyone had considered them worthy of being preserved after Schütz's death, the great fire of 1760 doubtless destroyed them all.

On December 7, 1622, Duchess Sophie of Saxony, mother of Johann Georg, had died and was buried in the Freiberg Cathedral on January 28, 1623. For the occasion Schütz composed the elegy *Grimmige Gruft (Grim Vault)*, which we shall discuss ot the beginning of the section dealing with his German secular works.[74] From the atmosphere of this work one surmises that Schütz was moved by more than a mere court duty. On Easter 1623 he doubtless gave the first performance, in the court chapel, of his *History of the Resurrection*, which he published soon thereafter. His *Psalm 116* appeared in the same year, in Jena. On November 28 his second daughter, Euphrosyne, was born. There was now much happy activity in the Kapellmeister's quarters, activity which lasted throughout the entire year 1624. On the other hand, life in Schütz's study must be pictured as the more concentrated and calm, since he was probably occupied with the forty *Cantiones sacrae, Op. 4*. The preface to this work is addressed to the minister of the emperor, Prince Eggenberg, with whose understanding of music Schütz had already become acquainted when the princes visited Dresden in 1617. It is dated January 1, 1625.

In order to understand this dedication to the emperor's counselor, Prince Eggenberg, who had become a Catholic, and also to understand the comparatively undisturbed situation in the cultivation of the arts at the Saxon court until nearly 1631, it is necessary to recall the attitude of Electoral Saxony during the first half of the turmoils of the Thirty Years' War. This attitude was strange enough. In a religious war of which the central theme was the existence or nonexistence of Protestantism as opposed to the destructive will of the counter-reformation imperialist Catholicism, one would have thought that Electoral Saxony, as the heir to the Lutheran movement, would have taken its place at the head of the anti-Hapsburg "Union." But such was not the case. For the war did not break out between Roman Catholics and Lutherans but was brought about through the union of the Bohemian Utraquists with the Reformed of the Palatinate during the winter regency of Frederick V. This challenged the imperial opposition of the Austro-Bavarian League, the union suffering a catastrophic defeat in the battle *am weissen Berg*. The denominational and political antagonism between

---

[74] Supra.

Lutherans and Zwinglians (or Calvinists) — one was wont to say "rather papist than Calvinist" — was so great at the time that Johann Georg could be tempted with the possibility of obtaining Lausatia as a possible booty of war and was drawn over to the side of the Jesuits. As genuine grand-nephew of the "Smalkald" Moritz of Saxony, Johann Georg undertook to obtain in this deal the return of the seven cities and Silesia by way of appeasement. In his *History of the Thirty Years' War* Schiller calls this a "wise policy of neutrality"; but he points out that the transaction was helped along principally by the imperial bribery of the Saxon court preacher, Hoe von Hoenegg, an evangelical, to be sure, but a Jesuit-educated Viennese. The elector flattered himself with the idea that he, as a Lutheran *tertius gaudens,* could play the part of the balance wheel *(Zünglein an der Wage)* between the Catholic war party and the opposing Reformed. But the peace of Lübeck of 1628, apparently so favorable to him after the withdrawal of Christian IV, nevertheless opened his eyes to the course which this policy must take. Ferdinand's edict of restitution of the following year was designed, through compulsory imperial executive order, to compel all the spiritual domains (which since the treaty of Passau of 1552 had been taken over by the Protestants) to return to the bosom of the only true church. While the edict did, to be sure, exempt the bishoprics of Meissen, Merseburg, and Naumburg, which had become part of Electoral Saxony, this was for the time being only, and Johann Georg could count on his fingers the days until, on the successful execution of Ferdinand's edict in the case of the others, it would be his turn for reincorporation.

In 1630, at the moment that the end of the Reformation had apparently come, Gustavus Adolphus stepped upon German soil. The elector sought an alliance with this powerful helper, an alliance which was granted by the Swedish king only with hesitation. It received its symbolical expression in the battle of Breitenfeld in 1631, after the Leipzig meeting of the two rulers. The Saxons, under General v. Arnim, who was then under Wallenstein, were completely routed by Tilly; but Gustavus Adolphus, in turn, put the imperial forces to flight, and thus the elector could only rather belatedly flatter himself as having been a co-victor. Of course, he had now finally become an unequivocal co-warrior, and when the great Vasa had fallen at Lützen, both the violence of the imperial forces and the depredations of the Swedes vented themselves upon the unfortunate Electoral Saxony. The Peace of Prague of 1635 only partially helped to end the brutal burning of the Saxon cities and villages. Fully thirteen further years of horror were required until Hapsburg with his Croatians, Spaniards, and Walloons, as well as the Swedish and French, could all be sent home as the result of the Peace of Westphalia, and the ploughing peasant could finally weed the swords, spears, bullets, and armor out of the poor German soil.

One can now begin to understand how, for the first twelve years of the war. Schütz could tolerate life in Dresden (a Lutheran city strangely chained to Catholicism) and how then, as a matter of spiritual self-preservation, his creative urge as an artist required his difficult migration to the court of Christian IV of Denmark.

Hans Ulrich, Baron, then Prince von Eggenberg (1568-1634), a rich Protestant heir of the Styrian nobility,[75] began his career as a captain in the Netherlands; then, as cupbearer of the archduke, who later became Emperor Ferdinand II, he became a Catholic and rose rapidly to the governorship of the Krain. He was the carrier of messages to the Spanish court for the emperors Rudolf and Mathias, and, on the occasion of the Frankfurt imperial election of Ferdinand, was elevated to the position of the emperor's High Dignitary (*Grosswürdenträger*). In the latter capacity he vainly opposed the dismissal of Wallenstein in 1630; but he finally achieved the latter's reappointment, only, however, to leave the imperial service shortly after Wallenstein's murder. On the confiscation of numerous Bohemian estates after the battle *am weissen Berg*, the emperor, in 1623, bestowed on him sovereignty of the region about Krummau and, two years later, elevated him to the dukedom of the same region. The emperor's address to the now hereditary Marshal of Austria was: "Our uncle and especially loved prince." Eggenberg was a brilliant though not a profound personality. He was all-powerful at the Hapsburg court, which might well have commended him to Schütz as one to whom a great work could properly be dedicated.

To the friends already mentioned who contributed their panegyrics to the *Psalms of 1619* — Seusse, Rüdel, Rüling — there is now added the Dresden school rector Georg Hausmann, who extols Schütz as the *arciger* — the bearer of the bow. As Wolfgang Caspar Printz had stated at the end of the century, Schütz's reputation throughout Germany may be dated from the appearance of this work.

In May of the same year, 1625, Martin Opitz came to Dresden, and the relationship with the Silesian who had just risen to the position of the most famous German poet of this time was to be extremely fruitful for Schütz from the artistic viewpoint.

Opitz, the son of a meat dresser who had connections in the council, was born in Bunzlau in 1597, being thus twelve years younger than Schütz. He attended the Magdalene high school in Breslau. At twenty years of age he published in Beuthen his Latin *Aristarchus,* in which he praised German as a possible vehicle

---

[75] Krones in the *Allgemeine deutsche Biographie.*

of poetry. He studied in Heidelberg at the time of the Winter King. Here he wrote many songs. Afterwards he visited Holland and Denmark to gather world-experience.

Called from Liegnitz to Bethlen Gabor, to Siebenbürgen, Opitz soon returned to the service of his Silesian duke at whose commission he composed his Epistle songs to the melodies of the Reformed *Goudimel Psalter*. In 1624, within five days, he wrote his *Prosodia Germanica*, or *Book of German Poetry*, which rapidly became famous. This Protestant, converted to Calvinism, was crowned as poet by the emperor in Vienna. He now entered, as private secretary, the service of the strict Catholic president of the chamber, Burggraf Karl Hannibal von Dohna, in Breslau. It was here that in 1625 his *Eight Books of German Poems* appeared. In the same year he visited his friend, the professor of poetry, August Buchner, in Wittenberg, and on the return journey associated in Dresden with Johann Seussius, Heinrich Schütz, and the court tutor, Ansorge. Again in Breslau, he completed on December 31, 1626, the preface to his *Paraphrases of the Song of Songs*, which, however, he had doubtless previously submitted in writing to his great composer. We shall speak later[76] of his collaboration with Schütz on Rinuccini's opera *Dafne*, which had perhaps been discussed on the occasion of his second (this time political) sojourn at the Albertinian court in August 1626. The fall of 1627 brought him the imperial title of nobility "von Boberfeld," and the year 1629, through the influence of Diedrich v. d. Werder, honorary membership in the Fruit Bearing Society.[77] In 1631 he translated into German for Dohna the proselytizing Jesuit document of Martin Becanus: *Manuale controversarium*. The fact that the thus carried water on both shoulders — according to political expediency — runs parallel to the Saxon policy in these years of being on both sides at once *(quer durch die Fronten)*.

We have no occasion here to renew the old controversy as to the value of Opitz' poetry.[78] That he "sufficed for the best of his time" and understood much of the meaning of these difficult years is at least indicated by his significant influence on the creative activity of Schütz. This comprehension also appears from the verses in his *Lob des Kriegsgottes* (1628), wherein, in 849 Alexandrines, he attempts by flattery to bribe the god Mars to retreat:

> Thou God of blood, I greet thee and I pray
> That if thy heart feels kindness still to this our land,

---

[76] Infra.
[77] *Fruchtbringende Gesellschaft.*
[78] H. Osterley's biography and selections in Kürschners *Deutsche National Literatur*, Vol. 27.

Then turn to others thy destructive hand,
And deal with Germans in a gentler way.

That Opitz must have had a relation to music beyond commissions from princes is indicated by the youthful poem *Echo oder Wiederschall* ("Echo or Reverberation"), *Dies Ort, mit Bäumen ganz umgeben* ("This Place Among the Trees"), the middle section of which is apparently intended for double chorus. Each couplet is followed by an echo syllable or syllables:

Ist denn niemand, der tröste mich,
Weil ich so trauer inniglich? — Ich,
O, Echo, wirst nur du alleine
Hinfort mich trösten, und sonst keine? — Eine.

Sie will er aber nicht verstehen,
Lest mich in Angst ohn Ablass gehen. — Lass gehen.

Unfortunately, Schütz's music which was formerly in Weimar has not been found. The song of the first shepherd in the opening act of his *Dafne, Umb diesen Wald und Schatten haben wir,* had the same echo effect.

Now, however, the year 1625, which promised so much for Schütz's art, took a tragic turn. This began with the early death of his sister-in-law, Anna Maria Wildeck. When still a bride of the Altenburg court counselor and president of the consistory, Dr. Martin Mende, she died on August 12 and was buried in Dresden four days later. Schütz composed for her funeral an *Aria de vitae fugacitate* for soprano and thorough bass, his setting of *Ich hab mein Sach Gott heimgestellt,*[79] which was also printed at the time (XII, Complete Edition, 33). He reworked the composition for his *Kleine geistliche Konzerte* of 1636.

The severest blow of his life befell him three weeks later. His wife died on September 6 and was buried on September 9. The details are contained in the funeral sermon of Hoe von Hoenegg:

"And though from the human point of view one might have wished that she had lived longer and continued to nurture her tender offspring, it pleased the Almighty otherwise. A week ago last Tuesday he permitted her to be smitten with sickness.[80] All possible remedies were applied, and no care was spared. As the pustules (pocks) had broken out considerably, it seemed that there was no further danger. But since, contrary to expectations, other complications set in and the fever increased, she died a blessed death on the following Tuesday at 2:30 in the morning. Several weeks before her end she suspected that the Lord God would soon summon her, and she informed her dear husband to this effect and told him that he would not live much longer. In anticipation of her death she requested certain hymns to be sung at her funeral. And as soon as the Almighty had brought the sickness upon her, she

---

[79] "I have put my all in the hands of God."
[80] Smallpox.

turned to him with childlike faith and prayed unceasingly, frequently repeating Psalm 6 and Psalm 130. With especial feeling did she utter the words 'My soul waiteth for the Lord more than they that watch for the morning.' In addition to this, her father confessor, Master Samuel Rüling, reports that she comforted herself with the words of St. Paul: 'None of us liveth to himself' (Romans 14)... Likewise the words of David: 'If I have but thee' (Ps. 73: 25)... Likewise the words of Job, the holy man of God, in the ninetenth chapter: 'I know that my Redeemer liveth' ... also that she prayed loudly and clearly the beautiful parting prayer *Herr Jesu Christ, wahr Mensch und Gott* ('Lord Jesus Christ, true God and Man'). And when he asked her whether in her extreme anxiety she still harbored the Lord Jesus in her heart, she replied in the affirmative and declared that she wished to live and die in Jesus Christ, which she then did and fell gently and blessedly asleep in the Lord at the age of twenty-four years, six months, two weeks, and three days — for herself a blessing.

> Her trouble, sorrow, woe are past,
> Have reached a blessed end at last.

But alas, alas for the bereaved and sorrowing widower! He laments: 'My lyre is turned to sorrow. To God be it lamented: my harp has become a dirge, and my pipe a weeping.' Among all the sounds of the harp he neither knew nor heard a lovelier sound or song than the voice of his beloved. He esteemed her his most valued harp on earth. But she speaks no more.

"Sorrow has descended upon the grieving, aged parents whom God has now several times afflicted thus by taking from them three dear daughters and a son, leaving but one son, to whom may God grant yet many years.

"Sorrow has overtaken the two poor little orphans, neither of whom can cut a mouthful of bread for the other, and who have lost their dear faithful mother almost before they came to know her.

"But what shall we do for him, my beloved? The Lord, the Lord 'turns man to destruction' (Psalm 90), and He who imposes the burden upon the widower is also 'the God of salvation' (Psalm 68). He is also ready to 'make his yoke easy and his burden light' (Matthew 11)."

In the sermon preached at Schütz's own funeral, Martin Geier recalls the sad event in the following words:

"But the sweetness of this welcome union was soon changed into bitter wormwood, inasmuch as in the sixth year of his love, on September 6, 1625, he was destined to see his beloved torn from his side by death, as the result of which he was overcome by no small measure of sorrow.... As the result of this, he entrusted his two aforenamed daughters at first to his dearest mother in Weissenfels, then to the wife of the tax recorder, Herr Christian Hartmann, as their nearest relatives."

The sermon at the funeral of Euphrosyne, the second daughter, reveals an error here with regard to the care of the two children by the Weissenfels grandmother. We read there:

"She was all too early deprived of the best disciplinarian, her beloved mother, since it pleased the Almighty to take this dear soul to himself on September 6, 1625, and thus to make this immature child, not yet two years of age, a little motherless orphan. It did not please the father to marry again and provide a stepmother for his children. Several years later he undertook a journey to Italy. After a safe return he accepted a call from His Royal Majesty in Denmark with the consent of His Electoral Highness of Saxony and, on account of the troublesome wars in this country, remained in Denmark for several years. Since he wished properly to provide for this his dear child and for her sister, Anna Justina, he entrusted them both to the hands of their esteemed (maternal) grandmother (Wildeck), under whose faithful tutelage she remained until her tenth year, when, in 1633, it pleased the Almighty to take her grandmother to the life to come. Thereupon a substitute for the blessed departed Frau Doctor had to be provided elsewhere; so she was placed in the care of her dear aunt, Frau Maria, beloved wife of the esteemed Electoral Saxon tax recorder, Herr Michael Hartmann, and of Frau Maria's mother, as the next of kin. But no abiding place of long duration was to be found here either, as her dear friend and aunt died in 1643, so that still another home had to be found. She came hither [doubtless to Leipzig], where for a considerable period she was educated by the dear wife of the esteemed Electoral Saxon tax collector, later bookkeeper, Herr Johann Hanitsch, her nearest cousin. After betaking herself to her cousin in the name of the Lord, she continued under her tutelage her virtuous Christian life until it pleased the Almighty to conduct her from maidenhood to wedlock."

Contrary to the custom of the time, the forty-year-old widower never married again. Sympathizing friends supported him in his overwhelming bereavement. Opitz wrote the following, which he included in the second part of his *Deutsche Poëmata* of 1628, on p. 417:

To Herr Heinrich Schütz
on the Departure of His Dearest Wife

O thou Orpheus of our time,
Thou whom Thalia has taught,
Thou whose songs and golden strings
Even Phoebus hears with pleasure,
What does our complaining serve?

Can our anguish banish death?
Tune again thy magic lute,
Let the organ better sound,
Let thy songs again resound,
If their magic yet remain.
She will leave the dark domain
And return to thee again.

Give to her thy pleasant singing,
Her whom death has snatched away.
Let the sweet tone now resound
Which the son of Oeagrus[81] made
And so artfully contrived
That he conquered night and day.

For your songs will still be honored
When we long have passed away.
What through them will not take root
Vanishes like smoke and wind.
He who dieth thus will perish,
And his praise with him be gone.

Praise the virtues of the loved one,
Sing abroad her kindliness,
Of her charming younger days
And the happy times now past
Which you so enjoyed with her,
Till it came her time to go.

We will join with you in singing,
Eagerly beside you climb
Up the azure vault of heaven,
That she live forever more
Through the magic of your art,
O thou Orpheus of our time.

It is possible that the plea expressed in the second-last stanza quoted — to tell of the pleasant days spent with Magdalene — may have found its subsequent fulfillment in one or another of Schütz's German madrigals.

It would have been more like Schütz to have set to music, as a memorial, one of the "last verses" spoken by his dying wife and mentioned in the funeral sermon. Psalms 6 and 130 are among the polychoral compositions of 1619. But *Unser*

---

[81] Orpheus.

keiner lebet ihm selber[82] (for five voices) and *Ich weiss dass mein Erlöser lebt*[83] (for seven) are in the *Geistliche Chormusik* of 1648. Perhaps they are related, as are other compositions, at least in their early form, to that period of mourning. The fact that the other texts — *Wenn ich nur dich habe*[84] and *Herr Jesu Christ, wahrer Mensch und Gott*[85] — are not at hand in settings by Schütz need not exclude the possibility that he may have set them too. The actual and demonstrable requiem for his wife was the *Cornelius Becker Psalter,* printed in 1628. This Schütz acknowledges in the preface of September 6, 1627, addressed to the Electress Hedwig of Saxony, the widow of Christian II and a sister-in-law of Johann Georg I:

> "... In view of this, I heretofore set for my house music and for the morning and evening prayers of the choir boys placed under me some few new melodies to the mentioned *Psalms* of Dr. Becker. After these had now and again reached other people's hands, I was advised on many sides both in writing and orally to continue and complete this work. Although this urging would have gone unheeded longer, both on account of other work at hand and in view of the fact that there is scarcely a musician who cannot compose a melody, it pleased God Almighty, according to His allwise cousel and gracious will, to have me forego such other work by reason of a special domestic affliction in the unexpected death of my dear wife, Magdalene Wildecken, and to give into my hands this little psalm book from which I could draw more comfort in my sorrow. Wherefore without further consideration of self I turned to this task as a comforter in sadness and have finally completed this little work with God's help, as it here lies at hand."

At the same time Schütz thanks the electress for being "most gracious heretofore in connection with the purchase of my present residence." Presumably it was the house at *Frauenstraße* 14, previously *Neumarkt* 12, which the records show to have been in Schütz's possession from 1629 to 1657. He may, however, have lived there previously as a tenant paying rent.[86] The house was distinguished by a beautiful bay window. The electress doubtless assisted him in 1627 by taking a mortgage or in some other way. In the same year, 1627, Schütz on not a few occasions was engrossed with outside occupations. From March 21 to April 24 he stayed in Torgau with the court choir for the wedding of Johann Georg's eldest daughter, Sophie Eleonore, and the Darmstadt Landgrave Georg II. Carlo Farina from Mantua, who since 1625 had been Schütz's concertmaster, wrote the banquet music, a specimen of which, the *Torgau Gagliard* for string orchestra, has been

---

[82] *No Man Liveth unto Himself.*
[83] *I Know that My Redeemer Liveth.*
[84] *If I Only Have Thee.*
[85] *Lord Jesus Christ, True Man and God.*
[86] Imparted by the council archives; cf. also Ad. Hantzsch, *Hervorragende Persönlichkeiten in Dresden und ihre Wohnungen (Mitteilungen des Vereins für Geschichte Dresdens,* Brochure 25, 1918).

preserved in one of Farina's five books of pavans, gagliards, and bransles (printed in Dresden 1626—28, a copy preserved in Kassel):[87]

One will note the great similarity to Gastoldi's *In dir ist Freude.*

The court lutenist (since 1618, or perhaps 1623), Johann Nauwach, provided the vocal part of the social entertainment. He was born ca. 1595 in the territory of Brandenburg, was a choir boy at the Dresden court until 1612, and was then educated at the expense of the elector in Turin and Florence. In 1623 he had published *A First Book of Arias Composed for Voice and Guitar,*[88] and now appeared with *Deutsche Villanellen* for one, two, and three voices (Freiberg, 1627). These songs were among the first Germain songs with thorough bass. Eight texts among nineteen are by Opitz. He may also be the author of the last number, *Glück zu dem Helicon,* which Schütz composed for two voices *in lode del autore.*[89] The *Bober Swan* (Opitz) also added here a paean to the "New Bach" *(neuen Bach)* and followed with a second one in 1629. The printed work is dedicated to the newly married prince and princess.[90]

---

[87] Performed in addition to 21 bransles at the Berlin Schütz Festival (November 15, 1930) and edited by H. Diener in my *Musikkränzlein* (Kistner & Siegel) as Brochure 1.

[88] *Libro primo di arie passegiate a una voce per cantar e sonar nel chittarone.*

[89] "in praise of the author."

[90] Cf. Hans Volkmann in *ZfMW,* IV, 553 ff., who also corrects a number of Ph. Spitta's observations in the preface to the *GA,* Vol. XV. Further, A. Einstein in *Sbd, IMG,* XIII and H. Kretzschmar, *Geschichte des deutschen Liedes,* pp. 13 ff.

We may gain the best picture of Nauwach's song style from the numerous new editions by W. Vetter,[91] as, for example, the following, with text by Opitz:

Most important of all, however, Schütz wrote the first German opera for the Torgau festivities — the first, if one disregards other little *Orfeo* and *Andromeda* attempts in connection with the Prince Bishop of Salzburg. The landgrave bridegroom was considered another "learned" Hessian to whom it was necessary to offer something special. For this reason Opitz, who at the time was visiting Buchner in Wittenberg, rendered Rinuccini's *Dafne* libretto (Florence, 1594) freely into German and had his verses printed[92] with a dedicatory poem:

"To Their Highnesses, the bride and the bridegroom, at whose nuptials *Dafne*, by Heinrich Schütz, was presented in music in the year 1627."

This great event, which perhaps made on but a few of the initiated in that court society[93] as sensational an impression as it was a sensational fact, is almost lost sight of in the court accounts. Hidden among extensive details of boar- and bearbaiting, one finds as the only evidence of a performance in *Schloss Hartenfels*, presumably in the dining hall, the journal entry: "the 13th (April 1627) the Dresden court musicians enacted musically a pastoral tragicomedy *(Pastoral Tragicomödia)* on *Dafne*." The work itself we shall discuss in connection with Schütz's *Opitz Madrigals*.[94] Schütz's score was doubtless completely destroyed in the Dresden fire of 1760.

Schütz had hoped, doubtless as an evidence of the appreciation of his artistic fidelity demonstrated anew in Torgau, to obtain a leave of absence for a trip to Italy which would tear him away from his domestic sorrow and make him conversant with the artistic changes there. But his request of May 30 was rejected.

[91] *Das frühdeutsche Lied,* II, No. 102 ff.
[92] In Oesterley, loc. cit., pp. 58 ff.; also in Taubert (Address Gymn.-Progr. Torgau, 1879).
[93] L. Schiedermair, *Die deutsche Oper* (1930), pp. 21 f.
[94] Infra.

The elector doubtless realized that he would soon require the services of his court Kapellmeister on another special occasion. So on August 17 he took him along to *Schloss Osterstein* near Gera. Here Schütz must have performed some music for the royal patron Heinrich Posthumus.

In October, finally, the court ensemble *(Hofkapelle)* set out for Mühlhausen, in Thuringia, where the electors were to assemble. For this occasion Schütz wrote a most remarkable double-chorus *Conzert.* It belongs among his "political compositions." An extensive note in Schütz's own hand, designating which musicians could be taken along to Mühlhausen "for performance both on the preaching days and at the banquet," has been preserved.[95] The list reveals the Saxon ensemble *(Capelle)* in all its glory. There are nineteen persons, traveling in two carriages and a stage. From among these fourteen are recommended to the elector in case it should be necessary to reduce the larger number. In this category we find Schütz, Farina, Nauwach; the singers Hasselt and Kramer, and the zither player Hans Beltz, about whom there still exist personal letters by Schütz. The organist Kaspar Kittel was then living for the fourth year in Italy under a grant from the prince.

Apparently the ensemble achieved a great success. Nevertheless, as the forerunner of many years of future misfortunes, the group found it necessary to forward through Schütz's hand, on Palm Sunday, 1628, a written cry of need *(Notschrei)* to the elector. For a year the petition stated it had scarcely received a month's wages and found itself in sore straits. At about the same time Schütz made a second request for permission to visit Italy. His modest assurance in connection with this request strikes one almost as touching: "as from the first I did not come upon this idea prompted by any frivolity, as a mere pleasure jaunt or desire to travel, but through the urge for an improvement in spirit."

However, as appears in a number of documents, Schütz had to arrange all kinds of trivial matters relating to the further education of choir boys whose voices were changing (among them Joh. Vierdanck), and the like,[96] before the elector finally permitted his departure. He was able to start his journey in August, and he arrived in Venice for the second time ca. November 1.

---

[95] M. Fürstenau, *Zur Geschichte der Musik und des Theaters zu Dresden,* I, 98.
[96] E. H. Müller, *Briefsammlung,* No. 27.

The Venice of Monteverdi

Geier's funeral address tells only briefly of Schütz's second journey to Venice. Furthermore, his words are not founded on complete accuracy. Geier said:

"As the pressures of war increased more and more in these lands, hindered that which in times of peace was wont to flourish, and thus also militated against the exercise of Schütz's profession, he resolved to undertake another 'peregrination,' and, after receiving from His Electoral Highness of most blessed memory the necessary permission for a certain length of time, he journeyed from here to Italy for a second time, on August 11, 1628." The address then speaks of events in connection with his return home.

Schütz's autobiographical memorandum of 1651 to the elector contributes no further material relative to this event. But the dedication of the *Sinfoniae sacrae* III, of St. Michael's Day 1650,[1] refers to it. We read: "Thus I remember very vividly the manner in which, during these past, long, wearisome thirty years of war, Your Electoral Highness did not altogether withdraw your favor and helping hand from noble music and the liberal arts. As far as possible you always came to their assistance. Especially, moreover, did you show all kinds of special favors to my unworthy person during the continuing unrest of our dear German fatherland. For the continuance of my profession you graciously allowed me, not only to undertake a second journey to Italy in 1628 and 1629 in order that I might there investigate the new advances and present practices in music which had developed there since my first sojourn, and for this purpose gave me a liberal allowance; but after the completion of this my journey. . . ."

But the most important documents relative to this event are the three letters of Schütz to the elector from Venice[2] and his Latin preface to the *Sinfoniae sacrae I*, dated *Venetiis XIV. Calend. Sept.* This was addressed to Crown Prince Johann George II,[3] who, although then but sixteen years old, had both artistic taste and talent for music. In Schütz's request of April 28 for leave of absence he had indicated the dangers of such a journey: "Since I am minded in this event to take

---

[1] E. H. Müller, p. 201.
[2] Dated November 3, 1628; June 29 and August 24, 1629.
[3] E. H. Müller's collection, Nos. 28—31.

good care of myself and to travel with strong company, of which I am somewhat
informed. . . ." In fact, when he finally departed, he was able to carry out his plans
only in the face of all kinds of difficulties. He had not been able to reach Venice for
a considerable time "on account of the closed passes, partly in Germany and partly
at the Venetian borders." Indeed, the journey consumed about ten weeks. He
requests that his position not be taken over by anyone else, and he hopes that this
journey "will be of marked advantage to him in many respects in his, to be sure,
modest profession." Although a continuation of his salary had enabled him to
undertake the journey, he nevertheless requests a further allowance, sufficient "for
the purchase of much new beautiful music, inasmuch as I already perceive that
since the time when I first visited these parts this whole art has changed much, and
that that music which is useful to royal banquets, comedies, ballets, and similar
presentations has now become markedly better and more plentiful. . . ." Thus in
November 1628. After nine months in Italy he is able to report that "that for which
I set out I have now accomplished according to my desire. I have procured a fair
supply of all kinds of music, which, together with some instruments, I have sent to
Leipzig." He will, therefore, soon set out on the return journey. He had become
acquainted with the best violinist (*Discantgeiger*) in Venice, Fr. Castelli, whom he
recommends to the elector as concertmaster. He likewise intends to bring back
home Kaspar Kittel, who had completed his Venetian studies.

The third letter is a request for an advance of salary, in order that he might pay
his debts before departing.

Most important from the point of view of the history of art are the observations
in the preface to the *Sinfoniae sacrae I*.[4] The passage concerning Gabrieli has
already been mentioned.

"Staying in Venice with old friends, I found the manner of musical composition
(*modulandi rationem*) somewhat changed. They have partially abandoned the old
[medieval] church modes (*antiquos numeros ex parte deposuisse*) while seeking to
charm modern ears with new titillations (*hodiernis auribus recenti allusuram
titillatione*). I have devoted my mind and my powers to present to you for your
information something in accordance with this artistic development (*norma*). . . ."
He appeals at the same time to the artistic understanding of Volrad v. Watzdorff,
the tutor of the prince.

The twenty Latin parts of the *Sinfoniae* were the first artistic harvest of that
stimulating visit. The preface to the *Sinfoniae sacrae II* (1647), with German texts,

---

[4] From which we present the following in translation from the Latin.

recalls it with the words: "Kindly disposed reader: I must tell you how in the year 1629, when I had arrived in Italy for the second time, I composed in a short period, in the prevailing musical manner, a little Latin work of one, two, or three vocal parts, together with two violins, or similar instruments, according to the modest talent (which I mention without boasting) bestowed on me by God, and how I published it in Venice under the title: *Sinfoniae sacrae.* After a number of the copies had been sent to Germany and had come into the hands of musicians, and I had heard good judgments pronounced on them, and had also heard that at certain distinguished places they had been repeatedly performed with German texts substituted for the Latin . . . ." he tells us that, as a result of this, he now also composed a German work "in the contemporary Italian style, which was still generally unfamiliar in Germany both as to composition and proper performance. In this style, according to the opinion of the keen-minded Herr Cl. Monteverdi, as he states in the preface to the eighth book of his madrigals, music has now reached its final perfection."[5] Schütz also honored the Cremonian (Monteverdi) in the second collection (*secunda pars*) by using in his *concerto Es steh Gott auf*[6] motives from Monteverdi's madrigal *Armato il cor* and the *ciacona Zefiro torna,* but with the remark: "I trust that no one will be suspicious of the remainder of my work, as I am not in the habit of adorning what I do with the plumage of others." The "keen-minded" Herr Claudius Monteverdi, therefore, who since 1613 was the new star of the first magnitude in the Venetian musical firmament, played for the forty-three-year-old Schütz a role as preceptor similar to that of Gabrieli when Schütz was twenty-three. At this time Monteverdi was sixty-one years old. According to a letter of Bentivoglio to the Duchess of Parma, of August 1627,[7] he was "the most lovable character and the greatest master in his field." Winterfeld (II, 192) called attention to the fact that Schütz was already so famous that the Kapellmeister at St. Mark's "scarcely dared deny him a personal approach."

Schirmer's "Elegy" (to Schütz's wife) tells us that Monteverdi, as teacher, took a definite and personal interest in Schütz:

> Who is there now can tell here of our Schütz,
> How, deep in sorrow, how, o'erwhelmed by woe,
> How he can drive away his loneliness?

---

[5] Strangely enough, nothing to this effect is mentioned in the printed preface by Monteverdi. Was Schütz perhaps acquainted with a fuller preliminary form of this in manuscript?
[6] "Let God Arise."
[7] Emil Vogel in *Vjschr. f. MW*, III, 385.

His healer was his Italy. For this he craved,
And this again the gallant man received.
The noble Mont de verd with joy did show the path
And with delight did chart the oft-sought course,
Until at last it came his time to soar aloft
And sing his sorrow unto Christ his Lord.

The rhyming "Elegy" by the Leipzig superintendent D. Georg Lehmann "to the godfather, brother-in-law, and esteemed old friend," "written with sad pen," has Schütz say:

Italia knows of me, in all of Germany my name is spoken.
In Denmark also I have long been known;
And Sweden, too, has offered me her hand;
So has my fame been borne to many a land.

Thus we have a reference here to otherwise unknown relations with Sweden.

Monteverdi's eighth book of madrigals consists of the *Madrigals of War and Love*[8] (1638), dedicated to Emperor Ferdinand, among which, with others, are to be found the *Ballo delle Ingrate* of 1608 and the dramatic Oratorio II, titled *The Battle of Tancred and Clorinda*[9] of 1624. The preface[10] describes the discovery of the *stile concitato*, especially the new tremolo — a most decisive innovation on the way to "modern" music. This Schütz had apparently followed with the keenest attention and probably had learned to know while Monteverdi's work was still in manuscript in 1629. If, however, one examines Schütz's *Sinfoniae sacrae* with regard to their instrumental style, it would appear that only seldom (for example, in the *Lament of David over Absalom*) did he use as his model the many-voiced style, concentrated into compressed ritornelles, of the corresponding numbers in Monteverdi's book of *concerti* (the seventh volume of madrigals). It would seem that he took rather that style which H. Riemann[11] calls "mixed style" *(Mischliteratur)*, consisting of voices and few instruments, like Francesco Turini's *Madrigali a cinque cioé 3 voci e 2 violini*,[12] or Paolo Quagliati's *Sfera*

---

[8] *Madrigali Guerrieri et Amorosi.*
[9] *Combattimento di Tancredi e di Clorinda.*
[10] Italian in E. Vogel,*Bibliothek der weltl.Vokalmusik Italiens*, p. 511; Torchi VI, 136; Malipiero's edition, VIII: German by Vogel in *Vj.*, III, 396.
[11] *Hdb. d. MG.*, Vol. II 2, p. 83 ff.
[12] Not contained for the first time in the volume of 1629, but clearly already in those of 1621 and 1624. From this collection of madrigals we have the madrigal *Mentre vaga angioletta* in an edition by Riemann (Langensalza).

armoniosa of 1623.[13] It may have some connection with Schütz's studies that a printed copy of the work of Quagliati (born in the region of Venice, and a Roman by choice) for one and two voices, with theorbos and in part with violin, has been preserved only in Dresden. Possibly an acquaintance on the part of Schütz with Turini's second book of concert madrigals (1624) might be inferred from the following similarity:

Turini, *Ardo mia vita*[14]

Schütz, *Ich lieg and schlafe* ("I lie and sleep") (1636)

But such figures are met with frequently since Caccini's time. "Mixture literature" by B. Marini should also be considered in this connection, as, for example, the *Scherzi e canzonette, Op. 5* (Parma, 1622). How unfortunate it is that we cannot find in some old library catalog a list of the music that Schütz brought back to Dresden at this time!

The *stile concitato,* however, which Monteverdi had made the principal feature of his eighth book of madrigals, did have for Schütz a certain, though limited, significance.[15] The object of this style in music is the presentation of states of emotional agitation, both through the heightening or enhancement of the text (as a special instance of the "monodic principle") and also by means of word painting (madrigalisms), expressive interpretation of the text *(musica riservata),* and descriptive instrumental features. This "agitation" is strongly limited in Monteverdi to the one affectual nuance of "bellicose anger" in the battle of the mounted Tancred with the armored knight, in whose armor Tancred's beloved pagan Clorinda suffers death at his hands — a half-dramatic oratorio, half-cantatalike madrigal and orchestral painting. In the case of words like *guerra, ira, furo,*

---

[13] From this collection the chamber duet with obl. solo violin, *O come dolce amore,* in Riemann's *Musikgesch. in Beispielen.* W. Schuh, p. 29, calls attention to the fact that the same scoring with two violins occurs in Joh. Staden's *Herzentrost-Musica,* 1630, and *Geistlicher Musikklang,* 1633; after all, then, later than with Schütz.

[14] Eugen Schmitz, Sbd. *IMG.,* XI, 517, *Zur Geschichte des ital. Continuo-Madrigals.*

[15] Cf. the Bern dissertation by Werner Kreidler, *H. Schütz und der stile concitato von Cl. Monteverdi* (Bärenreiter, 1934).

vendetta, or of tonal pictures or pictures of action, such as riding, fighting, the clanging of swords, the following means of expression are used: repeated melody leaps, fanfarelike triadic motifs, dotted rhythms, and sudden accentual changes; runs, tremolos, figures with trills, figures expressing emotion, linear reinforcement by means of parallel thirds and sixths; vigorous cadential displacements, frequent changes in harmony, but also simplifications through surface harmonies; long climaxes, close imitations, inversions, interval enlargements, contrary motion. In brief, we find here a new significance of the means of polyphony after the latter's decline to mere monody; interrupting pauses, insertions, filigree, *ostinati,* and repetitive enforcing measures; in short, the whole "modern" arsenal of all that builds itself up with tensions in strong contrast to merely gentle and elegiac songfulness.

We shall see that Schütz does not make much use of the *stile concitato* in the *Sinfoniae sacrae I,* that he still holds himself in restraint with regard to this style. He employs it much more pronouncedly in the *Sinfoniae sacrae II* and *III* since 1638, and after he had brought the problem of the monodic principle to a solution, according to his manner, in the *Kleine geistliche Konzerte.* To be sure, in the *Sinfoniae sacrae II* and *III* he employs the style in a strongly Germanized manner. More than this, he transformed it in his own manner, making it more profound, in that he mixes it with "traditional style elements" (Kreidler, p. 99), namely, the polyphonic motet technique and the polychoral technique of broad surfaces, and especially in that he drew it into the sphere of religion and spiritual symbolism (cf. p. 111). Monteverdi had approached this problem in a speculative manner, like an explorer in natural science, and, being an Italian, was fond of giving vent to extensive outbursts. Schütz, on the other hand, suffers *(erleidet)* it with the uncertainty of a Protestant wrestling with the meaning of existence and feels these outbreaks more as invasions of the inner recesses of one's being.

Schütz doubtless also absorbed another strong impression in the Venice of 1628-29, something not to be gained from volumes of printed notes — the development of the embellished solo song in the secular drama and the church cantata. To be sure, Venice did not become a city devoted to the public performance of opera until 1634, after which, of course, it rapidly took the lead in this field for an entire century. But it had long cultivated the opera privately, especially in the circles of the art-loving patricians in which Schütz moved. One need only remember what was performed in the way of opera by Monteverdi in the home of the Moncenigos, etc., for example, *La finta pazza Licori* (a parody) and the serious *Proserpina rapita.* Both of these scorces have been lost. One should recall further that these were the years in which a remarkably bold young solo-cantata art began to unfold itself, that of Benedetto Ferrari, Francesco Manelli, and Francesco Cavalli.[16] Besides the solo cantatas of those just mentioned and the earlier solo arias and madrigals with thorough bass by Caccini, we find sacred solo *concerti* by Monteverdi as well as by Saracini, Gagliano, Calestani, Alessandro Grandi, Giov. Rovetta, and Carlo Milanuzi.[17] We present one of the sacred solo *concerti* by Monteverdi, taken from L. Simonetti's *Ghirlanda sacra* of 1625 (36), the source also of the example by Martinengo, given above.

This example, which evidently is intended to represent the cooing of a dove, will be the more interesting since up to the present time new editions of the sacred music of Monteverdi are almost completely lacking, and also because we have here a text which Schütz also treated (in the *Symphoniae sacrae I*, Complete Edition, Vol. V, 42).

O quam pulchra es.

---

[16] In H. Riemann's *Kantatenfrühling.*
[17] Cf.Eugen Schmitz, *Gesch.d. weltl. Solokantate,* pp. 47 ff and *Sbde. IMG,* XI.

ter mu=li=e=res! E=gre=de=re, e=gre=de=re, e=gre=de=re et

ve=ni, Ve=ni, qui=a a=mo=re lan=gue=o. Ve=ni, ve=ni,

Ve=ni, ve=ni, ve = ni, Ve=ni for=mo=sa

me=a, ve=ni so=ror me=a, ve=ni im=ma=cu=la=ta me=a,

Ve=ni, qui=a a=mo=re langueo____, et a=ni=ma mea lique=

facta est, a=ni=ma, a=ni=ma me=a li=que=fac=ta____, li=que=fac=ta est.

Ambros has shown[18] how monody was also devoted to the service of the church. Monteverdi's *Lament of Ariadne* is imitated as a *Lamentation of Mary* by Radesca da Foggia (1616). Serafino Patta, in 1614, set the *Pietosi affetti* of Pater Angelo Grillo; and in the same year the singer at San Marco, Girolamo Marinoni, delighted the Venetians with motets for "one voice" which were entirely in the style of Monteverdi. The dramatic instinct of the time manifests itself in dialogs such as that between the penitent sinner and Christ;[19] or in the cantata between Christ and the Samaritan woman, which Goethe describes in the *Italienische Reise* and which Ambros bought in the streets of Rome as late as 1866. Here are the roots of Schütz's dialogs between Jesus and the Canaanite woman and between Jesus and the centurion; also those of the Hammerschmidt dialogs and Bach's duet cantatas.[20] The questionably coquettish tone of such dialogs is shown (Ambros, IV, 316) by the dialog *Dama, chi é patre* of Radesca da Foggia and by the religious operatic pathos of the *Penitent Magdalene* of Domenico Mazzocchi, with its purely vocal and close approach to the *stile concitato*. Ath. Kircher tells us that with the latter composition famous *castrati* of the day captivated the musical world. From this fervor the path is not a long one to Schütz's Augustinian monolog *Was hast du verwirket? (What Hast Thou Done?)*.[21] But for his solo works for high voices Schütz at first had at his disposal neither women nor *castrati* but only choir boys or *falsetti*. It was not until he was an old man that he came to deal — and then not with pleasure — with the *castrati*. The meager-voiced motets of Grandi, through their doubling of the upper voice in thirds, became of special significance to Schütz, as for example the *Missus est Gabriel* (Pirro, *Schütz*, p. 77), published for the fifth time in 1628. We shall see how Schütz later created a memorial to this master of St. Mark's[22] Above all, however, Monteverdi himself with his Mary vespers of 1610 had presented the most magnificent example of a spiritual concert, rich in contrasts, with soli and choruses.[23]

---

[18] *Musikgeschichte*, IV (*History of Music*), 310 ff.

[19] Text by Grillo, music by Batholomeo Pesarino, originally a conversation with Charon!

[20] When, however, Ambros (IV, 314 ff.) is somewhat properly incensed with regard to the saccharine bombast of a cantata for nuns, *Veni, veni, amo te, of* 1688, he has fallen prey to a mystification; for behind that anonymous Roman Clarissa stands the Göppingen Evangelical Cantor, Daniel Speer. The old vagabound (*Landstörzer*) (cf. my discussion in the *Euphorion,* 1933) published the collection *Philomela angelica* under his anagram *Res plena Dei,* and the place of printing, "Venice," is probably also a deception. Pirro, *Schütz*, pp. 73 f., enumerates further works in this connection.

[21] Complete Ed. Vol. IV, No. 4: *Quid commisisti.*

[22] Supra.

[23] Performed in Zurich by the Häusermann Chorus in 1934 in the practical edition of Redlich.

In Venice, Schütz himself wrote an opera of which we have neither the libretto nor a single note, but this has been little observed. On February 6 and 16, 1633, he referred to it in his letter to Friedrich Lebzelter in Hamburg in order to make his presence at the wedding of the Danish crown prince with Princess Magdalene Sybille of Saxony all the more desirable:[24]

"His Lordship, when the opportunity affords itself, should not allow His Excellency to be uninformed as to how on my latest visit to Italy I undertook a special form of composition, namely, how a comedy of all kinds of voices could be presented in recitative style and could be brought upon the stage and enacted with singing, which matters, according to my knowledge (in the manner which I mean), are still altogether unknown in Germany. On account of the difficult times in which we live, we have never practiced or encouraged this form. And because I believe that it is a pity that such very majestic and princely inventions have been neglected by other and better talents, I would not neglect upon my arrival to present such a work to Your Highness for the coming solemnities, I being at your service according to your wishes."

Since Schütz expressly states that since a work of this kind had never been presented in Germany, it must have differed essentially from his own pastorale-tragicomedy *Dafne*. The *Konzert* character of the latter may be inferred even more strongly from the above statement, since Schütz here speaks of a recitational comedy. This also harmonizes well with Schütz's first report to the elector concerning his journey, to the effect that the comedies and ballets especially had improved markedly in Italy.

Who knows what *Pranks of Old Age (Pazzia senile)* or *Juvenile Wisdom (Prudenzia jovenile)*, by Schütz, may not have gone up in flames in Dresden in 1760 or in Copenhagen in 1794?

During Schütz's absence an art-minded Augsburg patrician, Philipp Hainhofer, had come to Dresden as an ambassador to the elector in behalf of his evangelical fellow citizens, who were suffering as the result of the Edict of Restitution. We shall meet with him again as a correspondent of Schütz. We are indebted to the account of Hainhofer's journey[25] for a most vivid picture of the Dresden musical treasures. After he had visited Hoe v. Hoenegg, Georg Reichbrodt, and Friedrich Lebzelter, and had minutely described the art chamber *(Kunstkammer)*, library, armory, and cabinet of rarities, and had presented his requests in an audience

---

[24] Printed for the first time in Hammerich & Elling, *Die Musik am Hofe Christians IV von Dänemark (Vjschr. f. MW,* IX 83); according to this, E. H. Müller, No. 41.
[25] Oscar Doering, *Ph. Hainhofers Reisen nach Innsbruck und Dresden* (Vienna, 1901), pp. 217 ff.

with the elector, he visited the elector's summer house on the bastion: "When one dines in this upper hall, musicians are stationed in the lower hall, the doors are closed, and the resonance ascends pleasantly through the ventilators. Above, under the ceiling, there is also an arrangement for hidden music, so that one can hear such music from thirty-two different locations, all separated."

He then visits "the pipe and instrument chamber" on the third floor of the Dresden palace.

"In the *Pfeiffenkammer* Thomas Dax (Tax), musician and custodian of these musical instruments, together with two other attendants, showed us the following:
An octave trombone, which they consider a rarity
A quint-terce-tenor trombone
Some small discant trombones
Some bomars (Pommers, Bomharts). These are long and short wooden pipes. A shalmey. Some Turkish *Streitkolben* and *Axten mit Pfeiffen* (clubs or maces and axes or hatchets with pipes. Some cornets. Two kinds of *Bäugglein* with bells and cymbals. Large flutes. A triangle with bells. Bassoons. *Passembles (bassanelli)*. Eight *stammen Stimmpfeiffen (Stamentienpfeiffen)*, each with only three holes, etc.
On two pediments there are 14 figures of 14 famous Kapellmeisters and composers, such as: Andrea Gabrieli, Filippo del Monte, Giovanni Gabrieli, Cyprian de Rore,Claudio Monteverdi, Orlando de Lasso, Alessandro Stuchio (Striggio), Adrian Willaert Giovanni Croce, Claudio Merulo, Alessandro Orologgio, Gioan Peters (Sweelinck), Asmus de Klain (Erasmus de Glein). This last one was not a composer, but otherwise a good musician."

The almost complete predominance of Italian masters is very striking. This is also evident from the Dresden catalog of *musicalia* of 1595.[26] Hainhofer now continues:

"The electoral Kapellmeister, Hainrich (sic) Schütz, is now in Lombardy in order to purchase more musical instruments." Perhaps, then, Schütz went from Venice to Cremona, and it is fascinating to imagine him meeting there such distinguished masters of violin-making as Antonius, Hieronymus, and Nikolaus Amati.

"A number of these Kapellmeisters prospered; others, however, despite all their art, remained poor. Some among them indeed committed suicide *(mortui sunt morte Catoniana)*."

Then he describes a large number of ingeniously made claviers, organs, and the like which he found in the percussion *(schlagenden)* instrument chamber. These also fascinate him on the occasion of the electoral banquet: "During the meal we heard pleasing table music, first in the little enclosed room with the bay, *musicam vocalem;* then from without, *vocalem et instrumentalem:* on a clavier with one stop in front, four stops on the right side, and five on the left. Likewise on a long cypress instrument, on which one can play as on one instrument, or as on two with violins and harps, and on which there is also an octave coupler. Then

---

[26] Through the kind information of Prof. W. Gurlitt.

on the large bass viol alone, and then on the harp-lute *(harffenlauten)* alone. There was one performer who fiddled with one hand, piped with the other. Several glasses were also blown into, and according to the practice of high potentates the spirits of the guests were charmed by the stringed instruments. The elector's most distinguished musicians are Wilhelm Günther, Augustus Tax. These two excel on all instruments. Johannes Preus Anglus (Price) plays on the *viola di gamba* and pipes, as indicated, at the same time with the right hand on a little English pipe. I also heard him play this way in Stuttgart in 1615. There were also Elias Püncker, harpist, and Ernst Trost. The latter embellishes on the little trombone whatever he hears played for him on cornets and fiddles. Johann Kottwitz (Kökeritz), Gregor Hoyen (Hoyer), Johann Miller (Müller), court organist, were also there. His Excellency is reported to have in his employ about forty musicians." Hainhofer refers to the elector as very hard-working and, despite his large income, economical to the extent of niggardliness.

I am able to present the conclusion from the Wolfenbüttel Ms. 11. 22. Aug. 2, S. 526 verbatim for the first time:

"When then with God's help (for all undertakings are in vain without the assistance of God)[27] I had, thank God, returned home safely, I found awaiting me the following musicians who had come from Italy eight days before my return, namely, Herr Hainrich Schütze, Electoral Kapellmeister; Caspar Kittel, lutenist and theorbist, whom the elector had graciously sent to Italy for some six years of instruction there; and Francesco Castelli, formerly the excellent violinist of Vincentius, Duke of Mantua. They thanked me for exchanging their money, continued their stay here a few days longer, and, when I had invited them to my house, allowed me, together with some guests invited in their honor, to hear their praise-worthy art, to which we, in spite of the saying 'There is no song so good but that one tires of it,' could have listened for a long time. For as each little bird warbles according to its beak, so these musicians gave ample evidence that they had employed their time to good advantage."

---

[27] *nam frustra conatur, cui non DEUS auxiliatur.*

Years at Copenhagen

By the end of 1629 Schütz returned home to Dresden and at that time moved into his new house. He found his daughters grown taller, but he still left them under feminine care. With reinvigorated powers he might now plan to take the reins of the Saxon Kapellmeistership firmly into his hands. Many a friend must have spoken to him in friendly admiration of the *Sinfoniae sacrae I*, which had just appeared. But he was no longer destined to be happy. As Geier's funeral memorial states: "On his return not a few things were seasoned with sadness"; for "after his safe return he had to learn with sorrow that his dear father, Christoph (late burgomaster of Weissenfels), had departed this life on August 25, 1631, and that his dear father-in-law, Herr Christian Wildeck (late electoral recorder of taxes), had also died, on October 1 of the same year. He was thus overwhelmed by one affliction after another."

At the same time he lost a great fellow artist, a beloved companion of his youth, the cantor of St. Thomas, Joh. Hermann Schein. Schütz had visited him during his last illness at Leipzig in November 1630, and Schein had asked him to compose a funeral motet for him, using the text of 1 Tim. 1 : 15: "This is a faithful saying, and worthy of all acceptation, that Christ Jesus came into the world to save sinners, of whom I am chief." The fulfilment of Schütz's promise to his "dearest friend" *(amicus carissimus)* is indicated in the special edition which appeared in Dresden on January 9, 1631. This contained a preface by the publisher Wolf Seyffert addressed to Schein's widow and sons (Vol. XII, 21), to which Schütz added three Latin distichs:

> *Quod tibi, vivus adhuc Scheini dilecte, petebas,*
> *hoc cape supremum Funeris officium.*
> *Hactenus exsolvi sat-multis istud Amicis,*
> *quod sua Mors terris abstulit, ante diem.*
> *Quid restat, nisi munus idem ut mihi denique solvam,*
> *et sim Cantator Funeris Ipse mei?*[1]

---

[1] That which you, when still alive, beloved Schein, have asked,
  this receive, the final service of burial.
  Enough I have paid to his many friends until now,
  for what his premature death has taken away from the earth.
  What is there left for me but that I bestow the same
  gift upon myself and be the singer at my own funeral?

This conclusion is a vivid testimony to Schütz's baroque feeling of the Proximity to Death.

Schütz later included the revised funeral motet (for six voices) in the *Geistliche Chormusik* of 1648 (Vol. VIII, No. 20, p. 119). He regarded it, not only as a work of art but also as a memorial of devotion, the whole collection, indeed, being dedicated to the choir of St. Thomas, formerly conducted by Schein.

In the year 1632 anxiety again knocked at Schütz's door. Apparently his aged mother had suffered a stroke. The master hastened to her sickbed, and she improved as the result of his presence. We learn this from a poem found in the fourth *Book of Odes* by Paul Fleming, *Von Glückwünschungen* ("Of Felicitations"):[2]

"To Herr Heinrich Schütz, illustrious Kapellmeister at the electoral Saxon court."

1632

Your dear mother had already —
Is't not so, illustrious Schütz? —
Neared the brink of Lethe's pool
And the pale-faced Phlegethon:
Charon, too, of pallid face,
Already asked his ferry toll.

Consciousness was but a flicker;
She no longer was herself
When into her deafened ears
Someone called this cheering word:
Heinrich, your dear son, approaches.
See, he is already here!

Greatly this refreshed the dying,
Who had almost taken leave!
Flame of consciousness returned
From its slowly dying embers.
Come, son, spake she, come to me![3]
Of my death thou art the death!

What need is there, as of old
Thracian prince's famous son,[4]
Thou shouldst with thy songs and lyre
Fare into the gloomy shaft?
Schütz, at thy one name alone
Death yields up his spectral victims.

Thou mak'st subject with thy songs[5]
Realms of heaven and realms of hell,
Thou, whom powers cannot oppose
And nothing can deny,
Since even when thou dost not sing,
Thou dost subdue them both.

This a beauteous soul can do
Which calls the heaven "Father,"
Which from out this body's casement
Doth straightway rise to him
And through song prescribes a law
Through which His own remaineth here.[6]

---

[2] Lappenberg edition (Stuttgart, *Lit. Verein,* 1865) I, 351. See German edition for the text.
[3] Allusion to verse four of Luther's Easter song "Christ Lay in the Bonds of Death." "As one death devoured the other."
[4] Meaning Orpheus as the son of Oeagrus (king of Thrace).
[5] Doubtless only in a general sense as "compositions."
[6] The meaning is doubtless "and sing a verse to the heavenly Father, by which that which already belongs to heaven may remain for the time being on earth."

If God help and fortune favor
That in future I shall prosper,
That I need not yield my place
Nor be held in low respect,
Then I hope your prince's favor
Me, too, in good stead will stand.

Then one day I hope to journey
Where you kindly people are;
What already I have purposed,
This will its fulfillment see.
This is what I wish to say:
There doth lie my hope's objective.

Father Mars, desist from Meissen,[7]
And do grant to us thy peace!
And let strangers also battle
Who long since have looked on us!
Show thy might at last to him
Who doth still deride it!

Then indeed shall I exalt thee
When thou far from us wilt be,
And my Schütz shall in addition
Tune his lyre and sweetly sing
That the country far and wide
Will be glad at such a tide.

The beginning of the poem shows the very intimate and affectionate relation that existed between the aged Euphrosyne and her distinguished son.

His mother was spared him for three years more; but in 1635, when he himself was fifty years of age, he lost her. On the occasion of the recovery Fleming added the following dedication:[8]

> With this song we come to congratulate you on the recovery of your mother and the victory over the softened javelins of death.
> > We then come to offer to you every polished work that
> > expresses the mind in humble melody.
> > May the sun wish — or the great Apollo, who serves Pindus —
> > what I wish, what you also usually wish with me;
> > that I may live as guest soon close to your Albin.
> > Then I shall congratulate you more fully, but also myself.[9]

In 1630 the elector commemorated the centennial of the Augsburg Confession with considerable musical pomp. In the same year he celebrated the marriage of

---

[7] That is, from Saxony.

[8] Fleming's Latin poems, edited by Lappenberg, p. 395. Further music poems there: on the death of J. H. Schein (p. 48); David Gallus in Reval (p. 100); to Schein (p. 269); to the organist Samuel Michael (died 1632, p. 272); on the death of Georg Engelmann (died 1632, p. 274); to Sidonie Schein (p. 354); to Joh. Sam. Schein (p. 354).

[9] *Hoc tibi gratatum revalentem carmine matrem*
venimus et victa mollia tela necis;
tum per ut expressam tenui modulamine mentem
omne tibi cultus subjiceremus opus.
Sol velit, aut magnus, Pindum qui servat, Apollo,
quod volo, quod mecum tu quoque velle soles,
hospes ut ad vestrum vivam mox junctior Albin.
Tunc tibi gratabor plenius atque mihi.

his daughter Marie Elisabeth to Prince Frederick of Denmark. For the latter event Wallenstein came to Dresden as the representative of the emperor.[10] But apart from these events, because of the increasing burden of the war on the electoral treasury, Schütz experienced ever-mounting difficulty in keeping afloat the ship of the Dresden court chapel. In a series of communications[11] he was compelled to remind the court that he be paid his personal salary, which was in arrears to the extent of 500 gulden, that proper compensation be given the recently engaged violin *virtuosi* Carlo Farina and Francesco Castello,[12] together with their Dresden violin pupils and their families. who had remained behind in Venice; that there be brought to Dresden a splendid young tenor, the bachelor of arts Georg Hempel, whom Schütz had heard in Eulenburg on his journey to Leipzig; that Caspar Kittel's brother Jonas be appointed bass singer; and that arrangements be made for the lodging of the choir boys with Caspar Kittel. As a widower Schütz doubtless no longer wished to bring up, and act as preceptor for, these boys in his own home. He felt unable *(zu schwach)* to prevail upon the elector to do all this. Accordingly, he suggested that the house marshal, the treasurer, the court preacher Hoe, and the privy secretary of the prince sponsor his requests.

The entire chapel was required to be present at the Leipzig meeting of the elector with Gustavus Adolphus (1631), an occasion celebrated with the greatest musical pomp. In the notice giving the names of the choir boys the talented young Mathias Weckmann and Philipp Stolle appear for the first time. But the victor at Breitenfeld was soon killed at Lützen (1632). On account of the Swedish alliance, Saxony encountered the hatred of the imperial forces and, after the Peace of Prague, the still greater fury of the Swedes themselves. Since the poor harvest of 1617 there had been famine in Saxony. In 1626, 341 persons had died of the plague in Dresden. From 1630 to 1637 the black death reigned in the capital. In 1634 there were troublesome billetings of the foreign soldiery; the suburbs had become a desert and half the population had succumbed to the pestilence.

In a letter to his Augsburg friend Philipp Hainhofer, on April 23, 1632, in which he recalled the latter's expedition to Dresden[13] in 1629, when he sought aid from the elector, Schütz could take meager comfort in the fact that he could congratulate

---

[10] The bridegroom, the Duke of Holstein, at that time brought with him to Dresden his singer Gabiel Voigtländer, who formerly had served a Bohemian lord. B. Engelke, *Die Musik am Gottorper Hofe (Music at the Court of Gottorp)*, Vol. II.

[11] E. H. Müller, Nr. 32—35, 37, and Appendix, No. 6.

[12] He died as early as the spring of 1631 (letter of Schütz to Hainhofer).

[13] See supra pp. 111 and 137.

Hainhofer that Augsburg had at last been successfully freed of its imperial tor-
mentors. He continues:

> "In yesterday's sermon for Jubilate Sunday our first court preacher, Dr. Hoe, spoke about
> the great oppression and grief which up to the present time the Protestants had suffered at
> the hands of the Roman Catholics, but how now our Lord Christ had begun to gladden many
> thousands, even hundreds of thousands, of hearts in upper Germany and especially also in
> Augsburg. And he made a fitting application of the present situation to the Gospel. Hence I,
> too, am moved personally to congratulate my gracious lord and our fellow Christians in
> Augsburg on the occasion of the newly gained freedom of conscience and to wish them the
> blessing mentioned in the conclusion of yesterday's Gospel, namely, that the joy with which
> our Lord Christ has gladdened many thousands of hearts in Augsburg might never be taken
> from them by anyone. Amen[14]."

At the same time he requests Hainhofer to procure for him a long enclosed list
of new Neapolitan madrigals and church music, among them works by the Prince
of Venosa, Dentice, Macque, Trabaci, and others.

When, in 1629, Schütz returned from Venice with Caspar Kittel and the newly
engaged concertmaster Francesco Castello, he found a new situation confronting
him. In April 1629 the elector, despite his financial embarrassment, had engaged
the English violinist and flute player John Price, who had come from Stuttgart
with his brothers-in-law John and David Morell. As chamber musicians they were
to perform in the English, French, and, in case of necessity, also in the Italian style.
This undertaking on the part of the elector presumably was no unalloyed delight
for Schütz, as there was due him a considerable sum of money for boarding and
lodging in his house the choir boys whom his substitute master, Hestius,[15] had
instructed while he was away. As early as 1631 Price also, among other musicians,
had vainly demanded money from the elector. The distinguished singer Hans
Hasselt had, in fact, so vehemently demanded payment of the amounts due him
that the elector angrily wiped them out altogether, whereupon the singer left the
service. It was not long, however, before Johann Georg regretfully acknowledged

---

[14] The conclusion of the Gospel for Jubilate Sunday is from John 16:22: ". . . but I will see you
again, and your heart shall rejoice, and your joy no man taketh from you."
[15] R. Eitner (*Monatsh. f. MW*, IX, 196) expands and corrects his biography beyond Fürstenau:
Magister Zacharius Hestius, b. Oct. 8, 1590, in Unckersdorf near Dresden; d. June 1, 1669, in
Königstein. He was choir boy in the Dresden court chapel; was sent on October 12, 1607, to
Schulpforta, and, in 1611, at the expense of the elector, to the University of Wittenberg. In 1615
he became cantor in Luckau; on February 15, 1616, cantor of the *Fürstenschule* in Meissen. On
July 26, 1624, he became vice-Kapellmeister of the Castle Church in Dresden, and on January 1,
1641, he became pastor in Königstein — a typical biography for the German cantors and
clergymen of the seventeenth century.
A request by him in the year 1634 for a weekly "health potion" (*Stärkungstrunk*) from the
court cellars (Fürstenau, *Geschichte der sächs. Hofkapelle*, p. 61) emphasizes the difficulty, in the
absence of Schütz and the decrease in the musical personnel, even in keeping up the congregational hymn singing.

that he missed Hasselt's voice. It is very characteristic of Schütz that in a memorandum[16] to the house marshal he besought him to intercede in a friendly manner:

"I confidentially make known to Your Honor (E. E. Gestr.) not only that in my present position I personally felt the loss of Hans Hasselt to the company but that His Highness also lately indicated similar sentiments to me, from which I gathered that he, too, regretted his loss." Schütz suggests that an attempt be made through his brother-in-law to bring about a reconciliation with the elector — "his head could perhaps be set as straight in Dresden as elsewhere to conform with proper obedience."

The harpist Elias Pinckler[17] fared even worse. In his dire need he went so far as to sell his harp to King Gustavus Adolphus, who was in Dresden at the time. Pinckler followed the king in vain to Leipzig to receive payment and finally implored the house marshal for his dismissal, since he believed that his wife, who was living in Stockholm, might save him from utter starvation.

The situation became so threatening for Schütz, both as a practicing and as a creative artist, that on February 9, 1633, he resolved to ask the elector for a leave of absence. He accompanied this request with an informative letter to the elector's confidant, Friedrich Lebzelter, who was temporarily in Hamburg.[18] Schütz's proposal to his patron begins with a reminder of his frequent requests that he be permitted "on the near approach of spring" to make a journey to Lower Saxony. In explanation he adds: "On account of the war conditions prevailing at present I could readily get away, because the times do not demand or allow music on a large scale, and the more so because the company of instrumentalists and singers has at present considerably diminished. Some are subject to illness and to the infirmities of age; others are occupied with the war, or have taken advantage of other opportunities, wherefore it is now impossible to perform music on a large scale or with many choirs. Furthermore, if God, as is to be hoped, improved the times, and Your Electoral Highness desired my service, a considerable readjustment and improvement of our *Collegium musicum* would have to take place." Meanwhile, under the leadership of Inspector Caspar Kittel, the present status of the chapel could be maintained even in his absence, while his journey would give him inspiration for the "effective reorganization of the establishment." He would like to escape for a time from the difficulties and hindrances resulting from the war and "hampering me in the pursuit of my work, so that I might industriously

---

[16] Leipzig, February 28, 1631.
[17] W. Schäfer, *Sachsenchronik*, I, 434 ff.
[18] E. H. Müller's collection, Nos. 40 and 41.

and without interruption[19] continue my profession in Lower Saxony without dis-
turbance of my spirit." By Lower Saxony[20] he meant Sorö and Copenhagen, where
the Danish crown prince, Johann Georg's future son-in-law, had previously
invited him (through Friedrich Lebzelter) to participate in the coming ceremonies.
Schütz would travel at his own expense and would not pester the elector with
requests for money, provided only that "in the meantime something be paid the
Collegium musicum" and his quota be continued. He requested a furlough for a
year and said that he would leave his household in Dresden and that he would be
happy to serve the elector again at a future time.

He advised Lebzelter, the "chamberlain" (we would say "privy cabinet counselor"), in case his master was unwilling to grant the leave, to have the crown
prince himself appeal to his future father-in-law in the matter. His message to the
Danish successor to the throne is very significant. In it we note both modesty and
the urgent wish to be freed from the Dresden difficulties: "I have become well
aware of Your Highness' special inclination toward, and indeed love for, music in
connection with your presence here at the performance of my truly poor music,
and also have further information concerning the same. My qualities are modest,
and I can only say that I have worked with the most outstanding musicians in
Europe,[21] even though I have acquired only a shadow of their art. Nevertheless,
I would hope with the help of God to serve Your Highness in such manner (if my
work continued to please you) as to supply your chapel with a considerable number
of good compositions, not only of my own invention (as the least important) but
also with those of the most famous composers of Europe, which compositions I
have collected not without considerable trouble. I would also hope to bring your
chapel into a good state of order."

In reply to this Lebzelter wrote from Hamburg on February 15, 1633, to Prince
Christian: ". . . Your Royal Highness may certainly be assured that in the person
of this Kapellmeister you will have a thoroughly qualifed man, that few equals in
his profession are to be found in the empire, as a result of which his services have
been coveted by many, even by distinguished Catholic potentates, despite his and
their religion. . . ."[22] Actually the leave was finally granted after the crown prince,
on March 1, had already sent a pass to Schütz from Hadersleben, had written to

---

[19] Müller says *dero örter* ("such places").

[20] Christian IV, as King of Denmark and Duke of Schleswig-Holstein, was at the same time
head of the lower Saxon district *(Niedersächsischen Kreises)*.

[21] He means Gabrieli and Monteverdi, perhaps also M. Praetorius.

[22] This passage, which is missing in Hammerich, I owe to W. Gurlitt. Could there be a
reference here to a call to the imperial court in Vienna? "Despite his and their religion" means
that doubtless they had promised Schütz he would not be harassed because of his Protestantism.

the elector, and had asked his aunt, Hedwig, to act as intermediary. In the same letter to his father-in-law, Christian calls the master "a peculiarly excellent and at the present time almost unexcelled musician." Schütz seems, however, not to have left Dresden for the first of his three Copenhagen journeys until September 1633, after the crown prince had again personally requested him to begin his journey. At any rate, Lebzelter writes on November 18, 1633, that Schütz had betaken himself to Hamburg with his entourage (*Seinigen*) "two months ago" at his own expense.

A half year later there followed a great wedding train. Princess Magdalene Sibylle, accompanied by her mother and her brothers, journeyed to Copenhagen. The company included 532 persons, with 479 horses and 274 carriages. No wonder that after such royal lavishness virtually nothing remained for the choristers of the destitute Dresden court chapel. On the occasion of the fourteen-day wedding Denmark alone squandered two million *Reichstaler.*

Ph. Spitta's biographical sketch tells of the route: "He [Schütz] stayed in Hamburg a few months and possibly stopped before this at the court of Duke Johann Albrecht of Mecklenburg-Güstrow, since once in 1637 he mentioned to his elector that he still awaited revenues, not only from the Danish crown prince but also from other sources, and inasmuch as in 1640 Duke Adolph Friedrich of the same Mecklenburg royal house had had the Schütz *Becker Psalms* printed anew at his own expense. In November he continued his journey northward from Hamburg, stopped, it appears, for twenty-four days in Habersleben, where Crown Prince Christian was staying at the time, and then set out for Copenhagen on December 6. On December 10 he was appointed Royal Danish Kapellmeister with an annual salary of 800 *Reichstaler,* and on December 18 King Christian announced this appointment.[23] From this it appears that no mere passing contact was intended, but that a permanent relationship was to be established.

"Schütz was given very broad powers with regard to the training of the musicians, and he was treated with distinction. While he resided in the city, the rehearsals were conducted in Castle Croneburg, next to the apartment of the king. The preparations for the performances began six months before the wedding celebration in October 1634. It was Schütz's duty to provide music for plays (two comedies by Johann Lauremberg), ballet, and a masked ball. He had with him his pupil and nephew [actually cousin] Heinrich Albert, from Königsberg. Albert was allowed to contribute an aria to the festival compositions, with text by Michael Behm, on the entry of the Saxon princess into Copenhagen (September 30, 1634). The com-

[23] The assistant Kapellmeister was Jakob Örn (Ohren); the concertmaster, J. Foucart.

position appears with a different text as No. 8 in Vol. V, in the arias of 1642. After the festivities Schütz remained for seven months at the Danish court, where he was in high favor. On his departure on May 4, 1635, the king gave him a portrait, doubtless the king's own, a golden chain valued at 100 *Taler,* and a purse of 200 *Taler.* He also gave him a letter of greeting to the elector which said that he would gladly have retained his 'especially dear' Heinrich Schütz longer and that if the elector could spare him, the king would appreciate it if the elector would be good enough soon to grant Schütz further leave, to complete the organization of the music at the Danish court. A letter from the crown prince which set forth the 'most praiseworthy' services of Schütz followed on May 25.[24] The master himself, who had received his last monthly payment on May 10, had departed with a passport dated May 25 and with the certain expectation of an early return."[25]

The musical relations between Denmark and Germany were of long standing and manifold. The manuscript No. 1872 in the Royal Library of Copenhagen,[26] by the trumpeter Jörg Haider, dating from the year 1541, as well as the trumpet books from about 1598, numbers 1874 and 1875, 4° — from the same library — of the German (perhaps Electoral Saxony) trumpeters Heinrich Lübeck and Magnus Thomsen,[27] show that the lines of influence ran in part via Königsberg, in part via Nürnberg. Hammerich has shown how the coronation and wedding ceremonies of Christian IV in 1596 were enhanced by the importation of musicians from Dresden, Torgau, Coburg, and Danzig, and that trumpets were bought in Nürnberg. While the music-loving young king had sent his protégé Melch. Borchgrevinck, together with the latter's pupils Hans Nielsen and Magnus Pederson[28] (already known to us), to continue their studies in Venice,[29] John Dowland, the English master of the lute, graced his court. The extensive exchange of artists with Duke Ernst of Schaumburg-Bückeburg via Pinneberg, such as Brade and Simpson, has already been noted.[30] London, Wolfenbüttel, Dresden, and Kassel music celebrities met at the Copenhagen court, and at the court of the crown prince at Söra (Sorö) the old Lübeck minstrel, Gabriel Voigtländer, later sang his jovial ariettas. A large portion of Füllsack's and Hildebrandt's *Gagliards and Pavans* for five voices (1607-09) owe their origin to Danish court musicians. From 1615 to 1619 Joh.

---

[24] Printed, *Sachsenchronik* I, 542.
[25] The foregoing quoted from Ph. Spitta.
[26] See my contribution *Instrumentalismen bei L. Senfl* in the *Joh. Wolf-Festschr.*
[27] Cf. G. Schünemann in *Zeitschrift für Musikwissenschaft,* XVII, 147 f.
[28] Pedersön lived in Venice again for four years and in 1611 was sent for two years to the English court of James I (Hammerich and Elling in *Vj. f. MW,* IX, 74).
[29] See above, p. 66.
[30] Supra.

Schop served as violinist in the Copenhagen chapel. Nicholas Maas, who was subsequently town fiddler and composer of church hymns at Hamburg, brought an organ *(Orgelwerk)* from Stralsund. Esajas Compenius transplanted from the Brunswick Castle Hessen[31] to Fredericksborg his wonderful organ, which still preserves its silver tone. Though the chapel suffered at the beginning of the 1620's from the plague and from the king's participation in the war, M. Schildt, the Hanoverian pupil of Sweelinck, was employed there from 1626 to 1629. Two of his rare organ compositions have been preserved there. Apparently his successor was the elder Laurentz Schröder, who had fled from Germany on account of the war. Laurentz mentions as his father-in-law Georg Pfeil, the Anklam organist. Schröder, as organist of the Church of the Holy Ghost in Copenhagen, dedicated (1639) to Christian IV, "because of the great liberality of His Majesty toward the musicians," his *Useful Little Tract Relative to the Praise of God, or Music, the Heart's Delight.*[32] After the departure of M. Borchgrevinck, Schütz was summoned. The picture which shows Christian IV performing with his wife and son proves how great a friend of music awaited him in the person of the great king. From the standpoint of music history a splendid ceiling painting in Castle Rosenberg is still more enlightening.[33] This shows the king's instrumentalists in four groups consisting of three lutenists with a choir boy; three trombonists beside the composer; two cromorne players *(Krummhornbläser)* with several singers; and a contrabass, two fiddlers, and three singers, pictured in the work *Danmark, J Fest og Glaede* (therein Torben/Krogh, Teatret) I, 243.

To the king are dedicated, among other things, Oratio Vecchi's *Veglie di Siena* (1604). Another testimony to his devotion to music is the delightful report (originally in Latin) of the embassy secretary Charles Ogier,[34] who accompanied the representative of the French king at the wedding of 1634. It tells how, during the official audience of the embassy at Castle Rosenberg, the French were conducted into a rectangular room adorned with paintings beneath which the king was wont to place his musicians. Suddenly the legation was surprised by invisible music — instrumental and vocal. "It came to us through various openings and resounded now near, now far." When later the diplomats got into their carriages beneath the gateway, the "subterranean and invisible music" was again heard. From the manner in which Ogier relates the little episode one can see that it gave the

---

[31] This accordingly has nothing to do with Kassel and Schütz.
[32] *Nützliches Tractätlein vom Lobe Gottes oder der herzerfreuenden Musica.*
[33] Thanks to the kind information of W. Gurlitt.
[34] Cf. Ch. Ogier, *Det Storebälager i Kjobenhavn,* 1634, *Memoirer og breve udgivne af Julius Clausen og P. Fr. Rist,* XX, Copenhagen, 1914.

listeners genuine pleasure *(Vjsch.* IX, 90). At this time Johann Rist was probably also in Copenhagen and there attended a competition between the violinists Joh. Schop and Foucart.

Such was the "concealed music"[35] which Schütz recommended for his *History of the Resurrection.* It also played a role in his Copenhagen dramatic works. With regard to these lost scores let us hear what Hammerich was able to gather from the festival descriptions and the texts:[36]

> "The greatest musical interest was centered in the theatrical entertainments, especially the performance of the ballet, probably the first of the kind in Denmark. As the result of its development, the ballet had become a mixture of many different things, by no means merely dance or mime but also a kind of operetta *(Singspiel)* with recitatives, little arias, duets, and choruses, an 'opera ballet,' as it was quite properly called. The ballet, too, which the dancing master von Kükelsom had compiled, apparently with Schütz's music,[37] was a kind of mixture of pantomimic action, choreographic art, and interpolated episodes for solo or chorus. The text, in mythological garb, was a play dealing with the king as the happy monarch, and with the marriage of the crown prince, 'the son of Neptune,' with the 'goddess of wisdom, Pallas.'"

Here let us interrupt the summary by Hammerich and Elling with a very early account of such a performance:

In 1635 the Danish bookseller Jürgen Holst published a document titled *Triumphus nuptialis danicus,*[38] which relates:

> "After the meal a fine ballet was danced in the large hall. Its content and significance appeared in public print, but for the sake of information I should like to report about it briefly. First of all, a little song, inviting the gods to the dance, was played and sung by the entire group of musicians.
>
> "Thereupon appeared the god Pan with his satyrs, all clad in the garb of satyrs. They danced for some time before withdrawing. The god Pan danced into a cave, where he found Deianira sleeping and Hercules away. He was so inflamed by her beauty that he presumed to lie with her. Meanwhile Hercules arrives, discovers the god Pan, leads him to the dance floor, and treats him shamefully as an adulterer. Thereupon a fine song was sung by the entire chorus, a song in which the Muses rejoice greatly over the punishment meted out to the dissolute Pan for his lewdness. As the music continued, a hill appeared on which sat in order the nine Muses. The hill was moved about the hall until the goddesses descended and together danced a beautiful dance. After they had returned to their Parnassus and beautiful hill, the latter returned with them to its place behind the scenes. When it came to the ears of Orpheus how the chaste goddesses had rejoiced so greatly over the punishment of the adultery, he was again reminded of his lost spouse. He seats himself on a hill on which he is conducted through the hall as he sings a sad lament for his wife Eurydice, who had so nearly been delivered from the power of Pluto. He sang to the accompaniment of his violin in a voice that was as pleasing and charming as it was plaintive:

---

[35] B. A. Wallner mentions "concealed music" *(verborgene Musica)* in connection with the Stuttgart *Lusthaus,* 1584-93, in *Steinätzkunst (The Art of Stone Engraving),* 1912.

[36] *Vjschr. f. MW* IX, 87.

[37] May this perhaps not have been the opera-comedy which Schütz wrote in Venice and which Kükelsom then translated and for this occasion adapted for the dances?

[38] Royal Library, Copenhagen, No. 2358.

> Up, my viol, give me courage
> For my pleasure and renown.
> As my light is far from here,
> I shall raise my lamentation
> Over death's omnipotence
> Which has laid her swiftly low.
> (Ten additional stanzas)

"The wildest animals, such as lions, bears, and the like — as well as the trees came forth and, against the course of nature, were impelled to dance until finally Envy was no longer willing to grant Orpheus such alleviation of the pains as he experienced thereby. She accordingly presented herself dancing in the dress in which she is commonly pictured, and she summoned to her all the Bacchae and devil's wives who, clad in their appropriate dresses, drowned out with the noise of their cymbals and tongs the dulcet strains of Orpheus' violin, whereupon they tore apart and killed first the dancing animals, then Orpheus himself. When these women had gone, four angels appear. After performing a dance they carry away the murdered Orpheus. Thereupon three pantalones [39] appear, who gather the dead animals and cleanse the hall. The gods feel this gruesome deed very deeply and unanimously resolve to create a new love out of the ashes of Orpheus — and a new world. Thereupon Mercury appears and announces this to the audience in a very beautiful song:

> What sadness has overtaken
> You, the princes of this world?
> You should at once forget
> Him who was felled to earth.
> Orpheus lives and does not die;
> Orpheus' exploits will be sung;
> Orpheus' virtue will resound
> Till the final day shall dawn.

"This singer was a eunuch and knew how to use his voice so skilfully that he was listened to with amazement by all present. As he withdrew, lovely music was heard from the whole chorus. Thereupon a distinguished cavalier stepped forth. It was the king's natural son, Christian Ulrich. His excellent bearing and delightful dance received the praise of all. The Vices, such as Voluptuousness, Pride, and Sensuality, now appear and by their enticing manners lead away the cavalier, captive, as it were, and have him guarded by a dragon. Thereupon Fama, with her trumpet, emerges dancing. She describes the situation to the courageous goddess Pallas, who brings with her the four Virtues, Wisdom, Strength, Temperance, and Justice. They slay the dragon and set free the cavalier. Thereupon the Virtues go back and bring thankofferings to the gods on an altar intended for this purpose. Upon completion of the sacrifice Atlas appears with a large globe of the world on his shoulder. Out of this leaps Cupid, promised by the gods. He dances alone, indescribably well, with quiver and bow in hand. He wounds the young Neptune and Pallas. Thereupon Apollo is let down from above, and with the full power of his lovely voice he beseeches the gods to render assistance to these wounded persons and to attend the nuptials:

> O all ye gods above,
> My beams now no longer
> Shine as they have done of yore,
> Because Pallas now exalted
> With her brilliance and adornment
> Shines far beyond my sun.
> (Fifteen stanzas, followed by the author's monogram J. M. C.)

"The gods all appear together in a cloud and descend from above. They dance the grand ballet together in such a way that the names of Christian the Fifth and Magdalene Sibylle

---

[39] Masked characters in Italian comedy who wore breeches and stockings in one piece.

are constantly joined in felicitations. Thus ended this excellent ballet. After its presentation several sprightly dances (bransles) were performed. Herewith the day's joys and pleasures were concluded!"

To continue now with Hammerich (or Elling):

"In addition to this ballet, two plays with music and dance were presented. They were written by Joh. Lauremberg, at that time professor of mathematics in Sorö. Again the nuptials were celebrated in allegorical-theological fashion. The reports are silent with regard to the composer, but it may be considered as definitely established that here, too, it was Schütz. As intimated above, these works introduced the *stile recitativo* to Denmark. In other respects one may also observe a new practice: the chorus and the instrumentalists were placed behind the scenes and, as in the case of the first operas in Florence, were invisible to the audience.

"Both pieces are introduced with an overture in the form of a short chorus, probably in madrigal form. This is then continued in a special prolog with solo and chorus. In the case of both works every act, as a rule, concludes with 'chorus' and 'full music', that is, with chorus and instruments. In addition to this, every act has a solo, or, more often, a solo with ensemble and chorus, several of which we must mention especially. In the one piece — in the second act — there is a soloist who sings and plays. It is Cupid, who, having obtained Apollo's fiddle, cannot resist the attempt to discover 'whether Cupid may not have greater need of Apollo's strings than Apollo of Cupid's weapons.' He then plays a *sinfonia* on the fiddle and later sings, in not less than thirteen stanzas, a song in his own honor. This is followed by a brief hymn or pavan *(Hymne)* for chorus. In the third act the *finale,* an entire concert piece with soli, choruses, and ensemble parts, constitutes the climax. Three *amoretti* sing in glorification of 'the beautiful clan *(Volk)* of women.' But immediately satyrs enter and begin a song of derision. After some spoken replies the piece is continued antiphonally in different forms, now terzet, now solo, now duet, and, in conclusion, a triumphant chorus of joy, as the grim satyrs are driven to flight. In the fourth act there is a kind of 'dance song' for the heroine — a hymn to the sun and to life with changing and freer rhythm. The princess then enacts a pleasing dance with her attendants 'to the strains of her own sweet voice and to the echo from wood and dale.'

"In the second piece several ensemble portions stand out. At the beginning comes a hunting song to a lively text by Martin Opitz. This is developed into a larger concert piece: first a small chorus of shepherds, interrupted by the huntsmen's horns; then a duet and two soli by huntsmen; finally a general chorus of shepherds and huntsmen, who praise the free life in field and forest. A second ensemble presents an alternation of solo, chorus, duet, and terzet for female voices, and finally a chorus. Beside these, there is a solo for a woman's voice accompanied by two violins, praising the bridal couple in allegory; also a sailor song, sung by the leader of the Argonauts.

"Thus we find vidid and varied problems for musical treatment: soli in song form, recitatives in the new opera style, soli with obbligato instruments, different ensemble sections varied with duets, terzets, soli and choruses, and finally the introductory and closing choruses. But one sees at once that the music should be called concert music rather than dramatic music. It serves a purely decorative purpose and has no organic relationship to the content of the 'action'." So far from Hammerich-Elling.

At the beginning of the *Aequilo-Comedy*, reports the *Triumphus danicus*, there also appeared "Hymenaeus with a burning torch and a golden girdle and began to sing as follows:

> O worthy company! O folk famed beyond measure
> Which heaven's favor has now assembled here!
> Your inexpressible praise,
> Your glory, has brought it about
> That I have now descended from heaven to you."
>
> (eight stanzas)

And at the conclusion of the comedy, "as the harpies were chased away by two heroes from the north, and King Phineus was set free from them," Apollo turned to King Christian with this epilog:

> "On my exalted throne, on Parnassus' peaks,
> Where Aganippo arises and pours forth crystal clear,
> Which in times past welled forth from the hoof of Pegasus,
> I left my sisters, the Muses, seated there."
>
> (four stanzas)

From the festival music under discussion only a single fragmentary *canzonetta*, printed in 1634 in Copenhagen, has been preserved: *O der grossen Wundertaten*.[40] In H. Spitta's supplementary volume, XVIII, p. 135, discant 1, 3, and 4, and the continuo of the *4 Soprani con Sinfonie di duoi Stromenti* have been reprinted. Unfortunately, discant 2 (which H. Spitta has skilfully supplied) and both violin parts are missing. While the melody in itself is songlike, the interlockings of the boy quartet are so spun out and interrupted that the impression prevails of a non-periodic or non-cadencing madrigal. Here we have the point of departure, as it were, for the polyphonic quartet songs of Joh. Theile.[41] The continuo passages of

---

[40] "Oh, the Mighty Miracle."
[41] Cf. his *Du falsches Herze!* ("Thou false heart"); *Was acht ich deine Gunst* ("What care I for thy favor") in my *Corydon*, II, 40.

the instrumental ritornelles bear the designation "Bird Song" *(Vogelgesang)*. This was doubtless to be played, not as a violin figure but on a toylike organ stop called *Vogelgesang*. For the former there was scarcely sufficient space, nor would the songlike character of the whole have fitted this. The bass part in the interludes, with its descending and ascending scales, anticipates corresponding treatment in Adam Krieger.

The edition is dedicated to six Danish officials and property owners.[42] In the *Triumphus danicus* I also find the scenario. In connection with the huge festival train we read with regard to one group: "Thereafter came the throne or hill of Venus, drawn by four horses walking abreast. On the hill sat seven beautiful boys clad in white. They sang delightfully and beautifully the accompanying song: 'O the Mighty Miracles,' four stanzas, tossing this down from the hill among the people." This explains the separate print which is preserved. We also have the superscription *Thronus Veneris*, that is, 'The Highest Power of Love,' in which is proved the power of love over those who rebel against it, shown through four riders on the royal race track with the names Palmerion of Albion; Bellinus, Prince of Thrace; Pirrhus, Prince of Epirus; and Amorinus, Prince of Thessaly." In the same procession walked the dukes of Saxony with their singing mountaineers. Behind the triumphal chariot of Hercules and Omphale there then resounded from a group consisting of monk, peasant, and soldier (presumably, then, three-voiced) a song, 'Of the Power of Love,' that may perhaps at some time turn up as a work of Schütz. The first of the eleven stanzas is:

> Goddess who 'fore thousand years
> From the wild sea's desert waves
> First didst enter upon life
> And didst bring the true Love hither,
> Your own winged little child
> Is the strongest one can find.

Another small token of Schütz's first visit to Copenhagen has survived. In the *Album Morsianum* of the town library of Lübeck[43] there is an entry of Schütz dated January 21, 1634, as *pro tempore Serenissimi Daniae et Norwegiae Regis, alias Serenissimi Electoris Saxonii Capellae Magister* for Joachim Morsius, the peripatetic son of a Hamburg patrician — a friend respected and loved.[44] In addi-

---

[42] *Catalog of the Auction Sale Wolffheim*, II, 424.
[43] M. Seiffert in *Zs. IMG*, I, 28 f.; cf. in C. H. Müller, No. 42, without the signature *Henricus Sagittarius* and without reference to the discoverer.
[44] *Observantiae et amoris ergo lubens.*

tion to a *Cantabo Domino,* he adds in Latin the saying of St. Jerome: "For the believer the whole world is a treasure house; the unbeliever lacks even a penny."

When Schütz unwillingly left for Dresden, bearing a passport for a speedy return to Copenhagen, he is reported, according to Hammerich-Elling, to have left behind three of his best co-workers as members of the crown prince's chamber music group, namely, Philipp Stolle, Friedrich Werner, and the organist Mathias Weckmann. Inasmuch, however, as Weckmann was not born until 1621, and the three, according to the evidence, did not accompany the master on a third Copenhagen journey before 1642, the date given must be erroneous. As a matter of fact, they then remained in Denmark until the crown prince of Saxony urgently demanded that they return to Dresden, which they did in 1647.

When Schütz came home in 1635, it devolved upon him soon thereafter, in the midst of all the troubles of war, to compose a new important work, the *German Requiem,* or, as he called it, the *Musikalische Exequien.* This work Schütz wrote for his patron Heinrich Posthumus von Reuss. The *German Requiem* may indeed have been composed before the Copenhagen journey, since we are told that the prince heard it several times arranged for, and sung to, an organ with a soft *gedackt* stop.

In many ways Heinrich Posthumus von Reuss[45] deserves the surname "the Great," which later was generally accorded him. After some extravagant years he developed a wise self-restraint. During forty years of peaceful rule he transformed his neglected and insolvent country into one which was prosperous and free from debt. He brought order into the transportation system, the schools, the administration of justice, and the church; and he raised himself to be one whose advice was sought by three emperors. As a jolly companion in "tilting at the ring" and at court functions he showed an appreciation of the joys of life on earth, at the same time bearing in mind the life to come. As a student at the University of Strassburg ca. 1583 he may have participated in the rich musical activities of the Argentina (Jobin, Bernhard Schmid, Chr. Walliser). He was frequently a welcome guest at the electoral court of Saxony. He doubtless received musical inspiration during the visits he paid to Copenhagen. The "miners" of the Duke of Mansfield sang on the voyage to that place. He heard inspiring music at the imperial coronation in Frankfort on Main in 1612 (where H. L. Hassler died); also in Prague, where he

---

[45] Lit: Barth. Schwartz, *Zwo Christl. Leichpredigten,* Gera (1636) — Heinrich d. XXV. J. L., Heinr. Posthumus d. Grosse, *Zwei Gedichte nebst einer Lebensbeschr.* (two poems and a biography), Gera 1808 — *Reiseerinnerungen* (travel recollections) *Heinrichs Reuss Posthumus,* 1593-1616, ed. by Dr. Barth. Schmidt, Schleiz, 1890. — R. Büttner: *Gesch. des fürstl. Gymnasiums Rutheneum,* Gera, 1908.

was delighted with an Italian organist whose name we do not know. In 1608 he founded the famous School *(Gymnasium Rutheneum)* in Gera, which maintained a figural and a choral cantor as *Quartus* and *Quintus*. To the former position he summoned from Jüterbog Peter Neander (d. 1645), whose arrangements of Or. Vecchi's four-voice *canzonettas* for church use have been preserved in part (Gera, 1614-20).[46] To be sure, the cantor complains in 1619 that, as a result of the daily assemblies, of drinking bouts, and of serenades, the voices were ruined, and that they changed before their time; that there were actually few good voices at hand; that the pupils spent too much time drinking toasts, and that the choir-practice periods were often otherwise occupied. Posthumus, however, soon lent the cantor a helping hand. Neander was well liked. They were fond of calling the widely traveled "tall one" Ulysses, and people came from long distances to his Christmas matins. For these Posthumus himself graciously provided the equipment, personally directing (in 1623) that the choir boys should be clad as angels with green wreaths on their heads and burning torches in their hands. Among the choir boys Heinrich Albert, the godchild of Posthumus, was a pupil of Neander from 1617 to 1622. His brother, Joh. Albert, subsequently became chancellor of Reuss. Neander's successor from 1648 to 1693 was Andreas Gleich, a pupil of Schütz concerning whom we shall have more to tell later.[47]

Meetings between Schütz and Heinrich Posthumus in Bayreuth and on the Osterburg near Gera have already been mentioned. Close friendship must have existed between the unusually musical ruler and our master,[48] a friendship which, as the prince's death approached, produced the exalted memorial — the *Exequien.* In the first funeral sermon, according to the wish of the departed, Luke 2: 29 served as text: "Lord, now lettest Thou Thy servant" to "and the glory of Thy people Israel." The second funeral sermon was based on verses 7 ff. of Psalm 39. "And now, Lord, what wait I for?" Among the passages inscribed around the entire coffin were: "The souls of the righteous are in the hand of God" to "but they are in peace."[49] From these verses, together with those which the prince himself had placed on the lid of his secretly kept casket, Schütz created a grand *German Requiem* (to use Brahms's title). He dedicated the work — printed by

---

[46] Unfortunately, nothing remains of Neander's praised compositions, as the entire *Kantorei* was destroyed in the conflagration of 1780. In 1620 the *Gymnasium* had an "instrument room," also a room for musicians *(Musikantenstube)* in which *ein ganz stimmwerk (= positiv)* of violins, trombones, besides a closet for the *partes,* were to be found.

[47] Infra.

[48] On numerous occasions I have tried to obtain from the archives in Gera, Schleiz, Greiz the correspondence between these two; but so far I have not been able to find anything.

[49] Wisdom of Solomon 3: 1-3.

Wolff Seyffert in Dresden in 1636 — to the widow and the sons of the departed and prefaced it with a poem of his own in sixty German Alexandrines addressed to his late patron, a poem that laments his benefactor's departure as a sad supplement to all the horrors of the war and recalls his master's devotion to music:

"Why should I here announce how my modest singing and peasant tone you were wont to reckon among the most beautiful things and what kindness and favor and what benefit you often showed to me on account of such art, especially because I was born in your lordship's domain,[50] which you yourself considered an honor and, therefore, loved me all the more?"

R. Gerber[51] has sought to reverse somewhat this sequence of events, even though it is substantiated by Schütz himself when the latter says that in this musical work are to be found: "1. All those verses of Holy Scripture and verses *(Gesetzlein)* of Christian hymns which, during his lifetime, His Blessed Late Grace had recorded on the outside of the coffin he had secretly had made — on the lid and on the two sides as well as at the head and the feet." With regard to this Gerber thinks:

> "But herewith it is not stated that the prince selected all these texts himself, and certainly nothing indicates what points of view determined the selection. If it were merely a case of favorite verses, i. e., texts springing from a purely subjective state of feeling or from a definite disposition of the soul, it would be a singular, indeed improbable, coincidence to find these texts connected in so meaningful and profound a textual association In the Kyrie the three characteristic invocations, which one can scarcely designate as favorite verses, are introduced. More significant still, the individual chorale strophes in the Gloria summarize in concentrated and impressive form the thought content of the preceding solo sections. These facts point definitely to the conclusion that the arrangement of the text was the result of a conscious selection and an equally purposeful formulation. It would, therefore, seem obvious that Schütz did not compose a conglomerate of texts which were dear and precious to the prince and which he had determined upon as inscriptions for his casket. Undoubtedly the primary purpose of the prince was to have such a German-evangelical funeral Mass, and in all probability the situation was as follows: Heinrich von Reuss, in conjunction with Schütz, selected and arranged the appropriate texts which were to be a basis of the art work to be composed by Schütz. These verses the prince subsequently had engraved on his casket. We may assume this all the more because Heinrich Posthumus planned his funeral ceremonies, and especially their musical portion, in a thorough manner. This *German Requiem,* the textual organism of which develops a profound idea, betrays the most systematic planning. In his composition, Schütz brought the underlying idea to fulfillment in a unique manner."

We freely concede to Gerber the possibility that the choice of texts may have been the result of co-operation between the prince and the artist. And doubtless the addition of the chorale strophes was not an arbitrary choice on the part of Schütz, as I formerly believed. The question, however, arises whether the profound plan which Gerber sought to attribute to the verses and the hymn texts in the Gloria does not go far beyond the actual facts. If Schütz here had really wished to make the celebration of Communion the central theme (but even with the best

---

[50] Kösteritz is a mile from Gera.
[51] In *Musik und Kirche,* VI, 6.

of intentions I am unable to detect any evidence of this apart from the one word *Nachtmahl)*, and if, against all the purport and intrinsic significance of the Gloria, he had in later sections built in parts of the Credo — why, then, did he expressly form a *Missa Brevis* instead of a full Mass with Sanctus and Agnus Dei? The interpretation of Gerber seems to me to be fallacious. Consider this one thing alone: When in a funeral Mass one speaks of the resurrection of Christ and of the faithful, need one belabor the second article of the Creed? No. The Roman Gloria is tripartite, addressed to God the Father,[52] God the Son,[53] and God the Holy Ghost.[54] The tripartite division of the Schütz Gloria text also corresponds to this: God so loved the world;[55] the blood of Jesus Christ;[56] Lord, I shall not leave Thee.[57] Even though free in detail, further points of parallel relation can be found: *Das Blut Jesu Christi*[58] is related to the *Agnus Dei, Filius Patris;*[59] *Wenn eure Sünden*[60] to the *qui tollis peccata mundi;*[61] *Gehe, mein Volk, in eine Kammer*[62] perhaps to the *suscipe deprecationem;*[63] *Ich weiss, dass mein Erlöser lebt*[64] to the *qui sedes ad dexteram;*[65] *Der du vom Tod erstanden bist*[66] to the *Tu solus altissimus,*[67] etc.

As Bach divided the Gloria of the *B Minor Mass* into eight sections, so Schütz, according to Gerber's reckoning, made a similar division, each time a Scripture reading conjointly with a chorale strophe. But this, too, presents a difficulty: the fifth reading is three times as long and is made up of three separate Scriptural passages. The first two have the effect of a parenthesis.[68] Only to the last, *Herr, wenn ich nur dich habe,*[69] does the chorale strophe bear a relation. Therefore we are really confronted with nine parts, of which the middle one has no hymn. Should not the following then be the coffin-text arrangement?

---

[52] From *Gloria* to *Pater omnipotens.*
[53] From *Domine Fili* to *altissimus, Jesu Christe.*
[54] *Cum sancto Spiritu in gloria Dei Patris. Amen.*
[55] *Also hat Gott die Welt geliebet.*
[56] *Das Blut Jesu Christi.*
[57] *Herr, ich lasse dich nicht.*
[58] "The blood of Jesus Christ."
[59] "Lamb of God, Son of the Father."
[60] "If your sins."
[61] "Who taketh away the sins of the world."
[62] "Go, my people, into a chamber."
[63] "Receive our prayer." But it seems much more natural to me to view the verse group *Gehe hin* and *Der Gerechten Seelen* as an interrupting interpolation between the verses of the Jesus part. See below.
[64] "I know that my Redeemer liveth."
[65] "Who sittest at the right hand of God."
[66] "Thou who has risen from the dead."
[67] "Thou only art most high."
[68] Compare the preceding note 63.
[69] "Lord, if only I have Thee."

V.

Gehe hin, mein Volk (Is. 26: 20)

Der Gerechten Seelen (Wisdom of Solomon 3: 1—3)

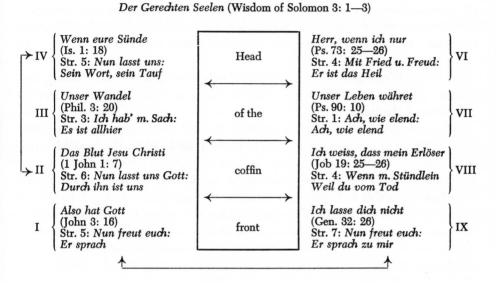

Thus there arises an organism that may be still more remarkable — one, how-ever, that is not forced and is intelligible at once. For the base of the coffin we could arrange the three Kyrie parts:

Kyrie Gott Vater	*Kyrie Gott Sohn*	*Kyrie Hlg. Geist*
Nacket bin ich (Job 1: 21)	*Christus ist mein Leben* (Phil. 1: 21) *Siehe, das ist Gottes Lamm* (John 1: 29)	*Leben wir* (Rom. 14: 8)

How these textual symmetries then evolved musically will be shown in the actual discussion of the work (infra). Here we are only endeavoring to state correctly the actual facts, as opposed to a somewhat forced interpretation, one which seemed to lead to questionable biographical and theological inferences.

Scarcely a half year later Schütz again appeared with a publication which at the time certainly had an effect much more far-reaching than that of the local and personal *Exequien*. I refer to the first part of the *Kleine geistliche Konzerte*, which he published in voice parts through Gottfr. Grosse in Leipzig and dedicated under date of September 29, 1636,[70] to Heinrich von Friesen of Rötha,[71] president of the Court of Appeals. Heinrich had entered the service of electoral Saxony in 1613. He became chancellor in 1640, and in 1653, at the *Reichstag* in Regensburg, he was elevated by the emperor (without his solicitation) to the rank of Imperial Freeman. The Castle of Rötha, which his father had acquired, is still in possession of the family.

Op. 8, the *Kleine geistliche Konzerte*, is both according to scoring and print a genuine product of war economy. Indeed, in his preface Schütz speaks of the difficulties of the times:

"Everyone can see how, as the result of the still continuing, dangerous vicissitudes of war in our dear fatherland of German nationality, the laudable art of music, among the other liberal arts, has not only greatly declined but at some places has even been completely abandoned, succumbing to the general ruination and disorder which unhappy war is wont to bring in its train. I myself am experiencing this situation with regard to a number of my musical compositions. Publication has had to be abandoned[72] until such time as perhaps the Almighty may graciously grant better days. Meanwhile, however, in order that the talent which God has granted me in such a noble art may not remain completely in desuetude but may create and present something, even though, on a small scale, I have composed and published to the honor of God as heralds of my larger musical works some small *concerti*, I have wished to have the first part appear under your excellent and illustrious name, not only because you have ever shown yourself to be my munificent and well-disposed patron but also because more than many others of the nobility you have been endowed with high ability and excellent qualities, being not a little experienced in, and a great lover of, the noble art of music, something I may say without any hypocrisy."

These pieces, most of which had German texts,[73] were small only in appearance. Actually, by means of them Schütz introduced into Germany a new species of monodistic solo *concerti*. They have no instrumental part other than the *basso continuo*. For German church music and popular musical culture they constitute an extraordinary achievement, as is further indicated by the comparatively large number of manuscripts. It was the gratitude of the public that enabled the second

---

[70] Some copies have "Michaelis 1636" instead of this, inserted by hand.

[71] 1578—1657.

[72] Apparently he refers to the large works composed for Copenhagen which appeared first in 1647 and 1650 as *Symphoniae sacrae II* and *III*.

[73] In Part I all the numbers have German texts. Three of these later received additional Latin texts, to be used *ad libitum*. In Part II ten of the thirty-one numbers originally had Latin texts, while subsequently Latin texts were added to three German numbers.

series, including thirty-one parts in contrast to the twenty-four in the first, to be produced in Dresden in 1639 despite the unfavorable times. Like the first series, the second was again arranged to proceed from solo to quintet. The Leipzig professor of poetry, Andr. Rivinus, added three poems of praise. The first praises Schütz as the best, because the most spiritual, of the electoral "master gunners." [74] The second is a play on his name, which is introduced in relation to the Scythian (= *Pfeilschützen* = archer) and also presents a musical evaluation: Plutarch, in his *Convivium septem sapientium*, says that the Scythians despised the instrumental music with which the Greeks called upon their gods, and that they were in favor of vocal prayer only. Schütz, on the other hand, held to the golden mean:

Mehr helt er vom Gesang, doch Instrument 'neinreichet.

"He esteems singing more, though instruments take part."

A certain P. H. M. H. profusely elaborated in German one of three Latin epigrams. The literal translation of the Latin distich would have sufficed to express the thought:

> Orpheus, Amphion, Arion tamed dolphin, beast and stone;
> Schütz has made the earth and sea and sky his own.

Preliminary forms of seven of the parts have been preserved in Kassel in manuscript, although these are not autographs. They show that at least these particular parts,[75] and perhaps still others, must have been begun quite a few years before. Even though they contain individual errors which Schütz did not correct until he did so in the Wolfenbüttel edition of 1664, they occasionally offer better readings than the published edition itself, readings which deserve practical consideration.[76]

The fact that Schütz dedicated the second part of his *Kleine geistliche Konzerte* (1639) to Prince Frederick of Denmark[77] indicates that the master viewed the sojourn in Dresden merely as an aimless makeshift. In a "Memorial" of February 1, 1637, to the court marshal for the elector, he shows this with pungent bitterness of tone:

"Inasmuch as at the present time, with the continuation of the war, I can be of no special service either to Your Electoral Highness or to your chapel (to speak briefly, can be of use neither to God nor to my fellow man, least of all to myself); in view of these circumstances so adverse to my profession, and since my God-given talent may diminish and die and I myself suffer unbearable distress through

---

[74] *Büchsenmeister* — a sort of pun on Sagittarius.
[75] I, 6, 15, 20, 21, 23; II, 11 and 26.
[76] As to this see Ph. Spitta's preface, VI, VIII ff.
[77] The preface in E. H. Müller, No. 47.

lack of a livelihood; and since, furthermore, my best musical compositions are still in Denmark, and I receive a honorarium from the prince and have other commissions there which, as I see it, urgently require my personal presence." Schütz, therefore, again asked leave to go to the court of King Christian IV at Copenhagen. He said that he would leave his children and his household in Dresden, would always gladly designate himself in his publications as Saxon Court Kapellmeister, and could, in case of need, return to his duties in Dresden within fourteen days.

Things looked bad enough in Saxony. In 1634 [78] the widowed Electress Hedwig, as the result of financial difficulties, had written to her brother-in-law Johann Georg: "Your Excellency will do me a brotherly favor and give me counsel according to your high wisdom as to what I should do. My subjects can give no more, as everyone knows." Two years later, in the battle at Wittstock against the Swedes, the elector lost his baggage, his silverware, and his entire staff; and his wife had to write to him: "I ask that I, too, may not be forgotten; fifteen ducats is all the money I possess." From the time of Johann Georg's return to Dresden in 1637 — after an absence of a year and a half — until about 1640 all the villages round about were laid waste with fire and sword by the Swedes. [79]

Further indication of the general atmosphere of distress in 1635 (the year Schütz's mother had died) is found in the title of a three-voice *concerto* on Josua Stegmann's *Lamentation on the Protracted War: When at Last Will My Grief Be Ended?* [80] This was composed by Schütz's pupil Martin Knabe, from Weissenfels, and was dedicated to Schütz, to Scheidt, and to six of the nobility. [81]

In the preface we read:

"It is unnecessary to speak at length concerning this long-protracted, wearisome war. Suffice is to say that its destructive fire is still burning at all corners of the Roman Empire. It is enough to observe how daily, yes, hourly, so many countless sighs are emitted with broken words by many thousands of souls: Oh, if there were only peace! Oh, if only the war would come to an end! Not to mention the collapse of studies which bloodthirsty Mars occasions in all the branches of the university and among the other liberal arts, and only to recall with a few words the state of music, how this noble art, even before the other arts, has sunk to the lowest level. It would appear as though Bellona had stormed the whole of Helicon so that Apollo with his sisters has had to set up his dwelling in the desolate wilderness. There are few indeed who have not lost every desire to follow Apollo's art. If indeed there are any left in whom the natural pleasure in art is so deeprooted that it is minded to abide by the art, then they must suffer more contumely and humiliation than art itself. They can comfort themselves only with hope for improvement."

---

[78] W. Schafer, *Sachsenchronik*, I, 437.
[79] M. B. Lindau, *Geschichte von Dresden* (1885), pp. 400 ff.
[80] *Wann soll doch mein Leid sich ändern?*
[81] In seven parts, *Unicum Stadtbibl.*, Breslau.

The first part expresses the atmosphere of distress, especially in the descending bass:

The second section has Saturn rage for a long time; the third has the winds blow:

until Favonius brings new refreshment. Finally, in the fourth part, the old color notation is utilized in order to give an obvious demonstration of "When night with its *black* locks saddens all." Here we have a real and very timely picture of the "bleeding ocean," and at the same time we have evidence of how the gifted young composers had learned, particularly from Schütz, the expressive elements of their style. But seldom does one find any traces of the furtherance of music on the part of those with whom Germany was at war. How they occasionally pilfered music is shown by the memorandum in the Lommatz *Kantorei* inventory: "Donfrid's Kyrie of five voices, which a Swedish regimental secretary left behind" at the siege of Meissen in 1645.[82] However, at the choral festival in Geringswalde in 1642 a calvary captain (*Rittmeister*) and a cavalry major (*Wachtmeister*) of the invaders took part.[83] Similarly, toward the end of the war two Swedish cavalry captains and an ensign assisted the Colditz *Kantorei* as honorary guests.[84]

In such circumstances it was not difficult for the elector to allow his Kapellmeister to return to the quiet island kingdom. Schütz departed in a sad mood, the news of the death of his beloved brother George Schütz having just reached him. Virtually nothing is known from the records about the second Copenhagen visit, but it is certain that the journey took place at the beginning of August 1637.[85] In Mattheson's biography of M. Weckmann (in the *Ehrenpforte*), after telling how Schütz had instructed him in voice and composition according to Gabrieli's method,[86] he goes on to say:

> "Our Weckmann sang a very good discant; however, after his voice changed to alto, the Kapellmeister advised the elector to dedicate his Weckmann to the organ, and at the same time suggested Jacob Schultz (son of Hieronymus Praetorius and a pupil of Sweelingk), famous organist at St. Peter's in Hamburg, as teacher, to which suggestion His Electoral Excellency

---

[82] *Wenn mit ihren schwarzen Haaren die Nacht alles traurig macht.*
[83] E. Simon, *Geschichte der Kantoreigesellschaft zu Lommatzsch* (1929), p. 63.
[84] Rautenstrauch, pp. 238 and 240.
[85] M. Seiffert, in *Sbd. IMG*, I, 218.
[86] Literally it says he was instructed by Schütz and Gabrieli, but since Weckmann was born in Niederdorla near Mühlhausen (Thuringia) in 1621 and Gabrieli died in 1612, the meaning must have been as presented above.

graciously consented and allowed him 200 *Thaler* annually. Kapellmeister Schütz brought his charge to Hamburg personally and delivered him, in the name of his gracious lord, to the tutelage of this man for three years, who instructed him diligently, not only in playing and organ registration but also in composition. Weckmann thus began, to the great delight of his teacher, to compose many parts of the vespers, German church songs, etc., in the manner of Praetorius, which gave him a great reputation. As he further had the good fortune to hear Scheidemann's pleasing style at St. Catherine's Church and to attend his vespers, he was influenced to moderate his Praetorian seriousness with Scheidemann charm and thus to introduce many elegant embellishments *(Erfindungen)*. He thus employed his three years in Hamburg in a most useful and praiseworthy manner. On his return to Dresden he was forthwith engaged and accepted as court organist.[87] The Italians[88] had never heard this type of organist, and they admired him greatly because he was proficient in all branches. He, on the other hand, in order to ingratiate himself with them all the more, studied the Italian language until he understood and spoke it quite well ..."

Weckmann's passport, however, from Dresden to Hamburg was issued July 31, 1637.[89]

We do not know whether the news of the death, at seventeen, of his daughter Anna Justina reached the master during his absence or whether, in 1638, he himself was at her deathbed. In this year, however (at least so reports the necrology of Geier), he was in Wolfenbüttel for the first time, perhaps on the return journey from Copenhagen. For many years thereafter many friendly relations bound him to the Brunswick court.[90]

The Guelph chapel, once so brilliant under M. Praetorius and still distinguished under D. Seelich, had completely disintegrated by reason of the vicissitudes of the war. However, Duke August, who took over the reins of government in 1634, re-established it three years later under the Kapellmeistership of Stephanus Körner.[91] In a decree of January 24, 1638, we read: "He, Stephanus Körner, however, should, above all, see to it that he engage exemplary musicians who are especially experienced in the science of art, who are beyond suspicion in doctrine, life, and conduct, and who are not given to drink or other misconduct." These appointments were made especially as a favor to the duke's third wife, who was versatile in music, even to the extent of composition, and who was a particular admirer of Schütz. This was Sophia Elisabeth, a daughter of Duke Johann Albrecht of Meck-

---

[87] Weckmann's engagement as court organist of the prince elector dates from September 14, 1641, according to Schütz's report in Müller, No. 49.

[88] This doubtless refers to the years from about 1653 on, when numerous Italians entered the Dresden chapel.

[89] Seiffert in *Vj. f. MW*, VII, 230. The autograph study-book *(Studienbuch)* of Weckmann in Hamburg has been preserved in the clavier tabulature A 1 of the castle museum of Lübbenau. I shall give a detailed report of this in the near future.

[90] Fr. Chrysander, *Geschichte der Braunschw.-Wolfenbüttler Capelle und Oper*, in his *Jb. f. mus. Wissenschaft*, I (1863), pp. 157 ff.

[91] Music by him for a ballet presented in 1653 has been preserved in Brussels (Collection Wagener).

lenburg-Güstrow, whose brother, in 1640, was responsible for the 8vo edition of
Schütz's rhymed *Psalter*. Apparently Schütz was to pass judgment on the newly
established chapel. The very lively correspondence between the master and the
duchess has been preserved only from October 1644 on.

When Schütz returned home to Dresden this time, it was his function to prepare
music for the wedding festivities of the Saxon Electoral Prince Johann Georg II
and the Brandenburg Princess Magdalene Sibylle. On the occasion of the wedding,
which took place on November 14, 1638, there was "excellent" music before and
after the sermon, the subject of which was the bridal Psalm 45: 11-18. It would
be consistent if the dialog-concerto for seven voices, *I Adjure You, Ye Daughters
of Jerusalem*,[92] dated from this occasion. On November 19 the wedding party and
the guests attended ten allegorical ballets presented in the great hall and, as Anton
Weck relates, also a well-arranged performance on the subject of Orpheus and
Euridice, referring to which Calliope as the head of the Muses threw out a
challenge in the form of a poem, "The Fear of God, Constancy, Heresy, and
Deceit," accompanied by fireworks. The libretto, like that of Orpheus and Euridice, was written by August Buchner, professor in Wittenberg.[93]

Content of the Ballet

The First Act

The faithful shepherd flock, / the pious bands of nymphs /
now wish good fortune to the newly wedded pair,
    and also to themselves. Orpheus goes to the temple
    to offer there his prayer; / meanwhile a dance begins
in further honor of the gods. Euridice leads off; /
before one realizes it, Envy undermines,
    and casts a serpent in the way; / Euridice, now stung,
    soon falls without the ranks / deprived of joy and light /
all things now burst apart; Iris descends from heaven /
cuts off the maiden's hair / that she may die; /
    then Charon, too, arrives / from pallid Acheron /
    takes on his dead and forthwith so sails away.
The fate of man shifts quickly like the wind /
so that in midst of joy sorrow is often found.

The Second Act

The nymphs raise their lament / for their dear playmate's death. /
Orpheus comes from the altar / and hears / to what distress
    he now has come: his heart enflames within him,
    misguided by his pain / finds neither ways nor means, /

---

[92] *Ich beschwöre euch, ihr Töchter zu Jerusalem*, published by Profe in 1641.

[93] Hugo Riemann (*Kleines Handbuch der MFS*) thought that these stanzas were sung by the
chorus. However, I think that they were only preliminary forms of the later libretto printed on
loose leaves for the purpose of being read during the performance. For the chorus sufficient
dramatic problems still remain in the ballet.

sets counsel all aside, / accepts no comfort now, /
seeks only Tenarus / there / where the sloping path
   goes down to Hell itself; / thither betakes himself /
   there to request again / that / which he loved alone /
from that one who can give it. If it be denied,
he then will stay, living even there, where his true Light did enter dead.
A mighty hero's heart has left the common path, /
and virtue seeks to go where there is fear and danger.

The Third Act

A festival of joy among his entire court /
doth Pluto now proclaim / since Euridice
   has increased his royal company in beauty, the like of which /
   one nowhere else doth find, / nor sees the light of sun;
one knows no whit of pain, / one knows no end of time, /
one practices but joy and naught but happiness. /
   Meanwhile doth Orpheus come, / plays, / begs, / and has his wish,
   and leads away with him / the prize that he has sought.
Where Virtue and Art have agreed, /
nothing can thwart them; and they win the victory.

The Fourth Act

Where no other doth go with a light heart /
and where, when once arrived, / none may return, /   .
   from thence doth Orpheus again retrace his step /
   in company with his love, / the wonder-working man.
His Thrace rejoices now, and he himself gives thanks
with lyre and song / to the Lord of all worlds, /
   who guided him. He sings, / and lo, forthwith
   the rocks are moved with life, / the woods also now hear,
the beasts and birds come forth. The crowd of wild women follow,
storming upon him in hate, / in fury; /
   but heaven protects / and sends its thunderbolt.
   Where virtue, there is hate: where art / is jealousy; /
but yet they stand their ground; / God bides own good time.

The Fifth Act

From heaven high above comes a messenger from gods,
and Orpheus learns from him their decision; /
   how from then on again he shall be one of them, /
   and his beloved taste the feast of mighty gods.
Then Amor doth appear, / Venus looks from above, /
and takes this noble pair to her in heaven.
   Then with a splendid glow their worthy names appear /
   and increase the number of the stars by a new jewel.
Ye heroes, hope and trust, / virtue will not succumb;
it rises high to heav'n / and shines throughout the world.

The words of the songs themselves, for which Schütz wrote the music—alas, again lost! — are printed in Hoffmann von Fallersleben's *Weimar Jahrbücher,* Vol. II, according to the Gotha ms. *J* 3, IV, 6, pp. 225—245. When Martin Opitz died in Danzig in 1639, the leadership of the German Parnassus devolved upon Buchner, with whom Schütz had corresponded since 1626. On the death of Schütz's daughter Anna Justina, Buchner sent Schütz a letter of condolence[94] together with a song. The latter[95] begins with the words "He a model who would have." Only the concluding strophe is at all barely endurable:

> Wisely will he measure his life
> who never can nor will forget
> its corruptibility;
> and will so comport himself
> that, although the corpse decay,
> and naught remain but ash and bone,
> he will enter as a spirit
> where no longer one will die.

Buchner's poem is so mediocre that its disappearance is no great loss, but we greatly regret not being able to see Schütz's solution of the many interesting dramatic problems which confronted him. For the instrumental music to the ballet scenes the following themes were intended:

1. Ballet of the Nymphs and of Jealousy. Euridice falls dead from the bite of the serpents;
2. Charon's ballet;
3. The ballet of Tantalus, Ixion, Tityus, and the three daughters of Danaus;
4. Ballet of the trees and of two rocks (with echo song);
5. Ballet of the birds;
6. Ballet of the beasts;
7. Invasion and ballet of the wild women of Thrace.

As for the ensembles and choruses, some were doubtless set in *concerto* form and others as madrigals. Thus as the opening there are two single stanzas by the shepherds in addition to a chorus of the shepherds and the same for the nymphs; there is a shepherd stanza with a shepherd chorus in the first act and an ensemble of the shepherds and nymphs at the end of the second act: "Go Hence, May Heaven Guide You, O Comfort and Hope of Our Time";[96] likewise the sequence "Three Spirits, One Spirit, and Full Chorus of Spirits" in the first half, and a

---

[94] Printed in Albrecht Merschens *Trostschriften (Writings of Comfort)*, Frankfurt, 1670. Unfortunately, this work was not traceable through the Information Bureau of German Libraries.
[95] According to the *Weimar Yearbook*, III, 173 ff.
[96] *Zie hin, der Himmel dich begleit, o Trost und Hoffnung unsrer Zeit.*

"Chorus of Spirits" at the conclusion of the third act; then the chorus rondo:

> All with life and being raise
> Voices here to sing his praise,[97]

with the inserted stanzas of Orpheus in the second-last scene; likewise in the closing scene, the chorus stanzas of the Cupids: "Love, All Ye Who Love Can Feel."[98] One can also without hesitation assign music to a few long strophic songs of Orpheus: "Nought Do I Seek But That Which Once Was Mine,"[99] "No Thunderbolt That Breaketh Through the Clouds";[100] or his free monologs, like the lament "Alas, Alas, Then Is She Dead"[101] as well as "Up, Rejoice Thyself,"[102] also the song of Iris, "How, Alas, Is Mortal Life."[103] But most of the others were probably not sung in the *stilo rappresentativo* but were spoken as a quasi-Shakespearean play.[104] Hence also the designation "ballet" instead of "opera." Otherwise a veritable monster score would have resulted, like that of Cesti's *Pomo d'oro* (1663 in Vienna).

There is a very strange report that a Dresden impresario, on February 9, 1673, only a few months after Schütz's death, presented the latter's opera *Orpheus* before the czar in Moscow. It is possible that the score was there until the conflagration of 1812.[105]

In Dresden the spring of 1639 was doubtless devoted to the compilation of the second part of the *Kleine geistliche Konzerte*, the preface to which is dated June 2 (Whitsuntide). In the spring of 1640 Schütz was in Hannover, as Kapellmeister *in absentia (von Haus aus)*. Duke George of Hanover had visited Copenhagen in 1638, had apparently learned to know the master there, and accordingly invited him for a visit. He had only a modest ensemble of seven musicians, for the most part gamba players. Undoubtedly he wanted to improve this ensemble. Schütz, however, appears only once in the Hanover accounts — on April 8, 1640, with a half year's salary of 250 Taler.[106] The next winter in Dresden, as Ph. Spitta reports, he suffered an illness that actually threatened his life. "But he recovered

---

[97] *Was nur Wesen hat und Leben soll sich seinem Lob ergeben.*
[98] *Liebe, wer nur lieben kann.*
[99] *Ich suche nichts als das gewesen mein.*
[100] *Kein Donnerkeil, der durch die Wolken bricht.*
[101] *O weh, o weh, so ist sie tot!*
[102] *Auf, auf, ermunter dich!*
[103] *Wie ist doch der Menschen Leben.*
[104] In the third act it expressly says: "The Spirit leads Orpheus to Pluto and says."
[105] Andrejewski: *Dilettanten und Genies*, 1951; according to Jakob Reitenfels, *Erinnerungen an Moscovien (Recollections of Moscow)*, Padua, ca. 1720.
[106] Dr. Georg Fischer, *Musik in Hannover* (1903), p. 2.

and left Dresden in March 1641, probably to go to Weissenfels, the old family seat, where a sister was still living and for which place he showed an ever-increasing preference." These reports come from a letter which Schütz wrote to the elector on March 7, 1641,[107] referring to "our music at present practically defunct," and in which, despite the "still apparent gloomy condition of our dear fatherland," he seeks to arouse the responsibility of the elector for the continuance of the orchestra. He asks *Perdon* "because I cannot refrain from seeking help for our *corpori musico,* which is in desperate straits, and from petitioning that you intervene as does a *medicus* in a serious illness before that illness becomes altogether fatal." If by looking ahead, he tells the elector, one does not now provide for the future of the ensemble, the organization will later be altogether incapable of revival, or at least only at great expense. There should, therefore, be installed as the "seed of the music" four boy choristers and four boy instrumentalists; among the former Joh. Klemme, Jr.; the latter from the best town-piper apprentices of the land, whom August Tax[108] should then give additional training. From this foundation one could very soon set up music to be played at mealtime *(Tafelmusik)* which, as soon as peace returns, could again be supplemented to the full *Collegium musicum,* this being both a ruler's obligation and a Christian's duty. And now a fine passage which shows Schütz's idea of the place of music among the other arts: "You will herewith preserve at your electoral court that profession which gleams and shines in the midst of the seven liberal arts not less than the sun among the seven planets." Perhaps, he states, life was granted and prolonged to him by God after his recent serious illness only in order that he might accomplish this work.

In the *Symphoniae sacrae II* of 1647 we find as Nos. 6 and 7 (Vol. VII, pp. 34 and 39) *concerti* for soprano or tenor solo, with the following text:

I

I shall not die, but live, and declare the works of the Lord (Ps. 118: 17).
The sorrows of death compassed me, and pains of hell gat hold upon me; I found trouble and sorrow. Then called I upon the name of the Lord; O Lord, I beseech thee, deliver my soul (Ps. 116: 3-4).
The Lord answered me and set me in a large place (Ps. 118: 5).

II

I will praise the Lord with my whole heart (Ps. 111: 1). For thou hast delivered my soul from death, my feet from falling, that I may walk before God in the light of the living (Ps. 56: 13).
Bless the Lord, O my soul, and forget not all his benefits, who forgiveth all thine iniquities, who healeth all thy diseases, who redeemeth thy life from destruction, who crowneth thee

---

[107] E. H. Müller, No. 48.

[108] Educated at the expense of the elector in Augsburg ca. 1610; beginning in 1612, in the Dresden court chapel; 1641, leader of the court music of the prince elector.

with loving-kindness and tender mercies, who satisfieth thy mouth with good things, so that thy youth is renewed like the eagle's (Ps. 103: 2-5).
     I shall not die, but live, and declare the works of the Lord (Ps. 118: 17).

One feels the strongly personal element in this selection of psalm texts. I consider this superb C major work Schütz's *Song of Praise to God* for his recovery.

Despite Schütz's persistent entreaty the elector apparently did nothing that was thorough. He allowed Schütz to go for a third time to Copenhagen, where on May 3, 1642, he was named *Oberkapellmeister* under the previous conditions. Apparently Schütz had to return to Dresden in July for a short stay in order to conduct the music at the Baptism of the eldest child of the Saxon crown prince, which was to be celebrated in September. It is humiliating to observe how, on this occasion, the greatest German musician of his time had to beg his ruler for a few choristers from Tob. Michael of St. Thomas', Leipzig, with a basso, Hermann . . . . from Halle, beside a "young fellow," Christian Krüger, who was passing through from the Hartenstein, since there was available in Dresden no foundation part, such as a contrabass, bass trombone, or contrabassoon. He would then have attempted to mold together the "now ill-harmonizing company" with repeated rehearsals. This time the elector must have understood that things could not continue thus, and apparently he commissioned Schütz to draw up an estimate for six plus six boys, of whom the six instrumentalists should be instructed by Tax, three singers by Kaspar Kittel, and three by Hans Klemm. The prince elector's musicians, Weckmann and Stolle, each had to board and instruct one discantist. Schütz transmitted the prince elector's command to these two virtuosi on July 15, 1642. Immediately after the Baptism (at the end of September) Schütz apparently returned to Copenhagen, this time accompanied by his pupil Weckmann,[109] by the theorbist and tenor singer Ph. Stolle, who later appeared as a composer of songs and conducted operas in Halle, as well as by the latter's pupil, Clemens Thieme, and the brilliant cornetist Fr. Werner.[110] There was also in the entourage Schütz's pupil Andreas Gleich, who was born in Erfurt in 1625 and who had transferred from the study of theology to music.

From Gleich's Gera funeral sermon[111] A. Werner[112] has taken the following:

"The town mayor at that time, D. (Benjamin) Schütze, recognizing his good knowledge of music, recommended him to his brother, the famous Electoral Saxon Kapellmeister in Dres-

---

[109] See supra p. 155.
[110] His funeral sermon is to be found in *MfM*, VIII, 5.
[111] Stolberg No. 10784.
[112] *Four Hundred Years in the Service of Church Music* (Leipzig, 1932), pp. 182 ff. His portrait is mentioned by Werner in *Aus dem Heimatlande der Kantoreien (From the Homeland of the Kantoreien)* (1933), p. 8, as No. 19.

den, Herr Heinrich Schütz, who became strongly devoted to our Herr Gleich on account of his ability in music and also took him along to Copenhagen in 1642, when he was summoned by His Royal Majesty to conduct the music at the impending nuptials. Gleich not only assisted with the music but also won for himself great renown. Nevertheless, despite the fact that His Royal Grace wanted him to stay in Copenhagen with the royal chapel, with promise of advancement, the deceased found it necessary, against his will, to return home in 1644, because the salt air and the habit of life *(Landesart)* did not agree with him. But he did not remain in his home long, since the Saxon general superintendent of the prince in Weimar, Herr D. Nikolaus Zapff, chose him as tutor for his children in 1643. In addition to this, he was invited to play the organ and supervise the church music in Mellingen, not far from Weimar. He conscientiously filled this position from Weimar for three years, until 1648, and made himself well liked by His Highness the Prince, Duke Wilhelm of Saxon-Weimar, and his court by his dexterity and excellent performance. However, in the year mentioned, on the death of the first *cantor figuralis*, Herr Peter Neander,[113] at the local school, he was unexpectedly summoned hither, and, after passing a vocal examination in the presence of His Late Excellency, Henry the Second of blessed memory, and his entourage, was inducted as *cantor figuralis* and *collega quartus* at the praiseworthy local school. He filled this position for forty-five years with faithful, tireless diligence."

Johann Rist, the "organiser of the German Parnassus," greeted Schütz on his passage through Hamburg with a poem "To Herr Heinrich Schütz, Royal Denmark and Formerly Electoral-Saxon World-famous Kapellmeister, When He Visited Him at Wesel on His Journey to Denmark."

Song[114]

(In dactylic meter)[115]

1.

See I not coming the excellent singer,
Schütz, the great master of pipe and of string, /
Who among Germans and all other people
So pleases princes of might and renown,
Putting to shame through the skill of his music
Most of the singers all over the world?

2.

Joyous Italia held him ensnared.
Opulent Venice, you have succeeded
In hearing Schütz in churches and chambers

---

[113] See above, p. 156. Another pupil of Schütz, Samuel List from Rosswein, applied as such in 1643 to succeed Demantius in Freiberg (R. Kade in *Vischr.*, VI, 525).

[114] In Rist's *Poetischer Schauplatz (Poetic Scene)* (1642), p. 269.

[115] Buchner wrote on November 19, 1639, to Prince Ludwig von Anhalt, the leader of the Fruit Bearing Society: "The famous musician Heinrich Schütz informed me that scarcely any other kind of German rhyme could be set to music in better and more flowing manner than this dactylic meter. Wherefore he especially asked me to arrange the libretto of the ballet *Orpheus* in such meter in order that the shout of joy and felicitation at the conclusion might be presented in this form of verse. And it was the almost universal judgment that this part of the music won the greatest approval." Ph. Spitta, loc. cit., p. 41. If one remembers that such letters circulated among the distinguished German academicians, one can easily understand that Rist meant to give a special pleasure to Schütz by the selection of this meter.

Singing his songs so delightfully
That the rocks in the waters
Began to sigh with joy.

3.

But after these times were past,
His name must be more widely known.
Saxony recovered this Arion /
And welcomed the singer with joy
When he came back again over the Alps.
Dresden was long resplendent with him.

4.

Since with the wars and their plunder and burning /
Virtue and art were but little regarded,
Murder and torture prevailed everywhere,
Especially, too, in Saxonland,
Schütz turned his footsteps again to the north.

5.

Christian, / the King of the Wends and the Goths,
Summoned him through his messengers /
That he should establish the art of singing
As the master of a praiseworthy band /
Which was graciously ordered to serve
The Danish King in his chapel.

6.

Glorious master, / I will now bear your singing
Past the clouds to the roof of heaven. /
Tomorrow you will prepare to journey
Across the often angry Belt
O'er which the royal Hero rules.
Worthy Herr Schütz, may God ever guide you."

The chief occasion for which Christian IV needed Schütz at this time was the double wedding of his twin daughters in November 1642 to Hannibal Sehested and Ebbe Ulfeldt. In the previous year the ensemble had been strengthened by seven men, among them six instrumentalists. Distinguished foreign singers, who were to perform works by Gagliano and Schütz, had been called. Specific details are not known. The master received his last Danish compensation on April 30, 1644. On his departure Schütz presented to the crown prince in manuscript the *Symphoniae sacrae II*, which he also dedicated to him in print three years later.

This was Schütz's farewell message to Denmark, where he, as creative artist, had found an inspiring asylum in trying times. After the king lost the war against the Swedes in 1645, he no longer possessed the same facilities to direct money and attention to the court ensemble. Its allowance was accordingly curtailed. In 1647 Agostino Fontana became Kapellmeister, but Christian V died in the same year near Dresden. In the next year his distinguished father died, and King Friedrich III, to whom Schütz had dedicated the *Kleine geistliche Konzerte II* of 1639, looked about for new musical forces.

As shown by a hitherto unprinted letter of Schütz to the Duchess Sophia Eleonore, dated Brunswick, October 22, 1644 (consisting of one and a half folio pages), the master again stayed in Hamburg, and then doubtless for some time cultivated the relation with his friend Delphin Strunck in Brunswick. The letter says:[116]

Her Serene Highness, right honorable princess
and woman among women, Sophia Elisabeth,
Duchess of Brunswick and Lüneburg,
born Princess of Mecklenburg,
my gracious princess and lady,
serene highness, right honorable princess,
gracious lady:

I have learned with humble and great thanks from the information given me through your servants that Your Grace has graciously seen fit to undertake the expedition in question to the princess, the widow in Schöningen. In connection therewith this little reminder seems in order, inasmuch as the *Positiv* in question, now in St. Peter's Church in Hamburg in the gallery beside the great organ, is on public sale and inspection under Jacob Praetorius and will, therefore, surely not long remain unsold. Therefore the esteemed lady widow, the princess, should come to an early decision. And if the price could not be agreed upon and paid in full, I would have to accommodate myself accordingly, though I would be better served with the full payment. I would ask Her High Excellency to let me know appropriately her intention, that I may humbly and obediently make remittance without any advantage to myself. Because during the present week, if at all possible, I plan to go to Hildesheim on a matter of business and hence will presumably have to remain away from Brunswick for a certain length of time, though contrary to my will and pleasure. I trust Your Grace will permit and be satisfied if I postpone my visit to the following week, in which case, after learning that this is satisfactory, I shall obediently present myself and shall humbly discuss without

---

[116] In 1932 in the possession of the Berlin *Antiquariat* Helmuth Meyer and Ernst; since then in the possession of Privy Counselor Dr. Hinrichsen in Leipzig. Our thanks to him for the permission to reprint; to Dr. Taut for renewed textual comparison.

delay and with the utmost diligence the completion of the musical work which we have in hand.

Meanwhile I herewith commit your gracious person to the divine protection for all princely well-being, and herewith commend myself and beg to remain

Your Grace's,
as long as I shall live,
most humble and faithful servant,
Heinrich Schütz mp
Brunswick,
October 22, 1644

We have safely received the new arias from the hands of your servant, and we note therefrom that Your Grace has markedly improved as the result of my modest instruction, and we shall hope that this little work will not only receive the praise of God but will also be an eternal memorial to His honor.

What persons or events enticed Schütz to Hildesheim at that time could not be determined from the information kindly given by the municipal archives.

Late Period in Weissenfels and Dresden

In 1645 Schütz entered upon his sixtieth year and thought that now he was entitled to look forward to retirement. The fact that this was not granted him is explained only superficially by the niggardliness and stubborness of his elector. In the case of a man as illustrious as Schütz one must attribute this to the destiny of a fate which again and again demanded from him new official activity. We find this to be the case even when finally the oft-requested leisure had apparently been granted. He thought that now he had time for the collecting and polishing of his works, and, behold, out of the revision come new creation, further development, and further conquests in hitherto unsuspected territory. Only in the case of Goethe does such recurrence on a higher turn of the spiral repeat itself. The parallelism might be illustrated in the following pattern:

	Schütz	*Goethe*
Early Period:	Individualistic artistry: Madrigals, *Cantiones sacrae*	Storm and stress: Original *Faust*, Original *Götz*
Middle Period:	Concentration toward (*Bindung zur*) the church: *Geistliche Chormusik*	Concentration toward classicism: *Iphigenie*
Late Period:	Second monolog isolation: Passions, *Psalm 119*	Second fantastic Gothicism: *Faust II*

Perhaps, after all, this is the normal course of every German artist who, like these two giants, enters the ninth decade of his life.

For Schütz the year 1645 was one devoted to arrangement and reconstruction of various kinds. He spent March in Brunswick and offered various suggestions[1] to Duchess Sophie Elisabeth as to how her husband, Duke August, could reconstitute his court ensemble (*Hofkapelle*) in Wolfenbüttel. To both he had recommended a Kapellmeister. Unfortunately, we do not know the name of the one

---

[1] E. H. Müller's collection, Nos. 54—55.

suggested. And now he is compelled to report with quiet, gentle humor "that this good musical bird whom I deemed worthy to be recommended to Your Highnesses is now about to fly past and abandon this locality." In connection with the appended questionnaire we must note particularly the elaborate systematization of all musical possibilities, neither *falsetti* nor eunuchs being overlooked in the court *Kantorei*. Characteristic of the times is the question: "What language should vocal music employ?"; and in paragraph five there is a reference to "secular, academic, and theatrical music" — we would say "concert and opera."

On May 21 Schütz (loc. cit., No. 56) sent a notice from Leipzig to Dresden, apparently as a preparatory reminder for the court marshal, to support "what I most humbly petition our most gracious elector and lord with regard to my person." Somewhat shocking in this connection is the blunt assertion that "the electoral court music in these troublous times has gone utterly to pieces, while I have been growing old." Even if a future restoration were to be planned, Schütz did not feel himself young enough to train the boys from day to day. He would, therefore, "like to live freed from all ordinary service" and receive only partial payment, which might be budgeted with the salary of the court preacher.[2] Schütz would still be glad to direct in church and at banquets on the occasion of high festivities. Finally he begs that the elector agree[3] to the annual compensation of 200 *Taler* established for him by Christian IV. Apart from the occasional duties involved in such a payment (which would not be "discreditable" to the elector), he would at all times be at the elector's disposal in Dresden.

Since apparently no decision followed, Schütz drew up a second petition (No. 57) on the evening before St. Michael's Day of the same year. He had to go to Leipzig for the fall fair and then had some legal matters to attend to in Weissenfels, and he asks that "if the winter should intervene and perchance detain me," he be allowed to remain in Weissenfels until Easter. Meanwhile he could, after all, be of no service to the Saxon court ensemble, and his Dresden house was occupied by "another good man," "with whom also my child is living." The occupant doubtless was the tax collector Hartmann. We have mentioned above how he wished to establish a household in Weissenfels with his sister. As the proposed Dresden pension of 200 *Taler* would not go very far, he also requested to be relieved of the beer tax, to receive an allotment of oats for some

---

[2] As a matter of fact, the chapel inspector Hoe von Hoenegg died at that time and was succeeded by Mathias Weller.

[3] Ratification; misprinted in E. H. Müller as "notification."

horses in Weissenfels, and to be given a reimbursement of four *Taler* per week for himself and his indispensable music copyist when he had to go to Dresden. For the plan of a reorganization of the ensemble he further advised first of all to provide for the choir boys and the instrumentalists and only secondly to take under consideration the more difficult problem of the supplanting of adult singers. But silence on the part of the elector with regard to the ensemble still continued. Schütz may have stayed in Weissenfels during the winter, occupied with the editing of the *Symphoniae sacrae II*.

Our next evidence of his activity is a letter from Calbe, near Magdeburg, to a certain Christian Schirmer, presumably in Danzig, in which Schütz gives an expert opinion at the request of the Danzig cantor, Christoph Werner, the brother of Schütz's best Dresden cornet player, Friedrich Werner.[4] Here we are dealing with a battle waged on several rather strange fronts.

The Danzig organist of St. Mary's was Paul Siefert,[5] who was one of the most distinguished German pupils of Sweelinck.[6] In 1640 he published the first part of *Psalms of David*. This was a collection of *concerti* undoubtedly ultraconservative in character, since for the most part he still used the Goudimel melodies as *cantus firmus* in the tenor. While Siefert was a most bellicose individual who incurred enemy after enemy, his principal Danzig opponent, the church-music director Caspar Förster, aligned himself behind the Warsaw court Kapellmeister, Marco Scacchi,[7] a pupil of Felice Anerio. At the time Scacchi was a highly esteemed composer who in an entire folio,[8] *Musical Sieve for the Syfert Wheat*, joined battle with Siefert against the latter's psalm compilation. Siefert answered in 1645 with a printed *Anticribratio*, whereupon Scacchi struck back with still heavier armor in a *Judicium cribri musici*, a collection of expert opinions[9] preserved in the *Liceo musicale* in Bologna. In this document the following correspondents are mentioned:

---

[4] Born 1621 in Gottleuba, where he became a town piper apprentice; 1634 with Schütz in Copenhagen; 1641 member of the prince elector's band of musicians; 1645 cornet pupil of Sansoni in Vienna; 1647 again at the Danish court; 1650 married in Dresden; 1663 head instrumentalist; died 1667.

[5] Born in Danzig in 1586; died there in 1666.

[6] Cf. Max Seiffert in *Vjschr. f. MW*, 420 ff.; Jos. Surzynski in *KMJb* (1890), p.77; H. Rauschning, *Musikgeschichte v. Danzig* (1930), pp. 140-167. Seiffert's organ works in the *Minorite tablature* in Vienna — discovered by me — had their first posthumous performance, by A. Sittard, at the Berlin Schütz Festival in 1930.

[7] Born in Rome about 1595.

[8] *Cribrum musicum ad triticum Syfertinum* (Venice, 1643).

[9] According to M. Seiffert, the title gives the name of the Warsaw court printer, Peter Elert; but up to the present time no printed copy is known.

H. Schütz, 1646 and 1648	David Cracowitta, organista,[10] 1646
Joh. Stobaeus, 1646	Christof Werner, 1646
Laurentius Starck, 1646	Math. Krinkovius, 1646[11]
Tob. Michael, 1646	Ambrosius Profe, organista, 1649
Benjamin Ducius, 1648	

Finally we should mention a Latin letter of Scacchi to Christoph Werner, which has been preserved in the Hamburg copy of the *Cribrum,* at one time in the possession of Selle and Chr. Bernhard.[12] I give the gist of both letters[13] of Schütz so far as — despite numerous errors in print — the sense can be deciphered.

"... I would have wished that Herr Siefert (sic) had not entered upon this controversy; at least my impression, gathered from a hasty perusal, is that Herr Scacchi is a thoroughly accomplished musician, although I have not yet seen any of his compositions. I cannot do otherwise than agree with him in many respects. I shall look through these documents more carefully when, after an absence of four months, I shall have returned to my new Weissenfels home and dwelling. If God should grant me health, I shall then answer Herr Syfert (sic) properly, which Your Excellency will kindly impart to him with my friendly greeting and apologies for not having written sooner. In any event, as much as I honestly keep my mind open to the wish of Herr Syfert, I would not care to constitute myself an arbitrator or judge in this controversy nor to inject myself into such far-reaching matters with anyone, and I trust that Herr Syfert will not take this amiss." In addition, Schütz asks Kaspar Förster to send him the recently published Masses of Scacchi, inasmuch as, so far, he knows virtually none of his compositions.

In the second letter Schütz says essentially the same thing again and more decisively by adding: "At all events, I must confess that I, too, was drilled and instructed in my youth by my teacher Giovanni Gabrieli of blessed memory in a manner similar to that in which Herr M. Scacchi in the *Sieve* sets Herr Syfert right. This I desire that Your Excellency will impart to Herr Scacchi on the proper occasion with my best regards, together with my request to let the controversy rest and to bury it in oblivion. Herr Syfert, too, whose works I likewise respect

---

[10] From 1626-34 he presided over the smaller organ at St. Mary's in Danzig; in 1633 he was court organist in Copenhagen; in 1634 he took his permanent leave from the Danzig council in favor of Denmark, having been invited by the Kapellmeister of Christian IV, H. Schütz, to co-operate at the wedding of the crown prince (Rauschning, p. 141).

[11] Perhaps a son of Valentin Cremcovius, who was a schoolmaster at Salza in 1603 and under whom the Latin translation of the *Becker Psalms,* to be discussed hereafter, appeared in Magdeburg in 1624.

[12] Reprinted by Erich Katz, *Die mus. Stilbegriffe des 17. Jhs.* (Dissertation, Freiburg/Brsg. 1926), pp. 81 ff.; also pp. 37 ff. Is this identical with the *Lettera per 1644,* preserved in Bologna in manuscript?

[13] The letter to Schirmer and that to Scacchi. Latin in E. H. Müller, Nos. 59 and 60.

and value, should promptly and honorably do likewise." With regard to the procuring of music from Danzig, moreover, he requested the Copenhagen Kapellmeister Agostino Fontana, who had recently stayed with him for a considerable period in Dresden, to act as intermediary. In conclusion, Schütz urges Scacchi "to complete and to publish the treatise on counterpoint which he promised us in his book. He would surely be of great service therewith to our German nation and would gain for himself undying renown."

It is somewhat tragic that Schütz, as an Italianizing modernist, should take the side of the Italian-Polish attacker. For H. Rauschning has clearly shown that here the controversy did not involve the opposition between reaction and progress (which Schütz imagined) so much as that between the North German Hanseatic and the Mediterranean musical point of view.[14] But, as so often happens when a distant authority is drawn into such a controversy and indeed is played up as such, it all depends on who marshals the opposing forces. Apparently Schütz was led by Chr. Werner into battle on the side of Förster-Scacchi against the somewhat enraged but basically and thoroughly German and able Siefert.

In a second case Schütz allowed himself to become engaged in a campaign in favor of the Italian musical ideal, and one feels — in view of the unfortunate experiences he himself underwent with the Italians a short time afterward — that had he been confronted with these questions a decade later, he would presumably have considered them from a different and more German angle. Schütz wanted his successor at the court in Copenhagen, Agostino Fontana, to be brought to Dresden as Vice-Kapellmeister. The latter must have been a great admirer of the master, as he preferred a secondary position and a smaller salary at the Dresden court to his Scandinavian independence. Schütz strongly advocated Fontana's appointment in the memorandum of September 21, 1647;[15] but apparently the elector delayed action. In the next year Christian IV died, and (as we learn from the second Scacchi letter) Fontana again stayed in Dresden in order to promote his appointment. But now the court cantor Hofkonz set up a violent opposition.

---

[14] Siefert concluded the controversy in a thoroughly dignified manner. In the *Anticribratio* he had asserted that the contemporary Italians could no longer undertake to act as judges of the great old school but were to be depended on only for the opera and the cantata; but when, in refutation of this statement, Romano Micheli, from Aquilegia, sent him his best works with a flattering letter, Siefert replied in February 1647 in a chivalrous manner and, recognizing such accomplishments, did full justice to the contemporary Italian school (Surzynski, loc. cit.). Scacchi returned to Italy in 1648 and died there ca. 1686 at a very ripe age (ninety-one).

[15] In the same year, in the company of the bass singer Christof Dyk, Fontana passed through Gottorp on the journey from Copenhagen to Dresden; cf. B. Engelke, *Musik am Gottorper Hofe*, II.

In a detailed memorandum to the elector[16] he himself sought to succeed Hestius as Vice-Kapellmeister and complained vigorously regarding Schütz. He insisted that Schütz had been hostile to him, and, in opposition to the will of the elector, had for years delayed his appointment and advancement. Schütz had intended, he reported, to place an arch-Catholic (the Italian Augustinus) in the position. While Schütz remained for three years in Brunswick, Denmark, and Weissenfels, he had obtained for the entire service the co-operation of the court organist Christian Kittel, "a man of distinguished musical ability."

"Although, most gracious elector and lord, it would be well, fitting, and praiseworthy for Kapellmeister Schütz, as the principal member and head of the ensemble entrusted to him, to remain at his post, to provide the ensemble with musical compositions, to serve it unswervingly with counsel and action, and thus to fulfill his official duties, it is generally known that he .... for many years has had little regard for his sheep but has deserted them and has traveled from one province to another oblivious to whether Your Electoral Highness was adequately served or was left in the lurch." Furthermore, during "the present four years" he [Hofkonz] has had to look after the festival services as well as daily prayers and thus "to earn for Kapellmeister Schütz his position and his bread." He appeals to Hoe and Weller, the court preachers, and inquires whether "since the title or the name of Vice-Kapellmeister is extremely distasteful to Herr Kapellmeister Schütz, you will allow me to be named a director, a court cantor, although Your Electoral Highness does not have a *Kantorei* but an electoral ensemble *(Capelle).*"

"Dresden, May 16, 1649

Joh. Georg Hofcantz." (sic)[17]

Schütz's undated memorandum[18] is to be interpreted as an answer to an attack similar to the one mentioned. It calmly shows "that all my most humble reminders were directed to the end that nothing subversive or incompetent might steal into Your Electoral Highness' court ensemble *(Hoffcapell)* but that it would be supplied with a thoroughly qualified and useful personnel and that thus, with

---

[16] *Hauptstaatsarchiv*, Dresden. Loc. 8687, 27 f. According to the kind information of Dr. R. Engländer.

[17] According to Eitner, *Quellen Lexicon*, Hofkonz was born on August 17, 1615, in Trautenau and died July 19, 1655, in Dresden. He studied at the universities of Königsberg and Frankfurt on the Oder, became cantor in Sagan, then in Guben, and, on January 2, 1642, tenor singer in the Dresden court *Capelle*.

[18] No. 58 in E. H. Müller. Weller's accompanying document is dated July 30, 1646; *Aktenstücke, Loc.* 8560, fol. 2 *(Schreiben von und an Weller, 1646-51).*

God's and Your Highness' help, it might again be raised to a praiseworthy status in order that it might shine forth as a light and be praised among other evangelical ensembles." With completely co-operative feeling Schütz advised that the salaries not be too unequal and that noteworthy achievement be rewarded with "a special gift of grace." Beyond this Schütz calls attention to the fact that "if excessive compensation should be given to one who is unqualified, what would properly qualified persons demand if such persons should be installed in the future?" So far as Hofkonz was concerned, he need not be ashamed of the title of court cantor, which Andreas Petermann had already held. Schütz makes a precise estimate of the salary proper for Hofkonz and hits upon 300 gulden. He recommends placing the choir boys with Chr. Kittel and Hans Klemme, "with whom they can best and most quickly be perfected and taught to sing true, which would in no wise happen if they were placed elsewhere." Apparently he places a meager value on the competence of Hofkonz as a teacher of music. "I would again recommend for the reasons given that the position of Vice-Kapellmeister be left vacant."

Somewhat later it becomes evident that the aging master is worried lest he be supplanted by a younger man. He praises Christof Kittel as court organist, composer, and choirmaster; but here, too, "Your Electoral Highness is reminded, in confidence, that it is to be hoped that as long as your Kapellmeister Heinrich Schütz is alive, it will not be desirable to engage a Vice-Kapellmeister."

Concerning himself Schütz says: "My chief and best accomplishment in my office consists, not in my constant personal presence and service but much rather in preparing and arranging all kinds of good musical compositions, overseeing the entire work, and taking care that the *collegia* of vocalists, instrumentalists, and choir boys be held in good order and practice." He requests once more to be allowed to reside in Weissenfels, and he concludes, not without irony: "N. B. Hofkontz can do little in this matter during my absence, except that in my place he can beat the time, which nevertheless will be a privilege *(Vorzug)* for him."[19]

The attacks of Hofkonz did have the result that there is no more talk about the candidacy of Fontana. On the other hand, the Danzig cantor, Christof Werner (who has already been mentioned in connection with the controversy concerning Sieffert),[20] received the call as Vice-Kapellmeister. Werner, however, died in Danzig before setting out for Dresden, and in 1651 Hofkonz who, as a capable singer, had had success in an opera presently to be mentioned, received the hotly

---

[19] (More than he deserves.)
[20] Supra.

coveted post. The fact that just at this time Christof Bernhard (a highly talented pupil of Sieffert, Chr. Werner, and Schütz) asked to be relieved from the electoral ensemble *(Kapelle)*, of which he had been a member for two years, may have some connection with his disappointment over the appointment of Hofkonz, especially as probably at about this very time he edited Schütz's *Theory of Composition*,[21] to which the master's preface to the *Geistliche Chormusik* of 1648 significantly points. Furthermore, the fact that in 1652 Bernhard applied for an appointment at the little court at Gottorp, where he had played a part three years before at the wedding of a princess in conjunction with Agostino Fontana,[22] is an indication of his desire to leave the Saxon court at all costs. The elector, instead of granting his leave, sent him to Italy a second time and appointed him Vice-Kapellmeister after the death of Hofkonz. How he then went to Hamburg (1664-74) remains to be discussed.

In the year 1646 the successor of Heinrich Posthumus, "Henry the other, eldest Herr Reuss," turned to Schütz with the request that he recommend a suitable successor to the figural cantor at Gera, Peter Neander.[23] A hasty letter by Schütz[24] to his Weissenfels factotum, Martin Knabe,[25] with whose *War Concerto* of 1635 we have already become acquainted, asks that he put off for some time the Gera court organist Kühnel.[26] Schütz then recommended (see reference above) his pupil Andreas Gleich.

Similar matters occupied the master in the towns of Lausatia. As court Kapellmeister, composer, and teacher of numerous talented pupils, he was the authority who organized musical matters during his century. Thus we read in a letter of March 9, 1646,[27] from the Dresden court organist Johannes Klemme to Johann Samuel Schein[28] in Bautzen:

"Honorable and high artist, very dear Herr Schein: The Herr Kapellmeister Heinrich Schütz sends kind greetings and at the same time would make known to you that when he was recently in Leipzig, though now again in Weissenfels, he recommended you to many distinguished persons and indeed brought it about that you will shortly be called to Leipzig.

---

[21] *Die Kompositionslehre Heinrich Schützens in der Fassung seines Schülers (The Instruction in Composition by Heinrich Schütz According to His Pupil)*, Chr. Bernhard, introduced and published by J. H. Müller-Blattau (1926).

[22] B. Engelke, *Musik am Gottorper Hof* II.

[23] Reprint of this writing for the first time through A. Werner, *Städtische und fürstliche Musikpflege in Weissenfels* (1910), p. 149; also in E. H. Müller, p. 340.

[24] October 30, 1646, from a place unknown.

[25] Organist and teacher at Weissenfels since 1635; died 1652.

[26] For the first time in Werner, *Weissenfels*, p. 150.

[27] Herbert Biehle, *Musikgeschichte von Bautzen*, Leipzig, 1924, p. 20.

[28] The son of Johann Hermann Schein, employed there as organist beginning in 1644.

When then your present position must again be filled, the Kapellmeister knows a fine man who was with him in Denmark and is still with him at the present time. He plays well; therefore the Kapellmeister would like to see him receive advancement.[29] In the event of the realization of your transfer (to Leipzig), he would be glad to have you refer to him and to have you recommend this person, in his behalf, to the council and its head, Martin Gumprecht, thus assisting in his call to Bautzen. Should the recommendation lead to a hearing, the Herr Kapellmeister would be glad to present him himself. He is ... about twenty-three or twenty-four years old. I have been asked to report this to you in behalf of the Herr Kapellmeister. He hopes you will do all in your power and offers, in return, to assist you in any manner when you come to Leipzig. May I have a reply from you, stating your intentions. May we herewith all be commended to the divine protection."

Inasmuch as Samuel Schein actually received the Leipzig position on the recommendation of Schütz, the Bautzen magistracy turned to Schütz with the request for an appropriate successor.[30] Schütz answered with letters[31] designed to obtain the position for Hering, his Dresden copyist. It was Hering who, with Klemme, ventured to publish the *Symphoniae sacrae II* and co-operated in the publication of the *Christmas Oratorio.*

Still a third matter of related nature: The Danish crown prince, Christian V, to whom Schütz had dedicated that large musical work, the *Symphoniae sacrae II,* died June 1, 1647, on a journey, not far from Dresden. Since he was the son-in-law of the Saxon elector, it was forbidden in all Saxony, as a sign of mourning, "to play the organ and all other stringed instruments in the churches or to indulge in joyful music" until further notice.[32] In December the council of Görlitz, which, with Zittau, had belonged to Saxony since 1635, inquired of the Dresden high consistory whether one might not at least play the organ again at Christmas. Schütz's letter, which accompanied this inquiry (loc. cit., No. 67) is not addressed, as E. H. Müller thinks (p.310), to the council of Görlitz but to the Dresden spiritual authority. The answer from Dresden (again via Schütz) seems to have been so late in coming and so ambiguous that the Görlitzers had to appeal further to the governor of Upper Lausatia.

Müller assumes that Schütz was in Görlitz for the dedication of the Church of St. Nicholas (April 16, 1649) because his *122d Psalm,* of the *Psalms of 1619,* was performed on this occasion. While Gondolatsch has shown that this assumption was erroneous, nevertheless the Görlitz researches have discovered two notices

---

[29] The reference is to Alexander Herig, who remained in Bautzen but two years, when he became organist of the Dresden *Kreuzkirche,* where he instructed young Kuhnau in 1669 and where he died in 1695. Cf. R. Munnich: *J. Kuhnaus Leben (Sbd.* III *der IMG,* pp. 480 ff.).

[30] Mar. 3 and Apr. 11, 1647. In Biehle and Müller, pp. 307-309.

[31] Mar. 14 and April 28, 1647. Müller Nos. 61/62.

[32] M. Gondolatsch, *Richtiges und Falsches um einen Heinrich Schütz-Brief (Zs. f. M. W.* XV, 428 ff.); facsimile according to the original (in the possession of Edw. Speyer-Ridgehurst) in Einstein, loc. cit.

from the local accounts: May 8, 1651: "To Herr Heinrich Schütz, electoral Kapell-meister, two ducats, because he honored the local churches with the third part of his *Spiritual Symphonies*"; and still earlier, February 6, 1648: "To Herr Heinrich Schütz, electoral Saxon Kapellmeister, four ducats on the marriage of his daughter."

We have now reached an event which, for a time, poured some sunshine over the life of the sixty-three-year-old musician, a life otherwise so solemn and serious. We have a detailed letter of invitation by Schütz[33] to administrator Duke August[34] in Halle requesting: "That you would graciously grant to show me your most gracious affection in a matter of honor close to my heart, namely, the marriage of my beloved only daughter Euphrosyne, who was recently engaged to the highly learned Herr Christoph Pincker the younger, twice doctor of laws, on January 25 of the year 1648, approaching, God grant, with happiness and peace. It would be an especially high honor for me if Your Grace most graciously con-sented to adorn and illumine the wedding day of my dear and only daughter and her beloved bridegroom with a representative of Your Excellency. This I most humbly request. . . ."

Martin Geier's funeral sermon for Schütz recalls the event as follows:

"In August 1647 the blessed departed had promised his sole surviving and youngest daughter Euphrosyne to the honorable, highly esteemed and highly learned Herr Christoph Pinker, J. U. Doctor, at the time practicing lawyer, now, however, Electoral Saxon counselor of appeals, assessor of the local court of Leipzig, and burgomaster there. The engagement was consummated with marriage by the pastor on January 25, 1648. The departed experienced great comfort and pleasure from this marriage, which made him five times a grandfather. But only one of the grandchildren has survived to the present day, namely, Frau Gertraud Euphrosina, who was married on May 18, 1670, to Herr Johann Seydeln, canon in Wurtzen and counselor in Leipzig. This marriage was blessed with two children; one of whom, how-ever, died soon after birth. The departed thus became a great-grandfather. The surviving great-grandchild is following her blessed great-grandfather to his final resting place."

Twenty-eight and a half years before, Schütz had sent invitations far and wide to his own wedding. He now sent out similar invitations, and in answer to them he received not a few acknowledgments, both material and spiritual. Among the latter there were a number of poems of felicitation — for example, one from Simon Dach in distant Königsberg — also a biographically fascinating one from Christoph Kaldenbach,[35] which he published in Tübingen in 1683 in his *Lieder und Getichte*.[36] It reads in part:

---

[33] Dresden, December 28, 1647; loc. cit., No. 28.
[34] Duke August was the son of Joh. Georg I, at whose Baptism, in 1615, Schütz had begun his conductorship at Dresden.
[35] Appointed in 1656 professor of rhetoric *(Beredsamkeit)* in Tübingen.
[36] L. H. Fischer in *Monatshefte f. Musikgeschichte XV*, 91 ff.

> Euterpe sang for you such lovely lullabies
> In gentle cradles,
> Which songs are widely known. . .
> No potentate was ever called to serve
> Who was not graciously disposed to you;
> But more than all the rest, the Saxon house esteemed you.
> Allowed you more and more to prosper.
> And then with kindness came the mighty Christian,
> Who likewise was delighted by your song.
> O Brunswick, I grow dumb. Your songs by heav'n inspired,
> Which 'round the Elb and Belt resounded here and there,
> Were later known throughout the whole wide world,
> And even now do gladden many a land.
> Yet you have not received the due reward
> Which your high art deserves. No northern church
> Has sung to me your splendid moving psalms
> But that my soul was overwhelmed with woe
> At your unhappy fate.

For Saxony lies destroyed by war; why does Schütz not seek another abode?

> See, Vistula flows on.
> Thank God; and Pregel, too, by quarrel not inflamed.

Here Opitz found a temporary refuge and Schütz's relative, Heinrich Albert, a permanent one. But peace will now return to Saxony also:

> To you will Nestor's peaceful days be given,
> To hold your grandchild on your honored knee,
> And someday, free from pain, to join the angel choir,
> With Asaph and with David evermore.

We have sketched the life of Euphrosyne Schütz from the death of her mother to her wedding. The funeral sermon for the son-in-law, Christoph Pincker, tells this about him:[37] He was born in Leipzig August 16, 1619, and was thus four years older than his bride, now twenty-five years of age. Through his great-grandfather on the maternal side he came from Lobenstein in Reuss, studied law in Leipzig, and especially in Basel, where he took his doctorate in 1644, then to return home to his native city.

"While he was living there, he, after reverent prayer to God and the approval of his dear parents, became engaged, in August 1647, to the honorable and virtuous Euphrosyne, daughter of the noble, esteemed, and highly learned Herr Heinrich Schütz, electoral Saxon praiseworthy Kapellmeister, the engagement being consummated in holy matrimony and with ecclesiastical blessing on January 25 of the following year, 1648. He enjoyed a peaceful and happy married life with his beloved for seven years. Two sons and two daughters were born to them, three of whom, however, died near the time of birth. Only one daughter remained living, namely, the noble and virtuous Frau Gertraud Euphrosyne, who was married in May 1670 to the worthy, noble, steadfast, and highly learned Johann Seidel, canon of the foundation of Wurtzen and distinguished counselor here. The marriage was blessed with four children, Henrietta,[38] Johannes, Johann Christoph, and Christiana Eleonora. God grant His grace to their further upbringing. . . ."

---

[37] Joh. Friedr. Mayer: *Ein löblicher Regent* (Leipzig, 1678, *Univ.-Bibl.* Halle, Collection Ponikau Z d 2900).

[38] Apparently so named in honor of her great-grandfather Heinrich Schütz.

Pincker lived for a time in Meissen, then again in his native city.

"As he was obliged to move his household to Leipzig, it pleased the Almighty, according to His inscrutable counsel, to make a widower of the blessed departed by taking from this world his beloved on January 12, 1655, after she had given birth to a young son six days before."

In the same year the widower, who had advanced to councilor of appeals (*Appellationsrat*), became burgomaster of Leipzig, and married, when the year of mourning had passed, Marg. Regine Oheimb, by whom he had six children. In 1673 he married a third time. On the occasion of his death (May 25, 1678) in Leipzig, L. Valentin Alberti lamented that in Leipzig, the city of lindens, the Whitsuntide birches had transformed themselves into mere mourning cypresses.

Thus in 1648 Schütz knew that his child was under the protection of a well-to-do, reputable, and apparently affectionate husband. Hence he could devote himself with greater concentration to his professional duties.

In February 1647 he had spent a week at the court of Duke Wilhelm in Weimar, and concerning this visit a small artistic memorial has been preserved in the library of the council at Zwickau. This is an aria by Schütz, printed in Gotha, on ten quatrains of Master Christian Timotheus Dufft, a hymn of thanks, *Princely Grace on Sea and Land*.[39] It is reminiscent of a multitude of masques, ballets, and musical performances — written 130 years before Goethe, at the same place, organized similar events. Here are a few of the stanzas:

> See, there were shining the seven bright planets,[40]
> Honor reflecting on God's gift of light.
> Songs of the Muses resounding so sweetly
> Silence the tumult of Mars with their art.
>
> Nightly did Vulcan appear on the mountain,
> Flashes of lightning and thunder his speech;
> Daedalus opened his opulent chambers.
> Oh, how abundant his closets and bins!
>
> Proteus himself would delight in disguises;
> Scarcely a person, yet many gay fellows;
> Roist'rously, boist'rously leaping and dancing
> Buildings half-builded that yet appeared whole.
>
> Life at the theater during the winter
> Kindled the yearning for breezes of spring;
> Flora, Pomona were resting in slumber,
> Whom the nymphs summoned with Echo's sweet voice.

---

[39] *Fürstliche Gnade zu Wasser und zu Lande*, Vol. XV, 86; with a new text, as a wedding song, in the *Volksliederbuch*, III, No. 645, Peters.

[40] Apparently a ballet, *The Seven Planets*, which until the end of the century was repeatedly given in Dresden.

> Grateful the arts with their strings and their voices
> Sing their approval of seasons all four; [41]
> Eleanora, in royal adornment,
> Takes us unworthy ones, leads by the hand.
>
> Skilfully Neptune did tame the Ilm's wavelets
> That the ships safely could sail on the stream;
> Tragic as told was the life of the Baptist; [42]
> As is continued, it ended a farce.

That portion which was not set by the Weimar house composer, Adam Drese, is presumably to be attributed to our master. Schütz's alto melody (in A minor) with continuo and a little ritornell for two violins, is one of his few *Lied* contributions. As a letter of the elector, dated July 17, 1648, to Duke Wilhelm of Saxony testifies [43] (loc. cit., 8561, 363), Schütz was again living in Weimar at that time.

> "First of all, be assured of our friendly service, great love, and good wishes, highborn prince, kind, much loved cousin and friend. With this our greeting we have wished to apprise Your Excellency that Kapellmeister Heinrich Schütz has opportunely informed us, in connection with his impending journey, that he would like to wait on you at your convenience. As nothing would please us more than to learn that Your Excellency, together with your esteemed household, is in good health and well-being, we have graciously bidden him learn of this and convey the news to us most speedily.
>
> Dresden, July 17, 1648
>
> Johann Georg."

At this time the master presumably had to provide all kinds of theatrical performances for the city on the Ilm (Weimar). The list of his lost dramatic scores, already so impressive, presumably becomes much greater when we consider his next duties in Dresden. Schütz doubtless presided with enthusiasm over the musical celebrations on the occasion of the Peace of Westphalia, having, from his thirty-third to his sixty-third year, passed through a world of blood and fire, pestilence, and destruction. But now, above all, young theatrical talent was astir at the Saxon court. For Joh. Georg's sixty-fourth birthday, March 6, 1648, there took place "toward evening by way of felicitation a musical presentation and a ballet presented by the Saxon princess Fräulein Erdmuthe Sophie. It was her first appearance." [44] Both a poetess and an impresario, she was doubtless the art-inspired princess who later married in 1662 and resided in Bayreuth, there becoming the founder of the early German opera of that district. [45] But who was the composer

---

[41] Doubtless a ballet, *The Four Seasons*.

[42] Apparently a sacred opera, *John the Baptist*.

[43] Through kind information from Herr Dr. R. Engländer.

[44] Fürstenau, *Zur Geschichte d. Musik u. d. Theaters am Hofe zu Dresden (History of Music and the Theatre at the Court of Dresden)*, I (1901), 169.

[45] L. Schiedermair, *Bayreuther Festspiele im Zeitalter des Absolutismus (Bayreuth Festival Plays in the Time of Absolutism)* (1908).

of the ballet? For a similar occasion, two years later, there was a *Singing Ballet,* performed by the prince elector's musicians. In 1650 a ducal double wedding took place in Dresden. The sons of the elector, Duke Moritz and Duke Christian, the founders of the lines Saxony-Naumburg and Saxony-Merseburg, married the sisters Hedwig and Christiane of Schleswig-Holstein. On this occasion "several pieces composed by Kapellmeister Heinrich Schütz for the royal wedding" were performed. There was also a five-act *Ballet.* The poet was David Schirmer; the subject, *Paris and Helen.* Later we shall note the artistic relation in which Schirmer stood to Schütz.[46] How extensive the musical numbers must have been is indicated by the preserved cast given in Fürstenau, p. 119: Hofkonz — Jupiter; Mars, Paris — Ph. Stolle; Mercury — Chr. Bernhard; Pluto, Priest of Venus — Georg Kaiser; Shepherd — Chr. Kittel; for the goddesses — the electoral choir boys and chamberlains. Joseph Nadler, in his *History of the Literature of the German Tribes and Countries,*[47] is probably the only Germanic scholar who up to that time fully evaluated Schütz as the spiritual center of the Meissen baroque and the Dresden court art of the seventeenth century. First he discusses Buchner's *Orpheus,* then the poet Schirmer. With regard to the former, he says: "Buchner was a professor of poetry in the electorate who supplied *Inventions,* set in German verse in the present new manner but composed in the Italian manner by the electoral Kapellmeister Heinrich Schütz and rendered into ballets by the dancing master, Gabriel Mölichen." There was no lack of commissions, and a happy workman whose productions flowed from his fingers was more valuable than a famous professor of poetry. One who was both tireless and always ready was found in David Schirmer. He was born in 1623 in Pappendorf near Freiberg, where his father was a clergyman. At first in Halle, then a pupil of Buchner in Wittenberg, he was brought to court by Johann Georg I in 1650. There years later he received a fixed salary, and in 1656 he became librarian. What was expected of him is related with gratifying clarity in the appointment: "We confess that we have engaged Schirmer as our servant with the understanding that he should work out to the best of his ability, both in poetry and prose, the material offered him, showing himself at all times subject and obedient to our commands." He had become acquainted with Heinrich Albert in Leipzig, and while in Dresden he attached himself closely to Albert's cousin, Heinrich Schütz. His *Poetic Stalks of Rue*[48] appeared in 1661. He died in 1686. Schirmer allowed himself to be made

---

[46] Infra.
[47] *Literaturgeschichte der deutschen Stämme und Landschaften,* II, 2 (1923), 329 ff.
[48] *Poetische Rautengebüsche.*

use of, and yet, despite speedy workmanship and much urging, his operettas and dance plays are quite excellent, as, for example, one of 1663, titled *Of Virtues and Vices*.[49] Konstantin Christian Dedekind, 1628-97, from Reinsdorf in Anhalt, Kapellmeister in Dresden, arranged, in addition to sacred songs,[50] the libretti for sacred music dramas. . . . An actual official with title and rank, called secretary of inventions, was Ernst Geller. The great dance play *Paris and Helen*, in five acts, 1650, offered practically everything: all the gods of Olympus and their offspring on earth; Greeks and Trojans; singing and dancing shepherds and shepherdesses; also tournaments. Between the stage action were pictorial dances, such as the seizure and abduction of Helen. The presentation began at seven and lasted until one in the morning. Besides Schirmer's dance play *The Triumph of Amor*[51] of 1652, *Paris and Helen* formed the starting point for all following pieces.

So much for Nadler. Perhaps, and indeed probably, we here have instances where dramatic scores by Schütz have again been lost.

In *Paris and Helen* we find included "a complete chorus of gods in honor of Peleus and Thetis, a song of praise by the six cupids on love, a prize song to wine by Chiron, the marshal of the gods; a recitative by Venus in connection with the judgment of Paris; after this a 'Duet of Wrath' by Juno and Pallas: 'Thunder, Hail, Lightning, and Flame';[52] a prayer of the priest of Venus; a prediction of Proteus against Paris on the sea; a lament by Hecuba, Andromache, Cassandra, and a chorus of the Trojans on the fall of Ilium; finally, a song of praise to the tribe of the rue[53] with Apollo as precentor and two cupids 'with the full chorus continually falling in.'"

The chief patron of these operatic ventures was the electoral Prince Joh. Georg II, who had appeared in person with his brothers in *Paris and Helen* and even had his little son Joh. Georg III (born in 1647) participate as Cupid in a small ballet, *The Prison of the Moors*,[54] while his companions sang a song with the accompaniment of the theorbo. We have a list of members of the electoral prince's ensemble *(Kapelle)* from 1651 (Fürstenau I, 29). It contains the names of the eunuch Giov. Andrea Angelini, called Bontempi, composer and discantist, as leader; M. Weckmann, as organist; Philipp Stolle, as tenor and theorbist; Friedr. Werner, as alto falsettist and cornet player; Christian Kittel, as bass and

---

[49] *Von den Tugenden und Lastern.*
[50] More correctly: Sacred and, especially, secular songs (H. J. M.).
[51] *Der triumphierende Amor.*
[52] *Donner, Hagel, Blitz und Flamme.*
[53] *Rautenstamm.*
[54] *Der Moren Gefängnis.*

violist; Friedrich Westhoff from Lübeck,[55] as lute player — altogether eighteen highly competent artists, a group far superior to that of the old elector and presided over by Schütz.

Bontempi, born in 1620 in Perugia, whose real name was Angelini, had adopted the name which he was to make famous in honor of his rich guardian. He studied voice and composition in Rome with the Kapellmeister of St. Peter's, Virg. Mazzocchi. From 1643-50 he was a discantist at St. Mark's in Venice under Monteverdi, Rovetta, and Cavalli, which would especially have recommended him to Schütz. He arrived in Dresden with fresh impressions of the Venetian opera and with friendly relations to the literati in the city of canals. He finally made his chief reputation also as an author, having written, among other works, a *History of the Rebellion in Hungary* (Dresden, 1672) and a *Latin History of Music* (Perugia, 1695). This latter work, though valuable in itself, by no means deserves the title of "one of the oldest histories of music" which belongs rather to the fine annals of Caspar Printz entitled *The Art of Singing and Playing (Sing- und Klingkunst, Dresden, 1690)*. The concept of origin and development properly characteristic of a real history is lacking in Bontempi's work. It is a learned presentation of two independent achievements: fully developed ancient music and, one might say, the doctrine of Palestrinian counterpoint, but without a real connection between the two.

Although the German Protestant musicians objected to serving under Bontempi — not only because he was a eunuch but also for national and religious reasons — the relation between him and Schütz was entirely cordial. This was apparent in their evident friendship and also from Bontempi's dedication to the old master of his work printed by Seyffert in Dresden in 1660: *An Introduction for Those Little Familiar with the Art of Music, by Which They May Acquire the Rules of Four-Part Composition with the Help of Numbers Instead of Notes.*[56]

Furthermore, there is preserved from his works the music to the opera *Paride* (Dresden, 1662) and to *Dafne,* the latter composed in collaboration with his colleague Peranda.[57] In addition to these, there is a secular cantata in Padua, and there are two pieces of church music, scantily scored, in Upsala. Bontempi's

---

[55] Formerly riding master of Gustavus Adolphus, later father of the violin virtuoso Paul v. Westhoff.

[56] *Nova quatuor vocibus componendi methodus, qua musicae artis plane nescius ad compositionem accedere potest.*

[57] Dresden, 1672-78; repeatedly performed.

countryman, Vincenzo Albrici,[58] was also viewed as a valuable acquisition for Dresden.

The electoral prince was sufficiently nonpartisan to use his influence toward the improvement of his father's music forces. This is evident from a document dated September 30, 1653, and addressed to the elector (Fürstenau I, 33). Schütz manifestly stood behind the attempt. The suggestion was to the effect that Johann Georg II would surrender a portion of his best musical forces to the elector. The lightening of his own economy doubtless played a part in the suggestion. On festive occasions both chapels would, in any event, often enough have united forces under Schütz's direction.

On a number of occasions we have relied on Schütz's memorandum of 1651 as authoritative. It was a document drawn up in connection with the presentation of the third part of the *Symphoniae sacrae*, dedicated to Johann Georg I. In it Schütz recapitulates for the elector his entire life up to the first Copenhagen journey.[59] The master requests that after thirty-five years of long service, now that all the princes and princesses have been married, he finally be pensioned. A reputable cantor advanced in years had recently complained to him that young counselors had criticized his old-fashioned music with the argument that "a tailor and a cantor who have served for thirty years are no longer of service to the world." To be sure, he, Schütz, did not expect such charges from the elector's sons but "from some newly arrived young musicians." "And inasmuch as indeed the prince elector's Italian eunuch, Andrea Bontempi, has on numerous occasions let it be known that even from youth he had devoted himself more to composition than to singing, and offered on his own initiative gladly to step in and direct the music, should I so desire, I would, therefore, at the conclusion of this writing of mine like to apprise you of such facts and obtain your opinion whether with your gracious consent I should accept the offer of Andrea Bontempi and should allow him on numerous occasions to conduct the music in my place?" He stated that the young man was well qualified and had demanded no increase in salary for such services. Schütz had also learned from Venice that on numerous occasions Bontempi had successfully substituted there for the Kapellmeister. The elector might then well make the attempt without any risk. One can discern in what he says both resentment at the bold

---

[58] Albrici was a Roman; in 1652 he stood at the head of Italian musicians in the service of Queen Christine of Sweden. He came to Dresden in 1654, where two years later the prince elector appointed him Kapellmeister. Concerning his sonatas and cantatas preserved in Upsala, see Pirro, *Schütz*, pp. 192 ff. Concerning his Dresden activity see R. Münnich, *Sbd. IMG*, III, 487 ff.

[59] E. H. Müller, No. 77.

rising generation and also a willingness finally to unburden on younger shoulders many of the duties which had long become irksome to him.

While Schütz, from the point of view of his court duties and annoyances, thus appears as an old man, the picture of the composer and the paterfamilias, on the other hand, is altogether different and by no means indicates a man weary with age.

The years 1647, 1648, and 1650 produced most brilliant publications by Schütz in his capacity as a creative artist. There first appeared, as already stated, the *Symphoniae sacrae II*, as a German counterpart to the Latin small *concerti* with instruments, of 1629. The *Symphoniae sacrae II* were dedicated to the Danish crown prince, who died soon thereafter. Then, in 1648, there appeared the *Musicalia ad chorum sacrum* or *Geistliche Chormusik*, dedicated to the singers at St. Thomas', Leipzig, or, more precisely, with a dedication dated Dresden, April 21, 1648, to "Their Excellencies Herren Burgomaster and Councilors of the Electoral City of Leipzig," as the trustees of the choir already famous at that time. This is Schütz's first and only dedication to the bearers of German municipal and civic culture, for Prince Eggenberg and Herr von Friesen were high dignitaries at the imperial or electoral court. Accordingly, in the case of these twenty-nine motets for from five to seven voices we are confronted with what was Schütz's essentially most German work, through which he became the greatest German cantor before and with Bach. In this preface[60] he recalls the manifold musical relations between Dresden and Leipzig; that his friend Johann Hermann Schein, later cantor at St. Thomas, had formerly been a choir boy in the Dresden chapel; and that the present leader of the choir of St. Thomas, Tobias Michael, was the son of his predecessor in the conductorship of the electoral chapel — Roger Michael. Above all, however, he wanted gratefully to show with this "modest gift" how the city of Leipzig, despite the difficult times, had never forgotten its noble instrument of *a cappella* song but had always maintained it with full membership. This was doubtless a veiled hint to his elector to compare therewith the decline of his own chapel! One may well say that with this glorious monument, fashioned from his innermost being, Schütz presented a patent of nobility for the cultivation of music on the part of the German cities in general, which now, after the ravages of the war, should and would turn again on all sides to cultural reconstruction.

The — as always — still more significant preface addressed to the "kindly disposed reader" will be considered in connection with the discussion of the musical works.[61] The wide circulation of the work, both as a whole and in parts, confirms

---

[60] *Collected Works*, Vol. VIII; E. H. Müller, No. 70.
[61] Infra.

the statement of Wolfgang Kaspar Printz that in 1650 Schütz "was considered the best of all German composers."

Even at this point we may briefly state that Schütz's warning in his preface that young composers should cultivate "the neglected counterpoint" apparently found a lively echo among the conservative German music theorists. At least I attribute to this preface the following passage in the *Cribrum musicum* (1700) of Andreas Werckmeister. He writes on page thirty:

"The famous electoral Saxon Kapellmeister and excellent composer Heinrich Schütz, of blessed memory, calls such unripe compositions *Bernheutereyen*[62] in a certain epistle." He continues on page thirty-nine:

"P. S. After concluding this letter I run across an epistle — lying among my *musicalia* — which H. Baryphonus wrote to the then famous Kapellmeister H. Schütz. In this he discusses, among other things, composition, of which discussion I herewith append the following. The reader can see both the original, in the handwriting of Baryphonus, and the answer of Kapellmeister Schütz, if he will please address me. This extract is as follows: 'It is no wonder that among many composers few good ones are actually found, for they have never reduced to score the work of composers of the first rank, have never executed them well nor recorded and committed to memory what was notable in them; nor have they arranged them according to their proper classification. They think the whole art of musical composition consists in producing consonances according to the obsolete old rules, in avoiding parallel octaves and fifths, whereas something more is required for the dance than red shoes. According to my opinion, true, proper composition requires the correct knowledge of three-voiced harmony and from this the joining-together of two voices, all of which, when properly taken into account, will constitute good harmony. If one does not attend to the three-voiced harmony, one will have dissonances in the two-voiced intervals; if one does not consider the natural position and the legitimate progressions, one will have a harsh harmony, which happens when one places a voice on top when it should be below, or a voice below when it should be on top, etc. Nowadays there is a great deal of this kind of composition, the composers of which I shall tactfully refrain from mentioning. Few contemporaries pay proper attention to the expression of the affections and the peculiarity of the text.

"As to the question whether a practical musician needs an exact knowledge of musical theory, certainly of mathematics, I would reply that there are two arbiters in matters musical, namely, reason and hearing (λόγος καὶ ἀκοή *ratio* and *auditus*). Now when a composer has written something, he must first consult his hearing to find out how it sounds. If one does not wish to place full confidence in this judgment of his ears, he will turn to the court of reason, which governs the theory, and will inquire into the causes why this sounds well, that bad; why this is to be used, that to be avoided. And this, then, is the correct judgment: when reason and sense harmonize and pronounce the same verdict, etc. For it is not sufficient to say with regard to a composition that this is good or that is bad. One must show reasons why it is good or bad.'" So much for Baryphonus.[63]

In the year 1650, then, there appeared, as the third and most comprehensive publication of this period, the third part of the *Symphoniae sacrae*,[64] dedicated to

---

[62] An obsolete expression meaning literally *Bärenhäutereien*, from *Bärenhaut*, the skin of a bear. It signifies a lazy, uncouth, or coarse being.

[63] With *triga*, Baryphonus' word for the sounding-together of three voices, and *syzygia*, Baryphonus' word for the sounding-together of two voices, compare the concepts *trias* and *dyas* in Lippius, 1624.

[64] Vols. X/XI. The prefaces are also in E. H. Müller, Nos. 74—75.

the Elector Johann Georg I. This constituted, as it were, an urgent and final warning to the elector to retrieve, at the twelfth hour, what had too long been neglected in the Dresden court chapel. Actually, at this time all kinds of new appointments were made, and choir boys were accepted.[65] Schütz indicates in his dedication that the elector had given a subsidy for the publication of this work. Here, too, it will be the purpose of the section dealing with the music to consider the further admonitions addressed to the musicians who use it.[66]

At this time Schütz was, as mentioned in the introductory chapter, corresponding with the Chemnitz trustees of the old Schütz legacy and even ventured to interest the electoral counselors in obtaining for his daughter and his son-in-law Pinckert a proper share of the income. In this correspondence he mentions the "domestic cross" that Euphrosyne had recently suffered, the stillbirth of a son. To the fact that Schütz was not able to visit Chemnitz in person we owe this insight into the energetic way in which the old gentleman managed his business and this indication of the former student of law. Here, too, he enjoyed the support of his patron, the elector.

The very animated series of confidential letters by Schütz to Christian Reichbrodt, Johann Georg's privy secretary, make it clear how the obstinacy of the aged elector in refusing to deal with his Kapellmeister's pressing musical problems necessarily aroused Schütz to fury and despair, which increased as the delay continued.

Schütz's direct and picturesque manner of expression is illustrated in the postscript to the first letter which referred to the biographical petition (see supra). One will recall his pithy report of September 23, 1616, concerning the runaway choir boy Bruno. Similarly, he now writes (February 29, 1651): "The lord marshal promised my pupil, the 'growler' [probably a choir boy who on account of change of voice had become a copyist], a suit of clothes on his recent arrival from Regensburg. As this has not yet been delivered, he has become impatient and threatens again to make his escape by the window through which the cows are driven to pasture. . . ." Or, as he once wrote in 1621 (No. 9): "As if, most benevolent lord secretary of the chamber, I and my colleagues in the profession did not think as much of good strings as a soldier does of a good pistol or another weapon. . . ." In

---

[65] For Schütz's notes see Müller, No. 72; for his letter to chamber secretary Berlich, No. 73, with postscript regarding Kittel's salary; for the suggestion regarding Christian Weber's appointment see Müller, pp. 364 ff; regarding Chr. Bernhard as preceptor of the choir boys, p. 374; regarding Clemens Thieme, p. 380. A *Konzert, Ich freue mich im Herrn,* and a *Magnificat,* both by Thieme, will be found in the collection of the Berlin cantor of St. Nicholas', Hermann Koch (*Singakad. Berlin*).

[66] Infra.

the letter No. 79 to Reichbrodt (11. 4. 51) Schütz even promises to live and die in Dresden; in other words, only to visit Weissenfels from time to time, if the elector supported him and his son-in-law in the Chemnitz matter, which, in fact, the elector did. Schütz also suggests that he has as good a claim to retirement as formerly M. Praetorius and R. Michael had, "both of whom, when first I came to Dresden, I still found in the electoral employ, but for both of whom I substituted, as I was still young, and, as it were, earned for them their salary. I do not, however, desire to be unoccupied; but I submit myself, while life lasts, to serve the electoral chapel *(Capell)* at all times to the best of my ability. . . ."

In the summer of the same year the pay of the musicians actually ceased. Therefore Schütz, together with Hofkonz,[67] had to appeal to the elector's son, Duke Christian, as the inspector of the chapel *(Capellinspektor)* at the time. Schütz describes "the running-about by the hour, the very great lamentation, distress, and wailing of the entire company of poor, deserted relatives of the singers and musicians, who live in such misery that it would move even a stone in the earth. Now I testify before God that their distress and their pitiful lamentation so touch my heart that I do not know how I can give them sufficient comfort and hope of any improvement." He said that rather than disgrace the elector by having to beg their bread, the musicians one and all were resolved to leave. Anyone who wished to pay their debts might then do so. Schütz begs that they be given at least a quarter of their back pay. Much more enraged, the master writes to Reichbrodt five days later that the whole music organization was in such a lamentable condition "that so far as I am concerned (disregarding the fact that even at my advanced age I might still choose a distant imperial or Hanseatic city for my last lodging place in this world), God knows that I would prefer with all my heart to be a cantor or an organist in a small town to remaining longer amid conditions in which my dear profession disgusts me and I am deprived of sustenance and of courage." He himself had finally advanced to the poor people cash in the amount of 300 *Taler* derived from "securities, portraits, and silver cups." But now he himself had reached his limit. For almost four years his musicians had received less than three quarter payments. His Austrian basso Georg Kaiser is especially badly off: "I learn that he lives like a sow in a pigsty, has no bedding, lies on straw, has pawned his coat and his jacket. His wife came to me yesterday and begged me for God's sake to render fatherly aid and help them get away.[68]. . ." Schütz's anger reaches tempestuous fury in the famous sentence: "I find it neither praiseworthy

---

[67] Nr. 80 of the 14. 8. 52.
[68] Out of this Ricarda Huch constructed a gripping scene in her novel *Der grosse Krieg*.

nor Christian that in a land so highly esteemed less than twenty musicians can or will not be supported, and I live in the most submissive hope that Your Electoral Highness will have a change of mind." In conclusion, he recommends Chr. Bernhard as his substitute, but if need be, he will agree to Hofkonz as Vice-Kapellmeister, if only he can be relieved.

In another of the further letters to Reichbrodt[69] Schütz reports that he had been ill for three weeks "on account of bodily humors (flüsse) which molested me in my head and finally took their leave from there and moved into both legs, with a resulting case of erysipelas or rose." He then returns to the bass singer who, because of necessity, had again pawned his clothes "and since then in his home has reverted to the life of a beast in the woods." The singer threatens to run away without saying goodby to his host (insalutato hospite). With delightful but grim humor the master continues: "It is a pity, a dire pity, that so splendid a voice should be lost to the ensemble (Capell). What difference does it make that his disposition makes him useless for much else and that his tongue requires daily to be moistened in the wine jug? Such a wide throat requires more moisture than many a narrow one. Even if the good fellow received his modest compensation promptly and properly, it would not suffice for large banquets. And if one properly considered this fellow's ménage and household, one should give him, as I think, his modest pittance at the right time. But as long as this does not happen, one cannot proclaim him a great spendthrift. But for my part I am through." And in a writing to the court marshal (Nr. 84, June 26, 1652) not a little bitterness springs from the heart of the aged master, "inasmuch also as all the old musicians have died, and I alone remain and find it difficult to adjust myself to the young world and the newest manner of music." In view of the lamentable financial neglect of the ensemble (Kapelle), he regrets "that I ever devoted so much diligence, toil, danger, and expense to the pursuit of music, so little understood and respected in Germany, and that I took upon myself the directorship at this electoral court." If only he might again be permitted to deal with a "happy company," he would gladly "offer my hand at all times for future arrangements and compositions."

In 1651 Johann Georg I gave his daughter, the widowed Crown Princess of Denmark, in marriage to Duke Friedrich Wilhelm of Saxony-Altenburg. On account of an intervening mourning the wedding festivities were kept within narrow bounds. Nevertheless, a small memorial of Schütz's art has come down to us in this connection: the ode "As When the Eagle Soars Aloft from His Rocky Crag," [70]

---

[69] No. 83 of May 28, 1652.
[70] (Vol. XV, 87.) Wie wenn der Adler sich aus seiner Klippe schwingt.

a poem of six stanzas by David Schirmer, which the latter published in 1663 in his collection *Poetische Rauten-Gepüsche*. To this Schütz wrote a monody in C with continuo, which with strict logic and rhythmic finesse developed an A-B *Bar*[71] from the structure of the first stanza. As Schirmer reports, the little piece with its music was sung at the electoral banquet on the day of the engagement.

For the same occasion Duke Johann Ernst of Weimar sent his court Kapellmeister Adam Drese (under whom J. S. Bach later served as court organist and substituting director of music) to Dresden to Schütz with a request for information regarding all kinds of questions. The questions on the list, still preserved,[72] include, *inter alia*, the following:

> 9. To extend greetings to Kapellmeister Schütz and to learn from him the number and names of the personnel in the electoral ensemble and music.
> 10. To learn the number and names of the personnel in the ensemble and music of the prince elector.
> 11. Who directs each performance, what instruments are used, and how many vocalists constitute each group. . .
> 12. Whether there is a very good organ builder there.
> NB. To ask Kapellmeister Schütz about these matters.

On a second Dresden journey, in 1656, Drese had in his possession a letter addressed to Heinrich Schütz which is preserved in outline. From it we quote: ". . . We would gladly and graciously learn on this occasion whether you are still well and in a tolerable condition."

The duke requests that Adam Drese be given access to the music. This was certainly granted.

October of the same year brought some sad news, which must have touched the master deeply. His nearest cousin, Heinrich Albert, had died in distant Königsberg. Schütz must have realized that of his generation he was the best master of the *Lied*. He constantly supplied Albert with "great" music from his pen,[73] and we

---

[71] See definition infra.

[72] Ad. Aber, *Pflege der Musik unter den Wettinern (The Cultivation of Music under the Wettins)* (1920), pp. 146 ff.

[73] In the preface to the sixth part of his *Arias* (1645), addressed to the Brandenburg upper-chamberlain Conrad von Burgsdorff, Albert had written: "I often observe with the greatest amazement what superb and ingenious compositions reach us from Italy, which may well be called the mother of noble music; likewise what vital and penetrating things have been written here in Germany by the highly renowed Kapellmeister Schütz, who acquired his knowledge there, especially from the excellent Johann Gabrieli. Many of his compositions (which for the most part have not yet appeared in print) he has entrusted to my hands. When I see such works, I am sometimes so overwhelmed and so fearful that I can scarcely prevail upon myself to write another song or melody lest it be interpreted by such highly experienced masters as a presumption on my part. However, inasmuch as I was not brought up in this art from my youth and did not intend to make music a profession, as is well known to many musicians, especially to the above-mentioned Herr Schütz, my dear cousin, I hope they will judge my modest melodies and whatever else I may present with good will and will view such compositions as a mere incident in my life."

can glean from the funeral address of Simon Dach how highly Schütz valued the younger colleague and dear pupil:

> How deeply will Herr Schütz be moved,
> When he shall learn that you are gone.

But Schütz also had warm sympathy for the work of other talented Germans. Thus in 1653 the Zittau Andreas Hammerschmidt[74] could preface with sixteen Alexandrines by Schütz his *Music for Chorus of Five and Six Voices in Madrigal Style*,[75] this title being apparently in imitation of Schütz's motet work of 1648.[76] With his Alexandrines Schütz declares to his most important popularizer "with good affection and friendship":

> The way has now been found,
> The road is open, and the goal in sight.

Apparently Schütz refers to "the madrigal-like nature" of the work when he acknowledged:

> 'Twas in this way I also had my choir to sing
> My Hammerschmied when I with music first began.

In other words, this is a recognition from one colleague to another; but when one compares the encomiums of the day, it is not without a trace of cool patronage.

How much warmer the two Latin couplets are with which Schütz congratulated the young Leipzig organist Werner Fabricius from Itzehoe (born 1633), a pupil of Selle and Scheidemann, when, in October 1662, Werner showed the master the manuscript of his *Geistliche Arien, Dialoge und Konzerte!*[77] Here is a somewhat free translation of the aforementioned verses:

> Ask you me, Werner, if I like your work? I say I do.
> For who could find a fault when even Phoebus praises you?
> Continue thus with sweetest songs, and they will shine afar,
> Renowned throughout the world and giving light to yonder
> Distant star.

> *(Nobilis inque solo, nobilis inque polo)*[78]

---

[74] Born in Brüx in Bohemia.
[75] *Chormusik mit 5 und 6 Stimmen auff Madrigal Manier.*
[76] Constituting the fifth part of his (Hammerschmidt's) *Musikalische Andachten.*
[77] R. Wustmann: *MG*, Leipzig, 219; E. H. Müller, p. 383.
[78] It is mentioned in the funeral sermon for Fabricius, who died at 45 years of age, in 1679, that Kapellmeister Schütz in Dresden honored him with his friendship.

We may add here the couplet that Schütz wrote on August 7, 1655, in the album
of the son of the Zittau organist Hernberger: [79]

> Opitz on Ps. 146
> God the Lord shall be my song
> Ever through my whole life long.

A certificate of approbation by Schütz — of which, however, only a fragment
has been preserved — apparently dates from the same year. In 1659 the Württemberg court Kapellmeister Samuel Capricornus [80] had to defend himself against
attacks by the local Stuttgart court organist Böddecker. In support of his ability
Capricornus cited Carissimi and Schütz. About four years previously, when he
was still cantor in Pressburg and when the *Konzerte* from his *Opus musicum* were
appearing in Nürnberg, he had sent them (through Dr. med. Zillinger) to both
Carissimi and Schütz for their approval. Carissimi presented the works with success in St. Apollinare in Rome, while Schütz wrote to the composer that "the
gentleman's good works *(opera virtuosa)* have been duly handed to me and have
delighted me greatly. May the gentleman continue thus still further to serve God
and his church." [81] One will note again that even in distant places Schütz was considered the ultimate criterion and the highest judge of his art.

As soon as the boundaries between poetry and music were involved, Schütz was
also regarded as a decisive court of appeal in literary matters. This is shown by the
letter of the master of August 11, 1653, [82] a letter dealing with matters pertaining
to the German "form of madrigal writing" and which the recipient, Caspar Ziegler
in Leipzig, was permitted to place at the head of his treatise [83] on madrigals. When
Schütz addresses him as "brother-in-law," this need not indicate any relationship,
since at the time this was a customary address of familiarity. [84] Ziegler says in the
text [85] that he had "at various times heard understanding composers, among them
Kapellmeister Herr Heinrich Schütz, well known in the world, favorably heard
and liked at the court of His Electoral Highness in Saxony," complain that they

---

[79] Thus in Ph. Spitta, loc. cit., p. 59; E. H. Müller, p. 314, writes: "Gottfried Hernberger."
Emil Vogel discovered the entry in the *Ratsbibliothek Zittau* in 1888.

[80] Born 1628 in Scharditz near Brünn, died 1665 in Stuttgart.

[81] Jos. Sittard, *Musik und Theater am Württembergischen Hofe*, I, 56.

[82] Quoted above.

[83] *Von den Madrigalen, Einer schönen und zur Musik bequemsten Art Verse (Of Madrigals,
a Beautiful and Most Suitable Kind of Verse for Music).*

[84] Just as at the present day the postillion is still frequently designated as *Schwager* (brother-
in-law) (see Schubert).

[85] Ph. Spitta: *Die Anfänge madrigalischer Dichtung in Deutschland, Musikgeschichtliche Aufsätze (The Beginnings of Madrigal Writing in Germany)*, pp. 62 ff.

could not always get on well with the German poets, because all verses were not adapted for music. Schütz fully confirms this in his letter, and he welcomes the suggestions given by Ziegler, together with the appended poetic examples.

Whether Schütz set these Ziegler poems to music is not known. Apparently, however, he did set madrigals by Ernst Stockmann (1634-1712), the first imitator along religious lines of Ziegler's poems, in which case we must again reckon such settings among Schütz's lost compositions. In the advance notice to his *The Joy of Writing Madrigals*,[86] of 1660, Stockmann relates that on numerous occasions the aged composer had exchanged letters with him and that he, at Schütz's request, had sent him some madrigals for use in church and at banquets. In his *Praise of City Life*[87] (Jena, 1683) Stockmann dedicated a madrigal to the great man himself:[88]

> "To Herr Heinrich Schütz, electoral Saxon Kapellmeister.
> As long as noble Schütz devotes
> His art to song, it will be pure;
> His music, with its silver notes,
> Unsullied, surely will endure.
> The music that they write today
> Goes piping on its worldly way,
> And though perchance it fills the ear,
> The harmony the heart would hear
> Is wholly lost. Its worthless strain
> The master's learned clavier doth disdain.
> Ah, well! Let th' noble swan
> Exalt his music linked with poetry
> In lofty choir to heav'nly harmony."

This innovation of writing madrigal texts for vocal compositions, which was welcomed by Schütz, was destined to assume the greatest importance in the history of music when Erdmann Neumeister introduced it (as a means of giving form to his rhymed prose) in operatic fashion into the libretti of the church cantatas for the secco recitatives of J. Ph. Krieger, Telemann, and particularly J. S. Bach. But one can also feel how this prosaically smooth "poetry"—so foreign to Schütz's spiritual nature — must be viewed as one of the gates through which the approaching rationalism of the eighteenth century might enter.

The death of Schütz's last daughter, Euphrosyne Pincker, on January 11, 1655, in the presence of her father, again overwhelmed the seventy-two-year-old master with deep sorrow. As stated in the printed funeral sermon,[89] she was "by nature not only of a very delicate and weak constitution but was also for a long time

---

[86] *Madrigalische Schriftlust.*
[87] *Lob des Stadtlebens.*
[88] Spitta, loc. cit., p. 47.
[89] Library of the Francke Foundations, Halle. Prof. Weiske kindly provided me with a copy.

disposed to hypochondria and scurvy *(Skorbut)* and, in addition, had sacrificed much of her strength in giving birth to her five children. Accordingly, sickness the more easily overcame her mortal vitality, humanly speaking." Three or four days after the birth of a son, who lived but a short time, she was seized by childbed fever *(der Friesel)*. Therefore she discussed the end of all things with her pastor. "With humility she took leave of her deeply moved father, her husband, and other friends present; she blessed them and comforted them in anticipation of a happy reunion in the eternal joy of the life to come. Shortly thereafter she commended her soul with fervent prayer and especially with Psalm 25[90] to the faithful hands of her Creator. God took her to Himself at one o'clock in the night without her experiencing any pain or fear — after she had lived in this world thirty-one years, five weeks, and two days."

Geier's *Köstlichste Arbeit*[91] says with regard to this sad event: "In January 1655, however, this his only daughter was carried away by death in Leipzig to the great sorrow of her father and her husband, the former having just arrived to pay her a visit. But here, too, the blessed departed one [Schütz] submitted to the will of God in the same way that he, as a gallant Christian, never exalted himself when he frequently experienced honor and good fortune, but rather let these be a spur to future Christian endeavor."

An unusually large number of sympathizers, almost fifty, sent elegies, which constitute the appendix to the funeral sermon. A number of these may well command our attention. In the Latin invitation to the student body the rector, J. Preibisch, mentions the father as

> "a most illustrious man, a musician very highly celebrated throughout all Europe, for a long time master of the electoral chapel *(capellae)*, the distinguished Dr. Heinrich Schütz, surviving the departed one not without great sorrow."[92]

Pastor Kromayer likewise expresses himself with reference to the father:

> The fatal arrow, though it reached its goal,
> To blessedness dispatched her gentle soul.
> Through ether's blue she flies on angel wings
> And in the courts of Heav'n with angels sings.
> One of the Graces verily was she,
> And rightly bore the name Euphrosyne.[93]

---

[90] "Unto Thee, O Lord, do I lift up my soul."

[91] *Most Precious Work.*

[92] *virum clarissimum Musurgum per Europam decantatissimum, Electoralis capellae a tempore multo magistrum praeclare meritum Dn. Heinricum Sagittarium pie defunctae non sine cordolio ingenti superstitem.*

[93] *Non detrimentum tamen hinc ex asse Beatae,*
quippe suum tetigit missa sagitta scopum.
Cum symphoniacis modulatur in aetheris aula
chromatice et veram se probat Euphrosynen.

The uncle, Benjamin Schütz, as well as Johannes Schütz, from Merseburg, and a Christof Georg Schütz, from France, also contributed tributes of sympathy. The poet August Buchner sent Latin verses of consolation "to the most excellent musician and our own German Orpheus, Heinrich Schütz, our true friend, who bitterly mourns his only daughter:

> As once the Thracian poet with his song
> Recalled Eurydice from Orcus' dark abode,
> Cannot thy strings, surpassing Orpheus, sound
> Thy sweetest song for deafened ears to hear? [94]

Schütz's colleague Bontempi adds a beautiful madrigal poem:

> This noble grace from heaven descended,
> To live on earth. [95]

The imperial poet Bohemus also turns to the grieving master whom all Europe knows:

> ... who contests the palm even with the Sirens themselves,
> whom Italy and France admire in awe,
> whom Denmark loves. By far the most famous Orpheus of
> the Saxon court, known in east and west. [96]

No less from the heart speaks the Dresden associate rector Benj. Stolbergius:

> Schütz, famous Amphion of our day,
> Whose melodies are sung both far and wide,
> E'en moving kings' and princes' hearts,
> He sorrows now, his face bedewed with tears.
> O sad calamity! Who will forbid the bard to weep
> Midst fate's hard blows and crosses manifold? [97]

Indeed, one could well speak of the aged man who "had experienced so many blows of fate and so many crosses." Christof Bernhard, Caspar Ziegler, Vice-Kapellmeister J. G. Hofkonz, C. Chr. Dedekind, Chr. Kaldenbach, and Joh.

---

[94] ... *Thracius Eurydicen revocavit carmine vates,*
atque Orci e mediis eripuit tenebris:
tu licet intendas numeros, quibus Orphea transis,
tu tamen hoc surdis auribus omne canes.

[95] *Scese dal cielo ad habitare in terra*
questa gratia gentile...

[96] ... *qui facit ambiguam palmam Sirenibus ipsis,*
quem stupet Italia et Gallia, Dania amat.
Orpheus Saxonicae longe celeberrimus aulae,
notus in Eois Hesperiisque plagis...

[97] *Schützius, Amphion nostri ille inclytus aevi,*
Musicus Harmonicis notus ubique modis,
Corda quibus regum solitus mulcere Ducumque
Nunc dolet et largis fletibus ora rigat.
O tristem casum quis jam plorare vetaret,
Hunc dira expertum fata crucesque Senem?

Georg Schoch rounded out the circle of the mourners. The funeral poem of the Weissenfels rector Albinus may be found in the researches of A. Werner, in the archives of Weissenfels and Zeitz.

But again this lonely man, now in his seventieth year, had little time to meditate on his personal sorrow. Dresden, Wolfenbüttel, and other courts demanded anew the counsel of this highly experienced and indispensable adviser. First of all, in order to brighten the scene of mourning, we may note his very happy relations with the Duke and Duchess of Wolfenbüttel. This Guelph duchess of the family of the Obotrites (aus Obotritengeschlecht), who was Schütz's pupil, initiated many festival plays during the decade from 1645 to 1655. No further letters have been preserved from this period. From such plays we may conclude that a goodly number of capable musicians were available.

From the Brunswick-Wolfenbüttel repertoire G. F. Schmidt[98] enumerated some thirty theatrical works between 1642 and 1665, the principal poet-author of which was, until 1656, Justus Georg Schottelius — later Duke Anton Ulrich. Chrysander's praise of the extant Joyful Felicitation[99] by Duchess Sophie Elisabeth (1655) would seem to be too meager. Pieces like the introductions to the spring, summer, fall, and winter sections are so excellent in structure and so well outlined in their emotional expression that B. Engelke[100] is inclined to claim them as well as the final chorus, which proceeds mostly in groups of duets, as the work of Schütz. Were this surmise correct, we would have recovered here the only surviving theatrical music by Schütz. But enticing though the thought is, the fact that the duchess has mentioned herself as the composer surely allows no further assumption than that Schütz's hand helped to polish them. As to this, we refer to the extensive musical supplements to the promised Engelke publication.

When it came to engaging musicians for the performance of her stage play, Sophie Elisabeth seems repeatedly to have requested the help of her great teacher. Schütz's reply of June 12 has been lost, but on June 22, 1655, the duchess discusses the lost letter with her characteristic vivacity:[101] There had been correspondence with "the well-known bass in Kassel"; but if the one suggested by Schütz was also "competent as an instrumentalist," all the better. In such case "a rotation would not be inexpedient." They were also looking forward to the prospective falsetto singer. Schütz answered on July 24 with manifest good

---

[98] Neue Beiträge (New Contributions), Munich, 1929.
[99] Glückwünschende Freudendarstellung. Literally, Felicitational Presentation of Joy.
[100] Geschichte der Musik am Gottorper Hof, II (History of Music at the Court of Gottorp).
[101] Fr. Chrysander, Mus. Jahrbücher, I, 161.

humor that he had started "on the march" his pupil Loewe,[102] as the suggested Kapellmeister, together with several discant singers. Schütz writes very picturesquely about his protégé: "This Johann Jacob Loewe, concerning whom I have written to Your Grace's husband, is an upright, honorable man in whom I never discovered any notable fault as long as he lived with me. Moreover, he has fresh Austrian humor and manners, likes to have all things in his own determined way, which causes me to worry a little, lest perhaps he work the boys too hard[103] and they then complain about him, or, as they intimated to some persons before their departure, run away. To avoid such trouble, it would be my wish that Your Grace, the Princess, if I may respectfully advance the suggestion, might take the matter somewhat under your gracious protection and occasionally allow them access to present their problems themselves." What a judge of people!

Or, as Chrysander writes so beautifully in this connection: "All the well-meaning solicitude, justice toward all, considerateness, understanding, humorous candor toward the nobility, and quiet guidance of complicated and disturbing matters toward harmonious co-operation — all these outstanding qualities in the character of the noble man are revealed by this one letter. From such conduct we can also understand the great and beneficent influence Schütz exerted on his contemporaries."

In this connection the postscript is especially characteristic. Schütz asks the duchess to remind her husband of his appointment as Kapellmeister *in absentia*[104] and of the attendant emoluments. And now what a strange transition from frivolity to deep seriousness —!

"Your Grace the Princess will recall that 100 gold gulden" (!) "were promised me. I shall still be humbly content to accept them, and — mindful of the old German saying that while, to be sure, one should enjoy great men, one should not starve

---

[102] He was born in 1628 in Vienna, where his father was Saxon ambassador. The family came from Eisenach. He was recommended to Schütz as a pupil from Vienna in 1652 (Eitner's *Qu. L.,* VI, 205).

[103] I. e., "to practice with them too ambitiously." A. Pirro, *Schütz,* p. 139. Footnote 1 presents an abundant list of side lights: "According to a remark of Seth Calvisius, the choir boys were forced along with words and blows *(verbis et verberibus)* and were everywhere roughly handled. In 1625 the Kapellmeister of Dole was accused of having thrashed one of his pupils to death; in 1564 the Kapellmeister at S. Marc in Bar-le-Duc punished one of the boys until he drew blood; in 1608 the little choir boys at Notre Dame in Paris aroused the sympathy of the traveler Th. Coryate. One also at times entertained the fear that the teacher loved his pupils 'too intensely' — cf. the *Diary* of the Canon Pepin (1586) at the Ste. Chap. in Dijon, and Rosenmüller's departure from Leipzig." One may further recall Pinello, who in 1584 was dismissed from his position as court Kapellmeister in Dresden because during the service he had threatened one of the choir boys with a dagger (my *Gesch. d. dt. Musik, I,* 476).

[104] *Kapellmeister von Haus aus.*

them — I could even be content to have the sum reduced to 100 *Thaler.* In this case, however, I would add a request that the matter be so arranged that one half, that is fifty *Thaler,* be paid at Easter, another half at Michaelmas, annually at the time of the two Leipzig fairs, the first payment to be made at Michaelmas. I make the request especially because, as director Löwe can testify, I am very hard pressed because of the funeral expenses connected with the burial of my late daughter in Leipzig." The Duke straightway raised his stipend from 100 to 150 *Thaler.*

Another letter of Schütz, of October 30, has been lost. The princess replied to this on November 10, 1655, that she and her husband were satisfied with Löwe. Schütz replied on the 27th that now he was also sending a theorbo player who was at the same time "a fairly good poet, showing considerable good invention, who recites his poetry and afterwards sings to his theorbo; something that fits in well at a court banquet and offers a pleasing variety to the other music." This is rather enlightening with regard to the prevailing practice of the thorough-bass monodists with literary ambitions! In other words, we have a phenomenon between the flourishing type of the court minstrel Gabriel Voigtländer and the type of Nauwach or Kittel. Unfortunately, we do not know who this many-sided artist was; he was also a falsetto singer and a painter. On January 2, 1656, the duchess again appears to be in accord with all of Schütz's suggestions, and she assures him that he will always receive his stipend punctually.

To be sure, her final promise often fell short of fulfillment. Schütz himself was in Wolfenbüttel at Easter 1660, not the least of his objects being to collect his over-due compensation. Through a receipt of May 21, 1663, for two years arrears in salary we know that Schütz then visited the warm baths at Teplitz.[105] At Easter 1665 he then again drew two years' salary in one — which was probably his last compensation from the Guelph court. But two letters of the master to the duke himself have been preserved. The first, of April 10, 1661, is sealed with a ring which Schütz had apparently received on the visit during the preceding year. Its essential function was to accompany the last edition of the *Becker Psalms,* which had just appeared. Schütz says that he had to remain in Dresden for nine months in connection with this revision. This was an exacting demand on the seventy-six-year-old master, who would so much rather have worked in Weissenfels, and doubtless it is an explanation for the somewhat strange preface to the psalm edition, which will be discussed later.[106]

---

[105] Schütz was probably in the entourage of Electress Magdelene Sybille, who annually spent at least four weeks here, arriving in the beginning of May with a large retinue (Pirro, p. 146).
[106] See infra.

More important is Schütz's letter of January 10, 1664, from Leipzig in which he notifies the duke that, as promised, he had now sent his complete printed works to the Wolfenbüttel court secretary through his friend, the Brunswick merchant Stephan Daniel. These are the copies, to a large extent preserved today, which, on account of the master's own revisions, contain so many valuable improvements. He is also sending them to the duke, as the founder of the library, doubtless to safeguard them as a record; at the same time he whets the appetite of the prince as a collector by leading him to expect still better music manuscripts:

"And first of all, I must express to Your Highness the Prince most humbly my heartiest thanks for having graciously shown my modest work the honor and high indulgence of granting it a little space in your library, which is most highly famed throughout all Europe. Wherefore I also had occasion to wish that I might have sent along the further works still remaining in my hands and copied with my pen — works which I consider better than those previously completed. You will doubtless receive them at a later time. I would have proceeded with the publication of these had I not lacked the necessary funds, or had I been able to use for this purpose, as I intended, Your Highness' salary or gratuities. I was, however, hindered from carrying out my intention on account of my otherwise frugal income. Therefore I had to resort to the aforementioned emoluments for my precarious livelihood."

When one recalls that under the really lavish Joh. Georg II Schütz was then receiving an 800-*Thaler* pension annually, in addition to other perquisites and presumably also other honoraria, as, for example, from Zeitz, one is tempted to assume that as a clever businessman[107] — or as the result of the well-known anxiety of old age with regard to security — he did not wish to give over the manuscripts without special compensation. Apparently the duke took the hint. We owe to this fact the preservation of the older form of the manuscript of the *St. John Passion* of 1664 in Wolfenbüttel.

However, this relation also waned in the same measure as Schütz himself became more and more "estranged from the world." In 1663 J. J. Löwe left Wolfenbüttel to move to Zeitz as Kapellmeister, where, to be sure, he did not get along especially well with his associate Clemens Thieme, a pupil of Schütz. In consequence, he went to Lüneburg in 1682 as organist, and here he doubtless spoke with a prefect at St. Michael's, Johann Sebastian Bach, about the patriarch Schütz.

---

[107] Thus Schütz had loaned the town of Erfurt a considerable sum. The balance of 120 *Thaler* was repaid only in 1657, on account of the "prevailing coinage confusion." In connection with this adjustment Benj. Schütz and a number of Erfurters visited the master in Dresden (information kindly supplied by Dr. E. Reinhardt).

This excellent man died in September 1703. As early as 1658 he is of importance in the history of music on account of his suites with their introductory sinfonias. He is also known to our domestic chamber musicians through the reprint of his *New Arias and Ritornelles*[108] of 1682 in Nagel's Archiv. Schütz wrote a commendation of Löwe's *Canons on M. Kempe's Festival and Moral Songs*,[109] which are still undiscovered. He addresses him as a "noble, constant, thoughtful, and especially much loved son and friend." He mentions in the preface "that he had acquired his knowledge and skill as well in 'theory' as in 'practice' with distinguished virtuosi at the imperial court in Vienna and at the courts of other princes."[110] Löwe wrote at least two early German operas for Wolfenbüttel. But with his departure the German operettas came to a standstill. Duke August died in 1666 at the advanced age of eighty-eight years. The duchess died at Lüchow in the year 1676.

In contrast to this idyllic and artistically fruitful relation of kindred spirits the circumstances in Dresden with which Schütz had to contend during the last years of Johann Georg I became more and more unpleasant for the master. This was not merely because of his constantly reiterated but disregarded wishes for retirement but principally now on account of the increasing tension resulting from the differences in nationality and in age between Schütz and the members of the ensemble *(Kapelle)* of the electoral prince, who were for the most part Italians.[111]

The battle blazed forth in connection with the arrangement made in 1653, according to which the leadership of the church music was to alternate from Sunday to Sunday between Schütz and Bontempi. Someone had doubtless informed the electoral prince that Schütz had indulged in violent expressions against his Kapellmeister. In a letter of August 21, addressed to the court marshal, to court preacher Weller, and to privy secretary Reichbrodt (a letter which accompanied his renewed request of August 21 to the elector to be pensioned),[112] he mentions that he had been compelled to write to the duke "for necessary vindication in an undeserved accusation." It was for him "well-nigh humiliating and painful" that "I should regularly exchange with the prince elector's director three times younger than I,[113] and a eunuch at that, and should have to argue with

---

[108] *Neue Arien und Ritornelle.*
[109] *Kanons über M. Kempes Fest- und Tugendlieder* (Jena, 1665).
[110] J. G. Walther, *Musiklexicon* (1731), p. 368. Concerning the missing works see also A. Göhler, *Musikkataloge II*, 887, f and g.
[111] *Cide:* Mattheson, *Ehrenpforte*, pp. 18 f.
[112] E. H. Müller's Collection, Nos. 86, 87, and 88.
[113] *3 mahl jüngern als ich.* Schütz was then sixty-eight and Bontempi thirty-three, which would have made Bontempi less than half as old.

him, as it were, on the spot in the presence of listeners and judges who are for the most part ignorant inferiors." He requests that in these circumstances the Vice-Kapellmeister might act as director. Quite vehemently he concludes with the remarks: "In conclusion, so far as I am personally concerned, I must protest that, after promising practically everything but the blood from my veins, actually advancing a part of my means to suffering musicians, it will be altogether impossible for me to continue here in Dresden any longer. With regard to this place I am not merely announcing but stating positively that I would prefer death to living under such harassing conditions."

Schütz's defense to the prince elector is also preserved. In it he states that the report was spread that he, Schütz, was responsible for the engagements of so many Italian musicians — a condition which had apparently aroused patriotic resentment that, as the persons in question are Catholics, he finds himself "discredited with the honorable spiritual *ministerium,*" and he requests that the successor to the throne testify before this body as well as before the elector to his innocence in this development. All that he recalls having done was once to have mentioned casually in a petition some twenty years before that an Italian "could instil a good method" into the choir boys and the German singers. But, he says, the contrary is not true, namely, that he ever opposed "the Italian musical directorate lately established by Your Electoral Highness, even though it served more for the humiliation than for the elevation of my own and other German standing here." He complains that now "all the planets and elements are, as it were, conspiring against me and want to make war on me" and that consequently such ill feeling has arisen.

On September 21 of the same year Schütz once more enumerates (No. 89) all the reasons why he should be pensioned. Thus first "my advancing age, declining sight, and other bodily powers; for while, without boasting, I venture with the help of God to develop my compositions as steadily and as well as ever before, all this proceeds more slowly and with more difficulty than heretofore, as may easily be understood." He alone remains of the generation long since departed. "Thus also the electoral ensemble *(Capell)* has now been filled altogether with young people among whom an old man cannot well stand on his own, since the young people are disposed to seek innovations and rather to disparage than to exalt that which is old."

The following paragraph, which speaks of the master's creative plans, is revealing. When Schütz here suggests that his works will outlast him, it shows how well he understood the fundamental significance of what he had accomplished. For the number of masters whose works were still performed posthumously was very small during the current generation, which in general was concerned only with the present. By the *Psalterbüchlein Beati Lutheri* Schütz probably means Luther's prose translation of the psalms, which — doubtless as a counterpart to C. Becker's *Rhyme Psalter* — he wished to make as singable through psalm tones or chants as they are in practice today in the apostolic congretations.[114] Perhaps he had in mind also four-voiced fauxbourdon settings. He says:

"So I still have to complete some musical works which I have in mind and have already begun, through which I hope after my death to serve God, the world, and my good name, and for which, however, I absolutely need a quiet and unhampered life. Among other things, it is my intention to attempt to put into music the *Psalter-büchlein Beati Lutheri,* the version in prose, in such form that the common people may readily learn and sing such melodies in the churches." He also intended "to compose and put on paper new things" for both *Collegia musica* — that is, the electoral and the prince-electoral *collegium.*

Schütz does not desist from this protest of his against the elector's decision not to grant him leave to move to Weissenfels. On May 29, 1655, he reminds the elector that he is in the seventieth year of his life and the fortieth of his service: "My musical vein has pretty well dried up when it comes to composing many new works requiring extensive labor. My pace has become slow and heavy." Friend Hein (death) was the first to give an answer to all these petitions by laying the elector low on October 8, 1665.

This, to be sure, meant the ultimate fulfillment of Schütz's craving to work in peace; but it must also have shaken him considerably, since he was of the same age as the deceased and had shared joy and sorrow with him through more than four decades. As an elegy for him Schütz composed the noble six-voiced double motet *Lord, Now Lettest Thou Thy Servant Depart in Peace (Nunc dimittis),* which is printed in the appendix to Volume XII (p. 201). The lost first discant was supplied by H. von Herzogenberg. Anton Weck has described the obsequies in

---

[114] Whether this plan was ever carried out is as uncertain as whether Schütz is referring to the rhyme psalms, prose psalms, or some third matter when on July 24, 1655, he writes to the duchess in Wolfenbüttel: "The copyist who in Weissenfels wrote out for me Your Grace's *Little Psalm Book (Psalterbüchlein)* is counting on a further remuneration of four or five ducats at the coming Leipzig fair." Or had the duchess composed them herself by way of a rough draft? What a prominent role the psalms played at that time, both theologically and liturgically, is indicated by the festival orders. For example, when, in 1655, the centenary of the religious peace was celebrated in grand style in Dresden on Sunday (for which occasion Schütz surely supplied new music), Psalm 138 was read in place of the Epistle, Psalm 125 in place of the Gospel. Similarly on the occasion of the dedication of the Castle Church in Zeitz.

detail. Schütz apparently walked in the funeral cortege, for we read (loc. cit., p. 423): "Then, according to an old custom, the basso of the court ensemble *(Hoff-Capella)* followed with the crucifix; then 200 pupils and thirty of the clergy; after these all the servants of the ensemble *(Capell-Bediente),* a tympanist, and twelve trumpeters." Weller preached on Rom. 14: 8: "For whether we live, we live unto the Lord; and whether we die, we die unto the Lord." In his festival, penitential, and thanksgiving hymns of 1658[115] A. Hammerschmidt published a setting of *Meinen Jesum lass ich nicht* as "the motto and last word of Duke Joh. Georg I."

The new elector[116] finally allowed the old master, whom he highly respected, to move to Weissenfels to his sister's. Accordingly, Schütz sold his Dresden house in 1657 and thereafter rented the house in which he died. He resided in the latter only when he had service at court. Such service was by no means spared him altogether, but it was lightened for him with every possible consideration. Thus, as already mentioned, he had to spend nine months in Dresden while supervising the new edition of the *Becker Psalter.* When, in 1662, in connection with the wedding of Margrave Christian Ernst of Bayreuth and Erdmuthe Sophie of Saxony, we read: "Splendid Italian and German music — beautiful music performed for some time" — we may assume that Schütz co-operated; for we meet him shortly thereafter in Leipzig. We assume, too, that he assisted at the marriage of the electoral prince Joh. Georg III with a Danish princess. We do not know whether the very aged master was again pressed into service in 1671 when the Darmstadt sister of the elector, Sophie Eleonore (at whose wedding in 1627 *Daphne* had been performed), was buried from the *Sophienkirche* in Dresden with "organ, singing, and figural music *(Figurieren).*"

But we read in the records[117] of 1658 that Schütz, who was to be summoned three or four times a year from Weissenfels for music, is each time to have two horses for the coach from stage to stage to Dresden. In 1663 he is assigned 200 gulden from the Merseburg taxes — doubtless as a nonrecurring gratuity. In 1666 he is compelled to turn to the elector three times with requests and complaints (Nos. 112-14), since the president of the chamber, v. Haugwitz, so often away, had neglected to give the necessary orders for payments. But Schütz received what was

---

[115] *Fest-, Buss-, und Danklieder.*

[116] He was so musical that in connection with the celebration of the peace in 1679 he had his own composition of the Latin text of Psalm 117, with trumpets and tympani, performed at the vesper service on the 20th Sunday after Trinity (J. G. Walther, *Musiklexikon).* The State Library in Berlin possesses as Ms. 8930, Score No. 15, under Giovanni Giorgio Secondo a *ciacona Laudate dominum* in cantata form. The same is also to be found in *Musiksammlung* (Music Collection), Dresden, D 7, I.

[117] Loc. 8297, p. 25. Information kindly rendered by Dr. R. Engländer.

due him, and indeed in 1669 he was presented with a gilded beaker as "a memorial of grace" — doubtless in remembrance of his fifty-five years of service.[118]

Truly different cultural conditions now prevailed in Dresden from those of 1651, when the basso "lived like a beast in the woods." Fürstenau (Beiträge, p. 92) gives a chapel budget (Capelletat) of the year 1666, according to which fifty persons are paid 25,800 Reichstaler. There were seventeen Italians as against thirty-three Germans, the former for the most part in the favored positions. We may enumerate the following prominent persons, with their salaries. Schütz's small salary is, of course, merely a pension:

Schütz, chief Kapellmeister		800 Taler[120]
Bontempi ⎫		1200 „
Albrici ⎪	Kapellmeisters	1200 „
Pallavicini ⎬		1200 „
Perandi ⎭		1200 „
Chr. Bernhard ⎫	Tenors and vice-Kapellmeisters	500 „
Novelli ⎭		800 „
David Töpfer, court cantor		300 „
Forchheim, violinist and head instrumentalist		400 „
Dedekind, concertmaster		400 „
4 sopranos, among them Melani and Sorlisi,[119]	each	800 „
J. J. Walter, violinist		600 „
P. von Westhof, trombonist		300 „
Kittel, sen. ⎫	organists	400 „
Kittel, jr. ⎭		200 „

In Dresden, as indeed in many places, the arrogance of the Italians toward their native German colleagues rose to such an extent that it constantly caused severe friction. Thus one is struck in the preceding list with how much worse Chr. Bernhard fared than the five Italian Kapellmeisters, although he was considered Schütz's most distinguished pupil and the head of the Dresden musicians. Here, too — as in the case of Kerll in Munich and Joh. Krieger in Bayreuth — this situation led to an insufferable injury,[121] so that Bernhard left, without obtaining leave, to go as cantor to his friend Weckmann in Hamburg.

On Trinity Sunday 1654 Schütz himself had made out the first voucher for the above-mentioned Christian Constantin Dedekind[122] as bass of the court ensemble

---

[118] Loc. 10441. No. 28, p. 179 (Geh. Archiv) and Loc. 8686, p. 63; information as before.

[119] It gave common offense to the Germans when the elector appointed this favorite of his to the position of "chief magistrate" and even had the eunuch married to a Dresden lady. In order to meet the resulting derision, theological authorities (Fakultäten) were compelled to give their approval. Cf. H. Delphinus, The Marriage of a Eunuch (Die Kapauner Hochzeit), Halle, 1685.

[120] From the table of honoraria in Petit.

[121] Ohnleiderlichen Torto.

[122] Born 1628 in Reinsdorf, in Anhalt.

(Hofkapelle), while Dedekind was still tax treasurer in Meissen. He then became leading German concertmaster and poet, crowned by the emperor, for whose splendid collection of songs, *Aelbianische Musenlust*,[123] Schütz wrote a favorable review on September 21, 1657, from Weissenfels (Müller, No. 100): "Now that I have given careful consideration to the music and have found that the melodies are handled artistically not merely according to the rules and methods of music[124] and are in themselves pleasing, I therefore wholeheartedly hold that the gentleman should not refrain from placing this little work in print and thus acquainting the world with it." As a matter of fact, this collection contains an abundance of charming parts,[125] and one can scarcely understand that in a second dedicatory writing Christian Bernhard from Rome felt obliged to defend his pupil against "defamers, vipers, and babblers." Dedekind himself, however, offers a song in answer to the "carpers"; he turns against the evil-tongued Zoilus with the lines:

> Klickety klack and pickety packle,
> So your carping couplets cackle.
> Know'st thou not the master hand
> Schütz all homage render?
> Bernhard, too, is in the land.
> Wilt thou him, too, slander?[126]

Kretzschmar has aptly sketched the subsequent influence of this pleasing form of song[127] up to the time of Sperontes.

The year 1657 was an auspicious one for the German lied inasmuch as at that time there appeared the first collection of one of Schütz's highly gifted pupils — Adam Krieger, from Driesen in the Newmark. After the death of his first teacher, Samuel Scheidt (1654), he had presided over the organ at St. Thomas Church in Leipzig (which Rosenmüller had left), but having had to yield to Seb. Knüpfer in the contest for the cantorship, he entered the chapel of the prince elector as court organist in 1657 and here cordially attached himself to Schütz. While in Leipzig he had been a protégé of Christoph Pincker. For the latter's second marriage

---

[123] *Muses' Delight from The Elbe.*
[124] *Regulis und modis musicis.*
[125] Four parts are reprinted in my *Alte Meister des deutschen Liedes* (Peters; expanded new edition, 1931) to texts of Dedekind, Tscherning, and Rist; cf. also: H. Kretzschmar, *Gesch. des dt. Liedes*, pp. 89 ff.
[126] *Klipdiklapp, dipritsch diprälle,*
  So klingt dein Geritornelle.
  Kenst du nicht den Herrn im Land.
  Unsern theuren Schützen?
  Ist dir Bernhard unbekannt?
  Willst du den beschmützen?
[127] Referring to Dedekind.

(with Regine Oheim) he composed to a German translation of Cervantes' novel *Preziosa* the famous melody which we still sing in church to the hymn "Now That the Day Has Reached Its Close." [129] Schütz doubtless had known Krieger in the latter's Leipzig days. While Schütz did not write an encomium for either of the two lieder collections by the young poet-composer (as Kretzschmar erroneously states), he surely must have felt the warmest sympathy for Krieger's captivating talent, which showed itself closely akin to the style of Schütz, not only in the strophic songs with five-part string ritornelles but also in the few preserved church works.[130] If the beautiful secular cantata *Adonis Tod*, in Krieger's second collection, owes its origin to the Dresden court ballet *Diana's Affianced*[131] (as from Osthoff's investigation would seem very plausible), this would mean an increase in our all too meager treasure of early German operatic music. Certainly Schütz must have been deeply saddened by the death of this young genius in 1666, in his thirty-second year. When it was deemed desirable to supplement the posthumous second collection of 1667 in a new edition of 1676 with a few newly discovered numbers, Schütz's "chief instrumentalist," Furchheim, composed the missing ritornelles for the last ten Krieger arias. Krieger's friend David Schirmer with full justice placed him as lyricist beside Opitz, Fleming, and Rist, and in his preface extended the "thunder-free laurel" *(donnerfreien Lorbeer)* to him. Schütz had already occasionally juxtaposed large ritornelles to the song strophes (as in *Fürstliche Gnade* of 1647, Vol. XV, No. 11, p. 86). Krieger's ritornelles of 1657 also show only this trio arrangement. We meet them occasionally in Heinrich Albert. Nevertheless, Krieger endowed them with a classical stature, and since then they have been steadily imitated in the Saxon lieder school of the Schützians: in Joh. Theile's arias of 1667 as in those of Joh. Pezel of 1672. Finally — in the collections of J. Caspar Horn, the Freiberg physician, those of Joh. Krieger, Kremberg, and, above all, Philipp Erlebach — the instrumentally pervaded cantata

---

[129] *Nun sich der Tag geendet hat.* GA of the arias of 1676 in *DTD* XX (A. Heuss); from this selections by M. Seiffert in *Organum*, H. Hoffmann (Kallmeyer), and in my *Alte Meister des dt. Liedes.* Particularly regarding the edition of 1657, most of which is lost, H. Osthoff, Ad. Krieger (B & H 1929); I can add a further source to the ms. sources cited by Osthoff, p. 28—29: the clavier tabulature, *Landesbibl.*, Weimar M 8, 29 b, with the arias *Seit das der Tugend Pfad; Ihr lieben Augen, du heller Glanz; Halt ein, halt ein, ich bin schon tot; Sie liebt allein der Tugend Schein — Jugend und Tugend ist selten beisammen; Ach mein Glücke, schläfst du noch; Ich habe mir die Welt so groß gemacht; Vanitatum vanitas; Amanda, darf man dich wohl küssen; Wenn ich mein Liebchen soll beschreiben; Soll denn die Jugend meiner Zeit; So hast du liebes Kind.* The last one, *Guten Morgen, Gartenmann*, we know from Seb. Knüpfer.

[130] Two in the *Staatsbibl.* Berlin; one in the collection of Hermann Koch. Regarding the former see Schering, *Musikgeschichte Leipzigs*, II, 135 ff.

[131] *Der Dianen Verlobter.*

form emerges supreme. This indeed Schütz had anticipated in his Opitz madrigals and his German secular duets.

The year 1657 was again fruitful for Schütz's own creative activity; for twelve sacred works by the master, which dated back in part to the time of the *Cantiones sacrae,* were issued. These were published in folio (four voices and optional continuo) through Wolfgang Seyffert in Dresden by Schütz's pupil Christoph Kittel, for use in the church service and in schools. This court organist Christoph Kittel was probably a son of the lieder composer Kaspar Kittel of 1638 or of the basso Jonas Kittel. In the employment list of 1666 he was already specified as "Kittel senior." *Op. 13* is again an offering by Schütz for the general cultivation of church music, as before it the *Kleine geistliche Konzerte.* Indeed, in the title (Vol. XII, 113) these pieces are expressly designated as "for small choirs."[132]

An entry in the genealogical record of a certain Joh. Georg Fabricius *(Staatsbibl.* Berlin) shows that in 1659 Schütz again remained in the quiet family home at Weissenfels. On the left side of the page Abraham Lichtenberger of *(zu)* Stolp, 1665, entered a canon in circular form; on the right one reads in Schütz's handwriting the beginning of Psalm 118 and beneath it:

> Witnessed, Heinrich Schütz, senior Kapellmeister of His Serene Highness the Elector of Saxony. In Weissenfels, St. Bartholomew's Day, 1659.

In 1662 Schütz was living in Dresden, since we know that Caspar Förster visited him here.[133] We have already accompanied the composer on his journeys from Weissenfels to Dresden, Teplitz, and Wolfenbüttel. From 1663 on he was in Zeitz on numerous occasions. Duke Moritz of Saxony, one of the sons of Johann Georg I, who had grown up under Schütz's eyes, in this year transferred his residence as administrator of the Naumburg chapter to the neighboring town of Zeitz. There he engaged the master as adviser, to participate with the chancellor and the president of the consistory in the organization of the new court ensemble *(Hofkapelle)* and in the regulation of its activities.[134] It has already been mentioned that Schütz's pupil, J. J. Löwe, was called there from Wolfenbüttel on the recommendation of his teacher. Cl. Thieme became concertmaster, and Gottfried Kühnel was appointed court cantor. Kühnel brought along with him two choir boys from Merseburg, while two others and an alto had been trained by Schütz in Dresden. Schütz, to be sure, had suggested[135] that he be allowed to train the dis-

---

[132] *Für kleine Cantoreyen zum Chor.* This work will be discussed together with other Schütz music for boy choirs in the musical portion of this work.
[133] Mattheson, *Ehrenpforte,* p. 75.
[134] A. Werner, *Städt. u. Fürstl. Musikpflege in Zeitz* (1922), pp. 62 ff.
[135] Letter from Dresden of July 14, 1663; Müller, No. 108.

cant singers as well, since they would acquire more and better experience in the
Dresden ensemble *(Kapelle)* in two months than elsewhere in four. The duke,
however, declined the suggestion; but he was grateful for Schütz's instrumental
arrangements. The famous gamba player August Kühnel became a special attraction. In addition to him, Schmelzer's pupil Aschenbrenner later appeared as
concertmaster. Schütz made arrangements for the building of an organ, which,
however, did not turn out to his satisfaction, as the organ builder sold the duke
a used "incomplete instrument" instead of a completely new one. Above all, the
master sent compositions by a special messenger and then became rightly out-
raged when he learned that the material laboriously produced by him was not
properly entered or taken care of. He complained about this in an angry letter
to the superintendent (No. 115), for whom he drew up an instructive index indicating into what categories such a music catalog should be divided. According
to a further statement by Schütz, his *Becker Psalms* were to be introduced in the
Schloßkirche. He sent four copies of the voice books for use by the municipal
cantor and also two copies of the text only (printed in Lüneburg), because he had
noted in Dresden, Merseburg, and Halle that the listeners at court, "noble and
otherwise," [136] were bent on getting the words in order forthwith to be able to join
in the singing. As a matter of fact, these *Psalms* were used here until replaced by
the *Schemelli-Bach Castle Hymnal* (1736). The chapel order *(Capellordnung),*
issued May 7, 1664, "at the Moritzburg on the Elster," [137] purports to state
specifically what music was to be performed at the services. Unfortunately, however, this statement is not sufficiently accurate to enable one to determine without
question the titles of works by Schütz, doubtless many in number. At all events,
there may be a connection between the direction "On Christmas Day at vespers
the birth of our Lord and Savior *figuraliter*" [138] and the fact that Schütz wrote
his *Christmas Oratorio* at just about this time. From the regulations for the minor
festivals we may quote: "On Trinity Sunday, after the sermon 'To Isaiah the
Prophet This Occurred' [139] by the choir boys, and the *Te Deum* in Latin *musicaliter;* further, for the Feast of the Purification, Simeon's hymn of praise in German or Latin *musicaliter;* and for the Festival of the Visitation, the *Magnificat*"
(always after the sermon). The distinction is made between *choral* Sundays and
figural Sundays, that is, Sundays on which there was simple music and Sundays

---

[136] *Edell undt Unedell im Hoffe.*
[137] Werner, p. 67 ff.
[138] *Figuraliter* and *musicaliter* signify a polyphonic setting.
[139] *Esaiae dem Propheten das geschah.*

on which there was polyphonic music. It is instructive to place the two beside each other, as the two kinds were then doubtless in universal use:

Choral Sunday	*Figural Sunday*
Chief service:	Introit, motet, town *Kantorei*
German hymn, town *Kantorei*	Mass, court ensemble *(Hofkapelle)*
Mass, German, town *Kantorei*	After the Epistle, German hymn
Allein Gott in der Höh	After the Gospel, *Concerto*
"The Lord Bless You"	*Credo*
Collect before the altar	After the sermon, *Concerto*, ensemble
Epistle	Brief German hymn
German Hymn	Collect, benediction
Gospel	"God Be Merciful unto Us and
Concerto	Bless Us"
Credo	
(Continuation missing)	

Vespers	
German hymn	German hymn
Prayer	
Concerto, ensemble *(Capelle)*	*Concerto*, ensemble *(Capelle)*
O Jesu Christ, dich zu uns wend	*O Jesu Christ, dich zu uns wend*
After the sermon, *Magnificat*	After the sermon, *Magnificat*
German or Latin, town *Kantorei*	or *Concerto*, ensemble *(Capelle)*
A short German hymn	A short German hymn
Collect, blessing, *Benedicamus.*	Collect, blessing, *Benedicamus.*

For general practice there are such further directions as: "The Kapellmeister should send to the honorable court preacher every Sunday and on holy evenings (doubtless the preceding evenings) a list of the music. After examination he will then approve it and have it taken to the Castle Church, or he may provide otherwise. According to his pleasure, he may also present texts to which *Concerten* and motets are to be composed."

Even in ecclesiastical architecture and in matters of acoustics Schütz was called upon for advice, which he, like Bach, was competent to give. The architect had arranged the choir space of the Castle Church so awkwardly that the musicians had to stand behind pillars, which interfered with the tone. Schütz advised the duke[140] to consider "whether through some carpentry and fine cabinet work the position of both choirs could not be moved by another ell and a half into the body of the church, that is to say, insofar as this was feasible without requiring supporting pillars. Only in this way could such choirs attain their proper perfection and receive due commendation. . . . At first my suggestion had been that the two choirs be placed in front, facing each other at the two pillars of the church." Basically, therefore, for Schütz the double galleries of San Marco were still the ideal, as will be confirmed in the case of his "swan song."[141]

At the dedication of the church, for which Werner Fabricius, according to his funeral sermon, had been called in as organist, the following music was performed (Schütz himself doubtless having composed most of it):

> "'All Glory Be to God on High,'[142] begun by the town cantor in the choir and then performed with organ, cornets, trombones, and other musical instruments."[143] Introit: *Veni Sancte Spiritus*.[144] Collect, *tutti*; complete Mass *musicaliter, Capelle*; *Concerto, Capella*, on Psalm 122: "I was glad when they said unto me".[145] In place of the Gospel Psalm 100 will be read; thereupon the same psalm will be sung as a *Conzert* by the *Capella*.[146] The Creed, with the organ and instruments.[147] At the conclusion of the sermon the organist will improvise until the court preacher has descended from the pulpit and has taken his place in front of the altar beside the other clergy; thereupon the *Te Deum* will be sung immediately, with organ, joined in by all musical instruments.[148] In connection with the performance of the *Te Deum* it is to be noted that at the words 'Holy is our God,' at which the entire congregation kneels, the music is to be taken very slowly. After the *Te Deum*, a *Concert* is performed until His Electoral Highness has taken his place in the Communion stall." During the preparation of the Communion table and during the distribution of the Eucharist there will be German hymns as desired; at the conclusion "God be merciful unto us and bless us."[149]

In the spring of 1665 Schütz was again in Zeitz to assist in settling the disputes which had flamed up between Thieme and Löwe. After this his advanced age doubtless prevented him from being present; then, too, his chief task of organization — getting the court music under way — had been accomplished. Perhaps his remaining at a distance may also have been due to his displeasure because Löwe could not maintain himself in Zeitz but had to move to Jena at the end of the year.

Most important of all is the fact that even when Schütz was in his eightieth year a new period of creative activity of the highest order again began. In the

---

140 Dresden, Michaelmas, 1663, No. 109.
141 Infra.
142 *Allein Gott in der Höh sei Ehr.*
143 No longer preserved in this form.
144 Vol. XIV, 16, polychoral; as solo quartet with continuo Vol. VI, 154.
145 Polychoral, Vol. II, 54.
146 Polychoral, Vol. III, 16.
147 Chorus à 4, Vol. XII, 129.
148 German, polychoral, Vol. XVIII, 140.
149 *Gott sei uns gnädig und barmherzig.*

years 1664 to 1666 he composed the *Christmas Oratorio* and the three passions: *Matthew, Luke,* and *John.* There followed, in 1668 (?), a "new composition" of Psalm 150, subsequently lost.[150] With such creative power at his very advanced age, from which there was still to blossom forth (in the year 1671) the great concluding work, *Psalms 119 and 100,*[151] with the German *Magnificat,* all for double chorus, Schütz towers far above Haydn and Verdi, the other great "productive patriarchs" of music history.

Half-blind and almost deaf, this tireless creator, producing in Weissenfels ingeniously fresh and new types of music, reminds one of Goethe's hundred-year-old Faust, whom Dame Care *(Frau Sorge)* had breathed upon:

> The night appears to pierce now deeper, deeper still;
> Within alone a light is glowing clear and bright.
> That which I planned I hasten to fulfill;
> The Word of God alone doth work the Right. . . .
> That be fulfilled the work that He demands
> One spirit doth suffice for thousand hands.[152]

To be sure, he is still disturbed now and then by the disorder of the world around him, as when in 1666 he is obliged to ask an unnamed Dresden patron to intercede for him in connection with a Naumburg beer tax and an overdue grain apportionment, and when he thunders in Latin: "I confess by God that I can neither perform nor wish to perform a miracle here, confronted by the credulity of the modern new world, which admires nothing but what is foreign, effeminate, childish, and foolish."

He finally settles down in Dresden in the house that formerly belonged to Countess Solms and, after 1657, to the electoral counselor and tax register Beyer, *Moritzstrasse 10.* It burned down in 1760. The present building bears a memorial tablet, as does the house with the beautiful bay window, *Frauenstrasse 14,* at the *Neumarkt,* which he occupied from 1629 to 1657.

---

[150] At least this work is mentioned in connection with the peace celebration of that year.

[151] This is doubtless referred to (and not the composition of 1619) when it says concerning the dedication celebration of the renovated Dresden Castle Chapel: "1. The priest before the altar intoned Psalm 100, 'Make a joyful noise unto the Lord, all ye lands,' the choir responding (with trumpets). The composition was by the old electoral Kapellmeister Heinrich Schütz, which he composed new for this occasion" (Fürstenau in *Monatsh. f. Mg.,* III, 59).

[152] *Die Nacht scheint tiefer tief hereinzudringen,*
Allein im Innern leuchtet helles Licht.
Was ich gedacht, ich eil', es zu vollbringen,
Des Herren Wort, es gibt allein Gewicht...
Dass sich das grösste Werk vollende,
Genügt ein Geist für tausend Hände.

Finally the sage meditated on the end of his pilgrimage. Of relatives there was left only his grandchild, Frau Seydel,[153] with husband and children, living in Wurzen and Leipzig.

No formal will and testament of Schütz seems to be preserved, but we have from the master's last year a Weissenfels testamentary contract which approaches such a testament fairly closely. From an intimate point of view, it gives the finest evidence of the warmth, sincerity, and tenderness *(Innigkeit)* which still distinguish his latest compositions.[154] Ca. 1651 Schütz owned a house in the Zeitz quarter of Weissenfels, the present Loricke house. It is one of the free houses *(Freihäuser)* presented by the elector to Secretary Rost in 1552. After his sister Euphrosyne, the widow Tünzel, had married again and had moved to Eisleben, Schütz made his home here with his widowed sister Justina, who in 1613 had married the Weissenfels superintendent Antonius Thörner. The testamentary contract of January 16, 1672, says that Frau Justina, born Schütz, widow of Thörner, "has given over, in the year 1662, to her dearly beloved brother Herr Heinrich Schütz, senior Kapellmeister in Electoral Saxony, on account of the many kindnesses shown her during her sad widowhood, all her fields, meadows, and property, with retention of usufruct for the period of her life; in return for which, the Herr Kapellmeister has given to this his dear sister residence in his house in the *Niclassgasse* in Weissenfels,[155] with an allowance for her support." This contract was never presented to the authorities for ratification. In the meantime the Herr Kapellmeister had again left Weissenfels. He now declared that inasmuch as, on account of his advanced age, he could not supervise his sister's properties, he does not wish to retain them but is satisfied that they be assigned to his beloved granddaughter, Frau Gertraud Euphrosyne Seydel. For this Herr Heinrich Schütz, as well as his granddaughter, Frau Seydel, promise their sister and aunt (Justina) that during her life they will provide her with ample support and will pay her in addition

---

[153] She was married on May 18, 1670.

[154] For this hitherto unknown document, discovered by the educational counselor Dr. Keil in Magdeburg, I am indebted to the kindness of Justice Dr. E. Reinhardt.

[155] Through G. Weisse we also learn something about the location of Schütz's study in Weissenfels: that it was in the rear of the house, on the top floor, facing north, and that there he always kept before his eyes, as an inscription on the wall, the text of his funeral sermon and funeral motet:

"'Thy statutes have been my songs in the house of my pilgrimage' (Ps. 109: 54). Which is thy motto verse. / We find it written there / In thy paternal town / high up in thine own room / In which I heard thee oft, O worthy man." The reference is to a room still standing, although considerably changed, in the Loricke house in the *Nikolaistrasse,* diagonally across from the *Gasthaus zum Schützen.* I am indebted to the Counselor of Justice Jung in Weissenfels for this information and for the picture of the stately patrician house with its Renaissance gables.

100 gulden annually. If, however, the good Lord should visit her with sickness, so that the 100 gulden would not suffice for the medicines and necessary treatment, they will assure her a sufficient allowance and will at all times see to it that she will suffer no want.

In an appendix 100 gulden are bequeathed to the still surviving sister, Frau Euphrosyne Fischer, in Eisleben. On November 26, 1673, Frau Gertraud Euphrosyne Pincker, with the consent of her husband, Herr Johann Seydel of Liebenau,[156] sold the entire estate which she had inherited from her grandfather and her aunt. It consisted of twenty-two acres in fields and nineteen acres, fifty-seven rods in meadows — in other words, a very large property. The price was 1,442 gulden, eighteen groschen, and the purchaser was the electoral Saxon chamberlain of rents, Heinrich Otto Mylius. Subsequently the house passed into the possession of the court counselor von Posern.

The master left his manuscripts to the electoral chapel (Kapelle). On the basis of manuscripts, doubtless Chr. Bernhard's posthumous notes, Mattheson tells us in his Ehrenpforte of 1740[157] how Schütz had given thought to the musical part of his burial ceremonies:

> "Furthermore, in his old age — he lived more than eighty-seven years — he wrote to Christoph Bernhard in Hamburg, his one-time pupil, requesting him to compose his funeral text in the style of Palestrinian counterpoint (for S.S.A.T.B.) 'Thy statutes have been my songs in the house of my pilgrimage.'[158] He received this motet in 1670, two years before his death, and showed great pleasure over it. In his reply, he also praised the work with these words:
> "'My son, you have done me a great favor by sending me the requested motet. I would not know how to improve on a single note.' It was used at his burial. . . . Thirdly, that his compositions are present in large numbers in the Dresden musical library, among which are admired to the present day his motetto à 8, 'To Isaiah the Prophet It Occurred',[159] etc., likewise the History of the Passion and Death of our Savior, which he, despite the marked decline in his hearing, nevertheless completed."

Eitner (QL I, 746) has stated that Bernhard's setting of Herr, nun lässest du deinen Diener (Nunc Dimittis)[160] was composed for Schütz's burial. Seiffert (loc. cit., p. IX) has shown this to be erroneous. The actual funeral composition referred to above has as text Ps. 119: 54: "Thy statutes have been my songs in the house of my pilgrimage." Unfortunately, it seems to have been lost.

Martin Geier's funeral sermon tells us of the peace enjoyed by the master toward the end of his life. He stresses the fact that despite all the trials Schütz had to

---

[156] Canon in Wurzen and distinguished counselor (Ratsverwandter) in Leipzig.
[157] Reprint by M. Schnieder, p. 322.
[158] Cantabiles mihi erant justificationes tuae in loco peregrinationis meae.
[159] Jesaia dem Propheten das geschah, Luther's versification of the Sanctus.
[160] Reprint in DTD, IV, 142, ed. by M. Seiffert.

endure, including the death of his daughter, he never allowed his faith to waver:

"He did not abandon his faithful God in the midst of the misery and sadness so frequently inflicted upon him, but ever trusted Him with his whole heart and placed all his actions and purposes under the will of the Highest, not doubting that He who had inflicted the wounds would also heal them and would direct everything for the best. With this confidence he won general praise, not only in the electoral residence but also at other places, such as where he was born, where he was educated, where he lived in foreign parts, and where he applied his time usefully to studies and other praiseworthy occupations. He also gained the praiseworthy Christian reputation of always acknowledging himself to be a penitent sinner who firmly comforted himself with true faith in the merit of his Savior and Redeemer Jesus Christ. He diligently heard the Word of God, went to confession, and partook of the blessed Sacrament — for the last time on the 15th of September last. In general, he faithfully practiced the obligations of a good Christian toward his neighbors. Moreover, he treated everyone according to the requirements of his status — with respect, discretion, friendliness, and courtesy. He showed much kindness toward his friends and others in need, rendering them assistance so far as was in his power. In return, on account of his upright conduct, his keen understanding, his peculiar skill, and his simple candor, he was greatly beloved and honored, praised and esteemed, by high and low to his old age. At all times he enjoyed the favor of the elector and the prince-elector, who also, even at his death, were unwilling to leave the blessed Herr Kapellmeister unattended by their distinguished representatives, etc.

"With regard to the last illness and the final departure of the blessed deceased, his powers, and especially his hearing, had declined for a number of years, so that he went out but little and could not attend the preaching of God's Word. But though for the most part he remained at home, he devoted much of his time to the reading of Holy Scripture and the books of distinguished theologians. He also continued to compose with great diligence outstanding musical works on a number of the psalms, especially the 119th; likewise the passions according to three of the evangelists. He led a very abstemious life, yet suffered a number of attacks of rheumatism, which, however, yielded to the use of proper medicines. On November 6 last he arose, apparently fresh and healthy, and dressed himself; but after nine o'clock, when he went to look for something in his chamber, he was overcome with dizziness and a stroke, which caused him to sink helpless to the floor. And although, after his household had come and had helped him to his bed, he recovered somewhat and spoke intelligently, the stroke nevertheless affected him so seriously that he was no longer able to speak after he had uttered these words: He placed everything in God's gracious will. Although the physician was immediately summoned and applied excellent medicaments and endeavored in every way to restore strength, it was of little avail. His father confessor was also summoned to his bedside. He offered numerous prayers and quoted many passages from the Scriptures in a loud voice. Several times the patient, with a nod of the head or a motion of the hands, indicated that he retained Jesus in his heart, whereupon the father confessor bestowed on him the last blessing. He lay as if asleep until finally the breath and pulse gradually declined and then ceased. The clock had struck four when he gently and blessedly departed this life without a tremor, with the prayers and the singing of those standing about. He had been electoral Saxon Kapellmeister for fifty-seven years and had reached the age of eighty-seven years and twenty-nine days.

"The place and date of death, then, were Dresden, November 6, 1672."

As the text for his funeral sermon Schütz had asked for the fifty-fourth verse of his favorite psalm, the 119th, called "the Christian's golden ABC of the praise, the love, the power, and the value of the Word of God." The words are: "Thy statutes have been my songs in the house of my pilgrimage." Court preacher Martin Geier spoke on the text with the following outline: "The most precious work: (1) wherewith it concerns itself; (2) wherein it consists; and (3) how it is accomplished." The discourse is printed in his *Miscellaneous Sermons* (pp. 137-177) and separately with Schütz's oft-cited biography, the contents of which are based partly on the accounts in Schütz's petition of 1651, in part on his oral conversations, and, for the account of his latter days, doubtless on information provided by his grand-daughter.

Concerning Schütz's funeral the court diary *(Fürstenau I,* 238) says: "The funeral service of the elector's senior Kapellmeister, Heinrich Schütz, was held in the Church of Our Lady. The elector was represented by the privy counselor von Wolfframbsdorff, and the funeral sermon was preached by the first court preacher Dr. Geyer (sic). Before and after the sermon the electoral German choir presented four compositions. The first was composed by the former vice-Kapellmeister Christoff Bernhardi, the remaining three, however — for voices and instruments — by the late Kapellmeister himself. A further piece by the master was sung by the *Kantorei* in front of the Solm house in the *Moritzstrasse* at the time of the taking up of the body." The farewell address in the Solm-Beyer house of mourning was delivered by Pastor *(diaconus magister)* Herzog.

Fritz Dietrich, in *Musik und Kirche*,[161] has given the following brief summary of Geier's sermon:[162]

"1. Schütz is a master of song. This is the title which we may confer on him from Holy Scripture. He may be compared with Chenanja, who instructed the Levites in singing. With the allusion to Chenanja's understanding the activity of Schütz as teacher is recalled. 2. Schütz's lifework was a precious occupation. It was dedicated to the praise of God. Therefore, too, it was a joyful and holy but at the same time also an arduous and endless task. 3. The object, the means, and the place of such a work are discussed on the basis of the verse chosen by the departed: 'Thy statutes have been my songs in my house.' 4. From all this there follows a justification of music. It is pleasing to God. High personages, such as emperors and dukes, have themselves joined in the singing in church. New songs have been written and introduced since the earliest times of the church. Augustine confirms this when he mentions the Ambrosian *hymnus, Veni redemptor,* in a Christmas sermon. 5. Power and consolation flow from church song. We need it on our life's journey, and especially in the hour of death. The angels, the heavenly musicians, are not far distant from the house in which the statutes of God are sung. Two hymn stanzas constitute the conclusion. What strikes us in this sermon today is the fact that the person of the departed is in no wise the central theme but is only the

---

[161] *Music and the Church.*
[162] One will also find there longer extracts from the sermon.

occasion, so to speak, for telling how a man like Schütz served his God. Ultimately the sermon speaks not merely of Schütz, nor of music alone, but of the connections which lead from Schütz to music and from this to things divine."

When the body was lifted in the house of mourning, Master Herzog concluded with the words: "Now you noble musicians, you virtuosi and faithful followers of this venerable old man, surround and accompany with tears the body of the blessed Herr Kapellmeister to his final resting place. Render now most movingly, according to the most gracious electoral decree, at his burial the music which has been chosen, and know that while he is thereby shown his final honors, yours will thereby increase and will make you the more beloved among high and low. Amen."

Copies of the special edition of the Geier sermon with the biographical sketch have apparently been preserved only in Stolberg and Wernigerode (now *Landesbibliothek,* Dresden). It has as its frontispiece the well-known black-and-white portrait which apparently was made from the superb oil painting[163] (probably belonging to the son-in-law Pinckert). Beneath it is his epitaph, hereafter described. There are appended poems by Dr. Georg Lehmann, superintendent, Leipzig; M. Joh. Bohemus, rector, *poeta laur.* (Latin); M. Joh. Aug. Egenolf, co-rector (Latin); David Toepffer, court cantor, Dresden (Latin); Jakob Beutel, cantor (Latin); Isaak Starck, Coll. III, Dresden (Latin); Andr. Kraut, Coll. V, *poeta laur.,* Dresden (Latin); Simon Vetter, Coll. VI, Dresden (Latin); David Schirmer, librarian, Dresden; M. Georg Weiss (e), pastor in Mutzschen.[164]

According to his wish, Schütz was buried in the outer hall of the old *Frauenkirche,* beside his wife, who had preceded him in death by forty-seven years. As we learn from Joh. Gottfried Michaelis' *Inscriptiones et Epitaphia* (Dresden, 1714, p. 82) a stately monument was erected at the expense of Johann Georg II, which, of course, disappeared when the new church was built. In Michaelis we read:

---

[163] A splendid six-color print was issued by the Bärenreiter-Verlag.

[164] It was in the spirit of the seventeenth century, as already demonstrated by Heinrich Posthumus Reuss, that Schütz himself arranged the details of his burial vault two years before his death. This is indicated in the elegy of Dedekind for which the master had arranged, apparently as a counterpart to Chr. Bernhard's motet:

The
Hearty Desire in Christ
for
Most Blessed Dissolution
of
Electoral Saxon Highly Deserving
Eldest
Kapellmeister
(Titul.)
Herr Heinrich Schütz

"From the church we pass into the hall by the entrance at the altar and find, immediately on entering, on the pavement a square tablet of black marble with the inscription:

Heinricus Schützius Seculi sui Musicus excellentissimus Electoralis Capellae Magister MDCLXXII; and in the same hall toward the south there was, above a square tablet of brass, in a wreath of rue, an open book with the inscription (Horace, *Odes,* III, 30, 7): *Vitabit Libitinam* (= "He will avoid the goddess of the dead," i. e., "He will arise"). Beneath the book is a skull; behind it two trumpets of alabaster. On the tablet is recorded:

D. V. S.

Heinricus Schützius
Assaph Christianus [165]
Exterorum Delicium, Germaniae Lumen,
Sereniss. Saxoniae Elect.
Joh. Georg I et II Capellae

Cui LVII annos praefuit
immortale decus.
Quod caducum habuit,
sub hoc monumento Electorali
munificentia extructo deposuit
Aetatis suae
Anno LXXXVII
aerae nostrae
MDCLXXII

That is: "The Christian singer of psalms, a joy for foreigners, for Germany a light, an immortal adornment of the chapel *(capellae)* of the two electors, over which he presided for fifty-seven years. That which in him was mortal he laid down beneath this monument, erected through the munificence of the elector, in the eighty-seventh year of his age, in the year 1672 of our reckoning."

Come, time! I long to go into this chamber
And there lay off mortality and all earth's woes
For all eternity. He who subdued the world
And who has triumphed gloriously over death
Will bid thee open. He will seal thee, vault,
Until on Judgment Day I fare with greeting forth.
Come, death! I wait for thee, come satisfy my longing!
For thou dost bear me hence to heavenly embrace.

At the request of the Herr Kapellmeister,
Constantin Christian Dedekind composed this.
On September 1, 1670, when
the burial place was completed.

[165] 1 Chron. 6: 31 and 39 and 15: 19: "And these are they whom David set over the service of song in the house of the Lord, after that the ark had rest. . . . And his brother Asaph, who stood on his right hand. . . . So the singers, Heman, Asaph and Ethan, were appointed to sound with cymbals of brass." Twelve psalms are attributed to him (Asaph).

The spread of Schütz's fame can be clearly traced. In 1620, a year after the *Psalms of David*, Michael Altenburg, in Erfurt, wrote a preface to the first part of his *New and Elegant Intradas for Six Voices:*[166] "For I shall not now speak concerning music at the electoral and princes' courts. It rises higher day by day, as is well proven by the glorious works of the excellent and highly endowed musicians Praetorius, Schütz, and others." In 1625 Daniel Selich of Wittenberg, court Kapellmeister in Wolfenbüttel, refers in the preface of his *New Treatise on German Concerti with Psalms*[167] not to his predecessor Praetorius but to Heinrich Schütz.

In the *Historical Description of the Noble Art of Singing and Playing*[168] of W. C. Printz (Dresden, 1690) one reads on page 136: "In this year (1623) Heinrich Schütz, the Kapellmeister of the Elector of Saxony, began to make a name for himself. He published not only motets but also artistically set *Concerten.*[169] About the year 1650 he was considered the very best German composer."

The preface with which the Nordhausen *Collegium musicum* introduced its collection of *Concerti* (Goslar, 1638) is very instructive. It puts Schütz at the head of all his German contemporaries:

> "What more are the present musicians, and especially the composers of *Concerti (Concertisten)*, than pleasant nightingales which arrived in Germany from Italy and France not many years ago and put themselves forward now and again with their charming compositions? Who does not know about Viadana, Finetti, and Poschio with what art they construct their compositions? Yes, the Germans themselves have learned this art from them, so that now some of the German nightingales surpass an Italian one. One need only hear and attend to the way in which the musically famous and experienced Schütz, Schein, Scheidt, Franck, Grimmius, Baryphonus, Trost, Heineccius, Rautenstein, Oehme, Selig, and others of their kind carry on so charming an art that one is most highly astonished at it and must imagine on hearing them that they all have the throats of nightingales."

Similarly, Heinrich Albert, in 1640, can write from distant Königsberg on the title page of the second collection of his arias: "Dedicated to the excellent and world-famous musician Heinrich Schütz. . . . his highly honored cousin." In 1650 P. Fleming had written: "When songs of Schütz resound, the Saxon's joy doth thrive."[170] A very significant statement is that of Elias Nathusius, when, in 1657, he applied for the position of cantor at St. Thomas', that he feared no other musician except Schütz, "the parent of our modern music."[171] We observed that

---

[166] *Newe und zierliche Intraden mit 6 Stimmen.*
[167] *Novum opus deutscher Konzerte mit Psalmen.*
[168] *Historische Beschreibung der Edelen Sing- und Klingkunst.*
[169] As this earliest German music historian for the most part bases his historical summaries on titles of *musicalia*, he doubtless refers to the *Cantiones sacrae* of 1625. He also mentions the "three famous S's: Schütz, Schein, Scheidt."
[170] *Wenn Schützens Lieder klingen, so wächst der Sachsen Lust.*
[171] *"parentem musicae nostrae modernae"*

the Danish crown prince praised the master as a phenomenon that did not have its equal in Europe. In his dedication of 1660 Bontempi says well and succinctly that no one could defend him against malicious criticism like Schütz, who "through keen cultivation in the art of music, through untiring work at night, by the fame gained through his merits, through labors long dedicated to the electors, was able to mount with the greatest splendor to a higher place of respect than any other." Michael Jacobi in Kiel and Lüneburg placed Schütz above all German masters.[172]

This, however, was only inside Germany. In the outside world Schütz seemed to have disappeared even during his lifetime. For when the French traveler Samuel Chappuzeau was visiting in Germany in 1669, he twice praised the Dresden court chapel *(Hofkapelle)* of Johann Georg II as the best and strongest in the whole of Germany, but beyond this he merely remarks that in it the soprano Sorlisi plays a role like that of Lully in Paris. Of Schütz there is not a word, and this three years before his death.[173]

---

[172] R. Mitjana, *Description of the Catalog of the Music Prints of the Royal Library at Upsala,* I (1911), col.
[173] A. Pirro in the *Riemann-Festschrift,* 1909, pp. 333 f.

Epilog

The German World When Schütz Died

The world into which Schütz was born was that of Cervantes and Shakespeare; that which he left; three years before Fehrbellin and eleven before the second siege of Vienna by the Turks, was that of Corneille and Racine. In the days of Schütz's boyhood and youth the Italian influence was dominant. In the days of his manhood a great wave of Netherlands culture spread through Germany. As formerly students went to Padua, now they sought learning in Leyden from Grotius, Vondel, Huygens, Boerhave. In the wide palace gardens in Dresden one wandered between beds of Haarlem tulips. In German music this movement surged through the Hanseatic organ pupils of J. P. Sweelinck, to one of whom Schütz had sent his favorite pupil, Christof Bernhard. In Schütz's old age Germany is flooded, both materially and spiritually, by the much higher wave from France.

In our master's sixty-second year his protégé, C. Chr. Dedekind, sang: "Every tailor praises clothing which is made in France," and a decade and a half earlier Moscherosch had complained in his *Gesichter Philanders von Sittewald* about the *neusüchtige Teutschlinge* — the novelty-seeking Germans — that if one could flap open their hearts, "one would find five eighths apparently French, one eighth Spanish, one eighth Italian, and the other one eighth hardly German."

In 1668 J. Jakob Becher[1] complains: "The clocks run better if they have been made by the Germans in Paris than if the same masters had made them in Augsburg, for the air of Paris improves them; their mirrors are clearer than the Venetian ones; their women's headdress, adornments, ribbons, necklaces, pearls, shoes, hosiery, even their chemises, are better when the French air has perfumed them a little (though before I would wear them, I would fumigate them with sulphur as one disinfects a letter in time of pestilence)." Such "Frenchism" was scarcely forgotten even after the devastation of the Palatinate and Baden by the hordes of Mélac, so that the great traveler Daniel Speer, cantor of Göppingen, wrote angrily

---

[1] Lamprecht, *Deutsche Geschichte*, 7, 1 (1910), p. 27.

1688:[2] "As nothing happens arbitrarily or without God's direction, so all these ench procedures may be a rod and scourge for Germany because of our sins ainst God for indulging in French glamor, garb, and other sinful hankerings for e things of that nation. Therefore as long as God wills, we must be scourged by em, but, let it be hoped, for our improvement." Or, as Friedrich von Logau grily mutters:

Deutschland bey der alten Zeit	Germany in olden days
War ein Stand der Redlichkeit,	Was a land of upright ways;
Ist jetzt worden ein Gemach,	Now it has become a place
Drinnen Laster, Schand und Schmach	Filled with vice, outrage, disgrace,
Was auch sonsten auss man fegt,	All else that is swept without
Andere Völker abgelegt.	By all other nations.

How far "Lullism" could turn musical heads is shown in the crassest manner in e case of the poor Württemberg court Kapellmeister Joh. Friedr. Magg. On ıristmas Day 1688 he, clad in a green hunter's habit and bribed by the French ıbassador, fired on the Stuttgart burghers from the ranks of the foreign pillagers[3] ·fore he took to flight with the French, and "thus, as it were, turned himself out office."

To be sure, this wave of French "civilization" did not as yet touch the master ınself; but it concerns us here insofar as, on account of the thorough change of ste, it helped delete his work from the consciousness of the nation even while he ıs still alive. Other changes in the point of view of people throughout the world ere responsible for similar effects.

After the great war the Germany which was bewailed at the time as being a ɔdern *Arabia deserta* and which Hegel called a "constitutional anarchy"[4] offered ıple opportunity for vigorous social upheavals. Most of all, the relation of the ısses to one another underwent radical changes. The fine old intimacy, when a ɔritz von Hessen and a Posthumus von Reuss sat side by side at the music desks th their musicians, had long gone by. The prince, according to the model of e despotic *Roi de Soleil* of Versailles, was windlassed to immeasurable heights. the year that Schütz died Bessel wrote in the *Smithy of Political Fortune:*[5]

---

[2] *Der durch das Schorndorffische und Göppingische Weiber-Volk geschüchterte Hahn (The oster That Was Frightened by the Women-Folk of Schorndorff and Göppingen).* Anonymous, :hout place and year.
[3] Speer, loc. cit., and Jos. Sittard, *Musik am Württembergischen Hofe* I, 65.
[4] Lamprecht, loc. cit., p. 8.
[5] *Schmiede des politischen Glücks.*

"Today the majority seek advancement through flattery, with which sweet pois
most of the courtiers are infected, and it is particularly in vogue at court."
ironic prose Father Abraham of Santa Clara laments in a similar vein. So do
Daniel Speer[6] in singable *quodlibet* lines: "In earlier times, and even in the si
teenth century, they called empty gossip 'fool's tidings'; now they call it the si
of wit *(marque d'esprit)*. It is a source of the bombast which so unfavorably chara
terizes the second half of the seventeenth century."[7] How disgusting is the tone
which Stefan Pallavicino, the son of the Dresden court Kapellmeister, address
Joh. Georg III in 1687, when presenting to him his father's opera *La Gierusalemn
liberata!*

> "I dedicate this drama to Your Electoral Highness and introduce you in it as a Maeand
> among celebrities, not only because it was he who made the journey hither from the scen
> of the Adriatic at the worshipful nod of Your Electoral Highness but also because your gre
> ancestors had a goodly share in this expedition which has here been cut short. There st
> sigh under the clods of Jerusalem those Saracens, now turned to dust, who felt their ste
> and the victories of the Christian world boast that they received the purple palms of glc
> from Your Electoral Highness' house. The Thracian experienced defeat at your hands on t
> Austrian fields when the fame of Your Electoral Highness, the preserver of the kingdom, w
> made purple with their blood. And now with the dagger of their terrible hordes this o
> hopes to conquer Hungary, that one the imperial Grecian coast. Here the pen grows dun
> to tell of the deeds of Your Electoral Highness, inasmuch as only heaven can find a wort
> page, and no youthful spirit is capable of describing superhuman deeds. In truth I have be
> altogether too bold to cover these pages to some extent with my unseasonable ink. But it h
> been done at the command of him who is my natural lord. Meanwhile I shall pay my vows
> Fortuna if she will allow your ear, accustomed to the clash of warlike metals, to hear t
> first wailing of my Muse, and I present myself as Your Electoral Highness' most submissi
> humble, and obedient servant."

From here it is but a short step to the "fine" *(schön)* words of Mattheson, a
dressed to Landgrave Ernst Ludwig of Hessen (1740): "Were God not God, wl
could better be God than our prince? To which David would reply out of yo
mouth: 'Lord, my heart is not proud' — an extraordinary statement for a prince

Similarly, there also develops the irresponsibility of the pompous *serenissin*
toward the resources of their bled countries. While in the good days before tl
war Christian II (d. 1611) kept down his total court expenses in Electoral Saxor
to 83,000 gulden, Joh. Georg I squandered 400,000, while under his son tl
amount rose to limitless heights; and this had no relation to the advance or declir
of their music, since the portion of the expenditures assigned to this was essent
ally dependent on the personal fancy of the prince.

---

[6] My *Corydon*, I, 75.
[7] Lamprecht, p. 45.

Nevertheless, this time of foreign spiritual domination was not one in which
erman culture was lacking. Quite the contrary! It was in the very time of the
aroque that each of the participating nations developed most clearly, by way
f opposition, its peculiar national style — Italy despite its *Spagnolismo*, Germany
espite its Italian-Spanish-Netherlands-French invasions: [8]

"Never was Italian art more Italian than in the period of the baroque — concerning which
Wölfflin said that its concept could be applied only to Rome — never the French more French
than with Perrault and Poussin, never the Belgian, Netherlands, Spanish more themselves
than with Rubens, Rembrandt, and the great painters of the golden century; finally, never
was German art more unreservedly the instrument of popular need and longing than at that
time when the mangling *(radebrechende)* [9] fashion of the Italians tainted architects and
painters, buried passionate dreams, and realized old and new German ideals. Beneath the
protective mantle of an apparent internationalism a European national consciousness developed
in the baroque period, just as the rights of the individual grew behind the bastions of absolute
monarchy, and as beneath the stark masque of a new 'theological century' the naturalistic
outlook on life received its philosophical foundation."

In a time so subject to foreign influence Schütz may indeed be counted as one
f the greatest representatives of a genuine Germanism, not, to be sure, as one of
ose who constantly and aggressively warned his countrymen against foreign
fluence — although we must ever remember that great summons in the preface
) the *Geistliche Chormusik* of 1648 on behalf of the old counterpoint over against
e decorative bombast of the Italian concert style. He was a true German in his
oility to assimilate within himself all the stimuli from without in order to deepen
em in his inmost being, to give them soul, and, having made them German
ithout this being apparent, to give them rebirth.

Soon after his death changes which rather directly influenced the fate of Schütz's
usic took place among the people. In the place of a self-assured aristocracy there
ose — in all but a few great imperial and Hanseatic towns — the privy counselor
r princely chamberlain who for his part aimed to be a lordly patron of numerous
rvile underlings. Everything beneath was *canaille,* and Daniel Speer became
dignant, in line with the remonstrance of Schiller's *Musicus* Miller, at how the
inisterial commissars made a "rabble" of the more simple burghers, something
r which he then had to atone by several years of imprisonment on the *Hohen-
euffen.* The result of this situation on music was that the "better families" now
onsidered themselves too aristocratic to sing in the *Kantoreien* beside the artisans
d petty merchants. Thus these ancient "homesteads" of motet and lied singing
ot only lost voices but also their status and their communal and economic strength
irtschaftliche Kraft), so that valuable music was no longer presented as a gift

[8] Hans Tietze, *The Baroque Style and the Protestant World (Der Barokstil und die protestan-
sche Welt). (Die Zeitwende* X, April, No., 1934.)
[9] To speak a language badly.

and could no longer be bought.[10] As early as 1655, it was felt necessary in th
Kantorei order in Frankenberg to remind the members: "Therefore he who ha
learned this art should not be ashamed to join the choir"; in Bitterfeld the friend
of art are accused of considering their service at funerals "as a very great disgrace"
and in Wurzen a chronicler complains at the end of the century that it is no longe
the fashion "to serve God with one's voice and other musical talents."[11] In 166⋅
in Pirna, they turned to the formation of a "genuine *chorus symphoniacus*" cor
sisting of schoolboys, because, apparently, the famous old *Kantorei* sodality ha
broken up.[12] For similar reasons it was ordained in Lunzenau in 1670: "Bot
spiritual and secular officials are requested to endeavor, by means of kindly exhor
tation and serious practical zeal, to direct those parents and artisans who hav
children gifted in music in no wise to deter their children from its practice but t
encourage them in it that the *Kantorei* may not be lacking in numbers." And i
Glauchau, in 1681, one "deliberated how in the future the *chorus musicus* might b
assisted by this society, because most of the members are unable to help with th
singing in church."[13] While up to that time even in small places bridal service
were accompanied by elaborate music, after 1666 the organist ventured to use onl
church hymns with organ accompaniment at weddings, against which the Grosser
hain *Kantorei*, for one, protested in 1694.[14] In a similar way the custom of givin

---

[10] It may be of interest to know what Schütz's printed works cost at the time. The Coldi⋅
Kantorei paid two gulden in 1620 for the *Psalms of 1619*, Vols. II & III, (Rautenstrauch, 299); ⋅
Weissenfels one paid two gulden, eighteen groschen for the *Symphoniae sacrae* II, Vol. VI
(Werner, loc. cit.); Chemnitz paid one and a half groschen for the aria *De vitae fugacitat*
Vol. XII, p. 33, (Rautenstrauch, p. 301); in Danzig one spent twelve marks for both parts of th
Kleine geistliche Konzerte, Vol. VI, (Rauschning, p. 190). The most extensive list of prices is tha
of the *Kantoreigesellschaft* in Pirna (Nagel in *MfM*, XXVIII, 158 ff.):

	Taler	Groschen
Cantiones sacrae, Vol. IV	1	12
Part I, *Kleine geistliche Konzerte*, Vol. VI		12
Part II, *Kleine geistliche Konzerte*, Vol. VI		18
Geistliche Chormusik, Vol. VIII	1	12
Symphoniae sacrae III, Vol. X	2	12

Apparently these were the official publishers' prices, which, of course, one would have ⋅
recalculate according to the very changeable purchasing power of the money at the time. As th
old Sprottau town piper Naucke jokingly said to W. C. Printz: "Before the war we had larg
notes and large money; now, however, small notes and small money." What the towns and th
princes paid to Schütz personally was often more halfway between a honorarium and a gift ⋅
appreciation.

[11] Johs. Rautenstrauch, *Luther und die Pflege der kirchlichen Musik in Sachsen* (*Luther an*
the Cultivation of Church Music in Saxony), 1907, p. 257.

[12] Rautenstrauch, p. 263.

[13] Rautenstrauch, p. 272.

[14] Rautenstrauch, pp. 285 f.

he singers a "bridal broth" was no longer observed. In Oschatz, in 1683, the
teachers request the inspector of schools, in appointing new teachers thereafter, to
look to their musical qualifications, "because the choir is already badly stripped
of helpers, and very few of those still present have voices, so that the chief burden
rests on the fellow members of the school faculty, as the others for the most part
neglect the choir for the pursuit of their livelihood." [15] What a chasm between such
a situation and the admonition of Luther: "A schoolmaster must be able to sing;
otherwise I will regard him as of no value"! On the basis of this statement unmusical teachers in the upper Palatinate were even driven from their positions at
the end of the sixteenth century. No wonder, then, that the cultivation of Schütz's
works also disappeared rapidly along with the old choir culture.

The genteel, cool, classically restrained Renaissance had warmed itself fantas-
ically to the baroque style and had become more Christian, so that the great
pedagog Amos Comenius, in his *Didactica magna* of 1632, stormed with the
violence of a medieval ascetic against the heathenish spirit of antiquity.[16] There
now appears, however, something like a tripartite division from the point of view
both of spirit and of taste: a first tendency exaggerates the superficial practice of
embellishment and the bombast of the baroque into the comic of the Eichendorff
Schreckenberger. At the end of the blind alley stands the insipid Herr von Lohenstein. A second path leads into the religious inner world, destined to assume the
most varied styles of pietistic subjectivity in P. Gerhard, Francke, Spener, Terstee-
en, and the Cherubic Wanderer (Angelus Silesius). The third incorporates itself,
as it were, in the educational ideal of the versatile man of the world, as already
represented by Balthasar Schuppius, and continues further to Leibniz, Thomasius,
and Christian Wolff. It carries great, but also many petty and unimaginative, pos-
ibilities of rationalism over into the eighteenth century. Viewed from all three
paths, Heinrich Schütz, who had been a powerful, organic entity, had become a
giant no longer quite understood. For the Lohensteinians he was a smooth
humanist; for the visionary followers of Angelus Silesius, an orthodox Lutheran;
for the followers of Thomasius, a furrowed and excited mystic. Thus from all
three directions he was a figure perhaps still viewed with great respect but nevertheless one that had been left behind. The *stylus luxurians* of Schütz, formerly the
natural focus of church music, is deemed by a new pietistic purism and asceticism
an empty series of roulades, no longer sufficiently "devotional." In the appendix

---

[15] Rautenstrauch, p. 343.
[16] Lamprecht, p. 113.

to Werckmeister's *Cribrum musicum*[17] (1700) there is a treatise by Kuhnau, *Th*
True Virtuoso and the Happy Musician,[18] based on his *Musical Quack*.[19] In para
graphs 53-54 we read:

> "Above all things, an upright *virtuosus* will aspire to employ his art for the honor an
> service of God in church. And how could he conduct his profession in a more praiseworth
> manner and with greater pleasure than by having his work heard, his voice resound, or h
> instrument play in the place where God is praised and served? In so doing he will take car
> not to appear in this holy place with any superficialities such as may be found in the theate
> or in gay company. If he is a Kapellmeister, he will avoid as much as he can the extravagar
> *(luxoriosen)* style and will oppose to it everything that is delicately touching, devout, an
> otherwise moving. He will not always obtrude with his own work but will also allow th
> inventions of other good masters to be heard and will realize that other able people are livin
> beyond the mountains. If he is a vocalist or an instrumental musician, he will adjust h
> performance in such a manner that one will hear no vulgar passagios or coloraturas or othe
> frivolous things. Such music is now and again introduced into the churches and gives offense.

All that was good at that time now gravitated toward Bach and Handel, i
whom the problems presented by the new age found their most exalted solutior
Certainly neither of these great masters was really aware of how much fruit he ha
harvested from trees which in former days the almost forgotten gardener Schüt
had wisely planted. The interval of two centuries with their manifold presents an
recent pasts had first to elapse before one descried that what rose gleaming lik
snow above romantic meadows, hills, and peaks was not a mere range of clouds bu
truly a gigantic Alpine chain with glaciers and snow-covered peaks — magnificer
and pathless, but nonetheless mightily enticing and exhilarating for the bol
mountaineer. The music of Heinrich Schütz reflects the purity of the eternal snow
but also the warmth and the dazzling light of the eternal sun. "I will lift up mir
eyes unto the hills from whence cometh my help."[20]

---

[17] *The Musical Sieve.*
[18] *Der wahre Virtuose und glückselige Musicus.*
[19] *Der musikalische Quacksalber.*
[20] Ps. 121. Schütz, *GA:* Vol. II, No. 10, p. 130. Vol. X, No. 2, p. 17.

Part Two: The Works

Introduction

The State of Music at the Time
of Schütz's Appearance

"All music without words is mere sound without meaning and hence impotent to arouse devout thoughts. When, on the other hand, divine words, so sung as to be easily comprehensible, are added, these then give the euphonious sound a devout emphasis. The music, on the other hand, gives the words a charming reverence and a reverent charm."[1]

As when one seeks to determine the position of a bright new star by relating it to a definite constellation, it would seem helpful here to relate Schütz's entry into music history to the dates of his most famous predecessors, contemporaries, and successors in the domain of art.

What, then, was the situation in 1585 — the year of his birth? The two old giants, Lassus and Palestrina, were still alive. They died, in Munich and Rome, when Schütz was nine years old. Outstanding talents had departed not long before his birth: Ivo de Vento in 1575, Jacob Meiland in 1577, the very aged Heugel in Kassel in 1584; during Schütz's childhood, the fine motettist Gregor Lange in 1587; the great Jacobus Gallus in Prague and the able Cornelius Freundt in Zwickau, both in 1591; in 1597 Friedrich Lindner, so active in introducing the Italian moderns into Nuremberg; finally, in 1599, the great madrigalist Luca Marenzio and, in Prague, the active master of the *villanella*, Jacob Regnart. When Schütz was a student at school in Kassel, the music world was moved by the death of the imperial Kapellmeister Philipp de Monte in 1603 and by that of the distinguished Leonhard Lechner in Stuttgart in 1606. Joachim a Burgk died in Mühlhausen in 1610, and as Sagittarius stood at the bier of Giovanni Gabrieli in Venice in 1612, the German music world mourned two who died much too early: Hans Leo Hassler and Johann Eccard. When we recall Melchior Vulpius (Weimar) and Seth Calvisius (Leipzig),

---

[1] Diedrich von dem Werder, *Vier und zwantzig Freuden-reiche Trost-Lieder (Twenty-four Joyous Songs of Consolation)*, Leipzig, 1653.

both of whom died in 1615, and Michael Praetorius (Wolfenbüttel) and J. P. Swee-linck (Amsterdam), both in 1621, we have a broad view of the departing generation.

Next let us take the births of Schütz's contemporaries. Hassler and Gregor Aichinger had come upon the stage of life in 1564. The mighty Cl. Monteverdi, of Cremona, and Chr. Demantius — both born in the same year — were but three years younger. Michael Praetorius was born in 1571. Chr. Erbach and Melch. Franck appeared in 1573, as did also the lesser lights Stobaeus and J. Jeep. The year 1583 (two years before Schütz) brought forth Frescobaldi. P. Siefert and J. H. Schein were one year younger than Schütz. Samuel Scheidt was born in Halle in 1587. In 1590 the Hamburg musician J. Schop and the Swabian Ulr. Steigleder first saw the light of day. In the next three years J. Staden, M. Schildt, and Tob. Michael began their life pilgrimage; before the turn of the century there were H. Scheidemann, Joh. Crüger, Th. Selle, and Jakob Praetorius. Heinrich Albert, Schütz's cousin, and the latter's South German spiritual pupil, Er. Kindermann, were both twenty years younger than Schütz. When Schütz began his work in Dresden (in 1615), Heinrich Bach and J. J. Froberger were in the cradle. Schütz's pupils Rosenmüller and Weckmann belong to the years 1620 and 1621.

Let us add some important new music publications to the dates of Schütz's first works, also some references to migrations of musicians. In 1585 Lechner went to Stuttgart. When Schütz was five years of age, Hassler's first work, the Italian *Canzonettes* of 1590, appeared; in the next year his excellent collection called *Cantiones sacrae* was issued. The Masses of Stadelmayr were a novelty in 1593. The next year Calvisius entered upon his duties as cantor at St. Thomas in Leipzig, and Peri's *Dafne* appeared in Florence as the world's first opera. In 1595 Demantius began his activity. The year 1596 was especially eventful. In Italy it produced the *Amfiparnasso* of Or. Vecchi; in Germany, the famous Gröningen Congress of Organists. On the part of the Hasslers, Hans Leo published the *Neue deutsche Gesänge* and the *Madrigals;* his brother Caspar, the *Sacrae sinfoniae* with similar Italianizing tendency. Cavalieri's first oratorio opened the new century. In 1601 the world was given Hassler's *Lustgarten* and Caccini's *Nuove musiche.* In the next year appeared Viadana's *Concerti ecclesiastici;* two years later Monteverdi contended with Artusi, while Cantor Bodenschatz published the extensive *Florilegium portense.*

1604 was a year of migrations. Hassler moved to Ulm; Demantius, to Freiberg; J. Eccard, from Königsberg to Berlin. In the following year the twenty-year-old Schütz could eagerly peruse the first volume of the *Musae Sioniae* of Mich. Praetorius, while Samuel Scheidt, in Halle, took up his knapsack to make his way to

Sweelinck, the great teacher of organists at Amsterdam. When Schütz was thinking of matriculating at the University of Marburg, Monteverdi's *Orfeo* was performed in Mantua; Gregor Aichinger had the first German thorough-bass part printed in Ingolstadt; Hassler published in Nuremberg his *Choräle fugweise;* people sang in Altorf from Jeep's new *Studentengärtlein* and in Greifswald from the *Centuria* of Dulichius. In the three or four years of Schütz's studies in Venice his fatherland was not without musical activity. Hassler moved to Dresden and published his *Choräle simpliciter;* Landgrave Moritz, his *Psalms;* Schein, his *Cymbalum Sionium* and *Venuskränzlein;* Demantius, the *Convivia* and the *Corona harmonica;* Schadaeus, his *Promptuarium;* Peurl, his *Variation Suites;* and M. Praetorius, his *Terpsichore.* Andr. Hammerschmidt and Wolfgang Ebner were still in their swaddling clothes. In the year when Schütz went to Dresden for the first time, B. Gesius wrote a splendid *St. Matthew Passion;* Th. Walliser, in Strassburg, composed his Christmas songs; and Henning Dedekind, his *Studentenlust.*

Even though limited to but a small number of the able composers of the day, the recital of these names and works presents a very imposing view of music as Germany then saw it. While the mere number of composers and music publications (which, for example, are almost overwhelming in the field of the madrigal) gives the impression of a period of a high artistic fruition, an appraisal of the substance of the compositions adds still more to this conviction. Viewed at large, one must go so far as to say that Schütz was born into one of the most brilliant periods of occidental music. He and Monteverdi added the glow of sunset to this bright day. It was a tragic feature of Schütz's career that he was to live almost too long — for decades after the music world about him had sunk into mediocrity and into one of those interim periods during which the world gathers breath for a vigorous new start. Of course, this was not a tragedy in the gloomy sense of the word, like that of an inglorious and long-forgotten composer of a former day, such as the later Viennese operetta composer Ferdinand Kauer, who outlived his reputation by a whole generation and ended his career as a viola player in a small theater. With Schütz there was the bitter consciousness of loneliness. He became an aged witness of great days that had passed. He was an awe-inspiring leader who commanded respect but was separated from his contemporaries by a veritable chasm. His loneliness was mitigated only by the knowledge that he had sown nearly all the seeds he saw still growing vigorously about him, and by the consciousness that only from his tireless and continued work would new power arise for the final assault by a future Bach and Handel on the Alpine summits then appearing on the horizon.

Three times Schütz received powerful incentives from without: ca. 1599, from the court in Kassel; in 1609, from the group gathered about Gabrieli; in 1629, through his visit with Monteverdi. Meanwhile, in 1619, his *Psalms of David* had given his German colleagues the first mighty stimulus. From then on he went steadily forward.

It would be possible to construct a further "group rhythm" based on the years in which his principal works appeared, but we shall leave this to the "theory of generation."[2] At all events, a golden glow must have pervaded the thoughts of the master as he grew old in the consciousness that he had spent his youth in an infinitely rich and beautiful culture. Schütz was too creative to whine over the *mutatio rerum* in the world about him. Such a prophetic genius as he was must surely have sensed the breeze which would spring up in the morning. It has recently been said (as by Dehio) that the great German masters of every period have always stood between the mountains of achievement in the matter of style, never on the summits of those mountains. In the century of Wallenstein and Seni our venerable wizard of world music must have looked on his last years as spent in the profound stillness of an observatory at night, or perhaps he received them even as a gracious punishment from God.

Thus, after an exceedingly rich harvest of achievement, Schütz's journey through life takes place during a period of vigorous breaking-off and breaking-away as well as of a no less energetic start on the way toward goals which, at the time, were, for the most part, unrecognized. To arrive at an understanding of his musico-historical mission, it is necessary to view this change from Germany as the observation post, even though Italy may have been the more decisive battleground.

Since about 1435 — exactly a century and a half before Schütz's birth — a more important German figural music (florid counterpoint) can be established. We might set up approximately the following chain of generations, based on the leading personalities or circles of those participating in the activity:

I.   1435-65: the Regensburg school of St. Emmeram and the Paumann circle at Nuremberg.

II.   1465-95: the Trent masters and circle of the Buxheimer *Orgelbuch*.

III. 1495-1525: the circle about Maximilian I and Frederick the Wise: Adam v. Fulda, Heinr. Finck, Isaac, Hofhaimer, Stoltzer.

---

[2] *Generationstheorie.*

IV. 1525-55: the early Protestants (Johs. Walter, S. Dietrich, M. Agricola); Senfl, Sporer, Heidelberg *Liederschule*.

V. 1555-85: the time of Lassus; the German villanellists (Regnart, Scandello).

VI. 1585-1610: Eccard, L. Schröter, Lechner, Hassler; the German-Venetian motettists.

VII. From 1610: the German composers of *Konzerte:* M. Praetorius and the three great S's: Schütz, Schein, Scheidt.

This very imposing development was, however, both furthered and hampered by strong and continued pressure on German musicians on the part of those from abroad: in the first period through the Burgundian school of Dufay and Binchois; in the second through the international influence of the English group (Dunstable, Bedingham, Power), the Italian (Ciconia, L. de Arimino, B. de Bruolis, Cornago), and the Netherlands-French (Brassart, Busnois, Comperes, Grenon, Ockeghem). Between these the Germans Driffelde, Frey, Krafft, Spiering, Tyling, and perhaps Joh. de Limburgia, have but a limited sphere of influence — this being the weak period of Frederick III's "imperial sleeping cap."[3] Nevertheless, in this second period we occasionally meet surprisingly strong, individual, and native German achievements, like the non-Dufay[4] *Salve regina* or the imposing *In Gotts Namen fahren wir,*[5] for eight voices. In the third generation Germans like Lapicida stand half in the class of Petrucci's frottolists, as Alexander Agricola stands in the Ockeghem-Obrecht circle; but Netherlanders like Isaac, Martini, and Adam Rener almost become Germans. One feels the spiritual drawing power of the *Last Knight.*[6] The fourth polyphonic "generation" — through Luther's great achievement and the expansive power of the "protesting" estates under Charles V — was the freest from foreign influence. This group could hold its own against the imperial chapels *(Kapelle)* under Gombert, Crequillon, and Peter Maessenus. Ludwig Senfl is the undisputed artistic head of this "generation." Altogether different is the situation in the case of the fifth "generation," which is characterized by a foreign inroad from all sides. The German masters are driven from the court ensembles *(Hofkapelle)* into the ranks of the municipal pipers. At best they are allowed to remain at the cathedral organs or as school choirmasters. Thus in Dresden, in 1524, Johs. Walter is followed by the Flemish Mathäus Le Maistre (d. 1577), Antonio Scandello from

---

[3] *Kaiserliche Schlafmütze.*
[4] K. Dezes in *Zf M W.*, X, 327 ff.
[5] *In the Name of God Do We Set Out.* In *D.T.O.* and my *Kantorei der Spätgotik (Kantoreien in the Late Gothic).*
[6] Maximilian I.

Bergamo (d. 1580), and the Genoese G. B. Pinello (d. 1587); then, after the brief interlude of the Zwickau and Annaberg cantor Georg Forster, came the Netherlander Rogier Michael (d. 1618), who was followed by Schütz. However, even under Schütz — and to the master's discomfiture — the Italians, such as Bontempi and Peranda, again prevailed.

In Munich the Senfl pupil, Ludwig Daser, was succeeded by the "Belgian Orpheus," Roland de Lassus, under whom for a while the two Guamis and G. Gabrieli and Zacconi served — perhaps also Cyprian de Rore; while at the same time Senfl's Antwerp pupil, Ivo de Vento, served in Landshut, Annibale Padovano and Johannes de Cleve in Graz, Alex. Utendal in Innsbruck, Christian Hollander in Heidelberg, the Dutchman Wessalius in Berlin, his countryman Johs. Wanning in Danzig, the Brescian A. T. Riccio in Ansbach and Königsberg. Augsburg, moreover, through Jacobus de Kerle from Ypres, became almost a second Palestrinian Rome.

At the imperial Hapsburg court in Prague and Vienna, Arnold von Bruck, thought to be the pupil of Heinrich Finck, was followed in 1545 by the Fleming Maessens, and he was followed by Jak. Vaet. From 1568 to 1603 Ph. de Monte from Malines was head Kapellmeister. Under him served Juan de Castro, J. B. Pinello, Aless. Orologio, Francois Sale, Charles Luyton, Pietro Joanelli, Gregorio Turini, Jasques Buus, J. and P. Melli, and especially the Flemish brothers Regnart, while the great "Prague-Venetian" Jac. Handl-Gallus is claimed as a Slovene. In contrast to these, Germans of high rank occupied cantor positions only in towns, among them being Joachim (Möller) a Burgk in Mühlhausen (Thuringia); Leonhard Schröter and his successor, Gallus Dressler, in Magdeburg; Wolfg. Figulus in Naumburg; David Köler in Zwickau; M. Vulpius in Weimar; Chr. Demantius in Freiberg; Seth Calvisius in Leipzig; and his pupil, Erhard Bodenschatz, in Pforta; Dulichius in Stettin; Batholomäus Gesius in Frankfurt on the Oder; Gregor Lange in Breslau; Joh. Stobaeus in Graudenz. These were posts of the second or third rank, and it was an exception when a Johs. Eccard advanced to the position of Königsberg and Berlin court Kapellmeister. Similarly in south Germany: Raselius as cantor in Regensburg; Glanner as organist in Salzburg; Mich. Tonsor in Dinkelsbühl; Jakob Meiland in Frankfurt on the Main, Celle, and Hechingen; Chr. Walliser in Strassburg. These musicians could have vied in talent with many a highly paid foreigner, but they did not attain to "great" court positions. Only two highly gifted men among them reached positions in imperial cities of the first rank and at important courts: Leonhard Lechner in Nuremberg and Stuttgart, where he died in 1606 as court Kapellmeister; and Hans Leo Hassler in Augsburg,

Ulm, Nuremberg, and, after 1608, at the Dresden court. Hassler, electoral Saxon chamber organist, died at forty-eight, while attending the coronation of the Emperor Mathias in Frankfurt on the Main in 1612.

These two, Lechner and Hassler, stand in close relation to our master in the course which their lives took. It is uncertain how much of their work Schütz consciously permitted to influence his artistic development. "Music of twenty years ago" was in those self-sufficient times already history. One did not esteem it highly as art, but at most one saved it from the flames "out of respect for the memory of the departed author's industry," as was once said in Breslau. Nevertheless, Schütz as a young man must frequently have assisted in the performance of works by both Lechner and Hassler. The most individualistic of the late works of the Faustian Lechner have all come down to us only through Kassel manuscripts — the *St. John Passion* of 1594, the *Song of Solomon* and the *Deutsche Sprüche von Leben und Tod*,[7] the last two copied in Stuttgart in 1606 shortly after Lechner's death. Schütz must have found Lechner's *Wedding Motet à 15, Laudate Dominum*, for the wedding of Johann Georg I (1604), in the chapel archives in Dresden, as well as his song *Saxoniae princeps o augustissime, salve*, preserved today only in Schwerin. In the case of such a cycle as that of the *Sprüche* it must surely have struck Schütz forcibly that here there was speaking to him the only closely related soul in the German music of the time — one who, coming from Lassus, possessed an enormous vitality in guiding his musical pen, but with this also the mystical fervor and the profound world-weariness of an intensely suffering nature. If Schütz had known Lechner's remarkable *Quid chaos*,[8] for twenty-four voices, which shows that toward the end of his life Lechner had adopted Gabrieli's orchestral technique with its telling dramatic group interludes, he would have especially admired Lechner's mastery.

Of Hassler's compositions Kassel possessed at least the *Cantiones sacrae* of 1591, the *Masses* of 1599, and, of course, the *Madrigals* of 1596, dedicated to the landgrave.

When Schütz indulged in musical get-togethers with his colleagues in Marburg in 1601, they must surely have sung, as a principal feature of their repertoire, Hassler's *Neue teutsche Gesäng* of 1596 and his *Lustgarten* of 1601. And when a year later he introduced himself to Giovanni Gabrieli, the first question asked him must surely have dealt with Gabrieli's friend Gian Leone. Schütz arrived in Dresden less than three years after the death of Hassler, who, at the time of his

---

[7] All published in the Bärenreiter-Verlag, edited by Ameln and Lippehardt.
[8] Unfortunately, without further text in the manuscript 40028 of the Berlin *Staatsbibliothek*.

death, was Dresden chamber organist and music librarian. Doubtless Schütz had access in the capital on the Elbe to the entire musical legacy of Hassler.

In this world of German music from 1586 to 1610 three principal styles vied with one another.

The first was that of the domestic German-Netherlands counterpoint, which, as developed by Isaac-Senfl-Jobst v. Brant, had reached a fine flowering in the secular song with tenor *cantus firmus*. In the domain of evangelical church music the heritage of Johannes Walter takes its place alongside this, with the church hymn and the verse motet, according to the genealogical table:

Johs. Walter

Johs. Walter, Jr.	Lorenz Schröter	Michael Schulteis	Georg Otto
	Leonhard Schröter	Mich. Praetorius	H. Schütz

With the strongest stimulation, especially from Clemens non Papa and Cl. Jannequin, the polyglot Lassus assimilated these two traditions and transmitted them to a rich circle of pupils (de Vento, Lechner, Eccard, Gosswin, etc.) among whom Eccard especially handed on to the opening seventeenth century a more conservative type. One may say that in this fundamental equalizing of all jagged individual lines, based on canon and imitation, there manifests itself the bit of latest Gothic which still flows over into Schütz and was indeed later *(Geistliche Chormusik,* 1648) developed by him to new significance.

The second stylistic center was the Roman, which today we designate briefly as the Palestrina style. From the technical point of view this *stilus gravis* is not so far removed from the conservative German style, because of the strict and common Netherlands foundation of both — in the German based more on Isaac and Obrecht, in the Roman more on Josquin. But the Roman style had passed through the Tridentine,[9] counter-Reformation purism, which shunned the world, and had already taken up into itself very much of the cool polish, the classical absolutism, of the Roman Renaissance (Rafael, Bramante). This Roman tendency found little conscious imitation in evangelical northern and central Germany. Nevertheless, it is not to be underestimated as a working ideal towering on the distant horizon. In the course of Schütz's own lifetime it canonized itself into a classical *stile antico.* We must regard as highly significant the fact that when, in 1670, Schütz asked Chr. Bernhard to write his funeral music, he requested this to be written in the Palestrinian style, not in that of Gabrieli, as he certainly would have done ca. 1620.

---

[9] Based on the decisions of the Council of Trent (1545-63).

It was the third style, however, the Venetian *stilus luxurians,* which became the great determining new experience of German musicians in the days of Schütz's childhood, but which developed very gradually — and for most German emulators with difficulty — from the motet-sequence or succession type to the monodic group type.

A brief but significant vanguard for the new fashioning of the melody was the Neapolitan *villanella,*[10] which, with the somewhat later wave of the *canzonetta,* won a determining influence on the compact, chordal style of Schütz's *Opitz Madrigals* with its parallel thirds. These little threefold double lines, with their harmonically close triadic and sixth-chord bantering, needed only to have the lowest voice transferred down to the thorough-bass region as was done in Schütz's student days,[11] and the type *Liebster, sagt in süssem Schmerzen* stands before us in its fundamental form.[12] Illustrative of this are the three-voiced *Canzonettas*[13] (Kassel), dedicated to Landgrave Moritz between 1598 and 1606 by the alto Christoph Schubhart, who was employed in Kassel and from 1612 to 1614 in Bückeburg. Here is an example of this type:

---

[10] In Germany especially the *Kurtzweilige teutsche Lieder (The Amusing German Lieder)* of Jakob Regnart (1576-77-79), reprinted in Eitner's *Publikationen,* Vol. 19. See with regard to this form my observations in *Petersjahrbuch,* 1928, pp. 54 ff.

[11] Compare the series of brochures by Willi Hermann, published by Tonger; however, with the misleading title *Deutsche Madrigale.* They contain villanellas and canzonets à 3 by M. Franck, D. Friderici, Harnisch, Brechtl, Haussmann, and Henning Dedekind.

[12] With regard to this the *Instructio pro simplicioribus* to Joh. Herm. Schein's *Musica boscareccia,* or *Waldliederlein (Little Forest Songs)* of 1621, is very significant: "Though I am fully aware that every experienced musician knows how best to use this kind of *villanella,* nevertheless I wanted to indicate something with regard to this for the less understanding. These songs of mine can be properly performed as follows: (1) All three voices, the bass and two sopranos at their natural pitch, either by solo voices or in chorus; (2) or the two sopranos or discants can be supplanted by two tenors; (3) soprano 1 may be retained as a discant, while soprano 2 is supplanted by a tenor; (4) the sopranos sing *viva voce,* while the bass is played quietly on a trombone, bassoon, or violon; (5) the soprano 1 may sing *viva voce,* while soprano 2 is played on a violin or a little flute," etc. Compare the villanellas of Marenzio (1584-87), published by Bärenreiter, edited by H. Engel.

[13] I owe the score to the kindness of Max Seiffert.

But this applies only to music on a small scale. Venetian art on a grand scale, concerning which more will be said in detail in connection with Schütz's study with Gabrieli, is based, in the first place, on the spreading-out of imposing chordal surfaces and on the use of contrasting tonal groups of varying brightness. The literature of the intermediate sizes is represented by the later madrigals of northern Italy, which depend on nerve-thrilling representations of human passions. For these madrigals, however, the same Venice remains the chief source of publication and the chief market.

While the Roman church style, under humanistic and philological leadership, limited itself to the *a cappella* form, the Venetian worked increasingly with all the magic of variously colored instrumental choirs. This constituted one more enticement to the happy participation of the German court *Kantoreien*, where the supporting instrumental accompaniment, despite apparent *a cappella* scores, had played an important part. This was doubtless true with Senfl as well as with Lassus; one need only look at the pictures and read the records. While the new multiplication of orchestral possibilities soon found in Monteverdi's *Orfeo* (Mantua, 1608) a one-time high-water mark for Italy, Michael Praetorius employed this instrumentation with inexhaustible pleasure in making clever combinations in the new "concert manner." Even a hundred years later the difference in instrumentation between Bach's *Brandenburg Concertos* and the *concerti grossi* of Corelli and Handel was to show how much more fertile was the soil which the enthusiasm of the German town pipers, delighting in their wind instruments, cultivated here over a long period than that of the seventeenth-century Italians, who adhered to their exclusive pattern of strings following vocal lines.[14]

The fashion of music composition as practiced in Venice during the High Renaissance,[15] with its ornaments and embellishments, its multiple choruses, and its emphasis on broad harmonies, found its chief German followers in Hieronymus

---

[14] The official records extensively reflect this penetration of "concert" music into Germany: in 1618 the cantor of the court school in Meissen had a controversy with the clergyman, who did not wish to tolerate having the pupils play the fiddle in connection with the German lieder (*in die deutschen Lieder gegeigt wird*). Th. Flathe, *Geschichte der Fürstenschule von S. Afra* (1879) p. 210. The Chemnitz funeral order of 1611 shows how the *Kantoreien* drew upon the town pipers. "Inasmuch as the town piper also assists the *choro musico* with his instruments, the society has consented, upon his request, that when, according to the will of God, he should die, he, too, should be accompanied by the society to his last resting place...." Rautenstrauch, p. 208.

[15] The expression "(Venetian) surface style" refers to compositions, primarily polychoral ones like many of those of Giovanni Gabrieli, in which there is no complicated intertwining of voices but in which longer (homophonic) "surfaces," resting on a common harmonic basis, determine the general picture of the composition.

Praetorius (Hamburg), Jak. Gallus (Prague), Friedr. Weissensee (Magdeburg), and especially in H. L. Hassler. In the case of Hassler we may mention in his *Sacri concentus* of 1601[16] the *Angelus at pastores ait,* for nine voices; *Psalm 46,* for ten voices, *Omnes gentes, plaudite (O Clap Your Hands, All Ye People); Psalm 8, Domine, Deus noster (O Lord, Our Lord),* for twelve voices — ravishing pieces brilliant in their effect. Their revival is still one of the great choral tasks of the future.

However, in spite of this impulsive renunciation by Venice of counterpoint as the principal feature of the musical structure, the power and importance of the melody did not become or remain permanently fused in the corporate structure of the compositions. It asserted itself in another way. Now no simple *cantus firmus* taken from the Mass any longer made sense. As a middle voice it would have been drowned irretrievably in the ocean of sound. But now the outer voices — high and low — were heard in a new way — as outlines of the pictorially blending tonal area. Perhaps one can even say that the *bel canto* instinct, so deeply embedded in the Italians, had to take this roundabout path, by way of the corporative chordal pillars, to win for itself the final "breakthrough to monody." The supremacy of the outer voices — the discant *(Generaldiskant)* and the thorough bass — is the result, together with the further rapid recession of the middle voices. The church concerto of Viadana and the solo cantata of Caccini (1601-02), with their slender-voiced structure, are to this extent legitimate heirs of the many-voiced style of Gabrieli. Nevertheless, fundamental differences exist between these representatives. For the most part Viadana still remains with the old "chain technique" of the text exegesis of the motet form, although technically he is scarcely any longer its master. Caccini, on the other hand, grasps the fundamentally new element of the monodic style, which makes it comprehensible but almost regrettable that Viadana at first exerted much more influence on the Germans than the more significant Caccini, although, to be sure, the latter did revolutionize the few ablest composers even in Germany.[17] As among the disciples of Caccini there arose from the ecclesiastical melody *(concentus)* the solo song and solo aria (along with its instrumental offspring, the solo sonata), so with the Florentine opera composers the ecclesiastical recitation *(accentus)* combines with the continuo to form the recitative. This result was doubtless reached also, to a certain extent, by the circuitous route via the polychoral psalm-*parlando* of

---

[16] Edited by J. Auer, as in *DTD-24/25.*
[17] Fr. Blume, *Das monodische Prinzip* (1926), pp. 67 and 74. Further, Ad. Adrio, *Die Anfänge des geistlichen Konzerts* (1935), pp. 96-120.

Gabrieli. Thus there arise the new domain of the expressive solo song and the new singing violin music. From the 1620's on Schütz will find here a broad field for his labors.

In this new period of the sovereignty of the outer voices the tenor *cantus firmus,* which Paul Siefert wanted to have dominant once more, must have seemed antiquated to Schütz. Wolfgang Caspar Printz, in his *Phrynis Mytilenaeus,*[18] presents the difference very clearly when he says: "When one composes a piece, one sets either the discant or the bass first. But it is more convenient to compose the discant first, next the bass, and then the tenor and the alto. The old composers set the tenor first, next the bass, then the discant, and finally the alto. . . ."

Behind the new orientation in the technique of composition and that of instrumental execution there was primarily a spiritual reorientation in the tonal world, a new music aesthetic. Josquin, who typifies the Renaissance, with his pupil and prophet Adrian Petit Coclicus, had felt the late Gothic art of the "old Netherlanders" as one based essentially on mathematical construction, and under the name *musica riservata* he had introduced a humanizing tendency in giving expression to the significance of the words which had found its first and principal field of activity in the setting of pathetic texts of lamentation.[19] Thereafter the problem of affectual music came ever more to the fore. In the case of Lassus this picturesque word exegesis had often become the determining factor in the motet. But it was in the field of the new, secular, gala *(Prunk)* madrigal that this striving for pictorial and affectual expressiveness became more pronounced with every new decade. The word "madrigalism" *(Madrigalismus)* is used to describe music's attempt, for about 150 years, even down through the Bach cantatas, to humanize, animate, and permanently relate the "I" of the composer to the "thou" of the listener by means extending all the way from pictures of movement to the symbolism of numbers.

To be sure, this early baroque music is characterized, on the one hand, by joy in the display of brilliance and power, which thus leads to the efflorescence of the psalms of praise. On the other hand, the awakening individualism allows the Scriptural understanding of the musicians to become ever more personal and subjective.[20] In the case of lesser artists the conflict between the world of great and of small things comes to be felt as an alarming chasm. The wide, inclusive point

---

[18] Dresden, 1696, I, 112.

[19] Cf. the section *Die Lamentomotette von Josquin bis Gallus* in my *Mehrstimmige Vertonung des Evangeliums* (B. & H., 1931) I, 14 ff.

[20] Fr. Blume, *Das monodische Prinzip,* pp. 51 and 54.

of view of a Schütz, a Bach, and a Handel was, however, to manifest itself in taking this small world of personal matters — which daily threatened to become more "subjective," more problematic, and thus ever more "microcosmic" — and perceiving it, encompassing it, and formulating it as a manifestation of the objective, the absolute, the macrocosmic, and, above all, the eternally divine. Perhaps in this very thing — the harmonizing of the seemingly irreconcilable antipodes, man and universe — Heinrich Schütz was the most astounding of the three.

A peculiar problem in Schütz's position in the history of music is that of nationality. Schütz personally possessed much of what Lassus called German daring *(teutsche dapfrigkeit)*. He was (also according to the Rutzian doctrine of type) in no way of an Italian cut *(Schlag)*, as were Mozart and Goethe; or, as Pastor Andr. Hirsch says in his German extract from Athanasius Kircher's *Musurgia:* "The Italians hate the Germans for the stuffy solemnity which they show in their musical style. . . . The Germans have a cold country, and thus a cold complexion and a rough voice. . . . The Italians have the superiority in music because they have the most tempered land and, therefore, also the most perfect and most tempered style, in conformity with their nature. . . . Germans like the motet style *(stylum moteticum)* and syncopations and fugues; the French like the hymnic style *(stylum hyporchematicum)*, with its skipping and dancing *(Hüpfen, Springen)*; the Italians have both." [21] Despite this, Schütz played a great part in ushering in "the Italian period of German music."

This touchingly simple-minded faith in the absolute superiority of Italian artistic taste had already enticed Albrecht Dürer southward in his search for the correct proportions of the body *(proportiones)*. It developed in the field of music, after the journeys of J. Meiland and H. L. Hassler, into the traditional pilgrimage to Venice and Rome which held our young artists in its spell up to the time of Otto Nicolai, although as early as 1647 the Nürnberger Paul Hainlein, in letters from Venice, did not find there much "of great importance." [22] Ever and again German music students felt themselves disillusioned by their visits to Italy. Schütz, however, under the magical influence of G. Gabrieli and Monteverdi, had learned to believe, in many respects, in the superiority of Italian music. He clung to this opinion in the controversy between M. Scacchi and P. Siefert,[23] although his fellow countrymen would rather have expected from him a recognition of German excellence. In the case of Schütz this attitude certainly did not reflect servility to

---

[21] Erich Katz, *Die musikalischen Stilbegriffe des 17. Jhs.* (Dissertation, Freiburg i. Br., 1926).
[22] W. Gurlitt in *Sbd. I. M. G.*, XIV, 494.
[23] Supra.

foreigners, which is so frequently found among our lackeys, but the serious conviction that a strong influx of Italian stimulus would at that very time be of the greatest service to German art. Relative to a similar situation 150 years later Romain Rolland remarked that the chimney of German music was badly "choked up." Schütz's task became the Germanization of this treasure from abroad, and he thoroughly fulfilled it.

On the other hand, Schütz always remained entirely faithful to the basic principles of Protestant German music even though at the beginning he seemed to be almost an ambassador to northern Germany of the trans-Alpine art. This is shown by his handling of the relation between word and music. The fact that he left behind no purely instrumental music, and very probably never wrote any, certainly plays a role in this problem. We recall the statement by Schütz's student colleague Diedrich von dem Werder, quoted at the beginning of this chapter. It also pointed in the direction of the interpretation of the "Word of God" as the kernel of all Christian being, under which "Word" the Augsburg Confession of 1530 had already placed all Protestant church music. Still more decisive is the attitude which Schütz took toward the "Word." Here we may well say that this differed essentially from the Tridentine humanistic view of merely understanding the text as well as from an affectual or emotional illustration of the text in the sense of the *stilus expressivus*. Schütz's fiery jolting of the hearer, his impassioned preaching of the Bible message, with sometimes almost excessive word repetitions, is more closely related to Luther than most of what the evangelical pastors and cantors had produced in the meantime. Although in the *Cantiones sacrae* of 1625 he paid fervent tribute to the mystical enthusiasm of his time, his adoption of the *stilus narrativus vel recitativus* and of Italian monody for spiritual purposes was certainly an important means of advancing from that prosaic, orthodox rigidity of the "Paper Pope" in the learned *stilus moteticus* to a fiery directness of religious experience approaching Luther. Though learned, cultured, and broad-minded in the highest degree, the consciousness of "Unless ye become as little children, ye cannot enter into the kingdom of heaven" often forced upon him the still fertile, youthful means of expression of the *nuove musiche* and impelled him, even in his old age, to bring about an astounding rejuvenation of the entire Protestant church music of his day.

With acute discrimination Hugo Riemann[24] delineated the peculiar position of Schütz:

---

[24] *Handbuch der Musikgeschichte,* II 3, p. 23.

"There is no doubt that in the creative activity of Heinrich Schütz there was to a large extent a fusion between the various new stimuli introduced from Italy and the firmly established practice of art in Germany during the preceding epoch. But precisely because of the strong influence which the Italians exerted on him one cannot say that he himself represents the transition of the musical hegemony from Italy to Germany. However, his independent assimilation of the new elements and the indisputably greater depth of his conception undoubtedly prepared the way for the emancipation of German art, since he does not merely imitate but continues and develops. The significance of his great colleagues Michael Praetorius, Joh. Herm. Schein, and Sam. Scheidt lies in their having built a broad foundation for the specifically German style of works based on the chorale, and of full-toned instrumental compositions. Schütz brings to German church music the highly significant and new leaven of free mobility by reducing the number of voices and by the variegated interchange between vocal and instrumental means, without, however, resorting to such primitive, childish stammering and to such elementary forms as are so noticeable among the Italians. Apparently Schütz at no time thought of relinquishing the achievements of the sixteenth century. Even the simplest parts of the *Kleine Geistliche Konzerte* and the *Symphoniae sacrae* do not give the impression of first attempts at walking on an unaccustomed terrain; but they are born of self-consciousness on the part of the young composer who had completely mastered the strict, imitative style of *a cappella* and double-chorus composition. . . . As Schütz was already twenty-four years old when he went to Giovanni Gabrieli in Venice, his own talent was apparently too far advanced to be carried away by the new stream without imbuing it with a reflection of himself. Then, too, the difference in the manner of composition between his master and the Florentine reformers doubtless drove him from the very beginning to the position of an intermediary."

As long as Schütz still stood in active co-operation with his surrounding German world, he occupied the strange position of the "affectionate opponent." During the first third of his activity it was necessary that as a creator he should make clear to his colleagues the difference which existed between their angular Nordic two- and three-part polyphony *(bicinia* and *tricinia)* and a true monody using but few voices. In the second third of his creative life he discovered that his colleagues had grasped and copied this all too quickly. Now, therefore, he had to lead them back to German counterpoint. The last third was that of solitude, in which the aged genius no longer reckoned with his colleagues but wrestled alone with God. The fact that the German musicians, usually sufficiently combative, did not take amiss this threefold opposition is the strongest proof of the compelling superiority of his person and his achievement. In contrast with the baroque man of power, Michael Praetorius, and with the musically effervescent J. H. Schein, Schütz stands forth as the representative of the aristocratic artist and craftsman who almost shamefacedly conceals the torrents of fire blazing within him and tends the flame in secret.

In his handwriting, in his patrician style of life, and in his university ideals, he is still thoroughly an adherent of the Renaissance culture of the sixteenth century;

but religiously and with respect to his artistic impulses he was just as much a man of the seventeenth century, and thus a leading prophet of the early and middle baroque — much more one who discovers and furthers a new style than one who completes and perfects an older one.[25]

---

[25] G. Weisse has very well summarized the kernel of Schütz's activity as a composer in the following verses. According to the parallel poem of D. Schirmer, the "three chief languages" which Schütz had thoroughly mastered were Greek, Latin, and French, though we would assume Italian to be referred to rather than French. The words "from numbers and from weights" refer to the legend of the Pythagorean discovery of all harmonic relationship in music. Phlegethon, the fire stream of the lower world, here functions as the devil.

> But in the art of song thy highest praise should stand.
> There should'st thou be the master and honored first of all.
> Three languages it served thee well to know and speak,
> And other arts and skills thou knewest to apply
> When thou didst undertake thy message for the ear.
> It all derived from art, "from numbers and from weights,"
> (Whatever came from thee, by thy wise mind indited).
> The texts thou knewest well to marshal movingly
> That every single word received its proper due.
> All that was heathenish and held impurity
> Was infamous to thee; thou stood'st on God's own Word,
> Which Father Luther taught; the others might proclaim
> In their own separate place what other spirits taught.
> Hence Phlegethon did howl and make lugubrious wail
> When joyous choirs began to sing thy songs;
> While, on the other hand, the angel host rejoiced
> With jubilation over thee, thou God-submissive man. . . .
> So didst thou, pious Schütz, send forth melodious songs.
> Thy many thousand works thy name do e'er extol.
> These never will be lost as long as notes remain,
> As long as organs play and Luther's doctrine stands.

And concerning Schütz's posthumous works he says:

> What still in cupboards lies, that I cannot describe;
> It is a treasure trove, so far as I can know.

The interment took place on November 17, on the Twenty-fourth Sunday after Trinity.

A. Early Master Years
Op. 1. The Italian Madrigals of 1611-12

The first work published by Schütz, then twenty-six years of age, and later designated by him as *Op. 1*, was issued through a world-famous publishing house and bore the title:

IL PRIMO LIBRO
DE MADRIGALI
DI HENRICO SAGITTARIO
ALLEMANNO
IN VENETIA MDCXI
Appresso Angelo Gardano & Fratelli.[1]

The chief space on the title page is occupied, just as in the case of Hassler's *Madrigals*, by the Hessian coat of arms of Landgrave Moritz, with its three lions, while a high-Renaissance edging, adorned with figures, forms the broad border.

The Italian preface by the young composer to the *Principe è Signore mio clementissimo*, dated May 1, 1611,[2] is a rather bombastic *Tabula dedicatoria* which one would more readily attribute to the rhetoric of the Venetian Augustinian *pater* (to whom Gabrieli entrusted the ring for Schütz) than consider it, when viewed in the light of his later German dedications, a completely personal testimonial by Schütz. He appends the madrigal text *Vasto mar*, probably written by him, in which, in baroque manner, he seeks to unite the sound of *Maurizio* with that of *mare* (the sea). Schütz also set these verses for eight voices as a closing climax to the compositions for five voices which comprise the rest of the volume. In the preface he varies and embellishes this thought, *Mare di virtu* and *di munificenza*, with the pompous panegyrics which the German prince of that day — the prince

---

[1] *The First Book
of Madrigals by
Heinrich Schütz,
a German.
In Venice 1611.
Press of Angelo Gardano and Brothers*

[2] With regard to the question of date see above, p. 56.

with the wide breeches — might well expect from his future privy secretary. Schütz indulges in an ocean of adulation *(oceano di devotione).*

In the biographical section we have already noted that among the pupils of Gabrieli the madrigal for five voices was considered the standard type of composition for testing the proficiency of a graduating journeyman.

A. Pirro has gone far beyond Ph. Spitta in determining the names of the poets of the texts of Schütz's work — the poets not named by Schütz himself. In the following table we present these findings together with the tonal designations, information concerning translations, and parallel settings:

I.   *O primavera, gioventù de l'anno*
     (prima parte)
     g—D (German by H. J. Moser in
     Seiffert's *Organum)*

II. *O dolcezze amarissime d'amore*
     (seconda parte)
     g—G

(Guarini, *Pastor fido*, III 1, Mirtillo on Amarilli). Cf. Monteverdi's *Madrigal Book*, III 1592; Spitta's Schütz Ed., Vol. IX, 88; Jaques Wert, 1595; Luzz. Luzzaschi (1601) *SbIMG*, IX, 538; the second one also in Marenzio, VII, 8

III. *Selve beate, se sospirando*
     g—G

(Guarini, *Pastor fido*, V, 8, Ergasto)

IV. *Alma afflitta che fai?*
     a—E

(Marino) (Cf. Joh. Grabbe 1609)

V.   *Cosi morir debb'io*
     a—E

(Guarini, *Pastor fido*, IV, 5; Amarilli: cf. No. XV)

VI. *D'orrida selce alpina*
     a—E

(Alessandro Aligieri in *Il gareggiamento poetico* of Carlo Fiamma, V, 157)

VII. *Ride la primavera*
     C—G

(Marino)

VIII. *Fuggio o mio core*
     C—G

(Marino); also set by Hans Nielssen (Giov. Fonteijo), 1606, No. 10

IX. *Feritevi, ferite*
     F—F

(Marino) Cf. also G. Priuli, II, 13 (1607)

X.   *Fiamma ch'allaccia*
     F—F

XI.   *Quella damma son io*   (Guarini, *Pastor fido*, II, 3
       a—A   *Dorinde to Silvio*)

XII.   *Mi saluta costei*   (Marino)
       G—G

XIII.   *Jo moro, ecco ch'io moro*   (Marino)
       g—G

XIV.   *Sospir che del bel petto*   (Marino)
       g—G

XV.   *Dunque addio, care selve*   (Guarini, *Pastor fido*, IV, 5;
       g—G   Amarilli, textual continuation of
                                       No. V

XVI.   *Tornate, o cari bacci*   (Marino) Cf. G. Priuli, III, 1 (1612);
       g—G   Monteverdi, VI (1620)

XVII.   *Di marmo siete voi*   (Marino)
       a—A

XVIII. *Giunto è pur, Lidia*   (Marino)
       A—A

XIX.   *Vasto mar*   (Schütz) Religious version in Ger-
       C—G   man by Heinr. Spitta (Sulzbach):
                                       Jauchzet Gott, alle Lande

Key combinations:

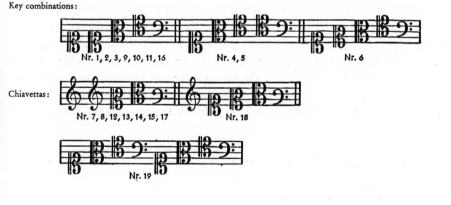

Nr. 1, 2, 3, 9, 10, 11, 16   Nr. 4, 5   Nr. 6

Chiavettas:

Nr. 7, 8, 12, 13, 14, 15, 17   Nr. 18

Nr. 19

In the preface to the complete edition Ph. Spitta expressed the opinion that the compositions were arranged according to key combinations. But this appears to be the case only at the beginning. If we consider the *chiavetta* transpositions[3] in Nos. 7 and 8, 12 to 15, and 17 and 18, it becomes clear that Schütz arranged the work according to tonal groups.

It is very significant that the arrangement of keys in the *Psalms of David of 1619* also takes essentially the same course as Glarean's *(Dodekachordon,* 1547), which we can here designate approximately as Dorian-Phrygian-Mixolydian-Lydian-Aeolian-Ionian, although the church tones for the most part already appear reshaped into forms of a now more authentic, now more plagal cadencing major and minor.

The importance to be attached to these key relations will be discussed later.[4] Ph. Spitta has persuasively shown that in the choice of texts from Guarini's famous pastoral piece Schütz surely did not think of its dramatic development but in each case only of the individual lyrical picture. Otherwise he would have placed Nos. 5 and 15 (Amarilli monolog), which belong together poetically, beside each other as Parts I and II, as in the case of Nos. 1 and 2. But even considering the *chiavette,* these two do not indicate a tonal unity, as No. 5 is attributable to the a-Aeolian, No. 15 to the Dorian tonality transposed to e. The two "halves" are also distinguished in the scoring. No. 5 is set for two tenors, No. 15 for two sopranos. Likewise, in Schütz's setting no consideration has been given to the question as to whether a man or a woman is speaking in the poem. As do most of the "madrigalists," Schütz relates the poetry to his own feeling, and the ardor of concentrating on the ego of the artist becomes the most fascinating source of power in this work of genius which Schütz called *Op. 1.*

In any description of the nineteen madrigals[5] as Schütz's contribution to musical form the first thing that strikes the attention is the composer's ardent delight in portraying the word, then in painting the emotions; in other words, the emphatic emphasis on what is called "madrigalism."[6] To be sure, this procedure might easily deteriorate into a superficial, pedantic, and tedious trifling if the extraordinary variety and the artistic elegance of his delineation did not ever and anew convince one of their inherent necessity. For the most part Schütz operates with

---

[3] We will show in the case of the *Psalms of 1619* that by the key transposition Schütz occasionally meant transposition to the fourth instead of to the third. The choice of the absolute chamber tone is another matter.

[4] See the discussion of the *Symphoniae sacrae II.*

[5] For the present without historical connection.

[6] See definition, p. 248.

rhythmic and melodic (diastematic) pictures of motion — themes which are imitated throughout, like

etc., constitute the "dictionary of Schütz's tone language." The impressiveness of such ocular symbols can be increased with their multiplication in several voices, as is demonstrated:

in No. 7, or

in No. 3. Schütz often begins with a word on a sustained note and then, after lively repetition, intensifies it by making it descriptive, as, for example,

in No. 7, as contrasted with

These last two motives reveal in full development one of the most striking characteristics of Schütz's personal style, which in large measure indicates the "baroque" element in his technique as a composer. This is his partiality for the sharpest contrasts between very long and very short notes, with the omission of intermediate values, as quarter notes would have represented these values in the above illustrations.

Concerning this change between long and short notes W. C. Printz (*Phrynis*, II, 72) says: "It is nevertheless to be noted that the change from shorter into longer or from longer into shorter notes creates a pleasant impression provided it does not occur too suddenly but gradually, as when *minimae* are changed to *semi-minimae*, these into *fusae*, and these again into *semifusae*,[7] etc. But a sudden change is also not to be rejected if it occurs at the right time and for a definite reason."

That these sharp contrasts do not belong to Schütz only but to a certain degree were or became the common property of the time is shown by an almost grotesque passage in a *Confitebor* by Monteverdi:[8]

Hugo Leichtentritt[9] called this "in bad taste." W. Kreidler[10] endeavors to save it as *stile concitato*, and, relying on the fact that Schütz would not write so crudely and superficially, he develops very plausibly the difference in the type of the religious experience of two masters: Monteverdi, the Catholic phenomenalist, for whom there are no problems; Schütz, the Protestant, wrestling with problems and transforming the sensory into the more abstract idea. While this manifestation almost disappeared in Schütz's *Geistliche Chormusik*, again to break out vigorously in his *St. Matthew Passion*, it especially dominates the youthful Schütz. As reflecting his character we here see great intensity and a tendency to abrupt changes, while from the artistic point of view we find a richly imaginative predilection for

---

[7] Notes of small denomination in the mensural notation of the late Middle Ages.
[8] In the Winterfeld collection in the *Öffentliche Wissenschaftliche Bibliothek*, Berlin, Ms. 89.
[9] *Geschichte der Motette*, p. 249.
[10] *Schütz and Monteverdi*, p. 212.

unprepared surprises. He is fond of developing tension by means of a long-drawn-out anacrusis,[11] which then discharges itself in many short syllables. Or, vice versa, there is a sudden cessation, as in No. 2:

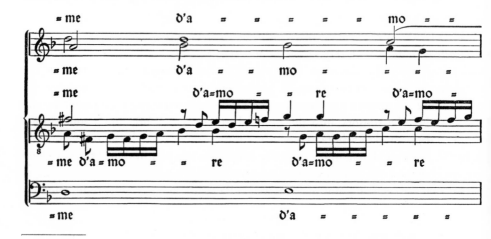

However, the strongest technical principle of form in Schütz's madrigals is the simultaneous combination of themes in antithesis. We might even call them "contrast-figure madrigals." We are confronted by the wide melodic contrasts in contrapuntal oppositions, such as are normally found in the double fugue. The way Schütz cleaves the word *amore* within itself in No. 2 is instructive: *O dolcezze amarissime d' a-mo- - - re!* ("O most bitter rapture of love"):

---

[11] A prefix of one or two unaccented syllables to a verse properly beginning with an accented syllable.

Both sopranos and the bass present the bitterness of "love as fate," while the alto
and the tenor present the sweetness of "love as fond delight," the briars and the
blossom clusters of the rose of love.

The process becomes very clear in the fourth madrigal, bars 3-5:

In contrast to the broadly flowing, pathetically dying-away question — to a certain
extent rhetorical — "Oh, my sad one, what can you do?" — there appears in

anxious, excitedly babbling eighths the counterquestion "How can you longer live?" Here we have a type of double movement like the instrumental introduction to the opening chorus of the *St. John Passion* by Bach.

Or the beginning of No. 8 *(chiavette* resolved):

One is tempted to speak here of a "solo *cantilena* over a rushing orchestra," although Schütz has completely dispensed with thorough-bass and instrumental support — already a bit conservative in the Venice of 1611. Elsewhere also the soprano assumes leadership of the chorus, as in No. 10 in connection with the beseeching *O caro, dolce vezzo d'amore* ("O dearest, sweetest spirit of love"). Occasionally in Schütz the madrigalist the bass clearly constitutes the foundation, as at the beginning of madrigal No. 9:

under the excited pressure of the contracted motives,

which then disembodies itself in sequences of eighth notes.

On the other hand, he also frequently employs the artistic device of letting the madrigal develop for long stretches at the start without a bass part, in order to have the bass enter with a special effect — in the most modern manner — and quite delicately and intimately, as in No. 14 (the *chiavette* resolved):

So = spir che del bel pet=to

So = spir   che del bel pet = to

Here there is a marked *villanella* sprightliness, a fluffy impressionism, for which the landgrave would have sought in vain in such works as Hassler's graceful madrigals, written fifteen years before. At the close of No. 16 the motive even sharpens itself to repeated

so   =   spi = ri   so   =   spi =ri

R. Wustmann (*Musikgeschichte Leipzigs*, I) has pointed out the imitation of this idea by J. H. Schein, but at the same time he has pertinently stressed its much weaker formation.

Furthermore, what an instinct Schütz shows for the color ethos of the different voices when in No. 18 the four upper voices dovetail into one another with inner

tension at the words "I leave you, Lidia,"[12] while to the bass is left only weary
sighing!

las=so   las=so   las = so   las = so   las = so

Perhaps the richest in such remarkable inspirations is No. 17, *Di marmo siete
voi*. The textual content is about as follows:[13]

> Thy heart, O lady, must of marble be,
> Who wilt not mark the burning tears of love.
> I, too, myself of stone may fancy
> When full of anger and defiant I thee see.
> Oh, love's a mad, capricious thing!
> For I'm as steadfast as obstinate art thou.
> Granite are we both, we both have iron heads,
> Mine of fidelity and thine of fury.

The opening *cantilena* of the first soprano enters with a broad Renaissance
ascent to the sixth, to be imitated by the tenor. The rhythmic variety is remarkable!

(M.M. $\rfloor$ = 70) Transposed down from a to f# through the *chiavette*:

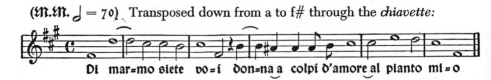

Di mar=mo siete vo=i don=na a colpi d'amore al pianto mi=o

Schütz's fondness for double themes begets for this passage a secondary motive,
very tenderly urging and variable. The relation between the two themes is shown
by the following contrasting juxtaposition:

di mar   =   =   =   mo sie=te vo=i

a le vostr'ire e a = gli stra=li suo   =   i

---

[12] *Giunto è pur Lidia.*
[13] The English text, from the Italian, is written to be sung with the music.

To this the bass, with the leap of an octave, cries out sorrowfully "and like marble," while the enlivening countermotive fervently intensifies itself to

Here one may speak of a deep metaphysical suffering caused by life itself — in the case of so young a man, to be sure, not one resulting from experience but from an inborn feeling of "proximity to death."

The next group of motives divides itself into bits of dialog

while a gigantic arch stretches above:

Again, for simultaneous contrast, the following figures are connected:

♩♩♩♩♩ and ♪♪♪♩♩♩
ambo siam sassi   e l'un e l'altro è scoglio

The poetic parallelism is very well reproduced by now having the rhythmic motive of the *io di fè* ("I with faith") associated with the *per amor* ("for in love") of the man, while that of *voi d'orgoglio* ("you to scorn it") is co-ordinated with the *e voi dura* ("but you are hard") of the woman.

For brevity's sake such a description may take the place of eighteen further madrigals. On merely leafing through the score, one is fascinated by the constant, sudden, and pliable changes. Closely woven imitations in impressive, fleeting, sharply contrasted pictures constantly succeed one another. As we hear it, we are fascinated by the fervor and the exuberance of expressions which manifest themselves in the use of wide intervals, as

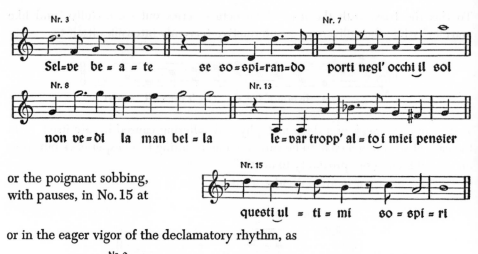

or the poignant sobbing,
with pauses, in No. 15 at

or in the eager vigor of the declamatory rhythm, as

or in the glowing fervor of altered chords, which sometimes involve the sharpest
cross relationships; also chromatic steps, such as

Schütz, as a born dramatist, divides his five voices into semichoruses, so as to be
able to carry on dialogs in groups, as in *Quella damma son io* ("What a doe must I
look like") (No. 11) and *Dunque addio, care selve* ("I must leave you, dearest
forests") (No. 15). Everything urges him subconsciously *(unterirdisch)* toward the
new solo song. Moreover, as a clever strategist, he knows how to husband his
forces: in No. 1 he first lets the whole bliss of spring unfold itself in all the voices:

> O lovely spring, youth among the seasons,
> Radiant mother of flowers, new-budding blossoms,
> Love anew awakened, you come not back; you come

Indeed; but with you does not come my springtime,
My days of sweet delight, serene and joyous. But with you
They return not. Alas, my treasure, so dearly remembered,
Yet lost, forever bringing pain and sorrow.
You still are fair as ever; you still are lovely, beautiful,
And charming. But I no longer, as in my
Springtime, am beloved by another.[14]

Now he withdraws the upper voices; the somber semichorus laments

In the last measure he lets the sopranos flicker forth smarting in a union of contrasting figures in which the first soprano raises the preceding bass to the position
of the melody:

One should observe the intervals marked *Nota bene* above: augmented fifth,
minor second, diminished fourth at the points of accent — bittersweet seasonings
for the affect word.

Note as particularly delightful how Schütz brings the motion to a standstill with
a solo voice; how, as often, he leaves the motion to a single "surviving" voice after
the others have subsided in the final chord. Both Lassus and Senfl were familiar
with this device, but with Schütz this last moving part always has something
fascinating to say, reflecting his personality, as, for example, in No.14, where the
tenor (with resolved *chiavette*) makes a short but complete descent into the hell
of suffering, during the sobbing syncopations of the second soprano.

And what daring leaps of the ninth into the depth; in the bass even a bold
death leap to the eleventh! (See music on next page.)

---

[14] The English text, from the Italian, is written to be sung with the music.

Similarly at the close of No. 13, immediately after all the voices had declaimed with great energy in equal pulse beats *non vò senza il tuo bacio* ("Alas, that I cannot die until you kiss me"), and then find themselves again in a sighing

, we have this motive twice in the alto during the broadly fading concluding chords.

Taking the *opus* as a whole, we find ourselves confronted by an almost insoluble dilemma in the problem of performance. On the one hand, the work is characterized by such driving power that we instinctively feel the urge to increase the "madrigal presentation" to a choral one. But then again, if we do this, everything becomes too heavy, too massive, too inflexible, and we are conscious of the fact that the almost-unheard-of difficulties of the work demand solo execution, with

but a quintet of singers. Yet where will such a group be found, combining the clearest mobility with ravishing sonority?

This score often has the effect of "music written for the eye" (*Augenmusik*), and even in the case of the best performance many an intended charm is lost. On the other hand, the music is no mere graph or design; it is conceived throughout for the way it is to sound. Perhaps we can distinguish the youthfulness of this work in the fact that it was born not really of "experience" but primarily and essentially from a conception (*Idee*) and musical volition. For a music group it will be fascinating to study these compositions to the point of masterful virtuosity. Yet even then, when they succeed, they will somehow feel that the pieces do not "sing" with complete satisfaction.

In order rightly to evaluate Schütz's achievement we must attempt to place it in its proper perspective in the history of the madrigal.[15] In contrast to the purely Italian species of the *frotolla,* the *villanella,* the *balletto,* etc., of closed strophic form we notice the Flemish-Nordic influence in the open type of madrigal, the music of which has been "through-composed" *(durchkomponiert)* for the entire text.

The elegant literary epigram (including extracts from lyrical epics and dramas), often in loose mixture of eleven and seven syllables, sprouting from the classical circle about Cardinal Bembo, produced serenades for the aristocracy as well as music for dedications, weddings, and festivals. But it also especially expanded its sphere into the salons of connoisseurs and aesthetes. It consists of ensemble art on a small scale, yet with most perfect polish, originally, for the most part, for male voices, later for mixed voices, and also intended for supreme vocal virtuosity. In the early period (ca. 1540, Arcadelt, Verdelot, Willaert, Festa, Alfonso della Viola) the setting for four voices predominates, as do homophony, "close coherence with the verse structure and the rhyme order of the poetry," the *a cappella* form, though also with the possibility of having only the upper voice sung and the lower voices played. A middle period is introduced by Willaert's *Musica nuova* of 1559. He elevated Petrarch to the position of chief poet and expanded the madrigal into the secular motet, while his pupil Cyprian de Rore sharpened it as a means of delineation and of spiritual expression. The chief masters of this art, now expanded to settings for five and six voices, are Lassus, Ph. de Monte, Palestrina, A. Gabrieli. Certain methods of subsidiary grouping now give the deceptive impression of double-chorus effects, while exciting changes of chordal harmony and polyphony dramatize the course of the composition.

The late epoch has as its chief exponents L. Marenzio (d. 1599), Gesualdo di Venosa (d. 1614[16]), and Claudio Monteverdi (d. 1643). The warmth of the preceding period now becomes a flame; the presentation seizes upon completely artful means of excitement, in which chromaticism permeates the voice-leading and the harmony is intensified with altered chords, while every textual possibility is called on for assistance to figurative music for the eye. Thanks to really great masters, enchanting individual effects remain possible; but mannerisms and

---

[15] Cf. A. Einstein, in Adler's *Handbuch,* 361—370; in *Ganymed,* III, 1921, and *Acta musicologica,* III, 1; Hans F. Redlich, *Ch. Monteverdi I (Das Madrigalwerk),* 1931.
[16] The murderer of his wife and the friend of Tasso.

baroque tendencies exceed the limits of good taste for chamber music. This either blossoms into a showpiece in double chorus, like the concluding part of Schütz's *Op. 1*, or transforms itself into a solo vocal *concerto* with instrumental accompaniment.

In this last blossoming of the madrigal[17] Schütz's compositions appear upon the scene. Einstein, a leading authority on the Italian madrigal, accords to this work by Schütz an illustrious testimonial: "There is scarcely a bolder, less scholastic, more characteristic work by Schütz. Moderation in expression is forbidden; the excessive, the overexuberant, has been elevated to a principle. Explosive feeling employs the strongest, freest means in declamation, in contrast of motives, in harmony. An immediate precursor can scarcely be found, even though there are not a few adumbrations in Andrea and Giovanni Gabrieli, Gesualdo di Venosa, Monteverdi, and Marenzio. These pieces by Schütz are better constructed, less playful, more closely interwoven, deeper than anything Italian."

One may perhaps supplement this as follows: With the boldest of the Italian madrigalists, the Prince of Venosa, extravagant chromatic displacements are certainly not ends in themselves but are introduced to serve the expression of deep emotion;[18] nevertheless, we have in him a more self-observing "art for art's sake," a cooly conscious, challenging experimentation; sometimes, in addition, a rough treatment of the bourgeois on the part of the grand seigneur, who otherwise also placed himself beyond law and statute. With Schütz, on the other hand (despite the lamentable absence of clearly authentic works of the kind antedating his visits to Italy),[19] we feel the madrigal to be an emancipation from the restraint of domestic tradition, like the blissful awakening to the fairy dream in the land of genius, where, free from all earthly bonds, we hover and soar, while before this transition we only stood or walked. If one wishes here to speak of "storm and stress," then it is entirely different from that of Klinger and Lenz;[20] it is not a giving vent to passion and thirst, but a supernatural glowing and burning in the flame-permeated region of the spirit.[21]

---

[17] An eighteenth-century echo of the madrigal gives the impression of historicity.

[18] H. Engel in the July issue (1935) of the *ZfMW*, XVII, has shown that the enharmonicism of Marenzio is, in large measure, purely a voice-book orthography.

[19] I see quite a drastic exception in *Ach, wie soll ich doch in Freuden leben* (Ah, how, then, shall I live in joy), Vol. XVIII; cf. the next chapter.

[20] Cf. Blume's *Chorwerk*, No. 35: *Neun 5stge Madrigale nordischer Gabrielischüler*, ed. by Rud. Gerber, which permits one to corroborate excellently the differences sketched by me between Schütz and his fellow student.

[21] Literally, "a supernatural glowing and burning in the spirit-enflamed region of passion per se."

Early Individual Works

Omitting for the present individual psalms for chorus when we gather together the works of Schütz which, on external or internal evidence, can be dated before the "political compositions" of 1621, we find the number fairly small. There is only one work which I venture to consider as definitely pre-Venetian or indeed (at least in its primary form) as belonging to the pre-Marburg-Kassel years. This is the composition printed in Heinr. Spitta's Vol. XVIII, 117 ff.: *Ach, wie soll ich doch in Freuden leben (What Indeed Can Be the Joy of Living)*. If the manuscript from the collection of the landgrave belongs to the third decade of the century, it would necessarily be a later copy, since this piece for three male voices (alto, tenor, bass), with the leading part in the middle voice (!), bears all the earmarks of an early. awkward attempt. The unusually large number of orchestral instruments[1] has a provincial and modernistic effect similar to the brass-armored orchestral lieder of Seb. Lemble-Agnello in Breslau[2] (1633-36). Schütz hardly knows how to assign to these instruments anything other than syllabic tonal repetitions and innocent thematic embellishments of the thorough-bass notes, as, for example, between the lowest trombone and the deepest gamba (p. 118):

etc., where a number of fifths and octaves creep in and the groups on repeated occasions merely strengthen one another in unison.

The text:

Ach, wie soll ich doch in Freuden leben,	What indeed can be the joy of living,
Weil ich von der muss sein,	Since I from her must part,
Die mir allein	My own true heart,
Tut Freude geben?	All gladness giving?

---

[1] A *capella* of violin and cornet, Chorus I of lutes, Chorus II of three gambas, Chorus III of three trombones.

[2] See also my *Corydon*, I, 8.

Lust ist fern von meinem Herzen,   Ah, in grief and woe I'll languish!
Denn dass ich muss geschieden sein   When her fair face I shall not see
Von der Herzliebsten mein,   Which e'er brings ecstasy,
Das bringt mir Schmerzen.   This thought brings anguish.

looks like a personal translation of an Italian madrigal and could well be a farewell
on the part of the twenty-three-year-old student about to leave for the university
to a young love left at Kassel. The setting is still surprisingly unskilled. Open chords
are quite predominant, and they are given little support by the thorough-bass
additions. Perhaps they are intentionally expressive of sorrow. There are awkward
crossings of the voices

denn daß ich muß ge = schie=den sein von der Herz=lieb=sten mein

an unmelodic descent into the depths in the gamba and trombone chords, and a
clumsy transition in tonality with cadence formation through the fifth:

Such things make it impossible to consider the piece as mature Schütz.

In view of the tonal emptiness, of the designation "à 15" with only twelve voices
at hand, and of the gap on page 120 that is filled in by the thorough bass alone, it
seems to me reasonable to question H. Spitta's suggestion that the three doubling
voices for the lutes were counted in and that the piece is thus complete. Either a
group of four flutes must be assumed, or a vocal terzet in close relation to the
violin and cornet of the *capella,* so that the vocal portion would become six-voiced
and would alternate only occasionally with the male voices in double chorus. But
even then the unprofessional construction of the piece remains to a large extent,
and one feels the justification of the sigh Schütz uttered later on when he discovered
through Gabrieli that his previous musical foundations were so incomplete that
he was almost driven to abandon in despair any further study of music. Apparently
Schütz was one of those who, like Beethoven and Haydn, mature slowly and attain

their craftsmanship by dint of prodigious struggle and effort. From this point of view an acquaintance with this youthful attempt is extremely valuable.

To the early period, when Gabrieli's influence was fresh, might be assigned the chorale setting à 6 from the *Geistliche Chormusik* of 1648: *Was mein Gott will, das g'scheh allzeit (The Will of God Is Always Best)*.[3] We may conclude that Schütz, at the time of publishing the *Geistliche Chormusik*, resorted to very old fascicles of his manuscripts; for we find that he mistook Andrea Gabrieli's *Angelus ad pastores*, with its German text *Der Engel sprach (The Angel Spake)*, as a work of his own — there given as No. 27, page 171 in Vol. VIII. Psychologically we can well understand his inclusion of such youthful compositions in a work expressly based on his own strict studies without thorough bass. For by means of these early compositions he intended to give to the rising German composers evidence of his own honest contrapuntal struggles. As a matter of fact, this vigorous and robust work for two male (chorus?) voices (Vol. VIII, No. 24) with manifest trombone foundation produces a somewhat strange and archaic effect as compared with the works which surround it, and its survival there could most easily be explained as indicated. The vocal duet works its way faithfully, though somewhat sluggishly, through the chorale, cultivating the lower voices with a ploughman's sullen defiance, as it were, so as to effect all the possibilities of imitation.

W. Gurlitt, in the unpublished portion of his *M. Praetorius*, has questioned whether Ph. Spitta's early dating of the *Veni, Sancte Spiritus* "ca. 1614" can be justified, inasmuch as the independent motival leading of the cornets, contrasted with the vocal discants which we meet here and for which the model is doubtless to be sought in M. Praetorius[4] is not found in the *Psalms of David* of 1619 but for the first time in the wedding music for Georg Schütz (likewise 1619). But the date might be correct if we assume that as early as 1613-15 Schütz had become acquainted with the festival music for Dresden gathered in Praetorius' *Polyhymnia* and that the reason he did not use this advanced orchestral technique was not the immaturity of his musical development but rather his strong desire for variety, causing him to reserve this for the wedding psalm. At all events, this question mark by Gurlitt is very worthy of consideration.

On the other hand, various things about the piece decidedly point to the period of Schütz's position as court organist at Kassel. This composition for four choruses on the Whitsuntide sequence[5] might have received several more instrumental

---

[3] Vol. VIII, No. 24, p. 152.
[4] So, for example, in the *Sleepers, Wake (Wachet auf)* setting of the *Polyhymnia Caduceatrix* of 1619; cf. H. Riemann's *Hdb. d. MG,* II 3, pp. 36 ff.
[5] Presumably by King Robert of France (d. 1031).

amplifications in the score of the collected works. Ph. Spitta reserved these suggestions, however, for his preface:[6] to Chorus I the *Positiv* is added as thorough
bass; to Chorus III, the virginal; to Chorus IV, the instrument (cembalo?), played
by the landgrave himself; while the designation *im Chor* in connection with the
violin *capella* II might indicate theorbos and lutes.[7] The fact that a vocal text was
not added to the two upper voices of the fourth chorus (violin and *cornetto*) until
later indicates that in this tonal group for six voices only the alto and the tenor
were originally responsible for the text. A second bassoon strengthens successively,
in verse one, the first bassoon; in verse four, the violone; and from the *tutti, O lux,*
the lowest trombone. In verse three the highest trombone was apparently doubled;
likewise the *traversa* (mezzo-soprano) to verse four, until it is relieved in the *tutti*
by an additional violin, soon to double at the octave a part of the third, then a part
of the fourth chorus. It is very instructive for us to note Schütz's practice of bringing up his reserve forces at all tonally important places. Apart from the instruments
supplying the continuo, the scoring — apparently conceived throughout from the
chamber music or solo point of view — is as follows:

  I: Sop. 1, sop. 2, bassoon 1;
 II: Cornets 1 & 2 (or violins), vocal bass;
III: Vocal tenor 1 & 2; three trombones;
IV: Violins 1 & 2 (or cornets, also *ad lib.*, with sop. 3 and mezzo), vocal alto, vocal
     tenor 3 (baritone), violone.

Schütz disregarded the old ecclesiastical, three-line sequence melody,

Roman version   German version
Römifche Faffung.   Germanifche Faffung.

Ve = ni sanc=te   spi = ri = tus.   Ve=ni sanc=te   spi = ri=tus.

as well as the six-line form in the *Crepundia* (playthings, rattles) of Joachim a
Burgk of 1596

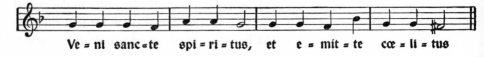

Ve = ni sanc=te   spi=ri=tus,   et   e = mit=te   cœ=li = tus

---

  [6] See p. VI of Vol. XIV.
  [7] C. Krebs in *Vjschr. f. MW,* VIII, 114, has in mind the church choir and is inclined to believe
that here the large organ was used.

Rather he invents a thematic model of his own, to the opening line of which
he adheres as closely in the first four strophes (each of which is presented by one
of the four choruses) as if he were writing a set of variations,[8] as, for example:

Ve = ni sancte spi = ri=tus, et e=mit=te cœ = li = tus lu=cis tu = æ ra = Di=um

But the second and third lines soon evaporate in a free exposition of the text.
Moreover, all this is like a long-spun-out and tonally frugal prolog for a *tutti* effect,
in the same vein as Haydn's "Let There Be Light." Actually, it has an enchanting
effect. All four tonal groups enter together and lead chromatically to a fervent
climax:

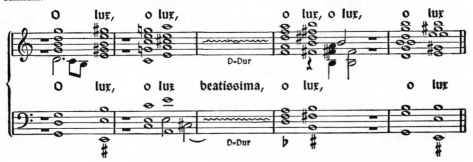

Note especially the transition from d to B. Here the spirit of a Mathias Grüne-
wald arises anew — and one could actually say that with these chordal pillars of
the "O Light, Most Blessed" of Whitsuntide 1614 (?) begins the second volume
of the *History of German Music*. The fact that the designation is retained despite
the three-part time is one of the clearest proofs that with Schütz ¢ 3 means "fast."
Here he really means "very broadly," and so through almost the entire fifty verses.
After four introductory sections *(Stollen)* this passage begins the conclusion *(Abgesang)*, which is now characterized by the rapid and more variegated sequence
of stanzas five to six of the *Graduale Romanum*. These are "variegated" *(bunt)*
through the complete, freely changing subordination to the immediate text of even
the opening themes of all stanzas and its illustration by means of virtuoso instrumental figures. Thus appropriate violin passages accompany the *Lava quod est
sordidum, riga quod est aridum* ("Wash what is unclean, moisten what is dry").

---

[8] It is a case very similar to the *Da Jesus an dem Kreuze stund* ("When Jesus Hung upon the
Cross") of the *Seven Last Words* — a fantasia, as it were, on an original theme not separately
noted.

From the beginning of the ninth stanza, *Da tuis fidelibus* ("Give to thy faithful ones"), the *tutti*-like singing in concert by the combined choirs, which flows broadly into *perenne gaudium* ("give joy forevermore"), replaces the smaller groups in a final climax. The final cadences of the ten stanzas are significant of the nature of Schütz's feeling for form: first, steadfast perseverance;[9] then, soaring-away aloft.[10]

Introduction *(Aufgesang)*   Conclusion *(Abgesang)*
G G G G   G C A *d* C G

Christ ist erstanden (Vol. XIV, No. 14, App. I, 167 ff.), à 11, with two instrumental *capellae*, surely belongs to this early period in which Schütz had come to Kassel saturated like a sponge with his impressions of Venice. The fact that the vocal bass is missing does not really make the composition "defective"; for Ph. Spitta has indicated how it can be supplied from the violone part, in doing which one might perhaps give the part a somewhat greater participation.[11] We see the inspired young court organist at his work when we note how the three choirs of viols, trombones, and voices (the last with *organo piccolo*, i. e., *Positiv*) are suddenly supplemented in the middle of the second stanza (p. 172) by a fourth choir as *capella* I with the large organ. The point at which this occurs shows the gifted master of the "storm and stress"[12] period, intent, just as before in the case of "O Light, Most Blessed,"on producing a tremendous effect. There is a fluttering-away (apparently in weary *decrescendo)* of the words of the text, *So wär die Welt vergangen, vergangen, vergangen* ("Then would the world have perished, perished, perished"), on page 173, then a general pause, and now for the first time the full *tutti* (pp. 173-174). (See music on next two pages.)

This mass entry is, therefore, intended actually and realistically to represent the resurrection of the Lord. Who does not think here of the soaring-up of the Easter Christ of the Isenheim altar, so strangely and independently repeated in Greco? Schütz again dispenses with the religious folk melody (a thoroughly unusual procedure with him!)[13] and retains only the text. This places him as a guest-

---

[9] *Beharren.*

[10] *Kurvenschwung.*

[11] A practical arrangement in manuscript by Rob. Unger (Bad Homburg v. d. H.) of the superb orchestral *concerto* deserves an early printing; he transposes the work from d to f Dorian and has supplemented the gaps in the *capella*, at least for the main chorus. Their independent restoration would not, however, be very difficult, as all the points of entrance are clearly indicated and can have been intended principally as echoes or supplementary voices in the upper register of the groups at hand. Compare my extract in the following music example.

[12] *Stürmer und Dränger.*

[13] See my statistics, *Schütz und das evang. Kirchenlied (Jb. d. staatl. Akad. f. Kirchen- u. Schulmusik, Jg. 3).*

visitor in that Renaissance century of the self-glorification of the artist (1550-1650), extending from the time when Le Maistre and Lassus ventured playfully to abandon the long sacrosanct *cantus firmi*[14] to the almost sacrilegious *ad majorem artis musicae gloriam* of the Roman Marco Scacchi in Warsaw.[15] But in the case of Schütz this happens only for the moment and as a youthful digression. He was indeed the one who was to ripen into a liturgical prophet "to the glory of God alone," his only successor in this role being J. S. Bach.

A third — probably early — work, the single-chorus *Psalm 19* in its first form, will be considered in connection with other psalms.

The next datable compositions of Schütz that have been preserved are three wedding compositions from his early Dresden years. The first, for Dr. Jos. Avena-

---

[14] See my *Gesch. d. dt. Musik*, I, 465.
[15] E. Katz, *Die musikal. Stilbegriffe des 17. Jahrh.* (Dissertation, Freiburg i/Br., 1926).

rius,[16] which appeared in Dresden as a special print in 1618 and has been preserved in the Kassel library, presents the passage from Ecclesiasticus,[17] "Blessed is the man that hath a virtuous wife." It is written in a clear rondo form, having three solo *intermedia* inserted between the double-chorus *tutti (ritornello)*. There are four introductory measures which, like the later *Motto Aria (Devisenarie)*, present the principal verse as a single chorus. This high-keyed *capella* (Chorus I) consists of three cornets, with a vocal tenor as the fundamental voice. Today two oboes, English horn, and baritone would be appropriate. But a purely vocal execution in the form of a quartet (SSABar.) is possible. To the normally keyed Chorus II Schütz has given a text throughout. In the intervening sections, obviously intended

[16] Vol. XIV, No. 11, 109.
[17] Ecclus. 26: 1—4 and 21: *Wohl dem der ein tugendsam Weib hat.*

as solo quartet, Chorus, II could be fortified in the rondo returns by a small chorus or strings. The thorough bass will be assigned to the organ or to the clavier, according to whether the piece is performed in church or in the home. In view of the scarcity of good wedding music, this piece may be warmly recommended for practical use. The contrast, between the pleasantly undulating *ritornello* and the three *intermezzi*, planned climactically, is very effective. Moreover, in the solo episodes we meet with rhythmic animation, typical of Schütz, as in the case of the contrast

In similar form[18] we have the *Concert with Eleven Voices* for the wedding of Dr. Thomae, Schütz's "fraternal friend" in Leipzig: *House and Riches are the Inheritance from Parents*.[19] The three-chorus form consists of the following tonal groups: Chorus I and Chorus II are apparently intended to be of greater volume. The one, keyed high, consists of three cornets or violins with the bottom voice given to the vocal tenor. This chorus, with its music so well adapted to the text, could be executed well by a four-voice boy choir. The other chorus, keyed very low, obviously for male voices, is here scored for three trombones or bassoons, with the upper voice (in the tenor clef) representing the vocal part. Both groups are a fascinating illustration of the fact that, despite the mixture of instrumental and vocal scoring, no Schering "split tone"[20] is intended[21] but a unified group effect with possible substitution between voices and instruments. It is only from

---

[18] From the same printing establishment.
[19] *Haus und Güter erbt man von den Eltern.* Vol. XIV, No. 12, p. 127; Prov. 19 : 14 and 18 : 22; copies in Königsberg and Kassel.
[20] *Spaltklang.* The co-operation of instruments whose tones do not blend well.
[21] A. Schering, *Historische und nationale Klangstile (Historical and National Tonal Styles (Petersjb. 1927).*

the time of the *Sinfoniae sacrae I* that the idea of the contrast between the voices
and the instruments comes really into its own. Chorus III is manifestly a vocal
terzet apparently for solo voices, in the late *villanella* scoring for two sopranos and
bass, which, like Chorus II in the preceding piece, fill in the episodes between the
tutti. Later, of course, the quasi-rondo gives way to a concertizing by the three
choruses on an equal footing. The lied style in the second episode, which apparently appears here for the first time (the *Psalms* to the contrary notwithstanding),
is witness to the expanding scope of Schütz's means of expression. The designation
Lautenchor (lute choir) in bar sixteen, for the thorough bass, emphasizes the
domestic nature of the piece. Now one may observe something very significant in
Schütz; the six-measure passage, before the other choruses take it up and continue
it climactically, is as follows:

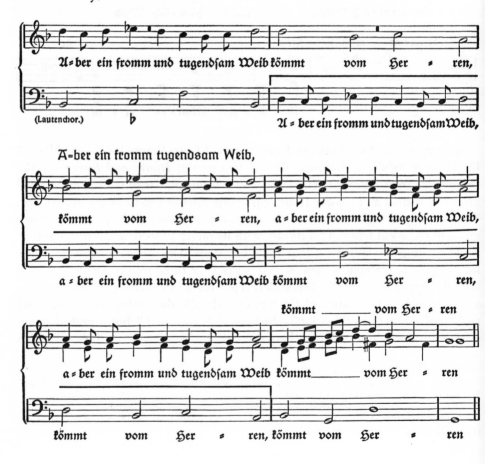

As the result of the smooth *(glatt)* half notes on the fourth beat (i. e., at the end of the measure) the individual measures are each time felt more strongly as motival units than they would be in the true polyphonic style.[22] Because of this, as well as on account of their inner contrast, one always involuntarily phrases two whole double measures as a little "theme." Through cutting across the half phrases *(Halbphrasenüberschneidung)* there again arises the technique of the "contrast madrigal"; but, as I have said, to a certain extent with the presence of the lied effect.[23] From where the triple time begins (p. 130) one strongly senses a new beginning (full terzet, setting out again from the tonic), and from the standpoint of Beethovenian periodic structure[24] the threefold descending sequence (which, to be sure, in the last measure but one receives as conclusion an energetic oppositional thrust) is musically open to question. This danger, however, of an annoying *rosalia* is at once obviated if we allow the text of the bass voice, *kömmt vom Herren*, to impress us strongly as an element of form, so that the first four (bracketed) measures of the vocal bass represent a period of their own (measures two to five of this section). Thus one will observe that Schütz's famous "adherence or nearness to the text" *(Wortnähe)* consists not only in the exposition of the text but also in the application of the text to the formal organization of the music. For him music serves not only for the better understanding of the words; the words also serve for the better understanding of the music. This presents an additional obligation to performers to devote the greatest attention to the clarity of the text. Characteristic, moreover, is the way in which Schütz simplifies the melodic thought as soon as a larger tonal mass participates in it:

He knows how to produce a climax by means of monumental simplicity where almost every other composer would have sought greater effectiveness by greater ramification.

The conclusion, actually in eleven voices, is magnificently developed, not only from the tonal point of view but also from that of countermotives in madrigal style. It gives us a "strong foretaste," in the language of Bach, of the secrets of

---

[22] The suggestion of Schubert's *C Major Quintet* is as surprising as it is nonsignificant.
[23] *Mit Liedfüllung.*
[24] H. Meersmann in his *Chamber Music Volume* to Beethoven's *A Major Quartet, Op. 18,* and in the Basel Congress report (1924), p. 255.

Schütz the harmonist. The piece as a whole is in g Dorian (g minor). After the last episode of the male chorus group has been presented in d minor, and the last vocal terzet episode has returned by way of D major to the key of the piece as a whole, the entire conclusion is unrolled in a great plagal cadence, g—c—G, into which, however, Schütz builds yet a b 6/5: g—d—b—c—G. With this our sense of tonality inclines so strongly to c minor that we interpret the final Picardy G major more as a half cadence of c minor than as a full cadence of g, and, as so often in old music, we have the feeling of being carried away prematurely out of a great stationary wave of tone.[25]

As the third wedding composition there should now follow Schütz's gift to his brother Georg, which has as its subject Psalm 133 in its entirety. But as we had better consider this work, which was subsequently revised, in connection with other chorus psalms, we shall add here a fourth and final wedding composition: *Rejoice in the Wife of Thy Youth*.[26] It has been preserved, without date, only in Königsberg. It probably reached Königsberg at the earliest in 1626, through Heinrich Albert. Stylistically it fits well into this period. Looking back, it is related to *Psalm 84* of 1619 — with the chromatic upward movement, related at the third *lieblich* ("amiably"). Looking forward, it is related to the *Kleine geistliche Konzerte* of 1636. One may compare *ergetze*[27] here with *Sela* there in *Ich liege und schlafe*.[28] *Cornetti* and trombones are placed alongside the four-voice chorus. The male alto in the melodic line, coupled with the trombones, creates the impression of a double chorus. The method of writing with six whole notes is doubtless to be conceived thus:

Freu-e dich, freu-e dich,   freu-e dich des   Wei-bes deiner   Ju-gend

This charming composition might well be supported today by a string quintet in place of the brass, as we have not learned again to play the cornets and our large modern trombones are essentially heavier and produce an effect more brassy than those of Schütz. The piece is in the form of a noble arch; the opening *tutti* reappear at the end, with an abbreviated form in the middle, thus:

---

[25] That is, we sense a semicadence instead of a full cadence.
[26] *Freu dich des Weibes deiner Jugend.* Vol. XIV, 156; Prov. 5 : 18-19.
[27] "Let her ravish thee."
[28] Vol. VI, Part II, No. 5, p. 99.

	sie ist lieblich		*Laß dich ihre Liebe*	
Formal parts:	A b	⅛ A	c	A
Tonalities:	a—A d—D,	a—C	a—D	a—A

I am able to present a hitherto completely unknown choral work of Schütz which is not mentioned in the *Collected Works*. In A. Göhler's *Musikalienverzeichnis nach den Messkatalogen 1564-1759* one finds, as 2, 1385, *I Am the Resurrection and the Life*,[29] for eight voices. This means a two-chorus single print, which the *Fair Catalog* of Gross announced for the Leipzig fall fair of 1620. From the work itself the general catalog of the *DTD*[30] could refer to two voices, the soprano of the first chorus being in a manuscript voice book in the possession of Prof. A. Werner (Bitterfeld). The tenor of the second chorus, written in 1652 by Christoph Lontzer, at that time cantor of the *Dreikönigskirche* in Dresden, was not rediscovered until October 1935.[31] Both are identical with those of an anonymous setting of the same text with corresponding scoring in the Breslau music manuscripts of the *17. Jhs., Hs. 21* (No. 210) and 23, 151.[32] On the basis of the latter I have published[33] the magnificent *a cappella* composition which apparently served as open-air funeral music. Two equal, normal choruses alternate (for the most part overlapping) in the presentation of the text (John 11: 25-26) and join each other in many passages for eight independent parts. The resurrection *(Auferstehung)* is indicated by rising figures. The dying-away of the chorus groups at "even though he die"[34]

reminds one of the *Verfolger* (persecutors) in the independent setting of Psalm 7.[35] The intimacy of the textual recitation

---

[29] *Ich bin die Auferstehung und das Leben.* John 11 : 25-26. *H. Sch., Kapm. in Dresden,* fol. G. 20 H. L.

[30] *Denkmäler deutscher Tonkunst.*

[31] Sincerest thanks to Prof. Werner for permission to use this; likewise to Prof. Seiffert as the custodian of the *General Catalog;* and to Prof. W. Vetter (Breslau) for the setting-down in score. Cantor Starke discovered the Dresden source. This presents a few minor improvements over the reading of my reprint, as in measures 66—67, in the second tenor: e/d.

[32] According to the numbering of E. Bohn, *Die Musikhss. der Stadtbibliothek Breslau.*

[33] Through the house of C. F. Peters, No. 4177.

[34] *ob er gleich stürbe.*

[35] Vol. XIII, No. 3, p. 46.

Und wer da lebet und glaubet an mich, der wird nimmermehr, nimmermehr ster   ben

is genuine Schütz. A great sectional repetition in the second half is based on an exchange of the voice parts between the two choruses. We shall meet with a similar situation in the double-chorus setting of Psalm 24 in Latin. The *coda,* with its *stretto*-like telescoping of the alternating choruses on *nimmermehr, nimmermehr* (word repetition) and the superb closing cadence on *sterben,* mark the piece as one of the most beautiful in its category. It will be well to transpose it to *e-* or *f*-Dorian, from *d*-Dorian.

Finally I can present a second motet for eight voices (which the Schütz research had so far not discovered) from the manuscripts Löbau 8 and 70,[36] as well as the *Kamenz Stadtbibl.*[37] This is a splendid Christmas composition, *Lift Up Your Heads, O Ye Gates.*[38] It deserves the very widest circulation in church music circles on account of its ease of execution. It is as though with this number Schütz had consciously given us a bit of musical folk art.[39] Up to this time only verses seven and eight of Psalm 24, announcing the entry of God Sabaoth, had been set to music.[40] After a richly antiphonal opening section in F major, Schütz, in a first interlude *(intermedium),* dramatically has the two sopranos and the tenor ask in a terzet: "Who is this King of Glory?" The double-chorus *tutti* answers with Is. 9: 6:

---

[36] The 6 plus 2 quarto volumes with 158 settings belong together. The town of Löbau had the collection planned in memory of two senators who had died of the plague in 1568 (Hier. Nostwitz and Thomas Amandus). The son of the former, Christophorus Nostwitz, was instrumental in bringing this about. From 1583 to 1682, almost exactly a century, the best-known Lausatian cantors and friends of music made contributions. The above setting was made in February 1625 by a Löbau student, Christoph Fibiger, between settings of Orlando and Giovanni Gabrieli. Further authors represented are Pfretzschner, Raselius, Vulpius, Schütz (a number of the *Psalms of 1619*), Andr. Cadener, Johs. Buchenserus, Bianciardi, Bassani, Castileti, Palavicino, Walliser, J. Gallus, Clavius, Gesius, Hassler, del Mel, Croce, H. Praetorius, Selichius, Grimm, A. Gabrieli, Siegfr. Bornensis, de Wert, Sam. Rüling, Abr. Riemer, J. Rainer, M. Lohr, Gg. Herbschleben, Richafort, Gr. Lange, Elias Grothkurtius, Stadelmayr, V. Judicius, Agazzari, Pevernage, Ruffo, Knöfel, Merulo, Dulichius, Erbach, M. E. Nathusius, Melch. Bischoff, L. Leoni, L. Senfl, Sulcius, N. Rosthius, Gumpelzhaimer, Grimm, Chr. Strauss, G. Leder, Elias Mathesius.

[37] Here the *General Catalog* likewise attributes the same piece to Schütz, but up to the present time the manuscript has not been found. Manuscript 23 of the Breslau *Stadtbibliothek* gives the same composition as No. 126 under the name of Sam. Rüling, who was cantor at the Church of the Holy Cross in Dresden from 1612 to 1615. But Rüling's biographer, K. Held, had expressed surprise (*Vj.* X, 293) at the advanced style of the solo terzets. Both from the content and the verification of the handwriting Schütz's authorship seems to me far more probable.

[38] *Machet die Tore weit.* Ps. 24 : 7—10.

[39] It has been published by Peters, No. 4176.

[40] There is also an anonymous polychorus *concerto* of the seventeenth century (Breslau manuscript 297). Unfortunately, the concert voices are missing.

"And His name shall be called Wonderful, Counselor, the mighty God, the everlasting Father, the Prince of Peace." Again the terzet makes inquiry. Now the full chorus in eight voices answers with a textual reference to Luther's *Vom Himmel hoch: Es ist das liebe Jesulein, das neugebor'ne Kindelein, das will unser Heiland und Erlöser sein* ("It is the dear little Jesus, the newborn Babe who will be our Savior and Redeemer"). In a second interlude the same brilliant soloists sing Luke 2: 14: "Glory to God in the highest," and the full double chorus brings the *Gloria in excelsis* to a brilliant conclusion in rapid six-whole-note time. Every note reveals Schütz's chorus mastery. Hammerschmidt's familiar six-voice chorus with the same title[41] is essentially later and only a modest reflection of this hitherto unknown major work, insofar as it merely appends a "Hosannah" to the Old Testament passage.

[41] Published by K. Thiel through Sulzbach.

Op. 2. The Psalms of David of 1619

The first important sacred work Schütz published is devoted to a form which up to that time had been cultivated more extensively in Venice than in Germany — the combination of the texts of complete psalms with the polychoral, instrumentally supported *"concerto* style" *(Concertenmanier).* Unfortunately, the history of the musical settings of psalmody is still unwritten.[1] Like the polyphonic treatment of the Gospel lessons, the Epistle lessons, hymns, and other texts, the settings grew out of the world of Gregorian song. They were a branch of the evolution of the motet, and they developed into the field of the cantata, the anthem, and the newer choral works.

The chief representatives of this form in the richly productive century before Schütz are, in approximately chronological grouping, Josquin, Stoltzer, Senfl, Johannes Walter, Päminger, Cl. de Sermisy, Clemens non Papa, Gombert, Berchem, Palestrina, Lassus, the two Gabrielis, Hassler, Viadana, Sweelinck. German, Netherlands, and French texts almost disappeared, even in the case of the Protestants, before the flood of Latin. We shall have something to say about psalm hymn settings in connection with the *Psalter* of C. Becker. Liturgically the psalms are most at home in the major hours of the Office, particularly in Matins and Vespers, where they are sung in groups of from three to five, with the small doxology (the *Gloria Patri*) at the end of each psalm. Each psalm is framed by its antiphon, which gives it its special designation according to its musical tone and the season and festival for which it was given. According to the Benedictine rule, all the 150 psalms are sung through within each week according to a well-thought-out plan; but the changing embellishment according to the church year gives them a constantly new environment and illumination.

Psalm composition for several voices begins long before 1300 with four-voiced expansion of the psalm melody in fauxbourdon style, as we still see it in Georg

---

[1] P. Wagner, *Einführung in die gregorianischen Melodien*, I, 83—287; Thalhofer-Eisenhofer, *Hdb. der kathol. Liturgik*, II, 533 ff; Schöberlein-Riegel, *Schatz des liturg. Chor- u. Gemeindegesanges*, I, 550—610 and 750 ff. The section in H. Kretzschmar's *Führer durch den Konzertsaal*, II, I, 316—342, treats chiefly only the time after Schütz. On the other hand, valuable practical contributions are presented in Vol. I of the *Handbuch der evang. Kirchenmusik* (edited by Ameln and others; Vandenhoeck & Ruprecht, Göttingen, 1934 f.).

Major in 1594, in Psalm 40, Tone II:

In contrast to this unemotional, utilitarian form the psychological aesthetics of the *musica riservata* enter upon the field. As early as 1559 Konrad Wolffhart says in the preface to the Basel *Gesangbuch* with regard to psalm composition: "From which it will properly follow that the singing of one psalm will be sad and low; of another, brisk and cheerful; of a third, in a moderate manner, each according to its content. In this, then, the industry and art of proper composition will be noticed" (W. Stammler, *Von der Mystik zum Barock*, 1927, p. 507).

Thus the Psalter reaches artistic heights of *a cappella* polyphony, as, for example, in the case of Lasso's *Penitential Psalms* (before 1565), which represent motets in several sections without the bond of a *cantus firmus*. Compare *Psalm 31*, part II:

Here we have a moving "tone poem" in monolog style, as a first turning to the spirit of the Counter Reformation.[2] The development now reaches the polychorus psalm *concerti* of the Gabrieli school, to which one can also doubtless attribute the following example of the Veronese G. Matt. Asola in Treviso and Vicenza,[3] *Psalms 126* and *127:*

The accompaniment by proper supplementary groups of instruments, in accordance with the practice of the day in upper Italy, is to be taken for granted. In this entire development one should further distinguish between the simple motetlike through-composition *(Durchkomposition)* of the entire text and the antiphonal

[2] H. Osthoff, *Einwirkungen der Gegenreformation auf die Musik des 16. Jhd.* (Peters-Jb., 1934), p. 41. G. M. Asola also arranges his *Vespertina Psalmodia à 4* (Venice, 1578 ff.) *juxta decretum sacrosancti Tridentini concilii.*

[3] Venice, 1599; poorly arranged in Torchi, II, 373.

treatment according to the structural parallelism[4] of the psalm form. Schütz, with many other masters, would occupy a position approximately between these two opposite poles of treatment. From an opposite point of view, the Venetian double-gallery technique and the antiphonal species of psalm composition became, as it were, fatefully welded.

Here, then, Heinrich Sagittarius, passing by a few almost contemporary examples of M. Praetorius, enters upon the history of this category. Of Schütz's "sacred *Op. 1*," according to his original counting, no manuscripts exist any longer; we have only the published voice parts in thirteen high-quarto brochures, preserved in several copies, according to which Ph. Spitta edited his scores in volumes two and three of the complete edition. In the biographical section we have already referred to the introductory panegyrics. The title page of the voices of choruses I and II, printed in black and red — the remaining choruses being more modestly set up — shows the coat of arms of the Elector of Saxony and says:

PSALMS OF DAVID

Together with

Sundry Motets and *Concerti*

with Eight or More Voices

Together with Two Other Choirs *(Capellen)* So That a Number of the Compositions
May Be Used Optionally in the Form of Three and Four Choirs *(Chor)*

Also with

Appended *Basso continuo* for the Organ

Lute, Cythara, etc.

Set Forth by

Heinrich Schütz

Electoral Saxon Capellmeister

Cantus I. Chorus

Anno   (Large Saxon Coat of Arms)   M. DC. XIX

Published by the Author.

Dresden,

In the Electoral Saxon Printing Establishment of Gimel Bergen

The German preface to Elector Johann Georg I,[5] dated June 1, 1619, but doubtless already forwarded in part in April,[6] recalls to the elector Schütz's appointment

---

[4] *Parallelismus membrorum.*
[5] Printed anew also in E. H. Muller, as No. 5, pp. 59 ff.
[6] See supra.

about three years before this time "with the excellent, distinguished, and far-famed chapel *(Musik)*." He dedicates this work to him as an indication of thanks "for the electoral grace shown my unworthiness throughout my service, in which before this I have composed some German psalms in the Italian manner into which I was carefully initiated by my dear and world-famous preceptor, Johan Gabrieli, while I dwelt with him in Italy." The "before this" doubtless means that Schütz wrote some of the psalms before his Dresden appointment. But his reference to Gabrieli, of course, refers merely to his acquisition of the "Italian manner," not to the composition of the psalms themselves. Therefore one may conclude that a considerable number of the compositions were written between the summer of 1612, when Gabrieli died, and the winter of 1615. It is further noteworthy that Schütz excuses himself for not having presented something to the elector before this, "because my incompetence at this time does not permit me to do more, however good my intentions may be." Surely this would appear to be no mere phrase; but, written by a thirty-three-year-old bridegroom, it sounds like a confession that the composer was not always fluent with his pen and that composition occasioned him difficulty despite the fact that twenty-six such *concerti*, from the viewpoint of mere bulk, present a very imposing accomplishment. But this is in accord with the innate, slower creative tempo of a master who was permitted to dedicate sixty-two of his eighty-seven years to composition. The fact that Schütz then further called the *opus* an "attempt" *(conatus)* and "my poor little work," which he is presenting "until in the near future something better may follow," of course, again indicates the "ocean of devotion"[7] which that Byzantine era demanded of its court servants.

As in general, here, too, the second preface,[8] addressed to "all those experienced in music," is more informative, since it discusses the method of execution. Translated into our modern language, it amounts approximately to the following:

1) One should distinguish *cori favoriti*, a vocal or instrumental solo ensemble ("which the Kapellmeister most favors and should dispose in the best and most pleasing manner") from the *Capellen*, the large choruses or orchestras ("for sonority and brilliance").[9] According to this distinction, the organist should register the continuo "quietly" for the *favoriti* and "strong" for the *Capellen*.

2) In the case of double-chorus compositions one should place the ensembles and the choruses crosswise, so that Grand Chorus I should stand with Ensemble

---

[7] *Oceano di devotione.*
[8] In E. H. Müller as No. 6, pp. 22 ff.
[9] *Zum starcken Gethön vnnd zur Pracht.*

II, and Grand Chorus II with Ensemble I. This will give the best tonal contrasts. We must remember that Schütz conducted his music from the middle of the nave,[10] which simplified such an arrangement.[11]

3) In the case of Nos. 10 *(Psalm 121 à 8)*, 12 *(Psalm 23 à 8)*, 18 (Vol. 3, No. 5:[12] *Lobe den Herrn à 8)*, and 20,[13] Chorus I is always the Great Chorus, while Chorus II is the small ensemble (the last with the omission of the orchestral groups). Where, however, both come into close competition, Schütz recommends that the smaller ensemble be fortified by doubling the voices to an equal grand chorus. In every instance Spitta has properly indicated this with the word *omnes*.

4) Where we do not have the designation "chorus" but "*capella*," the "orchestra" is meant, the upper voices as cornets, violins, etc., the lowest with

for contrabass, low trombones *(Quartposaunen)*, or bassoons. If one has singers available for such a group, so much the better. But then one should rearrange the vocal bass with

through octave transposition of the lowest notes so that they will be within the proper vocal compass. This may be elucidated by the following passage from No. 1:

---

[10] Cf. the picture in H. Spitta's supplementary volume, XVIII.
[11] M. Praetorius makes the same demand *(Syntagma,* III, 134):

Capella 2		Chorus 2
(*Tutti*)		(Select voices)
Chorus 1	✕	Capella 1
(Select voices)		(*Tutti*)

Cf. the valuable work by Max Schneider, *Die Besetzung der vielstimmigen Musik des 17. u. 16. Jahrhunderts (Archiv f. Musikwissenschaft,* 1, 218).
[12] The volume numbers referred to in this chapter are those in the Spitta edition (vols. 2 and 3); Moser refers to these as Vol. I and Vol. II.
[13] Vol. 3, No. 7, the church hymn setting of *Nun lob, mein Seel.*

5) High key groups do not represent transpositional chiavettas; they indicate the instrumentation.[14] In contrast to the orchestral groups, the *chori favoriti* are to employ voices. The compositions in the *opus* designated as motets and *concerti* (Vol. 3, Nos. 5-8 and Nos. 12-13) can be performed more instrumentally, while the psalms, on the other hand, are all conceived more vocally. However, in the case of Vol. 2, No. 6, *Psalm 8;* Vol. 2, No. 7, *Psalm 1;* Vol. 2, No. 8, *Psalm 84;* and Vol. 2, No. 9, *Psalm 128,* the disposition of the Gabrieli *Sonata pian e forte* recommends itself: the darker chorus with trombones, the brighter with cornets and violins; but in every group, of course, at least one part should be executed vocally[15] so that the text may always be heard.

---

[14] See the *Syntagma* III of M. Praetorius (reprint, Bernoulli, 122), who deduces from the keys of Lasso motets their instrumental scoring. I transcribe his deductions in score form (below).

[15] Similarly M. Praetorius' preface to the fifth part of the *Musae Sioniae:* "The *Cantus in primo choro,* the tenor in *secundo choro,* sing alone *viva voce* with the organ or the *regal.* One may omit the other voices or supplant them with violins *(Fiolen),* flutes, and other pleasing instruments as they are available. He, however, who wishes may have all parts sung by voices, either unaccompanied or with the organ, as each one may please."

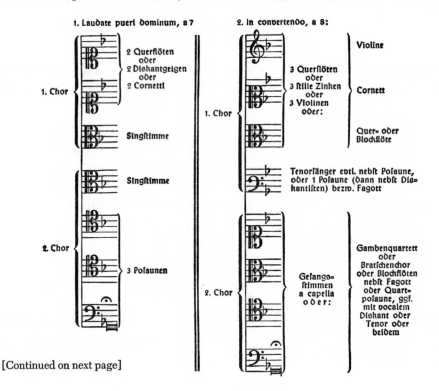

[Continued on next page]

Point six is developed so vividly and clearly that one must quote the passage verbatim:

"I have arranged these present *Psalms* of mine in *stylo recitativo* (to the present day almost unknown in Germany), which, in my opinion, is the most appropriate form for the composition of psalms. Because of the large number of words, one must engage, according to this method, in extensive recitation [16]) instead of in repetitions. I would, therefore, kindly request those who have no knowledge of this method that in presenting my *Psalms* they should not indulge in undue haste but should maintain a discreet mean, so that the words may be recited by the singers in a manner intelligible to the listeners. If this procedure is not observed, a very unpleasant discordance will result, and there will appear nothing other than a *Battaglia di Mosche* or 'battle of insects,' contrary to the intention of the author."

From these pungent words a general rule for the presentation of Schütz's works may be gathered. Present them, to be sure, in a lively manner (i. e., do not be misled by the long notes to use too slow a tempo); but first observe what is the smallest denomination of notes in the composition, and then regulate the tempo by the possibility of still presenting these denominations clearly! In No. 1, for

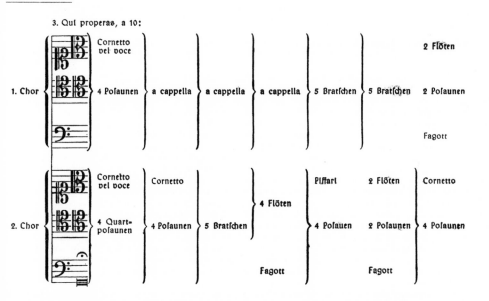

[16] Quite similarly W. C. Printz *(Phrynis*, III, 178) distinguishes the *genus luxurians* ("when the parts of the text are often repeated") and the *genus recitativum* ("when the parts of the text are either not repeated at all or only infrequently, and only when in the repetition there is a peculiar emphasis").

example, the combination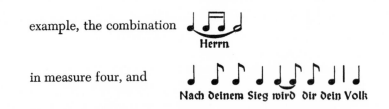

in measure four, and

compel one not to set a more rapid tempo than $\downarrow$ = 64, although there is no reason why this tempo should not be carried through very vigorously.[17]

In the final prefatory remark, No. 7, we see for the first time the distaste of the master (often referred to by him later) for the newfangled discovery of the thorough bass. This was, especially in the case of the solid polyphonic German cantors, in such disrepute that it had to be defended by Th. Selle in 1627 against the charge of "trash," by H. Albert in 1638 against the "hated cabbage chopping" (verhaßte Krauthackerei), and by Caspar Printz against the suspicion that it only instilled laziness and slovenliness. Our master really permits the thorough bass only for the settings of the psalms on a broad harmonic basis. He hopes that diligent organists will busy themselves from the motet Ist nicht Ephraim on with setting the music in score, carefully observing the middle voices as written, and, when more than one organ is used, drawing out the basses in the case of the

---

[17] Cf. in this connection the excellent, almost literally corresponding discussions of the Thuringian Georg Quitschreiber (1569-1638), which (what Bernoulli did not understand) M. Praetorius cites in his Syntagma, III (reprint, pp. 59 f.). The Latin passage is as follows: "One should not overspeed the delivery, for in doing so one will eradicate the impression of the most beautiful piece. With more moderate tempo the harmony becomes more pleasing and more understandable. One should also attend to the regularity of the beat in order that the harmony be neither distorted nor disturbed; for to sing without law and measure is to offend God himself, who, as Plato says, has arranged everything according to number, weight, and measure. But there is special dignity and charm in performing in slower or rapid tempo, according to the sense of the text — this serves as a wonderful adornment for the song. No less charm is given to the harmony and the melody by the interchange between voices and instruments, when the music is sung now more strongly, now more quietly." Praetorius makes the observation, very appropriate to Schütz's Psalms, that some rejected the change from motetlike to madrigalesque passages; "but I am not in accord with this opinion, since it gives to the motets and concerti a special pleasantness and charm and unity when in the beginning numerous tempora are set very pathetically and slowly, to be followed by more rapid phrases, soon again slowly and gravely, soon again to be intermingled with more rapid passages, that things do not always proceed in the same tono and sono, etc." Quitschreiber then further demands a closing ritardando at the chief sections.

Furthermore, the Protestant Church Orders of the sixteenth century say with regard to the choraliter rendition of the psalms in the subsidiary service: "The psalms should not be run away with but should be pronounced syllable by syllable with a good medium time, and one choir should not begin its verse before the other has concluded with its verse"; one should sing them "slowly and with fine reverence, in order that the rendition may not result in derision and howling instead of singing" (Schöberlein u. Riegel, I, 555).

psalms. In other words, he says that one should bring out the echo nature or effects of the *chori spezzati* even from the *bassus generalis,* which bridges without gaps all the changes of the component or part choruses.

Here we see Schütz, as master of tone between high Renaissance and early baroque, taking a hand in the great tonal masses, which he weighs and distributes with a view to their effectiveness according to nearness and distance, weakness and strength, darkness and light, for which purpose in the very same year (1619) Michael Praetorius, Schütz's older colleague at the court in Wolfenbüttel, wrote the great dramaturgy in the third volume of his *Syntagma musicum.*

Praetorius places the polychorus "concertos" *(Konzerti)* for voices and instruments, as "an immeasurably magnificent new invention," at the head of all music categories, where he defines:

"In specie a concertando. When, among a whole company of musicians, one selects a number, and especially the best and most outstanding, to alternate or contend with one another in groups *voce humana* or with all kinds of instruments — cornets, trombones, recorders and *flauti traversi; Krumbhörner,* bassoons, or colcians; racketts, viols de gamba, large and small fiddles, lutes, clavicymbals, regals, positivs, or organs, etc., as are their present names, or such as will be invented — especially, too, when the participants do this in such a manner that one group tries to have precedence and to make itself heard over the others, this is a *species a concertando....* This kind of composition, however, is preferably and really to be called a *Concert* when a lower and a higher chorus are heard antiphonally or together, which, even though it may be presented in compositions for six voices, will be much more effective when it is written for two, three, four, five, or more choruses."

When we examine the content of Schütz's *Psalms of David* as a whole, we see that among the twenty-six compositions only twenty conform strictly to the chief title, that is, are complete psalms. To be sure, one might add to this category, as No. 21, the crowning concluding composition of the work, insofar as it brings in Psalm 117 as a rondo refrain. This, of course, consists of only two verses, while otherwise, as a *concerto,* the piece consists of individual psalm verses from Psalms 98, 150, 148, and 96. No. 5 in volume three *(Lobe den Herrn, meine Seele)* is likewise only a *concerto* on Psalm 103: 2-4. No. 8 in volume three is a motet on Psalm 126: 1, 5-6. Two compositions have texts from the prophets: the motet, No. 6 in volume two *(Ist nicht Ephraim,* from Jer. 31: 20), and the *concerto,* No. 12 in volume three *(Zion spricht,* from Is. 49: 14-16). A setting of a church-hymn melody *(Nun lob, mein Seel, den Herren),* No. 7 in volume three, is called *canzone;* but the hymn by Johann Gramann (1487-1541 — melody from 1540) is a paraphrase of Psalm 103, thus preserving at least an indirect relation to the chief subject. This somewhat variegated interpolation of nonpsalm texts does not represent a personal laxity on the part of the composer — to be explained or excused on the basis of biographical accidents — but conforms to a widely prevalent practice of the sixteenth and seventeenth centuries. It is as if with such a "supplement not covered by the title of the work" the old publishers and authors wished to demonstrate to themselves and to their clientele something of the charming, lordly attitude of the Renaissance.

Another small irregularity confirms the natural spontaneity of the work. Two psalms occur twice: Psalm 128, as No. 9, p. 120 in volume two; and, more heavily scored, without doxology, as No. 9, p. 167 in volume three; Psalm 136 in two different compositions, as No. 11, p. 143 in volume one, and as No. 11, p. 182 in volume two.

The principal question now arises: Is the collection primarily a liturgical or predominantly an artistic work? The problem can be decided clearly from three points of view: (a) according to the choice of the psalms; (b) according to the relation of the compositions to the doxology; and (c) according to the inner arrangement of the work as a whole. So far as the author is aware, the eighteen *Psalms* — 1, 2, 6, 8, 23, 84, 98, 100, 110, 111, 115, 117, 121, 122, 128, 136, 137, 150 — do not belong together for any festival. But, on the other hand, the compilation is a collection of the most beautiful, poetically most outstanding, and musically most fruitful of the psalms. As one goes through them ("Why do the heathen so furiously rage"; "Out of the depths I cry to Thee"; "Lord, our Lord, how excellent is Thy name"; "How amiable are Thy tabernacles"; "I will lift up mine eyes unto the hills"; "The Lord is my Shepherd"; "Sing unto the Lord a new song"; "Rejoice in the Lord, all ye people"; "By the waters of Babylon," etc.), it is, of course, no mere coincidence that in the coming centuries these very texts recur again and again in compositions by Handel, Bach, Gluck, Schubert, Mendelssohn, Brahms, Reger, etc.

Next the matter of the doxology. In twelve out of twenty-one cases Schütz set the *Gloria Patri,* while in nine he omitted it. One is struck by the fact that the omission occurs either when the composition attains great length[18] or when the psalm in itself is very long.[19] But, above all, Schütz omits the doxology when the psalm text itself has a grandiloquent conclusion, as Psalm 121: *Omnes:* "The Lord shall preserve thee from all evil; He shall preserve thy soul. The Lord shall preserve thy going out and thy coming in from this time forth and even forevermore"; or Psalm 150: "Let everything that hath breath praise the Lord. Praise ye the

---

[18] Such is the case in the elaborately scored version of Psalm 128, while a *Gloria* is appended in the case of the more meagerly scored version of the same psalm.
[19] As in the case of the thirteen verses of Psalm 84, and twenty-six of Psalm 136.

Lord"; or Psalm 115: "But we will bless the Lord from this time forth and forevermore. Alleluia"; and in the case of the rondo psalm (136): "O give thanks unto the
God of heaven, for His mercy endureth forever." Here, too, then, the verdict leans
toward an artistic rather than a liturgical explanation.

In this connection it is astounding with what variety, in a comparatively small
space, Schütz presents these twelve settings of the doxology with the same text.
In a number of instances there is a clear thematic relation between the psalm and
the doxology:

Often, however, the connection is presented by means of the intentional contrast
between the setting of the psalm and that of the doxology. A polyphonically
divided slow psalm beginning may be answered by rapid triplets arranged as
chordal pillars, or vice versa. It is to be remembered as of fundamental importance

in connection with all of Schütz's compositions that he ordinarily recognizes "C" and "3" as measures of time only — "C" for slow and "3" for fast.

Thirdly, as to the arrangement of the collection: It is obvious from the preceding that it is not intended for a festival sequence, although in volume two, No. 1, *Dixit Dominus,* opens the psalm group of Sunday Vespers of the old church. It has also been mentioned in connection with the similar structure of the madrigal collection that the sequence of the pieces is not according to the scoring and the like but according to the tonalities. Here is the proof:

Vol. 2 - 1 and 2: *g* Dorian (with Picardy[20] G major close)
     3 and 4 in *a* (A) — E
     5, 6, 7, 8 in G (we shall speak later about the modulating Bb close of I 8)
     9, 10, 11, 12 in *d* (with Picardy D close)
     13 in *a* Phrygian — *D* Phrygian

Vol. 3 - 1 and 2 in F
     3 and 4 in *a* (with Picardy A close)
     9 and 10 in *d* (with Picardy D close; No. 9 with the intonation belonging
     11 in C   to Psalm 115 in the *tonus peregrinus)*

Even the group of motets and concerts follows this tonal sequence:
Vol. 3 - 5 and 6: *g* Dorian (with Picardy G close)
     7: G
     8: D
     12: *d* (with Picardy D close)

In itself this musical arrangement, or sequence, does not signify an outspoken break with the church tradition; it signifies only its transformation from the liturgical to the artistic, as these various major and minor tonalities merely represent descendants of the eight Gregorian psalm tones.

One need only consider[21] the collection of double-chorus *Vesper Psalms for All the Festivals of the Church Year,* by Willaert and Berchem, which appeared in 1550 from the house of Gardane, to recognize the principle: Each composition has the exact designation of the number of the psalm tone. In tone I, we have *Laudate pueri* (this also in the II, IV, and VIII tone) and *confitebor;* in II, *Lauda Jerusalem;* in IV, *De profundis* and *Laetatus sum;* in VI, *Nisi Dominus aedificaverit, In con-*

---

[20] J. J. Rousseau's *Music Lexicon* designates a "Picardy third" as the baroque brightening of the minor tonality through the use of a final major chord, a practice which J. S. Bach was still fond of following.
[21] Proske Library, Regensburg.

vertendo Dominus, and *Laudate Dominum;* in VII, *Dixit Dominus;* in VIII, *Memento Domine David* and *Lauda Jerusalem;* the *tonus peregrinus* in *In exitu Israel.*

The following co-ordinations of the harmonies resulted from the fauxbourdon harmonizations of the sixteenth century according to the different finals (the parenthetical cadential tonics appearing less frequently):

> Psalm tone:
>
> I F (*d*) — *d* (C)
> II *d* (F) — *d* (g)
> III *e* (C) — C (*e*, E, G)
> IV F (*d*, E, *a*) — E (*a*, C)
> V F (C) — F
> VI F — F
> VII F Mixolyd. (*c*—Dor.) —F Mixol. (g Aeol., *c*—Dor.)
> VIII C (*a* G) — G (C)
> *Peregrinus:* F (B) — *d* (g)

In Schütz this connection has already decidedly faded out of the picture, but the arrangement of his psalms in tonal groups of twos and fours becomes clearer. The result may be summarized thus: The master of 1619 still remains predominantly under the sway of the Italian Renaissance point of view of art for art's sake. It was a long road that he put behind him before emerging as the composer of the Gospel stories and the passions and the German cantor of the *Geistliche Chormusik* of 1648 — the road which led from the Parnassian fields of the "free artist" to the voluntary restraint of the great master of the middle-baroque church music.

Let us now examine the individual compositions comprising the *opus.*

The collection opens with *Psalm 110: Der Herr sprach zu meinem Herren* ("The Lord said unto my Lord").[22] The keys of the *capella* indicate cornets and trombones. Spitta's textual addition in the *capella* shows in how word-engendered *(wortgezeugt)*[23] but also in how singable a manner this five-voice Chorus III supplements the two four-voice vocal choruses of which the possible instrumental sections could be intrusted to such instrumental groups as strings against wood-

---

[22] Latin: *Dixit Dominus Domino meo,* set by J. Walter I., *toni à 4* (Rhaw, 1540); L. Päminger, *à 4* Petrejus, 1542); W. Mulner, *à 2* (Diphona, 1549); J. Berchem (Gardane, 1550); Lassus, *à 8* (1570, *Magn. op. mus.,* Nr. 728); Giovanelli, *à 8* (Conforti, 1592); Monteverdi, *à 6* (Gruber, 1615); Zucchelli, *à 8* with Bc. (Costantini, 1620); Rovetta, *à 4* v. 2V, Bc. (Profius IV, 1646); Stadlmayr 2v, 2V, Bc. (Havemann, 1659); anon. *Canto solo,* 3 Strom. Bc. (ibid.).

[23] To render accurately the word *wortgezeugt* it is necessary to employ such forms as "word-engendered," "word-generated," "word-begotten," "word-born," or "word-conceived." The term "text-inspired," of course, does not give the meaning intended.

winds. The very first four measures have the effect of an escutcheon, "I am Gabrieli's pupil," through the close leading of the fugal answer:

In the second musical group, which is declaimed in isorhythmic manner,[24] the inner restlessness of this style appears; for here it was surely Schütz's purpose to declaim less according to the rhythm of the musical measure

than according to the triplet rhythm inherent in the text:

whereas in the case of the next two half verses "emotional anticipations" *(pathetische Vorgriffe)* are rather to be assumed:

A third climactic degree of the declamatory principle on the chordal surface: Schütz has *Der Herr hat geschworen* ("The Lord has sworn to thee") with the parallel member *Du bist ein Priester ewiglich* ("Thou art a priest forever") recited

---

[24] That is, in such manner that all voices are subservient to the same rhythm, so that a strictly chordal style ensues.

like a fauxbourdon psalm, in thirteen-voice harmony. The change from D to B has about it something veritably mystic and romantic.

He then returns to the second, isorhythmic stage, and finally he has a doxology varying between double-chorus pillars in triple and *alla breve* time. The one in triple time may take approximately o = 84.

In No. 2, *Psalm 2, Warum toben die Heiden* ("Why do the heathen rage"),[25] we apparently have a four-chorus composition in which two high-keyed instrumental *capellae* are added to the two normally keyed choruses, without specific instrumental indication. But the four-chorus arrangement is only apparent, since *Capella I* merely strengthens Chorus I, as *Capella II* reinforces Chorus II where special dynamic climaxes, whether of textual or musical nature, are intended. One can, if need be, well limit oneself to the two vocal choruses with organ continuo. The vigor of this piece becomes evident after the first overlappings from the wildly incisive general pauses as well as from the brusque *parlando* style of the prose scansion, upon which then, suddenly again, extensions of the rhythm impose unwritten *crescendi*. We have sixteen or sometimes seventeen parts in the same rhythm.

(musical notation)
Und die Leute reden so vergeblich, die König im Lande lehnen sich auf / und die Herren
rat - schlagen mit einan—der

At the words *Bande* ("shackles") and *Seile* ("cords") the supplementary rhythms depict the binding. Also at the words *lachen* ("laugh"), *Himmel* ("heaven"), *Berge* ("hill of Zion"), *Zittern* ("trembling") figural madrigalisms are not disdained. The triplets at *und der Herr spottet ihr* ("and the Lord mocketh them") choose the dance rhythm in which the Jews in the previous settings of the passion also did their "deriding" *(spotteten)*. When God says: *Du bist mein Sohn* ("Thou art My Son"), the *tutti* entrance of the complementary registers, after these have been held in check for some time, is most effective. A great relief, after so much g Dorian,

---

[25] Pre-Schützian. I know only one German composition, a work by David Köler, *à 4*, 1554 (Zwickau, Hs. LII); Latin settings: *Quare fremuerunt gentes*, by Joh. Galliculus, *à 4* (Ott, 1557); Senfl (Zwickau, LXXIII, 1574); Gumpelzhaimer, *à 8* (Breslau, Hs. 24 and 29); Erbach, 1598 (Zwickau LXXXVII); Asp. Pacelli (Breslau Hs. 20).

is the brightening-up of the tonic by the Picardy major, while the subsidiary harmonies still persist in the region of B flat.

After this *furioso* we come, with the eight-voiced No. 3, *Psalm 6, Ach Herr, straf mich nicht* ("O Lord rebuke me not"), to the lyric and elegiac *a* minor sphere.[26] *Capellae* are dispensed with, but along with the *stylus recitativus* the extended mood of lamentation leads into strong emotional tensions. Note the syncopations limping along in three voices at *denn ich bin schwach* ("for I am weak"), the gloomy position at *Denn im Tode gedenket man dein nicht* ("For in death there is no remembrance of Thee"), the Monteverdi diminished fourth at *geängstet*. Schütz's fondness for letting a single voice serve as a counterpart to the rhythmic similarity of all the other voices, something which he doubtless took over especially from Lassus, leads to the strange passage on page 43:

If this is a madrigalism, introduced to depict the "evildoer" as an impudent interloper, it would indeed be a Lassus musical jest, which, however, we may hardly assume even in the "young" Schütz. It is more likely[27] an attempt to lighten up the too rigid, drill-like nature of the final solid *tutti* chord by infusing life into it by means of a solitary voice intervening.

---

[26] German by Val. Rab, 1547 (Zwickau, LXXIII); Scandellus, 1568 *(Das gesungene Bibelwort,* 7); Briegel, 1680 (Breslau Hs. 130c); Telemann *(Ges. Bibelw.,* 7). Latin: *Domine ne in furore:* Josquin, *à 4* (since Petrucci, 1519); Fr. de Layolle (Modernus, 1532); Verdelot, *à 4* (Rhaw, 1544); S. Molinaro *à 5* (Hassler, 1600); O. Bargnani, *à 3* and Bc. (Malgarini, 1618); A. Grandi, *à 4* and Bc. (Profe, 1641); St. Fabri, 2 C and Bc. (Floridus, 1647); Schütz also in the *Cantiones sacrae.*

[27] As in the same volume, pp. 35, 38, 53, 126, 136, 199.

The tonally related composition, No. 4 in volume one, *Psalm 130, Aus der Tiefe* ("Out of the depths"),[28] has the smaller scoring of the four plus four voices with figured bass and is characterized by the change between rapid scansion and embellished polyphonic lyricism. It was to be taken for granted that Schütz would not take the *De profundis lamento* lightly. But in the very first measures he surpasses what one ordinarily might have expected. Observe how Chorus I begins alone. Only after the suspense of a general pause is the word "Lord" introduced as an eight-voiced *tutti* cry. Note the woeful tensional chord at the word *Tiefe;* then the reaching-upward by all four voices one after the other at *ruf' ich;* now again the sudden and unprepared change from whole notes to eighths. The man of "storm and stress" has not grown milder in temperament since the days of the Italian madrigals! I add some obvious dynamic marks. (See next page.)

Here one sees how very closely Schütz's musical imagination is associated with the text. It is his most pronounced characteristic as contrasted with most other composers! How fine again from the rhythmic approach is his portrayal of the *Harren* ("await Thee")! One may recall the *io son costante* of the madrigalist. Let one sense how the entire piece clarifies itself inwardly until from agony and distress the definite assurance of future redemption is won. In a strange way the tonality still wavers in the doxology. A remains the fulcrum, and the E major final chord only gathers the tonal wave aloft in the Hypoaeolian semicadence.

An entirely different appearance is presented by the G major, No. 5, *Psalm 122,* p. 54, *Ich freue mich des* ("I was glad when they said unto me").[29] Again we have a double chorus, each with its reinforcing *capella,* which, however, is never silent. Therefore the entire piece rolls along in a constant *forte.* Without interruption the psalm proceeds in three-part time (six whole notes to a measure) until the doxology sets a contrast with its common time. This is not to be taken too slowly, as its only

sixteenth notes ♪♪♪♪ occur in the final *ritardando,* and then are in the instru-

---

[28] German also by J. Reusch, *à 4,* 1546 (*Gesungenes Bibelwort,* 5); anon. Zwickau XLVII; *à 8,* by B. Gesius (Breslau Hs. 24); S. Hossmann (ibid. 155); G. Geisler (ibid. 22); Latin settings of the *De profundis:* Josquin, *à 4* (Grimm and Wyrsung, 1520); L. Narbais (Modernus, 1539; *à 5,* published by Montanus, 1553); anon. in Rhaw, 1540; J. v. Berchem (Gardane, 1550); and anon. (Montanus, 1554).

[29] German, *à 5,* by Briegel, 1660 (Breslau Hs. 130); Roger Michael (Zwickau, LXXV); *à 8,* by D. Selich, 1624, and P. Schaffer (Hs. Breslau 36, 38 and 198); H. Schein, *à 14-26* (ibid. 20 and 200); Latin: *Laetatus sum, à 4,* by Andr. d. Silva, 1514 (Petrucci); A. Rener in Rhaw, 1540; J. v. Berchem and 5 *toni,* by J. Gero, 1550 (Gardane); J. Vaet, 1555 (Susato); Cl. de Sermisy, 1593 (Montanus); anon. in the *Thesaurus,* 1564; *à 3,* by Lassus in the *Meslanges,* 1577; *à 5,* by Goswin in Lechner, 1583; *à 8,* with Bc., by F. Costantini, 1620; *à 6,* with 2 V. and Bc., by G. Rovetta in Profe, 1646.

ments. The psalm, according to our present conception, has, therefore, a *presto* character. It is prevented from slipping into excessive speed by the repeated ritards that come about as a result of the change of its fundamental meter, which in the case of

leads to the hemiolas (2 x 3 = 3 x 2) still frequently found in Bach, Handel, and Mozart. The above notation is Spitta's resolution of the Schützian "warning color." The piece is one of those "unwearyingly jubilant" canvasses of colossal dimensions which express their exuberance, for example, in baroque pictures by countless palm-swinging angelic hosts. A breathless excerpt, such as (◼.= 56) (page 305) illustrates best the mad character of this Old Testament storm of jubilation which Schütz and his century frequently employed as a type of *stretto*. The many doublings show, to be sure, the still quite primitive but very auspicious technique of the Gabrieli instrumentation, promising much for the future. The setting remains fundamentally four-voiced. Everything in excess of this is of the nature of amplification or even with octaves added below and above. One recognizes that these pieces were by organists who transferred their four- and sixteen-foot coupling to their orchestration.

No. 6 in the second volume, page 72, *Psalm 8: Herr unser Herrscher* ("O Lord, our Lord")[30] is in G major, for three choruses, written in such a way that the five-voiced *capella* presents itself as a *forte* supplement to the four-voiced Chorus I. As the first chorus is keyed 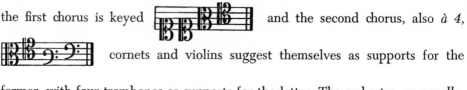 and the second chorus, also *à 4*, cornets and violins suggest themselves as supports for the former, with four trombones as supports for the latter. The orchestra, or *capella*, which is scored would then consist of woodwinds. As the thorough-bass voice has *à 8 ò 13 con una capella* (p. 13), it is clear that the *capella*, the purely instrumental group, is set merely *ad libitum*. Here one can follow Schütz's method of "register" disposition with regard to the text very well:

---

[30] In Schütz again, polychorus, XIII, 29; as *Sinfonia sacra* (Solo) VII, 16; *à 5* J. Staden (*Gesungenes Bibelwort*, 2); *à 4*, anon. (Cithara, 1625); *à 8*, by S. Scheidt (Breslau Hs. 19, 20); *à 4*, with Bc., Briegel, 1680 (ibid. 130); Latin: *Domine, Dominus noster*, *à 4* by Le Maistre (Munich, *Stb. Hs.* 28); J. Mouton (1538, Petrejus); *à 5*, by Josquin (Montanus, 1553); H. L. Hassler (Zwickau, LXXIV); *à 6*, Ph. le Dux (Joanellus, 1568); *à 8*, G. Gabrieli (Hassler, 1598); Chr. Erbach (ibid. 1600); H. Praetorius (Zwickau LXXXVII); with Bc., *à 1*, by Viadana; *à 4*, Finetti (Donfried, 1622); N. C. (Pace, 1646); *à 8*, Nanino (Costantini, 1614).

		Conclusions in	
Herr, unser Herrscher, wie herrlich ist dein Nam in allen Landen, O Lord, our Lord, how excellent is Thy name in all the earth,	*Tutti*	G	
da man dir danket im Himmel. Who hast set Thy glory above the heavens.	Ch. 2	G	
Aus dem Munde der jungen Kinder und Säuglinge hast du eine *Macht zugerichtet, um deiner Feinde willen, daß du vertilgest,* Out of the mouths of babes and sucklings hast Thou ordained strength because of Thine enemies, that Thou mightest still,	Ch. 1	C	
daß du vertilgest den Feind und den Rachgierigen. that Thou mightest still the enmy and the avenger.	Both Chs.	D	
Denn ich werde sehen die Himmel, deiner Finger Werk, den *Monden und die Sterne,* When I consider the heavens, the work of Thy fingers, the moon and the stars,	Ch. 2	G	
den Monden und die Sterne, die du bereitest. the moon and the stars which Thou hast ordained,	Ch. 1	C	
Was ist der Mensch, daß du sein gedenkest, und des *Menschenkind, daß du dich sein annimmst?* What is man that Thou art mindful of him, or the son of man that Thou visitest him?	*Tutti*	A	
Du wirst ihn lassen eine kleine Zeit vor Gott verlassen sein, For Thou hast made him a little lower than the angels,	Ch. 2	D	
aber mit Ehren und Schmuck but with glory and honor	Both Chs.		
wirst du ihn krönen. wilt Thou crown him.	Ch. 1	G	
Du wirst ihn zum Herren machen über deiner Hände Werk. *Alles hast du unter seine Füße getan,* Thou madest him to have dominion over the works of Thy hands; Thou hast put all things under his feet,	*Tutti*	G	
Schaf und Ochsen allzumal, darzu auch die wilden Thier; All sheep and oxen, yea and the beasts of the field,	Ch. 2	C	
die Vögel unter dem Himmel und die Fisch' im Meer, und *was im Meer gehet.* The fowl of the air, and the fish of the sea, and whatsoever passeth through the paths of the sea.	Ch. 1	C	
Herr unser Herrscher : / / : — wie herrlich ist dein Nam *in allen Landen : / / :* O Lord, our Lord, how excellent is Thy name in all the earth!	*Tutti*	G A G G	
Doxologie: Ehre sei dem Vater und dem Sohn und auch dem hlg. *Geiste* Doxology: Glory be to the Father and to the Son and to the Holy Ghost	Ch. 1	G	
: / / : wie es war im Anfang : / / :, jetzt und immerdar : / / :, As it was in the beginning, is now, and ever shall be,	Ch. 1 & 2 antiphonally	D	
und von Ewigkeit zu Ewigkeit. Amen. World without end. Amen.	*Tutti*	G	

One should observe the great threefold cadence of the psalms. Each time it expands itself, the psalm being firmly bound together by the repetition of the music with the repeated opening verse of the psalm before the *Gloria*. We shall meet the concatenation of the verses (indicated by brackets) again in Monteverdi's *Salve regina*. Even though there is nowhere a change to three-part rhythm, nevertheless a dancelike character asserts itself, in contrast to the more psalmodic manner of the main portion, through the very Schützian baroque rhythm, which occurs several times:

unð von Ewigkeit zu Ewigkeit. Amen!

Charmingly rocking triplets, on the other hand (C 3 = 6 ♩), begin *Psalm 1* (Vol. 2, No. 7, p. 91),[31] *Wohl dem der nicht wandelt* ("Blessed is the man that walketh not in the counsel of the ungodly"). It is written for two choruses. The key signatures would indicate cornets, violins, and bassoon with Chorus I, trombones with Chorus II. The select *favoriti* begin for a long stretch with continuo, also lying high:[32]

Wohl dem, wohl dem, wohl dem, wohl dem, der nicht wan-delt im
        wan=delt   im   Rat   der   Gott = lo = fen

    Rat   der   Gott = lo = fen!

after a brief double-chorus skirmishing in the "scoffer" rhythm *(Spötter-Takt)*, the *alla breve* takes charge of the trombone-colored second chorus, *Sondern hat Lust* ("But his delight is"); at *reden*[33] the polyphony broadens and becomes eight-voiced. True to the law of physics, the waters flow down (p. 94)!

---

[31] Again by Schütz as a duet (VI, 19). Latin: *Beatus vir, qui non abiit, à 4,* by Sermisy, 1534 through Atteignant; by Stolzer (Ott, 1537); *à 6,* by N. Gombert (Modernus, 1539); *à 6,* by Lasso, 1568 *(Magn. Opus,* No. 603, in 8 sections); *à 5,* by A. Pacello (Lilius, 1604); *à 8,* by Ph. de Monte (Schadaeus, 1611).

[32] In modern notation.

[33] "And in His law doth he meditate (the German has *reden)* day and night."

In each of the two chorusus the concluding formula, with its repeated note, is surprisingly archaic. This still haunts Schütz's *opus ultimum:*

The negation in the text, "his leaf shall not wither" (94-95), leads to a remarkable contradiction in the word-painting (which occurs similarly at times in J. S. Bach):

Here we have portrayed, not the still flourishing verdure, indicated by the sense, but the "withering" according to the word — a cleaving to the letter, which conceals the principle of illustration.[34] Magnificently all eight voices burst out together

---

[34] Thus about 1910 I heard a greatly admired reader declaim as follows in the role of Byron in Schumann's *Manfred:*

	(dolcissimo)	
hart, finster, tief	*Himmelsblick!*	*hart, finster, tief*
hard, dark, deep	glimpse of Heaven!	hard, dark, deep
Und die Götter stießen mich	*mitleids-los*	*zurück.*
And the Gods thrust me	back without	pity.

With regard to the "negative madrigalism" W. C. Printz, *Phrynis,* I, 114, says very pertinently: "When, however, an emotion of the spirit is to be expressed, the composer should consider more the general expression than the individual words, not, however, that he may be allowed not to consider the latter, but merely that he is not to give particular emphasis to words which conflict with the general emotion. For it would be foolish if I should set the following text in sad or gloomy manner: *Cede dolor, cede moeror, lacrymaeque flentium* ("Depart pain, depart sadness, tears, depart from the weeping ones") on account of the words *dolor, moeror, lacrymaeque flentium;* for the text as a whole expresses happiness."

at *Aber so sind die Gottlosen nicht* ("But the ungodly are not like this") on page 95. We have the same anticipatory syncopation as in Brahms's *A German Requiem* at *aber des Herrn Wort* ("but the Word of the Lord"). The "wind" driving away the chaff is painted with particular affection, and in the broad concluding cadence of the psalm we have a clear picture of how "the way of the ungodly shall perish" (p. 99):

This time the doxology takes the liturgical formula as the bearer of the melody:

then to let the declamations *(parlando)* of the leading voices of the two choruses concertize with great brilliance above the firmer rhythm of the lower voices.

One of the most beautiful and inspired numbers of the collection is *Psalm 84,* "How lovely is Thine own dwelling place." [35] Hovering between G major and g minor, it begins with a Bb—Eb circumscribing of the tonality (p. 104) which one might designate a "Riemann" anticipation of the substitutionary function of the tonic related tonalities at the third. The two tonal bodies are this time still more sharply distinguished as to height and depth than before — equal voices against

---

[35] No. 8 in Vol. 2, p. 104. Latin: *Quam dilecta tabernacula* is set, among others, by P. Certon, *à* 5 (Montanus, 1553); Josquin (ibid.); Mazucchi, *à 4,* with Bc. (Malgarini, 1618); Massari, bass solo with Bc. (Sammaruco, 1619); Patarto *à 6* (Bodenschatz, 1621); Finetti and Capella *à 2,* with Bc. (Donfried, 1623), etc. Since then very extensively as genuine baroque text. Reprint of Schütz's setting of *Wie lieblich sind* in *Das gesungene Bibelwort* (Vandenhoeck & Ruprecht), Brochure 23.

equal voices *(aequales contra aequales)*. The exposition shows the form of an
Alfred Lorenz *Kleinbargestalt*.[36]

One especially recognizes the "tone poet" in the beginnings of the *Stollen* — in
the *lieblich* ("amiable") with ascending chromaticism[37] and in the *Verlangen* and
Sehnen ("longing" and "fainting") in the basses:

Here we have the "principle" of monodic expression in both the height and the
depth of the tonal domain!

---

[36] The *Bar* was the most important strophic form of the Northern European Middle Ages. It
consisted of the *Aufgesang* or introduction, having two *Stollen*, each with the same melody,
and the *Abgesang* or conclusion, with a different melody, which, however, often returned to the
melody of the *Stollen* or its concluding portion. Briefly one may designate the form as AAB.
According to the researches of A. Lorenz, *Das Geheimnis der Form bei Richard Wagner*, Wagner
made the *Bar* the most important formal element of his music dramas by manipulating and
superimposing the *Kleinbar*, *Mittelbar*, and *Großbar*. They may be represented respectively by
Stollen: A

     B♭ major, corporative chordal / polyphonic conclusion / g major
     Wie lieblich sind deine Wohnungen, Herre Zebaoth (p. 104)
     How lovely is Thine own dwelling place, O Lord of Hosts

Gegenstollen: A

     G major corporative chordal / polyphonic conclusion / B♭ major
     Mein Seel verlanget und sehnet sich nach den Vorhöfen des Herrn (pp. 104-5)
     My spirit longeth, yea, fainteth for the courts of the Lord

Abgesang: B (conclusion)
     g minor   polyphonic   G major
     Mein Leib und Seele freuet sich in dem lebendigen Gott (pp. 105-6)
     My soul and body crieth out for the Living God

[37] H. Engel has shown that such passages are wont to be associated with *dolce* in the madrigal
since C. de Rore (*ZfMW*, XVII, 260). Likewise in Schütz's settings of the *Becker Psalter* at No. 84.

The *freuet* ("crieth out with joy") (p. 105) receives its arabesque; the *Vogel* ("bird") (p. 107), a most charming embellishment; even the swallow is recognized by its flitting rhythm ♩. ♫ ♩ ♫ (p. 107).

Blissful are the parallel thirds at *wohl denen, die in deinem Hause wohnen* ("Blessed are they that dwell in Thy house") (p. 109); picturesque the widely extending *von Herzen dir nachwandeln* ("in whose heart are the ways of them") (p. 111); tremendously moving the picturing by the male voices of those who "pass through the valley of Baca" (p. 112).

In the voice exposition imitating by pairs and in the cadence formation this is the sixteenth century at its best, but in the emotional chromaticism it is a path-breaker to baroque-romantic pieces like the *In hac misera valle* of Joh. Rosen-müller.[38] The chief demonstration of genius, however, Schütz prepares by ever freer or looser construction *(zerpflückteren Satz)*[39] with hocketlike punctuation in the three-voiced passages *der rechte Gott — sei zu Zion* ("there with the Lord in

---

[38] Reprinted in Seiffert's *Organum* (1935).
[39] Quick breaking-off and alternating of the voices.

His Zion") (pp. 114-115). Suddenly[40] there appears in three mighty chordal planes free, eight-voiced psalmody — this time in bold ascending steps, c minor, d minor, Eb major. In itself it is an old device, but it is employed here in a terrifyingly new way! Apparently the word *Gebet* ("prayer") (p. 115) ("O Lord God of Hosts, hear Thou my *prayer;* give ear, O God of Jacob. Sela.") inspired the vision of a host, many thousand strong, before the Holy of Holies in the temple. Again we see one of young Schütz's demonstrations of power as we have learned to know them in some early individual pieces. A fervently soaring double chorus, *quasi turba*, always with precentor, *Wohl dem Menschen, der sich auf dich verlässt* ("Blessed is the man that trusteth in Thee") (pp. 118-119), rapidly brings the glorious work to a conclusion, without a doxology. Here one feels the instinct of the artist, which after an inspiration like that of Bach's *Barrabas* will not let the music ebb away.

Schütz's fine setting of *Psalm 128*, from which Luther derived his praise of domesticity[41] ("Blessed is everyone that feareth the Lord"),[42] is characterized by a gentle anticipation and beginning, always in individual voices, which of itself implies or demands a *piano dolce* and gentle *crescendi*.[43] The hocket[44] at *fürchtet*

---

[40] We found only a brief example in *Psalm 110* (Vol. 2, No. 1).

[41] *Wohl dem, der in Gottes furchten steht;* No. 9, in Vol. 2 (p. 120), in *d* minor.

[42] Latin: *Beati omnes qui timent,* Senfl, *à 5* (Wyrsung, 1529; *à 4* in Ott, 1557) *à 4,* B. Ducis (Modernus, 1532); *à 3,* N. Gombert (ibid.); *à 4,* L. Hellinck and L. Pieton (ibid.); *à 4,* J. Walter (II toni, Rhaw, 1540); *à 6,* N. Champion (Petrejus, 1542); *à 5,* H. Matthias (Caluschus, 1543); *à 6,* Morales (Montanus, 1553); St. Zirler, *à 4* (Buchaw, 1559); *à 5,* Lassus (*Magnum Op.* No. 325-326, 1566; ibid. *à 3,* No. 46-47, 1577); *à 6,* Scandellus (Gerlach, 1568); *à 5,* M. Eckel and Th. Stoltzer, A. Schwartz, W. Figulus, W. Otto, J. a Burck (Buchaw, 1569); by 17 (!) different musicians, among them Meiland, *à 6* (ibid.); C. de Rore, *à 4* (in Lassus, 1569, II); R. del Mel, *à 6* (Hassler, 1598); Palestrina, *à 12* (GA, XXVI, 153); G. Gabrieli, *à 8* (Hassler, 1600); Nanino *à 8* with Bc. (Schadaeus, 1611); Hassler, *à 8* (Gruber, 1615); M. Praetorius, *à 8* (*Mus. Sion. Mot.,* Vol. X, 31).

[43] The delayed entrance of one voice after the seven others at *Siehe, siehe* ("Look ye, look ye") (p. 123) deserves notice; the somewhat unusual prolongations, occurring twice in all eight simultaneous voices, are to be explained by the same fundamental character of the declamation:

der Herr wird dich segnen

Obviously they are not intended to accentuate the article *(der)* and hence require correspondingly careful dynamics on the subsidiary syllable vowel. We are confronted by a case of those purposeful prolongations which absorb energy for that which is to come, as is the case also in the added doxology here:

und von Ewigkeit zu Ewigkeit

[44] See note 39 supra.

both times is intended to picture the heart faltering through fear. Giov. Gabrieli had given us models for this — for example, in the three-voiced madrigal of 1950, *Alma cortes e bella* (Torchi, II, 156) at

Very clearly, then, Schütz anticipates a favorite symbolism of Bach — the canon as a picture of obedience at *der Mann, der den Herren fürchtet* ("the man that feareth the Lord") (p. 123). The juxtaposed tendrils of eighths in the middle voices again reveal Schütz's madrigal-contrast technique:

The revised form of this composition (Vol. 3, No. 10, p. 167, without doxology) is not content with the mere addition of a five-voiced *capella* for each chorus [45] but distributes the fifty-eight measures of music for the whole unaltered psalm equally

---

[45] The first consisting of four cornetti and vocal bass, the second of violino, vocal alto, and three trombones.

among all four tonal bodies — therefore, too, the addition of a vocal part to the
new *capellae*, so that here, too, the text may be clearly heard each time. Even
within individual passages the master indulges in all kinds of deviations in the
free disposition of the parts. For example, the symbol canon to which we have
referred now occurs between the bass and the tenor, while above them, in the
soprano and alto, the eighth-note motives are plaited like flower garlands. In the
tuttis again organlike four-foot and sixteen-foot stops are drawn above and below.
Thus the fundamental character of the piece is transformed from the more intimate
into the monumental.

The tenth number of Vol. 2, the *Wander Psalm 121*,[46] "I will lift up mine eyes
unto the hills" (p. 130), is the first composition with solo song and with the positive
interchange between *favoriti* ensemble and full chorus and the complement chorus
on an equal footing. The disposition of this piece in *d* minor is very beautiful and
economical but intentionally climactic: [47]

Soprano solo	*d* — D
Corporative *tutti*	*d* — F
Alto solo	F — D
Alternating chorus *tutti*	*d* — D
Tenor solo	D — *d*
Alternating chorus *tutti*	*d* — A
Bass solo	*a* — *d*
Alternating chorus *tutti* on large scale	*d* — D
Solo duets and	*a* — A
Alto, soprano, tenor, bass solo	*a* — D, *d* — G, G — *c*, C — A
Favoriti quartet	A — A
Corporative *tutti* and	
Alternating chorus	D — D

It is astonishing how, despite the restricted harmonic frame, we meet in the
cadences of the subordinate parts nearly all possible functional combinations.

From the "lifting up" of the eyes to the "hills" and the "coming" of help all
possibilities of word painting are utilized in order to make the text pictorial in its
musical garb. The much-loved spatial antithesis between the high "heaven" and
the deep "earth" (used in the Mass, even by Bach and Beethoven) is here also
apparent both in the alto solo and in the choruses. In connection with this, in the
closing cadence at *gemacht hat* ("hath made"), the tenor is carried down surpris-

---

[46] Latin: *Levavi oculos meos, à 4,* Josquin (Petrejus, 1539); *à 4,* J. Berchem (Modernus, 1539);
à 4, Stoltzer (Rhaw, 1540); *à 6,* Clemens non papa (Montanus, 1553); *à 5,* Utendal (Joanellus,
1568); *à 8,* Lassus *(Magnum op.* No. 736, 1566); *à 4* voiced fugue, J. Paix (1594). Schütz's composition has been splendidly edited by M. Seiffert in *Musik am Hofe des Grafen Ernst* (Kistner
and Siegel).
[47] Schütz composed it again as *Sinfonia sacra* (X, 17).

ingly to the low A (p. 133) — significant for the problem of the pitch of chamber music in Schütz!

Again he uses motives representing the precise opposite of what the words mean:

With the four soli presenting the psalm in recitational manner on *Der Herr ist der Schatten über deiner rechten Hand* ("The Lord is thy shade upon thy right hand") (p. 137) an *ostinato* is announced four times in succession in the thorough bass, apparently suggested by the representation of the shadow. Probably in view of the rich development of the conclusion of the psalm Schütz foregoes the use of a doxology.

Psalm 136, Danket dem Herrn, denn er ist freundlich ("O give thanks unto the Lord, for He is good"), with every verse having the rondo refrain "for His mercy endureth forever," inspired the master to two settings in this work: No. 11 in volume two (p. 143), in *d* minor; and No. 11 in volume three (p. 182), in C major. The first is scored for a four-voiced, higher *(favoriti)* chorus and a deeper large chorus of four voices. The latter is supplemented by a normally keyed *capella* (I), doubtless to be played by strings, while a second high-keyed *capella*, doubtless for *cornetti*, is held in abeyance for the concluding climax of the *danket*. The structure is clearly divided into four parts besides a closing *stretto* by having the refrain proceed in groups from one chorus to another. But the "for His mercy endureth for ever" remains throughout with *capella I*:

Chorus I	*Chorus 2*	*Capella 1*	*Capella 2*
I: Verses (*Wechselverse*) 1-5 /	Refrain	Refrain	—
II: Refrain	6-9	Refrain	—
III: 10-15	Refrain	Refrain	—
IV: Refrain	16-25	Refrain	—

V: Verse 26: *Danket dem Gott vom Himmel denn seine Güte währet ewiglich* ("O give thanks unto the God of heaven, for His mercy endureth for ever"). *Tutti.*

Part one is concluded with a double-chorus passage of but two measures; likewise part two; in part three this conclusion is expanded to four measures; in part

four it is contracted into three measures; in part five it reaches its climax in fourteen *presto* measures in triple time. The number of measures of the subdivisions
also shows a well-constructed arrangement: I = 16, II = 15, III = 19, IV = 24,
V = 20 measures. All parts conclude in D major. A noticeable bit of word-painting
results in a change of the alternation of the choruses. At *der das Schilfmeer in zwei
Teil zerteilet* ("To Him which divided the Red Sea into parts") (p. 154) only the
two upper voices sing, and only the upper half of the antiphonal chorus replies.
Thus we have a case of space symbolism, as in the figural passions of the sixteenth
century at the words "one on the right and one on the left."

"To Him that stretched out the earth above the waters" (p. 147) is painted
figuratively. Likewise in the drastic speeding-up of the rhythm at *der Ägypten
schlug* ("to Him that smote Egypt in their first-born") (p. 151). It is worthy of
comment that Schütz, like Bach later on,[48] visualized the *Hinausführen* ("brought
out Israel") (p. 152) on a considerably elevated stage in the background (with a
similar figure in the second setting of this psalm, volume three, p. 200) and that
then "the law of melodic antithesis"[49] once again confirms itself very unequivocally:

Even the "remembered" (p. 162) receives a symbol of thoughtfulness in the
little canon at the third

and the *untergedrücket* ("our low estate") (p. 163) is likewise painted in graphic
manner.

---

[48] Cf. my *J. S. Bach* (1935), p. 119.
[49] *Jb. d. staatl. Akad. f. Kirchen- und Schulmusik*, Jg. IV, pp. 13 ff.

Noteworthy also is the inner structure of the final thanksgiving according to the progress of the cadences:

$\frac{4}{2}$ time: Bb — C; the same transposed: C — D
       Danket dem Gott vom Himmel
       ("Thank ye the Lord of heaven")
3 time: C, *d*, A; the same: B, C, *d*, *d*; the same: B, C, *d*, D — A — D
       Denn seine Güte währet ewiglich
       ("For His mercy endureth forever")

The C major setting of the same *Psalm 136* (volume three, No. 11, p. 182) shows a number of similarities, yet at the same time fascinating differences, the latter arising because of the different scoring: Chorus I: four bright *favoriti* voices; chorus II: vocal alto and three trombones; *capella I:* five-voiced vocal chorus; *capella II:* tympani and trumpets:

Part	No. of mss.	Verses	Of these: *tutti* conclusions: Measures	Chorus 1	Chorus 2	Capella 1	Capella 2
I	(17½)	1-5	4½	—	Alternating verses	Refrain	—
II	(37½)	6-12	10	Duets	Refrain	Refrain	Refrain
III	(15)	13-15	2	Duets Refrain (Duets)	Refrain		—
IV	(30)	16-24	8½	Duet- and Quartet- Refrain		Refrain	
V	(31)	25	25		Thanksgiving	*Tutti*	

Again there reigns the same persistence of key which Schütz apparently detected in the structure of this psalm, so that each of the subdivisions resolves its cadence on the tonic. Finally the two *Works of Thanksgiving* are as similar to each other as compositions based on the same text, written by the same master, and published in the same year can be without being identical. Both concentrate all melismas splendidly on the word *Himmel* (II, p. 166; III, p. 211). What Spitta has put only in the foreword really belongs in the score itself, at the conclusion, namely, the notice from the instrumental part *Parte per le Trombette à 13* ("With trumpets and tympani"): [50] "Hereupon an *intrada* is immediately blown as the *finale*" — in place of the closing notes in straight time, supplied by Spitta. Here, then, the

---

[50] Only the trumpets, however, have been noted in one voice, the tympani being left to improvisation.

Dresden court and field trumpeters came into their own in full brilliance under their imperial guild master.[51] We must agree that in the entire triple time of the thanksgiving section Schütz employs the trumpet voice "with boldest daring" (Ph. Spitta). His

against the operation of the three other choruses sounds hard, and yet, as in similar instances with Bach, as the result of the separated disposition and the different tonal color of the military group, it sounds splendid.

The pleasant shepherd psalm, the twenty-third (Vol. 2, No. 12, *d* minor, p. 171),[52] is arranged for antiphonal interchange between a brighter group of soloists and a darker full chorus. The soloists begin in straightforward time with a fugal and close interlacing of motives, which shows how Schütz at times still uses a purely mensural measure without strong accentuation, so that the accented upbeat fits into the full-measure notation:

In the alternating *tutti* a triple-time motive is formed:

3 ■. ○ ○ ○ | ■.
Der Herr ist mein Hirt

The upbeat is to be understood and executed more as a sustained anacrusis:

○ | ○ ○ ○ ○
Der Herr ist mein Hirt

---

[51] One will recall the above-mentioned festival program of October 30 to November 2, 1617. How such a Dresden trumpet *intrada* at the end of the sixteenth century looked has been shown by G. Schünemann in *Zs. f. MW*, XVII, 147 ff. (*Sonaten und Feldstücke der Hoftrompeter*); Dresden examples from the eighteenth century will be found in my *Tönende Volksaltertümer*, pp. 23 ff. Up to the time of Bach's cantatas the presence of trumpets and tympani connotes a festival occasion. Even today we say jocularly that one failed in one's examination "with trumpets and drums."

[52] Strangely enough, only seldom composed before Schütz; Latin: *Dominus regit me*, by H. Vinders, *à 4* (Montanus, 1553); Willaert, *à 4* (ibid., 1554); German by M. Praetorius, *à 4* (*Mus. Sion.* VIII, 34), as a lied.

The *er weidet mich* ("He leadeth me") (p. 172) is executed in solo duets in the rapid *parlando* style which in Schütz demands an unusually smooth-flowing delivery of eighths. The *frische Wasser* ("still waters") (p.173) receive their sixteenth-note painting; the *einschenken* ("cup overflowing") (p. 177) is also presented in a most pictorial manner:

und schen ket mir voll ein

The *Fürchten* ("fear") (p. 175), despite its negation, *kein Unglück* ("no evil") (p. 175), reveals the faltering of the heart by means of the insertion of pauses already made familiar to us in *Psalm 128;* and the *finstere Tal* ("the valley of the shadow of death") (p.175) is so well illustrated by the chordal sequence *g* minor — *c* minor — *d* minor that even at this time one could consider it a romantic tonal characterization. At the conclusion the oratorical rhythm subdivides itself into sixteenths, and after renewed solo duets the full quartets repeatedly toss the concluding line to one another in almost the manner of the psalm recitation, whereby the broad A major dominant, shortly before the Picardizing major tonic, changes in passing with strange cross relationship to minor.

Thanks to his inexhaustible riches of ideas, Schütz now expressed in music something similar to an autobiographical sketch. Here we see how he, a Nordic *Kantorei* pupil, had been transplanted into the concertizing[53] world of the Gabrielis, and how, after repeated attempts in the inherited technique, he had been completely carried away by the new southern style. For he begins *Psalm 111* (Vol. 2, No. 13)[54] like a good old German single chorus motet: *Ich danke dem Herrn von ganzem Herzen* ("I will praise the Lord with my whole heart") (p. 180); but at *im Rat der Frommen* ("in the assembly of the upright") (p. 181) there enter, most surprisingly, the similarly colored double choruses, each with its associated instrumental *capella*, so that the full, four-chorus Venetian brilliance is at once unfolded. At *der hat eitel Lust daran* ("sought out of all them that have pleasure therein") (p. 183) and *was er ordnet* ("His work is honorable and glorious") (pp. 183—4) this contrast between polyphony and flat harmonic composition on a large scale is repeated; a third time at *er hat ein Gedächtnis gestiftet* ("He hath made

---

[53] The word "concertize" is used by Moser to describe the practice — developed by the two Gabrielis and their baroque contemporaries in Venice — by which the voices and the instruments embellish, answer, and offset one another in contrast to the contrapuntal style of the Renaissance.

[54] He has treated the same text in two other compositions: as solo, Vol. VI, 7; à 4, Vol. XII, 140.

His wonderful works to be remembered"), each time with the other chorus at the
beginning, in order to introduce with the anticipatory syncopation chains a type
of expressive delineation[55] that was greatly beloved in Germany ca. 1585:

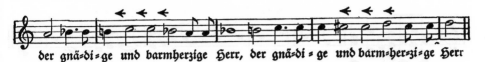

der gnä-di-ge und barmherzige Herr, der gnä-di-ge und barm-her-zi-ge Herr

And so again and again in this piece — for the fourth, the fifth, the sixth time —
until the principle of chordal painting wins the day and the linear delineation
disappears completely. Thoroughly in the sense of the above interpretation the
master here allowed himself a special obeisance to Gabrieli. He alters Gabrieli's
madrigal (see p. 200 of Vol. II) — or, more precisely, *Concerto per cantar e sonar
a 8 Lieto godea* — rather freely into a doxology, smooths out the special madrigalisms and the change to triple time, and expands the April bliss of Gabrieli's composition to general festal rejoicing. It is an invasion, seldom found in Schütz, of
the field of the "parody motet." Later he did a similar thing twice with varying
degrees of indebtedness to others, again to the works of two masters of San
Marco — A. Grandi and Cl. Monteverdi. Here the Phrygian character of the
model, which Spitta has happily added to the volume, has reacted on the psalm
to give it its Phrygian character.

The setting of *Psalm 98* for the Reformation festival of 1617, with which Spitta
opens his third volume (p. 3),[56] begins the "new" song with a genuine tonal fugal
answer, doubtless without this being intended as a play of the text on the Gabrieli

---

[55] Cf. in the case of Gregor Lange in *Ein sehnlich gross Verlangen:*

dir, die du mein Herz ge-fan-gen, niemand kanns glau-ben mir

Cf. also our juxtapositions in connection with Burckhart Grossmann's *116th Psalm.*

[56] *Singet dem Herrn ein neues Lied,* à 8 M. Roth (Bodenschatz, 1621); à 3, with Bc., Heinr.
Grimm (still in 1672 through Laidigen); Latin: *Cantate Domino canticum novum,* à 4, E. Genet
(Petrucci, 1519); à 5, J. Courtois (Modernus, 1532); à 4, anon. (Ott, 1537); à 4, J. v. Berchem (Pet-
rejus, 1542; à 3, Gardane, 1551); Cl. de Sermisy, à 4 (Montanus, 1553); à 5, Louys (Susato, 1553);
à 5, Lassus (*Magnum Op.* No. 327-328, 1566); à 5, M. Tonsor (in the *Theatrum,* 1580); à 6,
G. Gabrieli; à 4, Vecchi; à 7, Merulo (Hassler, 1598); à 4, G. Croce; à 5, Cavaccio; à 8, A. Neander
(Hassler, 1600); à 6, Bianciardi (1600, in Kaufmann's *Magnif.*); à 8, Bl. Ammon, Gallus, Orologio,
Berger, Anon. (Bodenschatz, 1603); à 8, H. Praetorius (1603); à 8, M. Franck; A. Pacello (Schadaeus, 1611); M. Praetorius (*Mus. Sion.,* Mot. No. 27); Nanino, Molinaro, St. Barnardi, Stadel-
maier, Allegri, and many others.

discovery. Two similar, normally keyed choruses carry the piece through — now in *tutti,* now in antiphony — as a freshly vigorous F major motet. The instrumental technique of the day is illustrated in appropriate instrumental motives:

Har • fen und Drommeten und Po=fau ꞏ ꞏ ꞏ nen.

The *Brausen* ("roaring") (p. 9) of the sea is painted in mighty overlapping melismas; the *Erdboden* ("world") (p. 10) has its deep place; the *Berge* ("hills") (p. 10) have their high places in the represented tone space through which the *Wasserströme* ("floods") (p. 10), of course, flow downward; and the *Völker* ("people") (p. 12), after first being mentioned in simple recitative, are pictured as a numerous and loquacious throng (p. 13):

die Völ ꞏ ꞏ ꞏ ꞏ ꞏ ꞏ ꞏ ter

This time the *Gloria Patri* develops its opening theme from that of the psalm and reveals Sagittarius as the complete master of eight-voiced form. For example, it is fascinating to note how, at the Amen (p. 15), he compresses the motives, which are by nature in 4/2 notes, to 3/2, in order to gain space in the penultimate measure for a "written-out *ritardando.*" (See next page.)

Schütz employs still another principle of composition in *Psalm 100* (Vol. 3, No. 2, p. 16, F major), *Jauchzet dem Herrn, alle Welt* ("Make a joyful noise unto the Lord, all ye lands") (p. 16), written for the same festival as the preceding. Here he uses the "echo" by designating Chorus I as *proposta* (the near chorus) and the same-keyed Chorus II as *risposta* (the far chorus). With reference to the early organs musicians used the terms *Vordersatz* and *Hintersatz* according to the fore or rear location of the registers. In this composition each of the two choruses logically has its own continuo. Today the two choruses will be placed at proper distances from each other, the echo chorus having a special harmonium for its support.

The play with echoes had been native to Italy for a long time.[57] The earliest German example seems to come from Kassel. It is Hans Heugel's ten-voiced *Colloquium hospitis et nymphae* of January 31, 1566, which graced the preliminary celebration for the wedding of the parents of Landgrave Moritz.[58] At first Schütz always gives the echo verbatim. Only in the case of longer passages does he abbreviate it to the last measure, now in direct sequence, now overlapping. From the bottom of page eighteen on he gives only an imitation that is similar to the original. He does this in order to obtain a canon in eight voices. The festal character of the work is determined by the fact that here we are concerned with matters neither of emotion nor of textual interpretation but with purely baroque tonal play.

The setting of *Psalm 137* (Vol. 3, No. 3, p. 25) moves one even more deeply. In the sixteenth century the text *An den Wassern zu Babel* ("By the waters of

---

[57] Cf. Th. Kroyer, *Dialog und Echo* (Petersjb., 1919).
[58] W. Nagel in *Sdb.*, VII, *IMG*, p. 99. Later we shall touch on the comic effects of the echo in the secular chorus song from Lassus to Opitz.

Babylon") had received a moving motet form through Johannes Wannemacher by way of the hymn by Wolfgang Dachstein and the melody by Matth. Greiter. The prose psalm inspired musicians again and again: in German, from Ad. Krieger's church cantata to the concert work by Kurt Thomas; in Latin might be mentioned settings by La Faghe (in Modernus, 1532, à 5), by Gombert (loc. cit., à 4); anonymously in Rhaw, 1540, à 4 (referred to B. Ducis in Susato, 1546, à 5); Lassus (Magnum opus, 1585, No. 152), à 4;[59] F. Regnart, 1590, à 5; by M. Vulpius, 1603, à 8; by Palestrina (1593, Vol. IX, 152), à 5, and 1604 (posthumously) à 4; by G. C. Gabutio (through Lucino) 1608, for two voices and Bc.; by Gavetta (in Schadeus) 1611, à 8; by G. B. Locatello (through Constantini) 1614, à 8, with Bc.; by St. Bernardi (symbolae 1620, à canto, Tenor and Bc.); by A. Morari (in Donfried) 1622, à 3, with Bc. From this compilation one sees how in the years of the early baroque the expressive content of this text repeatedly inspired musicians. Nevertheless, Schütz here — purely in the matter of composition — imposed some restraint on himself. To be sure, he paints the "weeping" (weinen) with a melancholy chord of the sixth (p. 25), e g# c;[60] the "cleaving" (kleben) (p. 29) of the tongue to the palate is indicated by

the "howling" (Heulen) (p. 27), and the flippant "Sing us one of the songs of Zion" (Singe uns ein Lied von Zion) (p. 27) receives pictorial portrayal by means of a significant general pause (p. 28). But for the most part the delivery is presented antiphonally between the two similarly keyed choruses in parlando style. Fortunately, however, a strong means of expression has been preserved in the printed

---

[59] On the other hand, his five-voiced composition of 1568 (Magn. op., 383-84) is a bold spelling jest. Cf. Corydon, I, 36.

[60] E. Kurth, Romantische Harmonik (1920), p. 179: "A noteworthy and bold anticipation of this (suspensions before altered chords) one can find as early as the seventeenth century. Heinr. Schütz uses augmented triads so frequently and with such telling effects as not to be equaled by any master before Wagner. Indeed, he did this often at the same time with strong suspension effects, and this even in unaccompanied choral works."

Berlin copy through a contemporary entry. In its convincingly climactic application
it may well be considered authentic. The dynamic indication of contrast should
not be omitted from any future practical edition. Even though it is inserted only
in the case of the second chorus, it certainly is intended to apply to the first also.
Thus *piano* at *An den Wassern* (bar 4), *forte* at *hiessen uns singen* (bar 15), *piano*
at *in unserm Heulen* (bar 20) and at the psalmody *Herr, gedenke* (bar 45), *forte* at
rein ab, rein ab (bar 47), *piano* at *Wohl dem* (bar 51), *forte* at *und zerschmettert
sie* (bar 53). This for once is a rare survival of a practice confirmed at the time by
Praetorius as a novelty[61] and, therefore, quite generally applicable, though it is
to be carefully distinguished from the now fortunately discontinued romanticizing
crescendo-decrescendo and *ritardando* directions in modern editions.

Schütz's grandiloquent and fascinating setting of *Psalm 150* (Vol. 3, No. 4, 35),[62]
Allelujah, lobet den Herrn ("Allelujah, praise ye the Lord"), leads again into
other regions of his tonal strategy. The composition is an *a* minor-A major work.
It has passed from an *ad libitum* instrumentation to a definitely prescribed
orchestration together[63] with an equally precise registration for the organ continuo, also a very clear (even if not precisely prescribed) distinction in the scoring
for solo voices and chorus in each of the two chief choruses. Finally we find in
places a change in rhythm which we have not met heretofore in Schütz and which
creates some difficulty in beating time for the four-chorus work. One should sub-
divide this long and elaborate composition by letters. As meager as is the harmonic
change, so variegated is the scoring that in this instance the musical architecture
(architectura musices)[64] rests on this scoring:

---

[61] Reprint Bernoulli, p. 87: "*Forté, Pian, Praesto, Adagio, Lento.* These words are used at
times by the Italians; and in the concertos and many different places, on account of change both
of the voices and the choirs *(Choren)*, they are printed with or beneath them, which does not
displease me. Although some think it is not good to employ these in church, it nevertheless seems
to me that such variation and change, when undertaken *moderate* and with good grace *(gratia)*
to express the *affectus* and to move man, are not only not unpleasant or improper but much
rather affect the ears and minds of the hearers and bestow on the concerto a special quality and
pleasantness. Moreover, the composition often requires this, as well as the text and the understanding of the words themselves. At times, but not too often and not too much, one should
conduct the tempo now rapidly, now again slowly; and one should let the choir sound now
quietly and gently, now strong and fresh; but in such and similar changes it will be proper to
employ a moderation in church much greater than one would employ at a banquet."

[62] Latin: *Laudate Dominum in sanctis ejus, à 4,* J. Mouton (Petrucci, 1514); *à 10,* A. Gabrieli
(Lindner, 1588); *à 8,* Hassler (ibid.); *à 8,* St. Venturi (Hassler, 1600); *à 8,* Anon. by Cantone,
(Bodenschatz, 1603); *à 8,* Gr. Aichinger and Palestrina (in M. Praetorius *Mus. Sion.,* 1607 and
GA XXX, 15); *à 2 voc.* and Bc., Gastoldi (Lucino, 1608); *à 8,* Croce (Schadaeus, 1611); *à 4,* Perini
(ibid.); *à 3* and Bc., Corsi (Victorinus, 1616).

[63] At least in the handwritten copy in Berlin.

[64] To use the title of a work by Wolfg. Schonsleder, Ingolstadt, 1631.

8 bars 6 ○, after the *fermata:* A, cadence: *a—A*	*Tutti;* now bassoon 1 & 2; solo soprano, 1 & 2; organ: *quintadena, Rückpos.* No. 4
10 bars 4 ♩, after the *fermata:* B, cadence: *a—A*	now: *tutti; Rückpos.* 2, 3, 4
9 bars 4 ♩, after the *fermata:* C, cadence: *a—A*	now: *cornetto* (today trp.) 1 & 2; bass. or trb. 1 & 2; alto solo 1 & 2; dulcian *Rückpos.; Oberw.* 1; BruSt. 10
11 bars 4 ♩, after the *fermata:* D, cadence: *a—E*	now: *tutti; Rückpos.* 2, 3, 4
11 bars 4 ♩, after the *fermata:* E, cadence: *E—A*	now: solo tenor 1 & 2; 3 trbni.; organ: dulcian, No. 1, 2, *grobgedackt,* after 3 bars: *Trbni.*
18 bars 4 ♩, after the *fermata:* F, cadence: *a—A*	now: *tutti*
18 bars 4 ♩, after the *fermata:* G, cadence: *A—A*	now: VI. solo, fl. solo, solo bass, 1 & 2; *Kleingedackt im Oberw.* No. 2 after 3 bars: *Rückpos. Spitzflöte* No. 7
8½ bars 6 ♩	now: *tutti; Oberw., Rückpos. grosses Werk klein*
10²⁄² bars 4 ♩, after the *fermata:* H, cadence: A—A	
12 bars 6 ♩	now: sopr. 1 & 2, tenor 1 & 2, *Rückpos. Grobged.;* after 3 bars. *Cymbel*
10 bars 4 ♩, after the *fermata:* I, cadence: A—A	
12 bars 4 ♩, after the *fermata:* K, cadence: *a—D*	now: *tutti;* solo episode: vla solo, cello solo; solo sopr. 1 & 2
10 bars 6-4 ♩, then letter L, cadence: F—A	now: *tutti*
13 bars 6-9 ♩, 3 bars 4 ♩, cadence: *a—A*	

Doubtless all other kinds of available instruments may be added to both choruses and to the continuo, and thus there may be as many additional instruments as are mentioned in the psalm itself, as indicated in part by Schütz with appropriate figures: harps (at least lutes and theorbos), psaltery, and pipes; most important of all, tympani![65]

The section after E contains in solos the motives to be used in the *tutti* after F; likewise the section after G for the *tutti* after H; and the *tutti* after L has at least the continuo in common with the introduction of the whole. Thus the apparent multiplicity is arranged to give unity.

As already stated above, there are two *Missae breves,* arrangements based on Schütz's *Psalm 150.* They are anonymous in that both the Breslau manuscript 201a and the Danzig manuscript 4012, No. 61b, say *Missa ad imitationem Hallelujah lobet den Herrn H. Schützen.* In connection with this the designation by the com-

---

[65] Joh. Schop, on the other hand, in his *Geistliche Konzerte* (1644) dispenses altogether with instrumental portrayal in the case of *Psalm 150, à 8.*

poser of the *Missa brevis* doubtless refers to the composer of the model (Schütz),
not to the settings of the *Missae breves*. Each of these is a different composition.
The fact that the Breslau composition, like the psalm in volume three, is written
in *a* minor, while the Danzig one, of which only the continuo voice is preserved,
is in *g* minor, is of little significance when one bears in mind the difference between
church and chamber pitch at that time, as the result of which Bach sometimes had
to write the same cantata in different keys for different churches. But the composition itself is totally different. The Breslau composition deals rather roughly
with the model of 1619 and reveals, especially where it purports to present something quite individual, a thoroughly commonplace style such as is found in rural
Masses, as, for example, in the

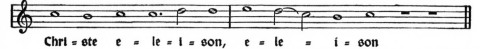

The beginning of the Schütz work is subdivided as follows for the beginning of
the Mass:

It continues in about the same manner until GA. III, p. 38, *seiner Macht*. In the *Christe* only a few appendices remind one of the model. The second *Kyrie* transforms the *tutti* (pp. 62—69), *Lobet ihn mit Pauken*. The *et in terra* again presents the model from beginning to end in a free manner; the *miserere* corresponds approximately to pp. 62 ff.; the *quoniam* to the *Lobet ihn* on pp. 68 ff.; the *cum Sancto Spiritu* to the *Allelujah* on pp. 74 ff. The work as a whole is surely not by Schütz.

In the case of the Danzig source, which, as noted, consists of only the continuo voice, the situation is still more problematical. The following is the thematic material:

Kyrie.

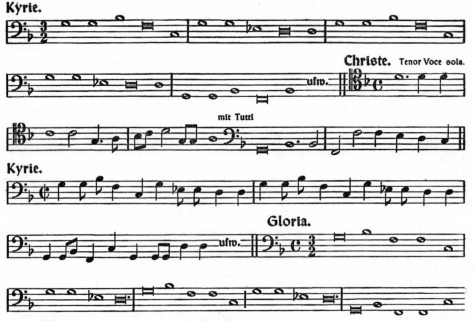

In the *Psalms of 1619* this threefold *ostinato* occurs nowhere, not even in transposed form. Unless the superscription is erroneous, it can refer only to Schütz's second setting of 1668, which up to the present time is still missing. In that case this anonymous source might be of assistance in discovering the missing work — provided again that the Danzig source is not too early for this. *Non liquet.* . . .

To continue the consideration of the complete *Psalms* we follow here with *Psalm 115* (Vol. 3, No. 9, 142), *Nicht uns, Herr* ("Not unto us, O Lord").[66] Here,

---

[66] Cf. the German setting by M. Praetorius, *Musae Sioniae*, VII, 126 (chorale by Greiter).

too, we see that Schütz's resourcefulness in making combinations is by no means
exhausted. At first he has choruses one, two, and three sing against one another on
an equal footing. Chorus II is strongly scored (chorus and strings); Chorus I is
scored (probably of necessity) for solo bass and three *cornetti;*[67] Chorus III likewise is scored, as a minimum, for solo alto and three trombones, the upper voice
possibly supported by a first bassoon. He who can do so will use in Chorus I a
full boys' choir with woodwinds; in Chorus III, male chorus and deep brass; in
Chorus II, mixed voices and strings.[68] Beginning with the solo bass intonation in
the *tonus peregrinus,* "Not unto us, O Lord, but unto Thy name give glory"
(page 142), from which the continuing Chorus III makes a cadence to the *d* minor
tonic, the composition is a peak achievement. The psalmody recitative frequently
has a rippling, dancelike effect *(allegro!):*

What a contrast of resignation after this the passage:

---

[67] Today possibly flutes, 2 trumpets, 2d bassoon.
[68] A. Sittard (*Jb. d. staatl. Akad. f. Kirchen- u. Schulmusik,* VI, 52) also shows an arrangement
with modulated mixed choruses.

In the slurring of the outer voices "heaven" *(Himmel)* spreads itself up and down like a ceiling (p. 152). Overwhelming is the presentation of the *Toten* ("the dead"), depicted only in the group of dark, low voices (Chorus III) with the empty acerbity of the Lydian *ars nova* chord of the sixth (pp. 159-160):

```
        g
e   f#  d
c   c#  h
a   a   g,
```

and the uncanny 6/4 parallels over the organ point:

Here is a stroke of genius that stands almost alone in the entire century. To this dark passage the contrast of the *Sondern wir loben den Herrn* ("But we will bless the Lord") (p. 161) strikes us at once as delightful. Finally we have a dance of joy, as if by a puppet show of angels. Today we hear the rhythm of the six whole notes about like

— a most ravishing work.

Schütz's setting of Psalm 103: 2-4 (Vol. 3, No. 5, 77), *Lobe den Herren, meine Seele* ("Bless the Lord, O my soul") is a *"concerto à 8* to be sung with the organ," doubtless intended "for two equal vocal choirs with organ continuo only" and without other instrumental support. By way of successive episodes Chorus I deploys from the full chorus its soloists, who indulge in correspondingly more mobile vocal technique. The chief scaffolding of the beautiful rondo is the powerful recurrent *tutti* refrain which appears four times with the same harmony, charmingly passing on, in its third recurrence, from triple to straight time. Indeed, at times the episodes give rather free rein to the solo voices, as at *Alle deine, alle deine Ge-brechen* ("all thy diseases") (p. 83).

One of the few compositions in the volume that have become "famous" today is the motet based on Jer. 31: 20 (Vol. 3, No. 6), *Ist nicht Ephraim mein teurer Sohn?* ("Is not Ephraim my dear son?"). This should be rendered faithfully according to Schütz's scoring: the brighter Chorus I with the vocal part in the soprano only and with cornets, which today would be best taken by two clarinets and a bass clarinet; the darker Chorus II should be led by the high solo tenor and supported by trombones. To be sure, all the other parts are "word-engendered" and singable, but it is a thoroughly German idea to entrust them "for better or for worse" to instruments. Added to this, we have in the final climax an eight-voiced double chorus, the one supported by string orchestra, the other by woodwinds: *Darum bricht mir mein Herz* ("Therefore my bowels are troubled for him") (p. 94).

The piece is so completely saturated with feeling to the very last note and is at the same time so utterly beautiful that it may be called a miracle.[69] It is difficult to refrain from setting down the entire piece, noting how, with its half-caressing, half-sobbing figure at *teuer* ("dear") (p. 89), it is born out of the most painful gloom; how it touchingly brightens to major at *mein trautes Kind* ("my lovely child") (p. 81) and rises imperceptibly to brilliance in the higher choir:

---

[69] Practical new edition by M. Schneider (B. & H.)

How tenderly warm the repeatedly raised *und mein trautes Kind!* Then equally superb in the second textual section the sympathetic support of the text by the rhythm:

This is the kind of thing one finds only in Schütz.

We must keenly appreciate the "Phrygian" emotional condensation, how an apparently altered dominant $\frac{6}{5}$ chord of C presents itself as a dominant $\frac{9}{7}\,_5$ of E major:[70]

[70] When here in the continuo we find merely the figure 5, we can understand doubly Schütz's request that from here on the organists should play all the parts *(intavolieren)* rather than merely fill in the notes designated by the figures.

How can he do so much with the smallest figural means at the word *Herz*
(pp. 92-93)? The piece certainly does not have a liturgical character but is an art
study on "the fatherly mercy of God" and is consummated with inconceivable
plastic, creative power! Here we again see illustrated that strange absence of
evolutionary development on the part of Germanic romanticists: the ability of
mature wisdom "to feel and say everything" with clairvoyance at thirty-four! It is
very instructive to compare the setting of the same text in the *Cymbalum Sionium*
(1615) of J. H. Schein, an eight-voice double chorus of noble tone about in a class
with Gallus' *Ecce quomodo*. Schein's composition shows not a trace of Schütz's
uncanny demonic power, a pleasing Tintoretto against an abysm-piercing El Greco.
Altogether different is a seven-voice setting of the same text by Sam. Scheidt[71] in
Pirna; it begins with a dialog between a deep three-voice and a high four-voice
group:

The repetitions of the phrases differentiate themselves in little exchanges of the
voice parts. Is this not objective mysticism, only strengthened somewhat by means
of almost monodic *espressivo*, as where the soprano at *trautes* goes to the high A?
At *denn ich denke wohl noch daran* ("I do earnestly remember him still") we have

---

[71] The added continuo is altogether superfluous.

more surface *parlando;* at *darum bricht mir das Herz* ("therefore my bowels are troubled for him") we have the broad descending, sobbing syncopations familiar to us from the contributions to Grossmann's *Psalm 116;* at *dass ich mich seiner erbarmen muss* ("I will surely have mercy upon him") again that approach to the *tonus currens* of the *stilus oratorius.* Scheidt's composition is a masterpiece. From the vantage point of these three compositions one could present a fine comparison of the three great S's.

As No. 7 of volume three Schütz presents his first example of the way in which he proposes to deal with a church hymn "in *concerto* manner" *(auf Concerten-Manier),* which, to be sure, from the viewpoint of content also has its origin in the world of the psalms.[72] Gramann's *Nun lob mein Seel den Herren* ("Now bless the Lord, my soul") was a favorite hymn for the Sunday after Christmas; for the Third, Fourteenth, and Nineteenth Sundays after Trinity; and for the Visitation of Mary. Because it is based on the hymn, Schütz calls this work a *canzone,* with much more justification for the use of the term than the contemporaneous Italians have. It is, as was also said at the time, a *concerto ad imitationem cantilenae,* the far-flung melody being carried through but once. In the *Kleine geistliche Konzerte* (Vol. 12, No. 3, 37), *Ich hab mein Sach Gott heimgestellt* ("To God have I entrusted all"), with many repetitions of the strophe, Schütz uses the term *aria.* He has treated both opening, musically repetitive lines *(Stollen)* in the same manner: every line of the congregational melody is first carried through in even time, in imitation, by the solo quartet with continuo, and then is rounded off *(abgeriegelt)* by the double chorus in broad harmonies which likewise take their thematic material from the church melody. As in *Psalm 111,* here, too, he carries out each time in narrow space an interplay between the "old German" and the "new Italian." J. H. Schein's treatment of the same melody,[73] with its rich embellishment and thematic resolution, certainly does not come nearer the original than does Schütz's setting.

Schütz has correctly noted the two *capellae à 5* as they should sound, with a # in G major. In this case the *capellae* are given completely without text, the first being written expressly for string orchestra, the second for cornets and trombones. Chorus I and Chorus II are placed a fourth too high, in C major. Ph. Spitta has

---

[72] An interesting counterpart to the composition is found in the *Polyhymnia caduceatrix et panegyrica* by the church hymn inspired M. Praetorius (also this work was published in 1619; *GA,* Vol. XVII). This collection, which otherwise contains nothing but chorale settings, presents, for princely gatherings, one prose psalm: No. 133, *Siehe wie fein und lieblich* ("Behold how good and pleasant a thing"). Praetorius set *Nun lob mein Seel* numerous times: *à 8, Mus. Sioniae,* I, 6; *à 16,* Urania 26, and XX, pp. 40-79. — A practical new edition of Schütz's piece by H. Spitta (B & H, 1935).

[73] Prüfer, GA. V, 78 ff.

very cleverly explained the reason for this: composers at the time hesitated to note vocal music otherwise than in the C or F system. If one wished to hear other tonalities, one wrote chiavettes. Here the instrumental parts prove that a transposition also took place at the fourth:

Perhaps, however, this has been plainly expressed in the case of this form of key combination, because for the mere transposition of a third the alto would have required the mezzo-soprano key instead of here, by using the soprano clef, having to stand a whole fifth too high. By calling attention to little oversights on the part of the composer regarding accidentals Spitta proved that apparently he had also written the vocal parts correctly in G major in the outline score (and did not write the instruments in C Ionian). According to the chamber music pitch of the present day, the piece had better be performed in A or Bb major.

Here Schütz made bold to employ a peculiar madrigalism for the concept of weakness. It is based on the dominant of the dominant (*Wechseldominante*), i. e., A:

And now a masterpiece, No. 8 in volume three (p. 135), which Schütz calls a motet, on the text made widely familiar by Brahms in his *A German Requiem,* Ps. 126: 5-6, *Die mit Tränen säen* ("They that sow in tears"). Each of the two groups of five voices consists of solo soprano, solo tenor, and three trombones. The other possibility for performance which suggests itself is that of a purely vocal chorus, as every part seems fully text-conceived. How greatly the expressive melismaticism of Schütz has diverged from the figural technique of, say, Lasso, is shown especially by the *bel canto*-like tenor part of each chorus:

in contrast to which the *werden mit Freuden ernten* ("shall reap in joy") (p. 134) is typically performed in rapid recitative style *per choros*. The Italian technique of contrasting motives is very beautifully employed by Schütz in order to set against one another the *sie gehen hin* ("he that goeth forth") (p. 136) in figures broadly descending and at the same time rising in notes of small denomination. The way in which he then portrays *Weinen ("weeping") (pp. 136-137)* and builds in the *und tragen edlen Samen* ("bearing precious seed") (p.137) with the old "agogic groups of threes" in four-part time, with *tempo rubato,* shows quite clearly the transition in style from the sixteenth to the seventeenth century:

The closing picture is especially vivid. It is based on *und bringen ihre Garben* ("bringing his sheaves") (p. 138): at first a heavy dragging of the burden in broadest descending syncopations, then the "sheaves" as such in a rich intertwining of the stalks:

and this in simultaneous integration or supplementation in four of the ten voices (p. 141): *Zion spricht: Der Herr hat mich verlassen* ("But Zion said, The Lord hath forsaken me"),[74] for four choruses. The relation between chorus and *capella* appears to be the reverse of the German norm: the six-voice Chorus I consists of three cornets, bassoon, vocal *cantus,* and tenor; the six-voice Chorus II of four trombones, *cantus,* and tenor; against this the two four-voice complementary *capellae* are set as purely vocal groups.[75]

In a practical arrangement[76] Max Schneider has shown how this scoring can be transferred to the modern orchestra: he assigns oboes and bassoons to the chorus *Capella I;* to the chorus *Capella II,* four horns *(Waldhörner)* and contrabassoon; the cornets of Chorus I are replaced by flutes, clarinets, and strings; the trombones and the tuba of Chorus II have remained, while the individual vocal parts of the *chori* are reduced to a solo quartet. Alfred Sittard,[77] however, has observed that the horn tone obscures the line in Schütz. He thinks the clarinets can be dispensed with.

The disposition is dramatic: the opening *Zion spricht* ("But Zion said") (p. 217) is presented in a powerfully lively *tutti* surface, so that the *Der Herr hat mich verlassen* ("my Lord hath forgotten me") (p. 217) in the solo duet and then in the interchange between the *semitutti* has a more subjective effect — a genuine *lamento* with stormy *affetti* gradually swelling to the *plenum (zum vollen Werk).* Thereupon we have the touching solitude of the solo quartet (p. 223), *Kann auch ein leiblich Mutter ihres Kindleins vergessen?* ("Can a woman forget her sucking child?"), which is again taken up *per choros* and is intensified by being declaimed in slow triplets in disregard of the bar lines:

---

[74] Vol. 3, No. 12, 217, from Is. 49: 14-16.

[75] The same text *à 8, a cappella,* by Dulichius in the Zwickau Ms. 10, No. 379; by J. H. Schein in the selection by Adrio (Blume's *Chorwerk*).

[76] B & H; cf. also the supplement to his essay *Die Besetzung der vielstimmigen Musik des 17. u. 16. Jahrh. (Archiv f. MW, I).*

[77] *Practical Experiences in Connection with Performances of Works of Schütz (Jb. der staatl. Akad. f. Kirchen- u. Schulmusik,* Jg. 4, p. 51) and orally.

daß fie fich nicht erbarmen,

daß fie fich nicht erbarmen, daß fie fich nicht erbar=

men über den Sohn,   über den Sohn

In the second quartet episode, with the most decided open work, or filigree, everything is reserved for the new entrance of the *tutti* at *Siehe* (twice three independent voices against the eighteen simultaneous ones!). Then the choruses shake, so to speak, the gently clanging tambourines of the surface chordal declamation against one another: *Siehe, in meine Hände* ("Behold, I have graven thee upon the palms of My hands") (p. 233) until the monumental cadence seals off the passage in heavy *tutti*. One may observe what Jakob Weckmann, under the quite general influence of Schütz's tone language, made of the same text in 1663: something very noble but removed from the monumental to an intimate, charming miniature.[78]

The last composition of the *Psalm Concerti*[79] is an expansive, far-flung piece in G major, *Jauchzet dem Herrn* ("Praise ye the Lord"). To a certain extent it towers textually as a "psalm above psalms." As *Psalm 117*, consisting of only two verses, it becomes a *rondo-ritornell*, between the returns of which are embedded, as episodes, the verses comprising Pss. 98: 4-6; 150: 4; 148: 1; 96: 11. Again we have a new combination of tonal sources: three *chori* as small ensembles of opposing tone color in the foreground and a large distant chorus *(capella)* in the background. The five-voice Chorus I includes solo alto, solo tenor; the discants are alternately scored for *flauti traversi* or cornets, with bassoon bass; Chorus II consists of only a solo soprano and solo tenor; its continuo is executed by lutes, perhaps also, for certain passages, by trumpets or trombones, respectively; the five-voice Chorus III has a vocal soprano, this time, however, supported by violin and three violas (gambas). Chorus III is probably to be supplemented with tympani.

It is interesting to observe at the beginning the relation of values of six whole-note to four half-note measures, for

---

[78] Seiffert's *Organum,* I, 17; for alto, tenor, bass, string quintet, and *basso continuo.*
[79] Vol. III, No. 13, 239.

is apparently intended. In modern notation it is:

Jauchzet dem Herren, jauchzet dem Herren, jauchzet dem Herren alle Welt

The piece resembles the setting of Psalm 150 in that Schütz has the individual choruses enter according to the instrumental groups mentioned in the text. Again handwritten entries in the organ part show how much extemporary embellishing was done at this instrument. Only for the divisional, structural complement-*ripieno* does the *capella* enter, until finally all four tonal groups, on equal footing, toss their alleluias to one another and conclude the entire work in bright festal light. We learn, moreover, from the organ entries how the organist worked with echo effects by means of *piano* and *forte* registration, at times almost to excess, as in the *concerti* of Scheidt.

If we again survey briefly the printed work of 1619 as a whole, we are impressed by the fact that these *concerti* represent a colossal achievement, both as to extent and especially as to content. As Spitta says: "With these Schütz addressed the world. From the viewpoint of their external compass these twenty-six polychoral compositions, in which the number of participating voices reaches twenty-one, constitute the largest work Schütz ever published. They represent the highest that he felt himself capable of achieving at the time." How quickly the *opus* advanced him into the front rank of the German musicians of the day we learn in the very next year from Michael Altenburg's preface to part one of his *Neue und zierliche Intraden* (Erfurt, 1620): "I shall not speak here of the state of music at the electoral and princely courts; for this mounts higher and higher from day to day, as is sufficiently indicated by the magnificent *opera* of the excellent and highly gifted musicians Praetorius, Schütz, and a number of others."

Michael Praetorius *(Creutzburgensis)*, who was a close friend of Altenburg, died in Wolfenbüttel on February 15, 1621. From then on Sagittarius was the chief musician of Germany, and this not least by reason of brilliant performances given under his direction. While printed editions of these psalms were available, manuscript copies of individual compositions — especially those still found in the libraries of Breslau, Königsberg, and Danzig — show how eagerly these pieces were seized upon by the musicians of the day.

The artistic effect of these psalms on other creative musicians must also have been very considerable. To be sure, we cannot be certain whether S. Scheidt's *Ist nicht Ephraim, à 7* (in Dresden), and his *An Wasserflüssen Babylon* (in Berlin) antedate Schütz's similar compositions; but this is highly improbable, since none of Scheidt's works can be dated before 1620. Be this as it may, it is not unlikely that the settings of Psalms 13, 121, and 43 in his eight-voice *Cantiones sacrae* of 1620 — Psalms 13 and 121 constituting the opening compositions — were inspired by Schütz's work. The fact that both Samuel Scheidt and his brother Gottfried set the text *Zion spricht* as elegies for their father may be mentioned in passing. The theory of Schütz's possible influence on Scheidt becomes still more compelling (also from the point of view of scoring) in the case of Scheidt's next work: the *Pars prima concertuum sacrorum* of 1622. It opens with a twofold setting of Psalm 150 (Latin): the first for two tenors with *basso continuo* and, at the close, full chorus with *capella;* the second setting is arranged for five voices with instruments. Then he presents Psalm 8, "O Lord, our Lord," à 8, for voices and instruments. In the second part of his *Geistliche Konzerte* Scheidt then added Psalms 148, 133, and 15. Thus he became one of the most industrious and outstanding concert psalmists of the time. Dan. Selich in Wolfenbüttel expressly refers to Schütz in 1624 in his *Deutsche Konzerte und Psalmen,* twelve compositions for from two to eleven voices.

Andr. Hammerschmidt was a man who learned especially from Schütz the brilliant possibilities of this genre, while the lyrically intimate, not to say "romantic," side was developed by few as extensively as by J. Rosenmüller, who also found later models for this category in Schütz. Both types finally converged to flower anew in Handel's anthems.

It is both strange and deplorable that up to the present time there have been so few new editions of Schütz's polychoral *Psalms.*[80] Perhaps this neglect can best be explained by the fact that in the evangelical church the psalms as a whole no longer occupy a regular liturgical status. Unfortunately, the minor services have for the most part lost their special character; and, in addition to this, those in charge of

---

[80] Apart from the above-mentioned practical editions of the nonpsalm works, I know of only three of the psalms, edited by Franz Wüllner through Rieter-Biedermann (now Peters) in 1878; all are transposed, with numerous dynamic indications, *a cappella* without continuo: *Ach Herr, straf mich nicht* (beginning in Db major); *Aus der Tiefe rufe ich, Herr* (E major); *Singet dem Herrn ein neues Lied* (Ab major). This revival long before the publication of the complete edition was most commendable. Since then *Psalm 84, Wie lieblich sind deine Wohnungen,* has been published in the *Handbuch d. ev. KM., Das gesungene Bibelwort,* p. 355. *Psalm 98, O Sing unto the Lord,* in G, *a cappella,* edited by Ameln and Mahrenholz, published by Vandenhoeck and Ruprecht (Göttingen, 1949).

them do not have elaborate musical forces at their disposal. If these powerful and deeply religious works, then, are again to be given a place in the liturgy, either the honored position of the psalms at vespers should be restored as of old, or the psalms should be used (as Schütz is proved to have used them in 1617) as Introits in the principal services, or — particularly those with a doxology — as concluding numbers. A "musical vesper service" would form a very appropriate frame for them. At Schütz festivals a number of them have produced the greatest effect, both when presented with large forces as well as when given with more modest ones. In the latter case some three singers or players to each part of the *complementum* against the *favoritae* produced the effect desired by Schütz. On all other festal occasions certain of these compositions are suitable, provided one wishes to allow the psalmist of the Bible to be heard.

In 1660 there appeared in Breslau the *Wohlwertes Lob der edlen Singekunst,* by Godfrid Lischke,[81] in which one reads:

> *Was der Schütze, Scheidt und Schein und der Selich abgesungen,*
> *Wie sie durch sinnreichen Klang bis gen Himmel sich geschwungen,*
> *Ist den Deutschen wohlbekannt. Jenen liebte diese Stadt,*
> *Wo der weltberühmte Sachs seine Kunstkapellen hat;*
> *Diesen ehret mancher Fürst in dem salzbelobten Halle,*
> *Der gab Meissens Pleissestrand überviel mit grossem Schalle;*
> *Selichens gelehrten Ton nahm das Wolfenbüttel an....*[82]

---

[81] A. Werner, *Vier Jahrhunderte im Dienste der Kirchenmusik* (1932), p. 167.
[82] That which Schütz and Scheidt and Schein, and, too, Selich have sung forth,
How through artful song they winged to the very gate of heaven,
This to Germans is well known. That one did this Dresden love,
Where the world-famed Saxon has his chapel known for art;
This one honored many a prince in the salt-famed town of Halle;
Schein abundantly did bless Saxon's Leipzig on the Pleisse,
While the Wolfenbüttel court Selich's learned tone did hear.

Individual Chorus Psalms

Apart from the larger works designated by *opus* numbers — i. e., *Op.2* of 1619; the *Geistliche Chormusik, Op.11;* and the *Sinfoniae sacrae III, Op.12* — Schütz wrote a whole series of individual chorus psalms, some *a cappella*, some with instruments. They may be listed here according to their number in the Psalter, and then they may be discussed according to the time of their origin or according to their scoring:

		Vol. of complete ed.
Ps. 5	*Herr, höre mein Wort* ("Give ear to my words")	[*à 8*, ed. by H. Engel]
Ps. 7	*Auf dich, Herr* ("O Lord, my God, in Thee")	XIII, *à 4*
Ps. 8	*Herr, unser Herrscher* ("O Lord, our Lord")	XIII, 2d comp.
Ps. 15	*Herr, wer wird wohnen*	XIII
	("O Lord, who shall abide")	
Ps. 19	*Die Himmel erzählen die Ehre Gottes*	XIV, 1st version
	("The heavens declare")	
Ps. 24	*Domini est terra* ("The earth is the Lord's")	XIII
Ps. 85	*Herr, der du bist vormals*	XIII
	("Lord, Thou hast been")	
Ps. 116	*Das ist mir lieb* ("I love the Lord")	XII, p. 3
Ps. 127	*Wo der Herr nicht das Haus*	XII
	("Except the Lord build")	
Ps. 133	*Siehe, wie fein und lieblich* ("Behold, how good")	XIV, 1st version

The funeral music for Jakob Schultes, Jr. (1625), on the last verse of Psalm 23, "Goodness and mercy," may be added here.

Psalm 133 (1619),[1] composed as a wedding gift for his brother George, towers above the occasional pieces in a similar category already described, not only in the compass of its two sections but especially in the fact that an orchestral part with its own motives[2] is developed in juxtaposition with a five-voice chorus (with two sopranos) in motet form.

---

[1] Cf. also C. von Winterfeld, *Johs. Gabrieli*, II, 209.
[2] *Cornetto muto (stiller Zinken);* violin or *flauto traverso;* bass viol or bassoon.

If I judge correctly, the primary function of these often very lively orchestral voices is either to present in diminution the interjections by the chorus, as that at *wie fein und lieblich ist's* ("How good and pleasant it is") (p. 145), or to afford contrast by antithetical motion and more agitated rhythms — assuming that no undisclosed allusions of a personal kind lie concealed in the themes which change in the different sections. For the anguished Monteverdi fourths at the beginning of the prelude are somehow surprising and extraordinary:

From the fact that when the second chorus is repeated (p. 144), it enters climactically a third higher we may surmise an allusion to Monteverdi's *Lamento d'Arianna* (1608); for even though this work was not printed until 1623, it is known to have circulated in manuscript copies after the first performance and to have produced a sensational effect. Perhaps this and some other things, which according to Schütz's standards would otherwise be almost devoid of meaning, were to remind George, the zealous author of Italian madrigals, of days spent together on the Rialto.

At the beginning of Part Two we have a fine confirmation of Schütz's feeling for form in the fact that the orchestral *ritornello* is now repeated in the lower third. The repeated notes *(Note radoppiate)* reveal the minute articulation in the organization of the parts. One should note the genuinely instrumental nature of the broken triads:

Now again the pictorial comes into its own in the chorus portrayal of the *Berge Zion* (pp. 152-153), and the *g—c—*G conclusion is felt as a genuine plagal ending. The reworking of this composition thirty-one years later will be discussed hereafter.

One of the most beautiful of Schütz's occasional pieces had its origin in a strange commission which he received in 1619. The tax collector for the prince, Burkhart Grossmann of Jena, had escaped a great danger in 1616 and had promised, after the manner of genuine numerical mysticism, to have Psalm 116 set by sixteen composers. The fact that he could not get this collection printed until four years later[3] was due to the debasement of the coinage and the lack of raw material connected with the outbreak of the war or, as he says in the preface, which has already given us so vivid a picture of the times:

"The distributor Mercury has delayed this publication at least two years in that he not only distributed all the gold and silver but also did not hesitate to create a scarcity of rags and make them very expensive so that paper mills, printing presses, and bookshops would close their doors and fall into ruin, and that therewith all praise, honor, and service of God, together with justice and the liberal arts, might be effaced and suppressed, while destructive Mars still follows in his footsteps."

Thus arose Schütz's six-part and five-voice *a cappella Psalm 116: Das ist mir lieb* ("I love the Lord") in Vol. 12 (No. 3, p. 3).[4] This work thus affords a unique and hitherto neglected possibility of comparing our master's textual and musical interpretation with that of several other masters who, superficially at least, stood near him. Though certainly the contributions of M. Altenburg, Nicolaus Erich, Andreas Finoldt, Abr. Genssreff, Joh. Groe, Joh. Krause, Christian and Daniel Michael (twin sons of Roger Michael), and Caspar Trost are in no wise comparable to his,

---

[3] *Unicum* of the Staatsbibl. Berlin: *Angst der Hellen und Friede der Seelen.* Note the opening page of the tenor voice part, which relates to this title drawn from the psalm. In a very excited woodcut it presents the light-dark, affectual antithesis so characteristic of the baroque and its musical ideals.

The sixteenth century already had occasional competitions on the part of various composers with regard to the same *cantus firmus* problem: so in the case of the Adam von Fulda tenor *Ach hülf mich leid* (Adam, Noel Balduin, Hans Schechinger; cf. *Jb. d. Akad. f. Kirchen- u. Schulmusik*, I, 12 ff.); so sometimes also as "nest" in the same handwriting, for example, in Munich, Staatsbl., 3155, immediately following one another: *An aller Welt*, by L. Senfl, Jörg Planckenmüller, and Arnold v. Bruck.

[4] Published by R. Holle through Schott. Those by Schein and Demantius appeared in Blume's *Chorwerk*, ed. by Ad. Adrio.

at the time Chr. Demantius, Melchior Franck, Roger and Tobias Michael, Mich. Praetorius, and Joh. Herm. Schein all had great prestige. The restless master of Wolfenbüttel[5] alone deviates from the ranks in that he was the only one who supplied his *opus* with orchestra and solo voices and used the modern *f* and *p* for the chorus *tutti* of the hallelujah conclusion, so that a comparison or co-ordination in this case becomes somewhat difficult. We shall also avoid evaluation of the works of the genuine masters, which, of course, because of their personal style and that of their particular generation, are difficult to reduce to a common denominator.

Nevertheless, a few textual passages reveal very characteristic differences of treatment, as, for example, in the case of the *Tränen*. Because of limitations of space we shall restrict ourselves to the discant:

Schütz, on the other hand, gives us expressive harmony tensions in place of the sob figures based on the pseudopolyphony of monodic recitative.

---

[5] Michael Praetorius.

Or the *Gleiten;* J. H. Schein paints

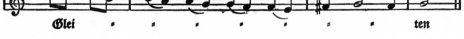

Tob. Michael has this phrase contracted to three voices, the second *cantus* being introduced as a canon to the first; the painting is vivid:

It is strange how some melody types seem to be characteristic of the period; thus we find (of course, entirely independent of one another) Schein writing:

Roger Michael:

Chr. Demantius:

The example *von den Tränen,* given above, from Joh. Groe, is almost the same; further Abraham Genssreff, superintendent in Freiberg, who in a neat distich excuses himself for having been able, on account of official duties, to compose only the first part:

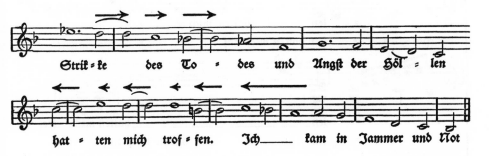

One actually sees this generation freely given to sobbing "wretchedly" with upstretched hands. How totally different Schütz is! While all the fifteen others pass over the word *Hölle* or, at the most, color it a bit with a shadow, he stages a furious devil's descent to the abyss. What spontaneous vitality also in his *hatten mich troffen* ("get hold upon me")! It is like a picturesque piece from his Italian madrigals; yet it is in no wise frivolous, but it is full of the deep passion of faith:

Here surely we see no mere talent, but we see genius that really paints the "tortures of hell" while employing supreme technique at the same time.

The excellent Melchior Franck, although considerably older, also proceeds in a genuinely expressive manner:

and the great vivacity of M. Praetorius shows itself in the wide contrast of the positions of the vocal phrases:

But where those other contemporaries are either pedantically dry or sentimental, Schütz strikes with the noble Damascene sword of his polished rhythm:

And altogether in the style of *der den Herren fürchtet* in *Psalm 128* of 1619 or of the *vitam aeternam* at the close of the *Cantio sacra XVII* of 1625 he lays down as a gigantic, double textual band at the close of the *seconda parte* in the second soprano and bass the *O Herr, errette meine Seele* ("O Lord, I beseech Thee, deliver my soul") (p. 6), with the other three voices anxiously knocking at the door with their eighth notes:

Certainly in this instance Grossmann's commission produced no mere secondary work, and Schütz's composition confirms the truth of what Goethe said so significantly:[6] "The occasional poem is the first and most genuine of all species of poetry...."

One should not underestimate the additional setting of Psalm 87[7] in g, even though the scoring is comparatively restricted — five solo voices and six instru-

---

[6] *Dichtung und Wahrheit,* II, 10.
[7] Vol. 13, No. 2, 29.

ments. The optional chorus-*capella* which enters at the climaxes merely doubles
the *favoriti* quintet. As the work is preserved only in Kassel, it was doubtless
written not later than the middle of the twenties. The striking preference for the
Florentine opera intervals, as, for example:

would fit well into the *Dafne* period. The way in which four trombones associate
themselves with the second alto in painting the moon and the stars is very romantic:

Significant of Schütz's impressionistic freedom in voice-leading is such a little
collision of parts as

and the extremely energetic upward thrust of the harmony, to indicate the renewed
exaltation of one temporarily forsaken by God:

There is much warmth in the sections *Was ist der Mensch* ("What is man") (p. 33) and *Alles hast du unter seine Füsse getan* ("Thou hast put all things under his feet") (p. 37). Cf. the *Seitenklang* chords of the sixth![8] Especially beautiful is the manner in which from the more meager scoring the repetition of the opening verse is developed at the conclusion. What the tenor soloist first sang with continuo accompaniment is now harmonized into a *tutti*. Note that according to the directions, the violins and cornets should be so placed as to frame the solo quintet, with the trombones and the complementary chorus in the background.

The comparison between this setting and that of the same text in the collection of 1619 is very instructive. One feels inclined to say that the differences are more unintentional than planned, or that they have arisen of themselves merely as the result of the different scoring and the different tonality (Ionian as against G Dorian). Otherwise, however, the same ideas *(Säuglinge — Sterne — krönen — im Meer gehen)* are also in characteristic figures; and after the passage *Alles hast du unter seine Füsse getan* has been declaimed both times in the same *tutti* and the same rhythm, the *Schaf und Ochsen allzumal* ("All sheep and oxen") is limited to the same lower semichorus without instruments. If we were concerned with two different composers, it might well be concluded that one had abundantly influenced the other. And yet the two pieces are as different in musical content and inspiration as two pieces by the same master in the same category, and composed within a few years of each other, could well be. The psalm of 1619 is monumentally static; the other, spirited, moving, flowing. Like Linnaeus in the case of the *Gentiana lutea* and *purpurea,* one could demonstrate from the two cases the unity of the *genus* and the variety of the *species.*

Psalm 7, Auf dich, Herr, traue ich ("O Lord, my God, in Thee do I put my trust")[9] has likewise been preserved only in Kassel manuscript voice parts. Set for two choruses with a *coro aggiunto di stromenti,* one may well view it as a representative of the second part of the *Psalms of 1619,* which Schütz had planned at the time. The seven-voice instrumental *capella* is treated now in *tutti,* now with a cleavage of two violins and viola from the quartet of cornets and three trombones as a semichorus. If we view briefly again the ground plan, we must realize that the eighteen verses of the psalm are constructed rather loosely and irregularly. One feels that in a whole series of instances Schütz has dovetailed the ends of the sentences into one another in order to declaim the lines expressively according to

---

[8] H. Riemann calls a chord of the sixth which has the same ground tone as a preceding chord and which may be viewed as a melodic gradation a *Seitenklang.*

[9] Vol. 13, No. 3, p. 45.

their inner meaning, with the lines, as it were, overflowing one another. The result is that he now combines two verses into one, now halves the single verses in order to accumulate new reserves before the *tutti* or tonal concentrations before solo passages.

A
- V. 1: As merely a superscription relating to the origin of the psalm, this verse has not been set.
- V. 2: Prolog: *Auf dich, Herr, traue ich* ("O Lord, my God, in Thee do I put my trust"). *Tutti;* further course antiphonal; finally also with antiphonally subdivided orchestra. Cadence course: G—G.
- V. 3: *Dass sie nicht wie Löwen* ("Lest he tear my soul like a lion"). Bass 1 & 2; Vl. 1; cornet — G.
- V. 4 and 5: *Herr, mein Gott.* Tenor 1 and 3; trombones — A.

B
- V. 6: *So verfolge meine Feinde, Sela* ("Let the enemy persecute my soul"). *Tutti* — G.
- V. 7 and 8: *Steh auf, Herr* ("Arise, O Lord"). Disc. 1 and 3, with Bc. only — D.
- V. 9 and 10: *Der Herr ist Richter* ("The Lord shall judge the people"). Alto 1 and 2, with Bc. only — G.

C
- V. 11-14a: *Mein Schild ist bei Gott* ("My defense is of God"). *Tutti* — G.
- V. 14b: *Seine Pfeile hat er zugericht't* ("He ordaineth His arrows against the persecutors"). Chorus I only, without orchestra — G.
- V. 15a: *Siehe, der hat Böses im Sinne* ("Behold, he travaileth with iniquity"). *Tutti* — C.
- V. 15b-17: *Mit Unglück ist er schwanger* ("He hath conceived mischief"). Tenor 1 and 2; with Bc. only — G.
- V. 18: *Ich danke dem Herrn* ("I will praise the Lord"). *Tutti* — G.

The general arrangement is clear: first, between the *tutti,* two chamber music quartets; then, between the next *tutti,* two vocal duets with continuo; now a quasi *finale* in the middle of which once more there is placed a vocal duet with continuo. The three tonal digressions to the dominant of the dominant, the dominant, and the subdominant also make the oscillations of the form clear.

Very picturesque is the disappearance of the *Verfolger* ("persecutors") (pp. 45-46), like the *wegsterben* in the *Ich bin die Auferstehung* ("I am the Resurrection"), a successive extinguishing of the voices of the one chorus. Similarly picturesque figures are used with *Erhaschen, Zerreissen* (pp. 48-49), *Sammeln* (pp. 57-58), and *Grimm* (p. 55); while *Zu Boden* (p. 52) and *Steh auf* (p. 54) have musical figures representing movement in space; note also the *Emporkommen* (p. 58). In the case of the *Nieren* ("reins") the madrigalism is not devoid of the comic, as Schütz employs the figure which he otherwise uses for "water" (p. 62).[10] Ph. Spitta has discussed extensively the change in harmony on page sixty-three, measures one and five, where D major follows Bb major, and E major follows C major, and yet despite this fact f and g, respectively, are continued in the higher octave, a tonal hardness which justifies itself by appealing to the Renaissance idea, contrary to what we actually hear, that f and f# (g and g#) are merely shadings of one and the same tonal root. In the course of the psalm the declamation achieves even greater compactness. The tenor duet, verses fifteen and sixteen, is one of the most picturesque passages that Schütz has written: *Seine Pfeile hat er zugericht't, er wird einen Fehl gebären, er hat eine Grube gegraben und ist in die Grube gefallen* ("He ordained his arrows against the persecutors; he brought forth falsehood. He made a pit- - - and is fallen into the ditch which he made") (pp. 68-69). The final *tutti* also, with its tonal masses in straight time and its dancelike triplets, can take its place beside many of his chorus psalms.

The house-building *Psalm 127* (Vol. 13, No. 5, 132) is seized upon with particularly fresh vigor. It must not be considered a biased, modern interpretation if we see indications of a quiet humor in Schütz's composition, which, to be sure, are even strengthened in the second setting *(Sinf. sacrae III, 1, X, 27)* by the episode with the night watchman's horn. The beautifully flowing piece (from Kassel voice parts) is intended, according to a remark in the violin part, to be presented in such a way that not only the five-voiced Chorus I but also the four-voiced Chorus II will consist of *voci concertati*, i. e., rather of solo voices; at any rate, not *complementum*. The general pauses after *umsonst* and the strong and pleasantly rounded conclusions, *die daran bauen*, establish a smug and cozy undertone; similarly the sole g minor tones within the C major composition at *lange sitzet* (p. 138) and *gibt er's schlafend* (pp. 140-141). In mentioning the *Kinder und Leibesfrucht* (pp. 142-143)[11] the sopranos have to do duty, and the comparison with *Pfeilen* ("arrows") is vividly painted in passages between solo bass and violins. The *Vollhaben*, the fullness of the quiver, brings the entire quintet *primi chori* upon the scene, soon

---

[10] The motet with which the anatomical amphitheater in Leipzig was soon thereafter dedicated may have presented a similar appearance: *Denn du hast meine Nieren in deiner Gewalt* ("For Thou hast possessed my reins").

[11] "Children and the fruit of the womb."

to be followed by the entire *tutti*. The *Feinde* ("enemies") are set forth chordally in the *stile concitato;* the *Handeln* (p. 155),[12] with reinforced figures. The composition is a concentrated work which one will gladly make use of at all kinds of dedications.

The question in verse one in *Psalm 15:*[13] *Herr, wer wird wohnen* ("Lord, who shall abide in Thy tabernacle? Who shall dwell in Thy holy hill?") receives in the original psalm its four brief answers: *Wer ohne Wandel* ("He that walketh uprightly"); *Wer mit seiner Zungen* ("He that backbiteth not"); *Wer die Gottlosen nicht achtet* ("In whose eyes a vile person is contemned"); *Wer sein Geld nicht auf Wucher gibt* ("He that putteth not out his money to usury"). In his *d* minor setting (XIII, 157), Schütz has not only extended this text but has also dramatized it most vividly by prefacing each of these answers with the same question, always with a variation in the scoring. He proceeds with amazing utilization of his means; for the two five-voice tonal bodies are selected in such a way that the vocal alto and bass with violins and *violone* simulate a full chorus, as do the vocal soprano and tenor with the three trombones. But the four solo voices also combine in duet and quartet groups, while in the introductory *sinfonia* the six instruments present a united chorus or antiphonal groups. One cannot achieve more with ten participants — or, if we add the thorough bass organist, with eleven!

Outline: { *Sinfonia:* 6-voice (*d*—D)
                V. 1: Tenor, alto, Bc. *(d—d)*
                V. 2: *Tutti*, antiphonal (*d*—D)

          { V. 1: Bass, soprano, Bc. *(d—a)*
             V. 3: *Tutti*, antiphonal (A—F)

          { *Sinfonia:* 4-voice (F—*d*)
             V. 1: Soprano, tenor, Bc. *(d—a)*
             V. 4: *Tutti*, antiphonal (A—C)

          { V. 1: Solo quartet, Bc. (C—*a*)
             V. 5: *Tutti*, antiphonal (*d*—D); coda: *Wer das tut* ("He that doeth these things"), with alto-bass, soprano-bass, alto-tenor, and soprano-bass as precentors (*d*—D)

---

[12] "Speak with the enemy at the gate."
[13] XIII, 157.

Here a few additional comments on *Psalm 19,* which Ph. Spitta printed twice.[14] From the viewpoint of composition it is almost too much to speak of two versions; for, apart from the opening note and one at *Landen,* almost the only passage that has been changed is the one at *zu laufen,* which in the later version was made still more mobile. From a biographical point of view it is interesting to note that pieces from the *Geistliche Chormusik* of 1648 may have their origin at a period at least twenty years earlier. But especially interesting are the great technical differences of presentation, and these allow conclusions with regard to some further numbers of the *Musicalia ad chorum sacrum.* Schütz originally bestowed a *concerto* character on the apparently smooth six-voice motet by the express separation of the *capella,* which he conceived as scored for large chorus with strong wind instruments, and the *favoritae,* for which he suggested delicate violas. The way in which, in addition, he presents the semblance of three- and four-voice semichoruses again demonstrates his skill in the use of his means. But we shall discuss the composition as such at a later point, where we shall also find added an *ad libitum* doxology for its use as an Introit or at Vespers.

Despite its strong scoring, the *e* minor *Psalm 85,*[15] *Herr, der du bist vormals gnädig gewesen* ("Lord, Thou hast been favorable unto Thy land"), is essentially a solo composition and, therefore, certainly belongs to a somewhat later period. Three large groups are represented by a five-voice *coro favorito* (two solo sopranos, two solo tenors, solo bass), a four-voice normal supplementary strengthening choir, and an orchestra of first and second violins and three trombones. So far as the orchestra is concerned, however, even in the introductory *sinfonia* the strings and the wind instruments perform antiphonally against one another as semichoruses.[16] The general plan of the architecture and the use of the text will show us that Schütz used the psalm to compose music for a political occasion. I consider it very likely that the piece served for the Mühlhausen Electoral Day of the fall of 1627.

Verse one of the German version of the psalm, *Ein Psalm der Kinder Korah, vorzusingen,* was obviously left uncomposed.

---

[14] XIV, as "earlier setting," according to voices in the manuscript looked through by Schütz himself; besides, an *Ordinanz* (Preface); and in the *Geistliche Chormusik,* VIII, 96.

[15] XIII, 80.

[16] Parts in Kassel. Ph. Spitta has splendidly supplied the missing continuo from engraved notes (*Stichnoten*), etc. He thinks that the trombones and the complementary choir (*Füllchor*) were perhaps composed by another hand, as they contain certain harshnesses. However, the trombones could not well be dispensed with in the opening symphony, and this is also true of the complementary chorus at *Ach, ach* (v. 9), and Schütz for once in no way shunned parallels between the groups so long as each group by itself was set correctly.

Sinfonia I *(e—e)*

A
V. 2: *Herr, der du bist vormals gnädig gewest deinem Lande* ("Lord, Thou hast been favorable unto Thy land"). Solo tenor and Bc. *(e—a)*

V. 3: *Herr, der du die Missetat* ("Thou hast forgiven the iniquity"). Solo tenor 2 and Bc. *(a—C)*

V. 4: *Herr,*[17] *der du vormals hast allen deinen Zorn* ("Thou hast taken away all Thy wrath"). Duet of both tenors *(a—a)*

V. 5: *Tröste uns, Herr* ("Be merciful unto me, O Lord"). *Tutti* with bass as precentor *(a—e* Phrygian)

B
V. 6-7: *Wilt du denn ewiglich über uns zürnen* ("Wilt Thou be angry with us forever?"). Bass solo with violins *(F—C—a)*

V. 8: *Herr, erzeige uns deine Gnade* ("Shew us Thy mercy, O Lord"). Soprano duet with trombones *(a—e)*

6-7: Tenor duet with Bc. *(c—d)*

8: Soprano duet, like the first (G—a)

V. 9: *Ach dass ich hören sollte* ("I will hear what God the Lord will speak"). *Tutti* led by the solo sopranos *(a—a)*

C
Sinfonia II: Violins only *(a—a)* as prelude to verse 10

V. 10: *Doch ist ja*[18] *seine Hilfe nahe* ("Surely His salvation is nigh"). Soprano duet with Bc. *(a—E)*

V. 11: *Lass Güte und Treue* ("Mercy and truth are met together"). Antiphonally solo sopranos and violins (E—G)

10: Solo quintet under the precentorship of the bass (C—E).

D
V. 12-14: *Dass Treue auf der Erde wachse* ("Truth shall spring out of the earth"). Solo quintet and violins, led by the tenors (E—C—G—E), the sopranos ever transposing thereto *(die Soprane immer transponierend)*.

From v. 11: *Gerechtigkeit und Friede sich küssen* ("Mercy and truth are met together"). Solo bass: *Ja, ja, ja!*

E
Doxology: *Tutti (a—a);* solo quintet, *Wie es war im Anfang* ("As it was in the beginning") *(a—a); tutti: Amen (d—E)*

---

[17] Schütz added this *Herr* on his own initiative in order to heighten the symmetry.
[18] Schütz always multiplied the *ja* 7 to 15 times. Spitta calls this *sächselnd* (Saxonizing); it would doubtless be better to call it "baroque impetuosity."

Thus the *Gloria Patri* (in itself a triptych) unites itself with the four psalm portions as a fifth part. The first part (vv. 2—5) is a *Bar* (AAB) with *tutti* conclusion; the second (vv. 6—9) an arch form *(Bogenform)* (ABA) with chorus *stretto;* here there is a main caesura. The third subordinate section (vv. 10—11) opens the second main division, again an arch form *(Bogenform);* the fourth is a *rondo* chain with a *rondo* arch. Ph. Spitta remarks with regard to this: "The entire work is extremely ingenious, being woven lightly and naturally like an opera ensemble." The doxology might be added to the fourth part as a choral conclusion if it were not in itself so extensively organized. And why a "state psalm"? Because the composer stresses in the most impassioned manner everything that might serve a council of peace: in the first *tutti* (v. 5) the *Tröste uns, Gott* ("Turn us, O God of our salvation, and cause Thine anger toward us to cease"); in the second *tutti* (v. 9), *Dass der Herr Friede, Friede, Friede* ("He will speak peace unto His people"). The passage takes its place with the greatest impressiveness beside the *Verleih uns Frieden, Frieden, Frieden gnädiglich*[19] of the Mühlhausen *concerto* of greeting, *Vivat Moguntinus*. And thus it continues: *Dass sie nicht auf eine Torheit geraten* ("But let them not turn again to folly"); *doch ist ja seine Hilfe nahe denen* ("Surely His salvation is night them that fear Him, that glory may dwell in our land"). And now again altogether Schützian:

But this greatest concentration of feeling in no wise deters the baroque court artist from introducing decorative echo plays — they begin in the concertizing violins at the bass solo, verse six (one hears the art of Carlo Farina!) — and then come fully into their own in the unison canon of the tenor duet in verse eight,[20] then, of course, completely to disappear in view of the full seriousness of the situation. An imposing piece for the times.

Among the anonymous Kassel manuscripts there has been discovered as a sure Schützian work *Psalm 5, Herr, höre mein Wort* ("Give ear to my words, O Lord").[21]

---

[19] "Lord, God, in mercy vouchsafe us peace."
[20] *In echo si placet e longinquo.*
[21] Ed. by Hans Engel as Edition Merseburger No. 924 in the *Evang. Verlagsanstalt,* Berlin, 1950.

The scoring reveals an architecture as original as it is impressive: there are four successive duets, each with varying singers: first two tenors, then two sopranos, then two basses, and then two altos. Finally the soloists unite in an antiphonal double chorus. One could, of course, employ groups of singers in place of the soloists. The whole is supported only by thorough bass, which will practically be assigned to the organ. At the final *tutti* strings or winds, or both, might easily be added. Engel has properly transposed the composition from *a* minor with *e* minor cadences (i. e., Hypoaeolian, according to the view of the time) to *b* minor-f# minor. The word-declamation (in No. 1, *Schreien;* in No. 2, *böse, Übeltäter, Falschen;* in No. 3, *in deiner Furcht;* in No. 4, *offenes Grab, heucheln, stosse sie aus)* is as full of Schützian preaching furor *(Predigerfurors)* as are the joy triplets of the concluding chorus which with unusual power of retardation institute hemiolas so that nine whole notes instead of six repeatedly constitute a measure:

The way in which this breathless *presto* transmutes itself *(sich fängt)* to a straight time *alla breve* at *Denn du, Herr, segnest die Gerechten* ("For Thou, Lord, wilt bless the righteous; with favor wilt Thou compass him as with a shield") — this constitutes one of the greatest climaxes the master ever succeeded in writing. One could even set the brief yet overpowering number a half tone higher and still have the alto duet sung by lyrical tenors, the tenor duet by dramatic tenors *(Helden-tenören)*, and the soprano duet by boys. Thus we would most closely approach Schütz's tonal intention. The composition constitutes a very valuable addition to Schütziana and lets us realize painfully how many similar glorious treasures must have existed beyond the number of those that have survived.

Finally, the only Latin chorus psalm by Schütz, *Psalm 24, Domini est terra* ("The earth is the Lord's and the fullness thereof"), reveals the richest scoring and the ripest mastery. This scoring and this mastery forbid us to view the work as a proximate result of the association with Gabrieli, despite its use of the Vulgate text. Ph. Spitta's surmise that it was only the Latin text which prevented the work from being included in the collection of 1619 doubtless dates the number with its formal organization too early. Furthermore, the fact that the only voice parts, some of them possibly autographs, belong to H. Albert's literary remains in Königsberg, suggests an origin scarcely earlier than 1630. It is conceivable that the festal piece was written as an Introit for a state occasion at which both Catholic and Protestant princes were present, like the Regensburg Reichstag of 1630, at which Wallenstein was deposed. The two four-voice normal choruses have in juxtaposition two orchestral groups, *à* 6 and *à* 7, the former consisting of four trombones and two violins, the latter of five (!) bassoons and two cornets scored very high. Today one might possibly employ violas in place of the highest trombone; a contrabassoon in place of the fifth bassoon; horns or, still better, bass clarinets for bassoons one and two; clarinets or oboes for the cornets.

Formally Schütz carried through a peculiar idea, one which we also meet in the Opitz madrigals. After a nine-measure orchestral *sinfonia* (G—G) the three lowest *favoritae* of Chorus I enter with *Domini est terra;* then the entire *tutti* continues with *et plenitudo ejus.* The three highest *favoritae* of Chorus I and Chorus II answer *Domini est terra,* and the *et plenitudo ejus* returns, but with exchange not of the *capellae* but of the choruses, then to be conducted further in the *tutti: orbis terrarum et universi qui habitant in eo,* i. e., schematized: a +A, b + A', C.

Now this opening verse returns twice, interpolated by Schütz after verse eight and verse ten for the sake of musical formal organization — but somewhat abbreviated, namely, the first time as b + A, in which case, however, the *cornetti* and the violins exchange at times, i. e., then, b + A' '; then, as final conclusion, a + A ' ' + A. Between these appearances the individual verses unfold themselves as changing episodes in the following manner:

V. 1: Solo terzet 1, *tutti*, solo terzet 2, *tutti*. G.

V. 2: *Quia ipse*. Solo bass 1 and 2 with descending motives *(maria, flumina)* for countermovement in short, embellished *(kolorierten)* duet interchanges of the *cornetti* and the violins. G.

V. 3: *Quis ascendet*. Solo soprano 1 and 2 *(steigend* and *stehend)* with the descent of the trombone quartet. G.

V. 4: *Innocens.* Solo alto 1 and 2 *(kurvisch)* supported by the five bassoons. G.

V. 5: *Hic accipiet*. Solo tenor 1 and 2 (more answering than in duet) with group interchanges between the trombones and the bassoons. G.

V. 6: *Haec est generatio quaerentium. Tutti* of the full choruses and *capellae* with interchange of both solo quartets. A.

V. 7: *Attollite*. Octet of both *favoritae* without orchestra, but then with very dramatic *tutti* interpolations: *Rex gloriae*. F.

V. 8: *Quis est*. Precentor (1; solo bass) and *tutti;* G.

(Interpolation: verse 1, abbreviated. Solo terzet and *tutti*). G.

V. 9: *Attollite.* Variation of verse 7 (same continuo, exchange of choruses). D.

V. 10: *Quis est*. Precentor (1; solo tenor, transp. of verse 8) and *tutti*. F. Then, spun out extensively, *ipse est rex gloriae (Penultima-Capriccio)*[22] as interchange between *favoritae* octet and chorus octet with orchestra). C.

(Interpolation and appendix: verse 1 as a + A '' + A). G.

Thus we have the most remarkable and ingenious development of the structure already present in embryo in the text *(tutti: generatio quaerentium)*, symmetries (verses seven and eight similar to nine and ten), and the utilization of the means. One should also note the genuine Schützian arrangement of the cadence procedures: G/GGGGG/AFGG/DFCG. What was noted in old handwriting on the voice parts is certainly correct: "very well and beautifully set." On this fine development *(Wohlgewachsenheit)* of the piece rests its chief value. It would make its revival — perhaps in translation — desirable.[23]

In order partially to compensate for the second part of the *Psalms of David*, which was promised for later years but never appeared, Ph. Spitta combinted six of these nine psalms in Vol. XIII of the complete edition. Perhaps Schütz, in view of the new visions pressing upon him, never arrived at writing anywhere near a

---

[22] Cf. my discussion, "The Fate of the Penult" *(Petersjb.,* 1934).
[23] The piece made a strong impression at the Schütz Festival in Dresden in 1935.

second group of some twenty-five compositions of that genre, and the compositions which have come down to us are scored in so variegated a manner that he would have wished to incorporate only individual compositions in this second part. But the residue that has come down to us is so rich and valuable that it deserves the highest consideration.

Supplementing the foregoing, we may discuss here also the six-voiced funeral motet with continuo for the young student Jakob Schultes (1625) on the final verse of Psalm 23, *Gutes und Barmherzigkeit* ("Goodness and mercy shall follow me") — apparently a special reprint as supplement to a funeral sermon. Unfortunately, only the first soprano, the alto, the first tenor, and two thorough-bass parts (written a fourth apart) have been preserved.[24] But fortunately the continuo permits to a great extent the reconstruction not only of the bass part, which manifestly has numerous long pauses, but also the missing second tenor and second soprano. Therefore I was able to reproduce the motet with considerable certainty.

The first part is dominated by long-drawn-out imitations, by harsh augmented chords of the sixth (g b e♭, etc.), and by suspensions of the ninth, and the like. Only in connection with the second thought, *und werde bleiben* ("and I shall remain"), does the music become joyous and show that the missing voices can be supplied from the thorough bass, as already mentioned. (See next page.)

With its melismatically far-flung conclusion, the composition is a splendid occasional piece which would well deserve to have been included in the *Geistliche Chormusik*. The work probably escaped Schütz's attention at the time he was gathering his material for this collection, because the occasion for its composition did not affect him as deeply as did the death of his sister-in-law or that of Joh. Herm. Schein. R. Wustmann, it is true, surmises that the collection of 1648 represents only the opening volume of a larger one which Schütz had in mind.

---

[24] Formerly Wolfheim Library, now *Landesbibliothek Dresden.* Also in the Dresden Ms. Schellenberg 35 only a few of the already known voices have been preserved. Unfortunately, my research among the most important collections of funeral sermons (Stolberg, Gotha, Halle, Leipzig, *Stadtbibliothek* and *Universitäts-Bibliothek*) were of no avail. Cf. *Letters,* pp. 362 and 385.

Op. 3. The Resurrection History of 1623

In the fifth year of the great war Schütz published an *Easter Oratorio*. This work, written according to Italian art form, with the recitative supported by chords, was almost a complete novelty in Germany. To be sure, one must except the small works, likewise in the Italian style, of the Mainz court organist Daniel Bollius. The latter compositions must have been produced between 1615 and 1628[1] and do not seem to have penetrated beyond the most limited circles in Mainz and Breslau.

In itself, neither the polyphonic setting of the *Easter History* nor the monodic oratorio was new. The novelty consisted in the combination of the two! I recently presented a type of the first class as the outstanding example dating from the sixteenth century: the unusually beautiful motet cycle in twelve sections by Leonhard Päminger, *Die drei Marien am Grabe (The Three Marys at the Grave)*,[2] which almost imperceptibly passes from the story according to St. John's Gospel into Wipo's Easter sequence, *Victimae paschali laudes*.

Just as this is an offshoot of the motet passion, so the *Auferstehungshistorie (Resurrection History)* of Nikolaus Rosthius of 1599 is similarly related as an Easter composition to the dramatic-choral (recitational) branch of the passion histories.[3] The Päminger work, despite its modest use of the customary church form, nevertheless directly prepares the way for that of Schütz. In the final chorus it even has the *Victoria!* which heretofore was attributed to Schütz as a singular stroke of genius. In fact, the use of this was traditional in Schütz's time. Above all, however, as can be demonstrated, Schütz used the *Easter History* of Antonio Scandello,[4] who brings in the *Victoria!* with all the voices at the conclusion. Schütz, then, did not create the work because no practical one of the kind was available. The *Leipzig Hymnal* of Vopelius of 1682 still printed the Scandello work as one

---

[1] C. v. Winterfeld, *Johs. Gabrieli*, II, 205 f.; M. Schneider, *AfMW*, I, 222; H. J. Moser, *Die mehrstimmige Vertonung des Evangeliums*, I, 54; cf. also *Musica moderna*, J. Andreas Herbst (1653).

[2] B & H.

[3] Berlin ms. 40016.

[4] Reprinted in Schöberlein and Riegel, *Schatz*, II, 619 ff. As to this see Julius Richter in MfM, 1882, pp. 37 ff.

sufficient for practical purposes. Schütz wrote his work because the form of those that were available did not meet his artistic requirements.

If again we look for examples of the monodic oratorio which might have served as models for Schütz, we find one even closer at hand than the famous *Rappresentazione di anima e di corpo* of Emilio dei Cavalieri of 1600,[5] such as the *Dialog of Abraham* from the *Motetti e dialogi* (Venice, 1615) of Giov. Franc. Capello,[6] who treats in solo song, without operatic pathos and yet with warmth, the story of the sacrifice of Isaac, interpolates short instrumental ritornelles, and presents the conclusion in a three-voiced chorus and strings.

Schütz took the text of his work — a Gospel harmony drawn from Luke, Mark, and John — faithfully from Scandello, his predecessor in Dresden; but he enclosed this text in a binding of his own. As Philipp Spitta remarks, Schütz shows on the title page the picture in which the risen Lord treads with one foot on death and with the other on the devil. The composer adds, in Latin, the verse from 1 Cor. 15:55: "O death, where is thy sing? O grave, where is thy victory?" He continues with the thanksgiving verse quoted also by Scandello as *gratiarum actio* from 1 Cor. 15: 57: "But thanks be to God, which giveth us the victory, through our Lord Jesus Christ."

Kade, in his *Ältere Passionkomposition* (p. 225), speaks briefly of resurrection histories by Benedikt Faber (1611) and Finolt (1621). A six-voice anonymous dialog, *Wer wälzet uns, Rabbuni* ("Who will roll away for us, Rabbuni"), is found in the Dresden manuscript, Pirna 23. Andreas Hammerschmidt wrote one for seven voices. Schütz's title page reads:

History
of the Joyous and Victorious
Resurrection of Our Only
Redeemer and Savior
JESUS CHRIST
In the Chapels or Chambers of Princes
At the Easter Season for Spiritual Christian Edification
Fittingly to Be Used
Set to Music
by

---

[5] Of Rome and Florence; see Schering, *Geschichte der Musik in Beispielen*, No. 169.
[6] Schering, *Beispiele*, No. 180.

HEINRICH SCHÜTZ
Kapellmeister
of His Serene Highness
the Elector of Saxony
(Picture of the risen Christ trampling
on death, and the Bible verse 1 Cor. 15:55)
Printed in Dresden at the printing press of the Elector of Saxony
by
Gimel Bergen

In the year 1623

Complete copies are preserved in the Berlin State Library,[7] incomplete copies in Grimma and Kamenz. A first reprint of most of the little duets (in which many of the mistakes of the first edition were corrected) is to be found in the *Fasciculus secundus geistlicher wohlklingender Concerten* (Nordhausen, 1637).[8]

In the preface to the reader[9] Schütz discusses the proper method of execution. He permits the use of the organ. The long-sustained chords, however, should be enlivened by improvising with "decorative and appropriate runs or passages"; otherwise the *falsobordoni*[10] will not attain "their proper effect." He prefers, however, to have in place of the organ a quartet of gambas, which would, of course, have to rehearse diligently with the evangelist. Therefore the text should always be inserted in the instrumental parts. Here, too, "one of the violas may improvise passages among the other instruments, as is customary in the case of the *falsobordon*. This gives a good effect."[11]

This would mean — when one consults the old gamba schools of Ortiz, Ganassi, and Girolamo della Caza (Venice, 1584) — that in place of the merely sustained *d* minor chord the second-highest (tenor) gamba would have to play. (See next page.)

This, of course, requires an artist with a sense of style and with the proper reticence — one who will execute only such passages as do not detract from the essential points of the narrative and neither delay nor hurry the *testo* (narrator). Schütz sets great store by the fact that the narrator *(historicus)* and the gamba

---

[7] A copy in Königsberg.

[8] G. A., I; practical new edition, Bärenreiter 22; there also, separately, the text.

[9] A royal dedication is lacking in this work.

[10] The term *falsobordoni (fauxbourdon)* is used not only to designate successive chords of the sixth but also for the improvisational chordal accompaniment of the psalm tones or recitatives.

[11] Cf. also C. v. Winterfeld, *Johs. Gabrieli*, II, 227 f.

group, as one choir, should be clearly separated from the other soloists, the choir of six voices, and the thorough bass (small organ), as the contrasting factor. He would like it especially if only the evangelist, book in hand, could be seen, while all the other performers stood hidden from view behind a curtain. These are the mystical operations of the Italian high Renaissance which we meet in Stuttgart in Lechner's late years (*Verborgen Musica*, 1599), in Schütz's biography in Dresden and Copenhagen, again in the life of Tartini, and once more in Goethe's *Wilhelm Meister*. With Schütz, however, they here have a pronounced Protestant coloring, as he wishes to see the real bearer of the Bible Word alone in the foreground. Finally, one more important direction by Schütz: He set the words of Mary Magdalene and the voice of Christ as a *duo*. Both parts, he suggests, can be presented vocally, as written; or one vocally, the other instrumentally; or, in case of necessity, even omit the one altogether. This last possibility will surely not be entertained by any who revere Schütz. The second, too — in view of the pronouncedly word-engendered character of the tonal color — is scarcely to be recommended. Extensive practice has taught me that for the voice of Christ — in place of the voices suggested by the pitch (tenor and female alto) — only the use of a baritone and a delicate tenor produce the effect desired by Schütz — both the mysterious transparency in the Person of the Risen One and the contrapuntal balance of the musical invention.

Schütz has done much more than place the choral, recitational Easter tone of Scandello over chords, although here, too, at the note *c* of the last music example, the resulting tonic minor seventh chord (d—f—a—c), without resolution, represents one of the master's boldest innovations and adds to the narrative an improbable, a mysterious, and, so to speak, a fairy-tale-like tone. But he also decisively reshaped the old melody formulas in a remarkable way and thereby gave the strongest impetus to the new Gregorianism of his later passion recitatives. In the first place, the master strongly limited the deviations from the tone "a" on which the evangelist recites *(tonus currens)* and thereby markedly accelerated the former tempo, a fact, however, which gives the evangelist no license to rattle off his part! But, above all, Schütz brought out melodically in the most striking degree the part sung by the evangelist at all those places which suggested emphasis, whether from the point of view of thought or of feeling. This applies not only to definite pictures or suggestions of motion, like the "rolling" *(Wälzen)* of the stone, the "weeping" *(Weinen)* of Mary, the "going out" *(Hinausgehen)* from the grave, the "falling down" *(Niederfallen)* of the disciples, the emphasis on the "other form" *(andere Gestalt)*, the "constraining" *(Nötigen)* on the part of the disciples on the way to Emmaus, and the "opening" *(Öffnen)* of their eyes — but also, to a large extent, to the handling of linguistic details. Compare:

(Madrigalismus)

Here one sees how, despite the continuance of the *d* tonality, Schütz presents, beside the chief reciting note *(tuba)* "a" with inflection on "f", also a darker one ("f") with inflection on "d" (here because of the words *zum Grabe,* "to the grave"); and a brighter one on "c," *und siehe* ("and behold"), with inflection on "a." He gives momentary enlivenment at *früh* ("early"), *bereitet* ("prepared"), *Engel* ("angel"); and at the cadences he always passes over to the definite compulsory time of mensural notation. The choral recitational tone is instructive in the case of Rosthius, who also has Jesus, Mary Magdalene, the youth, and "Cleopas alone" *(Cleophas allein)* sing on the note applicable to their respective registers, while he has set "Cleopas and his companion" and all the rest of the "multitude" *(turbae)* (two men, three women, the disciples) without exception for four mixed voices. Thus we have:

Even in Scandello we find the two-part setting for the "two" men and the three-part setting for the "three" women. When Scandello has Mary Magdalene, the angel, and Cleopas sing in two parts and Jesus each time in quartet form, Schütz arranges this as a duet, though, to be sure, with continuo foundation, while he even designates "Cleopas alone" as solo. Schütz's more-voiced treatment is a retrogression to the position of the motet passion from Obrecht to Demantius, a position which Schütz later abandons in his settings of the passion. The fact that Schütz has not already stripped off this old form shows him to have been much more closely associated with the German cantors than would have seemed likely in view of the Italian transformation of the *accentus* into the recitative. He apparently finds as most fruitful the constant self-development of the style of imitation, which, in addition, permits a number of word pictures to be carried out in exemplary fashion: *wer wälzt, auferstehen, hingelegt, verwundert sich* (= shaking of the head!), *wen suchst du?, ich fahre auf, geneiget, brannte, öffnet*.

But Schütz accomplishes his most astounding effects with the new means of sensitive harmony. If we recall the presentation of the concept *lieblich* in *Psalm 84* and *Psalm 133*, the same chordal sequence in the song of Mary Magdalene at once becomes a suggestive citation:

Then the twice-repeated augmented chord of the sixth (d—f#—bb, e—g#—c) at *Weib, was weinest du?* ("Woman, why weepest thou?"), which is darkened in the case of the same address on the part of Jesus to a—c#—f. Above all, however, there lies in such passages[12] as

something unutterable, mysterious, unreal, of the tone and bearing of those words of Angelus Silesius:

> *Mensch, so du willst das Sein der Ewigkeit aussprechen,*
> *So musst du dich zuvor des Redens ganz entbrechen.*
> Wouldst thou portray the essence of eternity,
> O man, all speech must thou abandon.

There is something indescribably gentle, intimately confidential, and tenderly pervasive in the mixture of sixths, as in songs, in the two-voice parts, and in the fleeting imitations of the *stile oratorio* in these Jesus duets, also the Schütz counter-rhythm, as, for example:

---

[12] Ernst Kurth (*Die romantische Harmonik,* 1920) sees herein most powerful predecessors of functional ventures of the nineteenth century.

At the end of the speech of the *Jüngling* — after the lively eighths — one should observe those broad, falling chains of syncopations, *siehe, ich hab' es euch gesagt,* which the Grossmann contributors to *Psalm 116* employed almost to excess *(Überdruss),* but which here in Schütz affect one not as sighing but as mysteriously soaring.

The scene at Emmaus also has similar passages of the greatest beauty, as, for example, the bold sequence from *f* minor to D major, in order to combine sadness with the question:

and again the combination of the liedlike tone (this time in thirds) with the fluent narrative tone in the speech of Cleopas and his companion,[13] a passage affecting one as being symmetrically parallel to the one quoted on the previous page:

---

[13] Both in the tenor clef; today use baritone and bass.

The sixteenths on the weak beat are, in the case of Schütz's style, essentially a preliminary figure or running start *(Ausholen)* intended to make the chief word, *Grabe,* strongly expressive. Likewise the fervor of the oft-repeated *bleibe bei uns* shows the baroque impressiveness of Schütz's repetitive words *(Häufungsworte),* as this device may be called. But perhaps the moving and the jolting effect of the Sagittarian form of presentation finds its most urgent expression in the liedlike words sung by the Lord, thrice repeated to a climax, and characterized by so wonderfully natural a rhythm:

The climax in the harmony, which ascends diatonically by seconds, F—G—a, reminds one of that *c—d—*E♭ succession in the mighty *falsobordoni* pillars in *Psalm 84* of 1619.[14]

What a warmth the *villanella* thirds of the monody have received, and how the *Fühlet mich und sehet* ("Touch Me and see") pleads itself into our hearts! How charmingly the remembrance of history smiles in the rapid triplets of the

---

[14] Sam. Scheidt's *Dialogus* of 1639: *Kompt her* (See Fr. Blume, *Monod. Prinzip,* Appendix, pp. 39 ff.) is a fascinating example of those psalm surfaces erected on one-voiced *tonus currens,* descending line by line, a type of setting that was in a vanishing stage.

in den Pro=phe=ten und in den Pſal   ʿ   ʿ   ʿ   ʿ   men

Above all, the final climax in the three final utterances of the Lord shows to what a height of expression Schütz has lifted the new solo recitative style. In view of this new birth and the complete maturity of this German modulation, who still thinks of Caccini? Two six-voice choruses, one at the beginning and one in the middle, as well as a nine-voice double chorus at the end, all in the more folklike and simple manner, serve as firm pillars for the whole composition. This is a work which, despite its stylistic roots so harshly opposing one another, nevertheless appears to have been welded together by Schütz's personality in complete harmony, and which, despite a novelty which even at the present day sometimes startles one but penetrates to the very innermost kernel of its subject matter and at the same time confirms the mysterious quality inherent in all that is artistically really great: the gift of being accessible in broad outline even to the simple man. So the devout master who in his thirty-eighth year contrived this mystery could place at its end in proud humility the Latin and German verses:

> *Christe! "Resurrexit" cecinit mea musica "Christus."*
> *Christe! Beatificum dic quoque "surge!" mihi.*
> *Sic nunc mortali cecini quod voce-resurgens*
> *Voce immortali tunc tibi, Christe, canam.*
> *Herr Christ, hieniedn hat mir's gelungen,*
> *Dass ich dein Urstend hab gesungen,*
> *Herr Christ, heiss mich am Jüngsten Tag*
> *Auch aufferstehn aus meinem Grab,*
> *So will ich dich mit ewigr Stim*
> *Im Himmel lobn mit Seraphim.*
> *Henricus Schütz Autor.*

O Christ! "Christ has arisen," sings my song.
O Christ! Say to me blessed, too, "Arise!"
What now with mortal voice I have sung
When I arise immortal I will sing to Thee.
Lord Christ, I have succeeded here below
In singing forth Thy resurrection.

Lord Christ, bid me on Judgment Day
From my grave also to arise;
Then with eternal voice
In heaven I will join in praise with the seraphim.

The liturgical environment in which this work stood in Schütz's time may be seen from an Order of the Christian German Songs for the Dresden Court Church. Fürstenau, to be sure, [15] places this order in 1521; but the content, for example, the verse referred to therein, *All Lob und Ehr soll Gottes sein*, which first appeared in 1539, proves that the date cannot be correct. 1621 is doubtless nearer the truth. There we read:

For Easter Vespers:

1. *Ich dank dem Herrn von ganzem Herzen*, etc. (= Psalm 9); *Da Israel aus Egypten zog* (= Psalm 114).

2. Then is sung the history of the resurrection of Christ.

3. The sermon to be introduced with the *Christ ist erstanden*.

4. After the sermon the *Magnificat* in German (= *Meine Seele erhebt den Herrn*), and thereupon *Jesus Christus unser Heilandt* (= Joh. Huss's hymn, paraphrased by Luther).

The Halle Church Order of 1640-60 gives the following direction with regard to vespers on Easter day:[16]

"The resurrection according to the composition of Herr H. Schütz should be performed."

Mahrenholz plausibly refers this prescription to the personal suggestion of Scheidt.

---

[15] *Geschichte der sächs. Capelle*, p. 32.
[16] Chr. Mahrenholz, *S. Scheidt*, p. 96.

German Secular Songs and Madrigals

H. Kretzschmar[1] attempted to answer in the affirmative the question whether Schütz wrote a large number of German solo songs which have disappeared. He wrote:

> "If the earliest development of the accompanied song in Germany is to be associated with the name of a definite musician, that of Heinrich Schütz, the chief pioneer of Italian art, the creator of our spiritual concert and of the first German opera, of course, lies closest at hand. And as a matter of fact, Paul Fleming, in his poem to Johann Klipstein, speaks of songs by Schütz, and in addition to Fleming, who might have been confused as to names, Christian Dedekind, in the preface to his *Aelbianische Musenlust*, also places Schütz among the song composers."

The passage in Fleming[2] reads — after he has praised the power of song in general terms:

> *Wenn Schützens Lieder klingen,*
> *So wächst des Sachsens Lust! Wenn Nauwach das Pandor*
> *Läßt hören und mit ihm den künstlichen Tenor,*
> *Da wacht mein Opitz auf, daß er des Künstlers Stimmen,*
> *So hoch, wo über uns der Leier Sterne klimmen,*
> *Durch seinen ersten Preis, die deutschen Vers' empört,*
> *Weil immer eine Kunst die ander' liebt und ehrt.*
> *Wo laß ich aber dich und deine schöne Laute,*
> *Herr Klipstein, welche dir von Hand zu Hand vertraute*
> *Apollo Phöbus selbst, der sich voreinst erdacht,*
> *Der deine schnelle Faust ihr griffreich hat gemacht? usw.[3]*

> When Schütz's songs resound,
> Then grows the Saxon's joy! When Nauwach the pandora
> Plucks and skillfully his tenor sings,
> Then doth my Opitz wake that he the artist's tones
> Through highest praise, through German verse, exalts
> To highest heaven, where lyres' stars do shine,
> Since ever and anon one art the other sings.

---

[1] *Gesch. des deutschen Liedes*, p. 9.

[2] Fleming addressed a whole series of poems to musicians; thus in Lappenberg's edition (Stuttgart, *Lit. Ver.* 1865): *Anagram auf J. H. Scheins Tod* (I, 41); *Auf M. Heinrich Lütgens, revalischen Musikantens Namenstag*, 1635 (I, 366); Mons. Bernhard Ostermannen, *Fürstl. Holsteinischer Gesandten Pandoristen aus Hamburg*, 1636 (I, 477); Mons. Christian Herpichen (= Herwig), *Fürstl. Holsteinischer Gesandten Violdigambisten* (from Heckstadt, Dukedom Mansfield), 1637 (I, 484); Ms. Joh. Hillebranden (from Hamburg) *dgl. Violisten*, 1637 (I, 485).

[3] The idea that Klipstein, who, as a matter of fact, celebrated his golden wedding in 1656 as Leipzig notary public, was "a famous lutenist from Prague" is doubtless one of the favorite fairy tales from Fétis, *Biogr. mus.*, V, 58. A Latin panegyric on him by Steinmetz is found in *Silvae juveniles*, pp. 65-66.

> But where do I leave thee and thy most beauteous lute,
> Herr Klipstein, which to thy hand entrusted
> Phoebus Apollo himself, who did the same invent
> And made thy hand so skillful o'er its strings? etc.

In another poem by Fleming, addressed to Schütz himself, the master's *Lieder* are mentioned, after he had compared him to Orpheus:

> *Du machest dir mit deinen Liedern*
> *Höll' und Himmel untertan.*
> With your songs
> You have subdued hell and heaven.

Quite similarly in the dedicatory verses addressed to Schütz by Kaldenbach. In my opinion, these passages are not so unequivocal; but they might refer to Schütz's Opitz madrigals or to his composing in general. In the case of Dedekind, Schütz, like Chr. Bernhard, is mentioned in the epilog only in general as an authority against the view of the critics, as both Schütz and Bernhard bestowed praise on Dedekind's collection. One may rather concur in Kretzschmar's further discussion:

"As against these witnesses, the mere circumstance that up to the present time no songs of Schütz have been found[4] does not appear decisive. Do the larger solo songs, such as the *Historie vom Absalon*, with its complicated harmonic construction, or the solo psalms, so rich in coloratura, really point to a special song talent? The matters mentioned indeed speak strongly for the fact that Schütz really composed songs, even though indications are lacking as to the time when he did so. But be this as it may, it is certain that indirectly Schütz furthered the new style of song writing more than any of the outstanding Germans of the seventeenth century. Clear evidence is found in the prefaces which he supplied for the song collections of Adam Krieger and Christian Dedekind. To this must be added the fact that a great number of the earliest German song composers stood in personal relations to Schütz: Heinrich Albert is his first cousin; Schein, Tob. Michael, Nauwach, Kittel, Reussner, Hammerschmidt, Röbel, Bernhardt, Dedekind, Ad, Krieger, Stolle, Theile, Kremberg are his subordinates, pupils, or friends. He recommends the restless Löwe for a position in Brunswick; Benj. Praetorius hails from Schütz's second home, Weissenfels. Possibly he, too, was a *Voigtländer* and can be shown to have had close relations with Rist. Even more than from the German opera of the seventeenth century the threads lead in most places from the song of the day to the faithful Eckart of sound musicianship. He may be counted as the first and most important patron of the new lied. This proceeded from the circle about Schütz, and Saxony is the home of the earliest demonstrable lied composers."

This influence of Schütz on the high-minded group of the early German masters of song (as contrasted with popular song, especially of the South German baroque)

---

[4] Appeared in 1911. But Ph. Spitta (*GA*, XV, 6) had already known of the *Lamentation* of 1623, *Grimmige Gruft*, through Eitner's *Werkverzeichnis* of 1886; Heinr. Spitta (*GA*, XVIII, 13) forgot to mention the first publication of the work by Karl Lütge, in the *Kretzschmar-Festschrift* (1918), p. 85.

I attempted to set forth further in the section of my *Corydon* (I, 1), titled "Heinrich Schütz As a Master of the Lied, and His School," where, especially in opposition to Kretzschmar's disparagement of Schütz's relative, Caspar Kittel,[5] I adduced Schütz as one of the very best forces of the new movement.

When we survey the pertinent Schütz material which has been preserved and disregard that early overpacked orchestral song, *Ach wie soll ich doch* (Vol. 18, No. 8), the list begins with a lamentation written and composed by him, a single printed page (through G. Hoffmann, Freyberg, 1623), of which the Prussian state library in Berlin possesses the sole copy:

> Sad farewell from the electoral vault at Freibergk,
> in which the Electoral Saxon Mother, the Most Serene
> high-born Princess and Wife, Sophia,
> Duchess of Saxony, Electress, Widow, etc.,
> who departed blessed in God on the 7th of last December in Dresden,
> was laid to rest and buried on the following January 28, 1623,
> with the most eminent electoral and princely following.

At the conclusion: "Author of words and melody: Heinrich Schütz."

Since K. Lütge's first reprint Johannes Wolf published the work in facsimile as the annual contribution for 1921-22 of the friends of the Bückeburg Institute. He also presented it in his *Sing- und Spielmusik* (p. 155) with the accompaniment copied from the score. Finally, H. Spitta included it in the complete edition in XVIII, 116. The melody to the six strophes is so characteristic of Schütz's position with regard to the song problem that we offer it here briefly. It is only necessary to omit the first strophe to obtain a generally excellent and useful solo composition for funerals:

---

[5] As already anticipated by Eugen Schmitz, *Geschichte der weltlichen Solokantate*, p. 213, and W. Vetter, *Das frühdeutsche Lied*, I, 181; II, 61 ff.

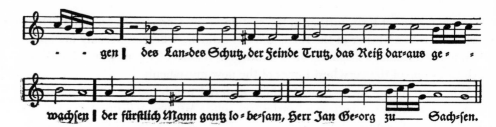

- - gen │ des Lan-des Schutz, der Feinde Trutz, das Reiß dar-aus ge - -

wachsen │ der fürstlich Mann gantz lo - be-sam, Herr Jan Ge-org zu——— Sach-sen.

This is, as can be seen by the sharp caesuras at the rhyming words, a real strophic song melody. In the first line the basses move from C to *d;* in the second. from G to *d;* in the third, from Bb to *a;* and in the last, from *d* to G. But the original *Bar* form (a—a—b couplet and conclusion) has been effaced through the monodic setting, inasmuch as Schütz, after the manner of a Monteverdi *lamento,* moves the second part of the distich up a third (from g' to b') and varies the cadence rhythmically. The changed position of the "shuddering" sixteenths (the sixteenths signifying a shuddering to represent the grave) in the second part of the distich, as against the three other occurrences, is sufficiently obvious. So, too, is the metrically altered beginning of the second part of the distich. But the parallelism of the descending chains of syncopations[6] is worthy of note. However, at the beginning of the conclusion *(Abgesang)* we do not have genuine syncopations but rather a case of "agogic"[7] groups of threes from the tenor style of the sixteenth century:

Des / Landes / Schutz / der / Feinde Trutz,	The country's protector, the enemy's
Das / Reiss dar / aus ge / wachsen	defiance,
Der / Fürstlich / Mann, gantz / lobe / sam	The scion from which grew
Herr / Jan Ge / org zu / Sachsen.	The princely man, all praiseworthy
	Herr Johann George of Saxony.

But they also obey the old melodist art rule that they must be merged into straight time "without remainder."[8] We must recall the words of Schütz in the second preface to the *Becker Psalms:* "As such arias or melodies can be sung much more agreeably without measure bars, according to the promptings of the words."

---

[6] One is tempted to speak of a "fashion of the year 1623." Cf. the B. Grossmann *Psalms.*

[7] "Agogic" *(Agogik)* is a word coined by H. Riemann to designate the small wavelike motions *(Wellenbewegungen)* of the tempo and rhythm in connection with a vital musical presentation in contrast to the mechanical rigidity of the metronome. At one extreme, in the case of strong affectual concentration, it can lead to an "agogic stemming of the flow" *(Stauung);* at the other extreme it can reduce the syllabic presentation in straight time to "agogic triplets." See H. J. Moser, *Lexikon.*

[8] I. e., without any part of a beat being left over.

While the bass, at the beginning of the third line, is so arranged rhythmically that it represents straight time, it passes over to the three-part grouping at *das Reiss* and remains in this form. One should also not overlook the new-sounding modernism in the chromaticism between measures one and two:

likewise in the Monteverdi diminished fourth from b♭—f♯ from measure one to measure two of the quasiconclusion, and the false relation here in the concluding line:

One should also note the dominant of the dominant in the final measure. The second line, in itself fascinating from the viewpoint of a problem in expressive variation, remains free from such seasoning.

In 1627 Schütz contributed a little strophic song in duet form, *Glück zu dem Helikon*,[9] at the end of the collection made by his lutenist J. Nauwach. The text may be by Opitz — written in order to greet the new colleague. Phoebus and Orpheus play, however:

> *Ein neuen Klang zuvor,*   A new note now doth sound,
> *Der nicht in ihrem Chor,*   Which they had not yet found;
> *Ein Jüngling fing mit an,*   A youth begins to play
> *Spielt auch auf diesem Plan.*   Who goes his own sweet way.

The Muses christen the youth; the river of the gods, Permessos, also "praises the affair." The whole thing is a play on *Neuenbach* = Nauwach. H. Volkmann calls

---

[9] As already mentioned in connection with the Torgau royal wedding.

the little piece of seven strophes a canon. But it is better to call it a fughetta, as the tenor, overlapping line by line, also in *stretto,* changes the phrases of the alto in the fourth-fifth reflection *(Quartquinten-Spiegel)* of the tonal answer.

With these compositions, however, Schütz takes his departure for the time being from the lied in the narrower sense and leaves its continuation to the young talents Heinrich Albert and Kaspar Kittel. In the preface to the *C. Becker Psalter* (1627) he observed somewhat disparagingly: "There is scarcely a musician who could not set a strophic song melody." For nearly all the rest of his life he is fascinated by a new problem: the German madrigal, whether and how the form of the chorus and chamber lied, composed throughout *(durchkomponiert),*[10] could also be mastered in his mother tongue. The outward occasion for this was constantly presented by his official position. When the court musicians in Zeitz had not drawn up a proper music catalog, the angry old master wrote a special rubric to the superintendent.[11]

Secular and Moral Songs for Royal Banquets. The entire question was, above all, a problem of texts, as German poetry almost completely lacked "German madrigals," that is, lyric epigrammatic creations of few, unequal lines, with the freest rhyme couplings possible. About 1635 Paul Fleming once attempted such little pieces,[12] but for the most part the German poets neglected this genre. When finally Caspar Ziegler, in Wittenberg in 1658, in his treatise *Von den Madrigalen,* energetically demanded the madrigal form for Germany, Schütz had to conclude his letter of recommendation to his "much-loved brother-in-law"[13] with the snarling remark: "Though I scraped together a little work containing all kinds of poetry, I know best what labor it cost me before I could mold this approximately into the form of Italian music."[14]

This "little work" must once have consisted of much more than the present few little rhyme *concerti* in Volume XV of the complete edition. This is indicated by the titles of lost Schütziana in the old Weimar, Kassel, and Lüneburg catalogs, and by the old Breslau covers of Schütz's *Madrigali à 6* and *à 7,* of which each one today contains but one composition.

---

[10] As was his *Op. 1,* the *Italian Madrigals,* which he so brilliantly wedded to the Sagittarian genius.

[11] A. Werner, *Musik in Zeitz,* p. 66.

[12] In Vol. 5 of his *German Odes,* ed. by Lappenberg I, 401.

[13] Dated Dresden, August 11, 1653.

[14] Cf. Ph. Spitta's fine discussion in *Die Anfänge madrigalischer Dichtung in Deutschland (Musikgeschichtliche Aufsätze,* 1894, pp. 61 ff.); further, my *Corydon,* I, 18 ff. where I showed the St. Thomas cantor Seb. Knüpfer, with his *Lustige Madrigale und Canzonetten,* to have been the chief fulfiller of Ziegler's hopes in the secular field, in Leipzig in 1663.

We mention fifteen such lost pieces:

Ach Liebste, lass uns eilen (Ah, Dearest, Let Us Hasten)	à 4 (Opitz; Catalog, Lüneburg)
Auf, auf, meine Harfe (Up, Up, My Harp)	à 10 (Catalog, Weimar)
Canite, psallite, placidite (Sing, Play, Win Applause)	à 12 (Cat. Kassel)
Der Wind beeist das Land (The Wind Doth Frost the Land)	alto, 2 tenors, in D (Cat. Lüneburg)
Dies Ort, mit Bäumen ganz umgeben (This Place with Trees All Surrounded)	soprano, continuo, in A (ibid.)
Dorinda	German secular madrigal (Cat. Weimar)
Ein wunder Löwe (A Wondrous Lion)	(Cat. Kassel)
Einsmals, in einem schönen Tal (Once in a Beautiful Valley)	2 voices, 6 instruments, in D (Cat. Lüneburg)
Einsmals der Hirte Corydon (Once the Shepherd Corydon)	2 sopranos, 2 violins (ibid.)
Geht meine Seufzer hören (Go, Hear My Sighs)	à 5 (Opitz)
Sag, o Sonne meiner Seelen (Say, O Sun of My Soul)	à 4, duplic. in G (Cat. Lüneburg)
So bist du nun, mein Lieb (So Art Thou Now, My Love)	à 6
Täglich geht die Sonne unter (Daily Doth the Sun Depart)	à 6 (Cat. Weimar)
Venus, du und dein Kind (Venus, Thou and Thy Child)	à 6 (Opitz)
Wenn dich, o Sylvia (When Thee, O Sylvia)	à 6 [15]

First of all Schütz attempted to set a German translation of *Anacreon*, by Opitz (1624). The only manuscript, in Kassel, designates the composition as set for male alto, tenor, and continuo *(Madrigale à 2)*. It is based on the famous old ‘Η γῆ μέλαινα πίνει, in Opitz's *Die Erde trinkt für sich* (XV). Schütz has spun an entire "small secular concert" from the eight-line poem, i. e., a series of wider, then narrower, imitations of the line motives in motetlike concatenation. Despite approaches to cheerfulness — "would then, ye friends, begrudge me the draught"

---

[15] The titles not mentioned with local catalogs were supplied to me by Heinr. Spitta in 1929; I do not know the source from which he obtained them.

(wollt dann, ihr Freunde, mir das Trinken nicht vergönnen) — it is a piece too much encumbered by the conventional endings of the polyphonic *tricinium*.

Likewise somewhat dry is the attempt (XV, 74) to put an Opitz strophic poem in the "form of Italian music," namely, that of a concert for two solo voices. Nauwach set it in 1627,[16] Joh. Weichmann in 1648, and Andr. Hammerschmidt in 1649, all in strophic form. This madrigal, *Tugend ist der beste Freund (Virtue is the Truest Friend),* has been preserved in voice parts in Kassel and so surely must belong to the third decade of the century.

Apart from a brief *sinfonia* at the beginning, the structure is as follows:

Ritornello I	Strophe 1;
Ritornello II	Strophe 2;
Ritornello I	Strophe 3 = 1 (with the omission of the *Wolken* coloratura at *in den Tod auch für mich geben* and a somewhat abbreviated ending);
Ritornello II	Strophe 4 = 2 (except for the last page, which deviates considerably)

The principle is that of free imitation of one voice by another, the imitating voice entering after lengths ranging from one to two lines to a single beat. The entire composition is conducted in a sprightly, *canzonetta*-like leaping of syllables in eighth-note style, which constitutes the basis of all these pieces. Schein's *Waldliederlein* of 1621 also have it, without, however, having passed, as Schütz does, from the corporate group to the free solistic and instrumental category. Coloraturas are infrequent; but when they are used, they effectively clarify the text. The changing imitations prevent too symmetrical a structure in periodic phrases, and this seems to have been almost the most important thing for Schütz in this artistic effort.

Most closely related in form, and with exactly the same scoring, is the setting of Opitz's madrigal *Liebster, sagt in süssem Schmerzen (Dearest, Tell in Sweetest Anguish).*[17] This is one of the paraphrases of the *Song of Songs,* which Opitz in 1626 combined into *Himmlische Hirtenlieder* and presented to a larger public in the second part of his *Deutsche Poematum.* The poems are genuine love lyrics and have nothing to do with "Jesus and the soul" and the symbolic interpretations as "church" or "wisdom." Indeed, on the contrary, they are gently enlivened by something quaintly buxom and baggily baroque.[18] They are pieces for use at wed-

---

[16] Reprinted in Ph. Spitta's preface to XV, xv, and in W. Vetter, *Frühdeutsches Lied,* II.
[17] Vol. 15, No. 4, p. 38; practical edition by Max Seiffert in *Organum,* 1935.
[18] *Putzig Dralles und barock Plustriges.*

ding banquets or for an amorous domestic idyl of infatuated newlyweds. We have already remarked that Schütz doubtless composed these works toward the end of his wedded felicity or in recollection of the happy years which he had spent with his Magdalene.[19] They are a paraphrased branch of the *Song of Songs* motets which were in high favor as bridal Masses and were to find a chief master in Schütz. In this case, at all events, a very delightful little work of art resulted. It is much nearer the lied than that little moralizing concert, since it is kept altogether homophonic and makes no use of coloratura except for a few emphases at the conclusion of strophes. The structural plan intermingles very charmingly *rondo* juxtaposition and *rondo* arch *(Rondo-Bogen)*, insofar as the large instrumental introduction returns divided into six little ritornelles (a—f), which always separate the two interchanging duet strophes A and B with *coda* strophe C, preceded by a little insertion (g), everything in G major. Thus:

abcdef   AaBbAcBdAeBfAgC[20]

Sinfonia

The chief prototype is the seventh *Book of Madrigals* by Monteverdi (1619), which contains nineteen duets among its thirty-three compositions. One of them is the *Canzonette* (XV, 91),[21] which doubtless, by reason solely of Schütz's translation, *Güldene Haare*, was designated incorrectly as one of Schütz's works. Its parallel thirds with voice exchange are, however, essentially more primitive than Schütz's bold construction:

How fruitfully, even though in a somewhat dwindling volume, this Schützian melody type continued its course may be seen from the examples compiled in

---

[19] Martin Goebel, *The Composition of the Song of Songs in the XVII Century* (Leipzig dissertation, 1914).

[20] In my *Corydon*, I, 5, I showed a similar structure in the case of the *Council of Trent Preces*, by Johs. de Kerle.

[21] Shown by A. Einstein in *Zf. f. MW*, V, 432 f.

Corydon, I, 6, from H. Albert *(Keine Nacht, kein Tag vergeht)*, J. M. Rubert *(Ein getreues Herze wissen)*, David Pohle *(Anemone meine Wonne)*, and Crato Büttner *(Wollt ihr wissen, soll ich's melden)*.

Considerably more important is a setting by Schütz in two parts of an Opitz poem which is found in manuscript in Breslau only. The composition is for soprano and bass with full string quartet and continuo, the themes of the quartet being richly worked out. It is entitled *Nachdem ich lag in meinem öde Bette (When I Was Tossing on My Lonely Pillow)*. There is a Part II, *Is Not the Bed of Solomon Protected?* That this number is in reality the second part of the former may be seen from a similarity in the scoring, style, and text form of 24 + 24 lines.[22]

Ph. Spitta astutely noted (XV, 11) that while Opitz has Solomon speak in the last four lines of the first part,[23] Schütz does not change the scoring. While the characters Sulamith and Solomon cause him to choose soprano and bass as soloists, he nevertheless does not divide the roles as in a drama. When Spitta interprets this to the effect that Schütz "then, morever, employs the voices solely as musical instruments,"[24] I believe he overstresses the formal side, since the division of the roles remains "poetic" throughout. Note, for example:

Ich sucht, ob ich den Liebsten bei mir hät=te

Ich fand ihn a=ber nicht

---

[22] At the end of Part I one may today take umbrage at the text:
> Although you have great delight in roebucks,
> So little shall you wake my dearest one.
> *So große Lust ihr habt zu'n Reheböcken,*
> *So wenig sollt ihr meinen Liebsten wecken.*

In place of this I would suggest:
> Though you such pleasure take in this pursuit,
> You shall not venture to awake my love.
> *So große Lust ihr habt, ihn aufzujagen,*
> *Zu wecken sollt mein Lieb ihr doch nicht wagen.*

A transposition from d minor to e minor will also commend itself. In the second example it is the bass who sings all the lines, twice in the treble and twice in the bass clef.

[23] Who can this be who comes in all her beauty
> That we may worship her,
> Like incense wafted far across the desert,
> With sweet spices and myrrh?

[24] *dann aber lediglich als musikalische Organe.*

In the first instance the soprano is the representative of joyful expectation; the bass, the expression of disappointed hope; in the second the bass is the portrayer of dark passion, the soprano indulges in an aimless running about *(Laufen)*. Both vocal oppositions are thus means of presenting antithetical affectual states. Formally the first part is divided into three similar and only slightly changed strophes, which, however, are introduced by three completely different quartet ritornelles. In precisely the same way — with new material — the second part is constructed, except that a *coda* is appended in which the voices and instruments are finally stratified instead of merely alternating with one another. In this concluding group we may agree with Ph. Spitta that we have merely a purely musical duet without any special purpose of poetical exegesis. In themselves, the strophes, by means of constant close imitations, are formed throughout in such a manner that they can be spun out. We feel the fundamental eight-measure phrase throughout and could restore it each time without difficulty by disregarding embellishments and polyphony. But there is a wonderful principle of natural organization in the way in which it is expanded to 9, 10, 11, 12 measures, which imparts the finest feeling of equilibrium between the static and the dynamic.

I follow most appropriately with the only German full madrigal by Schütz that has been preserved. I may be allowed to repeat my description of it from I, 2, of my *Corydon.*

"The madrigal *Vier Hirtinnen (Four Shepherdesses)* was one of the most outstanding successes of the Flensburg Schütz Festival (1932). We owe its re-acquisition to Max Seiffert's identification of the anonymous Kassel manuscript *Mus. Fol., 58 F,* and to Heinr. Spitta's publication.[25] The piece has the vocal scoring:

---

[25] XVIII, 127. (The Madrigal is published in the Association of American Choruses Series, No. 198, with English text.)

Here Schütz clearly intended to indicate by the clef employed the character referred to, in the same way as in Daniel Boll's oratorios.[26] Therefore we may assume a deep woman alto in the tenor part. The four singers present themselves:

---

[26] See my book *Die mehrstimmige Vertonung des Evangeliums* (B & H, 1931), pp. 54 ff.

However, as later the tenor is again associated particularly with the shepherd Coridon, the part may really be intended for a high male tenor. Since Schütz very probably did not plan his work for domestic music with female voices but for the chamber of the prince with boys and male voices, no particular problem in the distribution of voices would be involved. But from the above example many points can be deduced with regard to Schütz's principles of composition: the planned *tutti* as often as all four are mentioned; the solo form in the case of individual description, although the other voices may combine with the leading voice for purposes of figurative imitation in connection with such words as *Rosen, Kranz, Schatz.* The dynamic quality of the opening phrase by the "friendly Delia" heralds her ultimate victory. Note also how the taking-over of Delia's eighth-note passage by the second-highest voice anticipates the fact that Phyllis will be the first to show initiative.

Worthy of comment, furthermore, is the very great inward animation which prompts the master to employ all five degrees of note values from the ○ to the ♪, with notes of intervening values being often omitted, as, for example:

A corresponding "baroque restlessness" is also revealed by his harmony: the B♭ major — D major in the case of Phyllis; the E♭ — D major in the case of Angelica mounts to chromaticism in the case of the "potent" *(kräftiger)* kiss of the fair one, eager for the attack which thereupon finally wins the contest:

One cannot always speak of real polyphony; for in place of a contrapuntal inter-weaving of motives these are for the most part merely set forth loosely one after another on a broad harmonic bass (thorough bass!), while certain ones, purposely different, are excluded with intentional caprice from being taken over (at least literally) by other voices. This is a principle of contrast which is derived especially from Schütz's Italian madrigals. Occasionally, however, artistic structures build themselves up, as, for example:

Characteristic again, in remaining tied to the text *vor andern ihm zum*,[27] is the change of the motive a to a', i. e., from four descending half notes to four eighths[28] without the intervening quarter notes; and in the first soprano the brusque leap from the halves to the sixteenths without metrical transition.

As the last example we shall consider the *Madrigal à 7, Itzt blicken durch des Himmels Saal (Now Shining Through the Hall of Heaven)*.[29] Ph. Spitta has pointed out that Schütz composed only the plaintive little serenade, stanzas one to six, from Opitz's poem *Nachtklag. Auff die Melodey: Kehr umb mein Seel, usw. Aus eines andern Erfindung*, which concludes with the suicide of a student in Frankfurt on the Oder (1608). Schütz's pupil, Kaspar Kittel, followed this in 1638 with a continuation, stanzas seven to nine *(Aria XIV)*. Schütz enhanced the folklike nature of the poem with some textual variants *(Güldne Sternlein* instead of *Goldne Sterne*, etc.). Here, too, the disposition of the voices is very significant. One may call it a poetic-dramatic distribution, as the following extract will testify:

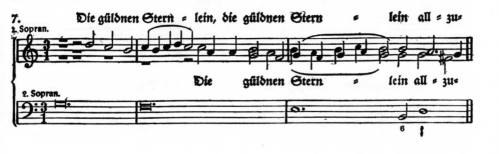

---

[27] "Will be his own; will be his very, very own."
[28] Second soprano.
[29] Five vocal parts, two violins, continuo. Vol. 15, No. 7, p. 58. There is also an edition of this by A. Schering (Verlag Kahnt).

Here the "objective" sopranos serve for the charmingly picturesque presentation of the starry heaven. The tenor is the bearer of the *lamento*. At NB. he sings clearly in the "pathos" of the new Florentine opera. Alto and bass alternate as his nearest shadows, against which he stands out with passionately subjective monodic rhythm. The figure for *schlafen* is a reproachful sobbing. In contrast, the deep bass paints the *in der Ruh liegen*. In anticipation, it was necessary for the tenor to join the alto. The violins shed their white light on the *Jungfrau*. The principle of the division of roles becomes very clear in the third stanza: as long as the lover speaks of *her,* the alto sings alone *(Du denkest nicht an meine Noth* — "Thou thinkest not of my distress"); as soon as he speaks of himself, the tenor sings *(ich lieg an deiner tauben Tür* — "I lie at thy deaf door"). Here, as at the beginning, a brief violin *sinfonia* has anticipated the word-engendered theme. Darting duet pairs in eighths paint the play of the fish in the sea. Only at *Die Tränen ruf ich Zeugen an* ("The tears I call to witness") do all the voices combine in equal rhythm for an impassioned *tutti.* We have in form a purely motetlike concatenation; the parts successively interpret the text with illustrations and madrigalisms, without considering unified songlike symmetries.

Finally we shall consider the *Pastoral Tragicomedy of Dafne.* The circumstances connected with the origin and presentation of this work have already been noted.

When we compare Opitz's text (which is all that is preserved) with the libretto of Rinuccini, we find that while he has in part translated literally, he has frequently, on the other hand, eliminated the dramatic and merely retained the lyrical elements, or has even enlarged on their idyllic nucleus. It is significant that while with the Italian librettist the people, in whipped-up consternation, are dismayed in the presence of the dragon and accompany the battle of Apollo with the greatest excitement, in the case of the Bober Swan (Opitz) the three shepherds urge the people to maintain the most discreet silence to keep from awakening the monster, whereupon a coquettish tonal play begins between the first shepherd and the echo. Perhaps after this the battle became a purely instrumental one. It would be interesting to know whether here Schütz was already employing the *tremoli* of Monteverdi's *Combattimento di Tancredi e di Clorinda.*[30] For the following solo song of Apollo we place Rinuccini's original according to Schering's literal translation[31] beside Opitz's text. Against the madrigalistic freedom of Rinuccini the German poet's line structure has been normalized to the newer Nibelung rhythm and only at the close succeeds in gaining more variety with a pair of Alexandrines and two trochaic eight-syllable lines.

Rinuccini:	Opitz:
See, finally it lieth wounded on (blood-besprinkled sod), This beast, my arrow's fortunate (prey).	Has there, then, now been stilled Through the power of my bow The gaping jaw of the monster?

---

[30] 1624; but not printed until 1638.
[31] In *Musikgeschichte in Beispielen,* No. 175, to Marco da Gagliano's music of 1608. The words here in parentheses are bearers of the rhyme in the original.

Go carefree to the wood,
Ye nymphs and shepherds, and occupy
    (the meadows);
No more with smoke and flames
Pollutes the pure air henceforth the mon
    (ster's breath).
Rosy and fresh now bloom Anew your
    cheeks.
Rest return to your heart, the
    Countenance (beam)
Since you my arm from the dragon's
    (fury freed).

Does night now envelop him
Who before was the pestilence of earth,
The dismay of the people?
Ye shepherds, bring your herds,
From danger you are free.
Ye nymphs, now wind your garlands,
And dance thanksgiving rounds,
Come boldly to the wood.
Sing till the heath resounds.
The beast no longer can
Pollute the air,
Bring sickness in its train.
Refresh your hearts and minds,
Your cheeks no longer must be pale, but
White like lilies and red roses;
For the dragon has been slain
Which brought you care.

How pedantic and how laborious! It is likely, too, that Schütz did not set this in the actual *parlando* recitative style but as a solo concert after the manner of *Tugend ist der beste Freund* (perhaps with an obbligato violin, associated with Apollo from the time of Rafael) until the shepherds conclude the first act with four song strophes. One could more easily imagine the genuine *stile oratorio* applied to the conversations between Cupid, Venus, and Apollo which occupy the second act and end in a comical six-strophic shepherd *canzonetta* (presumably in the style of the *musica boscareccia*). The scene between Apollo and Dafne, which, except for a strophic song of the shepherds, constitutes the third act, seems to have condensed itself into more concertlike dialog. Finally, the scene of the fourth act, Cupid-Venus, develops itself into six similar mournful monody stretches to which four shepherd-chorus strophes are opposed.

Even though in the Florentine Renaissance opera, to which this Torgau festival play belongs, the distinction between *secco* and *accompagnato recitativo* had not yet been carried through, nevertheless the beginning of the Apollo-Dafne scene clearly shows the fundamentally excited mood of the accompanied form, for which Schütz will surely have drawn all the registers of his chromatic harmony:

Apoll: *Bleib, Nymphe, bleib — ich bin dein Feind ja nicht,*
           Dass du so laufst, mein Licht,
           Als wann ein armes Schaf vom Wolfe wird getrieben.
           Mein Folgen kömmt vom Lieben.
           Ach, ach, dass für die grosse Brunst
           Kein Kraut wächst auf der Erden!
           Was hilft mich jetzo meine Kunst,
           Durch welche sunst
           Ein jeder Heil kann werden?

Daphne: *O Vater Peneus, nimm mich an,*
           Dein unbeflecktes Kind. O Vater, hilf doch mir,
           Im Fall ein Fluss auch helfen kann.
           Bedeck, o Erde, mich, nimm zu dir meine Zier,
           Verschling sie, oder lass sich meinen Leib verkehren
           In etwas, welches mich kann der Gewalt erwehren.

Apollo: Stay, nymph, O stay. I am not thine enemy;
           Thou hastenest, my light,
           As when poor sheep are driven by the wolves.
           My pursuit is prompted but by love.
           Alas, that for this passion
           No herb doth grow on earth!
           What helps me now my art
           Which otherwise
           Can make each sufferer whole?

Daphne: O father Peneus,[32] accept me,
           Thy spotless child. O father, give thy help
           In case a river now can be of service.
           Now cover me, O earth; O take my comeliness;
           Devour it, or else transmute my mortal frame
           To something to ward off this power from me.

Here Daphne changes herself into a bay tree. Apollo sings a lament which then develops into a three-strophe song on the chivalric wreath of honor won from the branch of the bay. The conclusion of the whole has a very realistically baroque

---

[32] A river god.

effect: the "Dance of the Nymphs and the Shepherds About the Tree" — a chorus-song of ten similarly constructed strophes, in which, beside the bay "never struck by lightning," the "supernoble wreath of rue" of the Saxons is celebrated in nuptial fashion as though one were dancing around a May tree or a village linden tree. A timely allusion is not lacking at the end:

> *Wir sehen schon, wie nach der Zeit,*
> *Wann Juppiter den harten Streit*
> *Durch Teutschland noch wird stillen,*
> *Wir sehen, wie der Rauten Zier*
> *Mit grüner Lust wird für und für*
> *Feld, Berg, und Tal erfüllen.*

> We see already how in due time
> Jupiter will still
> The bitter war throughout Germany;
> We see how the adornment of the rue
> With green joy forever and anon
> Will fill field, hill, and dale.

To be sure, the concept "opera" seems to be applicable only with some reservation in the case of Schütz's *Dafne,* since choruses and solo *concerti* seem to have far outweighed the real *stile rappresentativo.* Therefore one should almost speak rather of a concert and madrigal presentation than of an actual *dramma per musica.*

The next quasiopera score preserved in the German language is S. Th. Staden's allegorical and spiritual shepherd play *Seelewig,* on a text by Harssdörffer (Nürnberg, 1644),[33] a clumsily cadencing, stickily moving affair full of much unintended comedy. Schütz's genius and far higher culture must surely have produced something better than this — perhaps a work that could take its place beside those of Monteverdi. . . . It is useless to give rein to one's fantasy with regard to it. The score seems to have been irretrievably lost, and there are no textual clues to restore to us the music of Schütz. As a matter of fact, a remote possibility of this did exist,[34] inasmuch as the Görlitz manuscript (Milich fol. 129) possesses (among numerous

---

[33] For the most part printed anew by R. Eitner in *M. f. M.,* XIII, 55 ff.; cf. also my *Geschichte der deutschen Musik,* II, 5, 169 ff.

[34] H. Mersmann in the *Archiv f. Musikwiss.,* I, 251 ff. Cf. further M. Gondolatsch, *Beiträge zur Görlitzer Theatergeschichte bis 1800 (Neues Lausitzisches Magazin,* Bd. 103, 1927, pp. 122 ff.). But Gondolatsch states (1) that Abraham Lichtenberger was not the composer but the copyist; and (2) that the copartner was not Rector Funcke himself but his son Joh. Gabriel.

school comedies) one from the year 1667 with a table of contents by Rector Chr.
Funcke, a *Hymenäisches Freudenspiel* for Funcke's own second wedding, which
expressly refers to Opitz's *Dafne* and remarks: "There follow the melodies on the
shepherd songs as they were printed by H. Opitz in his *Dafne* and were arranged
in every act, though in a different manner." This might possibly indicate that these
melodies did not originate with a Görlitz musician but with a composer who had
been associated with Opitz. Such a one could doubtless only have been Schütz.
Therefore, in order to weigh the evidence, we submit the pieces here for the
first time.[35] During the first act of *Dafne* three shepherds sing alone:

Zwischen dem 1. Aktum der »Dafne« singen alleine 3 Hirten:

Du großer Gott, der du den Feu=er=wa=gen ringsumb den
der du den Tag, so oft es pflegt zu ta=gen, mit ei=nem

schö=nen Himmel führst, daß der hel=le Schein sich rin=get durch der finstren
gold=nen Mantel zierst,

Nächte Ruh, daß uns kla=res Licht umbringet, o A=pol=lo, das machst du

During the second act of *Dafne* three nymphs sing alone. N. B.: A violin is required in addition. ℀ The sign indicates that the last phrases (*clausula*) must be
repeated each time.

[35] Warmest thanks to Herr M. Gondolatsch in Görlitz for placing his copies at my disposal.

O du kleiner nackter Schütze, wann der Bo-gen, den du spannst,

gie-bet sol-che Lie-bes-hit-ze, daß du Göt-ter fäl-len kannst,

was dann wirst du nicht, o Kind, uns thun, die wir Menschen sind?

In the third act the shepherds again sing alone.

Lie-be, wer sich sel-ber haßt, a-ber wer sein gu-tes Leben

will der frey-en Ruh er-ge-ben, reißt sich von der ar-gen Lust,

su-chet für das sü-ße Leyden Fel-der, Wild, Gepüsch und Heyden.

In the fourth act the nymphs sing alone:

There follows — in the fifth act — the conclusion, with the shepherds and nymphs singing together and dancing about the tree:

N. B.! The alto may either sing or remain silent. If the part is not sung, the bass, the notes of which are crossed through, must be played on a violin; it is more effective, however, to have the alto sung and the bass omitted, so that the nymphs alone and the full chorus with the middle voices may achieve better euphony (*Konkordanz*).

M. Gondolatsch himself says that the manuscript contains many mistakes in writing. But even after discounting these, many false progressions in the middle voices remain, which certainly cannot be charged to Schütz. If one takes into consideration only the extreme voices, which are more correctly constructed, we perceive an agreeable song composer after the manner of H. Albert, Hammerschmidt, and Dedekind. Thus again the composer of these chorus songs was surely not Schütz but someone like Rector Funcke or one of the Görlitz cantors from the circle of his friends.[36]

Furthermore, it is probably no coincidence that the first Dresden complete opera, of the year 1671, a year before Schütz's death, again is based on *Apollo*

---

[36] As such, Gondolatsch (loc. cit., p. 133, and *Archiv f. MW*, VIII/3) mentions Andreas Theseus (in office from 1638-69) and Christoph Möller (1669-1714). The *Gymnasium Collegium Musicum* and the town pipers co-operated.

and Dafne, with textual dependence in part on Opitz.[37] This time the music by the court directors *(Hofkapellmeister)* Bontempi and Peranda has been preserved. To be sure, even this work contains, from the viewpoint of the year 1671, archaic things, with such a free collision of the voices that one involuntarily asks whether these might not have their origin in Schütz's score, as, for example, this quasi-strophic aria of Apollo:[38]

But despite such things the continuation is surely not by Schütz, and thus we shall doubtless finally have to conclude that the first great German operatic score is lost.

---

[37] Hereto H. Kretzschmar, *Geschichte der Oper,* p. 137; H. Riemann, *Handbuch der Musikgeschichte,* II, 471 ff.
[38] H. Riemann, *Musikgeschichte in Beispielen,* No. 105.

Op. 4. The Cantiones sacrae of 1625

In the Latin preface to this collection of Latin motets for four voices,[1] addressed to Prince Eggenberg,[2] Schütz confesses that from the beginning he had devoted his musical efforts primarily to the glory of God and only secondarily to the approbation of the great ones of this world. In dedicating these songs to the prince he says that he had begun them at an earlier time *(pridem inchoatas)* as a little work of a different kind, one that had changed as he grew older. Therefore the pieces belong partly to the old, partly to the new style of song composition. He confesses, however, to the "kind reader" *(benevolus lector)*, i. e., the professional musician, that it was the publisher only who wrested *(mihi extorsit)* the thorough bass from him, and that he was thus impelled to add at the end a few pieces especially adapted to thorough bass (namely, numbers XXXIII-XXXV, *Psalm 6*). These numbers alone show (in the Lüneburg manuscript, copied from the lost autograph) a thorough bass figuring which is more elaborate than that in the printed copy. "You organists, however, who wish to satisfy more sensitive ears I request not to spare the pains to fill in all the voices. If in customary manner you accompany only according to the *basso continuo*, I would consider this wrong and unmusical *(vanum et inconcinnum)*."[3]

The fact that the title page is also in Latin emphasizes the international and interdenominational usefulness of the work:[4]

Cantiones
Sacrae
Quatuor Vocum
Cum Basso ad organum.

---

[1] *GA*, Vol. IV; further, his edition of the parts (B & H, 1887), which has been published in form for practical use but used much less extensively than one could wish. Ten numbers in German, edited by Fr. Spitta, published by Schweers and Haake. Six numbers in the second series of Schütz compositions for chorus, edited by Johs. Dittberner, published by Schweers and Haake. Woyrsch's selection has *Verba mea, Sicut Moses, Domine non est exaltatum, Speret Israel, Cantate Domino.* Eighteen numbers have been published by Bärenreiter-Verlag, Kassel. New edition by G. Grote (Bärenreiter, appearing since 1943). All forty have recently been published in English by Henry S. Drinker through the Association of American Choruses, Choral Series No. 211, I and II.

[2] Cf. concerning him, above, p. 118. Concerning the dedicatory poems, p. 119.

[3] With regard to his disinclination toward thorough bass, cf. above, p. 294.

[4] Different the Lüneburg title page; see below.

Authore
Henrico Sagittario
Serenissimi Electoris Saxoniae
Capellae Magistro
(Saxon Coat of Arms)
Fribergae Hermundurorum
Typis Georgii Hoffmann
Anno 1625

The Wolfenbüttel copy of the printed work is important on account of personal corrections made in it by the master.

Schütz enumerates the individual numbers throughout and thus obtains forty in accordance with the Roman numerals in the table which follows.

A classification according to the subject matter and the texts by combining the parts into a unity is given under the Arabic numbers. Tonal groupings are indicated by brackets:

1. (I/II) *O bone, o dulcis* (St. Bernard?) *d* minor—A
2. (III) *Deus misereatur nostri* (Ps. 67: 1), *d* minor—A
3. (IV-VIII) *Quid commisisti*, 5 parts (Augustine, in part acc. to Psalm 115)[5]
   E—A, E—C, *e*—B, *b*—G, *e*—E
4. (IX/X) *Verba mea auribus* (Ps. 5: 2—5) *d* Dorian—Bb, *d*—G
5. (XI/XII) *Ego dormio* (Song of Songs, 5, 2 & 4, 9) *d*—F, F—*d*
6. (XIII) *Heu mihi Domine* (*Responsorium* from the *Off. defunct.*)[6] *d*—F
7. (XIV) *In te Domine speravi* (Ps. 31: 2—3) A—A
8. (XV) *Dulcissime et benignissime* (Augustine) A—A
9. (XVI) *Sicut Moses serpentem* (John 3: 14—15) C—C
10. (XVII) *Spes mea, Christe Deus* (Augustine) C—C
11. (XVIII) *Turbabor, sed non perturbabor* (pseudo-Augustine) C—C
12. (XIX/XX) *Ad Dominum cum tribularer* (Ps. 120: 1—4) *g*—D, *g*—G
13. (XXI/XXIII) *Aspice pater* (Augustine) *a*—E, *a*—C, *a*—A
14. (XXIV/XXV) *Supereminet* (Augustine) F—C, F—F
15. (XXVI-XXVIII) *Domine, non est exaltatum* (Psalm 131) D—A, D—F, *a*—D
16. (XXIX) *Cantate Domino* (Ps. 149: 1—3) C—C
17. (XXX) *Inter brachia salvatoris* (Augustine, Manuale) F—F

---

[5] About this see C. V. Winterfeld, *J. Gabrieli*, II, 170 ff.
[6] Also by Palestrina, first book of 4-voice motets (1581), No. 3.

18. (XXXI) *Veni, rogo, in cor meum* (Augustine, Manuale) G—G
19. (XXXII) *Ecce advocatus meus* (Augustine) G—G
20. (XXXIII-XXXV) *Domine, ne in furore tuo* (Psalm 6) *c*—D, *d*—Bb. G—G

Appendix:[7] Table Prayers for the *Kantorei* boys.

1. (XXXVI-XXXVIII) before the meal: *Oculi omnium* (Ps. 145: 15—16); *Pater noster* (Matth. 6: 9—13); *Domine Deus; g*—*g*, Eb—G, *c*—G
2. (XXXIX-XL) after the meal: *Confitemini* (Ps. 135: 1 and 146: 9—11) *Gratias agimus; g*—*d*, Eb—G, *g*—G

I have already emphasized[8] how in this work[9] Schütz renders homage in a singular degree to the fervent mysticism typified by Jakob Böhme. I have called attention also to the almost Jesuitical tenor of the whole, so that Elias Rudelius could say of it: If St. Augustine and St. Bernard could see these pieces, they would acknowledge Schütz to be one of their own.

It is noteworthy that here Schütz makes no distinction between the text of the Bible and that of devotional literature — indeed how even in the Vulgate text of the Psalms (as, for example, in *Psalm 6)* he allows himself to make transpositions according to his musical requirements. Being completely possessed by the "thought of pure inward devotion and immediate self-surrender of the individual to God" (W. Windelband), he allows himself even greater changes in the Augustinian texts for the sake of the enhancement of exuberant rapture.[10] One might say that while the orthodox Christian bowed before every kind of canonized dogma, there meet here, strangely, the artist still insisting on the Renaissance self-glorification of art and the pietist *(Neufrommer)* kindled to the love of Jesus — the pietist who, with Angelus Silesius, could bring himself to the condition of the tormenting and domineering lover:

> *Soll ich mein letztes End und ersten Anfang finden,*
> *So muss ich mich in Gott und Gott in mir ergründen,*
> *Und werden das, was er: ich muss ein Schein im Schein,*
> *Ich muss ein Wort im Wort, ein Gott im Gotte sein.*

---

[7] These occasional pieces are discussed later.
[8] Supra.
[9] Apart from No. 16, *Psalm 149*, and the appended table prayers.
[10] Anna Amalie Abert, *Die stilistischen Voraussetzungen der Cantiones sacrae von H. Schütz* (Kiel: *Beiträge*, No. 2) (Kallmeyer 1935, pp. 4-9). Thus in No. XII (Song of Songs 4 : 9) he ventures to substitute for *soror mea sponsa* the address *filia charissima*. As an example of a textual transformer J. Gallus should be added to the names of G. Otto and Dulichius, though I would consider instances in the latter two as resulting from free translation.

> If I would understand my final end and also my first beginning,
> Then I must find myself in God and God in me,
> And must become what He is; must be a glow within a glow,
> Must be a Word within the Word, a God within God.

In the case of the *Cantiones sacrae* we have an entirely unique phenomenon. A musician has built for himself an intellectual organism composed of motets in order to come to an understanding with his God in most personal and private dialog. With the exception of a few, and only a few, of the cantatas of Bach, we find nothing similar in the German language until we reach the spiritual section of the *Spanisches Liederbuch* of Hugo Wolf. These Wolf songs are indeed astonishingly similar to Schütz in their almost anti-Reformation, ascetic fervor.

In the case of such an emphasis on textual content it is to be assumed that here especially text and music must be in equilibrium. And this expectation is amply realized in accordance with the observation of W. Schuh[11] that the great impelling idea of Schütz's creative activity is "the endeavor to create a higher formal unity, a kind of synthesis, out of purely objective musical forms and personal organization." A. A. Abert has strikingly shown that while Schütz, to be sure, creates his larger divisions according to the dictates of the text, he nevertheless sometimes permits himself formal changes (expansions, etc.) when the inner balance seems to demand them. The beginning and end are generally more expanded than the intervening development. Nevertheless, the affectual high point, as Blume has also shown in numerous instances in the *Kleine geistliche Konzerte,* rests precisely on these middle sections. A. A. Abert has noted the same thing (pp. 65 ff.) in the case of the partly polyphonic-chordal, partly pseudo-polyphonic motets of the *Opus musicum* of G. Otto, whose example seems to be reflected in the stricter numbers of the *Cantiones sacrae.* There is, to be sure, the great difference that while Otto's declamation presents merely the general reverential or solemn atmosphere or meaning of the text, in Schütz we have an inspired presentation of the words which is always specialized in the highest degree.

Here let us refer to Lassus, the genius of the motet. With Schütz he shares the heights of spirituality, while with Otto he shares, at most, certain similarities in the styles of the times. Of Lassus it may be said that he comprehends and seizes upon the essential emotional nature and mood of the text, often even in opposition to the literal interpretation of the words, while Otto presents its reasonable meaning. It was no accident that in the atmosphere of Otto's *(seines)* court at Kassel the

---

[11] *Formprobleme bei H. Schütz* (Diss. Bern, Leipzig, 1928), p. 27.

western intellectualism of Calvin could find a footing. Schütz, however, exhausts the text both as to its meaning and as to its emotional content.

In the case of the detailed treatment of the themes in the *Cantiones sacrae,* that balance prevails which Christian Bernhard holds to be the distinguishing characteristic of the *stylus luxurians communis,* namely, that here the text is as important as the music. The word content forms the figures, but under the compulsion of the harmony these must subject themselves to constant changes.

This change in style — mentioned in the dedication to Eggenberg — from the old contrapuntal polyphony to the new monodic homophony leads to the conclusion that, according to my Arabic listing above, the following numbers are the oldest: 2, 4, 12, 15, 16, that is, mostly the psalm texts. Another psalm, *Domine, ne in furore,* being written in the concert style, also stands apart from the more usual forms. In contrast to these the real kernel consists of numbers with texts by St. Augustine. In the cycles 1 and 3 A. A. Abert (p. 52) considers the opening parts to be stylistically later arrangements of earlier pieces, an opinion with which, according to the evidence, I might ultimately agree. But perhaps here, as in the case of prologs, the composer's resources are merely held in reserve. Let us endeavor to become acquainted with the collection in approximately the order of their composition.

The small number of voice parts in the normal settings (without considering the continuo on which the publisher insisted) directed the master back to old German cantor traditions. In place of the alfresco decorative style of the many-voiced, polychorus *Psalms,* he now had to validate, in the case of the similar Latin texts, a "linear development per se," i. e., a clear design without pictorial assistance.

As the first piece of this kind let us consider No. 2 (III), *Deus misereatur nostri (God Be Merciful unto Us and Bless Us),*[12] written in *d* minor with semicadence on A-Phrygian but, on account of the high chiavettas (key signatures), doubtless intended as *b* minor-F#. With fugal exposition and many old strict cadences Schütz uses the madrigal double-motive technique at the transitional places, where the connected, individual themes overlap. Nevertheless, even in such an apparently "strict" composition, on closer observation many distinctive marks of Schütz's vivacity are noticeable, especially in the middle voices, as, for example, in the tenor in bars sixteen and seventeen:

---

[12] Ps. 67:1. Older settings: Stoltzer, *à 5* (Ott, 1538); Sermisy (Atteignant, 1534); Johs. Walter (Petrejus, 1538); Crecquillon (Waelrant, 1558); Moreau (Susato, 1557); A. Gabrieli, *à 12* (Joanellus, 1568); Zucchini, *à 12* (Breslau, Ms. 19); Lassus, *à 8* (1578, *Opus musicum,* 342); Utendal, *à 6* (Breslau, Ms. 1 and 15); Dulichius (1595, Ms. Zwickau XII); Stabile (A. Gualterii Motectae, 1604); M. Bischoff (Bodenschatz, 1603 and Breslau Ms. 20); B. Palavicino (Schadaeus, 1611).

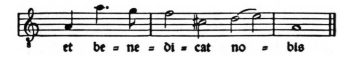

Or note the highly artistic motives in diminution built in above the broad Monteverdi motive.

And so again, quite similarly, at the close the passage constitutes the technical problem of the piece. This is not really counterpoint, since the rules of counterpoint with regard to the treatment of the dissonance are variously violated. It is something like the "art of motive adaptation" *(Motiveinpassungskunst)*, as the result of which there arises a mobile surface harmony which is thoroughly "modern."

The fourth, two-part motet (IX/X), on three verses of Psalm 5, *Verba mea*, in the cadential frame g Dorian—Bb, *d*—G, with normal key signatures, again begins with a fugal double form of the theme, from which one can detect how greatly Schütz admired Lassus. It is superb how he develops the entire first part with the changing, and in the bass gradually widening, overlappings of this idea, until in the second part he introduces the genuinely Sagittarian rhythmic change:

in = ten = de   vo=ci   o = ra = ti = onis   meae

For considerable stretches the Lüneburger score (hence also Schütz's autograph) has bar lines up to this point, always after three semibreves. This, however, apparently does not mean a speeding-up of the tempo but only an indication of large measure groupings.

The *secunda pars* becomes a genuine figural madrigal as Schütz paints the *vocem* in all the voices and at the conclusion formulates the *videbo* in the complementary rhythm of two linear pairs. The one who is praying wishes to mark God's word and thence to understand all the wonders of the world.

Of about the same dimensions but considerably more important is the twelfth motet (XIX/XX on Ps. 120: 1-4: *Ad dominum cum tribularer (In My Distress I Cried unto the Lord)*.[13] Note the sobbing *note radoppiate* at *tribularer* and the masterly linear build-up at

We are strongly reminded of Lassus' *Penitential Psalms* by the solitary high leading of the discant over the three deep voices closely grouped. Unusually harsh is the succession of chords at *a labiis iniquis* (Luther's *Lügenmäuler* — "lying mouths"):

Above all, however, the way in which, at the closing cadence of Part I, the "false tongues" are depicted is extraordinary. Where everyone expects C Major, D Major suddenly follows upon F Major. This almost surpasses the bounds of what is "musical":

13 Cadential frame: g-D, g-D. Other settings: Le Maistre, *à 4* (Munich, *Staatbl.* Ms. 28); Utendal, *à 5* (Breslau, Ms. 1); Palestrina *(Mot. fest* II, 1604); Lassus, *à 6* (*Magn. op.*, 628-29); H. Pfendner, *à 8* (Breslau, Ms. 29). For the formal construction of Schütz's work, see W. Schuh, p. 66.

In the second part, again begun with a *fugato*, Schütz presents for the same word further fascinating turns *(Wendungen)*:

ad   lín   =   gu=am   do = lo   =   sam

Most striking of all is the way in which the spiritual madrigalist shoots "the sharp arrows of the mighty" in five sixteenth-note figures and lets the "coals of juniper" flicker in strangely fluttering chains of syncopations.

The fifteenth motet (XXVI-XXVIII) embraces Psalm 131 in its entirety: *Domine, non est exaltatum (Lord, My Heart Is Not Haughty)*,[14] an outspoken D Major piece with persistent minor subdominant (D—A, D—F, a—D). The opening serves as an example of how Schütz, here apparently a spiritual disciple more of Lassus than of Gabrieli, builds up artistic structures with three motives, a rising and a falling *Domine* and a curved *non est exaltatum cor meum:*

Do = mi=ne,   Do=mi=.ne   non est   ex = al = ta = tum cor me=um

The last theme, as also at *neque elati*, is one of those "negative" madrigalisms whose "exaltation" Schütz, as so often in the basses, intensifies to the jagged

non est   ex = al = ta = tum cor   me = um

Confronted with such demonstrations of the art of weaving, I must retract what I said on page twenty-two of my *J. S. Bach:* that Schütz's music was historically fated to be "as distant as the sun from counterpoint." For even though the focal interest in Schütz is not to be sought in counterpoint, it must be admitted that he showed himself completely the master of this technique whenever he needed it. The *Mirabilia super me* ("things too high for me") again give him ample occasion to weave fantastic tonal skeins in contrary motion.

---

[14] Further settings: Schierrentinger, *à 4* (Petrejus, 1529); anon. (Rhaw, 1540); anon. (Vissenacus, 1542); anon., *à 5* (Ott, 1537); Clemens non papa (Susato, 1546); Jean Louys (Susato, 1555); O. Lassus *(Thesaurus,* 1564); Ferdinand Lassus (Lechner, 1585); Pytisous, *à 6* (Breslau, Ms. 30); G. Cocci, *à TT, B,* 3 instruments (Havemann, 1659). With regard to Schütz's first part see Schuh, pp. 51 ff.

The second part is again dominated by a contrast in spatial symbolism which Luther's translation almost obliterates. One must translate the Latin text literally: "If I did not feel myself abased, but exalted my heart." The *humiliter* receives its fall of a sixth, while the *exaltavi* in the tenor and later in the bass has three (!) successive leaps of a fourth:

The word *ablactatus* (the "milk-weaned") receives in a droll manner the usual coloraturas employed in the portrayal of fluids. . . . In the brief concluding verse we see again that with Schütz the same figure need not always be employed to produce the same effect. The long descending chain of syncopations in the discant at *ex hoc nunc et usque in saeculum* ("from henceforth and forever") does not sob here but is a symbol of the quiet dripping of eternity.

The one-part *C Major Motet*, No. 16 (XXIX) on Psalm 149: *Cantate Domino canticum novum (Let Us Sing to the Lord a New Song)*,[15] has a special peculiarity in that, with the exception of the last two *ritardando* measures, it is kept throughout in *presto* time (six wholes) — one of the compositions expressing frenetic jubilation, like *Psalm 122* among the *Psalms of 1619*. As a matter of fact, the present four-voiced setting has almost the effect of the extreme contraction of a polychorus setting. In its triadic interlacings, like trumpet flourishes and fanfares of *cornetti*, it is the ancestor of many a Handelian jubilation chorus, and for every capable choral organization it is certainly a rewarding field for cultivation. On account of the brilliance of the tonal effect one will refrain from resolving the *chiavetta*.

As the last of the psalm pieces of the older type it remains to consider the seventh motet (XIV), in A Major, *Psalm 31: 1-2: In te Domine speravi (In Thee,*

---

[15] As Psalms 95 and 97 also have the same textual beginnings, it was impossible for me so far to separate completey the tremendous number of settings that begin with the same words. As composers of the group we may mention briefly Berchem, *à 3; à 4,* Isaac, Genet, Sermisy, Berchem, Hassler, Vecchi Croce; *à 5,* Josquin, Courtois, Louys, Lassus, Tonsor, Boni, A. Patavinus, Molinaro, Cavaccio, Baccusi, Judex, Lütgemann; *à 6,* Lassus, Bianciardi, A. Fabricius, G. Gabrieli, Vulpius, Formellis; *à 7,* A. Perini, Cl. Merulo; *à 8,* Pacello, Nanino, M. Franck, H. Praetorius, Orologio, A. Berger, J. Gallus, Hassler, Ammon, A. Neander, Erbach, Pfendner, Pacelli, Utendal, Engelsdorffer, Asola, Bagni, Hackenberger, Dulcini; *à 12,* Hassler; with *basso continuo;* Viadana, Borsari, Finetti, Harzebsky, Merulo, Rovetta, Scacchi, Posch, Franciscus, Bruni, Marazzo, Balbi, Allegri, Stadelmayr, St. Bernardi, Loth, Perlacius, Scheidt. For a practical edition of Schütz's setting: H. Spitta, *Drei geistliche Chöre* (Peters). See also Drinker Choral Library, Choral Series No. 211, Vol. I, No. 14, p. 81.

O Lord, Do I Put My Trust).[16] It certainly must be confessed that there is little
to be found here of "older style." The piece is written for a boys' choir:

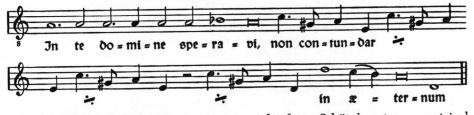 and is built up on a far-flung contrast. After first gliding

along horizontally in psalmodic fashion, it leaps downward at *non confundar* in
lively rhythm, with overlapping fourths, and then paints "eternity" in long-sustained notes. This is shown most clearly in the lowest voice:

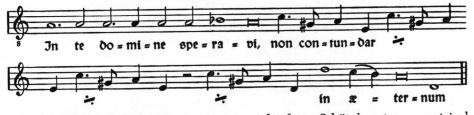

In   te   do = mi = ne   spe = ra = vi,   non con = fun = dar

in   æ = ter = num

A madrigalism which seems to come straight from Schütz's extreme metrical
sense dominates the second half of the fine contrapuntal piece: the "deliver me
speedily"[17] not only proceeds in a rising octave scale but drives the declamation
to syllables in sixteenth notes:

ac = ce = le = ra,   ut   e = ru = as   me

to which the "Bow down Thine ear to me"[18] presents the contrasting motive.

in = cli = na   au = rem   tu = am

It is as if King David sang the psalm especially for his greatest and most diligent
composer.

But now for the texts from the writings of the saints! Let us first consider the
powerful five-part cycle (IV-VIII) of the *Meditationes divi Augustini* 1-3, with the
addition of a verse from Psalm 116. On the whole Schütz treated the text in a
thoroughly autocratic manner.[19] Winterfeld has noted the common Phrygian

---

[16] Practical ed. in H. Spitta's *Drei geistliche Chöre* (Peters).
[17] *Accelera, ut eruas me.*
[18] *Inclina aurem tuam.*
[19] This *Quid commisisti, o dulcissime puer*, which Schütz also set as a German solo concert
soon afterwards, is found as a Latin cantata of the eighteenth century (ATB, 2 vls., continuo),
in the *Staatsbibl.* Berlin. With regard to IV see Schuh, p. 59; with regard to VII the same,
pp. 49 f.

foundation of this motet cycle. More specifically, the framing cadences are E—A, E—C, *e*—B, *b*—G, *e*—E. What splendid Communion music for the Lenten season!

The following English translation is the one used in the practical edition in the Drinker Choral Library (Choral Series No. 211, Vol. I, Nos. 4-8) which was made to be sung with Schütz's music.

One will observe here how El Greco fervor rises to lofty heights.

> IV. Why, for what transgression, O Thou sweetest of all youths,
> Hast Thou been judged in this wise? For what, O most
> Adorable flower of youth, that Thou shouldst be treated so ill?
> What wrong didst Thou do? What was Thy great guilt?
> For what didst Thou die, and what reason was there for
> Thy condemnation?

> V. I am he who has caused Thee Thy sorrow; I am the reason,
> O Lord, for Thy death. I, instead of Thee, deserve to die, suffer
> Thy sentence, and bear Thy shame. My life should have faded
> In Thine hour of Passion — passed away when Thou wert tortured.

> VI. For I only have been the sinner, yet Thou hast been punished;
> I did what I knew was evil, the retribution fell on Thee;
> I was vain and haughty, Thou art meek and lowly; I am
> Sound and well, Thou art pale and weary; I did what was
> Forbidden me, Thou sufferedst for my trespass the sting of death;
> I have sipped of the honeycomb, while Thou, O Lord, hast tasted
> The bitterness of death.[20]

> VII. How meek and lowly art Thou, Son of God in humility, how
> Humble Thou! Thy love, how it glows and burns for us and reaches
> Farther and farther! Thy compassion, who knows its end? What can
> I return to Thee for everything that Thy love has given to me — my
> King, Thou, my Lord and my God?

> VIII. Chalice of my salvation I gladly take and joyful call on
> The name of my Lord. I shall make my vows to Thee alone,
> My Lord, where Thy people all are assembled, and I there will
> Sing of Thy mercies everlasting forever.

The first ten measures show what a completely new harmonic world is opened up here. Even if we discount the harshness and the cross relations that have come in through the foreign injected continuo, there still remain the extraordinary boldness and austerity of the chords. Thus in measure three the leaping-away of the alto from the major seventh, followed by the rising chord of the second; in measure four, the diminished seventh and the augmented sixth chord; in measure seven note the empty seventh chord and its resolution to B Major, whereupon, with

---

[20] In the Latin "tasted the sweet apple (in Paradise), Thou the bitterness of gall on the cross." Winterfeld, *Gabrieli*, III, 139, under b.

cross relation, b minor enters in the soprano; then, in measures eight and nine, the altered six-four and sixth chords with which the basic color of the whole, the hand-wringing expression of the baroque, is established:

Then the chromatic sequence

or the austere

They all confirm this character through similar tendencies. In order fully to grasp how laden with feeling the prolog is, one must notice, at the conclusion of the first part (even without the themes having been especially developed by means

of intervals), the opposition between the rhythmic elements at

and the much more agitated

The opening theme of the second movement is most striking — with chiseled rhythm and yet full of *bel canto:*

Thus it proceeds in a closely knit octave and unison canon through all the voices. One might place beside this a "similar" passage from Schubert in order to grasp the complete difference between the two ("To Sylvia"):

With Schubert the sixteenths have something gently gliding and playful. They are not much more than a written-out *glissando.* With Schütz they produce a convulsive shudder, a pounding beneath sobs.

The second, third, and fourth motives are also formed with the utmost expressiveness, especially, too, from the viewpoint of rhythm:

The center of the piece and the most overwhelming part of it, the *mea maxima culpa,* so to speak, is the introduction to the fifth member of the motet chain:

If we also compare the next idea, which appears thus in all voices:

and note the following in the *St. John Passion* of Demantius:

we recognize that the sharps[21] in Schütz are doubtless also notation symbols with a deeper meaning. Pungently emphasized, there appears in the soprano, which, as a matter of fact, already receives much monodic predominance, the Monteverdi fourth:

At the close there is another imposing idea. Above the closely woven motives of *passio* and *cruciatus,* we have in the soprano, as a broad textual scroll, the organ point:

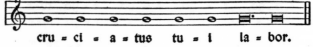

What Ph. Spitta wrote for his practical edition of the *Cantiones sacrae* is true of such a setting:

"And even if the music of Palestrina and of the madrigalists permits a more animated presentation than some would allow at the present day, there can be no doubt that in the case of most of the present compositions of Schütz the composer intended the most vital, the most varied, and the most individual expression of feeling. Not, to be sure, to the same degree in every case. There are numbers among them which endeavor to reflect more closely the manner of the sixteenth century. Even though in these Schütz does not altogether conceal his personal qualities, nevertheless they do represent the prevalance of a more objective feeling. In contrast to these, however, others are saturated to bursting with subjective passion, and the presentation must give expression to this if the true nature of the master is to reveal itself to us." (1887.)

In the third part the sixteenth-note shuddering figure is doubled to a linear *crescendo* countermovement

---

[21] The German word for sharp, of course, is *Kreuz* (cross).

and the portrayal of the one "smitten" through revenge (in the tenor) approaches
the instrumental

It is most amazing how Schütz harmonically expresses "the sweetness of the
apple and the bitterness of gall":

Such things are learned in no school of the world! Let me be rightly understood
when I venture to say that in such ingenious passages Schütz reveals himself as the
nobile dilettante who does not keep to the worn ruts of professional technique.

Like an outsider who is unencumbered by the prejudices and predispositions which bound his fellow craftsmen, he discovers and dares things which, transcending all the rubbish of rules, are wholly new and remain absolutely original. We can understand from such passages the peculiar consciousness of Schütz, that as a musician he was carrying burdens which once caused him to say:[22] "I had sufficient cause to regret that I ever devoted so much industry, labor, danger, and expense to the study of music — so little known and valued in Germany."

The fourth division, through much contraction of the voices, has a more intimate *trio* character — though here, too, there are a number of picturesque madrigalisms, from the "burning" *(flagravit)* to the briefly stressed *rex meus*.

The fifth and last section is characterized by flowing expression and doubtless a somewhat more rapid tempo. The joyful opening theme:

Ca = li = cem sa = lu = ta = ris ac = ci = pi = am, ac = ci = pi = am

has a symphonic *finale* swing; likewise the following theme, rich in tensions, doubtless to be rendered *piano*

vo = ta me = a red=dam ti = bi do = mi = ne

and the concluding theme of the whole series carries within itself a similar *con fuoco*:

Et__ mi = se = ri = cor=di = as tu = as in æ=ter=num can=ta=bo

being given a clarionlike *(zinkenhaft)* ending:

(Sopran u. Tenor.)

can = ta = = = = bo!
BaB A   E

_____

[22] June 26, 1952, to the Saxon Court Marshal.

Schütz was not only the German "tone poet" but a musician who can be compared to the aged Verdi in the subtlety of his sparkling inspirations. It is significant that in the old Lüneburg copy of the score (to be preferred to the printed copy) the work is designated as *Muteten von Enrico Saettario*. Thus in the autograph the master at that time still, with some reason, gives his name in the Italianized form of 1611.

H. Abert's daughter (see p. 99, n. 10) also thinks that the climax of the cycle lies in the middle section. She presents (loc. cit., p. 41) very well the harmonic functional plan which corresponds to the symmetries of the content:

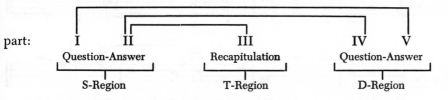

The text of the *G Major Motet*, No. 18, (XXXI), *Veni, rogo (Come, I Pray Thee)*,[23] is keyed for boy's choir and is taken from Augustine's *Manuale*. Technically it might be called a figural madrigal with a variable theme, as the descending opening theme constantly recurs in three forms, the second of which shows further numerous variations:

Ve-ni, ro-go, ve-ni, ro-go, ve-ni ro-go, ve-ni ro-go, ve-ni ro-go

The *inebria* has figures of eighth notes; the *laetitia*, a dance rhythm in three-part time. But the beseeching "Come to me that I may see Thee" finally restores the fundamental mood of suffering with a thematic Monteverdi fourth.

A showpiece of affectual presentation is the *St. Bernard Motet* I/II (*d*—A, *d*—A), which, with an appropriate text, constitutes the supplicatory prolog to the entire work. After the resolution of the *chiavette* it would be in *b* or *b♭* minor, but today it will sound best in *c* with semicadences in G. One need only observe

---

[23] In H. Spitta's practical edition, *Drei Geistliche Chöre*, for mixed voices, the work is transposed down to Ep. With German text *Komm, ich bitte*, MGkK, 15, pp. 175-182 (= Collection No. 111) in g.

the beginning of the soprano voice to become conscious of the expressional antitheses. Let us emphasize them here with the addition of expression marks:

What fervor of entreaty *(deprecor)* there is in the chromaticism of the upper voice!

The *effundere* ("pouring forth") is visualized in downward "dripping" eighths; the
adjicias ("casting aside") receives the same motion; the chromaticized chord of
the 6th—a—c#—f or d—f#—b (inversion of the augmented triad) reigns
gloomily into the concluding cadence.

The *secunda pars* also consists of music which, in the sense of the Josquin-Lassus
musica riservata, is in the highest degree expressive. The *Verachte nicht mich am
Boden (humiliter) Bittenden* ("Do not despise one who humbly entreats Thee") is
expressively presented by pairs of duets in a low register. The word "Jesus" twice
receives the aura of a balanced, hovering soprano, while beneath this the lower
voices picture the Aeon descending from the Father to the petitioner. What
mysteries may not be illuminated through music!

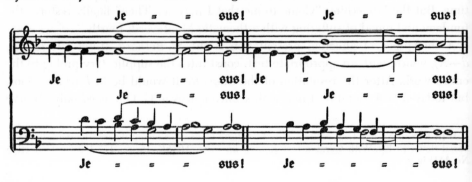

The sobbing bass suspension and the high extended *invocantem* tell of the one who bows beneath the consciousness of original sin.

After so much seriousness we now have an enchanting intermezzo, a roguish love madrigal from the Song of Songs, constituting the fifth motet.[24] Until the appearance of the seven-voiced wonder work in Ambrosius Profe *(Ich beschwöre euch, ihr Töchter)* this motet by Schütz was the most significant contribution to this type of madrigal, one which the seventeenth century treated with such favor[25] and which Schütz himself was still to supplement with four little *concerti* in the *Sinfoniae sacrae* I. The same *Ego dormio* is found in Gregor Lange in 1580.[26] If Schütz's piece did not have a Latin text, one might look for it, from the viewpoint of structure, among the madrigals of 1611. It has the virtuoso tendency of those early masterpieces and is probably to be conceived as a solo number when the bass sings that his heart is awake:

or when Schütz has the tenor coo tenderly about the

The themes are masterfully picturesque. They are often superimposed in an antithetical manner, like *Ego dormio* ("I sleep") and *Et cor meum vigilat* ("yet my heart is awake"), the one presented with the utmost repose, the other with throbbing restlessness:[27]

---

[24] XI/XII in *d*-F, F-*d*.

[25] Cf. my (Moser) collection in *Corydon*, I, 7/8, with contributions from Lechner, M. Franck (new edition by A. A. Abert in Blume's *Chorwerk*), J. H. Schein, Monteverdi, A. Colander, A. Ungar, Hammerschmidt, E. Kindermann, Th. Selle, St. Bernardi, G. Böhm, J. H. Krieger, D. Buxtehude. How popular this subject matter was at the time is indicated by the fact that some twenty continuo motets based on the Song of Songs are to be found in the *Viridarium* of 1627 (these by Nicolo Mezzogori) and in Donfried's *Promptuarium* of the same year.

[26] Eitner's selection, No. 21.

[27] A. A. Abert (p. 76) shows that Lassus extracted something very closely related from the text *Non moriar, sed vivam* ("I shall not die but shall live"), made famous by Luther's letter to Senfl.

Or the multiplication of the one motive is narrowly condensed, as in the illustration at *feritevi* on page 72 and here at *aperi*:

then the tenderly playful

in a canon at the fifth between two voices, while the *aperi* continues as counterpoint. One is almost tempted to call this pointed chamber-music filigree buffoonery. Then again how almost stupefied and in a reverie is the music for the phrase "for my head is filled with the dew drops"! The counterpart of the verse, "and my locks are wet and dripping with the mist of the night," is again completely inspired by the words:

The first theme of Part Two[28]

Vul = ne = ra = sti cor me = um

with its diminished fifth, no longer strikes us today as it must have struck Schütz's
contemporaries — as something quite special on account of this very interval.
They still heard the "wounding" in the dissonance of a "subsequent" time. But
we, too, feel the contrast in the color value of the vowels which Schütz has placed
in the tonal play of the polyphonically multiplied words

in u = no o = cu = lo = rum in u = no o = cu = lo = rum

("mit einem deiner Augen")

("with one of thy eyes")

in u = no cri = = = = = = ne

("und ein Härchen von deinem Halse")

("and a little lock from thy neck")

With him, too, the old rule from the imitation technique in the sixteenth century
still holds, under which that voice "is especially important" (hauptsächlich ge-
meint ist) which, in the web of the other voices, is the first to bring the new theme.

A charmingly delightful, heart-warming double composition!

But let us come back to the sphere of the spiritual penitent. . . . *Heu mihi, Domine* ("Woe, me, O Lord").[29] The text is from the responsory from the *Requiem*.
The Gregorian melody according to the Medicaea sounds but once perceptibly,[30]
namely, at

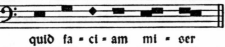

quid fa = ci = am mi = ser

---

[28] With regard to the form, W. Schuh, p. 58, points out that Schütz brings the textual beginning *Vulnerasti* as chief theme in connection with each of the three further sections (*Satz-
teile*) — Leichtentritt's *Geschichte der Motette*, p. 331, had referred to Monteverdi's *Lamento
d'Arianna* — and that, despite this, he has subsumed (*untergebracht*) this form idea under an
"intensified *Bar*," as conceived by Alfred Lorenz.
[29] Motet No. 6 (XIII, F Lyd.). A. A. Abert, p. 75, shows that Lassus (*Op. mus.* No. 359) also
employed "soulful" (*bëseelte*) declamation throughout the setting of the same text.
[30] Cf. Ph. Spitta, Preface, p. XVII.

Perhaps at first sight the composition does not promise much, but nevertheless it comes through powerfully. The rising motive of groaning, which suddenly breaks off

Heu____ mi - hi do - mi - ne

is very effective when properly and dramatically executed. The effect is intensified by the harmony, which generates sharp tensions, even cross relations. Especially effective is the passage when we have the leap into the diminished fifth, or when it expands in its progress to the octave or the twelfth. The tempo surely dare not be slower than $o = 40$, so that

u - bi fu - - gi - am

comes off rather smartly, and the sixteenth figure

in - vi - - ta me - a

vi - ta me - - a

glides along evanescently. Here we again meet, with uncanny effect, the *parlando* style of the *Psalms of 1619*

dum ve - ne-ris in no-vis-si-mo di - e, mi-se-re - re, mi-se-re-re me-i

Therewith the piece proceeds to its conclusion, palely illuminated in the atmosphere of the millennium at the world's end. *Piano* or *pianissimo* will be most appropriate for the close. Of course, the conductor will guard against supersentimentalism.

An especially moving composition is the short *Motet No. 8* (XV, Augustine), which Schütz again commits to boys' voices. From the viewpoint of tonality it is one of those pieces which, while always based on the major tonic (here A), still depend primarily on the minor subdominant and its relations at the third (here, then, *d*, F, B♭), which not only occasions many altered chords of the sixth but also gives rise to bittersweet harmonies, such as the following:

be = nig = nis = si = me Chri = ste

Incidentally, here we have the complete whole-tone scale (b♭—c—d—e—f#—g#)!
    The chief importance of the piece is in the second half with its change of tempo:

ut nihil terrenum, nihil carnale desiderem vel cogitem —
'*sed te solum amem, te solum habeam in ore et in corde meo.*[31]'

The bracketed passage is in 3/2 time. Today we would take a quiet 6/4 time with *dolce* written above it. Schütz presents the entire passage twice, the brighter part, *à 3*, in E—A, the second, darker, *à 3*, in A—D, schematically:

ut nil terrenum, etc.: I g-D *à 4*
sed te solum amem, etc.: II E-A *à 3*
    II' A-D *à 3*
    I' g-D *à 4*
    II' E-A *à 4*

Thus we find crystalline structures built from the smallest cells.
    The first Gospel text that we meet with in Schütz's present work is in the ninth motet (XVI, John 3 : 14-15), *Sicut Moses serpentem*. In accordance with the master's attitude at the time, he doubtless thought less of the solemn lesson for Trinity Sunday[32] than of the artistic, madrigalistic possibilities suggested by the words "as Moses lifted up the serpent in the wilderness," a passage in the presentation of which he succeeded splendidly:

Si = cut Mo = ses ser = pen = tem in de = ser = to ex = al = ta____ vit

---

[31] "that I may neither strive after nor think upon that which is of the earth or of the flesh, but that I may love Thee alone and may have Thee alone both on my lips and in my heart."
[32] It had received due treatment at the hands of Wanning, Raselius, Vulpius, Demantius. Concerning this setting see A. A. Abert, pp. 192 f. — M. Franck, V. Leisring (in German) and Dulichius (in Latin).

The words *oportet exaltari* ("so must the Son of Man be lifted up") are presented by a figure in the upper tetrachord, the figure beginning on the *sol* of the key in question and curving about the leading tone. In contrast to this loosely constructed polyphony we have a middle section of concentrated homophonic declamation for the purpose of expressing the assurance of the prophecy *ut omnis qui credit in eum* ("that whosoever believeth on Him"). And now there appears, with doubly animated polyphony, the painting of the "everlasting life." As a red thread there begins in the alto and the bass, accompanied by the lively little figures of the other voices, the canon with its giant tread:

A three-part Augustinian motet constitutes No. 13 (XXI—XXIII, *a*—E, *a*—C, *a*—A), *Aspice, Pater (Behold, O Father)*. As its principal characteristic we may perhaps designate the persistent and light oscillation of the dissonant emotional tensions which mark the very opening measures through the short steps in which the voices move:

Almost monodically the *pro me tam impia passum* ("who suffered such torments for me") stands out. Likewise, the *clementissime Rex, quis patitur* ("O most merciful King, who suffers") is dominated by the semitone step. Also the theme of seven eighth notes of the *et reminiscere benignus* ("and remember also in Thy mercy") moves along horizontally, dominated by the interval of the second. The jagged line which opens the second part is livelier. Here one clearly feels Schütz's fondness for pursuing the value of the bright vowel tones in the formation of his themes.[33]

---

[33] R. Gerber, *Wort und Ton in den Cantiones sacrae von Schütz (Abert Gedenkbuch*, pp. 57 ff).

With what a wonderful rhetorical effect the conclusion of the division develops with the songlike swinging curve in every voice at *ut servum redimeres, filium tradidisti* ("Thou hast given Thy Son that He redeem Thy servant")! The duet pairs enhance each other with their intimate thirds:

In the concluding part the climax becomes no less marked, despite the apparently quiet beginning. The "quivering" sixteenths at *dulcem natum* prove it. Then the tonal play at *toto, toto* (word repetition!) over Christ's body "extended" on the cross; the passionate rhythm at

cerne manus in—no—xi—as

Above all, however, the triplet tuttis, which are almost reminiscent of an opera *finale:*

In the same great style of the spiritual madrigal the movement ebbs out between the squarely hewn motives of the extreme voices for *ma—nus me—ae.*

Again Schütz has proved that he was one of the greatest rhythmicists, not only of German music but of all music.

The superb text of the fourteenth motet (XXIV/XXV), *Supereminet,*[34] deserves special attention. The following is an attempt to present the Latin original in English, the English text being constructed to be sung in the phrasing of the music:[35]

> XXIV. Far above all the knowledge of all mankind, O gentle Jesus,
> The devotion is supreme which Thou hast shown to us, though unworthy;
> For in Thy loving-kindness and Thy self-abasement Thou hast
> Become a man, coming not to earth among us as an angel,
> Giving to mortals thus the garb of Thine immortality.

---

[34] Likewise from Augustine, with cadence frames: F-C, F-F — in view of the high position *(chiavette)* doubtless Db-Ab, Db-Db.

[35] Version by Henry S. Drinker in *Choral Series* No. 211, Vol. 2, of The Association of American Choruses.

They bore Thee high above the heavens, over all the holy angel
chorus, over cherubim, over seraphim, to reign with the Father.
All angels honor (praise) Thee, on high they honor and adore Thee,
and all mighty powers in heaven tremble at Thy name, Thou who art
man and art yet God.

XXV. For this marvelous mystery I adore Thee,
And I magnify Thy name unto glory everlasting.
Lord Jesus, Thou Son of Mary, and the Father Almighty.
Glory to Thee and the Father, God, and unto the
Blessed Holy Ghost, forever and forevermore.

This blissfully transfigured strain of prayer fills every note of Schütz's tone
poem. As *pater seraphicus* and *ecstaticus* in one, he has the four voices begin one
after the other (I would surmise in restrained *piano*):

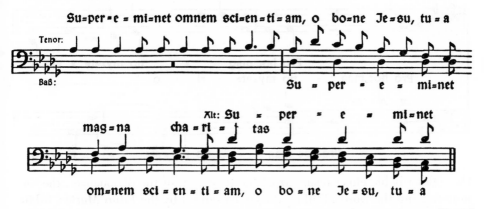

The fate of man and the nature of angels evoke, respectively, a "weighted" and
"hovering" rhythmic picture; and one can see Christ fly through the heavens:

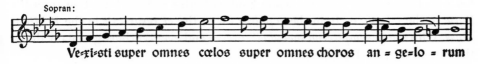

The trembling of the *virtutes coelorum* ("heavenly powers") is even painted in
baroque style with the high Renaissance trill, which we resolve according to examples by Monteverdi:

This presents an altogether wonderful picture, with pairs of duets overlapping four times in half phrases.

Schütz seeks to fathom the "great secret" at the beginning of Part Two in the following manner:

The indescribable effect results from the treatment of the dissonances, the tonal positions, and the words. Still mystically entranced by the *Filius Mariae,* Schütz, with baroque suddenness, reverses the helm and lets the *Tibi sit honor et gloria* ("To Thee be honor and glory") dance as if by buxom little angels *(von drallen Putten).* The contrast is of the same kind as Bach's sudden transition from the *Kyrie* to the *Gloria,* or from the *sepultus est* to the *et resurrexit* in the *B Minor Mass.* With the *in sempiterna saecula* ("forever and ever") Schütz gradually draws the curtain over his Danteesque vision.

Augustine's *Inter bracchia Salvatoris mei (Within the Arms of My Savior), Motet No. 17, XXX,* stands almost at the head of Schütz's affectual, expressive pieces.[36] It may have been the setting by Schütz, whom Paul Fleming highly ad-

---

[36] With regard to the content Ph. Spitta referred also to the alto aria, with chorus, *Sehet, Jesus hat die Hand, uns zu fassen, ausgespannt,* from Bach's *St. Matthew Passion.* W. Schuh, p. 43, shows that in the structure Schütz has peculiarly presented the form of "stretching out" *(ausspannen)* insofar as he brings the three sentences, first twice closely juxtaposed, then spread far asunder, thus

              ⌐ abc ⌐ abc ⌐
                  ⌐ a ⌐ ⌐ b ⌐ ⌐ c ⌐

mired, that prompted him at about this time to make a paraphrase of the text.[37] The contrast between *volo vivere* ("I wish to live") and *mori cupio* ("I desire to die") is presented first as a merely metrical difference (eighth notes against whole notes) and an affectual contrast of a melodic kind. Later he strengthens the contrast by way of opposite time juxtaposition: *vivere* ("to live") receives its floating *(federnden)* ⊕ three-part or 6/8 rhythm; *mori* ("to die"), the severe straight 4/4 measure. The *Ibi securus decantabo* ("Safe I will sing") receives the three upper tonal lines which intertwine in happy frills in order that the *tutti* may be reserved for the proper effect for the *exaltabo te, Domine* ("I shall exalt Thee, O Lord").

In continuous F major, the composition sails joyously into harbor with the words *nec delectasti inimicos meos super me* ("nor hast Thou allowed mine enemy to triumph over me").

The pseudo-Augustinian *Turbabor, sed non perturbabor (I Tremble but Am Not Confounded)* fascinated composers at different times. Thus in a single-voice manuscript recently acquired by the Berlin State Library [38] an anonymous composer wrote a six-voiced kind of church *quodlibet*,[39] or trope, by interpolating between the Augustinian text the second strophe of Hermann's *Wenn mein Stündlein vorhanden ist* ("When My Last Hour Is Close at Hand").

> *Mein Sünd mich werden kränken sehr,*
> *Turbabor, mein Gewissen wird mich nagen,*
> *Turbabor, denn ihr'r sind viel wie Sand am Meer;*
> *Sed non perturbabor,*
> *Doch will ich nicht verzagen,*
> *Quia, quia, die werden mich erhalten,*
> *Quia vulnerum Christi recordabor,*
> *Gedenken will ich an den Tod.*
> *(Herr Jesu, und dein Wunden rot)*
> *Die werden mich erhalten.*

> My sins will grievously distress;
> *Turbabor,* my conscience constantly will gnaw;
> *Turbabor,* my sins are like the sea's vast sands;

---

[37] *Sonnet I: German Poems*, edited by Lappenberg, I, 451.
[38] Appendix to the second disc. of Baumann's Collection of 1576, presented to his Pastor Barthol. Hörnigk in 1620 by the Leisnig organist, Erhard Müller; authors: J. B. Judex, Hassler, Georg Gross, L. Daser, Tonsor, Lassus, Mich. Episcopius, A. Grothusius *(Cantor Helmstadiensis)*, J. Siegfr. Bornensis, Vulpius, N. Rostius, R. del Mel, V. Haussmann, D. Thusius, H. Hartmann, etc.
[39] Christenius (Gera, 1624). Example, *Corydon*, I, 26.

> *Sed non perturbabor,*
> Yet will I not despair me,
> *Quia, quia,* they ever will sustain me,
> *Quia vulnerum Christi recordabor.*
> I'll ever think upon Thy death.
> (Lord Jesus, and Thy wounds so red)
> They ever will sustain me.

This compilation was really well conceived, for Nikolaus Hermann actually drew his famous death chorale from the patristic source.[40] In the present motet[41] Schütz, of course, uses only the medieval text. He presents the "distraction" drastically in pairs of canonic duets; but now, for once — for the sake of contrast — he must dispense with the negative madrigalism at the *non perturbabor* and must here paint the returning firmness of the soul. The concluding motive of this short verse-motet gives us another noble model of a musical phrase masterfully generated from the text.

Finally let us consider the group of those pieces which Schütz purposely created with a "necessary" thorough bass. With these the underlying instrumental part does not always follow the lowest voice; at times it goes its own way, occasionally forming a *terzet* with two vocal lines. This occurs for the first time in the last number but one, *Ecce advocatus meus apud te* (*Lo, My Intercessor Stands Before Thee*). Here the tonal position of the thematic ideas is determined, not by the principle of light tonal color but by that which directs that the notes bearing the accents shall alternate between the high and the low notes:

[40] The *Turbabor* as *Terzet Concert* by Erasmus Kindermann in *DTB*, XXI-XXIV, pp. 137 ff.
[41] No. 11 (XVIII, C-C).

After a threefold beginning with *Ecce* ("Lo"), the *Ecce* breaks forth three times
in all four voices in passionate summation — the tenor also reaching a climax and
overlapping the other parts in syncopation — is the number 12 a symbol? — in
order to point to the spotless Lamb that is dumb before its shearers. And now we
have the most meaningful application of the thorough bass, in order that above
it the individual voices can toss scattered bits from one solo voice to another:
"who, smitten on the cheek, spat upon, and subjected to insults"[42] — all this serves
to depict Jesus' loneliness. And what boldness in the chromatic presentation, that
Jesus literally "paid for our heart's indolence with blue spots" (*languores nostros
suo livore sanavit*)!

Confronted by such passages, we are reminded of what was said of one who
"threw his spear far into the future." Yet the figure of speech does not strictly apply
to Schütz; for his is not the case of one who had ideas which others later developed,
a case of accidental or incidental anticipation. This boldness of Schütz constituted
his constant present. Later on regressive developments took place. Art also, to be
sure, trod boldly forward along other paths. But this kind of venture even Wagner
did not attempt in his *Tristan*. Perhaps in the latter part of the twentieth century
someone may do so.

---

[42] *Cui alapis caesus, sputis illitus, opprobriis affectus.*

Finally Schütz tries out this *ars nova* on a grand scale in a three-part setting of the frequently composed[43] *Psalm 6; Motet No. 20: Domine, ne in furore (O Lord, Rebuke Me Not)*.[44] The composition consists of a cycle in the form of a tryptich, the middle portion of which is contracted to three voices. The bold tonal disposition, as in a romantic *concerto,* is in an unusual frame: *c*—D, *d*—B♭, G—G. This is not to be explained as mere G major. Rather it is a disguised *g* Dorian, which sends out its dominants and parallels in advance. This is also indicated by the *b♭* signature in the concluding movement, despite so many Picardian major variants. Only at *et conturbentur* does the true minor tonic break through briefly. Finally, despite so much *d* minor and *c* minor, the G major is victorious. The chromatic solo song of the soprano above the continuo immediately establishes this new tonality:

At the next soprano entrance Schütz, with the bravado of a conquistador, even ventures the introductory leap of a diminished octave (a most pronounced *mi contra fa!*),

which the alto imitates, from g'—g#. On such an occasion Schütz does not avoid even the ugly so long as it is "expressive". Here he truly stands nearer to Grüne-

---

[43] *A 4,* by Josquin (printed since the edition by Petrejus, 1538); Verdelot (Rhaw, 1544); Layolle (Modernus, 1532); *à 5,* Lassus (1565); Molinaro (Hassler, 1600); doubtful whether *Psalm 6* or the similarly beginning *Psalm 37: à 5,* J. Molitor (Manuscript Zwickau, LXXXVII), Gr. Lange (Manuscript Breslau 15); *à 4* with continuo, Grandi (Profe, 1641); *à 3* with continuo by Bargnani (Malgarini, 1618); *à 2* with continuo, St. Fabri (Floridus, 1647).
[44] Winterfeld, *Gabrieli,* II, 172 f.

wald's *Crucifixion* than to Lessing's *Laokoon*. There is much grandiose austerity
in the accidentals of this number, and there is a Dionysiac surchargedness of feeling in subsidiary syllables, as in the case of the motive

until in the repeated *salvum me fac* ("Save me") the *forte-piano* alternations appear
in solo form, and the *propter misericordiam Tuam* ("for Thy mercy's sake") shines
high like a rainbow above passing storms.

The *secunda pars,* for three voices, is one of the wonderful novelties in the
history of German music, which elsewhere is so prone to take a conservative stand.
In keeping with the *in inferno* ("in the grave") of the text, the soprano is silent,
while the bass has the precentor role among the three male voices. The tenor and
the alto like to proceed in thirds and sixths above, and here we are reminded that
in the sixteenth century, up to and including the time of M. Praetorius, passages
in sixths were employed as expressions of grief.[45] What connotation of deep
suffering there is when we hear:

One should note the sobbing effect produced by the rests at *laboravi in gemitu
meo* ("weary am I with my sighing"), whereupon the alto again enters dissonantly
and plays about the minor second, as does also the tenor, until the bass in the
tonus currens begins to murmur *lavabo per singulas noctes lectum meum* ("all the
night make I my bed to swim"):

---

[45] Th. Kroyer, *Die threnodische Bedeutung der Quarte* (Congress Report, Basel, 1924),
especially pp. 237 ff.

Thus it continues. But enough of words. One must perform the music of this remarkable piece!

The *ultima pars* in no way loses its boldness. Observe only how the idea *iniquitatem* brings about, horizontally, diminished thirds; vertically, diminished tenths or octaves, and diagonal cross relations.

But now the lamentation gradually turns to rejoicing. The *quoniam exaudivit Dominus vocem fletus mei* ("for the Lord hath heard the voice of my weeping") is announced in the *stile rappresentativo* of the young Florentine opera, and in connection with the *Exaudivit Dominus deprecationem meam* ("The Lord hath heard my supplication") Schütz has the *suscepit Dominus* ("the Lord hath received") hummed in a short measure occurring twice, each time by an imaginary congregation in rhythm-free *fauxbourdon* — a most impressive momentary picture. We have already spoken of the strangely Rembrandtian light-dark of the concluding part of the motet, from the viewpoint of tonality. One might say that the *convertantur velociter* ("turn back suddenly") and the *erubescant valde* ("let them be greatly ashamed"), as perceived by the enemies themselves, are portrayed in minor; but as viewed by the delivered petitioner they are portrayed in major.

I have intentionally and with reason described this *Op. 4* in special detail. It is one of the highest and also one of the least-known works of music in the modern musical world, although constituting a milestone in Schütz's development. It reveals the composer, before he visited Venice for the second time, as having passed beyond the boundary of the motet style deep into that of monody, and as having reached the artistic summit of his first great period. The *Becker Psalter*, as extensive as it became and as useful as it was for the spiritual domestic music of the century, was nevertheless for the artist in Schütz (who was still knocking with imperious insistence) but an incidental work by a sorrowing widower. His artistic main line goes directly from the *Cantiones sacrae* of 1625 to the *Sinfoniae sacrae* I of 1629, no matter how deep and dark the valley of the four intervening years of sadness was for Schütz the man.

Political Compositions

Actually, music used for festivals of state and empire has as natural and as important a function as that which is devoted to God and the church. The fact that so much more church music than music for the state has come down to us is probably to be ascribed to the superior power which the clergy exercised in medieval times. We must remember that the *Blick von oben* ("glance from above") gave to state festivities a consecration and a deeper significance, and that this was achieved primarily by means of what can be expressed in music. One need only recall the *Veni, Sancte Spiritus* in connection with the election of emperors and the coronation of princes, the *Christ ist erstanden* and the *Te Deum laudamus* in connection with victory celebrations. Thus today many compositions once used for state functions conceal their original purpose under the religious garb of what appears to be church music. On pages 357 and 361 I made it clear how in *Psalm 85* and in *Psalm 24* we probably have disguised state music. At all events, it would be a task well worthwhile to write a *History of Political Compositions* which would include such works (political also in the modern sense) as the *Templar Motets* of the *ars nova, In nova fert/garrit gallus,* presumably by Phillippe de Vitry, and *Plange regni / Tu qui gregem* of Guillaume de Machaut, Philippe Royllart's *Rex Karle Johannis genite,* the already mentioned *Stirps Mocenigo* of Antonius Romanus, and, in a certain sense, also Dufay's festival motet *Nuper rosarum flores* for the consecration of the Florentine Dom; furthermore, from the *Trient Codices* such compositions as the *Imperitante Octaviano* and *Virtute cujus praesideat.* An outstanding master of state music was Heinrich Isaac. On the death of Lorenzo Medici (1492) he wrote the elegies *Quis dabit capiti* and *Quis dabit pacem;* for the Imperial Diet of Constance of 1507, the works *Imperii proceres, Sancti Spiritus assit* and *Substinuimus pacem (DTOe, XIV, 1);* most important of all is his great work of homage to Maximilian: *Virgo prudentissima (DTOe, XIV, 1).* Ludwig Senfl, too, should be appreciated from this point of view with his Maximilian lament *Quis dabit oculis* (Ott, 1538), the eight-voice *Sancta Maria Virgo intercede* (Ms. Mü. St. 69); the four-voice psalm *Ecce quam bonum* for the Augsburg Diet of 1630; the five-voice *Oratio ex mandato principis Guilelmi mater digna Dei* (Ms. Mü. St. 90). One should also mention Hans Heugel with his "Hessian" pieces such as *Qua te voce canam* and *Felix illa dies,* in honor of Frederick II of the Palatinate; *Carolus Henricusque* (1545), in honor of Duke Henry of Brunswick; *Generosa vivat Hassia, à 6* (1566), in honor of Landgrave Philipp; *Pangite Castalides,* in honor of the wedding of Count Ludwig VI of the Palatinate (1560); *Inclitus Hassiaci,* in honor of the wedding of William the Wise (1566). Some of these compositions are on the borderline between state music and personal dedicatory *carmina,* as, for example, also Johs. Walter's Josquin imitation: *Vivat Johannes Friederich, vive Luther, vive Melanchthon!* In others the political character can scarcely be detected. To this category belong German songs for the weddings of princes, such as Hofhaimer's *Ich hab heimlich ergeben mich.* Or we have motets on royal mottoes, as, for example, the Wettin *Verbum Domini manet in aeternum,* as a twelve-voice canon by Mich. Gass;[1] or the Othmair *Symbola* (1527). This form is so extensive that Erdmann Neumeister[2] wrote a year's series of cantatas on royal mottoes,[3] while the princes of the Reformation period chose the beginnings of chansons at their mottoes.[4] A similar intermediary form is that of church-music compositions with stanzas interwoven in honor of some prince, such as Josquin's Mass *Hercules dux Ferrarie,* which, with altered subject, was recast in honor of Philip the Fair and Frederick the Wise. Likewise the motet *Ave mundi spes Maria,* with the tenor part a homage to Cardinal Matthaeus Lang, the chancellor of Maximilian I; also the Fugger motet by Gabrieli.

Three examples of secular state music by Schütz have been preserved *(GA,* XV, 1, 27, 17):

1. The *Syncharma musicum,* a homage by the Silesian nobility to Johann Georg of Saxony as the representative of Emperor Ferdinand, performed on November 3, 1621, in Breslau and printed there.[5]

2. *Teutoniam dudum,*[6] doubtless for the same occasion, the text probably likewise written by Schütz.[7]

3. *Da pacem / Vivat Moguntinus,* in nine parts, for Elector's Day, October 1627, in Mühlhausen in Thuringia.[8]

---

[1] In my *Kantorei der Spätgotik* (Sulzbach, 1928).

[2] Early in the eighteenth century.

[3] Manuscript in the possession of Freiherr v. Waldberg; the latter see in *Braune-Festschr.* (*Germ.-rom. Mschr.,* 1910).

[4] W. Gurlitt, *Johs. Walter,* p. 6. For example, *Tant que je puis,* for Frederick the Wise.

[5] Vol. 15, No. 1, p. 1. Incomplete in Kassel; complete in Breslau with text of *Psalm 124;* in German underlaid in handwriting; in addition, manuscript voice parts.

[6] Vol. 15, No. 3, p. 27.

[7] Printed in 1641 in the second part of Profe's *Geistliche Konzerte;* a manuscript score according to this in Lüneburg; likewise, subsequently provided with spiritual text, this time for Easter: *Adveniunt pascha pleno concelebranda triumpho.*

[8] Vol. 15, No. 2, p. 17. Preserved only in manuscript in Königsberg.

Both of the Silesian compositions have texts of equal length in distichs. For clarity I have given my own translations. Χάρμα means joy; σύγχαρμα, which does not occur in classical Greek, thus means, in substance, "a joyful rendezvous" (*freudige Zusammenkunft*).

1. Behold, to seats in Elysium there approaches anew the guest and friend,
   Saxon duke and swordbearer of the Roman Empire,
   That to the welcoming land he may bring the gifts of peace
   And secure the willing people in the Emperor's favor.
   Now that the enemy has been driven out, may there bloom in the whole
       congregation
   The work of noble piety and the adornment of righteousness.
   Rejoice, Silesia, over the good fortune that has been poured over thee so
       richly.
   Let the visiting prince hear thy devout vow.
   Hail to thee, lover of peace; hail to thee, thou glory of the Wettins.
   Thou towerest before us, and we praise thy happy work.

2. Dark dangers of war have oppressed Germany for so long a time,
   Most gracious peace, may from thee come to us thousandfold joy!
   All people dost thou refresh in the wide-open orbit of earth,
   And anew the fatherland happily blooms.
   Lower Silesia rings and Upper Silesia resounds.
   Most gracious peace, may from thee come to us thousandfold joy!
   Company of the nine Muses, raise thou new songs! Apollo,
   Sound thou with golden quill thy so precious music!
   Thus the genii of grace and blissful people call:
   Most gracious peace, may from thee come to us thousandfold joy!

Schütz does not preserve the original meter; but, by means of the accentuation, he converts it into free prose. In doing so he follows a practice current in music before the Renaissance. But even long after learning how to scan the ancient meters for the purpose of the composition of odes, the composers of the sixteenth and seventeenth centuries were understandably somewhat reluctant to put their polyphonic writing under the constraint of the hexameter and the pentameter, which lent themselves so easily to mere clatter.[9]

---

[9] With regard to this problem see my *Hofhaimer*, pp. 164 f., and *Evangelienvertonung*, p. 14

One almost feels that, after abandoning the scansion, Schütz is at some pains to develop a new way of forming musical accent.

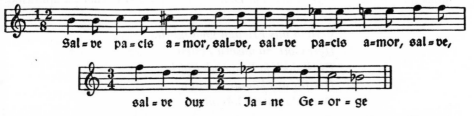

In neither piece did Schütz completely succeed in extracting himself from this difficulty, which doubtless also somewhat hampered inspiration. In the *Syncharma* the scoring is for an eight-voice double choir in such a way that in the high-keyed group three cornets, with the first vocal tenor as the lowest voice, are opposed to the low-keyed group, with the second vocal tenor carrying the melody over three bassoons — an instrumentation which sounds somewhat brittle. However, at *O tibi fortunam*[10] we have as a third factor a vocal chorus of three (!) sopranos with bass — an exceptional scoring (perhaps for the participation of school choirs) and one which the master turned to good account and validated by a close canonic leading of the three upper voices. The above distich is presented three times in the g minor piece as a *tutti* refrain, as it were, to flank the opening phrases *(Stollen)*, while the conclusion *(Abgesang)* is then introduced in the effective entrance of the supplementary chorus *(coro aggiunto)* and reaches its climax in the broad *tutti, Salve pacis amor*. Again the master of opera in disguise is detected in the chromatic soprano of the first chorus. In modern notation:

One might almost mistake this passage for a quotation from a Liszt offertory.

The idea of *rondo*like repetition carried out here led Schütz in the second Breslau festival piece *(Jam dudum)* to let the poem flow three times into the pentameter line *Omnibus o bona pax gaudia mille ferat*.[11] The frequent rep-

---

[10] P. 6.
[11] "Bring us all, O blessed peace, a thousand joys."

etition of the word *mille* produces a special baroque effect. The music of the
refrain, too, is extensively varied. In the five-voice chorus, to which but two violin
parts and the continuo are added, first a low, then a high semichorus is simulated,
and, by way of a third variation, the *mille, mille* is developed into a broad climax.
Meanwhile, vocal duet pairs and *terzet* groups, full of manifestly picturesque
madrigal figures, fill in the interstices, while the tonal summation *Tota Slesis
resonet*, with echo effects, stands forth impressively as the focal point.

The *Mühlhausen Congress Motet* is much more significant both in concept
and in imagination. Indeed, it is one of the most powerful of all of Schütz's compositions. Here the two choruses have completely opposite roles. This causes
us to admire Schütz both as dramatist and as a stage manager.[12] The four-voice
chorus is apparently placed in the foreground and is supported possibly by a
trumpet and three trombones, while a five-voice chorus is placed in the background. The latter Schütz has reinforced with five viols, which today would be
a string orchestra. The first chorus, as a happy throng of citizens, greets the
princes as they congregate before the church door: *Vivat Moguntinus, vivat Tre-
virensis, vivat Coloniensis, vivant fundamina pacis! Vivat Ferdinandus Caesar
invictissimus! Vivat Saxo, vivat Bavarus, vivat Brandenburgicus, tria tutamina
pacis!* That is: "Hail to the electors of Mainz, Trier and Cologne, the foundations
of peace! Hail to the invincible Emperor Ferdinand! Hail to the electors of
Saxony, Bavaria, Brandenburg, the triple protectors of peace!" The chorus in
the rear, however — apparently to be considered as within the church — sings
the medieval *antiphona pro pace: Da pacem, Domine, in diebus nostris, quia non
est alius qui pugnet pro nobis nisi Tu, Deus noster,*[13] which Luther paraphrased:

> *Verleih uns Frieden gnädiglich,*
> *Herr Gott, zu unsern Zeiten.*
> *Es ist doch ja kein ander nicht,*
> *Der für uns könnte streiten,*
> * Denn du unser Gott alleine.*

---

[12] Ideas like this, which in the case of M. Praetorius still remain chiefly in the sphere of tonal
effects, frequently receive at the hands of Schütz a picturesque poetic idea; so also in the concluding part of the *Exequien*, where a higher-placed ensemble carries the soul of the departed
toward heaven, while the mourners remain behind.

According to the kind information of the municipal archives of Mühlhausen, there is not
the slightest intimation that Schütz was present at the performance.

[13] With neumes in the *Codex Hartker*, of the tenth century (St. Gallen, 390-91), *Paleogr. mus.*
2d series I, 416; for the text see Marbach, *Carmina scripturarum* (1907), p. 374.

> In gracious mercy grant us peace
> In this our generation;
> For we no other helper have
> To fight for our salvation
> Than Thee, our Lord and God, alone.

Schütz did not use the ecclesiastical melody. His far-flung *d* minor lamentation excellently expresses the mood of the depressed multitude of petitioners and is in marked contrast to the lively rhythmical calls of the crowd which leap along chiefly in triads. The piece reveals a carefully planned climax. At first there is an interchange — but at higher pitch — between the two groups at the opening lines *(stollenartig)*. Then, at the conclusion *(Abgesang)*, *Quia non est,* the groups unite. At the very end there is a *tutti* for the petition of peace. Here there is a reinforcing chorus *(Verstärkungschor)*. But Spitta does not consider this chorus authentic. The preface *(Ordinantz)* says: *"Primus chorus 5 vocum* can be rendered by five viols and can be sung softly *(submisse)* by one or two voices; *secundus chorus* is to be rendered by four singers, who should enunciate the words with fine *gratia* and should otherwise sing strongly. This chorus may be placed in front of the first." The pace must be determined by the natural tempo of the *vivat* calls and, therefore, will be rather lively. On account of the rhythmically numerous insertions of these acclamations, the piece is not very easy to present; but with proper consideration of acoustical conditions it can be very impressive.

In addition, these Silesian compositions had spiritual texts, as did many secular works of the "Trent" period. In the latter case the spiritual substitutions were, to be sure, not very good. Of course, the additions or substitutions were meant to make the "occasional" pieces more widely useful. In the manuscript of the Mühlhausen music we find the name Ferdinandus crossed out and Leopoldus written beneath it. Apparently, therefore, the work was again presented in Königsberg after 1663 as a musical obeisance. We are reminded of the way in which Isaac's *Virgo prudentissima* was transferred from Maximilian I to Charles V and to Elector August of Saxony.[14] In such features one also sees the connection between Schütz's state motets and the older "political music."

---

[14] O. Kade in *Ambros*, V, 327.

Op. 5. The Becker Psalter of 1628

The thought of paraphrasing important parts of Holy Writ in the form of song in order to make them more readily remembered and more useful was practiced before the Reformation at least as early as the German mastersong and was then brought to the fore for the Psalter by Luther himself in his psalm paraphrases. Later there followed rhymed gospels — after the *Sonntagsbuch* of Martin Agricola of 1541[1] and the polished gospel songs of Matth. Seydel of 1565 — as well as rhymed epistles following the pericopes[2] for the entire church year. The fact that the rhymed psalm came to the fore had its simple origin in the reflection of the Reformer as to what the early Christians had sung in their assemblies before Christianity had been brought through popes and councils into the form of the medieval Roman Catholicism which he so vigorously opposed. The correct answer, of course, could only be: "First of all — psalms." The tremendous influence of the psalms of David on the composition of hymns and sequences will not be discussed here, though at some time it deserves a special presentation by a scholar in the field of the history of comparative literature. When in 1524 Luther undertook to create his own hymn book for the young church, he wrote seven hymn paraphrases: that of Psalm 12: *Ach Gott, vom Himmel* ("Ah God, from heaven, look anew"); the 67th: *Es woll uns Gott genädig sein* ("May God on us bestow His grace"); the 130th: *Aus tiefer Not* ("Out of the depths"); the 128th: *Wohl dem, der in Gottes Furcht steht* ("Blessed is he that fears the Lord"); the 124th: *Wär Gott nicht mit uns diese Zeit* ("Were God not with us here today"); the 14th: *Es spricht der Unweisen Mund wohl* ("The fool now in his heart doth say"); later, the 46th: *Ein' feste Burg* ("A mighty fortress"). In this way he made psalms the focus of hymn composition, so that the term *Little Wittenberg Psalms (Wittenbergische Psälmlein)* was used to describe the entire field of "evangelical church songs" despite many translations or paraphrases of hymns and other songs.

Similar considerations led to corresponding results elsewhere. Burchard Waldis had his rhymed Psalter printed in 1553 by Egenolph in Frankfurt on the Main. He had written it while in prison in Riga and had supplied it with 152 melodies of

---

[1] With regard to this, H. Funck, *Martin Agricola* (Freiburg, Br. Dissertation, 1933), pp. 70 ff.
[2] Selections from the Gospels and Epistles.

his own. Similarly, for the Netherlands the *Souterliedekens* (*Little Psalm Songs*) became signicant. They were psalm rhymes set to already existing folk tunes, as the result of which this collection preserved for us many treasures of folklore that would have been lost. Particular mention must be made of the collection published by Wilhelm van Zuylen van Nijevelt through Simon Cock in Antwerp, which, beginning with 1540, went through thirty-three editions and was set for three voices by Clemens non Papa and published by Tilman Susato 1556-57. Gherardus Mes produced a four-voice edition in 1561, while melodies from the *Souter-liedekens* found their way into the *50 Psalmen Davids* of Cornelius Boskop (1568).

Of greater significance for Germany were the rhymed psalms of the French Huguenots and the Swiss Calvinists by Clement Marot and Theodor Beza. Between 1551 and 1566 Claude Goudimel set these in three different ways, ranging in form from polyphonic motets to simple *fauxbourdon* compositions.[3] Through the German translation of these, first by Paul Melissus-Schede in 1572 and then especially by Ambrosius Lobwasser in 1573, these 150 compositions became the central hymn book of the Reformed Church in Germany. We have already seen what pains Landgrave Moritz took to enlarge and deepen this treasure of melody by doing away with duplications or repetitions. In opposition to the "Calvinistic" Lobwasser there arose a "Lutheran" rivalry on the part of the rather dry Leipzig Cornelius Becker, who supplemented the seven psalms of Luther with the missing 143 (Leipzig, 1602). Inasmuch as the Becker strophes did not show too great a diversity of metrical form, it was easy for the evangelicals to use the Becker texts with chorale melodies already in use.[4] Schütz now enters upon the scene. In the preface addressed to the widowed Electress Hedwig[5] he gave a fine appreciation of Luther's hymns and melodies:

"Most gracious Lady! Inasmuch as the little psalm book of the late Cornelius Becker, with its old melodies, has arrived at almost universal usage in many places, countries, and towns for Christian edification in churches, schools, and homes, a devout mind will perhaps consider it unnecessary or inopportune that I should now wish to provide these psalms with new and hitherto unknown melodies. First of all, however, with regard to those melodies which for almost a hundred years have been used in the advancement of Gospel truth, let me say that I have not only retained them, but, much more than this, I wish to add my public praise and

---

[3] Facsimile reprint edited by K. Ameln, Bärenreiter Verlag, 1936.
[4] Opitz also still wrote epistle and psalm songs. The latter, set to music, play a role in the Manuscript Löbau 10.
[5] Supra.

testimony. Some of them I consider to have been composed by the heavenly seraphim in praise of their Creator rather than by man. And indeed, such old melodies, together with the blessed words for which they were composed, have been preserved and commended also in the present psalm book. On the other hand, I did not think it appropriate that such old melodies by Dr. Luther and other devout Christians as are sung on special occasions or at special seasons should be borrowed for the present psalm book without distinction and that hence these equally devout songs of the late Dr. Becker should appear and have to be heard in Christian assemblies in borrowed clothing, as it were." [6]

Thus Schütz, as an old Saxon (Misnicus), not only testifies to the seraphic beauty and inviolable canonical correctness of the old Luther hymns; but, as a classical pupil of the *Gran Maurizio,* he opposes that obliteration of the affective content which results from forcing any hymn text upon a hymn melody of the same metrical structure, a custom still practiced today by many a lethargic congregation. As a fine-grained hymnologist, Schütz wishes to preserve the inherent significance of the *de tempore* songs from such universal insipidity *(Allerwelts-Verwaschenheit).*

Alfred Einstein wanted to give the impression that Schütz "had a very low opinion of this work, as he had of the invention of hymn tunes in general, even though this particular collection was his most successful one." [7] Apparently Einstein gathers this from Schütz's second preface of the year 1661, in which the master, then seventy-six years old, confesses: "I would rather have applied the remaining years of my life to revising and completing some other and more important of my creations." But we may not properly infer from this that Schütz meant to rate the expansion of this work as of small intellectual and artistic importance. The conclusion is otherwise. He means to say that he really wanted to continue his labors on works of high art. If, on the other hand, he had succeeded in something more modest to the glory of God, in the measure which the present work will show, the credit was due to the ceaseless prompting of his prince, who had persistently requested the revised and enlarged edition. One must, therefore, rather assume with Schering [8] that Schütz set great store by this composition. The first edition — 1628, in octavo — bears the title: [9]

---

[6] Carl v. Winterfeld gives particulars about settings of Becker psalms prior to Schütz *(Evang. Kirchengesang,* II, 220 f.). There are German settings by Seth Calvisius and Latin settings (the translations by Cremcovius) by the Magdeburg composer Heinrich Grimm. The latter's forty-two compositions of 1624 are in the *Stadtbibliothek Zwickau.*

[7] Loc. cit. (Bärenreiter), p. 26.

[8] *Zur Metrik der Psalmen Davids* (Peter Wagner-*Festschr.* 1926), p. 176. Schering says very correctly that one can find in these pieces the best introduction to the rhythm *(Rhythmik)* of the entire German song monody *(Liedmonodik)* of the seventeenth century.

[9] New edition by Walter Blankenburg (Bärenreiter).

Psalms of David
Heretofore Made into German Rhymes
by D. Cornelius Becker
and Now,
With One Hundred and
Three Original Melodies, Among Them
Ninety-two New Ones and
Eleven Old Ones,
According to Common Contrapuntal Art in
4 Voices, Set
by
HEINRICH SCHÜTZ
Kapellmeister at the Electoral
Court of Saxony,
Together, at the End, with Two Appended
Indices, the one According to the Alphabet, the
Other of the Old Familiar Melodies to
Which Each Psalm
Can Be Sung.
With Special Sanction of the Elector of Saxony
Printed at Freyberg in Meissen,
at Georg Hoffmann's
Anno 1628

As a matter of fact, there were not ninety-two but only ninety new melodies, as Schütz took over not eleven but thirteen old melodies.[10]

Heinrich relates in "two reminders to the kindly disposed reader" that when the work was already in print, Georg Schütz sent his brother the *Cithara Davidica,* which had just appeared. This was a Latin version of *Becker's Psalter,* with syllables divided, as in the German, by the Magdeburg rector Val. Cremcovius. In view of this, Schütz leaves it to the users of his arias to sing them, if they wish, with these Latin words. Furthermore, with regard to the agreement of the texts with the Epistles and Gospels he refers to the C. Becker text editions and concludes with a word of praise concerning the "pure doctrine." This proves how little the almost Catholic fervor of the *Cantiones sacrae* of 1625 was able fundamentally to

---

[10] Blankenburg kindly calls my attention to the fact that my statement in the *Jb. der Akademie f. Kirchen- und Schulmusik, Annual 3,* that only eleven old melodies come into consideration, is correct, as No. 2 is the same as No. 6, and No. 10 the same as No. 11.

shake his orthodox Lutheranism: "May the faithful God let His holy, pure, un-impaired Word in these last sad times dwell richly in churches and schools through pure, God-fearing teachers, and in every house through the father of the family, by means of spiritually strong and comforting songs and psalms, until the time of the wished-for appearance of His dear Son, our Redeemer and Savior, in order that we may await His coming in love, patience, and joyful hope, and shall ever be ready for it. Amen." A similar spirit was soon also to speak in Schütz's beautiful letter to Philipp Hainhofer in Augsburg.

The second edition of the rhymed psalter, which Duke Adolf Friedrich von Mecklenburg brought out in 1640 in Güstrow, is a duplication of the first edition, except that it appeared in quarto format. The third edition in folio (Dresden, 1661) is preceded by a word of commendation by court preacher Jak. Weller and a new foreword by Schütz himself, which represents the master's last version and, there-fore, forms the basis of the score of the complete edition (Vol. XVI). It provides all the psalms with special music, this time preserving only twelve of the thirteen old melodies. In the case of *Psalm 53* there is a reference to the music for the vir-tually identical *Psalm 14*, while Schütz's melody for *Psalm 15*[11] is replaced by a new one. A thorough bass part (at present very rare) was printed subsequently.

Inasmuch as the eighty-eight verses of Psalm 119, which were especially dear to Schütz, were now no longer sung to one tune but, following the form of the Roman Antiphonary, to eight different ones, the number of Schütz's melodies rose to 146 and the total number of melodies to 158, to which was added a *responsorium*, *Alles was Odem hat* ("All that hath life and breath"), with the Amen. The cost of this edition was borne by Elector Johann Georg II.

After Schütz's death Johann Georg II had a fourth edition published (1676) through Christian Bernhard, the master's favorite pupil, who succeeded him at Dresden in 1674. This fourth edition was published as Part I of the general Saxon hymn book, but only with the outer voices, melody, and thorough bass, like the Freylinghausen and J. B. König hymnals of a later date. Finally, in 1712, Duke Christian of Saxon-Weissenfels had the Schütz melodies according to the first edition of 1628 incorporated with continuo in his new local hymnal. Bach must have heard these when he attended the morning service in the palace chapel of Schütz's ancestral home, which throws doubt on the oft-repeated tale that Bach probably never heard a note of Schütz. A number of further circumstances also point to his acquaintance with the older master.

---

[11] This in Spitta's preface, p. VII.

Elsewhere the Schütz rhyme psalms are frequently to be met with in publications and manuscripts of the time. Thus Psalms 47 and 150 are found in the *Gotha Cantional* of 1647; Psalms 42, 84, and 85, in the manuscript Peltsch I (State Library, Berlin). To be sure, in Vopelius' Leipzig hymnal of 1682, despite several Becker texts, only one Schütz melody is given. On the other hand, Christian Drülle[12] (Drulaeus), pastor in Kellinghusen, in his *Liebliche neue Conzerte und Madrigale*,[13] included *concerti* on Schütz's melodies to Psalms 2, 4, 5, 7, 9, a fact which evinces a considerable vogue of Schütz's settings. Six of them are contained in the *Geistlicher Zeitvertreiber* of the Eilenburg organist Joh. Hildebrandt.[14] Indicative of contemporary thought is the fact that in each instance Hildebrandt distinguishes between *materiale C. Becker, formale H. Schützens.*" In other words, the poet gives the "content"; the melodist, the "form" of the song. Schütz also refers to Hildebrandt in his preface of 1661. Hildebrandt had remarked at the conclusion that he had occasionally changed some things in Becker's texts for the sake of the purity of the rhyme, "which I trust will not be attributed to superficial cleverness on my part but rather to a well-meant consideration of pure German speech and of the honor of God." Here one feels the influence of the German linguistic societies and the Buchner poetics. To this the master replied: "I cannot pass by in silence what I discovered after all the melodies in this work had been completed by me.[15] Yes, I myself even saw in print how the poetry of this book, which is the foundation of the music, was considerably changed in numerous places by several modern, present-day poets. This, to tell the truth, almost confounded me and caused me to delay the publication of this book for some time, until finally I was informed by distinguished and understanding people that in such church songs one need not consider the artistic, poetic structure so much as an intelligent paraphrase or interpretation, which here had the preference and achieved the mastery. In consideration of the fact that through such good exposition our thoughts would be inspired to a constant reverence so that we would not observe the poetry so minutely and could edify ourselves more in singing if the words appear in uniform German idiom than in a severe poesy in which the German idiom was not infrequently disregarded. . . ." This is very similar to Luther's rule with regard to translating: "One should look the common man in the mouth."

---

[12] Concerning Chr. Drülle and his Schütz paraphrase see also the article by Bernhard Engelke, "Christian Drulaeus," in *Zs. f. schlesw.-holst. Geschichte*, Vol. 59 (Neumünster, 1930), 476 ff.

[13] Hamburg 1650, Univ. Library, Königsberg.

[14] Leipzig, 1656, *Landesbibl.*, Dresden.

[15] Doubtless, then, as early as 1656, when the change on the throne between the two Georges was imminent.

Schütz is more concerned with a heartfelt proximity to Holy Scripture than with smoothly polished but basically unpoetic texts. Therefore inasmuch as the original version of Becker was practically available to all, he felt moved "again to lay his hands, which had been withdrawn for some time, to the work, the more so because his melodies would be found useful according to individual desire, in connection with other, thank God, highly developed German and Latin poetry and songs which were set forth in the same category as the psalms."

In connection with the continuo, which was added later, Schütz wrote detailed directions as to transpositions of his settings, since he presented these, in the voice books, according to the church tones in their customary *systemate* (we would say in the C tonality without accidentals) with chiavettes, while the voice compass in the practice of the *Kantoreien* demanded corresponding transpositions. Ph. Spitta carried out these key prescriptions extensively and gave precise directions (Preface, p. 8). Therefore we need not concern ourselves further with the matter, especially since, in any event, the present chamber-music pitch requires other transpositions.

When we consider the value of the entire work, we must make a distinction between Schütz as the mere harmonizer of old melodies and Schütz as the inventor and setter of his own new melodies. The first applies to thirteen old melodies as to which Einstein's observation that "Schütz has no great esteem for the traditional chorale" is hardly convincing.[16] A list of these thirteen melodies follows:

Opening line	Author	Oldest source of the melody used by Schütz
1. Ps. 12: *Ach Gott, vom Himmel*	Luther	*Erfurter Enchiridion*, 1524
2. Ps. 14: *Es spricht der Unweisen Mund wohl*	Luther	Wittenberg, 1524
3. Ps. 31: *In dich hab' ich gehoffet, Herr*	Ad. Reusner	*Psalter v. Sunderreiter*, Nürnberg, 1581 (Zahn 2461)
4. Ps. 46: *Ein feste Burg*	Luther	Klug, 1529
5. Ps. 51: *Erbarm dich mein*	E. Hegenwalt	Wittenberg, 1524 (Zahn 5851)
6. Ps. 53: = 19		
7. Ps. 67: *Es woll uns Gott*	Luther	Strassburg, 1525 (Phrygian)

[16] Pastor Engelhardt called my attention to the fact that Ed. Emil Koch, in his *Geschichte des Kirchenliedes*, 3rd edition, III (1867), pp. 266-269, was already guilty of the same misjudgment.

Opening line	Author	Oldest source of the melody used by Schütz
8. Ps. 103: *Nun lob, mein Seel*	Gramann (d. 1541)	Kugelmann, 1540 (Zahn 8245)
9. Ps. 124: *Wär Gott nicht*	Luther	Wittenberg, 1524
10. Ps. 127: *Wo Gott zum Haus*	Joh. Kolros (?)	Klug, 1535 (Zahn 305)
11. Ps. 128: *Wohl dem, der*	Luther	new melody by Schütz, 1661
12. Ps. 130: *Aus tiefer Not*	Luther	Wittenberg, 1524 (Phrygian)
13. Ps. 137: *An Wasserflüssen*	W. Dachstein	W. Greiter (Strassburg 1525)

The only case in which Schütz actually replaced an old melody was in a hymn the original tune of which must long ago have appeared unacceptable to others. For it is striking that Luther's Psalm 128 received, in addition to the major Wittenberg melody of 1524, another melody in Strassburg in 1526, in Walter in 1537, in the Augsburg hymnal of 1557, and from Joh. Eccard in 1597 — four very different melodies. Schütz's melody is, therefore, number six. It is needless to say that in their devoted care and hymnological fidelity (within the bounds set by normal church practice of the time) Schütz's harmonizations of the chief sixteenth-century psalm hymns are in every respect equal to the settings of M. Praetorius, of the Schein *Cantional* (Leipzig 1628), and the *Görlitzer Tabulaturbuch* of Scheidt (1650). Quite apart from the significant ideal "Luther and Schütz," these settings, on the basis of their own intrinsic value and in view of the polyrhythmic new hymnal, deserve to be introduced, together with the simply set chorales (the *simpliciter* ones) of H. L. Hassler, into the practice of church choirs and congregational singing. Let one observe as example merely the following number. Since Schütz employed bar lines only as phrase boundaries, we may use the customary modern bar lines *(Psalm 46):*

Der al · te bö · se Feind, mit Ernst er's jetzt meint, groß Macht und viel

List sein grausam Rüstung ist, auf Erd ist nicht sein's·glei · · chen.

The much more basic problem is that of the melodies composed by Schütz, and here an artist such as he is very dependent on his texts. So far as these texts are concerned, one must credit them with what Schütz said in their defense in 1661: that they reproduce the psalm content with fair accuracy. The Muse, however, but rarely bestowed her kiss on worthy Cornelius Becker.[17] So the melodies still await a new poetic ferment with a higher flight and more beauty.[18] The frequently

[17] Nevertheless, with several of his paraphrases, as, for example, repeatedly with Psalm 121, *Ich heb mein Augen sehnlich auf*, he entered the new hymnals by way of appendices for the provinces. In the Brandenburg-Pomeranian hymnal the Becker paraphrase is even coupled with the Schütz setting, while the Saxony-Anhalt book couples it with the Huguenot melody presently to be discussed. The Thuringian hymnal couples the Schütz melody with Julius Sturm's *Nun geh uns auf, du Morgenstern*. Frankfurt a/M, Holstein-Lübeck, and Thuringia combine Schütz's *Psalm 138, In meines Herzens Grunde*, with B. Schmolck's *Ich geh zu deinem Grabe*. The *Auslandsgesangbuch (Hymnal for Foreign Parts)*, following the example of the *Hymnal for Alsace-Lorraine*, couples it with E. M. Arndt's *Ich weiß, woran ich glaube*, all with the misguiding melody designation *Dieweil wir sind versammelt*, while the sole authentic melody to this hymn of C. Hubert (Zahn 5355, from Köpphl, 1545) is an altogether different one. Finally, Thuringia, Frankfurt, and Holstein-Lübeck combine Schütz's melody to Psalm 97, *Der Herr ist König überall*, with Friedrich Spitta's *Kommt her, des Königs Aufgebot (MGkK 3, 1898, p. 313)*.

[18] The head pastor at Flensburg, Heinr. Kähler, has been working for a number of years on new paraphrases. The examples offered so far give promise. It the attempt proves successful, our church choirs will have a highly significant possession; for they, too, were thwarted by the pedantry of the texts. Theodor Goldschmid in Dätlikon, who issued a practical selection of twenty of these psalms through Breitkopf & Härtel in 1900, has pursued a different course. In every case he supplied, beside the first stanza of Becker, better texts of similar meter by M. Weisse, P. Gerhardt, J. Zwick, B. Ringwalt, Hans Sachs, Tersteegen, M. Moller, Johs. Walter, and others. One should energetically cultivate this almost unused field! Johs. Dittberner issued twenty-one numbers in his two-choir selections (Schweers & Haake in Bremen). W. Blankenburg has issued a practical complete edition through Bärenreiter.

rough character of Becker's iambs (less frequently, his trochees) did, as a matter of fact, evoke what may perhaps be regarded as the most characteristic feature of the Schütz melodies: the vivacity and diversity of the rhythm. The changes made in Schütz's revision of 1661 were primarily those relating to long and short notes, which shows to what a great extent this particular feature of his creations occupied his attention. In his discussion of these alterations Ph. Spitta shows, to be sure, that in them Schütz did indeed occasionally bring forth an "ingenious trans-formation." Changes, however, are also the result of the "resignation of old age," which produced a smoothing-out where today we might prefer the original version. In connection with the planned practical new edition using Kähler's texts, and also in the selection of the tonalities, this deserves careful attention.

Schering's treatise *Zur Metrik der 'Psalmen Davids' von H. Schütz*[19] deals particularly with the problem of the placing of accent marks, a problem which also bears in an important manner on the question of rhythm. In the preface of 1628 "to the kindly disposed reader" Schütz himself made the statement, note-worthy from various points of view: "In place of pauses I used little strokes at the end of every verse, because in this kind of composition the pauses are not actually observed. Indeed, such arias or melodies can be sung much more satisfac-torily without bars according to the significance of the words. If, however, these melodies should strike some as too secular, or if a composer or organist should desire to improvise a chorale prelude on one of them, let him provide the discant, which has the chief, or chorus, voice, with long notes and then use interpolated pauses. I trust this will be deemed sufficiently satisfactory." In connection with this we must also recall his first reminder in which artistry and craftsmanship *(Kunst und Arbeit)* really mean "polyphony and counterpoint": "Although my new melodies to Dr. Cornelius Becker's psalm book do not reveal great artistry and craftsmanship, they were nevertheless not produced without difficultes. I was governed at first by the old church melodies. Yet I had to accommodate myself to the music of today. Instead, therefore, of constantly using breves and semibreves, I used, for the most part, minims, semiminims, and *fusae* in order that the song might not only be more vivacious but also that the words might not be drawn out too long, might be better understood, and that a psalm might thus be more likely to be sung through. These more rapid notes, when sung in the modern manner in an appropriate time, do not detract from the serious nature of the work. Yes, the old church songs themselves, even though written with slow notes, are nevertheless sung in Christian gatherings at a more rapid pace."

---

[19] *Festschrift* for Peter Wagner (1926).

Accordingly, fluent and flexible presentation is desired — one that adapts itself closely to the text. Schütz's *Becker Psalms* as yet know nothing of the isometric smoothing-out of the chorale melody which occurred during the course of the seventeenth century, in part since the publication of the *Praxis pietatis melica* of Joh. Crüger, in part through W. C. Briegel's *Darmstädter Gesangbuch,* and the like. This was the result of the transition from the figural music of the conducted *Kantorei* to the mass singing accompanied by the accentless organ and was an indication of the canonization of congregational singing, which came to be viewed as the orthodox method of rendering the chorale. Schütz still stands completely on the ground of J. Walter's polymetry in the sense of the old motet tenor, even though, obviously since Osiander, he has placed the melodies in the upper voice. Yes, still more, Schütz does not limit himself to the agogically[20] shortened and lengthened weak beats, groups of three's, and the pathetic anticipations which give to the German folk and church song of the sixteenth century its powerful and lively effect. On the contrary, apparently under youthful Calvinistic impressions gained at Kassel, he seizes upon—I should like to say—the "hyperagogic" type of the French Huguenot polymetry which our church song still preserves somewhat in the melody *Wenn wir in höchsten Nöten sein* ("When in the Hour of Utmost Need"):

Wenn wir in höch=ſten Nö=ten ſein und wiſ=ſen we=der aus noch ein,

und fin=den we=der Hilf noch Rat, ob wir gleich for-gen früh und ſpat

in L. Bourgeois (Lyon, 1547), originally a Ten Commandments hymn: *Leve le coeur,* and thus still found in Lobwasser *(Errett mich, o mein lieber Herre — "O My Dear Lord, Save Me, I Pray," Zahn, 750):

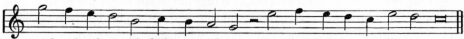

Er=heb dein Herz, tu auf dein Oh=ren, du Volk, das du ver=ſto=cket biſt,

merk auf und tu mit Fleiß an = hö=ren, was Gott's Ge=bot und Wil=le iſt.

A third source of sharpening the meter is Schütz's own pleasure in metrical contrasts, which results from the use of notes of different time values, as is

---

[20] See note p. 380.

especially indicated in his "writing out" of *ritardandi* and *accelerandi*, in which, as against corresponding manifestations of the sixteenth century, the baroque animation is sometimes increased, even though here he never passes over to the crass transitions of the madrigals.

Schütz's procedure can be easily and briefly illustrated by placing side by side the original text and the "derivative form." [21]

Psalm 18: GA, XVI, 23: [22]

---

[21] With regard to the use of the analytical indications see the discussion in my *Schulchoralbuch, Ein feste Burg* (Bärenreiter), larger edition.

[22] Thus also essentially *Psalm I.*

As in other church songs, one must also guard against adopting in the *Becker Psalms* an initial accent or emphasis as applicable to the entire hymn. The proper emphasis will become evident only after a further consideration of the remaining strophes. Thus, for example, in the case of *Psalm 19:*

Schütz's fondness for the choriambus[23] is strongly in evidence, as in *Psalm 3,* where, however, the isometric continuation brings about a very vibrant *animato:*

This has a splendid effect. The very irregularity of the five-syllable phrase preceding the cadence at the end of the first two lines, and also the irregularity, with nine short syllables before the final cadence, is much better, rhythmically and musically, than the somewhat mechanical symmetry of the melismas in his melody to *Psalm 97.*[24]

---

[23] A foot consisting of a trochee followed by an iambus (— ∪∪ —).
[24] *Der Herr ist König überall.* This has recently been revived rather extensively.

The pervasive and subjective feeling resulting from the meter and the rhythm at the beginning of *Psalm 6* is characteristically expressive. I transcribe the whole notes as halves with fermatas:

Here one can also note Schütz's mastery in the disposition of the church tones at the points of melodic retardation (*distinctiones*), which are occasionally enriched by pronouncedly modern harmonic cadences. Perhaps these melodies — in contrast to the more appealing popular style of the younger talents Crüger, Schop, Ebeling — were at the time too choice and serious to make their way among wider circles of congregations, despite the efforts of a number of the rulers of the day. Furthermore, some of the numbers, as the result of an excessive striving for expression (to be sure, mostly only with regard to the content of the first stanza),[25] became too complicated, like the predominantly choriambic melody to *Psalm 7*, which gives a good idea of how the choriambus developed from

---

[25] (Since Schütz's music to the *Becker Psalms* was the same for all the stanzas of each psalm, the word-painting could apply only to a particular stanza.)

This ruthless breaking *(niederreissende Mutation)* into the F system with the "impetuous" ascending minor scale, and still more the brief return to G Mixolydian, is not adapted to the singing ability of every congregation.

But one also continually meets melodies of unusually fascinating structure, such as this Dorian melody, which suggests still another time notation *(Psalm 10,* half mensuration):

Or this *g* Dorian with change between agogic double triplets and choriambs, where the *viel* of itself leads to a melismatic penultimate expansion *(Psalm 13):*

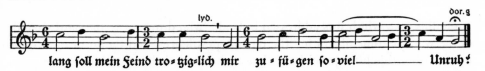

lang foll mein Feind tro=zig=lich mir   zu = fü=gen fo=viel—————— Unruh!

Peter Mortimer, in his book *Der Choralgesang zur Zeit der Reformation (Chorale Singing at the Time of the Reformation)* (Berlin, 1821), has shown by numerous examples that in this work Schütz was one of the last productive melodists in the field of the church modes. He emphasizes this mastery in the use of the customary subsidiary cadences *(distinctiones)*. Thus he says on page 101: "For a man like Schütz, who knew the old modes thoroughly, it was not difficult to compose 157 new chorale melodies for the psalms (for he divided *Psalm 119* into eight divisions, each with its own melody), melodies in which one finds no trace of his having exhausted his inventiveness. And yet he had to contend with the circumstance that Dr. Becker had paid little attention to metrical variety in his versifications. For example, the strophic form of *Allein Gott in der Höh sei Ehr* had to be set forty-four times by Schütz. Here, then, the modes came to his service, and thus we find that among these forty-four instances of the same meter five are set in the Dorian mode, five in the Hypodorian, two in the Phrygian, six in the Mixolydian, five in the Hypomixolydian, eleven in the Aeolian, seven in the Ionian, and three in the Hypoionian. There are ten instances of the meter of *Hilf Gott, daß mir gelinge;* eight of *Es woll uns Gott genädig sein;* seven of *Herr Christ, der ein'ge Gottes Sohn;* seven of *Ein feste Burg;* and seven of *Christ, der du bist der helle Tag.* These are all set with a most beautiful change of modes."[26]

But enough of the melody examples. The number could easily be increased to more than fifty equally valuable and fascinating ones![27] It is characteristic of the mysterious caprice of popular appeal that none of them has become a spiritual folk song which one can observe but never fully "explain."

The *Psalms* did, however, apparently play a role in school life. Thus I found Schütz's *150th Becker Psalm* in a form (*d* minor instead of *e* minor) which gives the music combined with a "prayer hymn of the pupils," *Grates agamus omnibus,* the latter admirably fitting the music. It is not likely that Christianus Steher, who entered the setting in the Manuscript Löbau 10 on March 31, 1670,[28] originally

---

[26] In the case of the plagal modes, however, Mortimer's assignment is erroneous.

[27] With regard to the strongly predominant *Bar* forms of this work cf. the analysis of *Psalm 84* in Schuh, p. 70.

[28] Five voice books in octavo, appended to J. Meiland's *Cant. Sacre.,* 1681, in the possession of Gottfr. and Benj. Schneider. Among authors are mentioned J. Handl; M. M. S. (R); Phinot; Clemens non papa; Carolus Mirus; Jhs. Walter; H. L. Hassler; Jos. Ad. Fiebiger; Christian Mauck, cantor; Benedictus Richter, rector; Martin Golbs; Joh. Georg Binder; Gottfr. Limmer.

wrote this text, which was addressed to God, "who drove away the hard wounds of the war, the funerals during the terrible pestilences, and the tortures of cruel hunger from this little jewel box." It is quite conceivable that here we have an original form that existed before 1628. Schütz had confessed to Electress Hedwig that he had written the first of these melodies for the early prayers of the choir boys who were entrusted to him.

Now let us consider a few examples of the Schütz method of harmonization. The way in which (especially in the case of archaic pieces) he likes to indulge in extensive angular diatonic progressions has already been apparent in connection with the Bb major of the *Mighty Fortress*. One can observe in *Psalm 52* that Schütz did not hesitate in the case of the triadic formations to present naive chordal repetitions. In accordance with the setting at *Trotzen* ("defiance") this could be interpreted as the typical harmonic simplification of the *stile concitato* of Monteverdi.[29] The more striking, of course, then, are the chordal changes in typical chorale manner in the conclusion. Let Schütz's thorough bass suffice. We may imagine ourselves to be listening to the Dresden court organist as he is accompanying the congregation (*Psalm 52*):

[29] Similarly in the case of *Es steh Gott auf* ("Let God arise"), *Psalm 68*.

What causes these harmonizations (as contrasted with those of Bach) to seem somewhat intractable and angular is the comparatively infrequent use of inversions and the almost complete dispensing with chords of the seventh. The extensive use of root position triads leads to frequent leaps of fourths and fifths in the bass. It requires the deliberate portrayal of a special word such as *Unglück* ("misfortune") to cause the introduction of a secondary seventh, as in the conclusion of *Psalm 57, Sei mir gnädig, o Gott* ("Be merciful to me, O God"):

The melody of the last text line, moreover, shows, after all, that Schütz did not always create melody and harmony independently of each other, but that he doubtless heard both at once, inasmuch as here the inner progress lies throughout with the chordal changes of the accompanying voices. These, too, are often in themselves so alive as to conform to Schütz's German nature and his widely announced antipathy to the continuo because of his fear of slovenly inner voices. Even if one can still consider the closing melismas of *Psalm 58*[30] as mere consequences of the movement of the outer voices:

we also find occasionally slight indications of motival imitation apart from the actual melismatic formations, as at the beginning of *Psalm 90:*

---

[30] *MGkK,* 15, 1910, p. 354, to the words *Wär Gott nicht mit uns.*

Or for the enlivement of rhythmic cessation, whereby, as if spontaneously, little similarities arise, as in *Psalm 100* (quarter mensuration):

Though here for once a very wide functional circle is traversed — from E to Bb to *g* — nevertheless, especially in the case of so continually inspired a master as Schütz, his almost constant restraint must be especially admired as an achievement of character.

If we view the *Psalms of David* as a part of that great rhythm that unfolded itself over Schütz's entire creative period between his two Italian journeys, we may perhaps venture the following epigrammatic characterization of the chief works:

Op. 1: *Madrigals of 1612:* first venturesome reconnaissance;
   2: *Psalms of David of 1619:* development to a large scale;
   3: *Resurrection History of 1623:* reconcentration into the intimate;
   4: *Cantiones sacrae of 1625:* second advance into the problematic;
   5: *Becker Psalter of 1628:* self-imposed restraint for the acquisition of new power.

Then the *Sinfoniae sacrae of 1629* could again allow the energies of independent invention to stream forth more richly and freely.

B. Middle Period
Op. 6. The Symphoniae sacrae I of 1629[1]

Ever since the Gabrielis wrote their *symphoniae sacrae,* the designation *symphonia sacra* — for "spiritual concert"[2] — was a term familiar to the world of music.[3] It was a noble and frequently chosen title. As a tribute to his one-time teacher, Schütz used it three times. He employed it first in 1629.

This work was composed and printed in Venice. When, on the title page, adorned with the coat of arms of Gardane, Schütz designated it as "his second ecclesiastical *opus*" *(opus ecclesiasticum secundum),* this was a Roman Catholic enumeration, his *Cantiones sacrae* (also in Latin) being reckoned by him as *Op. 1.* Herein we see clearly the inner line, the geometrical position of these twenty compositions. In the subsequently compiled list of Schütz's works this collection is properly put in the sixth place — between its evangelical neighbors, the *Becker Psalter* and the first part of the *Kleine geistliche Konzerte.* The Latin text was doubtless the chief reason why this highly important collection had to wait so long for the publication of new practical editions. Recently there have appeared, through the Bärenreiter Verlag: No. 1, *Paratum cor meum Deus;* No. 4, *Cantabo Domino;* No. 5, *Venite ad me;* No. 6, *Jubilate Deo, omnis terra;* No. 7, *Anima mea liquefacta est;* No. 8, *Adjura vos, filiae Jerusalem;* No. 9, *O quam tu pulchra es;* No. 10, *Veni de Libano;* No. 13, *Fili mi Absalon.* The alto composition, *In te Domine speravi,* No. 3,[4] was published by K. Lütge through Bote & Bock in 1928. In other words, half of the compositions are now available for practical use. In addition to the settings of psalms and other old Testament texts, which, beside their practical church use, also constitute glorious chamber music, there is a group of delightful pieces from the Song of Songs which, in view of the scarcity of good wedding music, should be extensively cultivated. In the first category belong I, *Paratum cor meum,* Ps. 107:

---

[1] Vol. V of the collected edition.

[2] *Geistliches Konzert:* Vocal, but especially also with instrumental participation.

[3] For example, in 1612 in Prague, for the motet collection of the imperial Kapellmeister Lambert de Sayve.

[4] This, in my opinion, was intended, not for a deep female voice but for a high male voice. The beginning of the composition is also found in Winterfeld, *Gabrieli,* III, 143-144.

2-4; II, *Exultavit cor meum,* the song of Hannah, 1 Sam. 1 and 2; III, *In te Domine speravi,* Ps. 30: 2-3; IV, *Cantabo Domino,* Ps. 103: 33; VI, *Jubilate Deo,* Psalm 90; XI/XII, *Benedicam Domino,* Psalm 33; XIII, *Fili mi Absalon;* 2 Sam. 18: 33; XIV, *Attendite,* Ps. 77: 1-3; XV, *Domine, labia mea,* Ps. 50: 17; XIX/XX, *Buccinate,* Ps. 80: 4 and 1; Ps. 97: 6; Ps. 150: 4; Ps. 87: 4. In the second category mentioned belong VII/VIII, *Anima mea / Adjuro vos,* Song of Songs 5: 6; 2: 14; 15: 8; IX/X, *O quam tu pulchra / Veni de Libano,* 4: 1-5, 8; 2: 10; XVI/XVII, *In lectulo per noctes / Invenerunt me,* 3: 1-4; XVIII, *Veni dilecte mi,* 5: 1. Finally there is also a Gospel number — V, *Venite ad me,* Matt. 11: 28-30 — for the Festival of St. Matthew.

Additional charm and excellency of the work are to be found in the extraordinary diversity of the scoring — for from one to three voices of different ranges and for from one to four instruments of the most varied kind. Violins, bassoons, recorders, shalmeys, *cornetti,* trumpets, trombones — all invite to joint participation. Here the explicitness of the instrumentation places Part I of the *Symphoniae sacrae* at an advantage over the *Symphoniae sacrae* II, which does not distinguish the instrumental parts according to specific instruments. Here Schütz takes a course similar to that of Monteverdi, who went from the richest orchestration in *Orfeo* to the impoverished and uniform instrumentation of the *Ritorno d'Ulisse* and the *Incoronazione di Poppea.* Although Schütz's groups are, for the most part, tonally similar, in one instance — the duet, No. XV, in the form of a double fugue — we find a clear-cut example of Schering's *Spaltklang,* the scarcely compatible combination of cornet or violin, trombone, and bassoon.

The basis of Ph. Spitta's score (Vol. V of the collected edition, 1888) were the six printed voice parts, the Wolfenbüttel copy of which shows the alterations that Schütz added in his own hand. Among contemporary manuscripts I know only the complete continuo voice (Pirna 54, *à 2),* which presents these twenty pieces instructively as No. 9 and Nos. 32-51 among 204 cantatas of those years. In the biographical section I have already outlined briefly how Schütz here used as his model the new Italian vocal instrumental "mixture literature" *(Mischliteratur).* At times the instruments are grouped together for ritornelles, preferably bridging over the pauses in the voice parts by overlappings rather than through alternations with them. Again independent elements set themselves against the vocal parts with specially exuberant themes and take over independent symphonic passages. These passages, in their thematic or tonal connection, serve either as reminiscent, preparatory, or (rarely) separating interpolations. Again the instruments unite with the voice parts in imitation, presenting unified chorus effects. This, however, is no longer in the primitive Turin *mentre vaga angioletta* form, where we really have but a five-voice madrigal in which instruments have replaced the two upper voices. On the contrary, here we can speak of a chamber-music equilibrium and personalization of the instrumental elements, which, as against the more illustrative and episodic collaboration in the *Psalms of David of 1619,* points definitely to the future and denotes a new epoch in the style of Schütz. Not only are the instrumental voices constructed in part in a highly virtuoso manner, but through exact indications of phrasing they call for very intelligent execution.

It would be wearisome and would exceed the bounds of this book to discuss and analyze in detail each of the twenty compositions in the collection. A sympathetic sampling and excursion through the treasure chamber must suffice. And indeed, not all the compositions are on the same level. For a master as dependent on the text as Schütz was, those among the psalm terzets, like Nos. XI/XII and XIX/XX, did not offer the inspiration presented by the atmospherically vivid pictures of the *Canticum cantorum.*

As an example of excellent practical music among the psalm settings we may cite the fresh *Paratum cor meum* (No. 1, p. 5), for soprano, two violins and organ continuo, with its joyfully repetitive and melismatically upward curling *cantabo;* the upward leaping *exurge* (p. 6); and the ringing *cythara* (pp. 7-8). The piece would not be Schütz if the concluding words, *in nationibus* (p.10), did not present musically the idea of multitudes by means of wide-sweeping coloratura figures.

The restless liveliness of No. II, *Exultavit,* strikes one at once as the voice part enters without instrumental preface, in distorted, strange rhythms. As the time signature in Schütz denotes tempo rather than accent, the note picture

is doubtless rather to be interpreted and executed as follows, without, however, eliminating altogether from one's consciousness the accentual system noted in the score:

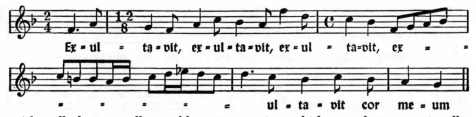

After all, these are all motetlike concatenations which treat the text sectionally.
They are not genuine monodies which generate new specific forms from the sound
of the words. Schütz, therefore, occasionally reverts, with variations, to the beginning in order not to let the form go to pieces, as, for example, in No. III,[5] *In te
Domine speravi* (p. 15). Here the beginning also shows what an important role the
old mensural measuring bar line still plays in Schütz. For when he notates:

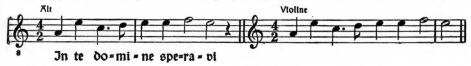

he means accentually:

which is also confirmed as he continues with a chain motive formed from the
baroque word repetition:

Of course, there are no rules for this; there is only an insight into the actual
situation.

Something new, which later plays a considerable role in Schütz, is met with at
the beginning of No. IV, *Cantabo Domino* (p. 20) (Winterfeld, *Gabrieli* II, 178 f.;
III, 82-86). Here we see the most varied treatment of the same word — to weigh
and test it from all angles:

---

[5] With regard to the sections A B C A, each of which is introduced by a *sinfonia*, cf. Schuh,
pp. 96 f.

and finally, as an extension of the second type, a fourth. Here we have a long coloratura passage in 3/1 time (in the violins) in order to give full effect to the voice part. From this figure there develops the instrumental accompanying motive to the *Alleluia*, which, at its return at the end of the second half, has the direction *passaggio* (embellishment of the cadence, *Zierkadenz*), to be executed about as follows:

The Gospel setting (No. V, p. 25) *Venite ad me* is especially impressive by reason of the contrast between heartfelt song style and pompous Florentine opera "pathos." By substituting a tenor for the liturgically traditional bass as Christ, the piece at once assumes a personal rather than an ecclesiastical atmosphere:

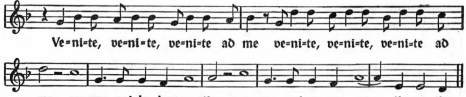

The voice entrance of the second "chain section" is very characteristic of Schütz's talent for building stately thematic arches by means of adding musical phrases to one another:

As this is built up much more fully than is the *venite* at the beginning, so now also the declamatory counterplay of the *quia mitis sum et humilis corde* (p. 27) is developed much more sharply. This finally unfolds itself as a sort of conclusion into an interplay between *suave* and *leve* (pp. 27-29) until the opening part returns (p. 30) in varied form as a free reprise section at the end or also a large three-part song form:

Form parts:	*a—b;*	A—BC;	*a—b'*
Cadences:	*g*—G;	*g—g—g*—C;	*g*—G.

No. VI (p. 31), *Jubilate Deo,* for bass, is warmly recommended for practical use. This is an effective Introit or presermon song for Jubilate Sunday. Even for a deep voice it should, I think, be transposed from F to Ab or A. In place of the *flautini* there may substituted two violins, which are suggested by Schütz as optional alternatives and create a better dynamic counterbalance to the powerful soloist as he storms through his entire range. In its successful alternation between singing melody and recitative the piece produces an electrifying effect.[6]

Here let us add the other two bass soli of the volume. The first of these is No. XIV (p. 70), *Attendite, popule meus.*[7] Schütz has given this text a moving tone of apprehensive warning, even of lamentation, which expresses itself especially in the two descending steps of a fifth following each other at the third. By subjoining the same melodic foundational outline to different words he emphasizes still more its intrinsic unity:

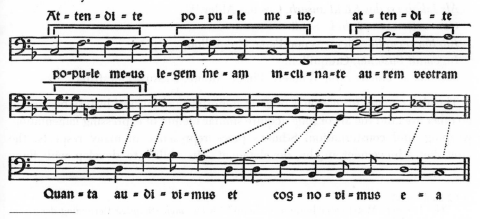

---

[6] Schuh analyses the *rondo*like disposition A₁ BA₂ CA₃ on pp. 97 f. (loc. cit.)

[7] The injunction of Asaph (Ps. 78: 1 ff.): "Give ear, O my people, to my Law: incline your ears to the words of my mouth. I will open my mouth in a parable: I will utter dark sayings of old, which we have heard and known and our fathers have told us."

At the *attendite* one should note the Monteverdi *lamento* climax, which, however, has another disposition of the members, consisting of an upward transposition at the second after an upward transposition at the fourth. In view of the thematic animation with which, in the concluding part, the sixteenths of the *narraverunt* are led through all four instruments (p. 76), one may question whether the four trombones suggested by Schütz are possible for this today and whether throughout we had not better use the strings which the master allowed in the superoctave as accompaniment for the two highest voices. It might be transposed from F to G.

Since Winterfeld's discovery No. XIII (p. 65), *Fili mi Absolon*, David's lament over Absolom[8] — scored exactly like the composition just discussed — is a culminating point of Schütz's lyricism. I have shown elsewhere that this *lamento* has a proud ancestry even as motet chamber music.[9] The chief compositions among these predecessors would be approximately:[10]

Didonis novissima verba: Dulces exuviae, by Josquin, LaRue, Mouton, Verbonet, Willaert.

Planxit autem David: Absalon, fili mi, Josquin, Ninot, Gallus.

Rex autem David: Doleo super te, frater mi Jonatha, Josquin, Clemens non Papa, Gascogne, L. Hellinck, A. Galli.

Videns Jacob vestimenta, Clemens non Papa, W. Breitengraser, S. Boileau, L. Päminger, Morales, Regnart.

Als Jakob nu das Kleid ansach, Cosmas Alder.[11]

Cum aegrotasset Job, L. Senfl.

Job tonso capite, Clemens non Papa, Crequillon.

Ingemuit Susanna, Crequillon.

Susanna se videns rapi, Willaert, Ph. de Monte, Lassus, Palestrina.

The above motet formation is of great importance in musical history because in no other area did the art of song acquire similar facility of expressing lamentation, weeping, and consternation. Schütz's piece represents, in many respects, the crowning achievement in this development. His ability to develop wide-flung

---

[8] 2 Sam. 18:33.
   [9] "The *Lamento* Motet from Josquin to Gallus" (in *Die mehrstimmige Vertonung des Evangeliums*, pp. 14-19).
   [10] As to the spiritual monody laments of Monteverdi's school immediately before Schütz see above p. 136.
   [11] From the Basel Joseph play by H. Rüti (1528) and not (Rhaw, 1544) by L. Senfl, as A. Gering has shown in *Die Vokalmusik der Schweiz zur Zeit der Reformation* (1933).

melodic arches from a mere nothing, as shown in the *Tollite jugum meum* (p. 468 above), marks new triumphs on his part. Here, according to the law of counter-thrust *(Gegenstoss),* he even forms a double arch. From rising, broken triads at intervals of a third, we find, with fascinating, vital irregularity, similar descending ones. The chromaticism of the augmented steps reaching upward and the diminished descending ones enhance the effect. Here the three-part time is intended to indicate, not a dance rhythm but agitation:

The twice-repeated closing motive, *Absalon,* is now taken up as an excited calling with a confirmatory closing cadence and with the climactic entrance of the trombone quartet, which, since its word-engendered opening symphony has remained silent, is a miracle in the exploitation of a musical sense of space. First the fifth is contracted, narrowed to a third, and repeated climactically at the interval of a fourth. Then the third is widened to a fifth followed by two fourths. The first fourth begins a third below the first note of the interval of the fifth, while the second fourth begins a second below the first note of the first fourth. Superb, too, is the logical sequence in which, after the repeated *Fili, fili mi, Absalon,* a double cadence seals off the section:

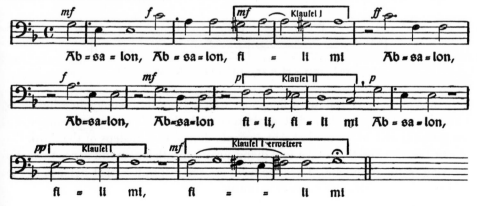

The dynamic indications added here result spontaneously from the melodic line, which is to be delivered with the greatest fervor.

The orchestral piece which precedes the second part — and is thematically independent — calls for an expression almost of savagery *(wilden Ausdruck)*. In its fugal overlappings of the voices and then in its mournfully throbbing parallel thirds it depicts the gesture of hairtearing, as it were, or at least of walking back and forth in despair:

In the second solo it is again worthwhile, as before in the case of the *Attendite, populue meus,* to place both halves under each other in order to observe the masterly points of correspondence:

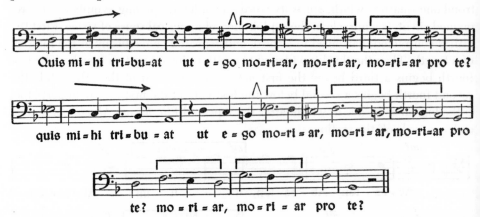

Immediately there follows a final solo which, from the manner in which it is formed from elements of the first, again reveals the highest art, as, for example, in the growing breadth of the last *Absalon* call, descending in steps of the third, the fourth, the fifth, and the octave, and dying away beneath a new and dense thematic weaving of the trombones. Here we have exalted inspiration that belongs to the highest achievements of the world of music!

There remain to be considered the pieces in Vol. V from the Song of Songs. While Schütz first presented these texts in the strophic form of Opitz, with small scoring, then in the *Cantiones sacrae* as motets, here he combines the Latin prose text with the intimate chamber-music organism. Nearly all the numbers in question, so far as the vocal side is concerned, are duets: for two tenors, for tenor and baritone, and for soprano and alto, both always representing one lover who is accompanied by the counterpoint-spinning shadow. Only No. XVIII is a *terzet* for two sopranos and tenor, constructed so as to place two dialog pairs in juxtaposition. In VII/VIII, *Anima mea* and *Adjuro vos*, for two "tenors," two *fifari* or *cornettini*, are prescribed. If one wished to retain the original position (*d* minor), then the instruments that would best conform to Schütz's tonal wishes — he notes his instruments in the mezzo-soprano clef — had best be two English horns, while the vocal parts, with a range c-f', would be given to a baritone and bass. It is better to transpose up to *e* minor so that tenor and baritone may sing and two oboes may play. There develops a most delightful play of two duet groups, of which at times the voices (as at *liquefacta)* take over the declamatory part, the instruments the illustrative, or the first group proceeds in homophonic thirds with the second in close imitation, as at *et facies ejus decora;* or the singers imitate each other at close distances, while the players imitate each other at a greater distance, as at *Adjura vos*, the voices imitating at low pitch, the instruments at high, as at *filiae Jerusalem*. Or again, a soloist declaims in a dramatic recitative above a sustained bass: *Wenn ihr meinen Liebsten findet, so saget ihm, dass ich vor Liebe vergehe* ("If ye find my beloved, tell him that I perish from love"), which is then confirmed by the *tutti* with all the forces. Here the vocalists give us excited figures; the players, songful lyricism.

Still more impressive in the invention of essentially songlike motives are Nos. IX/X, for tenor and baritone with two violins playing in high register. One can retain the *d* minor as indicated. In the first half the playful tenderness is reflected in the form, which one could designate as a *rondo* with a short and constantly varied refrain on *O quam tu pulchra, tu pulchra es*.[12] This theme, as the nucleus, is drawn from the introductory song, which appears first monodically, then in a dancing duet, and from its instrumental continuation (as *sinfonia*). Equally graceful and on a small scale are the intervening alternations in straight time, presented now in *parlando*, now in an embellished form: *Oculi tui columbarum, Capilli tui sicut greges caprarum, Dentes tui sicut greges tonsarum, Sicut vitta coccinea labia, tua, Sicut turris David collum tuum, Duo ubera tua sicut duo hinnuli capreae ge-*

---

[12] No. 8, p. 42.

melli,[13] where particularly the thoughts expressed in the latter statements are suggested by the music with captivating effectiveness:

and at the conclusion the ever heavenward-tending

as the introduction of the augmented *rondo* theme, is indeed graceful and elegant. The same idea crowns the conclusion of Part Two, and here with significant changes between *presto* and *adagio*. In this second part one is fascinated by the richly developed trio introduction with its fantastic intervals and rests. Observe only the two upper voices:

In measures three and six the unwritten phrase arches reach across the rests in a manner more compelling than in Riemann's disputed interpretation of the first theme of Beethoven's *Klavier Sonate*, Op. 7! In the second violin the diminished octave in measure three is as strange as the sudden pauses in measures four and six. After such witnesses to the great rhythmicist one must doubly regret that the ballet music, say, to *Orpheus* of 1638, has been lost. In the vocal parts of the composition under discussion the traversing of the directions in the conceived tonal

---

[13] "Thou hast doves' eyes within thy locks; thy hair is as a flock of goats. Thy teeth are like a flock of sheep that are even shorn; thy lips are like a thread of scarlet. Thy neck is like the tower of David. Thy two breasts are like two young roes that are twins."

space is especially picturesque. The *veni de Libano* ("come with me from Lebanon") (p. 48) as well as the *Surge, surge, propera, amica mea* ("Arise, arise, hasten, my friend") (p. 50) are made visual in the highest degree. At *Veni, veni* (p. 49) the tonal play previously presented in thirds at *sicut duo hinnuli* (p. 45) is repeated with climactic effect in fourths, and the

says with an impressiveness almost reserved for the tonal language of Schütz alone: "Come over mount and vale, come despite water and fire!" [14]

To this the numbers for soprano and alto, XVI/XVII (p. 83, p. 89),[15] stand in contrast. The three bassoons at the beginning indicate a dark, nocturnal atmosphere. With the exception of the one place, *inveni quem diligit anima mea*, which, however, also reveals an underlying tone of suffering, one could write above the whole the words: "Love is as bitter as death." But withal the gloomy instruments have in their symphonic motivation something of naive sincerity. C. von Winterfeld even says *(Johs. Gabrieli,* II, 180): "The accompaniment by deep instruments of gentle pleasing tone (for this reason the bassoon at that time was called *dulcino* and *dulcian)* points to a painting of a calm night." In the first part we are struck by harmonic functional characteristics or peculiarities, such as the minor cadence following the regular transition from the major dominant to the minor subdominant ♯ ♭ 4♯ | ♭ giving somewhat the impression of dark resolution.
V IV V | I

Then a predilection for the lower semitone before the fifth and a persistence on intense dominants, as, for example:

---

[14] *Komm über Berg und Tal, komm trotz Wasser und Feuer.*
[15] Winterfeld, *Gabrieli,* II, 180 f., III, 147-49.

Or the strange leaping from the seventh to conclude, after all, in minor through a Phrygian cadence expressing nonfulfillment and sadness:

In Part Two figures depict the restless tramping of watchmen. A grand climax leads from the timorous *paululum* to the jubilant *inveni,* and significant is the colorful harmonic change, G—c—A—F—D—g, which is used first for a chromatically upward-creeping line, *quem diligit anima mea,* and then in the quintet for *cantate dilecto meo.* The interlacing and joining of the rhythms at *tenui nec dimittam illum* [16] is, to a certain extent, a Tristan love-dream symbolism full of painful ardor that places the lonely forty-four-year-old Schütz strangely near the period of late romanticism.

The Song of Songs *terzet* [17] (No. XVIII, p. 96) expands, if we count the trombones (or gambas), into a sextet. The notice *tiorba* with the *bassus pro organo* for the solo episodes shows clearly (if indeed such indication were still necessary) that we are dealing, not with church music but with chamber music. Here we have a genuine situation dialog insofar as the first soprano, with the instrumental trio, represents Sulamith, while the second soprano and the tenor embody the wise, loving Solomon as the groups play and sing with one another in a concertizing manner. The piece produces an impression neither of suffering nor of ecstasy but rather paints the happy peace of assured love. The sheer pleasure of music-making keeps the piece at a medium level of expression, but some small flashes like the g—E at *mein König* or the repeated notes at *comedite* are delightful. The *tutti, Comedite dilecti et bibite amici,* [18] doubtless is the central feature of the piece, which might be viewed as somewhat related to the *Drinking Book* of the Persian poet Hafiz *(Schenkenbuch des Hafis).*

---

[16] "I held him and shall not leave him."
[17] With optional substitution of a voice for the second trombone it would be a quartet.
[18] "I bid you eat with me, beloved, and drink abundantly, my friends" (Song of Solomon 5:1).

This résumé will have shown that the principal compositions in the work have a vigor of feeling and expression that places the volume in the foremost ranks of Schütz's inspirations. Whatever compositions have not yet been published in practical editions should soon be added to the list.

This neglect is being atoned for currently by the gradual appearance of a new edition (1948-49) under the editorship of Rud. Gerber through the Bärenreiter-Verlag. Up to the present time Nos. 1 to 10 have appeared. The edition also has a German text.

Individual Church-Hymn Compositions

The chapter titled "Schütz and the Evangelical Chorale" deals with a moot subject, inasmuch as Ph. Spitta had somewhat undervalued this relation of Schütz to the chorale and Alfred Einstein practically denied that any such relationship existed: "Schütz severs that connection, utilizes the text of the hymn, and casts away the melody as a mere shell; or — seldom enough! — he chooses the melody in order to treat it freely in a motetlike or concertizing manner; it is not a firm, untouchable basis for him." In opposition to this I have emphasized[1] that such an interpretation approaches a tendentious uprooting of Schütz from the spiritual world of the Protestantism of his time, and I have pointed out that in about fifty cases Schütz has retained more or less strictly the traditional melodies and has rejected them in only three or four instances, where he has used only the poem. Although A. Heuss saw fit to contradict this, I must nevertheless for the most part maintain this factual report. We meet chorale strophes in the *Exequien* and in a dozen harmonizations of old chorale melodies in the *Becker Psalter,* while the remaining thirty settings are divided among the *Kleine geistliche Konzerte,* the *Geistliche Chormusik,* and the *Sinfoniae sacrae II* and *III.* Some occur in the passions, the *Zwölf geistliche Gesänge,* and in the *Psalmen von 1619.* Two have already been discussed as "early works" — the *Veni, Sancte Spiritus* and the *Christ ist erstanden.* The miscellaneous remainder, from Vols. XII to XVIII of the collected works, will be summarized here, as in these seven pieces we can conveniently study the types of Schütz's treatment of the church hymn. I have already stated that, of course, the church hymn represents a much more modest proportion in the case of Schütz than in the case of M. Praetorius; that Schütz for the most part approaches it in a somewhat freer, more Lassolike manner than, for example, J. H. Schein. Nevertheless, when Schütz uses the chorale melody, he stands well in the line which leads from Johs. Walter to Seb. Bach. The latter, both as organ composer and in his cantates, certainly allows himself similarly bold transformations of the old evangelical treasures of melody.

Among the seven settings referred to we have, in the first place, an incomplete, short, four-voiced setting: *In dich hab ich gehoffet Herr,* the alto of which H. Spitta

---

[1] *Jahrbuch der staatlichen Akademie für Kirchen- und Schulmusik,* III.

supplemented in Vol. 18, No. II of Appendix, p. 139. It is a double to the like-named setting of the *Becker Psalter*. Not only is this composition found in manuscript 40200 of the Berlin State Library, but here there is also a complete four-voiced setting: *Ach bleib mit deiner Gnade*, in a manuscript written by Caspar Peltsch between 1648 and 1661. The melody used by Schütz for Joh. Stegmann's hymn *Ach bleib mit deiner Gnade* has nothing to do with the one by C. Cramer, in common use since 1641, or with the one by Melchior Vulpius, in common use today and originally composed in 1609 for *Christus, der ist mein Leben*, I give the discant with modern bar lines:[2]

Because of a certain freedom it may well be an "occasional" piece by Schütz. The slight rising turns at *Gnade* and *schade* are not otherwise common in congregational song. As against the somewhat gloomy opening line, the concluding line forms an almost too trivial secular contrast.

More interesting is the six-voice setting, preserved in Königsberg, of Selneccer's melody for grace at meals to L. Helmboldt's words *Nun lasst uns Gott dem Herren*. It is especially effective because in the second-last line two of the voices are eliminated, the conclusion then appearing in full splendor in full setting (Vol. 16, p. 189).

The five-voice *madrigale spirituale, Ach Herr, du Schöpfer aller Ding* (GA. XIV, 105, manuscript in Kassel), is a free composition on the text of a church hymn. Here Schütz set the ninth stanza of Luther's Christmas hymn *Vom Himmel hoch da komm ich her*. Only at the close do we find an (accidental?) reminiscence of the melody of 1539:

The piece — devoid of signatures — which, on account of certain boldnesses, may be assigned to the beginning of the 1620's, is remarkable even from the tonal

---

[2] Volume 16 of the collected works, p. 188.

point of view. Its actual center is *a* minor, but it begins in *b* minor and concludes
on the dominant of the dominant, B major. Schütz would undoubtedly have spoken
of *b* Phrygian with the Dorian kernel *a*. From the composer's point of view we
again have a type that one could call "a motetlike expansion of an original model
with madrigalesque means." The "song theme not made known" would sound
something like:

Ach Herr, du Schöpfer al=ler Ding, wie bist du wor=den so   ge=ring, daß du da=

liegst auf dür = rem Gras, da = von ein Rind und E = sel aß.

A fine Christmas composition that has probably never been sufficiently utilized
for the occasion.[3]

In contrast to these choral compositions a fine example of the transformation of
a church song into a solo *concerto* with instrumental accompaniment is presented
by the quintet setting *Erbarm dich mein, o Herre Gott*.[4] It stands note for note in
the *Becker Psalter*. In the place of the second viola in the broad introductory
sinfonia the solo soprano enters in the actual *concerto*. While the first part of the
hymn *(Stollen)* — Psalm 51, paraphrased by Erh. Hegenwalt, the melody in Jhs.
Walter's *Chorgesangbüchlein* of 1524 —

Er=barm dich mein, o   Her = re Gott, nach dei = ner groß'n Barm=her=zig = keit,
wasch ab, mach rein mein Mis=se = tat,   ich kenn mein Sünd, und ist mir leid.

is played by the first violin in half notes, the solo voice develops a forefield of many
short *Erbarm dich*'s with a vivacity reminding one of M. Praetorius.[5] It then takes
over the melody itself, broadening it through numerous impressive individual
repetitions *(O Herre, o Herre, mein Missetat, mein Missetat)* into a subjective

[3] Published by H. S. Drinker in the Association of American Chorus Series.
[4] From Upsala and Danzig, in Vol. XVIII, *GA*.
[5] Settings by this master of the same chorale: *à 2, Mus. Sion.* IX, 71; *à 3*, IX, 72-74; *à 4*, VII,
39-43; *à 8*, III, 24; *à 12*, II, 28. Cf. also the *Concerto* by Schein (Prüfer ed. V, 76 ff.); and Hammerschmidt, *à 5*, 1641, in *DTD*, 40. Sam. Scheidt (*Geistl. Konzerte* II, 11, 1634) uses the text
without the church melody in an artistic experiment related to Schütz's *Wenn unsre Augen
schlafen ein*.

lamento. In the conclusion Schütz personalizes the *cantus firmus* especially through an increase of rhythmical liveliness. It will be useful to place the model and the setting side be side. Between the the two there may lie exactly one hundred years:

The fundamental melody, which in the *sinfonia* had constituted the bass, now, in the first violin, cuts across the lines of the voice part in half phrases — a strong proof of the way in which the baroque man Schütz still clings to the old evangelical foundations.

Now the eighteen hymn stanzas of *Ich hab mein Sach Gott heimgestellt*, the *Aria de vitae fugacitate*, which Schütz in that unfortunate year 1625 had sung for his sister-in-law Anna Maria Wildeck (*GA*. Vol. XII; again as the concluding number of the *Kleine geistliche Konzerte of 1636*). The comparison of the two settings gives a deep insight into the secrets of Schütz's workshop. From the viewpoint of composition he found but little to alter after eleven years — a few interchanges of the voices, at one point a short expansion, here and there a rhythmic change. The reworking, however, affects especially the system of embellishment.

In the first stanzas this is intentionally reduced to a minimum, and then it is added only here or there where he wishes to emphasize more vividly an individual word or concept, such as *Leben, gelöscht, Kreuz, Herrlichkeit*. In other words, we have a new tendency toward simplicity, a heightened striving for plasticity, a shrinking from merely mechanical ornamentation!

The Dresden separate edition of the first setting designates the piece *supra bassum continuum*, which means more than merely the addition of the chordal instrument for an obbligato part as in the appended *concerti* in the *Cantiones sacrae*. This, almost the most comprehensive of Schütz's chorale settings, is constructed as a chain of variations above a *basso ostinato:*[6]

This is doubtless conceived in the Italian manner, as an instrumental song body of the type of the *Ruggiero,* the *Romanesca,* the *Follia d'Espagna,* such as Francesco Turini, Biagio Marini, Salomone Rossi, and Stefano Landi took delight in writing at the time. As it progresses, Schütz's bass shows certain similarities to the *Aria di Ruggiero.* But need one, as Einstein does, call this a "surprising, strange, and almost disrespectful whim"? The tune *(Liedkörper),* appearing in 1589 in the *Frankfurt Liederbuch* for the text *Ich weiss mir ein Röslein hübsch und fein* ("I Know Me a Rose So Fair and Fine"), was used for the hymn of J. Leon for the first time in the hymnal of Landgrave Moritz (Kassel, 1601; Zahn, No. 1679), just at the time when Schütz first entered the *Maurizianum.* At first he sets this melody quite literally as a duet between the first soprano and the tenor. In the second strophe a variation occurs in that the beginnings of the lines are freely formed, while their conclusions flow back into the model as an imitative duet between alto and tenor. Stanza three is a terzet assigned to the three lowest voices. The thematic material (clearest in the tenor) is deduced from the last two lines of the church melody. In the duet of the discants which now follows the second soprano draws the melody line very freely, with only a slight reference to it. In strophe five the vocal parts depart entirely from the melody, but nevertheless the spiritual band remains tightly drawn. For precisely here it becomes manifest that the entire cycle stands under the law of the *ostinato.* The sixth stanza, which for the first time has

---

[6] Reduced to seven strophes in the selection by Woyrsch.

the four upper voices sound simultaneously, derives its short, folklike motives freely from the model. The alto-bass duo of the seventh stanza raises itself in noble melody above the *ostinato,* but in like dissimilarity to the ground melody. In strophe nine a first climax is reached through the first chorus *tutti.* The melodic relation to the model limits itself to the repeated circumscribing by the alto and the tenor of the notes g—e—f#—a—g.

The fact that in the second part the complementary choir (of which the original setting knew nothing) enters in strophes fourteen and eighteen is not so much required by the text but is, above all, a confirmation of Schütz's fine sense of musical space *(Raumgefühl).* The three sections which thus arise closely approach the relation of a golden engraving, a harmonious division; and this condition of rejuvenation prevents any tendency on the part of the listener to grow weary.

The first *tutti* enters after seven, the second after five, the third after three differently treated strophes. In strophe nine, a duet between first discant and the alto, the lower voice preserves the thematic material of the chorale at least at the two main divisions. In strophe ten the second discant follows the thematic material still more closely, as well as in strophe eleven, where the alto now follows, now precedes, like a shadow. In strophe twelve one must admire how the vocal bass, with very small changes, allows the *ostinato* to indulge in numerous madrigalisms. In the dark terzet of the thirteenth strophe the tenor has numerous points in common with the core of the melody. The *capella* setting of strophe fourteen arises freely (with preference for the rhythmic motive 234/1) over the firm foundation of the unchanging bass. Strophes fifteen, sixteen, and seventeen intentionally spin their duets and an outer-voice trio quite freely in order that the re-entrance of the chorale in the last *tutti* strophe may follow more effectively. Here the kernel melody lies first in the second discant, then in the alto; the first soprano and the tenor share the melody in line three; the fourth line dissolves itself into a broadening *coda.* One feels in the superbly far-flung piece that it was translated into music not merely for the purpose of condolence *(aus condolentz in die Music übersetzet)* but that it is a deep, personally felt clarification on the part of the master of the Christian interpretation of the idea of fate, as a religious "With forty years the mount is scaled" *(Mit vierzig Jahren ist der Berg erstiegen).*

Finally we shall take up Schütz's arrangement of *Wo Gott der Herr nicht bei uns hält* ("If God, the Lord, Doth Not Assist")[7] *à 10,* according to the Kassel manuscript, in which the "three violas" of the collected works are designated now as *viola bastarda,* now as *da gamba.* To the three strings a vocal soprano is added

---

[7] XIII, 169.

as Choir Two. Against these there is a similar vocal soprano with the three trombones as Choir Three. Choir One consists of a very high soprano with a lute bass that has been doubly preserved. In other words, we have a *concerto* of three often alternating discants with their assigned harmonic support. If one compares the setting with Schein's spiritual *concerto* of 1618,[8] the credit for the greater fidelity to the church pattern is decidedly in Schütz's favor. One can designate his work as the apotheosis of devout *cantus firmus* discipleship. The subject of the composition is not the earliest (Zwickau) melody to Justus Jonas' *Hymn on Psalm 129* but the Klug melody of 1535 (Zahn 4441a). To be sure, here, too, Schütz adds all kinds of free embellishments, but at no place without having introduced each line, word for word, three times — once for every one of the concertizing factors; this presentation is multiplied numerous times through instrumental imitations. Furthermore, every expansion or rhythmic variation — so beloved by Schein, Scheidt,[9] and Praetorius[10] — is here dispensed with. Every line is presented as a metrically clear unity in simple isometric form. At most only the intermediary embellishments *(Intermezzofloskeln)* derived from the respective lines and the *coda* attempt a certain variation of the regular rhythm. The piece is a little stiff and rather primitive in its transitions *(Verzahnungen)*. It is, therefore, perhaps older than its *canzona* sister from the polychorus *Psalms of 1619, Nun lob mein Seel' den Herren.*

All in all, when one reviews the Schütz church-hymn settings, one must confess that, together with the gospels, they occupy only a second place when compared with the psalms, both as to extent and in importance. But despite this fact Schütz nevertheless remains one of the most important setters of the treasures of evangelical hymnody.

Finally there remains to be mentioned the eight-voice setting of Luther's German *Sanctus, Jesaia dem Propheten* (unfortunately, still undiscovered). Besides the passions it is the only work of Schütz which Mattheson, in his *Ehrenpforte* of 1739, mentions as important. In 1658 Andr. Ungar presented the composition, besides twenty-two other works by Schütz, to the Naumburg Church of St. Wenceslaus. Fetis' placing of the work between the *Psalms of David of 1619* and the *Resurrection History* was doubtless based on mere surmise. Up to the present time I have not found even an anonymous copy of the work in this arrangement.

---

[8] Prüfer ed., V, 93.
[9] In Scheidt in the *Neue geistliche Konzerte*, II, 22 (1634).
[10] In M. Praetorius *à 2, Mus. Sion.* IX, 162; *à 3,* 163 ff.; *à 4,* VIII, 113 ff.;
à 8, III, 18.

Op. 7. The Musikalische Exequien of 1636

What led to the writing of this first *German Requiem* in our music — a work composed for Heinrich Posthumus, the excellent ruler of Reuss — and what the circumstances were with regard to the text — which is made up of Bible passages and stanzas from church hymns — has been related in the biographical portion of this book. Here, therefore, it is necessary to speak only about the composition itself. Soon after the first public performance — on February 4, 1636 — an edition of the voice parts appeared through Wolff Seyffert in Dresden, of which a single complete copy has been preserved in Königsberg, an incomplete continuo part in Reuss. In Ph. Spitta's complete edition the score stands in Vol. XII. A practical edition, edited by G. Schumann, was issued through Breitkopf & Härtel in conjunction with the Bärenreiter-Verlag.[1]

The general schematic outline of the work is:

I. *Teutsche Begräbnis-Missa, in e moll*
   German Funeral Mass, in e minor
   A. *Quasi-Kyrie:*
      a. *Nacket bin ich vom Mutterleibe kommen (e—E)*
         Naked Came I from My Mother's Womb
      b. *Christus ist mein Leben (e—a)*
         Christ Is My Life
      c. *Leben wir, so leben wir dem Herrn (e—E)*
         Live We, Then Live We unto the Lord

   } *à 6*

   B. *Quasi-Gloria:*
      Also hat Gott die Welt geliebt
      God So Loved the World
      Nine verses besides nine church hymn strophes *(e minor), à 6*[2]

II. *Parentationsmotette:*
    Funeral Motet:
    Herr, wenn ich dich nur habe, à 8, double chorus,
    Lord, If Only I Have Thee,

---

[1] An edition has been published (in 1957) by Arthur Mendel (G. Schirmer) with Latin and English text.
[2] To be sure, Spitta's score has seven staves; but only at two places does the bass divide itself into duets. The *tutti* never goes beyond six parts.

quasi A major (i. e., without signature and with constant
use of F major, C major, G major instead of f# minor,
c# minor, g# minor — i. e., more a Picardized a minor.

III. *Konzert für 5stg.en Grosschor*
Concerto for Large Chorus, à 5:
   Herr, nun lässest du
   Lord, Now Lettest Thou Thy Servant Depart in Peace
   and solo group, *à 3 (g minor):*
   Selig sind die Toten
   Blessed Are the Dead
   (2 seraphim, sopranos; *beata anima*, baritone)

In connection with the *Gloria* Schütz presents a kind of apology in the *Preface
(Ordinantz):* "Since I was to gather the verses of the German church songs into
one body from all kinds of modes, I trust understanding musicians will pardon me
for occasionally digressing from the bounds of the *noni toni* in pursuing such
melodies." Schütz, then, views the *e* minor as a transposed Aeolian. To our ears
conflicts between melody citations and tonal frames are doubtless no longer
perceptible. The master recommends that the work be presented also as a German
Mass on the Festival of the Purification of Mary or on the Sixteenth Sunday after
Trinity. The first suggestion was doubtless made because the appended motet on
the *Nunc Dimittis* might do service as the Gospel for the day; the latter suggestion
was doubtless due to the fact that the Gospel for this Sunday, Luke 7, dealt with
the story of the youth of Nain, for which the many death songs of the *Gloria*
section are very fitting.

The double-chorus motet was correctly described by Willi Schuh (p. 121) as a
potentialized *(potenzierte) Bar.* In the closing ensemble Schütz succeeded even
more remarkably in mastering the form problem. In connection with the "distant
inner" *(fernen Innen)* and the "near outer" *(nahen Aussen)* of the Mühlhausen
Electoral Motet we have already referred to this baroque "up and down" *(oben
und unten)* that finds a counterpart, as it were, in the Stettin *Lazarus Oratorio* of
Andreas Fromm (1649) with the division of the music positions in the church into
earth, hell, and heaven,[3] and which, of course, has its precursor in the old mystery
stage. Schütz himself says: "With this invention or *chorus secundus* the author
wanted to introduce and indicate the joy of the disembodied blessed souls in
heaven, in the company of the blessed spirits and the holy angels. *Primus chorus*

---

[3] Rud. Schwartz in *Petersjahrbuch,* 1898.

should be placed next to the organ, *secundus chorus,* however, in the distance and as each performer may deem most advisable. Anyone who would make one or two further copies of this *chorus secundus* for the sake of using them with the participants in different parts of the respective churches would augment considerably the author's hopes for the effectiveness of the work."

The poetic thought to have Posthumus conducted on high by angels is apparently derived from Luke 16: 22 — the Gospel for the First Sunday after Trinity: "And it came to pass that the beggar died and was carried by the angels into Abraham's bosom," which in turn is based on Ps. 91:11. Similarly, in the Epistle of Jude, verse nine, a battle between St. Michael and Satan over the dead body of Moses is mentioned, a scene that has something in common not only with paintings but also with the last scenes of Goethe's *Faust,* II. Schütz's double chorus, which, with its twofold texts, reverts to an outstanding characteristic of the old motet is, apart from the baroque spatial setting, one of the noblest developments of the so-called *Widerrufe* or "voices from the grave" which were prevalent at the time and, in the case of H. Albert, were often in rather bad taste. By designating the intonation with i, the textual divisions of the human choir with a—f, and those of the seraphim group with u—z, W. Schuh has set up a plan which, in simplified form, is as follows:

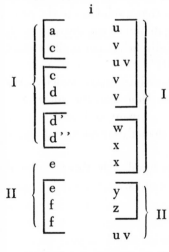

We have, accordingly, in the opening *(Aufgesang),* born of the text, a hemiolic contraction of two and three parts; in the conclusion *(Abgesang)* we have another kind of oppositional arrangement or telescoping. And while in the main we have a climactic dynamism of motetlike links, the repetition of the text u—v also gives a curved or arched static balance. In other words, we have *in nuce* examples of all the formative principles that occur in Schütz!

It should further be noted that "staticism" prevails in the case of the angels transfigured by their vision, while "dynamism" prevails in the case of the mortals still active under the sway of the will. Even if this were present only in the master's subconscious mind, it has a deep meaning. So Schütz succeeded wonderfully in distinguishing the stylistic expression of both groups: the text of Simeon is given with many syncopations and with metric restlessness, now loud, now soft; the words of the angels, on the other hand, are given in flowing uniformity (representing an undisturbed hovering) and without differences of dynamics.

The *Gloria* of the funeral Mass is one of Schütz's most significant chorale works. Out of a sum total of 293 measures, 117, almost a half, are devoted to eight stanzas of church hymns. They are all melodically faithful to the hymn-book versions, although the *Nun freut euch* ("Rejoice Now"), the first and the last episode, uses the rare Klug melody of 1535, while the second-last, *Wenn mein Stündlein* ("When My Last Hour"), uses the Dresden melody of 1593 (Zahn, 4486). Schütz thus pays his respects to a fashion of the time — that of presenting "church quodlibets," a fashion to which Johs. Christenius of Altenburg also paid homage with a Gera (!) music publication. Perhaps it was intentional that the chorale episodes amounted respectively to 14, 8, $16^1/_2$, 8, 15, $16^1/_2$, 19, and 20 measures. The two eight-measure episodes belong to the same short strophe, *Nun lasst uns Gott dem Herren* ("Now Let Us unto God the Lord"), and differ almost only in the exchange of the sopranos, a practice of which the master was fond in the case of a distich *(Stollen)* or similar members of a motet. He also used this exchange of sopranos in the case of the quasi-sixteen-measure portions. The fact that the second-last episode is nineteen measures long as the result of the rapid joy triplets becomes, so to say, contagious in the case of the last portion, with the result that it considerably exceeds its counterpart, the first portion. All the major melodies — I, II, IV, VII, IX — are in G and must be supplemented with a line that modulates to the principal tonality: E. On the other hand, III and VI, being in minor, can dispense with this supplementary line, as they begin with *e*. Typically Schützian is the climax in VI — *Es ist das Heil* ("Salvation Now Is Come to Us") — by means of a simple canon between the discants. In number VII — the Strassburg major melody, *Aus tiefer Not* ("Out of the Depths") — the imitations in almost all the voices and degrees are also Schützian. After the employment of so many technical devices Schütz wards off monotony (cf. pp. 325, 535) through the only entrance in *a* minor and a change of rhythm at the penultimate position.

Schütz knew well why he assigned a special *opus* number to this occasional piece, for *Op. 7* is one of the finest inspirations of his genius.

Oratoriolike Individual Works

The *Exequien*, with its conclusion similar to a mystery play, is a work closely resembling an oratorio. Each of the four compositions that we shall consider now can, for one reason, almost be classified as an oratorio: *Die Geschichte vom reichen Mann und dem armen Lazarus (The Story of Dives and Lazarus); Die sieben Worte am Kreuz (The Seven Words on the Cross);* the Easter dialog, *Weib, was weinest du? (Woman, Why Weepest Thou?);* and the dialog — recently discovered by me — between Jesus and the Canaanite woman, *Ach Herr, der Sohn Davids (O Lord, the Son of David).*

The first composition, on Luke 16: 19 ff., was discovered by Max Seiffert, on the basis of the old Lüneburg catalog, among the anonymous works in Kassel and was published by Heinrich Spitta in Vol. XVIII of the collected works and then by Seiffert himself in a practical edition in his *Organum.* Subsequently the attribution of the work to Schütz was confirmed by means of a Danzig copy made by Crato Büttner, a copy which contained Schütz's name.[1] Liturgically the work would be music for the Gospel on the First Sunday after Trinity. However, Schütz's treatment is pronouncedly in the nature of an oratorio, which would place this work of the 1620's between those of Bollius and A. Fromm, perhaps chronologically even before them all. The sequence of parts is as follows:

   I. Three-voice *sinfonia* (*a*—E)
  II. Dives (bass solo, 2 vls., continuo): *Vater Abraham* ("Father Abraham") (*e*—A)
 III. Abraham (tenor solo, traverse flute 1 & 2, continuo): *Gedenke, Sohn* ("Remember, son") (*g*—*g*)
 IV. Dives (bass solo, 2 vls., continuo): *So bitt' ich dich, Vater* ("So I pray thee, father") (*e*—F#)
  V. Abraham (tenor solo, 2 vls., continuo): *Sie haben Moses* ("They have Moses") (D—*g*)
 VI. Dives (bass solo, 2 vls., continuo): *Mein Vater* ("My father") (D—*e*)

---

[1] Büttner has made a number of changes for the worse. He has also made the two wind groups uniform and has introduced a theorbo bass. The Kassel readings are authoritative.

VII. Abraham (tenor, continuo): *Hören sie Moses* ("They hear not Moses")
(D—Bb)

VIII. IX. *Ritornello* (2 vls., continuo, *g—g*): Lazarus and two angels (alto, 2d soprano, continuo, *g—Bb*): *Sie haben Moses* ("They have Moses") *ritornello
da capo*

XI. *Tutti* (2 angels, Lazarus, Abraham, 2 vls., continuo, G—G): *Hören sie Moses
und die Propheten nicht* ("If they hear not Moses") to *Ob jemand von den
Toten auferstünde* ("Though one arose from the dead").

Schütz discarded all narrative connections. Therefore a purely dramatic *dialogus*
remained. The complete Gospel story[2] had been composed with a Latin text by
Leonhart Schröter and Homer Herpol for five voices, and by Vulpius for six voices.
At the time of Schütz's death it was set by J. C. Horn in an equally complete form
in German for four voices with instruments. In contrast to these, Lassus, in 1571
(GA Haberl, Vol. IV), was doubtless the first to extract the *lamento* only and to
dramatize it in a grandiose manner for five voices. How vividly the *intingat ex-
tremum digiti sui* is reserved by Lassus for the three upper voices in order that the
refrigeret might then swell forth polyphonically in a *tutti!* Or how mournful is the
effect of the fauxbourdons at *similiter mala!* How pointed the recitation of the
tu vero! Here one understands the meaning of a polyphonic setting of the Gospel
as a vivid coloring of the Biblical sketches.

The same extract was set for full chorus and as a duo by G. Otto and S. Calvisius,
by R. de Mel (1595), and by the Dutchman Wanning in Danzig with dramatically
repeated *Pater, Pater*. Among the German motets on *Vater Abraham* by Raselius,
Vulpius, Demantius, and Th. Elsbeth the four-voice setting by Melchior Franck
stands out by reason of the expressive power of its harmonies. The beginning will
suffice to show this:

Va - ter A - - bra - ham,   Va - ter A - bra - ham   usw.

---

[2] Cf. H. J. Moser, *Die mehrstimmige Vertonung des Evangeliums*, I, 23, 35 f., 46, 62.

The text of Dulichius was translated from German back into Latin for his two-part Gospel motet *Rogo te, pater Abraham, ut mittas. At ille dixit.*

H. Spitta has advanced the plausible argument that the scene in the netherworld in the third act of Monteverdi's *Orfeo* was modeled after Schütz's *concerto.* Schütz sharpens the tension in the dialog, not only by having the bass and the tenor soloist oppose each other in expressive recitative with contrasting instrumental groups but also through the irreconcilability of the keys. Abraham sings in the sphere of *g* Dorian; Dives, in *e* Aeolian. The oratoriolike nature of the piece is now particularly apparent in our master's new idea of developing from verse twenty-two, *Der Arme ward getragen* ("The beggar was carried by the angels into Abraham's bosom"), a song by two angels representing Lazarus, here of course in Abraham's tonality![3] The very simple opening *sinfonia* might be interpreted as the death of the poor man and the rich man. In the extended recitative of Dives the chromatic chords of the sixth on *erbarme* present the underlying atmosphere. The instruments, used at first only in echo effects, increase their participation as the piece progresses and enter the musical web on an equal footing at *dass er das Äusserste seines Fingers* ("that he may dip the tip of his finger in water"). The flames of hell are painted in powerful jagged arches extending through all the extremes of the voice range, and the Lydian chord of the sixth of the Florentine *ars nova* reflects vividly the passage:

Abraham's soliloquy is definitely characterized by the Monteverdi opera style, as, for example:

At the reply of Dives in hell the dramatist and psychologist Schütz steps brilliantly to the fore by letting the tortured Dives suddenly pause as he thinks of his brothers on earth, while the flames flicker alarmingly before his eyes. (See next page.)

The lively three-part time for the beginning of the answer of Abraham is splendidly effective. The *ritornello,* which frames the very simple harmonies of the

---

[3] Who is not reminded here of the redeemed soul of Posthumus between the two seraphim in the *Exequien?* Surely Schütz at one time must have seen the English comedians present the dialog between the good and the bad angel in Marlowe's *Dr. Faustus.*

terzet sung by the blessed souls, has the same rhythm, doubtless in order to paint the "hovering on the clouds." The concluding *tutti* then presents in polyphony the final words of the patriarch. While the instruments playing the melody were held in restraint before, they now flash more brightly above the texture of the voices. Here we have a little oratorio of strong impressiveness. It requires only seven persons for its execution. Felix Schreiber (DTB, XIII, 63) has shown by the dialogs of the Nuremberger Erasmus Kindermann of 1643[4] that this composition had contemporary imitators.

A work of the highest rank is the oratorio *The Seven Words on the Cross*.[5] The master prefaced it with the lines:

Lebstu der Welt, so bist du todt,	Liv'st thou to the world, then art thou dead,
Und kränkst Christum mit schmertzen,	And causest Christ so many a smart;
Stirbst aber in seinen Wunden roth,	But di'st thou in His wounds so red,
So lebt er in deim Herzen.	He liveth ever in thy heart.

---

[4] Especially in *Des Erlösers Christi und sündigen Menschen heylsamen Gespräch (The Healing Dialog Between the Redeemer Christ and the Sinner)*, printed loc. cit., pp. 155 ff.

[5] *Die Sieben Worte unsers lieben Erlösers und Seligmachers JESU CHRISTI so ER am Stamm des Heiligen Creutzes gesprochen gantz beweglich gesetzt von Herrn Heinrich Schützen Chur Sächsischen Capellmeistern (The Seven Words of Our Dear Savior and Redeemer Jesus Christ Which He Spake on the Holy Cross, Very Movingly Set by Heinrich Schütz, Electoral Saxon Capellmeister)*. Vol. I of collected works; student score ed. by Fritz Stein, Eulenburg; practical ed. by Alb. Hänlein, 1901, B & H; piano score by S. Jadassohn, B & H; new ed. by Br. Grusnick, Bärenreiter, 1577; English ed. by Frank Damrosch, G. Schirmer, N. Y.; Concordia Publishing House, ed. by Gore.

The source was a manuscript of the seventh century in the Kassel library, which Otto Kade discovered in the year 1855 and Fr. Chrysander arranged in score for the first time the following year. E. H. Müller recently[6] gave 1645[7] as the year of origin. If this is correct, the piece appeared almost exactly between the *Resurrection History* of 1623 and the group of passions (ca. 1664). From the viewpoint of content it stands to a certain extent, though not entirely, alone. The seven last words of the crucified Lord, culled from all the Gospels, were regarded by the Middle Ages as a sevenfold mystical unity. At the beginning of the musical settings in this category stands Ludwig Senfl's grandiose motet cycle on *Da Jesus an dem Kreuze stund (As Jesus Hung upon the Cross).*[8] At the end of the development stands the oratorio *The Seven Words,* by Joseph Haydn, which consists of string quartets.[9] For the sake of the completeness of the seven words Obrecht had already expanded his motet passion according to St. Matthew (a classic of the century) into a Gospel harmony.

The body of Schütz's work is preceded and concluded by a *symphonia,* an enclosing frame, which Schering describes as a "veil to shut out the world." We have the following plan of the work:

Introitus: Da Jesus an dem Kreuze stund ("As Jesus Hung upon the Cross"): Ch. à 5, with continuo, e minor

Symphonia: on motives of the preceding hymn, à 5, e—E

1st Word: *Vater, vergib ihnen* ("Father, forgive them"). Jesus — Tenor II, e—e

2nd Word: *Weib, siehe. Johannes, siehe* ("Woman, behold." "John, behold"), with 2 vls., E—G, e—B

3rd Word: *Wahrlich, ich sage dir* ("Truly, I say to thee"), with 2 vls., the thief: e—a

4th Word: *Eli lama,* with 2 vls.: a—E; Evangelist, à 4 with continuo; Jesus: *Mein Gott,* with 2 vls.: a—E

5th Word: *Mich dürstet* ("I thirst"), with 2 vls., E—B

6th Word: *Es ist vollbracht* ("It is finished"), with 2 vls.: e—E

7th Word: *Vater, ich befehle* ("Father, I commend"), with 2 vls.: e—e; Evangelist, à 4 with continuo

Symphonia: identical with the first

Conclusion: *Wer Gottes Marter in Ehren hat* ("Who Holds in Honor God's

---

[6] Index of the works preceding the collection of Schütz's letters.
[7] I do not know his authority.
[8] Ed. by Fritz Piersig through Schauenburg-Lahr.
[9] Cf. Ad. Sandberger's treatise in his *Gesammelte Aufsätze zur Musikgeschichte,* I, 266 ff.

Sufferings Sore"). The last stanza of *Da Jesus an dem Kreuze stund, Ch. à 5,* with continuo, *e—E*

It is noticeable that here the tenor evangelist (usually sung to the accompaniment of the continuo) is transferred to the four-voice chorus between the two presentations of the *Eli lama* and after the seventh word, making it apparent that Schütz has set up two separate climaxes. The fact that only the first word is sung without violins and that here the evangelist is an alto gives this scene an introductory or upbeat character. In the scene of the two robbers (alto and bass) the evangelist, by way of contrast, is sung by a soprano, a clear connection with the old motet passion.

Kretzschmar,[10] whose expositions are otherwise excellent, erroneously assumed that in the *introitus* and in the *conclusio* Schütz used the traditional church melody of *Da Christus an dem Kreuze stund.* Schütz's settings are, in fact, motetlike developments of an original model the twofold forms of which I attempted to set forth in the *Jahrbuch III der staatlichen Akademie für Kirchen- und Schulmusik.* It contains such evident and marked characteristics of the spiritual folk song of the sixteenth century as to make it seem plausible that Schütz used a local melody which had not passed into official church use. The melodic basis of the *introitus* would be as follows:[11]

The conclusion, with altogether different counterpoint, has a central melody which, at least in the disposition of the different cadences, strongly resembles the first. (See next page.)

---

[10] *Führer durch den Konzertsaal,* II, 1895, pp. 42 ff.
[11] One will recall the similar case in Schütz's early work, *Veni, Sancte Spiritus.*

Wer Gottes Marter in Eh-ren hat, und oft ge-denkt der sieben Wort, des will Gott gar e-ben pfle-gen, wohl-hie auf Erd mit sei-ner Gnad, und dort in dem e-wi-gen Le-ben.

In connection with the *Symphony of Lamentation,* the instrumentation of which Schütz left open, Kretzschmar has emphasized its resemblance to the Italian model (particularly to Gabrieli), although its form — in one movement — and its melancholy tone make it take on a style which is specifically Schützian. "From a hesitating step it soon assumes a livelier pace; and in the moment in which the drama must begin, it sinks back again into mourning." The words of Jesus are given in the noblest *lamento* style. At times the accompanying high melody instruments give only a halo characteristic of the Venetian opera heroes and *Ombre;* sometimes they depict the emotions; or, as at the end of the Hebrew and the German *Eli lama,* after imitative accompanying as tonal shadows, they enhance the impression of fading-out by subsiding before the end. Some of these little musical sentences are overwhelming in their tension and torture, as, for example, with the distressed return to *e* minor:

Mich dür - - - stet!

Then, after the vinegar has been given to Jesus,[12] we have, with wonderful realism, in a rhythm markedly Schützian, first uttered vehemently, then brokenly:

---

[12] It has been observed on numerous occasions that Schütz apparently quoted from memory, thus erroneously *einen Schwamm und füllet ihn mit Essig und Ysopen* ("a sponge and filled it with vinegar and hyssop"). But a phrase might be explained from an old and intended usage associated with Ps. 51:9.

Es ist vollbracht,   es   ist   vollbracht!

Likewise, in the last saying, the calls of "Father" which His distress wrests from the sufferer, those circumflex-seconds which in Bach[13] led to the type of theme found in *Schliesse mein Herze* ("Lord, to Thee my heart I proffer"); *Blute nur* ("Bleed and break"); *Buss und Reu* ("Grief and pain"); *Gerne will ich mich bequemen* ("Gladly would I be enduring"). In the last verse of the evangelist (S—A—T—B), after the natural falling of the line at *neiget, neiget er sein Haupt* ("He bowed His head"), it is most remarkable how, at *und gab seinen Geist auf* ("and gave up His spirit"), the voices rise urgently one after the other by major thirds. Schütz must have had in mind the picture of the sinking of the earthly head of the Redeemer while at the same time His immortal soul hastens aloft to the Father.

The declamatory impressiveness of the conclusion is magnificent. First the pillar-like *wer, wer* and then the surprising metrical shift in the two eight-bar phrases which are textually the same. The discant will suffice to show this:

Wer, wer Gottes Mar - ter in Ehren hat und oft gedenkt der sie = ben Wort

wer Gottes Marter in Ehren hat, und oft gedenkt, und oft ge=denkt der sieben Wort

Then the repeated energetic antitheses *wohl hie — und dort* ("both here — and there"). One need only observe the conclusion of the discant to obtain an impression of the wonderful vitality of the entire work:

und dort,   und dort, und dort in dem   e = wi = gen,   und dort,

und dort in dem   e = wi = gen Le = ben.

---

[13] *St. Matthew Passion.*

Although it takes barely twenty minutes to perform, today this work might well have a place in every Lenten vesper service instead of other and larger Good Friday compositions.

Thirdly, we have the *Dialog for Easter (Dialogo per la pascua), Weib, was weinest du? (Woman, Why Weepest Thou?)*, for four solo voices (SSAT, more practical for SATB) and continuo, which Ph. Spitta includes in Vol. XIV of the collected works (p. 60) according to the autograph score in Kassel.[14] Unfortunately, the beautiful manuscript, though apparently complete, is but a fragment, inasmuch as we have two continuos of an appended final chorus, the voice parts of which are missing. According to the rhythm, this chorus must have had a text somewhat as follows: *Ripieno forte*

Since the old Pirna *Kantorei* catalog designates the piece as *à 5 et 10 v*, the lost *capella* must have been for five voices.

Perhaps someday the torso will still be supplied from anonymous manuscripts.

This superb Easter dialog — based on John 20: 13, 16, 17 — is precious not only by reason of its sad, restrained, and mystical transfiguration scene but also because of its apparently hitherto unrecognized origin. For this work, which was written ca. 1624 and is still designated as by Henrico Sagittario, is nothing other than a *concerto* on the most beautiful motives from the first part of Schütz's *Resurrection History*.

As Daniel Speer, in his *Tafelschnitze (Table Cutlets)*, of 1685, worked over a number of pieces of J. Melch. Gletle in smaller composition *(in engerer Composition)*,[15] so Schütz here apparently did something similar with a work of his own — the *Resurrection History*. The extract became climactic because, by the omission of all narrative and connecting sections, the story of the *Resurrection History* has been stratified in a series of connected vocal phrases uttered simultaneously, one

---

[14] Practical edition by A. Hänlein in *Drei biblische Szenen* (B & H).
[15] Cf. my *Corydon*, I, 68 ff.

over the other, and has been concentrated to the last degree. This connection may readily be demonstrated by placing side by side a number of the motives. Schütz's extraordinary accomplishment consists not only in the atmospheric concentration but also in the fact that a wonderfully balanced new form has appeared,[16] the focus of which is the profound *Maria-Rabbuni!* The summary disposition would be: a preliminary frame of two "bars" (A & B), recognition scene; a concluding frame of two counter "bars" (type A B B), cadences *d—d*; E—E; F—*d*:

_____

[16] Cf. also W. Schuh, p. 93. With regard to the boldness of the chordal functions cf. Ernst Kurth, *Romantische Harmonik* (1920), p. 263.

The scoring, too, of the *Easter dialog:*

in addition to the continuo, is explained by the simple combination of the duet
pairs assigned to Jesus and Mary Magdalene in the *Resurrection History* over the
organ foundation. If everything Schütz wrote except this "Woman, why weepest
thou?" were lost, his position as the musical genius of his age would still be incon-
testably assured by this part of the composition.

Finally, in this connection I can present for the first time a work by Schütz as charm-
ing as it is significant, a work which I have published through Breitkopf & Härtel
with a supplementing continuo by Max Schneider. It also appeared in the *ZfMW,*
XVII, 335 (1935). This is the six-voice dialog *Ach Herr, du Sohn Davids (O Lord,
Thou Son of David),* the conversation between Jesus and the Canaanite woman
(Matthew 15), constituting the Gospel for Reminiscere, the Second Sunday in
Lent. The work is referred to as by Schütz in the musical catalog of Cantor Andreas Ungar. Unfortunately, all these documents of the Church of St. Wenceslaus
at Naumburg seem to have gone into the paper mill at the beginning of the nineteenth century, among them fourteen otherwise unknown works of Schütz! This
work — anonymous and very unobtrusive — was found in the *Breslau Tabulatur 46,* which also contains Schütz's *Kleines geistliches Konzert* titled *Bringet her
dem Herren (Bring unto the Lord),* but, in addition, has works by Schein, Scheidt,
Keifferer, Handl, Pratti, Dulling, Cifra, and Bl. Ammon.

When one adds the text missing on the manuscript, the deciphering reveals a
composition unquestionably by Schütz. As in the case of the Easter dialog, the
Annunciation Scene, and *Saul, Saul, Why Persecutest Thou Me,* only the direct

dialog is drawn from the Gospel lesson; there are no epical connecting links.
While A. Hammerschmidt presents the same scene in his *Musical Dialogs on the
Gospels*[17] with SATB and continuo, the scoring in Schütz is much more distinctive.
The chorus for the woman consists of two sopranos and a vocal bass; the chorus
for Jesus is formed by a third soprano, a tenor, and two basses — a somewhat
darker shading. Both are to be supplemented with a continuo. The anonymous
Silesian organist of the seventeenth century to whom we are indebted for the
preservation of the work did indeed follow Schütz's oft-uttered request and has
put the entire voice parts into the score and has not merely given us a continuo
sketch, although he does not carry this scheme through to the end. Inasmuch as
here the part of Jesus is taken, not by a tenor but by a second soprano, it is evident
that both choruses now united; but the one who wrote out the notation has indicated only the two highest parts and the lowest voice. Therefore I added, in small
notes, the three missing voices in order to obtain the complete six-voice setting.
The impassioned entrance of the Canaanite woman — where one should note the
beautiful difference between the declamation of the upper voices and that of
the bass:

is continued by a *lamento*like counterpassage (*Gegenstollen,* a third higher, which
is followed by an echo motive as a contracted conclusion:

A second small countermelody (*Kleinegegenbar*) opens with *Meine Tochter wird
vom Teufel übel geplaget* ("My daughter is grievously vexed with a devil"), to
which is again attached the above *erbarm dich mein* ("have mercy upon me").

---

[17] *Musikalische Gespräche über die Evangelia,* Dresden, 1655.

Jesus now takes up the chief tonality, *g* Dorian, which, in the initial address in the frame Bb—D, was at first encircled only indirectly. His words occupy a mean between imitation and *parlando*. One should note the mournful chord on *verlorenen Schafen* ("lost sheep"):

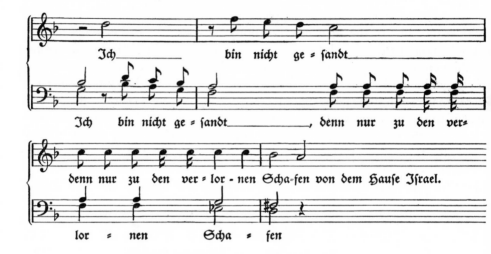

In three brief measures she answers in descending thirds: *Herr, hilf mir* ("Lord, help me"). Jesus replies in six measures: *Es ist nicht fein, dass man den Kindern ihr Brot nehme* ("It is not meet to take the children's bread and cast it to dogs"):

Again — with an echo phrase — the woman replies: *Ja Herr — aber doch* ("Truth, Lord; yet the dogs eat of the crumbs which fall from their masters' table"). Hereupon Jesus concludes *(tutti!)* with noble tenderness *(herrliche Innigkeit):* (See next page.)

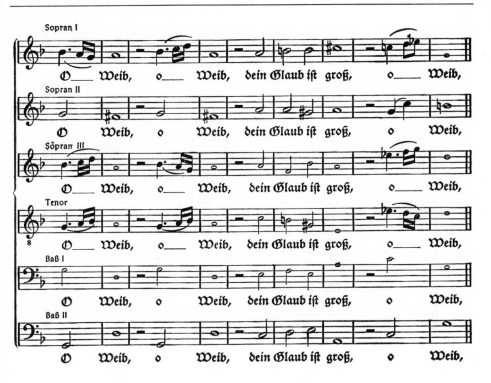

In pairs of thirds the chains of eights descend in all directions to close with *Dir geschehe* ("Be it unto thee"). (See next page.)

Despite its scant sixty-three bars, a regained Schütz work of the first rank!

The catalogs of Kassel and Naumburg report still another work of this kind by Schütz: *Dialogus: Herr, komm hinab (Lord, Come Down)*, in nine parts. It is the story of the nobleman of Capernaum (John 4: 47 ff.), the Gospel for the Twenty-first Sunday after Trinity. The text was as follows:

The nobleman: "Lord, come down ere my child die."
Jesus: "Go thy way; thy son liveth."
The servants: "Thy child liveth. Yesterday at the seventh hour the fever left him."

A work on this text and with the corresponding scoring is found as 18 in the collection of scores of Hermann Koch (Berlin *Singakademie*), but from the viewpoint of style and form it cannot be considered as Schützian. Pending a possible future discovery, this dialog must, therefore, be listed as lost.

Op. 8 and 9. The Kleine geistliche Konzerte of 1636-39

The *Kleine geistliche Konzerte* came into being between Schütz's second and third Copenhagen periods. Judging by the number of manuscripts through which the work was circulated[1] and the number of modern practical editions,[2] this collection is the most popular of all his works. And there is good reason for this. These twenty-four plus thirty-one thinly scored pieces, principally with German texts, represent a treasury most splendidly adapted to both church and domestic use. As compared with the *Symphoniae sacrae I* and *II,* which, respectively, precede and follow the present collections, the *Geistliche Konzerte* for the most part[3] dispense with instruments (except the thorough bass) and require but from one to five solo voices. Furthermore, the texts are very appropriate for church use.[4] Most of those in Part One are from the Psalms, two from Isaiah, two from the Gospels, and one from the Epistles; four are based on church hymns with the retention of their melodies, and two are taken from the *Meditations of St. Augustine,* thus forming a slender bridge with the *Cantiones sacrae.*

In Part Two there are only ten psalm texts; but there are three Gospel and four Epistle texts, a not unimportant turn in the direction of the New Testament pericopes. Six numbers are based on strophic texts: XI, *Wann unsere Augen* — the third strophe of *Christ, der du bist (Christe, qui lux);* XX, *Die Seele Christi,* a medieval text, probably translated into German by Schütz himself; XXI, *Ich ruf zu dir* — the hymn by Speratus; XXII, *Allein Gott in der Höh',* supposedly by N. Decius; XXIII, the Whitsuntide antiphon *Veni, Sancte Spiritus; and* XXXI, *Aufer immensam,* a new Latin *hymnus* by G. Klee-Thymus.

---

[1] VI, 110 *(Meister wir haben)* in Löbau; VI, 18 *(Erhöre mich)* in Pirna; VI, 164 *(Wer will uns scheiden)* in Berlin, *Akad. f. Kirchen- u. Schulmusik;* VI, 6 *(Bringt her)* Breslau 46; fifteen pieces in the *Altertumsverein,* Freiberg, Saxony, according to the kind information of the cantor there, Ernst Müller, etc.

[2] Nine numbers published by F. Blume (Kallmeyer, 1926); three by A. Mendelssohn (Peters, ca. 1910); five by H. Spitta (Peters, 1934); ten duets by Johs. Dittberner (C. F. Kahnt, 1921); six duets in Franziska Martienssen's *Duettenkranz* (Peters, 1930); four quartets by Woyrsch (Fritzsch); five duets in the *Chorbuch f. d. Kirchenchöre Sachsens,* D; six monodies by W. Stade (B & H); three quartets by Hans Hoffmann (Bärenreiter).

[3] Exceptions: I, 3; II, 28.

[4] The title in facsimile in R. Haas, *Musik im Barock* (Athenaion), p. 109.

The arrangement in both volumes is according to the increase of the vocal parts in the scoring and (within the individual categories) from the high to the low voices. The greatest variance in color is observed, a variety which is increased by the profusion of the chosen tonalities. In Vol. I, without ever counting the continuo, we have four solo numbers, eleven duets, four terzets, four quartets, and one quintet. In Vol. II, five soli, ten duos, five trios, seven quartets, and four quintets. These two parts then offer the following view, which shows that the master provided in a comprehensive manner for almost every practical combination of vocal forces, every tonal combination, and every liturgical festival need:

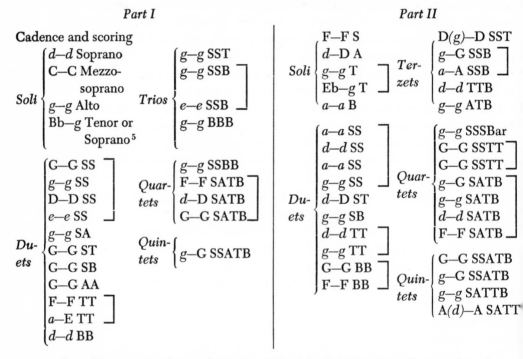

Since the prose texts predominate, Schütz had to decide with regard to these between motetlike sections and *concerto*like monodic structure. The designation *in stylo oratorio* to No. 1 indicates the second course.

---

[5] Here we find for the first time in Schütz the new conception of the "high and deep voices per se" (*schlechthin*), without respect for the absolute tonal region according to sex; thus in Joh. Staden, 1616; Schein, since 1621 (*Mus. boscareccia*); Kindermann, since 1643; Th. Selle, in the preface to his *Concertatio Castalidum* (1624), even allows an exchange of soprano and tenor in the case of duets, which thus implies double counterpoint in the invention.

This opening number, frequently heard today, consists of the entire 70th Psalm, VI, 3: *Eile, mich, Gott, zu erretten (Make Haste, O God, to Deliver Me)*.[6] Friedrich Blume[7] and W. Schuh[8] have considered the form which Schütz evolved and have determined that this "new Protestant verse monody" consists of two equally balanced halves sharply separated by the small dividing *symphonia*. Each half is tripartite, with the cadences ⎢DDD⎢ ⎢CAD⎢ , despite the *d* Dorian tonality. In the second half Schütz expanded the too short text by a rhetorical repetition of phrases so that a lengthened and a simple A A B passage oppose each other symmetrically. The tonal range is broadened in a well-planned manner: in the first subdivision of the preliminary part the melody sinks from d" to d', again to ascend to d" in the second subdivision (highest peak e"), finally to outdo both in the conclusion with a range from c — f". In the second part, *Ich aber*, the reciting tone d" rises to e", reaches the summit in the middle period on g", then almost to collapse, as it were, in the two appended measures (dramatic monolog!) and then, in the concluding section *(Abgesang)*, to lie, as it were, on the ground sobbing. The "classical" element of this Schützian baroque style lies in the equilibrium between the text-engendered declamation and, at the same time, the absolutely musical flowering. The feeling revealed in the realistic irregularity of the declamation of the text — rich in syncopations — is unusually strong. What holds it in check, both on the part of the listener and on the part of the performer, is an apparently subconscious realization of the skillful construction of this composition, both as a whole and in its smallest details.

No. 2 (p. 6), for mezzo-soprano, we would say is intended for a boy alto, as No. 3 (p. 7), in the alto clef, is probably intended for a high tenor. No. 2 is on verses one and two[9] of Psalm 29, *Bringet her dem Herrn (Give unto the Lord, Ye Mighty)* with *Alleluia*, and on Is. 6: 3.[10] It is constructed more in accordance

---

[6] In the practical editions by Blume, Stade, Spitta. As Latin 69th Psalm: *Deus in adjutorium*, *à 4*, by Tromboncino (Petrucci, 1505); anon. in Wyrsung, 1520; by Sermisy (Atteignant, 1534); Eckel and Senfl (Ott, 1537); Lemlin (Petrejus, 1542); Le Maistre *(München Stbl.* Manuscript 41); Päminger; Regnart (Theatrum, 1580); *à 5*, with continuo by Cazzati (Prof.IV, 1646); *à 6*, Clemens non Papa (Waelrant, 1535, and frequently); Lassus (1577, München, *Stbl.* Manuscript 11); *à 8*, Dulichius and J. Stoll (Manuscript Zwickau LXXXVII, 1598); anon (Bodenschatz, 1621); Gumpelzhaimer (Breslau Manuscript 20). German: anon., *à 6* (C. Freundt?; Zwickau LXXXIII); *à 7* by M. Vulpius (Breslau Manuscript 30); *à 8 and 16*, P. Schäffer (Breslau Manuscript 198); three years after Schütz, as duet with continuo: Hammerschmidt *(DTD*, Vol. XXXX, pp. 6 ff.) Hereto cf. Blume, *Das monodische Prinzip*, (pp. 94 ff.).

[7] Blume, *Das mon. Prinzip*, pp. 88 ff.

[8] Loc. cit., pp. 107 ff.

[9] A 7 by Hammerschmidt; as a six-voice cantata, Briegel, 1684; both also in manuscript in Breslau.

[10] New edition by W. Stade and H. Spitta.

with the older point of view. For while in No. 1 — a genuinely word-engendered melodic monody — the bass was but a foundation for chordal surfaces, here the voice part, in even time, has a much more independent theme motive. The bass, as in a duo, supplements this with imitations and complementary rhythm, while in the thrice-inserted *Alleluia,* in triple time, both parts seek to present, as in the polychorus *Psalms,* dancelike chordal masses.

No. 3, *Ich danke dem Herrn (Praise Ye the Lord)*[11] is a setting of the entire 111th Psalm.[12] The composition proceeds more or less parallel with the continuo in a more scansionlike manner. In view of several embellished and emphasized cadences, one feels its structure as essentially motetlike. The *symphonia* in the middle, sketched with its own melody voice (an unusual feature), indulges directly in thematic imitations. The power of the composition consists primarily in its rhythmic diversity.

Essentially more in profile is No. 4, the little concert piece *O süsser, o freund-licher (O Sweet, O Friendly),* translated from Augustine into German by M. Mol-ler.[13] Its designation *tenor vel cantus* has already been referred to. Blume[14] has shown very clearly how Schütz, both as a subjectivist as well as an organizer of musical form, has interpreted into this lengthy and quite uniform text an order according to differences of feeling and has so prolonged its last textual subdivision (emphasized by means of fermatas) that the ecstatic cry of longing, *O wie ver-langet meiner Seelen nach dir* ("Oh, how my soul longs for Thee"), becomes the center and climax of the whole.[15]

No. 5 (p. 11), *Der Herr ist gross (Great Is the Lord),* Psalm 145, verses three and four, with *Alleluia,* for two sopranos, is the first of the duets.[16] Its structure is duplex. In the first part the first soprano takes the lead, and the second soprano imitates at intervals, which, for the purpose of the climax, become smaller and smaller. In the second half, *Kindeskind* ("One generation shall praise Thy works to another"), the entrances are, for the most part, in reverse order. At the motival transitions the contrasts are of the nature of a double fugue, except that in place

---

[11] New edition by Blume, Stade, Spitta.

[12] Cf. also under *Psalmen Davids v. 1619,* and *à 4* in the *Zwölf geistliche Gesänge* (Vol. XII, No. 5).

[13] New edition by Stade and by Spitta.

[14] Cf. note p. 67 in *Das monodische Prinzip,* and also ibid., pp. 101 ff.

[15] Cf. similar things in the *Cantiones sacrae,* for the most part from Augustine. Very close is the relation of the melismatic "O" to the motet from the Song of Songs, *O quam tu pulchra,* in the *Cantiones sacrae.* As Blume has shown, Schütz has taken over from Viadana the beginning, *O süßer, o freundlicher,* with its major third relationships. These melismatic "O's" are found highly developed in J. H. Schein and frequently again in Schütz.

[16] In Dittberner.

of an answer at the fifth we have primarily imitation at the unison. In detail we meet *Kleinbar* elements again and again.[17]

Especially beautiful is the duet for two sopranos, No. 6, *O lieber Herre Gott (O Dear God and Lord)*.[18] Ph. Spitta (Introduction, p. XII) has shown how the text of this Advent collect by Joh. Spangenberg (1545) came to Schütz's knowledge through the *Dresden Gesangbuch* of 1625 and through him with a slight addition ("Thy dear Son") to Joh. Christof Bach. One could find in Schütz's opening words the following potentialized *Bar* form (A +, A', A", B):[19]

A large countercouplet brings the same thing in polyphonic duet form. The extended conclusion *(Grossabgesang)* begins at *Ihn mit Freuden.*

No. 7 (p. 16), *Ihr Heiligen, lobsinget (Sing unto the Lord, O Ye Saints of His)*, Ps. 30: 4-5, is in D major. The chief episode in *e* minor, *Lust zum Leben* ("His favor is life") (p. 16), is apparently intended as Dorian in an Ionian frame. The principal importance is in the second half, a study, as it were, in the affectual contrast between *Weinen* ("weeping") (p. 16) and *Freude* ("joy") (p. 16). This contrast problem fascinated the entire century from Schütz and Carissimi, with little cantatas on the "weeping Heraclitus and the laughing Democritus," to Joh. Krieger and Val. Rathgeber.

The text of the duet, No. 8 (p. 18), *Erhöre mich, wenn ich rufe (Hear Me When I Call, O God)*, is taken from Ps. 4: 1 and 5: 3.[20] This, too, like most of its sisters of 1636, is really a work in two parts. The chief caesura is the E major cadence at *Seid mir gnädig* ("Have mercy upon me"). But we can also divide the piece into

[17] Cf. *MGkK*, 18 (1913), p. 274 = Collection 135.
[18] Cf. also *Sächsisches Chorbuch (Saxon Choir Book)*, D.
[19] *MGkK*, 3 (1898), pp. 276—281 = Collection 13.
[20] In the collections of Blume and Martienssen. Cf. also *MGkK*, 3 (1898), pp. 126—129.

four parts: the first ends at the A major cadence at *Gerechtigkeit* ("my righteousness"); the last shows itself less from the harmonic point of view than in the metrical retardation at *mein Schreien* ("my prayer"), in order then to lead back to the broad measure of the prologlike beginning, *Erhöre mich.*

The soprano-alto duo (No. 9, p. 19) on Ps. 1: 1-3, *Wohl dem, der nicht wandelt (Blessed Is the Man That Walketh Not in the Counsel of the Ungodly),* is a delightful bit of music packed with good humor. The somewhat comfortable rest at *noch sitzet,* the melismatic painting of the "scornful" *(Spötter),* of the "tree" *(Baum),* the "waters" *(Wasser),* the "leaves" *(Blätter),* the "withering" *(Verwelken),* the dancelike *Wohlgeraten* (prospering), the pauses between the alleluias — all this leads to a smile of pleasure.

On the other hand, hearty, active joy and reverence characterize No. 10 (p. 23), *Schaffe mir, Gott (Create in Me, God),* Ps. 51: 12-14,[21] for soprano and tenor. The joy expresses itself especially in the triplets at *freudiger Geist* and in the final *coloratura* passages.

. No. 11 (p. 25), *Der Herr schauet (The Lord Looked),* Ps. 14: 2-3, is, somewhat unfortunately, declaimed; but one could easily correct this with a slight change of the text: *Du, Herr, schauest vom Himmel auf uns Menschen herab, dass du sehest* ("Thou, Lord, lookest down from Heaven upon Thy children, that Thou seest"). It is a pity if this piece is neglected, for it combines effectively the motet style in the first half and the *parlando* in the second.

No. 12 (p. 27), *Lobet den Herren (Sing Praises to the Lord),* Ps. 9: 11-12, is, to be sure, written for two "altos"; but it does not go above a'. Therefore it is surely meant for two light tenors.

While No. 12 remains on the plane of pleasant music making, No. 13 (p. 29), *Eins bitte ich vom Herrn (One Thing I Ask of the Lord),* Psalm 27,[22] for two baritones,[23] is one of the most fervent consecration pieces one can imagine. But instead of the "somewhat *con moto*" quarter notes suggested by one of the editors, one should doubtless count fluent halves.

No. 14 (p. 30), set for the same voices as the preceding, is the first hymn setting and one of high distinction: *O hilf, Christe, Gottes Sohn (O Help, Christ, Thou Son of God).*[24] It is the closing strophe of *Christus der uns selig macht.* Schütz added a Latin text *(Christe Deus adjuva)* in his own hand in the Wolfenbüttel printed

---

[21] Also in the collections of Blume and Martienssen.
[22] It is found in *Sächsisches Chorbuch,* Dittberner, *MGkK,* 1 (1896), pp. 34—37; and Gölz, *Chorbuch,* p. 132.
[23] Despite the tenor clefs it extends only to f'.
[24] See preceding note for editions.

copy. The setting is characterized by the fact that of the old melody of the Latin *hymnus*, *Patris sapientia*, in Michael Weisse's *Böhmisches Brüdergesangbuch* of 1531, only the beginning is retained literally:[25]

while the *bittres Leiden* ("bitter anguish") forthwith aroused in Schütz the independent and creative baroque chromaticist. During the further course of the composition only reminiscences of the chorale melody appear, such as the closing phrase:

as a kind of parallel curve to Schütz's final line.

The last duet of the first volume (No. 15, p. 32) has unusual individuality: *Fürchte dich nicht (Be Not Afraid, I Am with Thee)*, Is. 41: 10, for two basses. Up to the time of Bach's youthful works the vocal bass was extensively the foundation part, that is, identical with the continuo line. The latter had then merely to let its prismatic colors shine forth in order that from a motet for one voice a structure replete with harmony might emerge. It is fascinating to observe Schütz's restrained way of obtaining a climax. Three times, from merely two interchanging continuo voices, he arrives, beyond the duet between a melody voice and a continuo voice, at an *obbligato* trio between two melody voices and a special foundational part. The opening motive, with its flexible rhythmic changes, is indicative of a certain willfulness:

The interval of the fourth dominates the second theme, which must do service not only for the text of the second part, *Ich erhalte dich* ("I will uphold thee"), but also for the closing *Alleluia*, so that the form of the whole becomes a great *Gegenbar* with the structure A—B—B.

How this scoring rapidly impressed North Germany is shown in Franz Tunder's superb bass duet of 1641-42: *Herr, nun lässest du (Lord, Now Lettest Thou Thy Servant) (DTD*, III, 22).

---

[25] *MgkK*, 4 (1899), pp. 61—64.

Next the terzets. No. 16, festooned with hosannas, on Ps. 118: 25-26:[26] *O Herr hilf (O Lord, I Beseech Thee, Send Now Prosperity)*, for two sopranos and tenor, would be equally useful either on the First Sunday in Advent, on Palm Sunday, or as a brief *Benedictus* for a German Mass. Furthermore, with its very closely entwined calls of praise it is a most charming number for musical performance. We shall meet it again in an enriched form in the *Symphoniae sacrae III* as No. 5. As late as 1703 Joh. Beer copied it almost note for note.[27]

Similarly, No. 17, on 1 John 1: 7, *Das Blut Jesu Christi (The Blood of Jesus Christ)*, for two sopranos, bass, and continuo, with its moving warmth and its masterful fugal coupling of two countermotives, would be a most superb introductory composition for every Communion celebration. How much we allow to escape us through mere inertia!

While No. 18, on 1 Tim. 4: 5-8, *Die Gottseligkeit ist zu allen Dingen nütz (But Godliness is Profitable unto All Things)*, may suffer a bit from the prosaic nature of the text, the superb No. 19, on Luke 21: 33, *Himmel und Erde vergehen (Heaven and Earth Shall Pass Away)*, for three basses (better transpose from g minor to *a*, or even b flat minor), might well give to every sermon or Gospel reading its solemn and at the same time compactly pregnant closing confirmation. How tensely every word and every madrigalism stands out!

The series of quartets opens with a setting of Luther's *Nun komm, der Heiden Heiland (Come, Redeemer of the World)*, No. XX. In his own handwriting Schütz added the original text of the old Advent *hymnus, Veni, Redemptor gentium*. The old church melody is carried through in its entirety. Schütz worked all kinds of extraordinary figures into the continuo. The bass motives

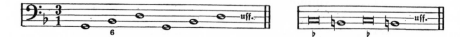

are surely heralds of the cradle motives in his *Christmas Oratorio*. Later the chorale is sung out in an impressive manner in the foundation part as an augmented *cantus firmus*. Above all, however, all kinds of canonic roguishness are developed from the unusual scoring (two sopranos and two basses); and the embellishments at *der Jungfrauen Kind erkannt* ("known as the Virgin's Child") make flourishes in their baroque festival joy, as does the extended *coloratura* of the first bass at *aller Welt*. The very naive motive in thirds:

---

[26] In Blume's collection.
[27] In the duet cantata, *O panis*; cf. Heinz Krause, *J. Beer* (Leipzig Dis., 1935), p. 26.

daß sich wun-dert al - le Welt [28]

which repeatedly swings back and forth above the bass *cantus firmus,* gives the impression of being sung from the balustrades by angel dolls, the impression of the domestic coziness of a simple chamber as portrayed in the old German paintings of the saints. The likewise constantly oscillating

ihm_____   be - ftellt

in the lower voices at the end forms an obviously intentional and pleasing contrast to the somewhat stubborn repetition of the soprano *cantus firmus* with its persistent Monteverdi fourth at *Gott solch Geburt ihm bestellt* ("God ordained this birth for Him"). In Schein's treatment of the same chorale, at the beginning of his *Opella nova,* each line is sung first by the tenor and then spun out in diminution by the sopranos. Praetorius *(Musae Sioniae,* VI) gives four simple harmonizations of it. The ninth volume of the *Musae Sioniae* begins with two duets and a terzet which preserve most faithfully the melody of the German *Veni Redemptor,* while in a second terzet it wanders in vigorous variations through the parts. Schütz's treatment is fundamentally different in that he introduces the melody in the first soprano line and then constantly expands it in the repetition of its constituent motives *(Teilmotive).*

A most charming *Christlabends-Ahlfanzerei* (as the Prussian soldier king later decreed with frowning brow) also pervades the next, normally scored quartet (No. 21, p. 44), *Ein Kind ist uns geboren (For unto Us a Child Is Born),*[29] which, despite its hymn character, is based on the prose version of the prophecy of Is. 9: 6—7. Here W. Schuh professes to detect two examples of the *Barform* but this is rather arbitrary. He himself confesses: "The tension of the *Bar* forms is weak; the will for grouping and symmetry predominates." I would call the work a simple succession of motets. What Schütz finds in the rhythm of the word *Wunderbar* is delightful. When one considers the polyphonic entrances of the subordinate members at *auf dass seine Herrschaft, auf dem Stuhle Davids, dass er's zurichte,* the imitations have the effect of *quodlibet*like distorted *fugati.* All the intervals are chosen for the entrances except the dominant-subdominant relation, and not until at the conclusion, *Solches wird tun der Eifer des Herrn,* does the normal interval relation appear.

---

[28] All the world wondered that.
[29] Practical edition in the selection by Woyrsch, Brochure 3.

No. 22 (p. 50) is the setting of another Luther hymn, the German *Credo, Wir glauben all an einen Gott (We All Believe in One God),* known in a German version as early as 1415. The fact that in place of an alto there is a second soprano is significant, so far as the tonal region is concerned, only in the initial canon. Immediately after this we have the boy alto going down to *a* (most unusual in the case of Schütz) in place of the falsettist. The entire thematic material is borrowed from the ecclesiastical melody with great fidelity. Despite this fact the sequence of the pictorial baroque figures derived from the melody is sufficiently variegated to surprise us constantly by their contrasting interpretations of the text. The method reminds one strongly of the changing series of figures, line by line, in the organ chorales of Samuel Scheidt's *Tabulatura nova.* The effect of the concluding phrase is rather surprising where the organ bass proceeds in restless eighth-note figures under the repeated *und wacht und wacht* and the last line, *Es steht alles in seiner Macht* ("Everything stands in His might"). Perhaps the riddle solves itself when one thinks back upon the tramping "watchmen" in the scene in the *Invenerunt me* of the Song of Songs in the *Sinfoniae sacrae I.*

The themes of the quartet, No. 23 (p. 54), *Siehe, mein Fürsprecher ist im Himmel (Behold, My Advocate Is in Heaven),* are in an unusually complicated rhythm. Schütz himself probably translated the Augustinian text into German. The music of this composition borrows some passages from the setting of the original text in the *Cantiones sacrae,* No. 32. It is a piece of almost whimsical, improvisational looseness, with arbitrary, sudden darkening in color, as, for example, the B flat in the soprano at *Erlösung erworben* ("gained redemption") (p. 53); again the harmonic climaxes at *Sieh, siehe* ("Behold") (p. 56); the retraction of the voices at *verstummet* ("is dumb"); and the surprisingly broad and harmonically warm solo *cantilena* of the tenor till the *capella* crowns the brief conclusion. But how incisively and inexorably here, too, the cross relation proceeds in the voice-leading!:

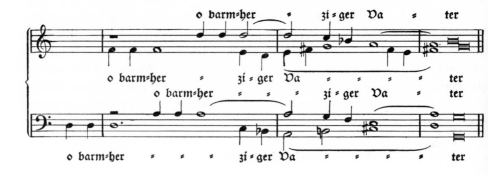

Quite similarly in Part II, No. 2, *Was hast du verwirket* ("What hast Thou done?"), at *Das todwürdige Laster* ("The deathworthy infamy"):

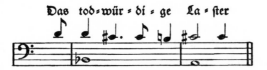

The conclusion of the first volume is the grand *Aria de vitae fugacitate* on all eighteen strophes of the hymn *Ich hab mein Sach Gott heimgestellt* ("To God Have I Entrusted All"), to which Schütz has added an optional Latin translation by the Altenburg rector, Jos. Clauder, from his *Psalmodia nova* of 1627. If one remembers that Schütz's first setting (1625) is dedicated to the fiancé of Anna Maria Wildeck, who was president of the consistory in Altenburg, it may well be that this *Meas dicavi res Deo* had its origin on the occasion of the Schütz elegy.

As was indicated, the second volume of the *Kleine geistliche Konzerte* (1639) is not merely a symmetrical repetition of the first with different texts. Volume II stands much closer to the New Testament. The opening composition (p. 93), to be sure — the soprano monody *Ich will den Herren loben alle Zeit (I Will Bless the Lord at All Times)*[30] — is based on verses from Psalm 34, which Schütz divides by four interpolated alleluia sections, with a fifth at the end. These are almost so identical with one another that here, instead of the *Barform* (A—A—B) adduced by W. Schuh (loc. cit.), we may accurately designate the *rondo* refrain as the prevailing formative principle.

For No. 2 (p. 94) we have a very impressive discourse of Augustine which had already been set in the *Cantiones sacrae (Quid commisisti,* Vol. IV, No. 4): *Was hast du verwirket, o du allerholdseligster Knabe?*[31] Here we have an alto (tenor!) monolog. It is fascinating to note everything that Schütz has brought here in motetlike juxtaposition, which is not merely to be explained as the *Barform*. The old rhetorical means of the *anaphora* helps him through melodically similar beginnings or even musically altogether similar portions to organize it all according to textually corresponding word groups, the whole having the following form:

---

[30] Edited by H. Spitta.
[31] Reprinted in Blume's collection; also ed. by A. Mendelssohn, transposed from *d* minor to *c* minor (seventh upwards!). Cf. also *MGkK*, 1, (1896), pp. 412—415.

Was hast du verwirket,	a
What hast Thou done,	
was hast du verwirket,	a'
what hast Thou done,	
o du allerholdseligster Knab Jesu Christe,	b
O Thou sweetest boy, Jesus Christ,	
dass du also verurteilt warest?	c
that Thou wast thus condemned?	
Was hast du begangen,	a"
What hast Thou perpetrated,	
o du allerfreundlichster Jüngling,	d
O Thou most friendly youth	
dass man so übel und kläglich mit dir gehandelt?	e
that one treated Thee so evilly and so wretchedly?	
Was ist doch dein Verbrechen und Misshandlung?	f
What is Thy crime and Thy transgression?	
Was ist deine Schuld, was die Ursach deines Todes?	g
What is Thy fault, what the cause of Thy death?	
Was ist doch die Verwirkung deiner Verdamnis?	f
What is the occasion of Thy condemnation?	

Climactie
Exordium

Beyond this the composition appears as a study of all that can be expressed in the illustration and enhancement of the text (madrigalisms) by melody and harmony: the Phrygian conclusion for the question; the threefold chromatic modulation to the parallel as an expression of the concentration of feeling:

Similarly, in II, 20 (p. 139) at the *tutti, O lieber Herr Jesu,* we have treasures of form that still belong to the heartfelt sincerity of the songs of Joh. Wolfg. Franck. How bold the harmonically foreign entrance is as a "pathetic anticipation" of the coming harmony! (See next page.)

This rising advance from the triad to the chord of the sixth with the same bass as the triad *(Seitenklang)* also belongs to the constantly employed treasures of

O ich, ich bin die Ursach und Plage deines Leidens.   h ⎫
Oh, I, I am the cause and torment of Thy sufferings.
Ich, ich, ich bin die Verschuldung deines Hinrichtens.   h'
I, I, I am the cause of Thy execution.
Ich, ich bin das Verdienst deines Todes,   h"
I, I am what was gained by Thy death,
das todwürdige Laster, so an dir gerochen worden.   i   Crowning
the infamy deserving of death, vented upon Thee.   Middle
Ich, ich bin die Öffnung der Wunden deines Leidens,   h"'   Section
I, I caused the opening of the wounds of thy suffering,
die Angst deiner Peinigung,   k
the anguish of Thy torture,
die Angst deiner Peinigung.   k
the anguish of Thy torture.

Ach, wohin, wohin, wohin, du Sohn Gottes,   l ⎫
Oh, how low, how low, how low, Thou Son of God,   Receding
hat sich deine Demut geniedriget?   m   Epilog
has Thy humility stooped?

l m varied four times!

form found in this piece. The bitter portrayal of the *todwürdigen Lasters* ("infamy deserving of death") we have observed above. The unexpected progress of the harmonic motion at the twice-pictured *Angst deiner Peinigung* ("the anguish of

Thy torture") connotes tormenting restlessness, and *geniedriget* ("stooped") receives its tonal picture in the sixth descending four times.

One will note an abundance of similar traits in the Latin tenor (baritone!) Nos. 3 and 4.[32] The *O misericordissime Jesu* (p. 97) belongs to the Augustine group,

---

[32] Both edited with German text by A. Mendelssohn in *MGkK*, 4, 1899, pp. 331-334. No. 4 edited by Blume with the Latin text.

while the *O Jesu nomen dulce* (p. 96) is, from the viewpoint of content, related to St. Bernard's hymn *O Jesu dulcis memoria*.

Blume very correctly transposed the beautiful No. 5 (p. 98), *Ich liege und schlafe (I Laid Me Down and Slept),* for bass, from *d* Dorian to *f* Dorian. At the very beginning the three phrases appear in unforgettable form in their vivid antitheses. Let the first as *vox unica* suffice:

The same thing is repeated, but it is transposed so that it again concludes on *a*. A second pair of varied couplets proceeds in lively *parlando* style and delights, with clusters of eighth notes, in repeating *für viel Hunderttausende* ("for many hundred thousands"). With focal importance there stand as the third zone the impassioned words *Auf, Herr, und hilf mir* ("Arise, O Lord; save me, O my God; for Thou hast smitten all mine enemies upon the cheekbone; Thou hast broken the teeth of the ungodly"). Schütz has filled this sentence with such intense indignation that it is a great pleasure to sing it. The fourth part has a pleasantly playful character, ebbing away as an afterthought: *Bei dem Herrn findet man Hilfe* ("Salvation belongeth unto the Lord; Thy blessing is upon Thy people. Selah"). The counter *Bar,* A—B—B, in which "Selah" receives three jubilant melismas, calls for extreme *coloratura* mobility.

The first of the soprano duets which follow (No. 7, p. 105) is on verse four of Psalm 37, *Habe deine Lust an dem Herrn (Delight Thyself Also in the Lord);* the second is on verse five of Psalm 13, *Herr, ich hoffe darauf (But I Have Trusted in Thy Mercy).* Both compositions, with regard to demands upon vocal virtuosity and lively recitative, constitute the most impressive works that we find in this category prior to the superb chamber duets of Ag. Steffani.

The two Latin counterparts, Nos. 8 and 9, make no smaller demand on musicianship and execution on the part of modern singers. No. 8 (p. 107), *Bone Jesu,* a pseudo-Augustinian text, and No. 9 (p. 111), on the Christmas antiphon *Verbum caro factum est (The Word Was Made Flesh),* are church compositions full of vigor and joy.

No. 10 (p. 114), also on a Christmas text, *Hodie Christus natus est*, begins in dreamy meditation but soon surprises us with its contrasting eighth-note alleluias and sixteenth-note passages, which require genuine virtuosity. Well rendered, the composition will produce an electrifying effect.

No. 11 (p. 117), a *Fantasieduett* for soprano and bass,[33] is a veritable Schützian stroke of genius. As its text it uses the church hymn stanza *Wann unsre Augen schlafen ein* ("When our eyes will close in sleep"), from *Christ, der du bist der helle Tag*. The master did not use the chorale melody associated with the hymn and based on the medieval evening *hymnus, Christe qui lux es et dies* ("Christ, Thou Who Art Both Light and Day"). He apparently wished to abandon himself freely to his affectual study. Because of the development of two antithetical pairs of lines plus a conclusion, this is a kind of companion piece to the composition with contrasting themes, *Ego dormio, sed cor meum vigilat*.[34] It is a work of the greatest impressiveness, as the following characterization will serve to indicate:

Wann unsre Augen schlafen ein, — quiet descending chromaticism
so lass das Herz doch wacker sein, — restless, throbbing eighth notes
halt über uns dein rechte Hand, — quiet diatonic descending scale
dass wir nicht fallen, — pointedly excited, afterwards stumbling in syncopations
in Sünd und Schand, — heavy whole notes

Next we have one of the most beautiful of Schütz's Gospel settings, No. 12 (p. 119), *Meister, wir haben die ganze Nacht gearbeitet (Master, We Have Toiled All the Night)*. Except for that descriptive work of art, *Sicut Moses*, and the composition from the *Symphoniae sacrae I*, the madrigalistic *Venite ad me*, fashioned essentially as a problem in melody, this composition is the first full-fledged number of that series, which contains such preciously devout and honestly painted histories as *Der Pharisäer und der Zöllner (The Pharisee and the Publican)* or *Der zwölfjährige Jesus im Tempel (The Twelve-year-old Christ Child in the Temple)*. The words of the brother fishermen, Peter and Andrew, at the sea of Gennesaret (Luke 5: 5) are given to two deep tenors (baritones). Wearily and yet wholeheartedly they tell what they have to say to the Lord simply, briefly, not a measure too much. The composition could well be inserted after the Gospel lesson for the Fifth Sunday after Trinity. It is developed directly from the lesson intonation:

Mei = ster,   wir ha = ben die gan = ze Nacht ge = ar = bei = tet

---

[33] In Martiens it is for soprano and tenor.
[34] See *Cantiones Sacrae* No. 11.

Note the effective pauses at *und nichts — und nichts — gefangen* ("and have caught nothing — nothing"); also how in the second half the motet group at *aber auf dein Wort* ("but at Thy word I will cast out the net") begins in antiphonal recitation tone and then becomes descriptive for the picture of "throwing out the net."

No. 13 (p. 120) has the same scoring as No. 12. Its text is derived from Psalm 111: 10: *Die Furcht des Herrn (The Fear of the Lord Is the Beginning of Wisdom).* From the formal point of view it evoked the interest of W. Schuh, who convincingly recognized an expanded *(potenziert) Bar* (A+—A—B) where the little *ritornello, Es ist eine feine Klugheit* ("a good understanding have all they"), varied according to plan, signifies the abbreviated conclusion *(Kleinabgesang).*

No. 14 (p. 122), an Epistle number, based on Eph. 3: 14-16: *Ich beuge meine Knie (For This Cause I Bow My Knees unto the Father of Our Lord Jesus Christ)* is for two basses. It begins in a highly picturesque manner. Let us place alongside it a similar though characteristically different curve from a later period:

Here the problem of the bass as foundation voice finds still another solution in that both solos regularly cross each other, while the continuo as *basso seguente* (following bass) regularly coincides in a somewhat simplified manner with the lower voice, so that here Schütz never goes beyond a two-line setting.

The same thing is true in No. 15 (p. 124), *Ich bin jung gewesen (I Have Been Young and Now Am Old)*, Ps. 37: 25.[35] This expressive piece arranges its text and its musical themes in several sections and then concludes with a very lively *concertante Alleluia.* One may well transpose it from F to A flat or A.

The series of terzets, impressive both as to number and as to content, begins with No. 16 (p. 120), a number from Ps. 73: 25, *Herr, wenn ich nur dich habe (Whom Have I in Heaven but Thee?)*, for two sopranos and tenor. Despite the B flat major beginning and ending, the piece really belongs in g Dorian. As the tenor is treated — now in its own range above the continuo, now as foundation with the

---

[35] English edition in Drinker Choral Library, No. 206, No. 2.

continuo — this heart-warming composition, primarily *parlando* in style, hovers between a trio and a quartet setting. This example again shows very clearly that Schütz's *stylus recitativus* — while, to be sure, it is to be presented fluently and with a clear pronunciation of the consonants — is also to be executed very *legato* in true vocal style in order that the fine linear drawing may come fully into its own.

No. 17 (p. 130) uses the beautiful Introit text for Advent, *Rorate coeli (Drop Down, Ye Heavens)*. Inasmuch as here we have two sopranos and a bass part (instead of a tenor) which but seldom, for solo stretches, varies from the continuo, the web, for the most part, remains a trio in form. A mixture of idyllic rest and delicate embellishment prevails. Toward the end the playfully oscillating figure work of dotted groups on *de-super* has a charming effect.

In No. 18 (p. 133) we again have a Gospel text. It is from the Christmas story (Matt. 1: 20) and has the same scoring as the preceding composition. I am referring to *Joseph, du Sohn Davids (Joseph, Thou Son of David)*. According to the clefs, we have a *chiavetta* combination in order to transfer the number noted in *a* minor to *f* minor. In view of the modern change in chamber-tone pitch, *g* minor will be the appropriate key today. The speech of the angel is set as a genuine polyphonic continuo motet for three voices. One might almost designate the piece as "in the old style," which, in view of such noble art, is not intended as a censure.

No. 19 (p. 135), *Ich bin die Auferstehung (I Am the Resurrection)*, John 11: 20, is for two tenors and bass. Schütz had already set this text as a funeral composition in 1620 for eight voices, and here we may have an "occasional" piece sketched at an earlier time.

No. 20 (p. 139), *Die Seele Christi heilige mich (May the Soul of Christ Sanctify Me)*, ranks high in the collection. With alto, tenor, and bass clefs the composition is conceived for three male voices. Schütz himself probably translated the text — so noble and genuinely "old German" in its effect — from the medieval Communion petition *Anima Christi*, which had its origin long before the like-named hymn of Angelus Silesius, the *Cherubinischer Wandersmann*. The frame is *g* Dorian, in which we find the opening calls of the beginning, to be followed by a crowning *tutti* stretch in B flat, *O lieber Herr Jesu, erhöre mich* ("O dear Lord Jesus, hear me"). This is followed by individual calls dying away in order, thus, according to the form A—B—C, to allow the first part to be concluded by the bass in *g* minor. (Tonality surfaces: *g*—*g*, Bb—Bb, *d*—*g*.) At *In meiner letzten Stunden* ("When comes my final hour") there begins the tripartite conclusion, the summit of which lies in the middle at the triplet section *Und mit allen Auserwählten* ("and with all the elect to praise and magnify Thee forever"). (Tonality sur-

faces: Bb—D, d—Bb, Bb—g.) The returning *O lieber Herr Jesu* ("O dear Lord
Jesus") rounds out the piece most impressively. The composition merits a revival
at the Communion table.

The quartets begin with a chorale setting, *Ich ruf zu dir, Herr Jesu Christ
(I Cry to Thee, Lord Jesus Christ)*, with the exceptional scoring for three sopranos
and bass[36] (p. 144) which we met with in the supplemental chorus *(coro aggiunto)*
of the Breslau "political music," *En novus Elysiis*. Schütz formed his quartet carefully on the pattern of the old melody. He carries on the melody version of Klug
of 1535 with minor divergences of his own time, using the text of the first stanza
only, in such a way that it is easily perceptible in the upper voice. The precentor
idea steps into the foreground not only at the beginning but also, and indeed
still more, at the conclusion *(Abgesang)*.

At No. 22 (p. 147) — set for two sopranos, two tenors, and continuo — Schütz
treats somewhat more freely the German *Gloria angelorum, Allein Gott in der
Höh sei Ehr (All Glory Be to God on High)*, supposedly by Nikolaus Decius.
M. Praetorius, in his *Polyhymnia*, treats the chorale as a terzet, the strongly canonic
discants of which can be freely diminished. In his *Musae Sioniae I* he presents
the chorale in a double chorus, interchanging line by line, almost note against note,
in simple triplets. In the *Musae VI* he harmonizes the chorale simply for four
voices. Schein (Prüfer ed. VI, 18) brings the chorale line by line in the form of a
freely polyphonic forefield of small motives for two discants with thorough bass,
and then always the entire line itself as a broad tenor *cantus firmus* with continuo
only — a kind of preliminary form of the Pachelbel chorale prelude. Schütz builds
up the hymn with its three stanzas in clear architecture.[37] Stanza one gives the
church melody in duet form, in part with intentional variants, as, for example:

in part with diminutions. The boys' voices are answered by a male duet with the
text of the second stanza and with the retention of the melody. The third stanza
is carried through altogether freely by the solo soprano and the continuo without
the church melody but with small motives from the preceding chains of embellishments. With its prayer content it constitutes the emotional high spot. From the
ecclesiastical and dynamic point of view, however, the climax is reached in the

---

[36] In M. Praetorius, *à 2, Mus. Sion.* IX, 122; *à 3*, 123-25; *à 4*, VII, 165-67; *à 8*, I, 10; *à 12*, II, 26.
and Urania, 16; by Schein, as *concerto* for SS and continuo, *Opella nova*, 16 (Prüfer V, p. 71).
[37] Cf. also W. Schuh, p. 110.

closing stanza, which brings the chorale melody faithfully as tenor, then as soprano *cantus firmus* with *tutti* accompaniment. In other words, Schütz employs the departures from the chorale melody for final climactic purposes, viewing the literal presentation of the church melody as the crowning climax to be attained. We may find this confirmed also in the increasing number of measures (16, 16, 17, 23). The large form *(Grossform)* would be that of the A—A—B *Bar* with *Stollen* return, that is, AABAA *(Rundkanzonen-Strophe)*. For the musician the spiritual bond of the whole remains the *ostinato* bass retained in all the verses.

No. 23 (p. 153), the quartet piece *Veni, Sancte Spiritus* (G major), is set in the bright radiance of two sopranos and two tenors. It is difficult to sing on account of the treacherous sixteenth-note progressions representing the "rushing mighty wind" and the fiery tongues at *ignem accende*. The composition does not deal with the Whitsuntide sequence, which Schütz set as an early work, but with the antiphon *Veni, Sancte Spiritus, et accende corda fidelium*. There is no objection to Schuh's interpretation of the work as a potentialized A—A—B—A *Bar* (p. 112). The far-flung alleluias, with their eighth-note arches standing in directional opposition to the embellishment chains of the introduction *(Aufgesang)*, represent the extended conclusion *(Grossabgesang)*.

The delight in harmonically foreign, unaccented melody syllables which stemmed from the Florentine declamatory-melodic monody (which syllables, as distinguished from suspensions, passing notes, and changing notes, one could designate as neighboring, adjoining, or juxtaposed notes) exerted a style-determining effect in the form of melodic unaccented *(Auftakt)* anticipations in II, 20 (at the solo passages, *O lieber Herr Jesu*). In the normally keyed quartet No. 24 (p. 160), *Ist Gott für uns* ("If God be for us, who can be against us?"),[38] the Epistle lesson for St. James's Day (Rom. 8: 31-34), with *Alleluia*, this pleasure in such syllables has the effect of a natural, lifelike descent of the voice:

In this composition, with its "intellectual" *(vernünftig)* and impressive recitational delivery at *Welcher auch seines eigenen Sohnes* ("He that spared not His own Son")

---

[38] In the collection of Woyrsch and in Winterfeld, *Gabrieli*, II, 187-189; III, 150-151.

(pp. 160-161) one could demonstrate a special Schütz Epistle style which stands in decided contrast to his mature Gospel settings: in the histories we have the devout legend atmosphere; in the Pauline letters, on the other hand, something like a "systematic, theological discussion," as, for example, in this cleverly ingenious passage:

Scarcely anywhere does one seem to hear Schütz's voice so personally as when he then carries his solemn affirmation

in lively manner through all the voices. It is in just such apparently insignificant passages that one can observe how at that time the artist in Schütz remains more and more in the background, while the light of the evangelical church glows more and more brightly and perhaps reaches its greatest intensity in the *Geistliche Chormusik*.

We have a similar situation in No. 25 (p. 164), which is a textual continuation of the preceding and from the viewpoint of tonality also represents the second part of it. The text, *Wer will uns scheiden (Who Will Separate Us from the Love of God?)*, Rom.1: 35, 38-39, is treated as two varied couplets with the cadence on the dominant D major, whereupon a second couplet, *oder Hunger oder Blösse* ("or famine or nakedness"), leads to the dominant of the dominant, A major, until the conclusion *(Abgesang)* begins in *d* minor at *denn ich bin gewiss* ("for I am persuaded") — a highly spiritual and intellectual piece full of the best Lutheran Paulinism.[39]

Next a German and then a Latin psalm quartet. The former (No. 26, p. 168), in *d* minor, from Psalm 29, *Die Stimme des Herrn (The Voice of the Lord)*, forms the textual continuation to the C major monody *Bringet her*, I, 2. The Latin composition (No. 27, p. 174) in F major, *Jubilate Deo*, presents Psalm 100 in its entirety. Both works are full of pictorial splendor and of Old Testament eloquence — powerful echoes of the monumental style of 1619.

No. 28 (p. 184), in G major, the blissful *Annunciation Dialog, Sei gegrüsset, Maria (Hail, Mary)*, shows of what unheard-of multiplicity of expression Schütz is capable. Blume, in his collection, appropriately interpreted the alto clef used for the voice of the angel as a tenor voice. Even if the soprano of Mary may, in Schütz's day, have been sung in church by a boy, in domestic circles it was surely sung by a woman even at that time. Schütz placed this miniature oratorio among the quintets because he has a *sinfonia à 5* precede and follow the solo dialog above the continuo, which, of course, constitutes the kernel of the number, and also because he concludes the work with a five-voice homophonically declaimed chorus, *Siehe, ich bin des Herrn Magd, Allelujah* ("Behold the handmaid of the Lord. Alleluia"), for voices and instruments. The twice-played *sinfonia* naturally recalls the *Seven Last Words*.

That we really have an oratoriolike scene and not merely the Gospel for the day is shown by the bold way in which Schütz bent the text, Luke 1: 28-38, to his purpose. Not only, as in the *Easter Dialog*, does he omit all epical connecting links while expanding Mary's brief interjections, *Welch ein Gruss ist das — wie soll das zugehen, sintemal ich von keinem Manne weiss* ("What manner of salutation is this — How shall this be, seeing I know not a man?"), through repetitions so that they counterbalance the address of Gabriel; he also strikes out the heavenly messenger's references to David and the house of Jacob in order, after Mary's *Wie kann das zugehen?* ("How shall this be?"), to introduce a second *Fürchte dich nicht, Maria* ("Fear not, Mary"). In contrast to the tenderly soaring ecstasy of the

---

[39] English ed. by Ulr. Leupold, Chantry Music Press, Ltd., Fremont, Ohio, 1949.

"angelic greeting" the hemiolas of the Virgin's *Welch ein Gruss ist das?* ("What manner of salutation is this?") have the effect of noble reticence. How delightful, on the other hand, is the involuntarily impetuous *sintemal ich von keinem Manne weiss* ("seeing I know not a man")! What an observer of man and what a painter of saints Schütz was! The preceding hemiolas accompany the third speech of Mary only in the bass, and one might suspect that in their twofold

there lies that bit of holy eroticism which the old German painters of this scene were wont to indicate through the mystically symbolical position of the hand of the announcing angel; or, as the old folk song has it:

> *Sie schloß wohl auf ihres Herzens Fensterlein,*
> *Wohl zu derselben Stunde der heilig Geist ging ein.*
> The window of her heart she opened wide.
> The Holy Spirit entered in, forever to abide.

In the Appendix to Vol. VI of the collected works there is Schütz's own Latin version of this truly glorious composition. How much weaker is the *Dialog* of Hammerschmidt (DTOe, VIII, 1, p. 123), which at one time was frequently performed and which the good Zittauer worked out in 1645 apparently as a copy of Schütz!

The vocal quintet (No. 29, p. 191), *Was betrübst du dich? (Why Art Thou Cast Down?)*, Ps. 42: 6-12,[40] has at the head of its opening couplet a motive which one might designate as the essence of the Dorian in its harmony:

which then unfolds itself in splendid motet style, superimposing contrasts of half and eighth notes above one another.

Surely it is not merely an accidental relationship of scoring that causes a quintet, No. 30 (p. 197), likewise g Dorian, *Quemadmodum desiderat*, to come next. Even

---

[40] New editions by F. Woyrsch, Hohmann, Ansbach; also in Winterfeld, *Gabrieli* III, pp. 87-91.

though the words are from Augustine's soliloquys, chapter thirty-five, Augustine refers verbatim to Ps. 42: 2-3, from which No. 29 is derived. One feels how, as soon as Augustine's subjectivity *(Ichtümlichkeiten)* begins, Schütz turns from the psalm world to the style of his *Cantiones sacrae,* as in the downward thrust of the parts at *clementissime* (p. 198) and the falling chromaticism at *misericordissime* (p. 198). When, on the other hand, Schütz colors the *aquae dulcedinis tuae* (p. 200) by rising progressions, we may assume that he views the *Wässer deiner Süssigkeit* ("waters of thy sweetness") as a fountain in Paradise. The work is of great emotional power. The massed *Ich dürste, Herr* ("My soul thirsteth for God, for the living God") serves as the central theme. It is full of a dramatic division of roles, as each time Schütz deliberately contracts the number of voices in order to prepare a new point of brilliancy, as, for example, at *O gaudium super gaudium!*[41]

No. 31 (p. 207), the conclusion of the second volume, is a quintet *concerto* with two tenors on the entire new Latin *hymnus* in Sapphic measure by George Klee (Thymus), of 1541:[42]

> *Aufer immensám, Deus, iram*
> *ét cruentatúm cohibé flagéllum,*
> *néc scelús nostrúm properés ad aéquam*
> *péndere láncem.*

Freely in English:

> Take away from us, O God, Thy mighty anger,
> And restrain Thy bloody scourge;
> And let not our offense
> Disturb the balance of Thy scales.

Again, as in those Silesian state *concerti* from distichs, Schütz here dissolves the antique verse meter entirely in favor of prose declamation. He allows the eight strophes to cadence on $\lfloor a, C, A \rfloor \lfloor a, C, E \rfloor \lfloor a, A \rfloor$. The presentation by bass, alto, *tutti;* second tenor, soprano, terzet; tenors, *tutti,* also confirms the *Grossbarform.*[43]

One might designate this great prayer of contrition as Schütz's exorcism against the massacre that lasted for thirty years. There are a number of fascinating points: in measure six, the augmented second f—g# at *cruentatum* (p. 207); the wavering

---

[41] From this Latin text there probably comes the Silesian Christmas folk song which Hammerschmidt cites: *O Freude über Freude.*

[42] With regard to the almost liturgical use of this so-called *Kleine Litanei* cf. R. v. Liliencron in *Monatshefte für Musikgeschichte,* Jg. XXIX, pp. 30 f.

[43] I am unable to find the four divisions postulated by Schuh, p. 112.

between triad and chord of the sixth at *Si luant justam mala nostra poenam* (p. 208) with the unusual prolongation of seventh chords related at the third; the movingly distressing *rigidam mortem* (p. 213) and *mala nostra* (p. 210); sharp cross relationship at *sanguis et unda* (p. 214); delightfully picturesque the number symbolism of *trinus et unus* (p. 216).

As that mighty chorale work *Ich hab mein Sach Gott heimgestellt (To God Have I Entrusted All)* concluded the first volume, which so profoundly pierces the relation of the individual to things eternal, so Schütz crowns the second part with a *hymnus* on the equally powerful theme *God and His People in Sore Distress.* Glance back to his preface of 1639, where he hopes that "the arts now strangled by weapons and trodden in the soil might again be raised through the grace of God to their dignity and value." If any work could contribute to such a resurgence of musical culture, Schütz's *Kleine geistliche Konzerte* doubtless did so in highest measure.

Individual Church Concerti

It almost seems as though for a time Schütz considered writing a third volume of *Kleine geistliche Konzerte*. The two individual continuo parts to little solo *concerti* titled *Ego autem* and *Veni domine,* which were discovered by W. Gurlitt in Helmstedt and published by H. Spitta in Vol. XVIII, p. xvii f., might well belong to the beginning of such a volume. Inasmuch as Schütz's relation to Brunswick-Wolfenbüttel and to Hildesheim became more active after 1644, it may be proper for us to assign them to this period.

A *concerto* for five choirs on the Emmaus responsory *Surrexit pastor bonus* (Vol. XIV, No. 1, p. 1)[1] has been preserved only in Kassel parts. However, I do not venture to say whether they date from about 1620 or a dozen years later, because, in addition to an apparently orchestral treatment, we meet in the six-voice chief chorus *(favoritae)* fine points in harmonization which border on the most fully scored of the *Kleine geistliche Konzerte.* The alleluia measures of the complementary chorus also savor more of the desire for formal organization on the part of the mature master than of a desire for surprise effects on the part of the younger one. The peculiarly interrupted and scattered passages in the voices at *qui pro grege suo mori dignatus est* apparently represent the "scattered herd."

Beginning at the second *sinfonia,* the alleluia conclusion is organized with special beauty. We have the *sinfonia* and chorus *tutti* with the same bass as a kind of couplet and then, as conclusion, an A—B *Bar* consisting of solo groups with *tutti* endings. The little repetitions

remind one strongly of the *Erbarm dich* (Vol. XVIII, III), the *paravit,* and the *exultavit cor meum* at the beginning of the *Sinfoniae sacrae I,* and of the *non*

---

[1] The Emmaus responsory is found transformed into a *Magnificat* in M. Praetorius, XIV, 3. This composition is based on a motet by Lassus.

confundar or *Venite, venite*, there as Nos. 4 and 5. Even later Schütz never ceased to feel and express himself with vehemence like this.

To this "permanent chapter of Schütz's storm of jubilation" there belongs, in the first place, the St. Michael composition *Es erhub sich ein Streit*. It has been preserved anonymously in Kassel since ca. 1620. Heinrich Spitta, with convincing reasons, printed it in Vol. XVIII of the collected works, although the Lüneburg Catalog gives the corresponding title in Latin. Versions of Schütz's works in two languages are, of course, not infrequent, and no one but Sagittarius could have written this piece at that time. For a long time Joh. Christoph Bach's composition, the piece with the C major fanfares, was the only great forebear on the part of the old Bachs of Sebastian's famous *Michaelskantate*, which is based pictorially on the same text from the Apocalypse. Now, however, we see that Joh. Chr. Bach, with his Biblical double-chorus work, was only the most outstanding intermediary between Schütz and J. S. Bach, although he almost surpasses Schütz from the point of view of scoring. We shall come to recognize him further as one of the greatest of the Schützians. To be sure, what we have just said with regard to the instrumental scoring does not apply to the writing for voices. For while J. Chr. Bach presents two five-voice choruses, Schütz, in addition to his two four-voice choruses, has specified an additional vocal tenor part for his instrumental groups as the bearer of the Word. One of the tenors is the lowest voice under the three *cornetti*, against which, however, the ingenious Eisenach composer has four trumpets with tympani. The other tenor appears with a choir of one trumpet and three bassoons, to which, however, Joh. Christoph opposes two violins, four viols, and bassoon. Ultimately, however, the value of a work does not lie in the profusion of its scoring, and, so far as inner content is concerned, the work of Schütz is clearly superior to the later composition.[2] Although Joh. Christoph's work stands forth with surprising vitality in its day (ca. 1680), it produces a somewhat restricted effect from the viewpoint of thematic invention when compared with Schütz's "Bruckner breath" *(Atem)*.[3] In practice one will transpose the score up to D. Even if it were transposed to E, the dark basses at *grossen Drach* and *alten Schlang* would scarcely attain the intended effect. One had better render them in the higher octave and add a bassoon each for the lowest position despite the sixteen-foot organ bass. In spite of the thoroughly primitive surface nature of the beginning *(stile concitato* before Monteverdi!), the descriptive function of the solo voices appears at once

---

[2] M. Schneider presented the beginnings of the themes in the *Bachjahrbuch*, 1907, pp. 144 ff.
[3] Bruckner's *Te Deum* is perhaps the composition of our time which, unconsciously, most closely approaches the spirit of the *Psalms of 1619*.

in their portrayals of *im Himmel, ausgeworfen,* and *verführet.* The *capella* enters as with cudgels at *auch ward ihre Stätte nicht mehr funden* ("nor was there any place for them any longer"), and the heavenly voice resounds mightily against the nine voices singing the part of the quasi-evangelist. This heavenly voice also, in the narrowest space, likewise has nine voices singing, four against five, *Nun ist das Heil und die Kraft* ("Now is salvation and might")[4] with a terzet *intermezzo* of the counterchorus and a second intervening section, which expands into a quartet, after which the double chorus sings *Und haben ihr Leben nicht geliebet* ("for they did not love their lives"), this last in five sections, being the heart of the whole. The conclusion, however, is crowned by the *coda,* a *Bar* (A—A—B) with an octave leap which makes us feel fully the youthful intoxication:

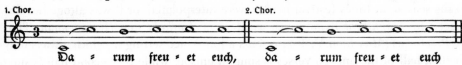

The *Magnificat* from Upsala, printed in Vol. XVIII, is likewise for five choirs. Eitner's *Quellenlexikon* had called attention to it in 1903 before Pirro did so in 1913. When Eitner says for four voices and five instruments, the latter is correct despite the six instrumental voices of the H. Spitta score, inasmuch as the *violone* beneath the two violins and the third trombone sound in unison almost throughout. The two vocal *capellae à 4* function only in a supplementary capacity. We must distinguish the following settings of this *Canticum B.M.V.* (Luke 1: 46-55):

A. Latin: the present piece from Upsala (Vol. XVIII; piano score by H. Spitta, Peters);

B. German: *Meine Seele erhebt:* (1) For soprano and instruments *(Sinfoniae sacrae II,* VII, 23), without verse forty-nine and without the doxology; (2) for four-voice chorus *(Zwölf geistliche Gesänge,* XII, 149); (3) for double chorus (last work, 1671; promised for Vol. XIX; practical edition by H. Spitta, B & H); (4) for three voices and two violins (Catalog Weimar, lost); (5) *à 10* (STB, *capella à 4,* three trombones, bassoon, in D major, Catalog Lüneburg, lost).

When H. Spitta (XVIII, 11) is of the opinion that since Schütz composed the Latin text throughout, "he therewith consciously lifted the piece out of the sphere of ecclesiastical usage (by way of comparison, Scheidt's *Magnificat: Geistliche Konzerte,* IV, 3),"his conclusion is not quite correct but could at the most be applied to the solo number in the *Sinfoniae sacrae,* which for formal reasons lacks

---

[4] One may glance from here to that unique double chorus of Bach as a most grandiose remainder or torso of a second *Michael Cantata.*

a verse, as well as the *Gloria Patri* at the conclusion, which all the other Schütz magnificats that have been preserved have. They, too, are all "through-composed" *(durchkomponiert)* and would thus also have to be "lifted out of ecclesiastical usage," which is scarcely credible in view of the practical purpose of the *Zwölf geistliche Gesänge*. To be sure, the antiphonal usage was ancient and widely practiced according to which alternate verses were set in choral polyphony or for the organ, while the others fell to the liturgist, whether this most important *Canticum majus Novi Testamenti* of Vespers was sung in Latin or in German. But the execution was also very much varied. Occasionally the canticle was performed in alternation between altar and congregation in the *tonus peregrinus* instead of in one of the eight psalm tones; at times it was framed by an antiphon appropriate to the season; at times festival hymns were interpolated, or it was altogether displaced by *Magnificat* hymns such as *Mein Seel erhebt den Herren mein*. Thus M. Praetorius *(Mus. Sion. V, 46)* presents a four-voice setting in which always only the first half of the uneven verses is sung in unison, while the second half is sung in parts by the first chorus. The alternate verses are sung, in polyphony throughout, by the second chorus. In the *Megalynodia* by the same composer[5] we have magnificats for the most varied festivals set now to Gregorian, now to madrigal, *chanson*, or church-hymn models. At times the chorus enters with the *anima mea*, at times only with the *et exultavit*. In the eight-voice setting *super chorale melos Germanicum* (No. XII), with the exception of the intonation of the word *magnificat*, the entire text is in polyphony throughout, divided between two choirs merely according to the inspiration of the composer. Exactly so in XIII and XIV, only that now often merely the *sicut erat* of the doxology is assigned to the choir. And surely Praetorius coined all this for liturgical use. So also the "through-composed" magnificats of Schütz.

To be sure, in another sense the G major piece from Upsala shows its creator's purpose to have the old hymn of praise appear in a new artistic spirit: the precentor role of the liturgist at *magnificat* is not continued by the choir but is emphasized by *tutti* reiteration. So, too, at *anima mea* and *Dominum*. The *anima mea*, repeated twice by the choir, emphasizes the subjective warmth of the church life of the time; but since the tenor, and not the soprano, acts as precentor, the clergyman at the altar is indicated, from the stylistic point of view, and not the Mary of the annunciation scene (as in the piece of 1639 for soprano solo). Only after this monumental prolog do the participating groups perform in contrast with

---

[5] 1611; in Blume's *GA*, ed. by H. Zenck. Further ones in *Mus. Sion*, V, 44, *à 5*; V, 45, *à 6*; I, 5 and Urania 6, *à 8*; Urania 22, *à 12*; Polyh. Caduceatrix 40, *à 19*.

one another. A word-engendered trombone trio presents the *exultavit* as a *sinfonia*, which is followed by the verse itself as a soprano-tenor duet above the continuo until both tonal groups unite in conclusion. The *quia respexit* is answered by the foundational bass soloist with both violins concertizing. The *Ecce enim ex hoc* flashes through all four *favoriti* voices, with *beatam* shining forth in *tutti* pillars in Bb—G—*c*—A contrasts, until the *omnes, omnes generationes* effervesces in eighth-note cascades as in the *Magnificat* of Bach. Again a new tonal picture: *Quia fecit* climbs aloft with alto and bass as leaders of the chorus, then to coax out their companions at *qui potens*. The *et sanctum nomen* creates a mystical momentary picture in the soprano-alto duet in whole and half notes which thrusts itself upward chromatically above the three trombones. God's *misericordia* is praised fervently in the solo quartet, in which the lowest parts lead off. The "children and children's children" *(a progenie in progenies)* grow and thrive in the score like a genealogical tree. The *fecit potentiam* opposes itself symmetrically to the beginning of the *Magnificat* (like the head of a giant countercouplet), inasmuch as now the alto, as quasi-liturgist, always sings in advance of the *tutti*. As God "destroys" the proud, the enunciation of the text is ground into sixteenth particles. Long-sustained trombone tones give a gloomily fateful, shadowy background to the excited virtuosity of the duets of the soloists. Finally the five choruses crush the *superbos* as in a mortar. The verse *deposuit potentes de sede et exaltavit humiles* shows how Schütz is able to vitalize the dimension of tonal space and the segments of time. The *deposuit — potentes — de sede —*, torn asunder by general pauses, becomes actually breath-taking. How solitary and pale after the beaming *tutti* is now the solo terzet: alto, tenor, bass! What a descent from the high C major to the deep, narrow A major — but out of a still deeper *d* minor God *exaltavit humiles* until they tarry glittering in the high E major of the alto and the soprano, while over the tenor solo the violins glisten in the high C! Again a new possibility sprouts from Schütz's inexhaustible fantasy — he paints the "hungry" by having the single solo bass (surely *piano!*) restrainedly echo the *esurientes*, while the same soloist (surely in a pronounced *forte!*) self-consciously lets the *divites* precede the *plenum*. When now, in concord with the trombone group, the bright solo soprano takes over the strophe *Suscepit Israel puerum suum, recordatus misericordiae suae,* the word of Isaiah doubtless passed through the mind of the master: "I will comfort you as a mother comforteth her children" (for the boy soprano often takes the place of the female discant), while the masculinity of the solo tenor shows us the Lord *sicut locutus est*. The violin passages which accompany this paint the Holy Word — one will recall the crisp figures at the beginning of the *Resurrection History: Wie uns die von den vier Evangelisten beschrieben wird* ("As they were written by the four evangelists").[6] The *Gloria* forms the *tutti* head of two couplets of the structure ABB, the first of which modulates from G—C to C and F. The second is transposed to *e*—B (!), *a* and G, until the *sicut erat* constitutes the conclusion, exuberant in its power, with the jubilant solo soprano in the front rank. And this entire unheard-of plethora of ideas in the simple large frame of the verse cadences GCGDG/CGGG/G—G. . . .

Of the two litanies of Schütz that have been preserved the composition for four voices will be discussed under the *Zwölf geistliche Gesänge*. Here we shall speak of the six-voice setting (XII, 185) which has been preserved in manuscript in Königsberg only. The age-old ecclesiastical petition which still lives today in Catholicism in three forms (All Saints, Lauretanian [Mary], and Name of Jesus litanies) Luther called *valde utilis et salutaris*, and in 1529 he translated it into German metrical verse. People were fond of singing and praying this text on days of penance and at Vespers before festival days in place of the *Magnificat*, but occasionally also in the chief service of the Advent and Lenten seasons after the Epistle,[7] as Bach noted on the occasion of his visit to St. Thomas' in Leipzig in 1714. The performance took place in most cases by having "from four to five boys with good pure little voices" intone the invocations at the altar according to the formula f—g—a, with the congregation or the choir answering antiphonally. For this manner of execution Michael Praetorius *(Musae Sioniae* VIII, 296—298) made three 4—5 voice harmonizations. Two of these are found in Schöberlein-Riegel I, together with a 5—6 voice setting by M. Vulpius. They uniformly lead every little line from the F major harmony to a *g* minor (or Picardian G major) cadence. We find an essentially closer approach to Schütz in the hitherto scarcely noticed seven-voice *German Litany* of Hans Leo Hassler that was printed in 1619 *(Nat. Bibl.,* Vienna).

In the case of the six-voice composition Schütz retained the customary practice of execution mentioned above, in that the first soprano presents the invocations while the remaining voices follow chordally with their *erhöre uns, erbarm dich über uns, behüt uns, hilf uns.* Only in a few chief places do both factors unite. In the case of the conclusion this was a regular ecclesiastical practice. What is new in Schütz is the thorough bass which persists even throughout the portions sung at the altar. Most important of all, he further supplants the traditional simple

---

[6] An amusing misprint occurs, twice each time, not only in H. Spitta's score (XVIII, 85-86) but also in his edition for piano (Peters); *femini ejus* instead of *semini ejus.*

[7] M. Praetorius, *GA,* VII, 295-297, and the litanies in Vol. XX.

fauxbourdons of the conventional accentual formulae with a completely new type of composition which combines boldly and yet carefully, in the Dorian frame, all the impressiveness of the invocation with congregational reference. Here we have one of his creations of quasi-Gregorianism, as in the *Resurrection History* and the passions. The little chorus lines pursue the paths C—A, E—*e*, F—*d*, *a*—*d*, *d*—F, C—C (these with polyphonic beginnings), C—*a*, G—*a*, *a*—D, F—D, *a*—C, *d*—A, *d*—D, G—A, D—G, *a*—A, F—C, *d*—E, B—C, *g*—D. In brief, they present all the imaginable combinations in order to avoid tediousness and to formulate a climactic, artistic whole.

The concert piece *O bone Jesu, fili Mariae* (XVIII, 93) again represents a fascinating addition from the Düben treasure-trove in Upsala. Schütz himself doubtless put together the text from verse and prose. As the source of the former, H. Spitta was able to refer to strophes of the *Jubilus rhythmicus de nomine Jesu,* which is ascribed to Bernard of Clairvaux.[8] As for the prose texts of the soloists, interpolated between the chorus passages, only some mystical writer of the pseudo-Augustinian group can have been the author. As the chorus strophe is repeated verbatim three times, we have a *rondo* form in the middle. A *sinfonia* by the seven viols precedes, while at the end we have a *coda* (beginning at *Redemptor mundi)* in which the six upper voices, with two entering solo terzets, concertize with the orchestra. Between these pillars there constantly swing the light recitative garlands of alternating solos and duets. The piece is one which shows exemplary planning and is so capable of general appreciation that it could well serve, if presented in the vernacular, to further the Schützian cause far and wide.

Next let us consider the ingeniously constructed dialog *Ich beschwöre euch (I Adjure You),* which the Breslau organist at St. Elizabeth's, Ambrosius Profe, published in 1641. This fantasia on very freely treated texts from the Song of Songs stands as the crowning concluding number in Profe's *Anderer Teil geistlicher Concerte.* We have already conjectured that this piece may owe its origin to the wedding celebration for Johann Georg II, which took place three years before Profe published it. Sulamith speaks passionately through four sopranos; the "daughters of Jerusalem" answer with the three male voices: alto, tenor, and bass. Apparently, then, Schütz was not concerned with a realistic painting of the actors but with the inner tensions between the contrasting colors of the voices represented in the dialog.

----

[8] In Johs. Arndt's *Paradiesgärtlein* (1612). W. Bremme's monograph *Der Hymnus Jesu dulcis memoria* (Mainz, 1899); thereto W. Nelle, *MGFK,* 5 (1900), pp. 37-45.

Instead of unrolling the extensive history of the madrigal dialog at this point,[9] let us simply refer to a few German love contests of a related kind which Schütz might have taken as his point of departure, and which doubtless paved the way for a better understanding of his compositions by his contemporaries. Thus we have the primitive but at the time widely circulated strophic song of Joh. Staden, *Ich bitt euch Jungfräulein* (DTB, VIII, 1, p. 88); then, from 1608, a *Dialogus metricus, à 7*, by Melchior Franck; from 1622 a six-voice dialog by Daniel Friderici; the dialog between the maiden and the *Postillon vom Venustron* of H. Christof Haiden;[10] H. Albert's *Gespräch der Jungfrau mit dem Rosenstock;*[11] and Joh. Jeep's *Aussprache zwischen Gesell und Jungfrau.*[12] But all these impress one as exceedingly modest beginnings when compared with the Schütz dialog.

The most charming of these compositions, the most highly developed, and the one which approaches Schütz most closely is Melch. Franck's *Metrischer Dialog* of 1608. The *juvenis* always inquires *à 4*, while the *virgo* answers *à 3*, in Latin distichs. Thus at the beginning: (See next page.)

Schütz's piece requires — as practical experience at the Berlin Schütz Festival of 1930 showed — a lively tempo. The little four-voice groups have about them something cooing, humming. The work as a whole possesses intoxicating tonal splendor. It exudes a certain voluptuous, oriental, stupefying atmosphere. The dynamic contrasts *in seinen Garten — zu den Würzgärtelein — und Rosen breche*[13] must be rendered with genuine pleasure in the tonal play, till at the end all seven voices unite in the most colorful tapestry: *Lasst uns gehen und ihn suchen* ("Let us go and seek him").

One might like to think that this septet signifies Schütz's farewell to the Song of Songs, the charming eroticism of which he so often set to music and had here once more put together in a crowning manner, and that after this he left it to younger blood to eavesdrop on Salome and Sulamith. Erasmus Kindermann and Dietrich Buxtehude stand at the head of the post-Schützian Song of Songs composition, which then received a new transfiguration in Bach's dialog cantatas.

However, the Naumburg catalog of Andr. Unger of 1658 (A. Werner in *AfM*, VIII, 413) shows that Schütz set still more texts from the Song of Songs,[14] as it

---

[9] Cf. Th. Kroyer, *Dialog und Echo* (Peters *Jahrbuch*, 1909).
[10] In W. Vetter, *Neudeutsches Lied*, II, No. 7.
[11] In Moser's *Alte Meister des deutschen Liedes* (Peters).
[12] Likewise, Vetter, No. 45; also there, No. 57 a and b, the dialog song *(Wechsellied)* between *Adolescens* and *Puella* by Erasmus Widmann; in manuscript Löbau 15, a twelve-voiced dialog of Latin distichs between bridegroom (six-voiced) and bride (six-voiced) from the six-voiced madrigals of Camillo Zanotti (1590).
[13] "To his garden — to the little garden of herbs — and pluck roses."
[14] Cf. also a Schütz bridal Mass *à 6: Mein Freund komme,* which the *Kantorei* in Pirna possessed.

mentions a Schütz work (subsequently lost): *Stehe auf, meine Freundin (Arise, My Friend)* in eight parts. To be sure, a work with a similar scoring and a similar title is also ascribed there to J. H. Schein. I also know a rather heavy-footed third work in Joh. Schop's *Geistliche Konzerte*. But the anonymous *Stehe auf* of the manuscript of Joh. Gräffenhain, of 1646 (BB 40345, No. 138), the greater part of which I presented in the *Z.f.MW.*, XVII, 339 ff., would seem to point much more clearly to Schütz than to Schein, so ingeniously are the interweavings of the four-voice boy choir and the four-voice male choir placed in juxtaposition to one another, and with such charming lightness is the text (Song of Songs 2: 10-13) treated.[15] Note the beginning:

---

[15] Presented over the radio for the first time on October 20, 1935, by the Bremen Dom Choir (Cantor R. Liesche) together with other Schütz motets newly discovered by me.

The structure is ABACA, i. e., *rondo*like with two middle sections, certainly a most delightful piece. It is to be hoped that the name Schütz can soon be unequivocally applied to this composition.

Schütz's name could definitely be associated with the following single-voice part (tenor II) from the *Voice Book 474* of the Dresden *Dreikönigskirche*, written between 1628 and 1652 by Christof Lonzer and marked *à 6*, v. Heinrici Sagittarj *C(apellae) M(agistri) D(resdensis):*

Fortunately, I have just discovered this glorious work: *Ich weiss, dass mein Erlöser lebt (I Know that My Redeemer Liveth)* in Freiberg in Saxony. This composition could readily have appeared in Ph. Spitta's complete edition had Otto Kade not made an unfortunate mistake. For in his supplement to the *Monatshefte f. Musikwissenschaft*, 1888, titled *Die älteren Musikalien der Stadt Freiberg i. Sa.*, he writes, p. 25:

"(1648) *Ich weiss, dass mein Erlöser lebet, à 6 vocum*, No. 27 in the *Sammelband XI.*, 8° 47; immediately following the twenty-six motets of Albinus Fabricius. The piece is taken from the *Musicalia ad chorum sacrum*. There it is found as No. 25 for six voices, in addition to *basso continuo*."

In view of the single voice of the Lonzer manuscript my suspicion was aroused that O. Kade was in error here, for the setting of the same text in the *Geistliche Chormusik* is actually for seven voices. I turned to Herr Studienrat Wilh. Löhner, teacher of singing at the *Gymnasium Albertinum* in Freiberg with a request for verification. To my great pleasure he confirmed the correctness of my conjecture: the Freiberg setting corresponds to the Dresden voice part and has nothing to do with the print of 1648. My hearty thanks to the Freiberg *Gymnasium* for kindly forwarding to me the complete manuscript.

We are concerned with a *d* Dorian composition in two parts which maintains the Dorian character so clearly that only a few flats appear. The above-cited theme of genuine Schützian antithetical rhythm begins in the second soprano, to be most closely followed by the alto, soprano one, and tenor one, until our Dresden sixth voice *(sextus)* and the bass mingle in the surprisingly dense web of the chordal chains which crisscross for the most part in parallel thirds. The first soprano looms up broadly above the dark flood of these other voices:

At measure sixteen the harmony turns to F major. Here the second section of the text is introduced: *Und er wird mich hernach aus der Erde aufwecken* — ("He will hereafter awaken me from the earth"). The last word, *"awaken,"* with amazing intertwinings of four and five voices, on F, G, d, G, is led pictorially upward. See bars 25-28. (See bottom of this page and top of next page).

The conclusion follows on page 34 in F major *(erwecken)*. The second part (39 measures d—d) begins in an almost greater contrast of slow and fast time, with the mysteriously drawn-out *und ich werde,* to be followed immediately by precipitant groups of eighths in the first soprano and the alto at the words *mit dieser meiner Haut.* The *tutti* at the words *umgeben werden* ("enveloped with my skin") is doubtless intended to portray the completeness of the envelopment. The second

line of the couplet is abbreviated and has the same words. The conclusion has joyful triplets. They whirl first in the four uppermost voices, then in all voices. The
words are: *und werde in meinem Fleische Gott sehen* ("and in my flesh shall I see
God"), G, D, F. There is a retardation in G to even time. Then the dance rhythm
breaks forth again: *denselben werd' ich mir sehen* ("Him shall I see for myself"),
this section cadencing in A Phrygian, then in E. The wonderful, closely woven
conclusion is built as a kind of double fugue on the madrigalesque subject and
countersubject:

This fine newly won work has appeared in the Bärenreiter-Verlag. The date
"1648" is an arbitrary, erroneous addition by Kade. The Freiberger part books say
nothing about it. However, as the Dresden voice part is followed by a date, "We-
senstein 1628," we are doubtless justified in dating the work "before 1628." This
is also confirmed by considerations of style.

Op. 10. The Symphoniae sacrae II of 1647

The *Symphoniae sacrae II* of 1647,[1] which constitute the German continuation of the Latin work of 1629, was presented to the Danish crown prince in manuscript in 1645 on the occasion of Schütz's third departure from Copenhagen. It appeared in print two years later with the following title (red and black alternating):

Symphoniarum Sacrarum

Secunda Pars

Wherein Are to Be Found

German

Concerted Pieces

with 3, 4, 5. Namely, One / Two / Three

Vocal and Two Instrumental — Voices /

as Violins or Such Kind

Together with Added Doubled Basso Continuo

the One for the Organist, the Other

for the Violon

Set to Music

by

Heinrich Schütz

Capellmeister for the Elector of Saxony

With Roman Imperial Majesty's License

M D C.   (Coat of Arms)   XLVII

Opus 10

Printed in Dresden at Gimel Bergen's Electoral Saxon

Court Printer's / Blessed Heirs / Published by Johann Klemmens

Court Organist There / and Alexander Hering

Organist in Budissin.

A notice states further that the work can be obtained not only from the persons mentioned but also from the organists Delphin Strunck in Brunswick and Johann Rosenmüller in Leipzig.[2]

---

[1] Vol. VII of the collected works.

[2] Joh. Rosenmüller refers to the direction with regard to the presentation, which is found in the preface to the *Sinfoniae sacrae of 1647*, when he says in his *Mitteilung* (information) preceding the second part of his *Kernsprüche* (1652): "Where Herr Heinrich Schütz, Electoral Saxon Kapellmeister, reports sufficiently, according to my judgment, with regard to this."

In the dedication of May 1, 1647, to Crown Prince Christian, we find the important information that between the first conclusion of the work and the present publication "a diligent revision on my part" has taken place. Schütz confirms this in the preface "to the kindly disposed reader" with the supplementary information that this publication occurs for the additional reason that for a number of years some of the pieces had been circulated in corrupt form. That, as a matter of fact, older pieces are to be found among these *symphoniae* is indicated by the presence of the bass solo *Herr, nun lässest du (Lord, Now Lettest Thou)*, dedicated to Schütz's Kassel colleague Christoff Cornett. Four more of these pieces have been preserved in Kassel in manuscript in their original form (see Ph. Spitta's *Revision Report*), so that one can follow precisely Schütz's final corrections. Schütz complains that the Germans frequently showed that they were not precisely acquainted with the "black note" notation, with the result that "settings thus recorded were often so badly performed, maltreated, and distorted that they must create nothing but disgust and annoyance in an intelligent listener, indeed also in the author himself, and must bring unjustified disrepute upon the honorable German nation, as though the last named were lacking in skill in the noble art of music (as indeed such charges are not wanting among some foreigners) . . . ." Schütz asks of those "who are not familiar with the proper method of keeping time in the aforementioned music of the present day and are not acquainted with the black notes" that before a public performance "they might not be ashamed to obtain instruction in such matters from those acquainted with them, and might not be wearied by private practice therein, in order that neither they nor the author, without the latter's fault, might obtain derision instead of thanks."

In the case of the "black notes" the reference is doubtless not the change in color, which indicated a change to three-part time, a matter long known in Germany, but to the now increasingly used sixteenth and thirty-second notes in the coloratura style — in other words, to the "chromatic play" *(das chromatische Spiel)*, as the Italians said at the time with reference to the *chroma* = 1/32, which was to be counted exactly instead of being hurried through *ad libitum*. Very important, furthermore, is Schütz's remark (omitted by us above) that this request was made also to those Germans to whom "the constantly drawn-out musical stroke or bow on the violin" was not known — who, in other words, still "scraped" *(schrabten)* like the old dance fiddlers instead of drawing from the violin a noble *bel canto* — a remark which present performers of Schütz's works might also well bear in mind. After this "singing on the violin" under the influence of the Schützian and the Viennese violin school had to some extent gained a footing in Germany, it was again threatened with extinction through the Lully "pointed" method of playing, which the petty princes, bewitched by the luster of Versailles, wanted to force upon their violinists. In this connection the protest of the Ansbach concert-master, J. Andr. Mayer, is instructive. In 1683 he besought his ruler, after he had learned from Schmeltzer in Vienna the Italian long bow strokes, to preserve him from the "quite short strokes" desired by young Cousser.

The relations of Schütz to Monteverdi, which are referred to in Schütz's preface of 1647, were mentioned in connection with his second Venetian sojourn of 1629. Noteworthy, however, are two further observations in the printed edition relative to Schütz's further creative plans. In the first place, he offers in the *violone* voice a table of contents of his works or "specification of the musical works published hitherto by the author for the information of the well-disposed reader," wherein he desig-nates the *Psalms of 1619 (Op. 2)* as "First Part," which was not the case on the original title page. According to this, Schütz had in the meantime apparently created so much new music of this kind that he could plan a second volume.[3] In the second place, he rounds off his preface to the reader with the promise: "Finally, I would like to offer, if God will grant longer life and His gracious help, to publish in the near future more of my works, unimportant though they are, and among them especially such also as those who are not, and do not plan to become, musi-cians *ex professo* can nevertheless use to good purpose."

Such willingness to be of service to the layman could best be interpreted as a plan for a third volume of *Kleine geistliche Konzerte*. Later we shall consider how during Schütz's last years such a wave of popularity spread over Germany.

Now let us examine Vol. VII of Ph. Spitta's collected works. The twenty-seven pieces divide themselves, according to their scoring, into twelve solo numbers descending from soprano to bass, ten similarly arranged duets, and five terzets. Of twenty-two numbers with texts from the Old Testament sixteen are based on the Psalms; the remainder are divided chiefly among Sirach, Ecclesiastes, and the Proverbs. Against these we have only three New Testament texts: the *Magnificat*, in German; the *Nunc Dimittis;* and one specifically Gospel number, *Hütet euch (Take Heed)*, Luke 21: 34, for the Second Sunday in Advent. Three numbers are based on church hymns.

There is provision for ample variety of tonalities. Many remarkable instances which occur here may present occasion to view, in the context of one work, as a brief digression, the subject of Schütz's tonal conception, which has already been

---

[3] A considerable portion of this material opens the *Symphoniae sacrae III,* of 1650.

touched on several times. As Schütz himself occasionally makes known (for example, in the remark in connection with the *Gloria* of the *Exequien*, namely, that it caused him difficulty to provide quarters for all church melodies *in nono tono*, i. e., in *e* Aeolian), he still reckoned with the twelve church tones of Glarean of 1547. If, however, we consult the composition textbook of Chr. Bernhard of 1650, which perhaps was made under Schütz's very eyes, we find that Bernhard no longer counted *à la* Glarean the Dorian as the first and the Hypoionian as the twelfth tone, but the Ionian as the first and the Hypoaeolian as the last tone, just as Luscinius reported 120 years earlier with regard to Hofhaimer. The clavier, of course, suggested the Ionian to the organists[4] as the first tone.

The following places side by side the two forms of reckoning:

Glarean:		Final	Bernhard		Final
1. *d a d*	Dorian	} D	1. *c g c*	Ionian	} C
2. *a d a*	Hypodorian		2. *g c g*	Hypoionian	
3. *e b e*	Phrygian	} E	3. *d a d*	Dorian	} D
4. *b e b*	Hypophrygian		4. *a d a*	Hypodorian	
5. *f c f*	Lydian	} F	5. *e b e*	Phrygian	} E
6. *c f c*	Hypolydian		6. *b e b*	Hypophrygian	
7. *g d g*	Mixolydian	} G	7. *f c f*	Lydian	} F
8. *d g d*	Hypomixolydian		8. *c f c*	Hypolydian	
9. *a e a*	Aeolian	} A	9. *g d g*	Mixolydian	} G
10. *e a e*	Hypoaeolian		10. *d g d*	Hypomixolydian	
11. *c g c*	Ionian	} C	11. *a e a*	Aeolian	} A
12. *g c g*	Hypoionian		12. *e a e*	Hypoaeolian	

Undoubtedly the Bernhard arrangement is more modern and logical than the *Dodekachordon* of H. Loris of Glarus, which latter evolved historically from the tetrachord or the *oktoechos* and was expanded in a supplementary manner only by appending the major and the minor scale. For Bernhard's system, rising from the fundamental tone C *(Systemton)* in the *hexachordum naturale*, ranks every *authenticus* with its *plagalis*. Bernhard, remaining conscious of the original nature of the tones as purely melodic, emphasizes (p. 98) "that the tenor is really the voice on which one should base one's judgment as to the tonality of a particular composition" — something that made real sense only during the time of the tenor *cantus*

---

[4] Edition Müller-Blattau, p. 93: "So the *musici* are still at variance with regard to the order of the modes, insofar as some consider the mode on C as the first, others that on D. But the former have the better arguments."

firmus with its primary cadences *(Primärklauseln).* The transition to the determination of tonality according to that of the harmonic final cadence he obtains through the concept of the association of the modes *(consociatio modorum),* inasmuch as in the concluding chord the finals *(finales),* fundamental and octave, the quint *(confinalis principalis),* and the terce *(confinalis minus principalis)* combine with one another *(consociantur).* The concept *confinalis* must likewise submit to a reinterpretation as the modern "functional," insofar as Bernhard understands under *cadentia confinalis principalis* the semicadence and recommends that we place this, in the case of works in two sections, at the end of the *prima* and, in the case of works in three sections, at the end of the *secunda pars.*

Now he also knows the "transposition of the modes" in that intermediate position — characteristic of the seventeenth century — between medieval and modern: as normal, only the transposition into the subdominant, thus from the C system without a sharp or flat signature to the F system with a b♭. When he calls this "a transmutation *(Verwandlung)* of the *cantus durus* into the *cantus mollis,*" this has nothing to do with our major and minor tonalities but refers to the solmization concepts of the transition from the *hexachordum naturale* (c—a) to the *hexachordum molle* (f—d), where the flat (b *molle*) prevails and not the natural (b *durum*). He considers all other transpositions "unusual" *(seltsam),* and he does not arrange them — corresponding to the signatures — according to the circle of fifths but according to intervals: from C Ionian upwards to D and E, downwards to b♭, A, and G major.

When Schütz begins nearly all his major collections with (according to our designation) *g* minor or *d* minor pieces,[5] he does so because, according to his old reckoning, these tonalities were *tonus primus transpositus* or *naturalis.* Already, of course, the six authentic tones reduced themselves to two kinds of tonalities. Bernhard says that the Lydian and Mixolydian often coincide with the Ionian,[6] that the Aeolian has affinity with the Dorian and even with the Phrygian. Rosenmüller expressed this forcefully at the time in the observation preserved in Fuhrmann's *Trichter* of 1706: "*Nimasch rosmye* (Wendish approximately for "Rosenmüller can't help it") — Jonicus and Doricus are my two modes, of which the former has

---

[5] The *Italian Madrigals,* the *Psalms of David of 1619,* the *Cantiones sacrae,* the first volume of the *Kleine geistliche Konzerte,* and the *Symphoniae sacrae II* and *III.*

[6] Significantly, Bernhard, who for the chief tones refers to church melodies as examples, has no further example of the Lydian in his stock and hence refers to the Roman altar song; even Luther's pronounced Lydian *Jesaia dem Propheten* was at the time already polished into Ionian, as, for example, its notation in the manuscript Peltsch (BB 40110), leaf 487v, proves. So, too, in Rhaw's *Enchiridion* (1530).

a major third, the latter a minor third, and both go through all tones and semi-tones. The remaining ones are contained in these two just as many sparks are contained in steel and stone." Here the way becomes clearly evident to the twenty-four *triades harmonicae* of the *Well-tempered Clavichord.*

The question whether a transposed minor is to be derived from Dorian or Aeolian was determined chiefly according to the smaller number of sharps or flats required in the signature: *e* minor, for example, Schütz liked to regard as Aeolian; *g* minor, as Dorian. Tonalities further removed were arrived at through chiavettas. When even a *c* minor piece, as *Sinfoniae sacrae II*, 10, *Lobet den Herrn in seinem Heiligtume (Praise Ye the Lord. Praise God in His Sanctuary),* receives the so-called "double Dorian" signature of only one B flat, this occurs from the same disinclination to use more signatures than in the *genus molle* of the F system.

Beyond this, "Picardizations" play a great role, that is to say, the major form in the final chord of a composition in minor, which we have often met with. Examples from the *Sinfoniae sacrae II* would be No. 2, *Singet dem Herrn (O Sing unto the Lord),* and No. 26, *Von Gott will ich nicht lassen (From God Will I Not Part),* in *g* minor with a G major conclusion; No. 12, *Was betrübst du dich (Why Art Thou Cast Down, O My Soul);* No. 20, *Zweierlei bitte ich (Two Things Have I Required of Thee);* and No. 27, *Freuet euch in dem Herrn (Rejoice in the Lord, O Ye Righteous),* in *d* minor with a conclusion in D major.

However, we also have "Picardization" of the opening chord with a transition after this to the minor subdominant, which retrospectively brightens the opening chord as the dominant major, so that that above-mentioned "Hyperdorian" *Lobet den Herrn* (II, 10) despite the opening and closing C major chord is really a composition in *c* minor, according to the scheme:[7]

f: ♮V (♮) I   c: V   ♮I

This is also confirmed in the same composition at *Psalter und Harfe* by the cadence with the bass tones *c* G Eb G C. Likewise No. 25, *Zwei schöne Dinge sind (Two Fine Things Are),* begins and closes with the G major triad and yet stands in *g* minor! Even though such "Picardizations" occur very frequently during the course

---

[7] In Nikolaus Zangius, *Kurzweilige newe teutsche Liedlein* (1603, British Museum), No. 8 *(Kein Handwerk gilt mehr in der Welt)* is a g Dorian composition; but it begins with the transition G major-*c* minor and concludes in G major.

of a composition, Schütz nevertheless uses them as frugally as possible from the viewpoint of their further expansion or connotation. The terzet from the *Sinfoniae sacrae II* offers a repeatedly drastic confirmation of this fact. The passage sounds thoroughly dissonant!

We also meet remnants of the Mixolydian.[8] If Schütz, for example, had written the G major piece in the *Sinfoniae sacrae II*, No. 23, *Lobet den Herrn, alle Heiden (Praise the Lord, All Ye Nations)*, as Ionian, with the signature of one sharp, a number of f naturals would have appeared as foreign to the tonality. Inasmuch, however, as he writes in the Mixolydian mode, we have the constant vacillation between the C and the G system:

Or we find the strange mixtures of tonalities, as toward the end of the *Psalm 2* (1619), in which the tonic alone has long been "Picardized," while the dominants, the subdominants, and the mediants still remain in the shadow region of the minor tonic relation. Conversely, passages in F and Bb major show Lydian tendencies. As even in the music of the fifteenth and sixteenth centuries, the unconscious and unwritten tendency prevails: When in doubt, always resort to the *musica naturalis* of the C—F system, poor in signatures, rather than to the *musica ficta* of higher accidentals! However, Schütz did not shrink from B major and g# minor if the occasion demanded. But with him the matter does not end with the Ionian and Dorian (Aeolian), with Picardizings, and transpositions. The concept of the plagal

---

[8] For example, in the *Zwölf geistliche Gesänge*, in part three of the *Credo, Der mit dem Vater und dem Sohne* (Bb major triad in C major!).

tonalities, like that of the authentic modes, led to strange formations from the melodic field into the harmonic. On the one hand, in this, that not only — as Bernhard recommended — was the *cadentia plagalis principalis* employed in the conclusions of inner divisions but this half close is also used at the end of one-movement settings. Thus in the *Sinfoniae sacrae II, 4, Meine Seele erhebt (My Soul Doth Magnify the Lord)*, which is in *a* minor, we have the dominant E major:

According to the old rule, *Cujus toni videtur in fine*, the end of the piece is, to be sure, tonally determined by the final or the cofinal cadence; the beginning, however is essentially freer. Thus *Psalm 84* (No. 8 of the *Psalms of 1619*) began in B flat major despite its *g* Dorian tonality, and *Psalm 115* (II, 9, loc. cit.) in F major despite its *d* minor bearing.[10] Similarly, extended dominant stretches abound as introductory regions: so, for example, in *Sinf. sacr. II, 21*, the bass duet, *Herr, neige deine Himmel* ("Bow Thy Heavens, O Lord"), has a broad *a* minor forefield despite its *d* minor conclusion — a piece which Schütz, therefore, would probably have designated as Hypodorian. In this way there arise those strangely distorted tonalities, mentioned several times, as in *Psalm 130* of the *Cantiones sacrae* (XXVI-

---

[9] It is instructive to note how here at first we still have "Dorian" f # g, while the *subsemitonium* g # is first chosen between the boundaries of two *a*'s, the *erheben* ("magnifying") occurs subconsciously step by step!

[10] In Zangius, loc. cit., No. 16, *Daß ich den Worten dein*, begins in F major but is a *d* Dorian number with a D major conclusion.

XXVIII): a Picardizing *d* minor cycle which, to be sure, plays strongly with the major dominants and related dominants but on the subdominant side operates primarily with *g* minor, B flat major, E flat major, *c* minor, and thus contains the entire riches of Schütz's harmonic colors. The situation suggests the interpretation as the Hypo-form of the *g* Dorian and yet rather represents a "D major dwelling deep in the B flat tonal kingdom."

If we wished to expand these observations on tonality to the theme "The Harmony of Schütz," to which subject we have offered copious contributions, we would certainly have to refer further to his freedom in the use of the more distant quint- and third-related functions, likewise still half-grounded in the modal system, as, for example, in a *g* Mixolydian setting the application of numerous intermediary dominants (E major — A major).[11] But such observations would take us too far away from the subject.

It is certainly not by accident that the opening composition in the *Sinfoniae sacrae II* (VII, 7) has, by its very text, Ps. 57: 7-10, a prologlike character: *Mein Herz ist bereit (My Heart Is Fixed, O God, My Heart Is Fixed)*. The manner in which these words, through partial repetitions, are formed into a period of five and a half double bars; the way in which *Gott, bereit,* and *lobe* receive their full characterization both as to development and as to pitch; the way in which the motive *dass ich singe* four times receives the "new Landino cadence" of the Florentine opera and the obbligato instruments are held in reserve as echo for the second motive, *Wach auf, meine Ehre,* which is introduced in dance rhythm — all this can be viewed as setting the tone for the entire volume, not to forget the pictorial slurs on *Psalter*. The composition is a genuine *Kleines geistliches Konzert,* determined in part by a word-engendered monodic unity, in part by a motetlike juxtaposition of divisions. The imitative nature of the co-operating violins confirms polyphonically the latter principle of construction. The conclusion, *Denn deine Güte ist,* which is to be taken slowly, has received in the published edition, as distinguished from the preserved manuscript, a beautiful expansion of the passage on *soweit die Wolken gehen*. There is so much Teutonic feeling for nature in this passage that because of this very "field solitude" *(Feldeinsamkeit)* the composition is worthy of being known and sung.

Similarly No. 2, Ps. 96: 1-4 (p. 11), *Singet dem Herrn (O Sing unto the Lord a New Song),* must be a delight for every singer who is a master of the baroque. Like the preceding and the following composition, it has the optional scoring

---

[11] P. Dickermann, *Die Entwicklung der Harmonik bei Skrjabin* (Bern, 1935).

cantus vel tenor, familiar to us from the compositions of 1636. The notes marked with the sign "t" on *alle Welt* are to be executed as inverted mordents, as thus indicated:

On the other hand, in No. 3 (p. 16):

unless in both instances he means merely *espressivo* or *vibrato;* for in Caccini *trillo* indicates merely the *vibrato* on the prime, while our trill with the second was called *gruppo.*[12]

Splendid is the way in which in No. 2, on page twelve, the music for *Singet* in straight time vies in virtuoso manner with the violin passages; jovial is the always brief phrase conclusion, *einen Tag dem andern,* wherewith energy is stored up for a long time until it finally streams forth at *sein Heil.* Note also the passage at *erzählt,* with its little breathing pause between the groups of eighths. Finally, the last motive, at *Wunderbarlich, wunderbarlich* ("He is mighty; there is none beside Him"), ringing with its repetitions and with its scintillating accentual changes — what fiery musicianship still remained in the "wise and highly learned man"!

Psalm 8, *Herr, unser Herrscher (O Lord, Our Lord, How Excellent Is Thy Name),* which Schütz had already set twice in large scoring, now receives its extensive chamber-music setting as No. 3 of the present collection (p. 16).[13] It is fascinating to observe how here the same words that lend themselves to pictorial representation — *Säuglinge, Mond und Sterne, Ehren und Schmuck, krönen, Fisch im Meer, gehen*[14] — now receive their special figures from the present scoring. The representations are exactly the same in the instruments as in the voices; yet in the instruments they do not have a vocal effect, nor do they have an instrumental effect in the voices. Each time they appear as though conceived according to the intrinsic nature of the executing tonal instrument. How this is done is Schütz's secret. And

---

[12] C. v. Winterfeld, *Johs. Gabrieli,* II, 131, with musical examples.
[13] Practical edition by H. Birtner, Bärenreiter-Verlag, 1933.
[14] "Sucklings," "moon and stars," "honor and adornment," "crown," "fish in the sea," "going."

so Birtner's statement (in the preface, loc. cit.) is fully justified: that the full significance of the work of 1647 is due directly to the fact that "in it the purely tonal and formal musical values are fused together with the sung word into a characteristic and convincing unity. The synthesis of vocal solistic form construction with an enhanced instrumental diction, also the fusion of the vocal and instrumental tonal groups, and, beyond this, the sovereign mastery of all musical means and tonal effects in the service of an exposition of the Word, all concentrated into the greatest intensity — this stands out with special clarity in this work." W. Schuh (loc. cit., pp. 98 ff.) has shown the archlike form of *Psalm 8* about the purely homophonic focus D, *Was ist der Mensch* ("What is Man"):

$$
\begin{array}{ccc}
 & \text{D} & \\
\text{BC} & & \text{EF} \\
\text{A 1} & & \text{A 2}
\end{array}
$$

in connection with which the *da capo* part A is also further characterized by a three-tone quasi-*ostinato*.

In the case of No. 4 (p. 23), the German *Magnificat*,[15] Schütz deviated somewhat from the style of scoring in the *Sinf. sacr. II* in that for the violins he substitutes at intervals two violas or trombones, two cornets or trumpets, two recorders, two *cornettini* (soprano cornets). He doubtless indulges in this departure, on the one hand, to bring more variety into the somewhat lengthy composition and, on the other hand — in part at least — in the interest of the textual exposition. Thus in connection with *Er übet Gewalt* ("He showeth strength") there appear the royal trumpets, as in the case of Herod in the *Christmas Oratorio*. To be sure, at *Er stösst die Gewaltigen vom Stuhl* ("He hath put down the mighty from their seats") the small flutes are less fitting than they are for *Er erhöhet die Elenden, die Hungrigen füllet er mit Gütern* ("He hath exalted them of low degree. He hath filled the hungry with good things"), which words, after all, occupy the greater portion of this section.

As already remarked, Schütz omitted the verse *Denn er hat grosse Dinge*, etc. ("For He that is mighty hath done to me great things; and holy is His name"). With regard to this omission Karl Lütge says: "While presumably reasons of structure lie at the basis of this omission — the introductory part would otherwise have become too long, and this textual omission occasions a most insignificant hiatus — one may also recall that Schütz wrote this composition in the midst of the

---

[15] Practical edition by Karl Lütge, Bote and Bock, 1928.

Thirty Years' War (perhaps between 1630 and 1640) and, when confronted by these words, faced a conflict between the most difficult personal experiences and his artistic conscience." The latter consideration would have been absolutely impossible for Schütz. A Schütz who had withheld from God this paean of praise on account of personal misfortunes would have appeared to himself as being in the very clutches of the devil! Certainly here we are confronted solely by architectural considerations. There is also a textual omission in his swan song of 1671. The passage at pp. 23-24:

is a fine confirmation of the fact that progressions in fifths can become absolutely correct if they have proper harmonic supports. Quite similarly in No. 7, at the passage conducted through all the voices:

An indication of bold energy of expression is the c# at

And the playful baroque double echo at *Er lässt die Reichen leer* ("The rich He hath sent empty away") (p. 27):

is apparently presented very seriously to suggest unfilled space. Every mezzo-soprano and (when transposed up to *b* minor) every soprano should sing this superb number. Indeed, a tenor also, Spitta to the contrary notwithstanding, may well sing the piece if one remembers that for Schütz the *Magnificat* was not merely a Mary legend but even more so a liturgical canticle.

Again a canticle, but now the song of praise of Moses (Ex. 15, 2), is No. 5, *Der Herr ist meine Stärke (The Lord Is My Strength)*, with a supplement from Ps. 104: 33. The somewhat fanatical passage, even heightened the second time: [16]

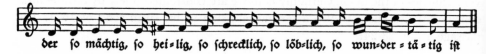

der   fo mächtig, fo hei=lig, fo fchrecklich, fo löb=lich, fo wun=der = tä = tig ift

is characteristic of the piece, which is built up very effectively in three terraces: stratified, as it were, as *secco, accompagnato,* and dance *stretta.*

Nos. 6 and 7 (pp. 34 and 39), *Ich werde nicht sterben (I Shall Not Die But Shall Live),* together constitute a unity. The second part seems to have been composed as an afterthought, as the Kassel manuscript (which, with its strong deviations, indicates an older version) [17] gives only the first part. I have already shown that this composition is apparently Schütz's *Thanksgiving of a Convalescent* of March 1641 after a serious illness. The diversity of the text verses [18] — which, however, are all included in the contents — is welded together by the *non moriar sed vivam* at the beginning of six and the close of seven. It will be recalled that it was with this text that Senfl comforted Luther when he was psychologically so distraught at Coburg at the time of the Diet of Augsburg. W. Schuh, with his tendency to consider Schütz's compositions from the viewpoint of individual sections, probably underestimates the situation when he says: "Scarcely more than a spiritual connection is indicated here, inasmuch as we are confronted merely with reminiscences and not with a form covering both pieces. There can be no question of a recurrence of the chief and opening motive. In the case of Schütz, so far as I see, this formal idea is completely lacking. In the case of his *da capo* types we are confronted throughout primarily with the will for symmetry, a rounding-out, an archform, not with dynamic forms." Granted the predominant staticism of Schütz's architecture, we are nevertheless confronted with much more than mere reminiscences. Thus the opening theme. (See next page.)

---

[16] Ed. also Hohmann, Ansbach.

[17] This older version is distinguished by the following: Before *Aber ich rief* (C major) Schütz had already landed in this tonality, the entrance of which he now introduces more effectively by means of a preceding semicadence; for this *Aber ich rief* he had formerly chosen a leaner motive than the one finally chosen; in the printed version he tightens the conclusion of the *prima pars,* where originally the violins had the last word, to a more concise *tutti.*

[18] Ph. Spitta's derivations are not altogether accurate.

against the beginning of the *coda* with violins:

From here on, however, both sections are identical to the very end, note for note, only strengthened by violins. One can almost discern an artful procedure on the part of Schütz. What he previously presented consecutively as solo and *sinfonia*, he now presents simultaneously in climax — Ossa on Pelion!

The text which Schütz set for the first time at the request of Burckart Grossman at the time of the latter's convalescence now affords ever-new material for the convalescent Schütz himself. The *Stricke des Todes* ("The bonds of death")[19] are embellished with all their windings; the *Angst der Höllen* ("the pains of hell") is portrayed in the bass by the interval f—g#; *Jammer* ("trouble") receives a g minor coloring in the midst of C major. At *Not* ("sorrow") the voice leaps down an effective sixth in connection with a Phrygian change of chord. What baroque restlessness lies in the *presto* at *Ich rief an* ("Then I called") and in the *tarde* at *den Namen des Herrn* ("the name of the Lord")! One feels that these were the years of the first invasion of the *tempo rubato*, as Frescobaldi taught it in Rome for his toccatas, so that soon the Cologne Cathedral organist, Caspar Grieffgens, wrote

---

[19] Compare the passage *Stricken meiner Sünden* in Bach's *St. John Passion* (alto aria, No. 11), which is related in thought but altogether different in stylistic execution.

to the Württemberg Duchess Sybille concerning Froberger, the greatest pupil of
Frescobaldi, that he had learned his *memento mori* from him measure for measure
(grif vor grif), "because he who did not learn the matters from the late Herr Froberger himself could not possibly play with proper discretion." Froberger himself
had been in Dresden in 1649.[20]

Then one must attempt to perceive the symmetry which formulates the next
section into a dramatic dialog:

> *Ich rief an den Namen des Herrn:*
> *O Herr, O Herr, O Herr,*
> *Errette meine Seele, errette meine Seele!*
> *Und der Herr antwort mir,*
> *Und half mir*
> *Aus allen meinen, allen meinen Nöten.*

> I called on the name of the Lord:
> O Lord, O Lord, O Lord,
> Deliver my soul, deliver my soul!
> And the Lord answered me
> And saved me
> From all my, all my troubles.

This makes itself felt each time through the third member by means of the now
suspended, now anticipating steps of eighths. The frequently noted chromatic
mediant modulation produces in the second part, at measures three and four, by
means of a number of repetitions, a strong accentuation of feeling of the diatonic
succession which proceeds but slowly in measures one and two:

The extract from Ps. 103: 2-5 (p. 40), *Lobe den Herrn (Bless the Lord)*, belongs
to the most deeply felt music that Schütz has written. It is a great Hypoaeolian
episode, after which the concluding portion in C Ionian then comes as a sort of
outburst *(Hervorbruch)*.

The eighth *concerto* (Psalm 18: 2-7), for falsetto alto in *a* minor, *Herzlich lieb
(I Will Love Thee, O Lord)* rests in the first of its three subdivisions on a strange
dualism of the motival forms: a static, linear, descending thought and a progres-
sing, angular, expanding one, after which the former concludes in abbreviated

---

[20] As Pirro computes in his *Buxtehude*.

form. This construction is so free and doubtless so unique among the great masters that it is worthwhile adding here this "A, b b b, 2/3 A" theme:

The somewhat more extended countercouplet, strengthened by the addition of the violins, is followed by a *symphonia* as "the conclusion." This *symphonia* confirms the deliberate purpose of the procedure, inasmuch as it is derived from motives which repeat this conflict on a smaller scale (with a directional change of motive A):

A middle portion, constructed tonally within the same frame, *a—a* as the outside wings, proceeds in the *stylo recitativo*. Whatever pre-eminence this section has by reason of the power of its text is counterbalanced, again with violin accompaniment, in the third or closing section, *Wenn mir Angst ist* ("In my distress"), by means of the plasticity of the thought in the melody. But a new antithetical couplet

becomes almost a bit wearisome with its manifold, even though transposed, repetitions.

The same zigzag type of linear formation[21] that formerly evolved on the arsis-thesis melodic line of a darkening sequence of fundamental vowel syllables and is now primarily merely a musical echo also dominates the initial portion of the tenor (baritone!) piece, No. 9 (p. 49), *Frohlocket mit Händen (O Clap Your Hands)*. This composition varies the idea of Nos. 6-7 — "Solo, *Sinfonia*, Combination of Both" to "*Sinfonia*, Solo, Supercoupling with Voice Exchange." No. 9 consists of the first six verses of the Ascension Psalm, 47, which Schütz set nowhere else.[22] It is a fresh, useful piece for this festival.

The *Hymn of Praise*, treated previously on account of its tonal characteristics, No. 10 (p. 54), *Lobet den Herren (Praise Ye the Lord)*,[23] Psalm 150, is a most effective creation; but it demands a virtuoso tenor. As in the polychorus composition of 1619, Schütz knows even in this incomparably more modest creation how to portray with impressive tonal pictures[24] the instruments called for in the text. In so doing he does not merely figure but writes out the organ part fully for "psaltery and harp" — a most unusual procedure. There has been speculation as to the reason for this. To me it seems perfectly clear. Here Schütz has in the organ bass the succession "octave, quint, fundamental" at intervals of half a measure; but he wanted to have the harmony held over, unchanged, in the right hand for the same duration in order that the real "harp motive" might stand out prominently. Accord-

ingly, the figuring $\begin{smallmatrix} 6 \\ 4 \\ \text{g d G} \end{smallmatrix}$ would not have guarded against lively chordal changes in the manual. Thus no other alternative remained for him than the definite notation:

---

[21] Leopold Mozart calls it *anaphora* in his violin school.

[22] Other compositions of this psalm I know only with Latin text *(Omnes gentes plaudite)*, à 4, Eustachius de Monte Regali (Petrucci, 1519); Senfl *(Mü. Stb.*, Ms. 25); de Grandi (Donfried, 1623); A. Rigatti, 1654; anon., 1562 (Manuscript Breslau 92 E); à 5, Stoltzer (Petrejus, 1538); Senfl (Mü. 25); à 6, Massaini (Zwickau Manuscript LXXIV); à 8, Lupi, 1580 (Breslau 18); Massaino (Lindner, 1585); H. L. Hassler (Breslau 20); H. Praetorius (ibid.); Bagni (ibid.); Balbi (ibid.); Steuccius, 1618 (Bodenschatz); anon., 1651 (Zwickau XCVII); à 16, G. Gabrieli (Breslau 21); with continuo, à 2: anon. (Breslau 46); à 3, Scacchi, 1650 (Breslau 197); Montano (Victorinus, 1616); à 4, G. F. Capella (Donfried, 1627); à 5, R. de Lassus *(Philomela)*.

[23] Practical edition and piano reduction by G. F. Walter (his own publication, 1920).

[24] That the use of several successive instrumental groups is intended here, even though not definitely specified, follows from the use of two alto clefs at the passage *Lobet den Herrn mit Posaunen*, for which there is no occasion for higher pitch; in connection with this one is amazed at the mobility demanded from the slide trombone at this time.

A procedure exactly like this confronts us in the notated passage of the closing *concerto,* No. 27, on page 184. The four eighth-note groups are not to be individually harmonized but merely constitute figurations beneath sustained harmonies. Conclusions from such examples that Schütz "regularly indicated his thorough bass in this primitive manner" are in no wise justified. We might much rather conclude the very opposite, as we are here manifestly concerned with a definite exception. The octave organ points (in No. 10) at *Pauken,* (p. 57), the agitated tremolo at *Cymbalen* (p. 58), the filigree work at the *Alleluia* (p. 59), which probably demands the phrasing[25]

are very fascinating. The confirmatory and at the same time further modulatory instrumental refrains at the subdivisions of the expanded A—A—B *Bar* (Schuh, p. 103), which, stemming from the double-chorus technique, overlap with artistic interlacing, delighted Hugo Riemann, who introduces a detailed analysis of this particular composition with the significant words:[26] "The composition perhaps shows Schütz's style at the pinnacle of its development, at least with regard to that which distinguishes him from Gabrieli and gives him his importance for further development. Doubtless a number of his polychoral works in the *Psalms*

---

[25] H. Riemann errs when he thinks he finds this motive for ten measures in the second place in the *Sinfonia.*

[26] *Handbuch der Musikgeschichte,* II, 3 (1913), pp. 16 f.

of 1619 or the *Symphoniae sacrae III,* with their rich apparatus, are more grandiose and more imposing. But exactly the manner in which here, with modest means, he knows how to achieve such rich effects exalts him without any doubt above all his contemporaries, such as Giovanni Rovetta and Francesco Cavalli, the two famous pupils of Monteverdi and his successors as Kapellmeisters at San Marco. Although in Schütz we also occasionally find Monteverdi's mannerism of bringing lengthy series of measures in transpositions, this nevertheless does not manifest itself in so unconcealed and bald a form as in the case of Rovetta and Cavalli *(Musiche sacre,* 1656). The general development is essentially freer and is designed more along great lines, not welded together in mosaic fashion. The motives used are taken throughout from the voice parts, but they reach their full significance only in the instrumental parts . . . ."

We now come to two highly significant New Testament bass solo compositions (XI and XII). The first, *Hütet euch (And Take Heed to Yourselves),* a Gospel address from Luke 21: 34-36, had better be transposed from *d* minor to *e* or *f* minor. The second, the *Canticum Simeonis* for Christof Cornett, had also better be transposed from *g* minor to *b* minor. No. XI (p. 60) has a gloomy, threatening mood which receives a wild chiliastic expression through the furiously rapid *parlando* in sixteenth-note syllables *und komme dieser Tag schnell über euch* ("and so that day come upon you unawares") — the severe Christ of the Byzantine mosaics.

The second composition (Luke 2: 29-32, p. 65) fascinates by reason of its fantastically extravagant melismas on *fahren* ("depart hence") and *allen Völkern* ("all Thy people") because of the intensive chromaticism of the *wie du gesagt hast* ("as Thou has promised"), and because of the fervent fourth-interval motive in eighth notes, *welchen du bereitet hast* ("which Thou hast prepared for us"). At almost the same time Franz Tunder in Lübeck undertook similar things *(DTD,* III, 22).

To what extent in Schütz the 3/1 designation has to do with a rapid tempo rather than with thematic formation (even though, to be sure, the whole must add up to a three-part reckoning) is clearly shown by both of these compositions. In the first there is a second motive group:

So seid nun wacker al = le = zeit,   so seid nun wacker al = le = zeit

in which doubtless, when viewed purely musically, the triple rhythm does lurk in a dancelike manner, but in which, on the other hand, according to the word accent and the melody formation resulting therefrom as well as according to the imitational intertwinings of the violin voices, the two-part time decidedly predominates:

The pauses in square brackets are the remaining surplus beats (*Zählzeiten*), in order that $4 \times 2 + 1 = 3 \times 3 = 9$ results! Soon thereafter genuine triple motives enter, expressly designated *presto* (i. e., "still faster"!), like the following, which is to be given in a blood-drawing *portato*:

Similarly, in the next work, *Herr, nun lässest du (Lord, Now Lettest Thou)*, the passage:

Licht, zu er = leuch=ten die Hei - = den

We come to the group of duets! No. 13, on Ps. 42: 11, *Was betrübst du dich (Why Art Thou Cast Down)* (p. 69),[27] is for two sopranos or tenors. Here the master shows decided "instrumentation instinct" in that, after an impressive trio prelude, he has the strings sustain only *submisse*, that is, "softly," deep-lying fundamental chords for the first voice, while then for the second voice, now in duet setting, the violins proceed *fortiter* into the upper octave. The way in which he places a *d* minor surface alongside a B flat one sounds remarkably romantic, and in the "restlessness" of the conclusion baroque and romanticism meet in the common dynamic principle: not the "being" of the Eleatics but the "becoming" of Heraclitus! So, then, also the very brief return of the beginning, *Was betrübst du dich, meine Seele*, at the close (without an intervening section) is most certainly a spontaneous and outspoken poetic and atmospheric reminiscence which, by means of the twice-repeated modulation in the circle of thirds, takes on a Schumannesque dreaminess. The question on the semicadence confirms this still more:

(und mein Gott ist.) Was be = trübst du dich? Was be=trübst du dich, was be=
trübst du dich, mei = ne See - - le

Next, with the same scoring (Nos. 14-15, in g minor, pp. 77 and 83), is a two-strophe church hymn setting on the *antiphona pro pace* with Luther's text, *Verleih uns Frieden gnädiglich / Gib unsern Fürsten (Lord God in Mercy Grant us Peace /*

---

[27] Easily available in Dittberner's collection as a piano reduction.

Grant unto Our Rulers).[28] Schütz set this text also in the *Mühlhäuser Kurfürsten-konzert* and later in the *Chormusik* as a New Year motet. In Part One lines one to three of the church melody are presented verbatim. The first line is given in the first discant, then in the second; then, after free interpolations in the lower plagal, the second and third lines are presented in the first, then in the second soprano. The word *streiten,* however, without *obbligo,* is reminiscent of the *stile concitato*

The little violin fanfare also manifestly leans on the corresponding chorale line:

In the lowest part there are *ostinato* elements. The second part (No. 15, p. 83), in which the theme

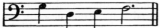

plays a noteworthy part as *basso quasi ostinato,* begins surprisingly in the opening line in free style but then flows at once into the old melody, which, exclusively and unchanged, does service for the further melodic invention. Again we have (a year before the Congress of Münster and Osnabrück!) a passionate plea for peace. Above and beyond the numerous interpolations there is a passionate tension that calls to mind the concept of a Bruckner *Pausensinfonie (Symphony of Pauses).* The numerous halvings of the syllables *(es ist doch ja kein andrer nicht, Gib unsern Fürsten);* also in No. 23 *(Alle, alle Völker)* remind one of Beethoven's *O namen-, namenlose Freude.* Schütz shares with him the "German" *Rutztypus,* even though ostensibly not the *Beckingkurve* (Becking curve).[29] The wish for a "peaceful and quiet life" *(ein geruhig und stilles Leben)* is emphasized each time through the indicated *piano.* One senses Schütz's personal longing for the creative solitude in Weissenfels which "prince and authority" should obtain for him.

No. 16, Ps. 68: 1-3, p. 87, *Es steh Gott auf (Let God Arise),* is the composition in which Schütz, as an act of obeisance to Monteverdi, uses the latter's secular thorough bass duet for tenors, *Armato il cor,* from the *Scherzi musicali* of 1632. The relation of the two pieces, which can easily be observed from Spitta's reprint

---

[28] Individual edition in the *Handbuch der Ev. Kirchenmusik (Geistl. Konz. No. 6),* Vandenhoeck and Ruprecht (Göttingen, 1947). *MGkK,* 21 (1916), pp. 97-108, 237-248.
[29] N. Danckert, *Ursymbole melodischer Gestaltung (Primal Symbols of Melodic Formation),* Bärenreiter-Verlag, 1932; R. Steglich, *J. S. Bach* (1935), pp. 52 f.

of the Monteverdi setting in the appendix, is rather free, somewhat as in the case of Gabrieli's *Lieto godea* (not to be compared with the close dependence in the case of Grandi's *Lilia convallium*). One can say that by adding the very lively instrumental parts Schütz essentially overtrumped his model in the manner of the *stile concitato*. Or, as W. Kreidler (loc. cit., p. 130) expresses it:

"This case is remarkable not only in the fact that Schütz here aligns himself with the *stile concitato* but that in this work he at the same time shows the most ingenious demonstration this has received. Schütz not only presents a personal acknowledgment of Monteverdi but, beyond this, the possibilities of expression which he sees in the *stile concitato*. He clearly shows the profounder significance he detects in this technique." There "is revealed the fact that in this piece Schütz has found the most far-reaching adaptation of Monteverdi's *stile concitato*. He subordinates himself in order to be merged completely in Monteverdi's style — another indication of his superiority to all technical restraints. Thus one sees here in fact all the characteristics of the *stile concitato* in pure form without any clouding by personal formative tendencies. For the first time we meet the foundation chord sustained through many measures, the 'fast-nailed' harmony, which regularly, at the end of long climactic waves, is terminated by V-I cadences. The driving power of the climaxes and the anticlimaxes lies, as with Monteverdi, in the chordal shift of position. In measures four and five the typical rest technique *(Pausentechnik)* of the *stile concitato* shows itself. The melody, with syllabic setting, consists throughout of triadic motives which are characterized by numerous repeated notes. From measure seventeen on, at the climax of the development so far, the *ostinato* repeated 'g' appears, which is formed by a crossing of all four voices. In the case of the melismatic formations we frequently have the coupling of thirds. . . . the dotted rhythms, numerous runs, and closely conducted imitations here, too, point directly to the faithful picture of the *stile concitato*."

Under the impelling impression of the text an altogether free, powerful piece flowed from Schütz's pen in its further course, for which, in the third (closing) section, *Aber die Gerechten* ("But let the righteous") (p. 93), Monteverdi's *Zefiro torna* provided essentially only the *ciacona* theme. The middle portion. *Für ihn fliessen* ("for him flow"), consists of four parts which each time present the structure: text-interlude-text.[30]

The position of this composition is very significant in contrast to the preceding prayer for peace. It is a religious battle piece with scarcely an equal. One might say that Schütz mirrors the fate of his time with the desire for peace in one's heart while being pursued by the fanaticism of the most terrible of all religious wars.

When we find now in immediate juxtaposition a soprano-alto duet on the Sirach (Ecclesiasticus) passage 32: 6, *Wie ein Rubin* ("As a ruby"), there doubtless existed for Schütz and his readers something not noted before — the connection with *(Gedankenbrücke)* Monteverdi. For the latter's *basso continuo* madrigal *(concertato nel clavicembalo)*, *Una Donna fra l'altre*,[31] was popular in Germany with the text

---

[30] Schuh, p. 103.

[31] From the sixth madrigal book (1614) published earlier in Latin as *Una es* in Coppini's collection *Il terzo libro della musica di Cl. Monteverdi* (Milan, 1609).

Wie ein Rubin. This is shown by the old Lüneburg choral catalog, which notes the piece as "*à 4:* C C A T (E major)." I found it in the Pirna Manuscript 8. The bass is missing.

Despite its Biblical original this text as well as that of the next composition inspired some jolly table music in praise of song and wine. Schütz extracted from it a most remarkable effect. As new lights ever appear when the facets of a polished gem are revolved, so Schütz, with the help of a quiet bass scale, rapidly turns the tonality from C to G to D to A and then again by way of *d* to F and down to *g*, and thus ever again with variations, while the violins follow along with sportive, teasing motives.

The soprano-bass duet, from Eccl. 9: 7, *Iss dein Brot mit Freuden (Eat Thy Bread in Gladness),* issues from the same bucolic spirit. Both this and the preceding composition have in common the idyllic figure motive

which in the *stretto* portion is transformed into the theme (here noted in shorter time values):

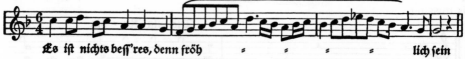

The exuberant *Ich lobe die Freude* ("Then I commended mirth") should be well noted in connection with drawing a portrait of Schütz, lest his picture be distorted into that of constant gloom. The man who at fifty composed the most charming scenes from the Song of Songs and at sixty wrote these jolly pieces, who reports so amusingly about the tipsiness of his best bass, and who probably illustrated so many bacchantic scenes in his lost opera scores was surely not a sour-tempered kill-joy.

In No. 19, Ps. 27: 1-3, 5, 6, *Der Herr ist mein Licht und mein Heil (The Lord Is My Light and My Salvation),*[32] for two tenors,[33] the role of the violins in the ensemble can almost be designated as the antiphonal technique of two duet groups. In the middle sections Schütz's trust in God *wenn sich Krieg wider mich erhebt* ("though war should rise against me") expresses itself powerfully. As in the *Sinfoniae sacrae II,* Schütz likes to take a thought drawn first from the meaning of the text and then develop it once more purely musically, so here again he uses this pendulum of the circle of fifths as found in the "ruby" composition in cupola-arched bass passages. In the "ruby" composition, No. 17, incidentally, it is very characteristic of the energetic swing of the whole that Schütz omitted the one "placid" verse, *Eins bitte ich vom Herrn* ("One thing have I desired of the Lord"). The cadences of the division are: ⌐G—C, G—G⌐ ⌐G—C, G—G⌐ G—G, which corresponds to a *Grossbar.*

Just as *Drei schöne Dinge (Three Lovely Things There Are),* No. 25, p. 155, is set as a terzet, so it is a matter of course that, according to the old number symbolism, *Zweierlei bitte ich (Two Things Have I Required of Thee),* No. 20, for two tenors,[34] Prov. 30: 7-9, should be scored as a duet. Both pieces doubtless were not intended primarily for church use but could rather be titled *Schütz's Domestic and Life Wisdom.* How sharply the *verleugnen* ("deny Thee") and the

---

[32] To be found also in Dittberner's collection. But a piano reduction, of course, misses the situation noted above. Furthermore, Dittberner has omitted the entire middle sections also referred to above.

[33] Latin settings *(Dominus illuminatio mea):* à 4, Senfl (Manuscript Munich *Stb.* 25); anon. (ibid. 26); anon. Montanus, 1553; *à 7,* Chr. Erbach (Schadaeus, 1611); with continuo, *à 4,* Or. Tarditi (Profe, 1641).

[34] Schuh, p. 101, reports on the fourfold division of the piece.

Spötterrede ("vanity and lies") are etched, and how the secrecy of the *Stehlen* ("stealing") is branded until the circle of the whole work is closed by means of the repetition of the opening part!

Next we have two powerful duets for two basses.[35] From this genre there was later to emerge *Der Herr ist der starke Held (The Lord Is a Mighty Hero)* in Handel's *Israel in Egypt*. What singers Schütz must have had at his disposal for such songs! They have a range of more than two octaves!

No. 21, Ps. 144: 5-7 and 9, *Herr, neige deine Himmel (Bow Thy Heavens, O Lord)*, of which a preliminary version, not yet so tightly woven, exists in Kassel, had today better be transposed to *b—e* minor from *a—d* minor. Sufficient has been said above with regard to the tonal peculiarities of the piece. From the connections *(Bindungsformen)* and directions which the passages take *(Passagen-richtungen)* in this number one could deduce a whole theory of pictures of movement in their extent from high to low, for which the text here provides an occasion in almost every word; even the ten strings of the psaltery have ten notes for the word "ten."

A similar showpiece of tonally jovial chamber music and textual musical space measurement is No. 22 (p. 134), which had better be transposed from F to A. It is based on Ps. 113: 2-9, *Vom Anfang der Sonnen bis zu ihrem Niedergang (From the Rising of the Sun unto the Going Down of the Same)*. Verse three, so well adapted to the arched form, is placed at the beginning. The number of older settings is large because of the musical adaptability of the psalm.[36] The motive which rises in triads to the octave and then sinks stepwise occurs here again and again with a repeatedly changing text. But beside it we have forceful separate themes, such as:

und er = hö = het, er = hö = het den Ar = men aus dem Roth

[35] Tob. Michael, in 1637, in the second part of his *Mus. Seelenlust,* had already written for this scoring; but his composition cannot even distantly be compared with Schütz's piece, as one can convince oneself from the reprint in R. Wustmann, *MG., Leipzig,* I, 451 ff.

[36] German: *Lobet, ihr Knechte, à 8,* Vecchi; *à 10,* A. Haeckelshoven in Breslau Manuscript; Latin: *Laudate pueri, à 4,* Isaac (Munich *Staatsbibl.* Manuscript 29); Josquin (Montanus, 1553); anon. Rhaw, 1538 and Petrejus, 1539; Johs. Walter (Rhaw, 1540); Unterholtzer (Petrejus, 1542); *à 5,* Heugel (Ott, 1537); Berchem and Willaert (Gardane, 1550); Vinders (Susato, 1557); anon. (Breslau 103 & 108); *à 6,* Demantius (Breslau, 105); Fr. Regnart, 1590; Nucius (Breslau 12); *à 7,* Lasso; *à 8,* Hassler (Zwickau, LXXIV); Anerio (Conforti, 1592); *à 9,* Fritsch (Breslau 21); *à 10,* Selich; with continuo, *à 2,* Cima (Lucino, 1608); *à 3,* Binago (Victorinus, 1616); Prenatale (Breslau, 49); Tarditi, Profe, 1642); *à 4,* Viadana (Donfried, 1622); Sabbatino, Rovetta, Rigotti, and Merulo (ibid. 46); *à 5,* Cazzati (Profe, 1646); *à 6,* S. Vesi (Havemann, 1659); *à 6,* Rovetta (Profe, 1646); *à 8,* Nanino (Constantini, 1620).

In the great *presto* conclusion the 9/1-6/1 measure is not to be construed as three-part but is rather to be mastered through subordinate straight time, at best with an elastic *(schwebend)* prose accent of the theme

Finally, there are five pieces for three voices!

In the case of the first terzet (XXIII, p. 142), Psalm 117, *Lobet den Herrn, alle Heiden (O Praise the Lord, All Ye Nations)*, W. Schuh (p. 104) noted its "strongly motetlike nature." I would like to go a step farther and assume that, as a matter of fact, the piece was originally a five-voice motet in which Schütz subsequently gave the discant parts, with a few octave transpositions, to the violins. Here everything is completely word-engendered.

In the case of No. 24 (p. 148) the situation is somewhat different. Here the three male voices — alto, tenor, and bass — after a solo beginning *Die so ihr den Herrn fürchtet* ("Ye that fear the Lord"), Ecclus. 2: 7, form a closed group over the continuo and are interrupted in the middle by a genuinely instrumental *ritornello*. Where the violins enter in the concluding part in a concertizing manner, they again unite with the voices to form a highly unified quintet.

While these two compositions, with their more objective character, create the impression that they were written at an earlier time, No. 25 (p. 155), for bass and two tenors, *Drei schöne Dinge sind (Three Lovely Things There Are)*, creates the impression of being a very personal work and one of later origin. With evident satisfaction the master, who was well grounded in the Bible, chose and put together six passages from the Old and the New Testament. The work is apparently intended for the double wedding of two brothers who seem to have wooed their brides because of faithful neighborliness. Perhaps a Dresden or Leipzig antiquarian will at some time disclose the occasion for the composition.

We spoke above of the number symbolism of the scoring. The thought can be further pursued through the entire work: the compressed simple terzet leading at *Wann Brüder eins sind* ("when brothers") and *einträglich bei einander wohnen* ("live together in unity") (p. 156); then the duets at *beide, Gott und Menschen* ("both to God and mortals") (p. 155); a deep and a high voice answering each other at *wenn Mann — und Weib* ("when man" — "and wife"); then, of course,

the flowing down of the balsam (p. 156); and finally the gratifying return of the
beginning with a new *Bar coda* (A A B) after the text refrain had twice interpolated itself in *rondo* manner with a vigorous variation. Here, too, we feel the
pleasure of the creative urge.

In No. 26 there unfolds itself a large church-hymn setting for two sopranos and
bass, *Von Gott will ich nicht lassen (From God I'll Not Be Parted)*. Ludwig Helm-
bold's hymn was associated (Erfurt, 1572) with an originally secular tune. Since
the opening couplet variants in Schütz's piece can be found here and there in
congregational use a little later (Zahn, 5264b), it would seem fair to assume that
the remaining lines did not originate with the master either. He brings in the
original form of the closing line in strophe two and uses it extensively as the theme
in strophe three. Again, as in the case of *Ich hab mein Sach*,[37] the entire hymn has
been set. This time the strophic chain is ingeniously organized in that, after a
longer *symphonia*, strophes one, two, and three are separated by little instrumental
ritornelles; then, however, stanzas three, four, five, six, eight, and nine are combined into three double strophes without interludes between the individual stanzas. However, the ritornelles between four and five, between six and seven, and
between seven and eight receive special weight: the one between four and five by
means of the energetic leaps of sevenths in the bass; the one between six and seven
by the tremolo of the violins; and the one between seven and eight by the pictorial
passages at *Irrens* ("erring") (p. 175) and the early entrance, after one strophe.
Two *ostinati* provide the chief cement for the variation cycle: the one is the accompanying voice to the soprano entrance and recurs three times after being introduced in a prevariant and original form in the *symphonia*:

Much more important is the other *ostinato*, which is derived from the second
half of the first as well as from the opening line of the hymn. One should note again
the three "successive parallel fifths":

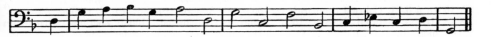

---

[37] Vol. VI, No. 24.

Altogether this second *ostinato* appears fourteen times with only minor deviations and most noticeably also contributes to *(speist)* the instrumental interludes which are so apparently different from one another. In general the middle strophes move quite freely above this representative of the chorale idea. In strophe eight one feels the rhythmic and metrical return to the church hymn. In the concluding strophe the original melody dominates and does not return to the second *ostinato* until the *coda*.

The *tremulus* (on p. 168) is to be carefully distinguished from the *tremolant* of the next piece. It is no modern rapid improvisational tremolo hither and thither, as Monteverdi invented it as "numerous *Pyrrichien*" for depicting the trampling of horses in battle, but a light *portato* (four quavers *[Flocken]* under one stroke of the bow) to paint the ethereal path of the soul to Abraham's bosom. Ph. Spitta pointed out (Preface, p. 21) the imitation of the underlying thought which occurs in Buxtehude's soprano cantata *Herzlich lieb* in connection with "Ah, Lord, let Thy dear angel bear my soul when from this world I fare straight forth to Abraham's bosom." The piece, which, with its friendly eighth-note syllabification, should be rendered quite fluently, shows in the music an abundance of textual reflections which will be evident to sympathetic interpreters and listeners.

Finally, the concluding composition, published by H. Birtner (Bärenreiter edition 631), Ps. 33: 1-3, *Freuet euch des Herrn, ihr Gerechten (Rejoice in the Lord, O Ye Righteous)*, for alto, tenor, and bass,[38] which again evokes all possible brilliance from this scoring. A veritably playful freedom disports itself with delight in the first great section (A B B), where the *Freuet euch* ("Rejoice") again and again rushes ecstatically from the depths to the height by repeatedly forming irregular measure periods through now shorter, now longer instrumental reminiscences or anticipations. Then the thrice repeated, temperamental surprise of a choral intonation, *Singet, singet dem Herrn*, which the first two times evokes the magical effect of double-stop violin *tremoli* (perhaps *ondeggiando* and to be played in simplified one-voiced "hither and thither," which was also permitted by Schütz). While they mark the peaks of the opening lines *(Stollenspitzen)* of a *Grossbar*, the third intonation, presented mensurally by the alto, gives the climax

---

[38] It is striking that this jubilation psalm has played a role in figural music only since the days of the Gabrielis. Latin: *Exultate justi*, à 5, Fr. Regnart (1590); à 6, S. Ertel (Manuscript Breslau 29, 1631); à 8, A. Gabrieli (Bodenschatz, 1603); Bl. Ammon (Breslau, 15); J. Gallus (Zwickau, LXXXVII); G. Gabrieli (Hassler, 1600); Dulichius (Bodenschatz, 1603); Zucchini (Schadaeus, 1611); anon. Breslau, 29; à 10, A. Gabrieli (Lindner, 1588); à 16, Hassler (Gruber, 1615); with continuo, à 2, G. de Civita (Donfried, 1622); Banchieri (Victorinus, 1616); à 4, Viadana, à 5, Grandi *(Symbola*, 1626). German: à 9, Seelich, 1624; à 9-18, J. H. Schein (Breslau, 200).

of the conclusion *(Abgesangsspitze)*, the chief theme of which is a tumultuous alleluia quintet.

Thus the second volume of the *Symphoniae sacrae* reveals itself as an entire cosmos of scintillating and spirited music with extensive variety and charged with deep personal feeling — a wonder garden of art, now seriously religious, now joyously half-secular. After perusing the work one can well understand how ten years later the Silesian Elias Nathusius,[39] as cantor of St. Nicholas at Leipzig, gave our master the illustrious designation "father of our modern music."

---

[39] A. Schering, *Musikgeschichte v. Leipzig*, II, 144.

Miscellaneous Gospel Settings

It is striking that Schütz, the Christian Asaph of the Psalms, wrote the greater part of his Gospel settings in later life — apparently an indication of his turning toward a Christological ideal of piety and to the special needs of the evangelical liturgy in general. Since I have treated the history of this category of motets and concerted vocal works in an entire volume,[1] I may summarize briefly here.

Since the thirteenth century the liturgical chants of the church have always tended to present the Gospel in a rich and solemn manner (Council of Grado). In the fourteenth century these readings are set in two- or three-voice arrangements, a moving example of which is afforded by the *pulchrum evangelium* on Luke 10: 38-42, ca. 1417 (Manuscript Breslau, U-B., I 4° 466), printed in Johs. Wolf, *Alte Sing- und Spielmusik* (pp. 1 ff). At the end of every sentence the chant becomes *organum* polyphony. From this practice there then branches off the dramatic and then the motet passion, which reaches its first classical example in Obrecht ca. 1500,[2] while the polyphonic settings of Old Testament readings, such as the laments of Jacob, David, and Job, become a chief field for the *musica riservata* of Josquin.

Many narrative sections of the New Testament are set polyphonically as responses, a chief exponent of this being B. Resinarius with his two-volume series for the year: 118 numbers for four voices, published by Rhaw in 1543. In Rhaw's publica-

---

[1] *Die mehrstimmige Vertonung des Evangeliums,* 1. Bd. *Geschichtliche Darstellung* (B & H, 1931); of Vol. 2 (*Partitursammlung, Scores*) there has appeared so far only Brochure I, L. Päminger, *Maria Magdalena et altera Maria* (1935). Though O. Ursprung (*Acta musicol.,* VI, Brochure II) may be correct with regard to the Catholic liturgy when he denies that the Gospel motet could have taken the place of the Gospel lesson, it is nevertheless questionable to me whether his rejection of this custom is also valid with regard to the Protestant Church, because as early as 1539 Johs. Galliculus, through Rhaw, polyphonized the entire lesson, including *Dominus vobis-cum-Et cum spiritu tuo-Sequentia Scti. Evangelii,* etc., in the Mass between the sequence and the *Sanctus,* and countless polyphonically treated text passages would have no sense as independent motets without textual environment. Nevertheless, this type would not lose much in importance if it had been performed only as a motet between the lesson and the sermon. At all events, in the sixteenth-eighteenth century it belonged among the most important *de tempore* pieces of the evangelical chief service, as proved by the numerous special prints. One should also remember that at that time music was performed either at, or immediately alongside, the altar.

[2] The passion of Longheval (reprinted in *Evangelienvertonung,* I, 12 ff.) is identical with this. It was a novelty in Rome when in 1499 three priests "in Spanish manner" presented the passion song in three parts, at four points in the Gospel story (A. Schering in the *Johs. Wolf-Festschrift,* 1929, p. 173).

tion of the Offices, which so peculiarly amalgamate the ordinary and the proper into a mixed form of polyphonic missal and gradual, we then meet gospels by Resinarius, Lupi, Morales, and Galliculus, which carry the lection tone through as *cantus firmus*.[3] There are others by Bruck, Isaac, and Josquin. Dulichius and Demantius have given in polyphonic settings, as a supplement to their Gospel settings, the prefaces that remain unchanged. This, too, speaks for their liturgical function and not for their use merely as a motet. Inasmuch as a large number of evangelical church orders provide for a double reading of the Gospel (first sung solemnly in Latin from the altar, then read in German from the pulpit for the common man), the polyphonic settings, which also on Lutheran grounds used the church language almost exclusively until toward 1590 and in at least half of the cases until 1620, will have been intended for the Latin presentation.

In comparison with fifteen Gospel motets of Lassus and more numerous individual works by Clemens non Papa (which are found with settings by other composers in the Nuremberg collection of Gospels, consisting of several volumes), published by Johs. Montanus (1554-56), we then find whole series of gospels for the year by individual masters: 1565, Homer Herpol; 1573 ff., L. Päminger; 1584 and 1590, Johs. Wanning; 1586-90, J. Handl; 1594-95 (German), Raselius; 1595 and 1599 *(bicinia)*, Seth Calvisius; 1599-1600 *(Novum opus)*, Philipp Dulichius; 1601 *(bicinia)* and 1604 *(à 4-8)*, Georg Otto; 1610, Chr. Demantius *(Corona harmonica)*; 1616-21, Th. Elsbeth (German); 1619, M. Vulpius (German); thereto 1625, a third part by Johs. Christenius; 1623, M. Franck *(Gemmulae evangeliorum)*. Since the motet collection of Ott of 1537, which provided the foundation for the Gospel prints of Montanus, these works are for the most part called *Novum opus musicum*.

One branch at ca. 1606 passes from the Gospel motet[4] to the liturgical oratorio,[5] while another leads to the cantata, for which, after Schütz's examples, the numerous instances by A. Hammerschmidt, K. W. Briegel, and J. R. Ahle provide ample evidence. In contrast to the greater strictness of Schütz they relax and transform

---

[3] The Catholic clergyman Eisenring, in *Zur Geschichte des mehrstimmigen Proprium Missae (Veröffentlichungen der greg. Akad. Freiburg,* Switzerland, ed. by Peter Wagner), p. 118, calls these *evangelia* a "substitute for the omitted offertory"; this, too, O. Ursprung should bear in mind.

[4] I present here some supplements to that book: p. 20a: *In convertendo Dominus* is not a Gospel, but the beginning of Psalm 125 (126); p. 39a, *Christmas Gospels*, supplement, Martin Mayer, 1678, for S A, 2 vlns., organ (published by Fr. Koschinsky, Breslau, 1931); p. 40a, supplement for Epiphany, Matt. 2:1-12; p. 41a, Hassler's 16-voice *Nuptiae factae sunt*, reprinted in DTD, II, 173 ff. P. 44b: to B. Musculus read: *40 schöne geistliche Gesänglein*, 1597. P. 51b: *O Jesu, fili David*, by Josquin = *Wolauff gut gsell von hinnen* (by Isaac, DTOe, XIV 2, No. 40).

[5] Which was demonstrated above both by the *Zacchaeus* and the *Baptist History* of Daniel Bollius and by the *Father Abraham* of Schütz.

the Biblical text step by step even to the point of a madrigal libretto. Finally, the complete Gospel sets for the year by J. Casp. Horn (Dresden and Pirna, 1680), by Petzel (lost), and twenty pieces by W. Brückner represented the last attempt to restore the Bible text. But the madrigal tendency is finally victorious and flows by way of Erdmann Neumeister (1700) into the Gospel cantatas of J. S. Bach.

The list of Gospel settings by Schütz may be repeated here briefly with some additions in order to make available a survey of the impressive collection and at the same time to give a reference to the *de tempore* use:

Ach Herr, du Sohn Davids (O Lord, Thou Son of David), à 6, Matthew 15, *Reminiscere*, published by me for the first time in the *ZfMW*, XVII, 1935; cf. the chapter *Oratorienhafte Einzelwerke* ("Oratoriolike Individual Works").

Also hat Gott die Welt geliebet (God So Loved the World), John 3, Pentecost and Advent, VIII, 53.

Auf dem Gebirge hat man (In Rama Was There a Voice Heard), Matthew 2, Sunday after New Year, VIII, 177.

Das Wort ward Fleisch (The Word Was Made Flesh), John 1, Christmas, VIII, 89.

Du Schalksknecht (O Thou Wicked Servant), Matthew 18, 22nd after Trinity, VII, 184.

Entsetzet euch nicht (Be Not Affrighted), Mark 16 : 6, Easter (Catalog Kassel).

Es begab sich aber (And It Came to Pass), Luke 2 = *Weihnachtsoratorium* I, 165; XVII.

Es erhob sich ein Streit (And There Was War in Heaven), Revelation 12, Feast of St. Michael, XVIII (and Latin, Lüneburg).

Es ging ein Sämann aus (A Sower Went Forth to Sow His Seed), Luke 8, *Sexagesima*, XI, 3.

Es gingen zween Menschen (Two Men Went Up into the Temple to Pray), Luke 18, 11th after Trinity, XIV, 55.

Es sei denn eure Gerechtigkeit (Except Your Righteousness Shall Exceed), Matthew 5, 6th after Trinity, à 8 (Catalog Naumburg).

Freuet euch mit mir (Rejoice with Me), Luke 15, ed. by H. Engel.

Herr, nun lässest du (Canticum Simeonis), Circumcision, VII, 65; XII, 104; XII, 201, 204.

Hütet euch, daß eure Herzen (Settle It, Therefore, in Your Hearts), Luke 21, 2nd Advent, VII, 60; XI, 75.

Herr, komm herab (Sir, Come Down), John 4, 21st after Trinity (Kassel, Naumburg, à 9); scarcely the same as the anon. cantata à 9 in the collection of Hermann Koch (Berlin *Singakademie*), I, 8.

Ich bin ein rechter Weinstock (I Am the True Vine), John 15. Between Epiphany and Easter or Whitsuntide, VIII, 130.

Jesus trat ein in ein Schiff (And When He Was Entered into a Ship), Matt. 8 : 23, 4th after Trinity, à 8 (Naumburg).

Joseph, du Sohn Davids (Joseph, Thou Son of David), Matthew 1, Sunday after Christmas, VI, 133.

Lobsinget Gott, ihr Männer (Praise God, Ye Men), Acts 1, Ascension (Lüneburg).

Mein Freund, ich tu dir nicht unrecht (Friend, I Do Thee No Wrong), Matthew 20, à 6, *Septuagesima* (Weimar).

Mein Sohn, warum (Son, Why Hast Thou Thus Dealt with Us?), Luke 2, 1st Sunday after Epiphany, X, 42.

Meister, wir haben die ganze Nacht (Master, We Have Toiled All the Night), Luke 5, 5th after Trinity, VI, 119; à 8, Catalog Naumburg.

Meister, wir wissen, daß du wahrhaftig bist (Master, We Know That Thou Art True), Matthew 22, 23d after Trinity, XI, 86.

Pater Abraham (Father Abraham), Luke 16, 1st after Trinity, XVIII, 37.

Saget den Gästen (Say to Them That Are Bidden), Matthew 22, 20th after Trinity, XIV, 43.

Sammelt zuvor das Unkraut (Gather Ye Together First the Tares), Matthew 13, 5th after Epiphany, VIII, 36.

Saul, Saul, was verfolgst du mich? (Saul, Saul, Why Persecutest Thou Me?), Acts 9, Conversion of Paul, XI, 99.

Sehet an den Feigenbaum (Behold the Fig Tree), Luke 21, 2d Advent, VIII, 163.
Seid barmherzig (Be Ye Therefore Merciful), Luke 6, 4th after Trinity, XI, 25.
Sei gegrüßet, Maria (Hail, Mary), Luke 2, Visitation of Mary, VI, 185.
Sicut Moses serpentem (For as Moses Lifted Up the Serpent), John 3, Trinity, IV, 56.
Siehe, dieser wird gesetzt zu einem Fall (Behold, This Child Is Set for the Fall and Rising),
   Luke 2, Sunday after New Year, XI, 39.
Siehe, es erschien der Engel (Behold, the Angel of the Lord Appeareth to Joseph), Matthew 2,
   Sunday after Christmas, X, 58.
Venite ad me omnes (Come unto Me, All Ye That Labor), Matthew 11, St. Matthew's Day, V, 25.
Verbum caro factum est (The Word Was Made Flesh), John 1, Christmas, VI, III.
Viel werden kommen (Many Shall Come), Matthew 8, Epiphany, VIII, 32.
Weib, was weinest du? (Woman, Why Weepest Thou?), John 20, Easter, XVIII, 60.

Of these forty-one pieces on texts from the Gospels (not counting the passions, the *History of the Resurrection*, and the *Seven Last Words*) thirty-five have probably been preserved, while six have been lost. Presumably the number originally was considerably greater. Therefore despite the most diverse scoring not much was lacking for a complete yearly Gospel cycle by Schütz.

Ten compositions are to be found in the *Geistliche Chormusik*, seven in the *Sinfoniae sacrae III*. They will be discussed in connection with these collections. The others are distributed among the works already discussed as well as among the oratoriolike pieces, composed as dialogs without intervening texts. So there remain only a few extant works to be discussed here.

The first composition (XIV, 43) is the Gospel verse Matt. 22: 4, for the Twentieth Sunday after Trinity: *Saget den Gästen (Tell Them Which Are Bidden)* — in other words, a passage from the parable of the wedding of the king's son. The setting is found in a Kassel manuscript. Surely here we are not confronted by a central portion of the parable, to be inserted as a climax in the Gospel reading, but at most with a "supplementary" Gospel motet, since in this composition Schütz apparently merely indulged his artistic impulse to portray the joyful wedding hubbub *(Hochzeitslärm)*, for which purpose, in the first place, two exuberant sinfonias by two violins, bassoon, and thorough bass do service, then four voices, doubtless intended for chorus. The structure of the whole is as follows, all being in F major:

Sinf. 1: soprano and bass duet.   *Sinf.* 2: quartet with the parts

A B C / / : C' : / /

This repeated subdivision C' adds the full instrumental part to the full chorus. Furthermore, one feels everywhere in the case of this spontaneous piece the technical problems which fascinated Schütz: primarily the fuller development in a four-voice setting, by means of richer combinations, of the pictorial motives of the duet text linked together in motet manner; and finally, during the developing course of the concluding part — which is significantly repeated — to bring the joyous tumult to a static conclusion *(zu statischem Drehen auf der Stelle).* In the case of the almost overrich use of this verse, in itself not at all so essential for the Gospel narrative, it may well be that Schütz (despite the *de tempore* note on the director's continuo part, which is not in his own handwriting) thought more in this case of a festal wedding Introit. In connection with such a question it is always instructive to observe the settings of the older masters *loco evangelii* for the corresponding Sunday.[6] As a matter of fact, Schütz here stands completely alone with his excerpt. Therefore the conclusion remains: Either we have an early artistic study or a bridal Mass introduction. Perhaps, and most probably, we have both.

Also in Vol. XIV, No. 4, p. 55, and likewise in a Kassel manuscript, we have *Es gingen zwei Menschen hinauf (Two Men Went Up to the Temple to Pray).* Because of the high alto-tenor part A. Hänlein, in his practical edition in the brochure *Drei geistliche Szenen* (B.&H.), transposed the piece from G to F. Schütz, to be sure, called the work a *dialogus* because the chief emphasis rests on the antithetical statements of the Pharisee and the publican, whom the master then allows to concertize against each other simultaneously. Nevertheless, it is not an "oratoriolike work" with additions or omissions but the literal parable spoken by Jesus (Luke 18). One must, therefore, imagine that on the Eleventh Sunday after Trinity the altar lesson was sung as follows:

And now follows the Schütz Gospel music, sung immediately beside the altar. Anyone who has once experienced this, as we did in 1929 at the Schütz Festival in Celle, has the impression that Schütz could never have intended the presentation

---

[6] Of the entire text, vv. 1-14, which only Wanning and Horn composed completely and verbally, while Elsbeth paraphrased it, G. Otto and H. Herpol begin with vv. 4-7, *Dicite invitatis,* then follow this with a *secunda pars* at v. 8, *Nuptiae quidem paratae.* Calvisius and Otto present only the first part in their duets. Raselius and Demantius, in their motets, enter at the moment of the dramatic nodal point: *Da sprach er zu seinen Knechten.* Vulpius, à 8, 1619, passes still somewhat later from the Gospel to polyphony at the climax, *Die Hochzeit ist zwar bereit.* Dulichius directs everything to the scene with the unbidden guest by composing v. 11 as part one, and vv. 12-13 as part two.

to be otherwise. The narrative of the two men is assigned to two boy discantists. The publican is a tenor, noted in the alto clef; the Pharisee is a bass. The moral application by Jesus, *Wahrlich, ich sage euch* ("Truly, I say to you"), is then scored for all four voices (as in the *Ach Jesu, à 6*, the concluding words also become a *tutti*). A. Hänlein, the editor, sensed correctly that, according to Schützian usage, a *capella* might enter *ad libitum* to give additional volume. In the introductory report the going up "together" is pictorially portrayed by homophonic thirds, after which, in immediate, vivid contrast through alternation of the voices, we have *einer ein Pharisäer — der ander ein Zöllner*, the latter three times in order to underline the despised publican as the chief personage. Again in contrasts: *Der Pharisäer stund* ("The Pharisee stood and prayed thus"), *und der Zöllner* ("and the publican, standing afar off, would not lift up so much as his eyes unto heaven"). Here Schütz gives emphasis by letting the other discant repeat *wollte auch seine Augen* ("would not lift up so much as his eyes unto heaven"); then the second soprano joins the first to emphasize the words "to heaven" with all the intensity of religious longing and continues the association in order to paint most impressively the *schlug an seine Brust* ("smote upon his breast"). *Und sie sprachen* ("and they spake") is the only slight liberty which Schütz takes with the words. These are separated in the Bible by *betete bei sich also* ("prayed thus with himself") and the *und sprach* ("and spake"); but in order that the contrast between the two prayers might appear fully, Schütz has the Pharisee and the publican sing this passage together. The manner in which Schütz now portrays the self-indulgent, self-satisfied boasting of the Pharisee in essentially rising lines (*a* minor with f# and g#!), and the sigh of the publican, weighed down by his guilt, nearly always only with

Gott, sei mir Sün=der gnä=dig!

this, in its simplicity and impressiveness, belongs to the most inspired passages in all religious music. At first the concluding chorus gives very concisely and impressively the summary of the Lord, *Ich sage euch, dieser ging hinab* ("I tell you, this man went down to his house justified rather than the other"). Then it lets the

---

[7] Matt. 18:21-22, and Luke 17:4, *siebenmal vergeben*. W. Schuh, p. 93, finds in the closing chorus a partial, potentialized *Bar* form. The sevenfold use of the phrase may be symbolic.

tension relax in motet form in the tonally spatial presentation suggested by *denn wer sich selbst erhöhet* ("for everyone that exalteth himself shall be abased; and he that humbleth himself shall be exalted"), as many a master had previously set this passage.[8]

As already shown in connection with the *cantio sacra* titled *Sicut Moses serpentem* and the *Sinfonia sacra I*, titled *Venite ad me*, this is no denial but a development of the conception of Gospel music on the part of Schütz. At first these passages from the New Testament are for him essentially only musical texts; but later — from about 1630 on — when his grievous war experiences begin, the relation between text and music deepens to the very opposite. His music now becomes the serving medium with the function to enhance to its greatest luster the delivery of the Gospel text. Accordingly, we may place the *Saget den Gästen* ("Tell them which are bidden"), which indeed still has the Italian designation *Del Sigr. Henrico Sagittario*, at the beginning of the 1620's (but, on account of the rich and independent instrumental treatment, not before 1620!), the *Dialog of the Pharisee and the Publican* about ten years later. The greater part of the superb examples of the *Musicalia ad chorum sacrum* will demonstrate that this became Schütz's individual and central Gospel form.

We have discussed Hans Engel's discovery, among some anonymous works in Kassel, of a setting of Psalm 5 which he properly assigned to Schütz. A second anonymous setting, which Engel discovered in Kassel and which is undoubtedly by Schütz, presents verses six, nine, and ten of the fifteenth chapter of the Gospel According to St. Luke: *Freuet euch mit mir* ("Rejoice with me").[9] The verses have to do with the parables of the lost sheep and the lost penny. The composition is a spiritual *concerto* for two solo tenors or possibly two sopranos; more precisely, *Cantus I* might be assigned to a tenor or a soprano; *Cantus II*, to a baritone or mezzo-soprano. The extracting of the direct words from the context and the conclusion, *Also wird auch Freude sein über einen Sünder, der Busse tut* ("likewise joy shall be in heaven over one sinner that repenteth"), with the confirmatory alleluia, are genuinely Schützian. The declamation varies impressively between

---

[8] Johs. Galliculus has set, *à 5*, *Duo homines* (Manuscript Proske-Butsch 4°, 1538); G. Otto, in two parts, *Pharisaeus haec apud se orabat / Publicanus stans a longe bis mihi peccatori;* H. Herpol and Otto, in his *Bicinia*, continue the same to the end of the Gospel extract; M. Vulpius (German) limits the four voices to the concluding summary, *Ich sage euch, dieser ging hinab.* Raselius and Demantius concentrate on *Denn wer sich selbst erhöhet;* Calvisius and Wanning proceed similarly in Latin; Th. Elsbeth presents one of the earliest prose paraphrases, *Den Pharisäer verdammt sein stolz Gebet;* but Caspar Horn, with his characteristic thoroughness, treats the entire Gospel account in German.

[9] Published by the *Evangelische Verlagsanstalt,* Merseburger edition, No. 925.

stationary (or revolving) triplets of joy and even time, which is the bearer of the urgent announcement. The whole work is borne along, as it were, by an impetuous flood and reveals superbly the intensity of the master's feeling, even to the d—f#—b♭ for the word *Busse* ("repentance").

Engel also found among the anonymous pieces in Kassel a *Friede sei mit euch* ("Peace be with you"). As Engel has shown, we have here a portion of the *Resurrection History* of 1623 in the form of an independent *concerto*.

Op. 11. The Geistliche Chormusik of 1648

The *Geistliche Chormusik (CollectedWorks,* Vol. VIII), dedicated to the Council of the City of Leipzig and to the St. Thomas Choir of that city, is the motet collection with which, in the year of the Peace of Westphalia, the important process was completed by which the Gabrieli pupil became German again. It bears the following title:

Musicalia ad Chorum Sacrum
That Is,
Spiritual Choral Music /
With 5, 6, and 7 Voices / to Be Used /
Both *vocaliter* and *instrumentaliter.*
Set
by
Heinrich Schütz /
Kapellmeister to His Electoral Highness in Saxony
In Which the *bassus generalis,* According to Advice and Desire /
Not, However, from Necessity / at the Same Time
Is Also to Be Found.
First Part

M. D. C.   (Coat of Arms)   XLVIII

Opus Undecimum
Dresden /
To Be Purchased from Johann Klemmens / Electoral Saxon Court
Organist There. Printed by Gimel Bergen's / Electoral
Saxon Court Printer's Heirs.

Again, on account of the exigencies of the time, a "First Part," despite the further material which was certainly available, could not be followed in print by a "Second Part."

The preface to the "kindly disposed" reader is one of the most comprehensive Schütz ever wrote. Schütz is particularly eager to explain the title of the work: *Chormusik.* To be sure, the motets as a whole can be strengthened by instruments; indeed, Schütz expressly arranged Nos. 26-29 in such a way that they are intended for only a few voices, with instrumental parts predominating. He also suggests that individual compositions be presented as solo motets or with the chorus entering only for contrasting sections. Nevertheless, *Chormusik* here signifies "without *obbligato basso continuo.*" Schütz rebels against the idea of presenting his works as models. He much prefers to refer for such models "to the old and new Italian and other classical authors who were canonized, as it were, by all the most distinguished composers." Nevertheless, he is prompted by a great pedagogical concern to place before the eyes of the rising generation of German composers examples of music without thorough bass and thus to stimulate them to take this same path. Herein he shows a striking similarity to the educational purposes of J. S. Bach. One will recall the title pages of Bach's *Inventions, The Well-tempered Clavichord, The Art of the Fugue.* Schütz observes that concertizing music with the thorough bass had gained a larger following in Germany than any other category. But he notes that in Italy "in the true high school of music (when in my youth I began for the first time to lay my *fundamenta* in this profession) it was customary for the beginners each time to work out properly their little sacred or secular work without the *bassus continuus.*[1] . . which good custom is presumably still practiced there." On the other hand, this procedure no longer seems to be followed by the young German composers, and this implies the decline of counterpoint. For there is little doubt on the part of all musicians "educated in good schools that no one can successfully undertake other kinds of composition unless one has sufficiently devoted oneself to mastering the most difficult study of counterpoint by way of the method without the *bassus continuus.*" Further, the sixty-three-year-old master demands that one "should make up the *requisita* necessary for a well-regulated composition," such as the *dispositiones modorum* (disposition of the tonalities), *fugae simplices, mixtae, inversae* (imitation — simple, free, and in contrary motion),[2] double counterpoint (linear writing with exchange of voices), *differentia styli in arte musica diversi* (different styles according to the different genres), *modulatio vocum* (voice-leading), *connexio subjectorum* (intertwining of antithetical themes), etc. To be sure, even music without these techniques may seem to uneducated ears to be a "heavenly harmony," but by experienced composers it will "not be valued much higher than an empty nut." Thus Schütz would like to rouse the rising German composers "before they proceed to the composition of concertizing music to crack this hard nut (wherein the true kernel and the right

---

[1] Schütz himself thus explains the absence of the thorough bass in his *Madrigals of 1611.*
[2] Cf. Chr. Bernhard's *Musiklehre,* chs. 57-63. So Nathusius also cites "His Excellency, Herr Kapellmeister Schüzze," 1657 (Schering, MG. Leipzigs II, 124).

foundation of good counterpoint is to be sought) and to pass their first tests in this category."

One might be tempted also to chide Schütz — as happened frequently enough with other German masters — for becoming "reactionary" in his old age. As a matter of fact, however, we observe in his case the breaking-through of a thoroughly German tendency to a sense of responsibility for one's craftsmanship. He speaks, like Wagner's Hans Sachs, with affectionate concern, as a wise Ekkart, to all young Stoltzings:

Die Meisterregeln lernt bei Zeiten,
Dass sie getreulich euch geleiten
Und helfen wohl bewahren
Was in der Jugend Jahren
In holdem Triebe
Lenz und Liebe
Euch unbewusst ins Herz gelegt,
Dass ihr das unverloren hegt.

The master-rules do learn in season
That they e'er faithfully may guide you
And help you well to treasure
What in your youth's awakening,
In blissful passion,
Spring and rapture
Unknown within your heart did place,
There to be cherished evermore.

It is a small tragedy, as it were, that this work, written almost in opposition to the thorough bass, nevertheless had to add the continuo "upon advice and request." While at the same time it seems like a quiet, ironic vengeance on the part of fate that the figuring turned out to be very bad, as if Joh. Klemme had had some amanuensis *(famulus)* add it hastily and more poorly than correctly. Thus it is wise that the new editions (W. Kamlah, Bärenreiter; K. Thomas, Breitkopf & Härtel)[3] present the choral settings without this once fashionable supplement, and here clearly contrary to Schütz's inclination. We saw that the Saxon *Kantorei* practice had transferred even the polychoral psalms and the like to the *a cappella*

---

[3] *Selig sind die Toten,* ed. by H. Holle through Schott (Mainz); in Woyrsch, II: *Die mit Tränen säen, So fahr ich hin, Also hat Gott die Welt, Die Himmel erzählen, Herzlich lieb, Das Wort ward Fleisch, Selig sind die Toten.* The complete series of the *Geistliche Chormusik* has been published by Bärenreiter.

style again. Thus the work of 1648, from the point of view of scoring, approaches closely most of the compositions of the *Cantiones sacrae of 1625;* but in their musical content there is scarcely a relation between them. For all delight in artistic experimentation, every Jesuitical ecstasy of the former work, has disappeared. The fundamental attitude has become a serious, simple, and plain-spoken Lutheranism, which places itself joyfully and unequivocally at the service of the community of the living church. While in the case of the earlier work one had to consider the similarly contrapuntal, more absolute compositions as earlier and to regard the problematic ones as later and "more advanced," we find here a noble example of the classic without sugar or spice, which, nevertheless, in its timeless nature, radiates vigorous warmth and represents in its unobtrusive polyphony something which in kind and power[4] is eternally German.

It is a remarkable spiritual parallelism that Rembrandt, Schütz's greatest contemporary in the field of art, made the same transition that Schütz made when the latter passed from the almost Jesuitizing *Cantiones sacrae* to the thoroughly Protestant *Chormusik.* Both made the transition approximately between their thirty-fifth and fifty-fifth years. Of Rembrandt's transition Hans Tietze[5] writes:

> "F. Schmidt-Degener has shown that Rembrandt's closest approach to the Italian-Catholic baroque took place ca. 1640. In 1638 he etched 'St. Catherine with the Wheel'; in 1639, the un-Protestant 'Deathbed of Mary'; in 1641, a pathetic *Mater dolorosa;* and in the same year a 'Madonna on the Clouds,' surrounded by the glow of flashing, quivering beams related to Federigo Barocci's engraving of the glorification of Mary. It is no mere coincidence that Sandrart's slander (with its aftereffects continuing through centuries) that Rembrandt painted his backgrounds so dark in order to mask his poorly drawn contours gained its support likewise in the year 1641, the year of Sandrart's sojourn in Amsterdam. Rembrandt was never closer to the baroque than shortly before 1642. Never was his feeling *(Pathos)* more pronounced, his composition richer in contrasts, his coloring more scintillating. The last quarter-century of his activity overcame and repudiated this kind of manifestation of the baroque. And just at the point where that which at first unfolded itself outwardly turned inward he fulfills most deeply the idea of a Protestant baroque."

Schütz arranged the collection of twenty-nine compositions according to the progression in the number of voices: Nos. 1-12 for five voices, Nos. 13-24 for six, and Nos. 25-29 for seven voices. Each division represents, as Ph. Spitta thought,

---

[4] Similarly also H. Leichtentritt says in his *Geschichte der Motette*, p. 338: "These motets are German, not because they are written on German texts but rather on account of the expression of the sentiment which they contain, an expression quite different from the manner in which Italian masters presented the same texts. No rapturous mysticism but greatness, simplicity, and a warm honesty of feeling speak here with compelling power. To gain a conception of this thoroughly German nature, glance through No. 11: *So fahr ich hin zu Jesu Christ;* here one is reminded of the power of a Joh. Seb. Bach. The wonderful piece will bear every sort of comparison."

[5] *Der Barokstil und die protestantische Welt (Zeitwende,* X/4, April 1934).

a journey through the church year from Advent to All Souls Day, or at least into the late fall. Of the texts four (five settings) are derived from the hymn book; only six are from the Old Testament, and even these are for the most part prophecies or use ideas that have completely penetrated the thought world of the New Covenant. Three texts are from the Epistles, ten from the Gospels; there is an Advent Collect and also an antiphon. When one examines the tonalities, one observes occasional group formations: 3-6 *g* minor, 7-9 F major, 13-14 and 18-19 *g* minor, 24-25 *a* minor — but these do not predominate to an extent which would warrant the assumption of a conscious structural principle. However, instead of the above *de tempore* interpretation of Spitta, something must be said for R. Wustmann's view, since a number of the texts could lend themselves to a double usage. In his *Musikgeschichte Leipzigs*, I, 470, Wustmann acknowledges here only the quarter of the church year from Advent to January, this then followed by numbers for special occasions; finally he sees pieces of a special musical kind appended. From all this he ventures the engrossing conclusion that Schütz planned a four-volume work. He attempts to establish the following plan:

"1-12: 12 five-voice motets; 1-8 for Advent to Epiphany; 9: wedding motet; 10-12: funeral numbers, the last in special form *(aria)*.

"13-24: 12 six-voice motets; 13-18 for Advent to New Year; 19, 20, 22, 23: funeral numbers; 21 and 24: wedding numbers, the last in special concertizing form.

"25-29: 5 seven-voice compositions; 25: funeral motet; 26-28: duets with five participating instruments, for Advent to New Year; 29 (Matt. 18: 32-33) in special form: tenor solo with six deep instruments, today perhaps best with viola, three 'cellos, and two basses.

"The compositions designated here as funeral and wedding music were composed in part for such purposes, as can be proved in the case of the one for Schein; in part they are based on texts used in Leipzig for such purposes. The numbers to be used according to the church year in the general church service embrace only the first quarter of the church music year. One may conclude from this that, as Schütz designates the collection on the title page as Part One, his supply of similar numbers was fourfold or even greater. He also speaks of this part as 'my present little work now given out, with few voices.' He had probably composed many other motets for eight or more voices. We may dream of an eightfold motet supply of this splendid quality as once existing in Dresden ca. 1650."

Let us add the further remarks of Wustmann in their laudable conciseness:

"Schütz himself distinguishes two styles in this *Geistliche Chormusik:* the chorus type, which permits presentation by one or more voices for each part as well as optional instrumental substitutions or reinforcements, that is, the old style of the baroque motet; and another style, in which vocal and instrumental voices are to be definitely separated.[6] This second style is the one which approaches the concertizing style. It can also 'be performed with the organ with good effect': Nos. 24, 26, 28, 29. No. 27 entered the collection only through an oversight on the part of the aging Schütz. It is a composition by Andrea Gabrieli which Schütz copied in Venice and to which, by way of practice, he may have attempted to add a German text, something which he later forgot. The treatment of the text, despite the opinion of Spitta, would have been quite impossible for Schütz in view of his other compositions."

---

[6] Note by H. J. Moser: "Here we stand at the crossroads where the paths leading to Bach's motets and to Bach's cantatas separate."

With the scores as found in Vol. VIII of the collected works (1889) before us, let us now go through the individual compositions of the *Geistliche Chormusik*, a work which Ph. Spitta properly called "the most beautiful motet collection of its time."

At its head (VII, 71) stands the two-part motet on the Advent prophecy, Gen. 49: 10-12: *Es wird das Szepter von Juda nicht entwendet werden (The Scepter Shall Not Depart from Judah).*[7] The cadential frame of the Aeolian composition is *a*—E, *a*—A. It will be useful here to place together in continuous sequence the opening motives of the discant. We omit bar lines:

One will observe that while differences have been intended and achieved in the different numbers (indeed, even very characteristic ones!), nevertheless such sharp contrasts as characterize the madrigalistic technique of word painting have been intentionally abandoned. The horizontal lines have also something fluent from the rhythmical point of view. Their character is no longer violently excited and intended to surprise but is nevertheless very impressive, expressive, and emphatic. Corresponding to this is the interweaving of the voices. The harmony glides along in a noble "maze." The simultaneous employment of contrasting motives is dispensed with. Within the individual members of the chain the exposition of the

---

[7] For the first part compare W. Schuh, pp. 56 f., who particularly emphasizes how Schütz, in this No. 1, has raised the shorter second half of the text to an inner and outer equilibrium with the first.

voices proceeds in all kinds of free fugal development and with all the old master-ship of the early sixteenth century. The delivery is strongly impersonal and yet full of inspirations, as the three connected motives in No. 2 (p. 11) demonstrate:

The first composition of the g Dorian group (p. 15), *Es ist erschienen die heil-same Gnade Gottes (For the Grace of God That Bringeth Salvation Hath Appeared to All Men,* Titus 2: 11), the Epistle for Christmas Day, Kamlah transposed up to *a* Dorian.[8] Here Schütz, after all, cannot quite deny his innate baroque impetuos-ity. The joy over the grace of God that has appeared to "all, all, all men" is too great! Furthermore, his keen, rational genius for interpreting the Epistle, already evident in the *Symphoniae sacrae II,* comes fully into its own in his setting of *züchtiget uns* ("teaching us"), *die weltlichen Lüste* ("worldly lusts"), *züchtig* ("soberly"), *gerecht* ("righteously"), *gottselig leben* ("live a godly life"), *warten* ("looking for"), *Herrlichkeit des grossen Gottes* ("the glorious appearing of the great God"). He does not, however, digress from the motet style to the decorative style of the *concerto.* Note the tonal and extraordinarily spiritual climax as the central concept, *unsers Heilands Jesu Christi,* is built up. Then also the vigorous joy in action at *reiniget ihm selbst* ("purify unto Himself"), *fleissig wäre* ("zealous of good works"), the melismatically powerful and far-flung *guten Werken* ("good works")! In this motet one can read an entire Lutheran exposition of grace, which, without work-righteousness, nevertheless does not consist in mere passive recep-tivity but in the task "how man may work to please God in his faith" (Luther, *Von den guten Werken,* 1520).

Next we have a New Year motet in two parts (Nos. 4 and 5, pp. 20-22) on *Verleih uns Frieden gnädiglich,* Luther's paraphrase of the *Da pacem.* I think I have demonstrated[9] that, on closer examination, Schütz, after all, did not depart nearly as far from the church melody as has been commonly assumed. At times he conceals the lines in a subsidiary voice, at times he allows their motional thrust to exhaust itself with some baroque exaggeration. Even in the case of an apparently rather free tone picture like *ein geruhig und stilles Leben* ("a quiet and peaceful life"), on page twenty-five, Schütz held most closely to the original; so also at *aller*

---

[8] Likewise in *Das Gesungene Bibelwort,* Brochure 20 (Vandenhoeck & Ruprecht).
[9] *Jahrbuch der Staatl. Akad. f. K. u. Schulm.,* III, 21.

Gottseligkeit und Ehrbarkeit ("devotion to God and honesty"), so that, despite all free interpolations, we can count this motet among the settings of church melodies.[10] We also find here tendencies toward fugal contrasts and to linkages of free momentary pictures that characterize the figural madrigal — perhaps indeed as a subconscious contrast or counterweight to the, to be sure, very loose restraint of the church melody.

No. 6, on the text Rom. 14: 7-8, *Unser keiner lebt ihm selber (For None of Us Liveth to Himself)*, is both the Epistle for New Year's Day and a funeral text. Kamlah likewise gives this last of the five-voice *g* Dorian pieces in *a* minor. W. Schuh (loc. cit., p. 62) has astutely sensed the framework *(Rahmenform)* which allowed Schütz to develop a fourfold division from the tripartite text:

	I	II		III
	A	B	C	D
	Frame	*Bar*	*Bar*	Frame
		Leben	*Sterben*	
No. of measures	8½	10½	14	13

How vividly the phrases representing motion at *leben wir* dart at one another, and then how restrained the feeling as the voices for the most part sink down at *sterben wir!* We have two dynamically pregnant pictures and, in conjunction with them, as the static wings of the triptych, the declarations *unser keiner* ("none of us liveth to himself") and *darum: wir leben* ("whether we live, therefore, or die, we are the Lord's"). Countless fine points might be observed in counterpoint and also in declamation and tone painting. Frequently all three features are simultaneous, mutually calling on, and enhancing, one another. Herein, too, there is a tremendous difference between the present work and nearly all the preceding collections of the master in that Schütz now no longer displays ingenious caprice in the treatment of the dissonance but, both in preparation and resolution, proceeds as the strict instructor of Germany who displays his genius in an altogether different direction, as the precursor of Goethe's dictum "And only the law can give us freedom."[11]

No. 7 (p. 32), on Matt. 8: 11-12, *Viel werden kommen (Many Shall Come)*, is the Gospel for the Third Sunday after Epiphany[12] (transposed in Kamlah's edition

---

[10] Cf. the use of the same chorale in VII, 77, and of the *Da pacem* in XV, 17.
[11] *Und das Gesetz nur kann uns Freiheit geben.*
[12] So in Latin by G. Otto as a duet.

from F major to G). The duality developed from the text is very clear: in measures 17-18 the mighty *aber* is the little tongue between the two arms of the scale: the seventeen-measure picture of the strangers who are permitted to sit in the fields of the blessed and the nineteen-measure picture of those who are thrust out of the kingdom — first the idyll with the patriarchs, then the "darkness" with the weeping and gnashing of teeth. Of course, all this is also "painted," no longer, however (as in Psalm 116) in Danteesque antithesis between *Paradiso* and *Inferno* but with restrained severity, which goes back even beyond Lasso's delight in vivid story telling to the more general picture language of a Clemens non Papa. Perhaps the best example of this is the simple —◦——◦— without chromaticism or melismatic outthrusts and the like. *Heu - len*

No. 8, Matt. 13: 24-30 (p. 36), is the Gospel for the Fifth Sunday after Epiphany.[13] At the beginning of this brief piece, as well as in No. 11, the *basso continuo* ventures on its way alone for a stretch in order to expand the discant-alto duo to a terzet, and in its subsequent course it also remains somewhat more independent than otherwise. The text offers nothing on the emotional side, so Schütz can devote himself the more unreservedly to contrapuntal values which show themselves in the very artistic interlacings and group alternations of the voices. W. Schuh[14] has called attention to how well Schütz has maintained the equilibrium of the two halves of the piece by means of textual development.

How very differently our master is enabled to pluck the strings of human feeling in the last of the three pieces in F major (Kamlah, G major)! Since at that time the religious lyric passed almost generally from Luther's "we" to Paul Gerhardt's "I," this No. 9 (p. 39), based on the first antiphon for the Sixth Sunday after Trinity,[15] reveals the most personal expression of faith: *Herr, auf dich trau ich* ("Lord, in Thee do I put my trust [C, A], let me never be ashamed [F, C]! Deliver me in Thy righteousness [Bb, Eb] and help me [C, F]. Bow down Thine ear to me, deliver me speedily [g, D]! Be a strong defense [F] to which I may ever flee [C], who hast promised to help me [Fg]. Be a strong defense [Bb] to which I may ever flee [FC], who hast promised to help me [Bb], a strong defense to which I may ever

---

[13] Only J. C. Horn set the entire parable of the tares among the wheat. The words of the servants, "Sir, didst not thou sow good seed," are placed at the head by Herpol, Otto, Dulichius, Wanning, mostly with a second part, "Gather ye together first the tares." Calvisius and Otto, in their *Zwiegesänglein,* present this answer of the householder only; likewise all the German Gospel motets by Raselius, M. Franck, Vulpius, Demantius ("Gather the tares") — so also Schütz. Elsbeth alone begins somewhat earlier: "The householder said to his servants: Leave the tares."
[14] Loc. cit., pp. 36 f.
[15] Ps. 71: 1-3, and so also as funeral text.

flee [G], who hast promised to help me [F]").[16] While I have thus given the
cadential finals for the individual sections, it must be added that, on account of
the flood of feeling here, there are no points of rest interposed by means of which
the piece is clearly subdivided — although one can find a beautiful A—A—B *Bar*
in the first phrase of the text. Likewise in the second, and so on. Much more important in this case is the wonderfully passionate declamation of the word content.
Observe, for example:

First the repose of the "strong defense," then this sudden venting of feeling which,
surely, as a rhetorical connection, also remarkably interprets and illumines the
text. This antithesis dominates almost the entire second large portion, which one
may view as a free A—A—B *Bar* with differences in the cadences and member
repetitions that are captivating in the highest degree.

It is interesting to compare the *d* minor composition, *Die mit Tränen säen (They
That Sow in Tears)*, No. 10 (p. 44),[17] with Schütz's double-chorus composition on
the same text in the *Psalms of 1619* (III, 133) and to place both beside the same

---

[16] *Herr, auf dich trau ich* (C, A), *laß mich nimmermehr zu Schanden werden* (F, C)! *Errette
mich nach deiner Barmherzigkeit* (Bb, Eb) *und hilf mir aus* (C, F). *Neige deine Ohren zu mir und
hilf mir* (g, D)! *Sei mir ein starker Hort* (F), *dahin ich immer fliehen möge* (C), *der du hast zugesaget, mir zu helfen* (Fg). *Sei mir ein starker Hort* (Bb) *dahin ich immer fliehen möge* (FC), *der
du hast zugesaget, mir zu helfen* (Bb), *ein Hort, dahin ich immer fliehen möge* (G), *der du hast
zugesaget, mir zu helfen* (F).

[17] Also in Woyrsch; Kamlah gives it in e.

text in the opening number of Brahms's *A German Requiem*. From such a juxta-position one could establish decisive differences in interpretation and form between the seventeenth and the nineteenth centuries. Let it suffice here to indicate briefly the treatment of the texts in Schütz's two pieces. While in 1619 *säen* ("sow") is almost disregarded, and while the *Bringen der Garben* ("bringing of the sheaves") is painted broadly and picturesquely, the very opposite occurs in 1648. In 1619 the *mit Tränen säen* ("sow in tears") is treated as a couplet with the *werden mit Freuden ernten* ("will reap in joy") as a rich conclusion *(Abgesang);* in 1648 both contrasts are presented as a b / a b', these then being followed by *sie gehen hin* ("they go forth") as conclusion. In 1619 the *edler Samen* ("precious seed") is more important, while in 1648 everything is pointed toward *Freuden,*[18] as indicated in the expanded second couplet. Here, too, we may say that the delivery of the second, the later, piece seems to be more restrained, more cool, more sober — until one notes that the less picturesque may be psychologically more moving.

No. 11 (p. 49), in C major, is also a funeral composition: *So fahr ich hin (So Fare I Forth to Jesus Christ),* a setting of the concluding stanza of Nikolaus Hermann's hymn *Wenn mein Stündlein vorhanden ist* ("When My Last Hour Is Close at Hand").[19] W. Schuh (p. 48) challenged Ph. Spitta's opinion that Schütz denied himself the use of the church melody. However, I do not agree with him that Schütz derived the g a b c from the Ionian melody

by abandoning the very characteristic opening note (C), according to which interpretation the abbreviated accompanying voice would represent the contrary motion of the first phrase. I hold that Schütz derived this directly from the Görlitz melody (Zahn, 4484)

So fahr ich hin

which was in use in Leipzig in 1603, while Dresden used the tenor part of the Görlitz melody for that of the congregational tune. But the enlarged A—A—B *Bar (potenzierte Barform),* maintained by Schuh, can be definitely confirmed, as also his conclusion that the emphasis (as often in Schütz) lies with the conclusion. The

---

[18] W. Schuh, p. 42.
[19] Edition by G. Schreck, *Thomanermotetten* (B & H); also in Woyrsch's collection.

pictures, *So fahr ich hin zu Jesu Christ, mein Arm tu ich ausstrecken* ("So fare I forth to Jesus Christ, with open arms betake me") and *so schlaf ich ein und Ruhe fein, kein Mensch kann mich aufwecken* ("I fall asleep in slumber deep, no man can then awake me"), are nothing more than foregrounds *(Vorfelder)* — though, to be sure, wonderfully blooming ones — till the clouds burst open for the radiant vision at *denn Jesus Christus, Gottes Sohn* ("for Jesus Christ, God's Son is He, will open heaven's door to me, and lead me to life everlasting"). We may say that here mere decoration and illustration of the melody have been left behind, while the stanza has been reborn into a dramatic picture of the *iterum venturus*, the life to come. The problems of intonation which are presented to a chorus by relationships at the third, C—A, G—E, at *So schlaf ich ein* ("I fall asleep") have been pointed out by Max Planck in the *Vjschr. f. MW*, IX, 434. And how warmly expressive is the ⁶ chord on *ruhe!*

Schütz carried out an unusual idea in the last of the compositions for five voices (No. 12, p. 53).[20] He transformed the prose verse from John's Gospel, *Also hat Gott die Welt geliebt* ("God so loved the world"),[21] John 3: 16, into an E major *aria* of the structure //:A://:B://c. It is an *aria* not merely on account of this structure but also because the setting is primarily homophonic, with emphasis on the soprano. Even the detailed rhythm is surprisingly like that of a song, with its preference for agogic groups of three's. One need merely arrange the "couplets" with proper bar lines. The first *Also* (p. 53) is like the index finger of John in the "Isenheim Crucifixion":

And in the conclusion, despite extending elements, it continues similarly:

---

[20] Also in Woyrsch.
[21] The Gospel for Whitsuntide and also for Advent.

It is as if in this way Schütz wanted to show "the rising German composers" how, just as it is possible completely to resolve a hymn text into musical quasiprose, so it is possible, with the proper utilization of the text, to transform prose to "formal" music. It is, at all events, a thought that does not have many counterparts in the field of music.

At the head of the six-voice motets stands one in *g* Dorian on the Advent Collect, *O lieber Herre Gott*, which Schütz had already set as a *kleines geistliches Konzert* for two discants. The structure of this very important composition will doubtless be best clarified by the following outline:

Couplet	⎰O dearest Lord our God (g—G)
	⎱rouse us from sleep that we be prepared (g—F)
Couplet	⎰O dearest Lord our God (F—D)
	⎱rouse us from sleep that we be prepared (d—g)
Middle member:	when Thy Son comes (g—Bb)
Couplet	⎰with rejoicing to receive Him (F—A), triple time
	⎱and with clean and pure heart may e'er serve Thee (d—F)
Couplet	⎰with rejoicing to receive Him (Bb—D), triple time
	⎱and with clean and pure heart may e'er serve Thee (d—Bb)
Conclusion	⎰this we ask Thee through Thy beloved Son (Bb—
	⎱Jesus Christ our Lord and Master (g—Bb—G—g)
Coda	Amen (—G).[22]

Note how *Jesum Christum* is peculiarly imbedded in the soprano, like a tonally changing scroll above the texture of the lower voices.

No. 14 (p. 63), again in *g* Dorian, is a study in double-chorus composition. It is from Isaiah (40: 1-5) for the Feast of John the Baptist: *Tröstet mein Volk (Comfort Ye My People)*. One may note that in four-part measure, beside the six-voiced *tutti*, the most varied combinations of four voices against four are introduced.

---

[22]

Stollen	⎰*O lieber Herre Gott* (g—G)
	⎱*wecke uns auf, daß wir bereit sein!* (g—F)
Stollen	⎰*O lieber Herre Gott* (F—D)
	⎱*wecke uns auf, daß wir bereit sein!* (d—g)
Middle member:	*wenn dein Sohn kömmt* (g—Bb)
Stollen	⎰*Ihn mit Freuden zu empfahen* (F—A), *Tripel*
	⎱*und dir mit reinem Herzen zu dienen* (d—F)
Stollen	⎰*Ihn mit Freuden zu empfahen (Bb—D), Tripel*
	⎱*und dir mit reinem Herzen zu dienen* (d—Bb)
Conclusion	⎰*durch denselbigen, deinen lieben Sohn* (Bb—
	⎱*Jesum Christum, unsern Herrn* (g—Bb—G—g)
Coda	*Amen* (—G)

Here we have an example of that "illusion of more voices" at which the masters of the Lassus period were so skillful. In the triple time, however, Schütz divides his forces much more primitively into three high against three low parts. This is doubtless due less to conscious number symbolism than to subconscious recognition that in the dancelike triple time the world actually simplifies itself.[23] Here, too, as in the preceding composition, the middle section in three-part time is the center of the whole. The prolog presents a beautiful example of the fact that the designated 4/4 measure in Schütz is often merely a mechanical measuring rod (*Zollstockmensur*). The fresh, vigorous harmonic changes also show that the superimposed order of accents is the correct one and that the whole is to be understood as iambic:

As in the three-part time section F major and D major vie for supremacy, so we also note the, at the time, double nature of the g minor as Dorian (with Ionian as its most important offshoot) and as minor, with major dominant.

Exactly the same "shying-away from the upbeat" creates misunderstanding in the notational picture at the beginning of the fifteenth motet (p. 71), which is likewise dedicated to John the Baptist. The accent should be

an example of folklike plasticity which might easily mislead some to place it in the period of the Romantic oratorios of Loewe and Spohr. While in the preceding motet the "uneven" (*das Höckerige*) was drastically portrayed, so here the "way" itself is painted in an astonishing six-skeined web, which one must also admire in the case of *Schuhriemen-Auflösen* ("loosening his shoe's latchets") (pp. 77-80) at the end. Not less picturesque is the *Taufen mit Wasser* ("baptizing with water") (pp. 74-75). When one considers the horizontal *parlando* style at *aber er ist mitten unter uns getreten* ("but he has come among us") (p. 75) together with the suite-cadence of the style of 1620 (see next page)

---

[23] So again also in No. 16 (*Ein Kind ist uns geboren*).

and the somewhat naive

we would be inclined to believe this thoroughly charming and valuable piece to belong to the treasure Schütz had kept concealed in his chest for decades, finally to present it to a larger public in this distinguished company.

The Christmas composition, No. 16 (p. 81), *Ein Kind ist uns geboren (To Us a Child Is Given)*, with its F major tonality, often employed in such connection, and its captivating musical verve *(Musikanterei)*, looks very much like the "young" Schütz of the period of the *Psalms of David of 1619*. This is suggested by the phrase which revolves around in little duets

while accompanying gigantic sustained notes indicate the type of the madrigal. The latter is also indicated by the automatic textual disposition of the repeated motive

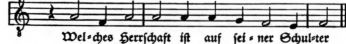

Finally, the hemiolic treatment of the three-part time is altogether in the style of the *Psalm 122* of 1619 (Vol. II, No. 5) or the *cantio sacra* titled *Cantate Domino* of 1625 (Vol. IV, No. 29). The passage *Und des Friedens kein Ende* ("and of peace no end"), with an anticipatory oppositional voice *(Konflikt-Stimme)*, reminds us of Schütz's early concert style. What inspiring animation we have when, after different groups of parts of the chorus, all unite (p. 87) at the end in *Solches wird tun* ("The zeal of the Lord Sabaoth will accomplish it")!

On the other hand, the six-voice motet No. 17 (p. 89) on the Gospel for Christmas Day, John 1: 14, *Das Wort ward Fleisch (The Word Became Flesh)*,[24] rather

---

[24] Also in Woyrsch's collection and in *Das gesungene Bibelwort*, Brochure 21.

embodies the mild, noble simplicity of the sage of 1648, although its *da capo*, with a mere interchange of voices,[25] which here leads to a large *Gegenbar*, A B B (c), has its counterparts in Schütz ca. 1620.[26] This *da capo* repetition is, of course, no mere formal conservation of power; neither is it a mere play of tonal nuances. But it is a means by which to bring to bear all the emphasis, all the coloristic climax, upon the appearance of *Herrlichkeit* ("glory") (p. 90).

In No. 18, Ps. 19: 2-7 (p. 96), *Die Himmel erzählen (The Heavens Declare)*, Schütz carried out the following major division into four parts:[27]

	Verse	
Introduction	2	
Barform (A A B)	3-5a	*(an der Welt Ende)*
Archform (A B A)	5b-7	*(Er hat der Sonnen)*
Conclusion	2	

The use of verse two at the beginning and at the end thus form a frame for the entire work.

In addition, as a supplement, there is a small doxology "in case one wishes to use the piece as an Introit or with the Vesper prayers."

The middle of the archform (A B A) is occupied by a six-voice climactic tone picture on *laufen* ("run"). Even though there is no great variety of cadences, this is a radiant and powerful New Year composition.

Next we have a comprehensive composition based on a church hymn, No. 19 (p. 106), in g Dorian, covering three stanzas of the New Year hymn *Herzlich lieb hab ich dich, o Herr* (M. Schalling). Even in the case of this *aria*, ostensibly altogether independent of the congregational melody, the connection in thought with the hymn can be felt at least in its general progression

Paſch. Reiniglus, 1587:

Herz=lich lieb hab ich dich, o Herr... in Schanden laß mich nim=mer=mehr

Schütz, Disc. 1.

Herz=lich lieb hab ich dich, o Herr ... in Schanden laß mich nimmermehr

---

[25] *Und wir sahen seine Herrlichkeit, eine Herrlichkeit als des eingeborenen Sohnes, voller Gnade und Wahrheit* ("And we beheld His glory. ...").
[26] Thus in the six-voice motet *Ich bin die Auferstehung*, first edited by me.
[27] Schuh, p. 63. The piece is also found in Woyrsch.

In the mottolike *Herzlich lieb,* in the *tutti,* the piece reminds one of the prose *aria Also hat Gott* ("For God So Loved the World") (No. 12). In a peculiar way Schütz shifted the architecture of his music as contrasted with that of the text: both are A A B *Bar* forms, but, instead of setting both text couplets with the same music, the master, with a mere interchange of voices, repeats the music of the first couplet, transfers the textual countercouplet to the conclusion, and again doubles the last lines of the conclusion by repetition with voice exchange *(Stimmentausch-Wieder-holung),* thus:

Music Divisions	*Text Divisions*
Introduction: A A	A⎫
Conclusion: B C	B⎭Introduction
Final conclusion: D D	C D conclusion

The entire piece, with its almost isometric line presentation, is characterized by an indescribable simplicity and by deep feeling. It is, in fact, like a fantasy on a funeral chorale.

No. 20 (p. 119) is the funeral music for Joh. Herm. Schein, which has its special significance in this *St. Thomas Choir Volume,* while at the same time it is the Epistle for the Festival of the Epiphany (1 Tim. 1: 15-17), *Das ist je gewisslich wahr* ("This is a faithful saying, and worthy of all acceptation"). When one compares the version of 1631 (XII, 25) with that of 1648, one finds much greater restraint with the *Jesus Christus kommen ist* ("that Jesus Christ came into the world") and the addition of a middle voice in the original terzet, *Aber darum ist mir Barmherzigkeit* ("Howbeit for this cause I obtained mercy"), which also begins more closely interwoven with what precedes. Above all, the former very intricately colored *Amen* has become extremely simplified — again a sign of Schütz's mature classicism. Corresponding to the three Bible verses, the work is tripartite: *a—A: der fürnehmste bin* ("of whom I am chief"); *A—G: zum ewigen Leben* ("to life everlasting"); *C—A.* The first part is constructed in five sections: two pairs of couplets, the second pair in joyous triplets with exchange of sopranos and tenors, and in place of the conclusion rather a transitional member: *unter welchen ich der fürnehmste bin* ("of whom I am chief"). The second part begins with a threefold arch. In the middle the motives of the first and the third part are joined together. Then there is an outer and an inner dynamic crest in A major at *Barmherzigkeit widerfahren* ("I obtained mercy"), whereupon the music gradually ebbs away to the G major *fermata* at *ewigen Leben* (p. 128). The powerful concluding part, *Gott dem ewigen König* ("God the King eternal"), is built block against block (C—C) until in shorter supplementary phrases the general tonic A is reached again.[28]

The following composition, No. 21, in F major (p. 130), is the mystical word of Christ (John 15: 1-2, 4-5), *Ich bin ein rechter Weinstock (I Am the True Vine)*. With the exception of the spiraling, groping *Reben* ("branches") (p. 135), the work has been given a comparatively restrained presentation. With its delivery almost exclusively in quarter and half notes, it would seem to belong to the ripest among the late works of the collection. The closeness of the imitations is often astonishing. It would be a mistake to sing the composition in a purely objective manner. Such phrases as *wird er wegnehmen* ("He taketh away") (p. 132), *wird er reinigen* ("He purgeth it") (p. 133), *also auch ihr nicht* ("no more can ye, except ye abide in Me") (p. 135), were spoken and must be spoken very impressively!

No. 22 (p. 137) (g Dorian), *Unser Wandel ist im Himmel (For Our Conversation Is in Heaven)*, Phil. 3: 20-21, is the Epistle for the Twenty-third Sunday after Trinity and at the same time one of the most important funeral texts. Here we have a very clear example of Schütz's fondness, when the text permits, as it does here, of concentrating his spotlight on the middle portion, *Warten des Heilandes* ("we look for the Savior, the Lord Jesus Christ, who shall change our vile body"). After this the passage on *nach der Wirkung* ("according to the working whereby He is able even to subdue all things unto Himself") (pp. 143-144), despite the ingenuity of Schütz's Epistle declamation, is, after all, merely an echoing conclusion, while the beautiful picturing of the *Wandeln* ("walking") at the opening is merely a reconnaissance. The twofold D G c F Bb in the bass at *Jesu Christi des Herrn* strikingly illumines the unique Protestant nature of the *Geistliche Chormusik* in the suprasensuous and clear fidelity of the Christian to his God.

One of the most famous settings of Schütz is No. 23 (p. 145), *Selig sind die Toten (Blessed Are the Dead)*.[29] This text, from Rev. 14: 13, and Schütz's new sacred style *(Sakralstil)* have happily met. Not only are the words presented with infinite dignity and austere tonal beauty, but they are dealt with in a remarkably exhaustive manner according to their tonal poetic content. Note, for example, the passage at *die in dem Herrn sterben* ("who die in the Lord"). (See next page.)

---

[28] Cf. also the charming analysis by W. Kamlah (Bär. ed. 292).
[29] In Woyrsch; also Hugo Holle (Schott), C. Thiel (Sulzbach), etc.

Observe the *Ja, ja — der Geist spricht* ("Yea, yea, the Spirit speaketh") (p. 148), as if breathed forth mysteriously; the vigor of the *Werke* ("their good works") (pp. 149-151); finally the, so to speak, Brahmsian atmospheric

and the splendid brilliancy of the *coda* with its pictorial *folgen ihnen nach* ("follow ever them") glowing in both discants:

Finally, there is the group of pieces for instruments with but a few voices. As the last of the sextets we have a church-hymn setting (No. 24) which carries through the church melody completely: *Was mein Gott will das g'scheh allzeit (Whate'er God Wills Let Come to Pass)*. A quartet of trombones and a baritone-tenor duet (or also small chorus) will best do justice to this archaic and compact composition based on the old Huguenot melody. The work is an A. Gabrieli study, so to speak. In the chapter on "Early Individual Works" it was indicated that here we may have a Venetian student work of Schütz.

At the beginning of the septet group, No. 25, p. 156, we again have a purely vocal composition, from Job 19: 23: *Ich weiss, dass mein Erlöser lebt (I Know that My Redeemer Liveth)*. The composition is doubtless another funeral motet; but it is characterized by that joyful ecstasy, which, for the baroque Christian, almost converted the departure for heaven into a festival. The piece can serve as an example of "affectual presentation by means of rhythmic variety." Here, too, the date — 1620-25 — may be suggested as a hypothesis for discussion, notably on account of the four concluding measures, marked *tarde,* with their pronounced oppositional, antithetical madrigalism. In the face of this threefold canon in the outside voices in a rhythm with large note values, plus the tenor against a whirring of eighth notes in the four other parts, one is reminded strongly of passages such as the conclusion of *Sicut Moses (Cant. sacr. XVI)* or of *Reduc domine* or of stretches in the *Psalm 128* of 1619 (II, 123). Also the leaps of the voice — the lowest one at the time — which give the harmony of the four- and seven-voice opening groups so much restless diversity, do not seem to point to the time when Schütz had reached his sixtieth year.[30] However, the master of 1648 certainly had no reason to be ashamed of this well-organized seven-voice setting. How genuinely Schützian is the threefold homophonic *tutti* at *Und meine Augen werden ihn schauen* ("And my eyes shall behold Him"), the supreme promise the devout can receive![31]

Outwardly No. 26, *Sehet an den Feigenbaum (Behold the Fig Tree),* Luke 21, for the Second Sunday in Advent, for soprano and tenor with five instruments, might remind one of the Gabrieli study, No. 24. But despite this fact it is surely not its sister so far as the time of composition is concerned. In the first place, we have no second example of Gospel music[32] by Schütz with so early a date of composition. In the second place, the text declamation of the vocalists is much more mobile; it is genuinely word-engendered and rhetorical, and on listening more carefully to the instrumental scoring (string quintet with two violoncellos?) one will find this more facile, more slender, and more elegant than the one referred to. In the matter of counterpoint it is less studied despite the occasional virtuoso canon technique.[33] It also shows greater consideration for the euphony of the whole. How delightful is the joyful picture *dass itzt der Sommer nahe ist* ("that now the summer is near at hand")! How inevitable the passage *Himmel und Erde vergehen* ("Heaven and earth will pass away, but My words will not pass away")! It is more easily conceivable that the master, remembering his early setting of *Was mein Gott will,* felt moved to see what he might accomplish with the old scoring but with the technique he had acquired at this time.

Since No. 27 (p. 171), *Der Engel sprach zu den Hirten,* was composed by Andr. Gabrieli, it does not come into our present discussion. On the other hand, No. 28

---

[30] However, such leaps again play an important role in the introduction to the *Passion According to St. Luke.*

[31] For the newly discovered six-voice setting see the Appendix.

[32] Latin settings by Herpol, Dulichius, Otto, Wanning; German settings by Raselius, Musculus, Demantius, Franck, Vulpius, C. Horn.

[33] For example, between the two highest voices.

(p. 177), in C major, from Matt. 2: 18, for the Sunday after New Year, *Auf dem Gebirge (In Rama Was There a Voice Heard)*,[34] is a most original example of Schütz's workmanship. It may belong to the end of the 1620's. Trombones and bassoons intermingled may be used for the five lowest voices. Two high tenors may sing the parts written in the alto clefs. The entire composition is to be performed in very vigorous tempo (◯ = 56). Even though the abundance of the cadences may be somewhat reminiscent of a past style, the general disposition and expression have turned out to be surprisingly modern. It is difficult to perform; but when well rendered, it is a most impressive piece.

And finally, another Gospel lesson, No. 29, p. 184, *Du Schalksknecht (O Thou Wicked Servant)*, Matt. 18: 32-33, for the Twenty-second Sunday after Trinity. Schütz has fashioned the words of the Lord into a wide-flung monody for tenor with six deep instruments. At the Berlin Schütz Festival we gave these parts to three violas and three 'cellos in addition to an organ, and we had the piece presented immediately after the reading of the lesson at the altar. The instrumental voice at the beginning

has the effect of a confirmatory cadence to the accentual song of the evangelist. Here, too, one will certainly be permitted to count in whole notes *(Ganze zählen)*. The first part ends clearly with the tonic cadence (G major) on *weil du mich batest* ("because thou desiredst me"). We must note the ardor of the words, which works itself out rhythmically in larger *(alle)* and smaller *(batest)* anticipations *(Vorgriffe)*. How heartily reproachful now the second half, which is constantly governed by the word *erbarmen!* It is a profitable study in itself to note how Schütz presents this concept in a manner ever new and more passionate, and how the instruments also contribute their full participation to this affectual climax.

When one reviews the collection as a whole, it appears, as does Bach's *Well-tempered Clavichord*, to put together in a somewhat motley array precious examples from all creative periods. Determinative, however, for the collection as a

---

[34] The antiphon according to Isaiah, *Vox in Rama: à 4*, by Clemens non Papa (since Salminger, 1549); *à 5*, by Crespel and Luys (Susato, 1554); *à 6*, by Schultetus (1621); also by G. Otto, and as second part of *Herodes rex iratus*, by Saine (Joanellus, 1568); as *bicinium*, by Calvisius; as thorough-bass duet by Urban Loth in Donfried, 1622. Schütz, accordingly, seems to stand alone with a German setting.

whole are those late compositions which reveal Schütz as one who perfected a new personal style of greatest dimensions, as the evangelical Christian whose music had emerged into a fine classicism, as one who has put far behind him all self-willed artificiality *(Artismus)* as well as all self-indulgence in religious debasement, and who, like the devout patron of old German paintings, kneels in devout reverence before the presence of the Crucified One.

C. Creations of Old Age
Op. 12. The Symphoniae sacrae III of 1650

The first part of the *Symphoniae sacrae* (1629) contained only Latin *concerti* for few voices with two *obbligato* instruments; the second volume (1647) was devoted to works of the same nature with German texts. But in the third and last part (1650) Schütz presents German compositions which, in addition to from three to six vocal parts and two instrumental parts, frequently have optional vocal and instrumental supplementary choruses, as is stated in the title:

Symphoniarum Sacrarum
Tertia Pars
Wherein Are to Be Found
German
Concert Pieces
in 5, 6, 7, 8, Namely / Three / Four
Five / Six Vocal and Two Instrumental Voices /
As Violins / or Such Kind / Together with Some *Complementa*
Which from the Index of the Herewith Appended Doubled
Bassi Continui May be Seen / and According to Pleasure,
Can Be Used Along / with Them
Set to Music
by
Heinrich Schütz
His Electoral Highness' Kapellmeister in Saxony
With Permission of His Roman Imperial Majesty
M. D. C. [Saxon Coat of Arms] L.
Op. 12
Printed in Dresden Through Christian and Melchior Bergen / Broth-
ers / Court Printers to His Electoral Highness in Saxony.

We have already considered the dedicatory address to Johann Georg I, wherein Schütz, among other things, thanks him "for those gracious means granted me some time ago by Your Electoral Highness / through which the publication of my musical work has again been furthered / and made easier." He recalls the thirty difficult and disastrous years and hopes that the elector will enjoy, after such heavy burdens of war, the peace granted to his worthy lands by the grace of God. From the brief preface to the "kindly disposed dear reader," which, according to Schütz's own admission, is merely added "because otherwise this page would have had to remain vacant or empty," the only point worthy of mention is the fact that the thorough-bass figuring is not by the author himself but probably by a not wholly infallible pupil. He says that while the Italians now freely dispense with the figures, despite the fact that organists versed in counterpoint do not need them and inexperienced ones will not be helped by them, he nevertheless will abide by the rule, since "excessive caution does no harm."

In connection with the organ registration one should note carefully the entrance or cessation of the supplementary choruses.

The arrangement of the twenty-one compositions in the work, ten of which are to be found in Vol. X and eleven in Vol. XI of the collected works, is such that five terzets and seven quartets in Vol. X are followed by four quintets and six sextets in Vol. XI. Within the four divisions it is scarcely possible, as it is in the first two parts or in the *Kleine geistliche Konzerte,* to determine a liturgical or tonal connection, although the latter is very similar in the terzet and the quartet group. Tendencies toward groups of the same tonality seem unmistakable, as the following survey may show:

Vol. X　　　　　　　　　　　*Terzets*

1.	*Psalm 23*	SAT (3 trombones)	*d–D*	4-voice *compl.*
2.	*Psalm 121*	ATB	*F–F*	"
3.	*Psalm 127*	SSB	*a–A*	"
4.	*Luke 2* (1st after Epiphany)	SMB	*a–A*	"
5.	*Psalm 118*	SST	*g–G*	without "

Quartets

6.	*Matt. 2* (S. after Christmas)	STTB	*d–D*	4-voice *compl.*
7.	*1 Cor. 5* (Epistle for Easter)	SATB	*F–F*	without "
8.	*St. Bernard,* Transl.	SSAT	*g–G*	4-voice *compl.*
9.	*St. Bernard* (tr. by M. Moller)	SSTT	*g–G*	without "
10.	*Sirach & Psalm of Psalms*	SSTB	*a–A*	4-voice *compl.*

Vol. XI X

(1) 11.	*Luke 8 (Sexagesima)*	SATB	G–G	"
(2) 12.	*Luke 6* (4th after Trinity)	SATB	*d–D*	"

Vol. XI (Cont'd.)	*Quintets*		
(3) 13. *Luke 2*			
(Purif., Sun. after N.Y.)	SSATB	G—G	without
(4) 14. *Lord's Prayer (Vater unser)*	SMTTB	*g*—G	4-voice *compl.*
(5a) 15a. *Psalm 133* (Wedding no.)	SSATB	*g*—D⎫	2-voice instr. *compl.*
(5b) 15b. *Psalm 133* (Wedding no.)		*d*—G⎭	
(7) 17.[1] *Matt. 22* (23d after Tr.)	SSATB	*g*(G)—G	4-voice instr. "
	Sextets		
(6) 16. *Luke 21* (2d Advent)	SSATTB	*a*—A	without
(8) 18. *Acts 9* (Conv. Paul)	SSTTBB	*d*—*d*	2 4-voice *compl.*
(9) 19. *Psalm 13*	SSATTB	*e*—E	4-voice *compl.*
(10) 20. *Sequence* (Whitsuntide)	SMTTBarB	C—C	2 4-voice *compl.*
(11) 21. *Sirach 50*	SSATTB	F—F	"

Thus we have Old Testament numbers (six and a half from the Psalms and one and a half from Sirach), ten New Testament numbers (among these eight Gospel numbers and one Epistle), two church hymns, and one prayer text, corresponding to the tendency of the later Schütz. Five numbers are without *complementa*, one with only two-voice, thirteen with four-voice, and two with eight-voice supplementary parts. With regard to its external compass the work is the most comprehensive and powerful since the *Psalms of 1619*. According to its internal value, it also takes a position in the foremost rank. Here, too, we have a collection of pieces from different decades, as is proved by the presence of three numbers known from earlier Kassel forms and by the presence of the *Wedding Psalm* of 1619 for brother George. Perhaps Schütz wanted to call forth directly a comparison with the equally strongly scored *Psalms of 1619*, for it is striking that he now places at the head three psalms which he had already set.

Volume 10 begins with a setting of Psalm 23,[2] *Der Herr ist mein Hirt (The Lord is My Shepherd).* The three trombone parts in the Kassel copy have been omitted. It does not follow from this that they were written by another hand. If we add them to the two violins and the three vocal parts, we might have here the same composition "in eight voices" that the Frankfurt fall catalog of 1675 (Göhler II, No. 1397) announced as a single print of *Psalm 23* by Schütz, published by Friedr. Spoor in Strassburg. However, this lost publication might equally well be

---

[1] Doubtless interchanged because of a technical oversight in printing. Schütz has established a number of such oversights in the Appendix.

[2] Practical addition by Karl Friedrichs (Eutin) as Supplement No. 2 to *Der Musikant* (ed. by Fritz Jöde, Kallmeyer, 1924).

the double-chorus setting of 1619 (II, 171). The intermediary may have been
Valentin Strobel, the native Thuringian who was with Scheidt in Halle, then at the
Darmstadt Court, and, at least after 1652, in Strassburg in the capacity of lute
player and lieder composer.[3]

There are a number of surprising similarities (something not heretofore pointed
out) between the two *d* minor numbers, that of 1619 and that of 1650. As examples
we may merely cite the following:

---

[3] M. Vogeleis, *Geschichte der Musik im Elsass* (1911), pp. 514 ff.

Despite these similarities we have different compositions — not only in their scoring but also in their broader construction as well as in their architecture, which in the setting of 1650 very beautifully reverts to the beginning with a *symphonia* of independent motives, for which it holds the instruments in reserve. We should note in the composition of 1619 such charming details as the delightful development of the motives at *Er weidet mich auf grüner Aue — und führet mich zum frischen Wasser* ("He maketh me to lie down in green pastures" and "He leadeth me beside the still waters") in their expanded returns. The later work is in no wise less colorful in its picturesqueness. One could well date it ca. 1625 — especially since the instrumental parts are still held in restraint *(zurückhaltend).*

No. 2, p. 17, the *Wanderpsalm, Ich hebe meine Augen auf (I Will Lift Up Mine Eyes unto the Hills),* has its counterpart in a setting of 1619, and here, too, there are points of resemblance between the two despite the fact that in this case there is a difference of tonalities. The present setting is in F major; that of 1619 is in *d* minor. In both cases we have the melismatic solo beginning to describe "I will lift up mine eyes"; in both a tenor solo for *Er wird meinen Fuss nicht gleiten lassen* ("He will not suffer thy foot to be moved") and

But herewith the similarities (almost accidental) are exhausted, and in every other respect the work of 1650 reveals itself as an independent one. With its unusually smooth flow of lines and the happy relation of the relaxing and tightening of the tonal web, it is undoubtedly the composition written much later. The statement and immediate continuation of *von welchem mir Hilfe kömmt, meine Hilfe kömmt vom Herrn* ("From whence cometh my help? My help cometh from the Lord") is outspokenly original. Here the elegant and anything but conventional melody is of great charm, as is the other closely related solo passage in triple time, *Der Herr behütet dich* ("The Lord is thy keeper"). The piece, with its majestic *tutti* parts, may be warmly recommended for performance.

In the case of the setting of 1650 of Psalm 127 (No. III, p. 27) the "House-Building Psalm," *Wo der Herr nicht das Haus bauet (Except the Lord Build the House)*, the humorous element strikes us more forcibly than in the setting of 1619. In the present version Schütz has the second instrument (cornet?) which accompanies the soprano duet *wo der Herr nicht die Stadt behütet* ("except the Lord keep the city") play the old call (p. 31) "in imitation of the night watchman's horn":[4]

How comically the bass now comes in to deride the "stay-at-homes" *(Hocker)* while the instruments underline "in vain" *(umsonst)* with their mock echo! —:

Subsequently the roles alternate exactly between the sopranos and the bass. What a touch of humor we have when, after the expressly prescribed *tutti forte* (with *complementum)* at *Denn seinen Freunden giebet er's* ("for so He giveth His beloved"), the word *schlafend* ("sleep") is marked *piano* and is to be sung by but a few voices! In the upper parts two are sleeping, while the bass gropes his way in the dark hallway. (See next page.)

---

[4] Buxtehude renewed the same jest in a cantata from the Song of Songs (Pirro, *Buxtehude,* p. 363). A night watchman's horn is met with in Staden's *Seelewig;* but, above all, it blows an *ostinato* in the *Chaconne* of 1673, which forms the third movement of a *Serenade à 5* by H. J. Fr. Biber (P. Nettl, in *Studien zu DTOe,* VIII, 175), published by him and Th. Veidl through Nagel, 1935.

The liveliness of the "children" is portrayed in an equally gay manner: in the discants we have intervals of thirds at *Kinder sind eine Gabe* ("children are an heritage"); then the "arrows" *(Pfeile)* whiz in rushing *coloratura* passages; the "full quiver" is painted in a nine-voice *tutti*, and a very merry *finale* is developed from the bellicose theme

This is doubtless the most roguish composition Schütz ever wrote in the category of spiritual music.

Next we have one of the most beautiful Gospel scenes: the twelve-year-old Christ Child.[5] Here the structure of the text borders on that of an oratorio. All narrative connections are discarded, so that the answer of Jesus follows at once upon the words of his parents. The *muss ich nicht sein* ("Must I not be about My Father's business?") (p. 46) is immediately followed by a *tutti* with a supplementary chorus (p. 48) on Ps. 84: 1-2, 5, *Wie lieblich sind deine Wohnungen* ("How

---

[5] Winterfeld, *Gabrieli* II, 199 f. (III, 153-154). Practical edition but without the complementary instruments by A. Hänlein (*Drei biblische Szenen*, B & H). Lassus and Herpol composed from Luke 2:41-52 the *communio: Fili, quid fecisti nobis sic;* likewise Joh. Schultetus, 1621, with the Protestant deviation *cur* instead of *quid* (Luther, *warum*), all these à 5; Dulichius also gives essentially the words of Mary supplemented by the introduction *Videns Maria puerum Jesum.* Calvisius *(duo)*, on the other hand, limits itself to the answer of Jesus, prompted doubtless by his setting for boys' voices. Raselius and Otto begin with the dramatic passage *Und es begab sich nach dreien Tagen* ("And it came to pass that after three days") or *Post triduum invenerunt.* Similarly Joachim Gotthardt, à 6 (Breslau, manuscript 15), *Et apprehendentes;* while Demantius turns to the lyrical kernel of the *communio* with *Mein Sohn, siehe,* as does Vulpius with *Mein Sohn, warum.* G. Otto's duet cleverly concentrates the scene on *Fili, quid fecisti nobis sic? Ego et pater tuus dolentes quaerebamus te. . . . Et ait illis: Quid est quod me quaerebatis? An nesciebatis quia in his, quae patris mei sunt, oportet me esse?* Rudolf Lassus presents through Donfried, 1622, a thorough-bass duet, *Puer Jesus proficiebat;* Horn begins *Da Jesus zwölf Jahre alt war* and carries the entire story through to the end; likewise W. Brückner (1656). Elsbeth, however, summarizes briefly in a paraphrase, *Und Jesus sass zu Jerusalem im Tempel.* The beautiful six-voice motet by Demantius has been reprinted in my *Die mehrstimmige Vertonung des Evangeliums*, I, 33 ff.

lovely is Thine own dwelling place"), a wonderful, crowning conclusion. To be
sure, Schütz himself did not conceive this textual sequence, which belonged to
theological tradition. The entire work is, of course, a shining example of Schütz's
way of depicting man in the language of music. In the instrumental prelude one
can observe how the parents search restlessly for their child. Then the simple and
kindly reproachful words of Mary (mezzo) and Joseph (bass), *Mein Sohn, warum*
("Son, why hast Thou thus dealt with us?"), Luke 2: 48 (p. 43), *a—G, g(!)—d,
D—A*, tripartite. Note the almost annoyed excitement at *Siehe* ("Behold") (p. 44);
the chromaticism at *Schmerzen* ("sorrowing") (p. 44). Observe also that the violins
are held in reserve for the words of Jesus. The early form in Kassel[6] not only
lacks the *complementum*, but the duet of the parents is three measures longer.
Accordingly, the final form aimed at greater compactness and concentration and
also elaborated a number of rhythmic details more impressively; *g* minor is the
subdominant. The way in which, after these essentially descending lines, the quiet
innocence of the God Child[7] is pictured in the rising fifths:

The words of the Child are presented in tripartite form *(a—C, C—C, a—e)*,
the first and third parts, in turn, both forming a little triptych. The concluding
chorus, again tripartite (which has its counterpart in a *Psalm Concerto* of 1619
(II, 104) is of exemplary simplicity and has the character of folk music. One can
scarcely speak of seven and nine voices, since the complementary voices merely
underscore the solo trio, which retains the leadership. A blissful light spreads itself
over the entire painting.

No. 5 (p. 54), the last of the compositions for three voices, is based on Psalm 118:
25-26, *Herr, hilf (Save Me Now, Lord, I Beseech Thee).* The "Hosannah" added
by Schütz apparently allocates the work to Advent or to Palm Sunday. We already
know the composition as a *kleines geistliches Konzert* of 1636 (VI, 33). Schütz
has now added the two instruments, which form a symphony of their own as a
framework about the entire composition. The repetition of the *symphonia* at the

---

[6] Surely before 1632, printed in the Appendix to Vol. X, 111.
[7] This part must unquestionably be sung by a boy soprano. Regarding the form cf. also
W. Schuh, p. 92.

conclusion is stricken out in the Wolfenbüttel copy and in the one printed in Berlin, indicating that ultimately Schütz wanted to conclude at the *fermata*. The "Hosannah" has been essentially expanded, as befits the development of the richer concertizing ensemble. One notes with admiration the masterly manner in which Schütz wove the violins into the instrumental fabric. In such a revision (here, for once, demonstrable) the master may often have molded and embellished his original version.

The fivefold symmetry of the form is evident from the scoring (W. Schuh, p. 91):

> a violins only
> b vocal without violins
> c vocal with violins (climax)
> d vocal without violins
> e violins only

As the first of the quartets (No. 6, p. 58)[8] there is a richly scored and outstanding Gospel setting[9] for the Sunday after Christmas: *Siehe, es erschien* ("Behold, the angel of the Lord appeareth to Joseph in a dream, saying"). This introduction by the narrator is given in full *tutti*, as later also the narrative part: *Und er stund auf* ("When he arose, he took the young Child and His mother by night"), in order that the words of the angel — in solo form — may form a contrast between the two. In this solo part the violins co-operate in the first half as an echo to the *Steh auf* ("Arise");[10] in the second part they illustrate the far-flung *und fleuch* ("and flee"). In a charmingly vivid way there is pictured the manner in which the blessed foster father arises with difficulty, as with stiff limbs: a whole series of general pauses between *und — er stund auf — und — er stund auf* ("and — he arose — and — he arose")! (p. 61.) It is the "St. Joseph" of R. M. Rilke:

> *Und da nahm er seine dicke Mütze . . . .*
> (Then he took his heavy cap . . . .)

The strange thirty-second-note figures in the violins after the departure into Egypt, *und entweich* ("and flee"), the instruments being divided imitatively on account of the "flight" *(Flucht)* and continuing thus until the words *und blieb allda* ("and was there until the death of Herod") (p. 62), caused Carl v. Winter-

---

[8] Winterfeld, *Gabrieli* II, 200; III, 155.
[9] Matt. 2:13-15.
[10] Ph. Spitta has attempted by means of little strokes to interpret the *Steh auf* as iambic, for which, however, there is scarcely any reason; Schütz doubtless emphasized *Stéh auf* in trochaic form (as, for example, today we still call some beakers *Stéhauf-Männchen*).

feld to ask why. Naturally, he was unable to answer the question.[11] The method of execution will, of course, depend to a great extent on the manner of interpretation. W. Kreidler (loc. cit., pp. 128 ff.) considers it "probable that the presentation springs from the condition of secrecy that was necessarily observed both on the flight and during the sojourn in Egypt. Joseph naturally feared discovery, and so it may have been the intention of the composer to express this threatening fear by the way he wrote this part of the composition." In contrast to this view I prefer to consider the gentle, rising little trills which concentrate themselves on the passage *und blieb allda* ("and bided there") (p. 62) as figures of joy, as if we were to interpret the passage as meaning "and he remained there in peace — while the Child played undisturbed." At all events, they disappear with "Herod" and, therefore, could in no wise refer to him.

The Easter Epistle (No. 7, in F major, p. 67)[12] from 1 Cor. 5: 5, *Feget den alten Sauerteig (Purge Out, Therefore, the Old Leaven),* has the normal voice distribution, S—A—T—B, after the preceding composition had the unusual scoring STTB. It is a fresh, joyful work from the very beginning of the *symphonia,* which anticipates, but in $\frac{3}{1}$ time, the motives of the first chorus portion. The antithesis between the old leaven *(Sauerteig)* and the new *(Süssteig),* the former paired with *Bosheit und Schalkheit* ("malice and wickedness") in the Lombardian rhythm,[13] produces the inner tension in the external wings, between which *das Osterlamm Christus, geopfert* ("the Easter Lamb, Christ, offered") receives full illumination, like an altar painting, in eighteen, twelve, and seven and a half measures, with cadences F—A, F—F, F—F. In a second main division, after another *ritornello,* the spotlight is peculiarly shifted: that which in the first part was the concluding last third: *Darum lasset uns nun* ("Therefore let us keep the feast, not with old leaven, neither with the leaven of malice and wickedness, but with the unleavened bread of sincerity and truth") in the restatement is elevated to the chief position, is expanded from seven and a half to twelve measures, and is strengthened in its texture with a fourteen-measure alleluia. Thus a kind of "chain type" *(Kettentyp),* A B C, C D, results.

As No. 8 (p. 77) we have the *Jubilus S. Bernhardi, O süsser Jesu Christ (O Gentle Jesus Christ),* in a German version by an anonymous author in the bright scoring for two sopranos, alto, and tenor, which obviously does not call for *chiavetta* transpositions. The most varied duets, in the nature of folk songs, are combined

---

[11] "All kinds of gay passages, as in Monteverdi's *Vespers* of 1610, distracting and meaningless."
[12] Practical edition in G major by Heinrich Spitta in *Drei Chöre mit Instrumenten* (Peters).
[13] Quantz and others designate as Lombardian "taste" *(Geschmack)* the rhythm (Scotch snap):

with great tenderness. One is reminded of the style of the Opitz madrigals or of the little prose compositions from the *Song of Songs* of 1629. But after the duet groups have attached themselves to one another ever more closely — what an elemental outburst there is of all solo and complementary voices together!

„Was Jesum lieben heißt, kann keine Hand be = schreiben, kein Mund kanns sprechen

aus, nur der, nur der kanns gläuben, der es erfahren hat, der Jesu hat ge=

liebt, der ihn noch liebt und sich in seine Lieb ergiebt."

This is a glorious composition, one that deserves to be counted among the most famous of its kind!

To No. 9 (p. 89), *O Jesu süss, wer dein gedenkt* (*O Jesus Sweet, Who Thinks on Thee*), for two sopranos and two tenors,[14] Schütz gives a supplementary note in an appendix: "This composition should have as its caption *On A. Grandi's Lilies of the Valley* (*Lilia Convallium*), to which this composition was set by the author, who by no means wishes it to be considered as his invention." As the result of an error in the Kassel voices *(lilium convallium)*, Spitta thought that we are confronted with a setting from Song of Songs 2: 1: "I am the rose of Sharon and the lily of the valley";[15] but he added: "I would have liked to have presented this composition by way of comparison, but so far I have been unable to find it." We can now carry out such a comparison, since the model by the master of Venice and Bergamo (1630) is in the Municipal Library of Breslau.[16] We now observe that Schütz retained the composition of his friend of 1609-12 throughout and, with the exception of an expansion of the conclusion, merely embellished it considerably. Thus what we have lies almost precisely between what was a mere translation of the *Angelus ad pastores* of A. Gabrieli and Schütz's *Gott stehe auf,*[17] constructed freely according to two Monteverdi compositions. Here we have one of those examples of the very close attachment to a model, as in the case of Handel with regard to Urio, Erba, and Carissimi. Schütz wove the German trans-

---

[14] Winterfeld, *Gabrieli* II, 209 f.

[15] *Ego flos campi et lilium convallium.*

[16] *Canto Primo MOTETTI / A UNA DUE / et quattro voci / Con Sinfonie d'Istroment' Partiti per cantar, & / Sonar co'l Chitarrone / DI ALESSANDRO GRANDI / Novamente ristampati, & corretti. / CON PRIVILEGIO / LIBRO SECONDO / (l. e.) / IN VENETIA / Apresso Alessandri Vincenti. MDCXXV. A. -* Professor W. Vetter was so very kind as to put the work in score for me.

[17] See Vol. XII, No. 16, p. 87, LXVIII 1-3.

lation of the *Jubilus S. Bernhardi* by Martin Moller[18] into the composition in a
most skillful manner. [19] Carl v. Winterfeld *(Joh. Gabrieli, II, 210)* knew that
Grandi's composition is concerned with a picture of the Madonna. Thus in Schütz's
text selection we have its conversion into Protestant form in a way similar to that
which we have in the case of Hans Sachs when he converts the German *Salve
regina, Wilkom lobes werde,* of Heinrich Loufenberg into his *Silberweise: Salve
ich grüsse dich schone, Rex Christe mit der Krone.* Let us observe first the beginning of the *sinfonia:*

Then the first solo (the basses are almost the same everywhere):

---

[18] W. Nelle, *Geschichte des deutschen evangelischen Kirchenliedes* (1909), pp. 80 ff.
[19] The idea that Schütz omitted the line *Du Licht der Welt und Gnadensonne* is an oversight
of W. Schuh (p. 91). In the case of this text, too, one cannot assert that Schütz rejected a congregational melody, for in his day there was as yet no such melody; at least, the earliest one, by
Joh. Staden, 1625 (Zahn, 550-60 and 1759) had no more entered the congregational song of
Saxony than the one by Trümper (Gotha, 1648).

In the second solo the two versions balance each other in their figuration:

Let us also add a brief example of style from the third solo:

The concluding part of Grandi's work, *de quo triumphans et laeta canit ecclesia*, consisting of fourteen measures, Schütz expanded to eighteen measures with the text *Jesus, du engelische Zier, all Himmelsheer lobsingen dir* ("Jesus, Thou Glory of the angels, all heavenly hosts sing Thy praise"). He apparently utilized the happy coincidence that both texts speak of "singing."

While this *g* minor composition is fascinating from the viewpoint of technical workmanship, No. 10 (p. 96), *Lasset uns doch den Herren, unsern Gott, loben (Let Us Sing to the Lord, Our God, and All Praise Him)*, an *a* minor prayer of thanksgiving from Ecclus. 50: 22 and numerous individual psalm verses, captivates one by its splendid rhythmic liveliness, which, to be sure, as the result of its ceaseless chains of eighths *(alles, alles)*, almost borders on the buffo-comic. Indeed, this musical *(musikantische)* unconcernedness of the

and the drastic portrayal of *Jauchzen, Regen, Triefen, Kriege, Pfeifen* (jubilation, raining, dripping with fat, wars, and pipes) point to the period ca. 1620, as does the manner in which, in the radiant concluding *tutti*, the interlacing oppositional voice is simply chiseled in octaves between the alto and the second violin, then between the tenor of the *favoriti* and the soprano of the *complementum*. Here we still find in Schütz a bit of the theatrical Kapellmeister who carries his *finale* to a climax.

What another world speaks out of the Sexagesima Gospel, the parable of the sower (Luke 8: 5-15), *Es ging ein Sämann (A Sower Went Out to Sow His Seed)*, with which Spitta's Vol. XI begins![20] Here Schütz has beautifully developed a *rondo* form by concluding each of the four parts most impressively with a variation on a three-part refrain that approaches the Gospel tone:

The last time he indulges in a most imposing multiplication of the elements (from ten to thirteen and ten to thirty measures)![21] Inasmuch as parts two, three, and four can be omitted, according to Schütz's own statement, either completely or individually, it apparently was to be optional how much of the Gospel one wished to render in polyphony. The remainder of the story — verses nine to fifteen — at all events belonged to the liturgist at the altar. With the perfect simplicity of 1650

---

[20] Practical new edition by H. Hoffmann (Bärenreiter, ed. 827), transposed up from G major to B flat major.

[21] Detailed analysis in Schuh, pp. 84 f.

Schütz treats the opening account, despite the intervening polyphony, in genuinely narrative manner. How pictorial is the music at *fiel etliches an den Weg* ("some fell by the wayside; and it was trodden down"); *und frassens auf* ("devoured it"); *und etliches fiel auf den Fels* ("and some fell upon a rock"); or the waywardly rhythmicized *Dornen* ("thorns")! One should note how, by way of symbolism, the briars, allotted to the three instrumental parts, actually "choke" *(erstickt)* the vocal lines. Then comes the regular cadence at *ein gut Land,* the baroque word repetitions at *hundert-, hundertfältige Frucht,* and finally, in connection with this, one of the boldest examples in all music for the eye and also for the ear, as one stalk outgrows the other:

When we note how this piece concludes: *der höre, der höre* ("let him hear") — beseeching in a solo voice, with *piano* and *forte* alternation on the part of the instruments, then bursting forth monumentally in the brightest light, with rushing violin passages — we see before us a figure of the Christ, a painting in music that could scarcely be matched by any artist in the late seventeenth and in the entire eighteenth century.

On the same level of perfection stands No. 2, the Gospel parable of the mote and the beam, Luke 6: 36-42 (p. 25), for the Fourth Sunday after Trinity, *Seid barmherzig (Be Ye, Therefore, Merciful).*[22] Here, too, Schütz has left it optional whether to perform the entire work or only the first half, which itself is subdivided into two clear halves: a *Bar* (d—F) with precentors — couplet: *seid barmherzig*

---

[22] The first half was set by Wanning, Raselius, Demantius, Elsbeth, Vulpius, Herpol, Otto, Calvisius; very important the setting by Lasso, *à* 7; *Nolite judicare,* by Oscolati in Schadeaus (1611); Dulichius gives the second half only; Caspar Horn gives the entire Gospel.

("be merciful"); conclusion: *richtet nicht* ("judge not"), *verdammt nicht* ("condemn not"), *vergebet!* ("forgive"), *gebet* ("give"); and again a *Bar* in *tutti* scoring at and on account of the "good measure pressed down and shaken together and running over"[23] (F—A). While in the former *Bar* one is impressed by the penetrating seriousness of the admonitions, with their neat symmetry, as

so in the case of the *tutti Bar* one is struck by the free, homorhythmic declamation uttered by all, which must be understood as disregarding or crossing the bar lines as it hammers in the words of the Savior

Then one actually sees the blind leading the blind. They suffer their catastrophe in three groups of duets:

All this is sketched with the simplicity of a *biblia pauperum;* especially where

and

are placed against each other. Deeply moving now is the way in which, in the *tutti,* the angry Christ breaks in with *Du Heuchler* ("Thou hypocrite"); the eighths within the tonal pillars paint the indignation; all speak as one man: *Zeuch zuvor den Balken* ("Cast out first the beam out of thine own eye, and then shalt thou see

---

[23] *Volles, gerütteltes, überflüssiges Mass.*

clearly to pull out the mote that is in thy brother's eye"). If only many of the "righteous" would ponder this sermon as Schütz presents it with such powerful emphasis!

And next we have, as No. 3, p. 39, a third Gospel setting, for the Feast of the Purification of Mary or for the Sunday after New Year, Luke 2: 34-35, *Siehe, dieser wird gesetzt (Behold, This Child Is Set for the Fall),*[24] with two sopranos, the first of the vocal quintets. The peculiar rhythm of the first theme, which enters immediately — as Simeon is speaking, the bass begins — is to be understood as a succession of two agogic groups of threes with a *ritardando* as the objective on the second, and it is to be emphasized accordingly:

The rising lines at *Auferstehung* ("rising") present the fruitful countermove to the *Fall;* the two together form the first part of a couplet. The second part of the couplet is begun symmetrically by the alto. The conclusion *(Abgesang)* begins with *Siehe, dieser wird gesetzt* ("Behold, this Child is set for a sign"). Then a second part is formed by *Und es wird ein Schwert* ("Yea, a sword shall pierce through thy own soul"), again in the melody form $\diagdown\diagup$, to which the countertheme, *auf dass vieler Herzen* ("that the thoughts of many hearts may be revealed"), shows the reverse course $\diagup\diagdown$. Both also supplement each other splendidly in a metrical manner, in that the first half reduces itself from the broadest note values to ♩ ♪ ♪ ♩ ♩ , while the second passes from ♪♪♩ ♩.♪♩ ♩ to very quiet rhythms.

A piece of the first order is *The Lord's Prayer (Vater unser)*[25] (No. 4, p. 51), in which Schütz alters the architecture of the text in a peculiar manner by prefacing almost every petition with the call *Vater* and developing *denn dein ist das Reich* ("Thine is the kingdom") by an expansion to four lines. This is one of the first beginnings toward the gradual transformation of the composed Bible texts into

---

[24] With regard to the earlier composers of settings of this prophecy of the aged Simeon, which for the most part is interwoven into the entire history of the presentation in the temple, see my *Mehrstimmige Vertonung des Evangeliums,* p. 40. Practical edition of Schütz's composition in Heinrich Spitta's *Drei Chöre mit Instrumenten,* with transposition from C major to D. Oboes, not violins, are here plausibly suggested as instruments.

[25] Practical edition by Fritz Sporn, 1922 (B & H). With regard to the form see Schuh, pp. 85 ff.

the madrigalistic paraphrases.[26] At all events, this encroachment gives to the four-part whole the strongly subjective undertone of the trusting, even passionate, supplication of a child. For this reason, too, we doubtless have the soprano in the role of precentor in the first petition as well as, during the further course, the repeated *lux in tenebris* effect of the discant entrances *Vater, Vater!* At the beginning the chromatic chordal sequence *à la* Marenzio: E flat major — C major; F—D, G—E flat in the four lower voices is to be interpreted as a caressive *(lieblich)* petition. Judging from the frequently rather nervous rhythm, we are probably again confronted with an early rather than a late work. We should note the very effective economy of means: the instruments enter for the first time only at the tenor solo *Vater, denn dein ist das Reich* ("Father, for Thine is the kingdom"), where again they develop a livelier motion only at *Amen*. Not until the repetition of this section does the same soloist, with instruments and full *complementum*, appear in brilliant antiphony to the full quartet of the remaining *favoriti*. It is to achieve the intoxicating fullness of the double plagal ending that at *Amen, Vater, Amen (c* minor — G major), with a sustained $^{g}_{e}$ flat, a portion of the voices passes by way of $^{a}_{f}$ to $^{b}_{g}$.

The wedding composition for Georg Schütz, which follows, gives, to some extent, the effect of a stranger with its scoring for six instruments. The work has been discussed previously.

As the last of the quintets we add here No. 7, the Gospel parable of the tribute money, Matt. 22: 16-21, *Meister, wir wissen (Master, We Know)*, for the Twenty-third Sunday after Trinity.

While Caspar Horn later set the entire lesson, verses fifteen to twenty-two, as did also Th. Elsbeth — though with the briefer beginning "The Pharisees and the servants of Herod" — Vulpius begins with Jesus' question, "Why tempt ye Me, ye hypocrites?" Demantius begins with "Whose is this image?" Most musicians feel that the beginning of the dramatic tension lies between these passages and accordingly begins with "Master, we know that Thou art true." [27] Thus do Herpol, Wanning, Dulichius, Otto, Calvisius, and also Schütz. Since the concluding verse, "When they had heard these words," is felt as anticlimactic, it is for the most part not polyphonized.

After a somewhat prattling trio symphony, which doubtless is intended to represent the malicious counsel of the Pharisees, the latter enter with the tenor as leading voice in the quintet. One should fully appreciate the hypocrisy which lies in

---

[26] Cf. my *Evangelienvertonung*, pp. 64 ff.
[27] *Rabbi (Magister) scimus, quia verax (verus) es.*

this tenor part — in most cases answered canonically by the soprano. Especially should one observe the hypocritical genuflections at

After the manner of the motet passion, the evangelist and the people are presented polyphonically. The "one penny" which is presented appears only in the alto! Jesus, as tenor, is the sole soliloquist against the crowd. That which in the Gospel of the "mote" was superimposed at *Ihr Heuchler* ("Ye hypocrites") — four eighths and halves — is now presented in sequence with complementary rhythm in the organ bass:

The lower sequence has the effect of sad indignation! It is glorious to note what feeling Schütz draws from Jesus' apparently so entirely reasonable answer (p. 92-98):

That is, in reality he laughs at the emperor as a colossus with earthen feet — but he thinks of God with the most joyful devotion. And this antithesis hovers over the entire *tutti* development of Jesus' answer, as though all Christendom were confirming the Savior's meaning.[28]

No. 6 (p. 75) opens the series of sextets with the words of Jesus from Luke 21:

---

[28] The form analysis in Schuh (pp. 89 f.) is excellent, though the concept *Rahmen* (frame) for the first words of the Pharisees and the completely differently functioning *finale* does not seem to be quite appropriate.

34-36, *Hütet euch* ("And take heed to yourselves lest at any time your hearts be overcharged with surfeiting"), the Gospel for the Second Sunday in Advent.[29] We have already met the text in the *Symphoniae sacrae II* as a bass monody with instruments (VII, 60). This time, despite the polyphony, the tenor, to a large extent, has the leadership. There are also numerous other relations between the two compositions:

Also the rhythmic similarity at *und komme dieser Tag....* ("so that day come upon you unawares, for as a snare shall it come"). Furthermore, one should note:

---

[29] Practical edition by H. Spitta (*Drei Chöre mit Instrumenten,* Peters) with transposition from *a* minor to *b* minor.

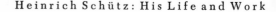

be ≠ tet, be ≠ tet, daß ihr wür≠dig wer≠den mö≠get___

Finally, at *und zu stehen für des Menschen Sohn* ("and to stand before the Son of Man")[30] the correspondence is nothing less than startling. This is a case neither of "recomposition" nor of conscious borrowing; but it is instructive from the creative, psychological point of view, since it shows how even in the case of so unusually imaginative a spirit as Schütz invention follows related paths when one deals with the same text. It was not otherwise with Handel, Gluck, and Schubert. Moreover, the sextet is as significant and as beautiful as the solo number; indeed, quite naturally, it is developed in a still richer and more florid manner. It is remarkably suitable as an introduction to Schütz's characteristics.

Finally, No. 8, p. 99, the very famous setting of the lesson for the Festival of the Conversion of St. Paul, Acts 9: 1-19,[31] *Saul, Saul, was verfolgst du mich? (Saul, Saul, Why Persecutest Thou Me?).* L. Päminger polyphonized the quite detailed account as an effective four-voice, four-part motet: *Saul adhuc spirans / Dixit autem: Quis es, Domine? / Erat autem quidam discipulus / Et introivit domum* to *quod is esset Christus.*[32] Similarly, there is a setting for five voices by Copus (in the *Thesaurus* of 1568 and in a Zwickau manuscript) and another five-voice setting by Wanning; there is a six-voice composition — *Et cum iter faceret* — by Chr. Hollander and an eight-voice setting by Leoni in Schadaeus, 1611. G. Otto limits himself to *Dixit Dominus ad Ananiam.* Both Renaissance and baroque were attracted to the text excerpt used by Schütz, *Saule, Saule, quid Me persequeris?* as having the merit of illustrating the emotional emphasis of the *musica riservata.* Lebrun offers a quartet published by Giunta in 1526 and a quintet published by Attaignant in 1554; L. Balbi, a septet published in Schadaeus III. Urban Loth presents a thorough-bass duet through Donfried, 1627; Viadana, a duet through the same publisher, 1622, and, above all, a soprano monody which Ph. Spitta includes principally[33] because its repeated echo effects may have inspired Schütz's work.[34] If this should be the case, it was surely only to do something better *(per oppositionem);* for basically Viadana's work is quite a sorry creation! If Ludovico Grossi had in mind in this connection a powerful *soprano castratus,* such an unnatural

---

[30] Afterwards in the first soprano this is even quite literally like *Sinf. sacr. II!*
[31] Practical edition ed. by Siegfried Ochs with clavier (B & H, 1925).
[32] Examples of style in my *Evangelienvertonung,* I, 27.
[33] GA XI, p. 8, acc. to the Nordhausen *Fasciculus* of 1638.
[34] As Schütz echo effects Ph. Spitta places together there III, 16 ff.; VII, 27; XIII, 92 f.

effect *(Nympheneffekt)*[35] is certainly to be rejected in view of such a textual content. Observe merely:

cur me   per = se = que = ris,   = se = que = ris   cur   me_____,

me_____,   quis es tu,   quis   es tu, tu

Equally incomprehensible is the fact that in Grossi the words of Saul and of Jesus are presented immediately after one another with the same echos.

On the other hand, what has Schütz accomplished with his precisely indicated dynamics *(forte, mezzopiano, pianissimo)*? In reality these are not echoes at all but the representation of "frightfully near, half-distant, gruesomely vanishing!"

Respect demands that we let Carl von Winterfeld speak at this point.[36] It was he who rediscovered Schütz more than a hundred years ago, and he knew full well how to describe what he discovered!

A six-voice chief chorus, accompanied by two violins and organ, constitutes the nucleus of the whole. Two four-voice choruses are associated with this for purposes of filling out and strengthening. The master has distinguished two things in this text: the call of the Lord to the persecutor and the warning directed to him. By means of the opposition of these two parts and their ever richer and more significant development, he formed his tone painting. At the beginning he divides his principal chorus into three vocal pairs, allowing the voices lying next to one another to associate themselves. Two basses, a tenor and an alto, two sopranos, finally also, as a kind of echo, the two violins, are thus heard successively. In the deepest tones of the two basses the stern call begins to the one who rages heedlessly along on his wicked path. More keenly, more impressively, it raises itself more and more into the heights. It seems to disappear again in the tones of the violins. But now, unexpectedly, it repeats itself with full power in the union of all three participating choruses, where before it was heard by but two voices at a time. But it is not this strengthening of the mass alone by means of which the master strove for a heightening of the expression or the surprise of the listener. The relation of the entrances of the choirs to the measure selected for the song serves him in bringing about a still more powerfully moving effect. The 3/1 measure lies at the basis of the beginning of the song. The call is now heard at first on the second beat of this measure, then on the first and the third beats, proceeding along the steps of the minor triad, finally to rest again on the first beat of the measure. In similar manner it thus repeats itself in the voice pairs which follow one another. As soon, however, as the choirs unite, this relationship of vocal entrance appears in reverse order. And thus we hear with increasing strength of tone, with heightened

---

[35] From Lassus by way of the Opitz opera echoes and Gluck's *Orpheus I* to the present-day children's jest, *Wie heisst der Bürgermeister von Wesel?* - *Esel*. Cf. recently also the treatise by Johs. Bolte, *Das Echo in Volksglaube und Dichtung* (Treatise of the Prussian Academy of Sciences, Philos. - histor. division *(Klasse,* 1935) and the postscript.

[36] *Johs. Gabrieli* (1834), II, 197 f.

emphasis, that call on every beat of the measure, from changing sides or directions. The words "Why persecutest thou me?" [37] attach themselves to the call with the full power of all three choruses. Then the subordinate choruses become silent. Only the chief chorus repeats the question twice more in decreasing strength and abbreviated rhythmus, which transform the 3/1 to 3/2 time. Now the 4/4 time takes the place of the hitherto uneven time and remains the regulating measure to the end of the song. The warning admonition begins: "It is difficult for thee to kick against the pricks," [38] and it, too, is driven home more emphatically as the composition proceeds. For at the beginning we hear the admonition with organ accompaniment only, presented successively by the tenor and the alto of the principal chorus. After the preceding call has repeated the reproachful question exactly as before in all the choirs, with the exception of the changed time, two voices, the first soprano and the bass of the principal chorus, are united for the admonition. The four lower voices now also seize upon it in its main outlines. The highest voices also unite in the full concert, the violins also finally joining in. After the warning words are thus heard ever louder and more powerfully, they finally fade away in the lower voice, besides which only the two accompanying instruments are still heard. But then the call and the question again, and unexpectedly, break into these separate tones. Three other voices again take up the admonition; but the latter is overpowered by the strength with which those two former ones are repeated, by means of the new and unexpected manner of this repetition. . . . From the point described Schütz assigned the call "Saul, Saul" only to the tenor of the principal chorus. In sustained tones, with ever-increasing strength, he ascends the scale with this call through three whole tones (c, d, e). On the part of the remaining five voices, on the other hand, we hear the words "why persecutest thou me?" in the gradations already described. As the tenor now rises ever higher, their pitch also rises, so that we hear them in threefold change as they proceed through the major tonalities of F and G to *a* minor. While, however, their song gradually fades away at each repetition, we hear out of this recession, in inverse ratio, the call of the tenor with ever-greater power, ever more threatening, powerful, and overwhelming. Associated with the bass alone, he appears to wish to end the whole with the question, "Why persecutest thou me?" But once more, unexpectedly, he seizes upon his former call; and after the remaining voices have interpolated themselves in the manner described before, the composition fades away in softest tones, with dying breath, the alto alone associating its voice with that of the tenor.

As a pictorial presentation the master shows us by his music the whole power of a supernatural phenomenon which moves one's innermost being. The overwhelming power of a voice which, like distant thunder, arises from the depths, which seems to dissipate itself in the heights like a repressed foreboding, then to return with full power, shakes us to the depths; it again fades away, but even though repeatedly warded off — ever resounds anew with solemn, urgent warning, intensifying its call, ever approaching closer to the sinful, blinded persecutor till, to be sure, it fades away, but only after effecting a complete reformation in the shattered spirit, after turning within the eye blinded to the outer world, then again to open it for this world, too, with strengthened, illuminated, brighter vision, that it might see the time and place where the unknown God, who had revealed Himself to him, was to be preached to others who have gone astray.

A classical presentation filled with the culture of Goethe and the care of a Schinkel drawing board!

Only a few individual points remain to be added. On viewing the opening motive we find each time in two individual instances liberties which indeed almost violate the rules of the time — liberties that were characteristic of Schütz ca. 1625:

---

[37] *Was verfolgst du mich?*
[38] *Es wird dir schwer werden wider den Stachel zu löcken.*

the leap from the held-over ninth to the sixth, and the parallel seconds resulting
from the fact that the middle voice gives the resolution of the suspension, while
the upper voice simultaneously gives the melodic anticipation (quarter measure):

From such liberties one has a presentiment of the creative tonal chaos out of which
such phenomena in Schütz must have detached themselves with demonic power
and as though superrationally dictated from above.

Between this first call and the second text phrase, *es wird dir schwer werden*
("it is hard for thee"), there stands in the original *Er aber sprach: Herr* ("And he
said, Who art Thou, Lord? And the Lord said, I am Jesus, whom thou persecutest").
As Viadana had omitted all narrative connections, so Schütz, doubtless in subconscious recollection of the corresponding omission, introduced that single
general pause (pp. 100—101) except for the *basso continuo*. I no longer believe
he introduced this to serve intentionally for the interpolation at that point of the
altar song.[39] The composition under consideration, though doubtless intended for
the service, was a concerted piece to be sung before the sermon, but not in the
middle of the lesson, and this kind of textual omission is well known to us from
Schütz's dialogs. Considered from the formal point of view, the work stands
between a *rondo*like, five-divisional structure (R A R' A' R") and *Bar* form, in

which $\begin{smallmatrix} \overline{RA} & \overline{R'A'} \\ T & SB \end{smallmatrix}$ would be the *Stollen* and the self-expanding *Gegenstollen*,

while R" r plus R''' would be the conclusion, in which "r" represents that peculiarly lashing tenor voice "Saul, Saul, Saul."

But one almost feels ashamed to apply the plumb line and the measuring rod
to such inspiration. We have before us a pinnacle of the entire older music;[40] a
piece of spectral dramatic art; a distant whispering and rustling, the approaching
threat, the roaring, the nightmare of a colossal cloud shadow finally dissipating
itself specterlike into the mist, as it had begun mysteriously like the inescapable
voice of conscience — all this reminds one of the colossal style of P. P. Rubens'
"Last Judgment."

---

[39] *Die mehrstimmige Vertonung des Evangeliums,* I, 60.
[40] My *Geschichte der deutschen Musik,* II, 1922, p. 63.

The setting of Psalm 13 (Vol. XI, No. 9), *Herr wie lang (How Long, O Lord)*, which follows, for a choir of six strings and a chorus of six voices, may have belonged (like Nos. 1—3 in Vol. X and the individual works discussed above) to the scattered planetoids that were intended for the second volume of polychorus psalms to which Schütz still looked forward in 1647. Even if parts of a preliminary form, differing only slightly from the later one, have been preserved in Kassel, the piece, despite this fact, may have originated at the beginning of the 1630's. For the individual voices which enter after the compact and definitely text-engendered instrumental prolog *(e—E)*, with their *stylus oratorius* developed from the repercussion tone and in the textual formation of the repeatedly injected "Lord, how long, how long?" strongly recall the *Kleine geistliche Konzerte* of 1636-39. They constitute only the terzet foreground to the artistically woven *Bar*, *Schau doch und erhöre mich* ("Consider and hear me"), with the conclusion *Dass sich mein Feind nicht rühme* ("lest mine enemy say") *(C—a, a—D, D—a)*. Only here does the string choir again enter to concertize with solo, duet, terzet, and finally sextet of the vocal parts, now in full chorus, now in semichorus. This *finale* is likewise of *Bar* form: C—G, E—E and C—E, in connection with which at the juncture between *Auf-* and *Abgesang* (before the sextet entrance), there is peculiar preliminary modulation:

In the concluding concerted passage one should note the fine and variously grouped phrases overlapping one another — a valuable composition, but, when compared with the others, without an "emphasizing asterisk."

Such an asterisk, on the other hand, everyone will doubtless grant without hesitation to the Whitsuntide *concerto, Komm heiliger Geist (Come, Holy Spirit, Lord and God),* based on the church melody. The three stanzas, varying radically, with an alleluia refrain after each and expanded after the last, represent an expanded *Bar*[41] with a tendency to a *rondo* structure. This brief example will illustrate Schütz's use of the model:

Thus we have now embellishment, now a playing about the melody or a slight transposition or paraphrase, now expansion, now contraction of the model, yet always perceptibly along the lines of its contour, even though at times altogether free lines are interposed as counterpoints. A fourfold chordal *O, O, O, O* before *O Herr, durch deines Lichtes Glanz* ("O Lord, through Thy descending fire"), or threefold before *O Herr, behüt für fremder Lehr* ("Lord, from strange doctrines keep us free") belongs to the heartfelt characteristics of Middle German baroque. In the last stanza there is even a sixfold repetition before *O Herr, durch dein Kraft uns bereit* ("O Lord, through Thy strength us prepare"). Even in such small differences we perceive Schütz's sensitive and delicate spatial sense, as he also well knows how to paint *ritterlich Ringen* ("nobly striving") with the power of a Sicking! The last three alleluias show what an ingenious harmonist he is. After he has already arrived at the C major tonic by way of G major, he cadences by way of E A D D, D G C C, *a* E⁶ F C. The ecclesiastical cadence is far more festal for him than the universal V—I!

No. 11, *Nun danket alle Gott (Now Thank We All Our God)*[42] doubtless comes from Schütz's *Festival Music for the Peace Celebration*[43] (1648); for the phrase *und verleihe immerdar Friede, Friede, Friede* ("and grant us ever peace, peace, peace") is presented with such a gleam of joy that it stands in most significant contrast to the preceding cries of longing. Here Schütz did not set Martin Rinckart's *Tischgebetlein* (little table prayer) with the same title, the prayer which Rinckart

---

[41] Schuh, p. 82, likewise. The practical edition by Fritz Sporn (B & H) transposes from C to D; an ed. by Rob. Unger (Bad Hamburg), which transposes to E flat, offers the advantage that three voices can be sung by a female chorus and simplifies for the trombone choirs the complement support.

[42] Practical edition by Fritz Sporn (B & H).

[43] *Festmusiken zur Friedensfeier.*

sang so touchingly during the horrors of the war at Eilenburg; he set its prose model from Jesus Sirach. Nevertheless, as often as the beginning of the text returns with the full power of the complementary choir, he approaches the Crüger melody very closely. I alter the bar lines in a manner already indicated in Ph. Spitta's score:

Here we may subjoin the description of the form by W. Schuh (p. 83):

> A *sinfonia* (with its own motives) for the two violins with continuo serves as introduction. Then follows a little *tutti* section which further on is repeated as refrain. Between the four appearances of the refrain there are three differently worked-out sections. The first of these has two parts; the second has two with a tendency to the formation of a third subdivision (as *Abgesang* or conclusion); the third section is set as *Bar* form. These three main divisions show a climactic arrangement insofar as the first part is not more than two-voiced, the second not more than four (with two violins), while only the third part is six-voiced (with two violins). After the last repetition of the refrain an alleluia, set as *Bar* form (six-voiced, with two violins and complement), constitutes the conclusion of the piece.

Symphonia (with own motives) (two violins)
Refrain *(tutti)*
1. Part　(two-voiced, without violins)
Refrain *(tutti)*
2. Part　(four-voiced, with violins)
Refrain *(tutti)*
2. Part　(four-voiced, with violins)
Refrain *(tutti)*
3. Part　(six-voiced, without violins)
Alleluia *(tutti)*

It is noteworthy how in the inner structure of the parts the *Bar* forms become more and more evident toward the conclusion, in the second part as a striving toward this form, but in the third part and in the alleluia clearly.

The two violins in the second part adhere closely to the motives of the voices; likewise in the refrain; in the alleluia they are presented in freer instrumental leading, without, however, gaining essential significance of their own.

Despite the dissimilarity of parts one, two, and three with respect to scoring, length, and inner structure, the form of the entire piece is extremely clear, thanks to the refrain and the climactic arrangement. Freedom in details is compensated for by strictness in the form as a whole, primarily by means of the introduction of fulcra which substantiate the general outlines.

The second part has a certain predominance by reason of its extent and the co-operation of the violins, but it is not so great as seriously to disturb the equilibrium of the structure determined by the refrain and climactic arrangement.

When we view the *Symphoniae sacrae* III in its entirety and from this point look back upon the totality of the three works with this title — 1629, 1647, and 1650 — we behold a proud and royal picture:

German instrumental music, which in the future was to become so powerful (if we disregard the worthy old domestic organ tradition), here undertook for the first time a task which spiritually and intellectually went essentially beyond the popular art of the suite. And it fulfilled this role brilliantly. From the general situation of German music of the day it is understandable enough that its function stood first of all in the service of spiritual vocal music; and the fact that it took as its point of departure the slender-voiced art of Italy is reflected very clearly in the little Latin *concerti* of Schütz's *Symphoniae sacrae* I, which, however, even in 1629 revealed a perfect equilibrium between the instrumental and the vocal elements. The second part developed the linguistic and theological Germanization without surrendering the small intimate form. Only the third part allows the new art to develop all the means of attaining monumental structure whereby the circle returns to the polychoral *Psalms of David,* although at a higher level. Even where the instrumental introductions of these *concerti* and the interwoven, accompanying violin voices show independent material, the latter is nonetheless word-engendered or at least permeated by the representations of the Biblical words. The idea of Schütz's contemporary, Samuel Scheidt, to compose seventy trio symphonies according to the seven chief tonalities, these symphonies to be used according to choice in connection with vocal works at hand,[44] would doubtless never have occurred to Schütz. On the other hand, Schütz's *Symphoniae sacrae,* by means of their structural and antithetical *(kampflich)* insertions of the instrumental groups — which remain now vocal in character, now sprout forth in bold technique according to need — won a new freedom and mobility which allowed these works to become a strong propelling power along the important path "from the motet to the cantata." But entirely apart from such a historical mission, the three volumes contain, like precious vases (from all decades of Schütz's creative activity), not only fresh, green branches but an almost overwhelming abundance of the most brilliant blossoms of his God-given creative power.

---

[44] Concerning this work of 1645, published through Ambrosius Profe, see Mahrenholz, *Scheidt,* pp. 34 ff. As early as 1642 Scheidt had offered the manuscript in vain to the dukes of Brunswick and Weimar.

Late Occasional Works

In the present chapter we include five additional works composed on various occasions, some in the capacity of Court Kapellmeister, others by Heinrich Schütz as "man and friend." While this category is the one which has suffered the greatest loss, doubtless some things may still come to light in the examination of funeral sermons and contemporary prints. Following is the list:

Fürstliche Gnade zu Wasser und zu Lande — *Princely Grace at Sea and on Land* (Vol. XV, No. 11, p. 86), 1647[1]

Wie wenn der Adler — *As When the Eagle* (Vol. XV, No. 12, p. 93), 1651[2]

O meine Seele — *O My Soul* (Vol. XVIII, No. 6, p. 115), 1652

Gesang der drei Männer — *Song of the Three Men in the Fiery Furnace* (Vol. XIII, No. 8), 1652 (?)

Canticum Simeonis, à 6 — *Canticle of Simeon* (Vol. XII), 1657

Herre Gott, dich loben wir — *Te Deum laudamus* (questionable), 1668 (?)

The first, for male alto with a *ritornello* (printed only in Gotha), dates from what was probably Schütz's first visit; the second, set for a discant without melody instruments, was written for the Altenburg wedding and was included in Schirmer's *Rautengepüsche*.[3] Both are worthy successors to the monody *Grimmige Gruft*, of 1623, which, however, offered us more inducement for detailed consideration.

The poem for *O meine Seele, warum betrübst du dich?* (*O My Soul, Why Art Thou Cast Down?*) was written by the widower of one Anna Margarethe Voigt in September 1652 and was given a simple four-voiced setting by Schütz, a setting that reminds one of the *Becker Psalms*. The Dresden print exists not only in Göttingen, where Mahrenholz discovered it, but, according to A. Werner, also in Stolberg. If provided with a better text, the quartet would be a most welcome funeral composition even today. Even Zahn knows of no chorale strophe to its "iambic" meter 11, 10, 11, 10, 5, 5, 9, 11.

---

[1] With different words, as a wedding song, in the *Volksliederbuch*, III, 645, p. 156.

[2] *MGkK*, 29, 1924, p. 174. *Volksliederbuch*, III, 646.

[3] The arias *Fürstliche Gnade* and *Wie wenn der Adler* have already been briefly described in the biographical section.

The date "March 1652" on the only surviving copy, in Königsberg, of the *Gesang der drei Männer im feurigen Ofen (Song of the Three Men in the Fiery Furnace)* refers to the date of the copy, not to that of the composition of the comprehensive work for five voices with its three instrumental choirs (five strings, two *cornettini*, three trombones). However, as this copy was made a half year after the death of Heinrich Albert, the work doubtless was not composed much before 1652; otherwise Schütz would undoubtedly have sent it to his cousin long before this. The litanylike text, with its refrain repeated thirty-four times — chiefly *preist und rühmet ihn ewiglich* ("praise and magnify Him forever") — suggested to Schütz a formally very artistic arrangement, which will be apparent from the following plan:

Scoring of the little solo parts	*Tutti Refrains*	*Cadential Frame:*	
T, T, TA, B, TA, TAB	6 x Type I	*d*	— D
S, SS, AT, SBS, BT, SS	6 x Type II	F	— G
AT, SSATB, SA, ATB, SS, SB	6 x Type III	*d*	— F
S², T, S¹A, B, BT, S²A	6 x Type IV	F	— D
SS, TB, B, TA	6 x Type V	C	— A
SST	6 x Type VI	C	— A
A, T, B, SS	6 x Type VII	E flat	— G
T, SS, TAB, SSATB	6 x Type VIII	*d*	— Bb

with dominant conclusion on F *(Quintabschluss)*. (The entire work reminds one strongly of the structure of a gnomic poem *[Priamel]*!) And now comes (p. 210) a solo quintet without orchestra, *denn er hat uns erlöset aus der Höllen* ("for He hath redeemed us from hell") *(d—G)*, as an introduction to the magnificent closing *tutti* on verses sixty-seven and sixty-eight of the Bible passage in the Apocrypha, *Danket dem Herrn* ("O give thanks unto the Lord") *(d—D)*. The choice of the kind of soloist is to a great extent dependent on the text: *siehest in die Tiefe* ("seest all beneath Thee"), *Erde* ("earth"), *Walfische* ("whales"), *Priester* ("priests") call for a bass; *ihr Himmel* ("you heavens"), for the first soprano; *Licht und Finsternis* ("light and darkness"), for a soprano and bass; *alle Winde* ("all ye tempests"), for the entire quintet; *Sonn und Mond* ("sun and moon"), *Feuer und Hitze* ("fire and heat"), *Tag und Nacht* ("day and night"), each for a duet; *die Schlossen* ("hailstones") and *der Hagel* ("hail"), for a terzet; likewise, at the end, the three men mentioned by name (p. 207). As some of the refrains also show a tendency toward polyphony, we are protected against monotony not merely by a change of tonality; and the piece, somewhat frightening at first sight, might merit a performance at a festival service.

The two motets on the *Nunc dimittis,* for the death of Johann Georg I, Ph. Spitta placed in the appendix to Vol. XII, p. 201, as the discant is missing in the only printed copy *(Stadtbibliothek,* Leipzig). Heinrich von Herzogenberg, however, supplied this with "the fine and experienced hand of an artist." The title page tells us that the work was not sent to the printer by Schütz: "Printed and published by Wolffgang Seufferten," who doubtless wished in this way to commend his court printery to the new ruler by means of such an offering of devotion. This fact, however, also explains the numerous mistakes, especially in the doubly added continuo, which Spitta had to correct.[4]

Schütz, of course, set the *Canticum Simeonis* several times: as a bass solo for Christof Cornett in the *Symphoniae sacrae II;* as a double-chorus number in the *Exequien;* and now here, twice, as a chorus for six voices. Demantius had already chosen the same scoring. In the first of the last two settings the first member of the couplet, in the four higher voices *(g—G),* and the second member, in *tutti* with the same cadence, are opposed to each other after the passage on *wie du gesagt hast* ("according to Thy Word") has led to A major *(fermata!)* as a brief conclusion. Now, in the process of development, the structure is lightened to three- and four-voice interchanging groups with intervening *tutti* by all seven on G major *für allen Völkern* ("before all people"), *d* minor, B flat major, *d* Phrygian, g minor, finally to flow, after a row of closely cadencing anapests ♩♩♩♩♩♩♩♩♩♩ to G major.

In the second motet (the two were probably intended to frame the funeral sermon) the tone pictures also limit themselves to painting Simeon's "departure" *(fahren).* On the base of a finally Picardized *a* minor the darkness grows brighter, not merely by reason of the higher tonality but also through the triplets introduced for the pictorial delineation just mentioned. This madrigalism constitutes a little *Barform* in the introduction, which progresses with uniform heaviness. The continuation, *denn meine Augen* ("for mine eyes"), entering after an E major *fermata,* passes over to a three-part climactic stretch after the A major conclusion at *für allen Völkern* ("before all people"). This climactic passage in three-part time presents in a very fervent and joyful manner *ein Licht zu erleuchten die Heiden* ("a Light to lighten the Gentiles and to be the glory of Thy people Israel").

---

[4] See p. XV of Vol. XII.

A *Barform* A A—B[5] concludes this nobly restrained pair of motets with a return to the beginning of the first motet.

Finally, we may add here the German *Te Deum (Herr Gott, dich loben wir)* in Vol. XVIII, pp. 140 ff.,[6] for which we have but one, and that not a very accurate, copy, from the Erfurt St. Michael's Church. It was made in 1677 by Joh. Chr. Eppelmus.[7] Heinrich Spitta is perhaps correct in surmising that the present form[8] is merely a pupil's arrangement of a more simply scored composition by our master, one written for the peace celebration of 1668. For this festival Schütz had to present as the principal number a "new" setting of Psalm 150,[9] while his *concerto, Nun lob mein Seel,* of 1619, was apparently performed during the course of the festival.

Since from 1617 on the Dresden *Oberkapellmeister,* during his long life, frequently had to provide a *Te Deum,* it is idle to speculate whether under the crude final direction stating "for which the trumpets and tympani are used and with which three salvos are presented" we may refer the origin of this composition to 1617, 1630, 1648, or some other date. Still other fanfare parts to Luther's paraphrase of the Ambrosian chant have been found among the notes of the Dresden court trumpeters. But they would fit another composition of this period.[10]

The work under discussion is a simple harmonization of the Lutheran melody version in antiphony between soprano and *clarino* with trombones, against the four-voice chorus with *clarini.* Or it may be that the *cantus pro organo* was to embody the continuous congregational song with the violins above it and organ continuo in which, always only as second chorus, the *Kantorei* joins with fanfares as a change from the trombone support. And yet when we note, during the sixfold repetition of the melody in the second and fifth sections, the constant return of the same harmony with but very minor variations by the *clarini,* we must have serious doubt that Schütz is the real author; for elsewhere he so well understands how to present variations. One may recall the litanies and the *Canticum trium puerorum!* Where, in Part III of the present work, there is some variation, the harmony of the opposing members remains extremely feeble. Probably for this

---

[5] Five plus five measures and five plus five measures, both times in D major and a seven-measure *Abgesang.*

[6] See *Handbuch der d. ev. KM., Der Altargesang,* Bd. I, Teil 2, p. 486. Vandenhoeck & Ruprecht, Göttingen, 1942.

[7] Now B. B. mus. ms. 20, 374.

[8] Even if we disregard the *trombetta* 1 and 2 as having perhaps been otherwise added for Erfurt alone.

[9] So far, this setting is lost.

[10] A view was kindly granted me by chamber virtuoso L. Plass.

reason we have here merely the laborious workshop attempt of an apprentice or pupil.

It is precisely when we meet such inferior work unjustly current under Schütz's distinguished name that in reverence we come to realize his true greatness and recall the splendid description of his character by Herbert Birtner (*Lied und Volk*, August 1935):

> Heinrich Schütz, the most spiritual of all musicians, was a character of unassailable firmness. By reason of the inner harmony between his work and his personality he rises above historical limitations as does scarcely another musician. His will and his creative urge are steadfast and unfaltering. But at the same time he points as scarcely another does beyond himself to the nearer and farther reaches of history, not because he is imprisoned and enmeshed in the laws of historical time but because, in aggressive analysis and in the consciousness of his divine mission, he molds these historical laws, and as the result of his conquest of himself he seeks to point the path for German music. The figure and the work of Heinrich Schütz grow uniquely from the tension between the laws of history and its circumstances and the law of his own life of art. There is scarcely a work in the history of music which to such a degree as that of Schütz is the expression of a conscious and consistently pursued path, the conscious formation, consummated step by step, of a plan of life which, at the same time, involves a constant coming to terms with the historical forces that meet and oppose him as he progresses.

Op. 13. The Twelve Religious Songs of 1657

In the biographical section we have already discussed the publication of this church music, intended for specific occasions, through the court organist Christoph Kittel in his capacity as vocal teacher of the Dresden choir boys. In the preface to Vol. XII (p. xv) we again learn of Schütz's aversion to the thorough bass apart from the concertizing style, insofar as Kittel emphasizes, in the first place, "that these compositions for a full chorus are really intended and arranged to be performed by voices and instruments without organ," and that, in the second place, the continuo was "published at the suggestion of the publisher, to be used at the discretion of the performer." The organists are expressly urged to fill in the parts in the *Mass* and the *Magnificat*.

The works are for four voices, and are in Vol. XII of the collected works, as follows:[1]

I	*Kyrie, Gott Vater in Ewigkeit* (G—E)	
II	*Das teutsche Gloria, All Lob und Ehr* (G—G)	
III	*Der Nicaenische Glaube, Ich gläube* (G—G, Hypoionian)	
IV	*Abendmahlseinsetzung (Institution of the Lord's Supper), Unser Herr Jesus Christus* (g—D, g—G)	
V	*Der 111. Ps., Ich danke dem Herrn von ganzem Herzen (I Will Praise the Lord with My Whole Heart)* (d—D)	Church Music
VI	*Danksagen wir alle Gott* (d—D)	
VII	*Magnificat: Meine Seele erhebt* (a—E = a Dorian)	
VIII	*Jubilus S. Bernhardi: O süsser Jesu Christ* (d—D)	
IX	*Deutsche Litanei, Kyrie eleison* (F—F)	
X	*Das Benedictite vor dem Essen (Grace Before the Meal), Aller Augen (All Eyes Wait upon Thee)* (d—D), *mit Vaterunser*	School Music
XI	*Das Gratias nach dem Essen (Grace After the Meal), Danket dem Herrn* (d—D). Another *Gratias, Wir danken dir* (d—D)	
XII	*Hymnus: Christe, fac ut sapiam* (a—A)	

---

[1] Nos. 1—5 ed. by Rudolf Holle as *Die deutsche Messe* (Schott, Mainz); No. 1 also separately; No. 4 as *Passionsmusik*, ed. by Hugo Holle (ibid.); also No. 5, *Neujahrsmotette* (ibid.); No. 4 and several parts of the other pieces in Woyrsch.

As this list shows, the first nine numbers are intended for the church service, Nos. 1-6 for the chief service, No. 7 and No. 9 especially for Vespers, for which No. 8 is also probably intended. Nos. 1-4 constitute even tonally (G major) a close unity as a Mass of the catechumens in addition to the celebration of Holy Communion. Nos. 5 and 6 (*d* minor) then doubtless present a choice for the end of the service. It is to be noted, on the other hand, that Nos. 4, 5, and 8 are distinguished by *chiavettas* for certain parts (A, T, B are keyed higher).

As the school pieces, Nos. 10-12, correspond in part to the similar Appendix of the *Cantiones sacrae* of 1625, these present pieces constituting the younger German draft of the latter, we shall discuss them in conjunction with some other school music by Schütz.

The present preview shows a double connection with the two older motet works of the master. With the *Geistliche Chormusik* these numbers have in common the fact that they are intended for the service and their mature, strictly evangelical bearing; with the *Cantiones sacrae* they have in common the fact that they are for four voices and in part are also school music.

First, as to the *Deutsche Messe (German Mass)* — *Kyrie, Gloria, Credo, Communio*. It is a veritable calamity that the once famous *Deutscher Sanctus, Jesaia dem Propheten*, which would fit in so well here, although for eight voices, is still missing.... Schütz conceived the *Missa brevis* here as a *Lied* Mass, as M. Praetorius in his *Polyhymnia caduceatrix*[2] did by binding together the *Kyrie* song, *O Vater, allmächtiger Gott*, and the *Gloria* song, *Allein Gott in der Höh*.[3] Chr. Kittel's designation of the opening number, *Kyrie, Gott Vater in Ewigkeit super missam Fons bonitatis*, is shown to be misleading in Ph. Spitta's preface: "From whom this *Mass* stems and whether it still exists I have not been able to determine up to this time." It would have been more correct for Kittel to have printed:

"*Missa. I: Kyrie, Gott Vater in Ewigkeit supra Fons bonitatis*," for which we do not have a polyphonic model which can be identified as the basis of Schütz's composition, but a German church hymn which arose with the Erfurt *Teutsch Kirchenamt* of 1525 and M. Weisse's *Brüdergesangbuch* of 1531 as the German paraphrase of a troped *Kyrie* syllabizing with *Fons bonitatis* and which had passed over into evangelical congregational usage. The melody as quoted in Zahn No. 8600c shows how faithfully Schütz has taken over this tune in the discant (or, in the case of pausing of the discant, in the tenor) according to the version of the *Dresden*

---

[2] Edited by W. Gurlitt in Blume's *GA*.
[3] Cf. also later the third part of J. S. Bach's *Klavierübung!*

Gesangbuch of 1622-25, No. 187. The following juxtaposition will be instructive:[4]

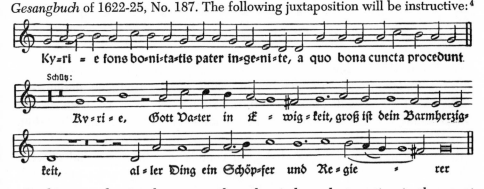

In this case, despite the apparently rather independent section in three-part time, we may speak of a strict church-hymn *cantus firmus* composition by Schütz. The origin and the treatment of the *Gloria* hymn are both related to the *Kyrie* number. Recently O. Albrecht, on the basis of Nik. Medler's *Naumburg Church Order*, wanted to ascribe this to Luther himself.[5] Schütz faithfully takes over from the *Dresden Gesangbuch* of 1625[6] the prescription that the first two lines should be intoned only by the boys. His version, which wanders through the voices more freely than in the case of the *Kyrie*, apparently departs somewhat from the official readings; but it was unmistakably as follows:

---

[4] J. Wolff, in the *P. Wagner-Festschrift* (1926), pp. 228 ff., presented three two-voice *Kyrie Fons bonitatis* of the fifteenth century; P. Dom. Johner, in the *Bericht der Reichsschulmusik-woche*, Hannover (1929), p. 178, presented a version for one voice from the fourteenth century. See also: Ameln, *Hdb.*, I, 1; for a version with Latin text, M. Praetorius, VII, 1.

[5] Weimar Luther ed. 35, 287 ff.; thereto also, pp. 530 ff., my derivation of the melody from that old church *Gloria angelorum*, from which also the *Allein Gott in der Höh*, ascribed to Nicolaus Decius, is derived.

[6] May he not have been a musical coeditor of this? It was expressly intended for the Dresden *Schloßkirche*. Both editions have been preserved in Darmstadt, the second also in the *Stadt-bibliothek* in Leipzig.

wir an = be = ten dich, dein Ehr wir rüh = men e = wig = lich.

According to this "technique of a *cantus firmus* wandering from voice to voice, with free imitations" (as such a treatment would be most accurately designated), the hymn *Gloria* takes its place close to the Schütz settings of *Da Jesus an dem Kreuze stund*, whether its model was a current melody or one invented by Schütz himself.

Before inquiring into the psychological content and the emotional effect of Schütz's *Missa brevis* we must attempt to determine the time of origin of the work, since H. Rolle speaks of an "early work" which Schütz "probably wrote soon after his return from Italy." This seems to me to be an improbable date. In my opinion, there is scarcely a work of Schütz that shows such a wonderful maturity, balance, and perfection of counterpoint as this one does! All descriptive trifles are limited to a minimum; chromatic lines, altered chords, or bold and forced transitions do not play a special role. The rhythm, with very few exceptions, which are well supported by the text, has a simplicity which prevails in the late works of the *Geistliche Chormusik* without arbitrary shifts and the like. There is nothing of *parlando* or mumbling *fauxbourdon;* but there is a linear construction of the purest equilibrium in gently swinging curves, a veritably Ockeghem flow in the contrivance of the cadences. To be sure, there are many archaic final cadences, but none of them appear to have been used because the composer was behind the times; they seem to have been employed only as a result of his conscious study of the classic composers, such as Lassus and Palestrina.

What so fascinates one in the youthful Schütz — his defiant rising above the rules, his unintentional dumbfounding through liberties resulting from exuberant fantasy — has given way here to the cleanest treatment of dissonances and accidentals. An occasional false relation, an occasional cadence at the fifth in the Lydian mode, are not inconsistent with this. And yet we are forced to admire the greatest vitality of presentation from line to line.

To be sure, with regard to musical expression the Schütz of 1640-50 was never an insipid purist or a washed-out effete. On the contrary, his strict style is a model of luminosity and flowing line. Thus while I would gladly forgo in the Holle edition as too anticipatory many a *flehend* (beseeching), *drängend* (urging), *dim. e ritard.*, *ff, pp, breiterwerdend* (becoming broader), *beteuernd* (assertive), *dumpf* (gloomy), *geheimnisvoll* (mysteriously), *schneller* (more rapidly), *wuchtig* (weighty), etc.,

I would gladly retain his *feierlich* (solemnly), *innig* (fervently), *zart* (delicately), *schlicht* (simply), *leicht* (lightly). This will doubtless suffice to answer the question, touched on above, as to expression.

Of the three statements of the *Credo* the Apostles' Creed was used for the most part in connection with Baptism; the Athanasian Creed was used less frequently, as at Trinity or in the minor services, while the Nicaean Creed (prescribed, as generally assumed, by the Synod of Nicaea in 325) was a regular part of the principal service between the lessons and the sermon. The increasing infrequency of its use since the time of Bach is one of the indications of the liturgical decline in the eighteenth century. Though as a rule (as in the Catholic Mass) the opening line was intoned in Latin or in German at the altar, the choir then continuing, Schütz begins polyphonically. He apparently has held himself aloof from any use of Protestant Gregorianism. Nevertheless, here, too, the tone of absolute churchliness prevails — even to the extent of archaic features, as

Here also madrigalisms are exceptions, though we find them employed with purposeful frugality, as at *begraben* ("buried"), or the g minor in the G major framework at *Toten* ("the dead"), the augmented chord of the sixth at *leibhaftig worden* ("became flesh") (pp. 130-131), and at *geehret* ("glorified") (p. 133).

We could much more easily imagine that the institution of the Lord's Supper, No. IV, p. 135, or at p. 137 (which at least since the time of L. Senfl's *Discubuit Jesus* was often composed separately), with its Dorian mode,[7] might have come from Schütz's problematic period (1625?); for here we are confronted with the evidences of his glorious individualism, as at p. 135

oder

---

[7] *Chiavetta* = *e* flat minor; today *f* minor.

which E. Kurth[8] correctly praises as "mystical darkening" and the "impression of the most extreme awe," or

The aged Schütz would scarcely have written *trincket alle, alle, alle daraus* ("drink ye all, all, all, of it") (p. 137) if he had intended the work as a "liturgical" composition. It savors more of a passion motet than of a work originally intended for the act of consecration, the more so as Schütz used none of the three customary consecration melodies.[9] W. Schuh (pp. 54 f.) has very neatly shown how in the second half, *Desselbigengleichen* ("In the same manner"), two inner frame sections full of painful expression and two exterior ones group themselves about the central idea *dieser Kelch ist das heilige Testament* ("this cup is the holy Testament in My blood") (p. 138), with its transcendent psalmodizing,[10] whereby corresponding elements arise in the similar structure of B and D, and A and E, thus

A   B   C   D   E

This is also confirmed tonally:

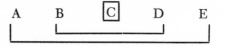

g—D,   d—D,   C—A,   d—G,   g—G

---

[8] *Romantische Harmonik* (1920), p., 431. See also *MGkK*, 8 (1903), pp. 113—118 = *Sammlung* No. 47.

[9] Schöberlein und Riegel, I, 361 ff.

[10] Three high, then three low voices, with a *tutti* conclusion.

where the fore parts lead away from the tonality and the concluding parts lead back to it, while the central part draws about the dominant-tonic region the next successive arc of the circle of fifths.

During the distribution of the Lord's Supper the congregation sang appropriate songs, such as *O sacrum convivium* or *Jesu dulcis memoria* in translations, or, according to numerous church orders, Psalm 111. Therefore here we have this Psalm 111 appropriately chanted in the first thirteen large measures of the discant. Despite its uniformity the composition is a work of unusually fresh inspiration. This has not weakened, even though this is Schütz's third setting of the text.[11] These nine little sections, with doxology, again show a clear symmetry in their cadences: *d d* G F *D* B flat B flat *d d*. Throughout a sincere tone of joy prevails; only in the *Gloria Patri* are the dancing triplets abandoned for an instant, immediately to return, however, giving the impression of folk music at the *Amen,* which is constructed from broken triads (p. 146).

The little d minor piece, No. 6 (p. 147), *Danksagen wir (Let Us All Give Thanks to God),* included as an alternative to the preceding, is like a precious wood carving. The division into two parts is clear: an A—A—B *(barförmig)* prose section leads to C major, *von des Teufels Gewalt* ("from the power of the devil"). A second A—A—B *(Bar),* with the joyful rhyme, *alle — Schalle,* which Schütz supplements with an echo at the couplet endings, leads in the introduction from C to A major, after which its conclusion, *Singen: Preis sei Gott in der Höhe* ("Singing: Praise be to God in the highest"), subsides in *d—D.*

The *Magnificat* (Vol. XII, No. 7, p. 149) is, as is known, one of Schütz's favorite texts. In this version the tonal relationships are peculiar. All the verses conclude in E major, which is arrived at now in Phrygian, now as V-I. Despite this there is a signature of only one sharp. The mystery is solved by the fact that *a* minor is the point of departure, more precisely, *a* Dorian. Schütz would have called the composition transposed Hypodorian, or, speaking in terms of Glarean, "in the tenth church tone." This also is a composition which Schütz has sung for everyone, as illustrated in the unexaggerated clarification of words like *erhebt* ("magnify"), *freuet sich* ("doth rejoice"), *elende Magd* ("lowly handmaiden"), *mächtig* ("mighty"), *heilig* ("holy"). In happy contrast, the three-part time enters at *er übet Gewalt* ("He hath showed strength"). The tenor foundation, taken over by the soprano, splendidly illustrates the putting down of "the mighty from their seats". (See next page.)

---

[11] Vol. II, p. 180, for four choruses.

er ſtö-ßet die Ge-wal-ti-gen vom Stuhl

The *Niedrige* ("those of low degree") are "exalted" *(erhöhet)*, and the rich, who are sent away empty *(leer)* (p. 154), have to content themselves at first with *unisono,* then with hollow fifths and octaves. The composition is one of the master's most widely significant works!

The *Jubilus S. Bernhardi,* No. 8, p. 158, which Schütz had set twice before, he now presents in the German version of Joh. Heermann. The translator,[12] mentioned here expressly as pastor in Köben, wrote a total of fifty four-line stanzas, which were frequently sung in their entirety during Communion. Schütz, however, combined five stanzas into a large strophe, so that one would have to sing his composition through ten times — as is indeed made possible by the fact that the original voice books add the complete text. Spitta transferred the last forty-five strophes into the foreword. Schütz himself, however, intimates the possibility of concluding before the completion of the entire text (depending doubtless on the number of communicants) by introducing the *coda, Nun sei dem Vater Dank* ("Now thanks be to the Father") (p. 161). Schütz utilized the fivefold division by always having the first and third lines of the four lines sung by the first choir and the second and fourth by the antiphonal choir, while at the fifth little strophe both groups unite in triple time without abandoning the four-voice setting. The cadences of the *d* minor frame are D, A, *d*, F, *d,* with *coda* D. The exceedingly numerous ways in which Schütz came to terms with the hazardous babble of the Opitz Alexandrines present a very charming chapter. Only twice in twenty instances did he surrender to the feared middle caesura; elsewhere he succeeds in compressing the thirteen-syllable iambic line to four arses or to expand it to ten. One need only scan according to halves:

O süsser Jesu Christ, wer an dich recht gedenket   = 6

Dem wird sein Herze bald mit Freud und Lust getränket.   = 6

But: Nichts kann des Menschen Zung und Mund so lieblich singen   = 4

or: Was ich mir wünsch und was mir mag erfreulich sein,   = 8

---

[12] Concerning the renowned hymn writer (born 1585 in Raudten, N.-Sch., died 1647 in Lissa in Posen) see W. Nelle, *Geschichte des ev. Kirchenliedes,* 99 ff., and, recently, Alfred Wiesenhüter, *Johann Heermann* (Schloesmann, Leipzig, 1935).

O gentle Jesus Christ, if one but knows Thee rightly,   = 6

For him his heart will soon with joy and peace be sated.   = 6

But: Naught can the tongue or lips of man so sweetly sing us   = 4

or: for whom I long, what fills my heart with constant joy.   = 8

Also in the case of a double-value arsis he shows himself as a master in the treatment of verse, one who knows how to adapt the Roman monotony to a Germanic style:

Was Jesum lieben sei, kann keine Hand beschreiben.   = 8

Nur der kanns sprechen aus, nur der, nur der kanns gläuben,   = 8

Der es erfahren hat, der Jesum hat geliebt,   = 6

Der ihn noch liebt und sich in seine Lieb ergiebt.   = 7

What loving Christ may be, no hand of man can picture,   = 8

No spoken word describe; he only can believe it   = 8

Who for himself has learned by truly loving Him,   = 6

Who loves Him still and to His love surrenders all   = 7

The way in which Chr. Kittel transformed and expanded Schütz's work into a solo *concerto* can be seen in the musical example in Ph. Spitta's introduction (XII, xii ff.).

As No. 9 (p. 163) we have a four-voice "German general litany, brought, as the style requires, into an appropriate rhythm." [13] In the preface the author remarks that, while he did not wish to find fault with the singing of the litany, it is rendered "at some places so slowly and tediously, without any appeal, that, according to his opinion, one must lose all pleasure and reverence while listening to it." He states that for this reason he has arranged the prayer in such a manner that it is to be rendered, not indeed by the congregation but by the choir and organ, "at times in alternation and without the loss of much time," and yet can be followed by the

---

[13] *Teutsche gemeine Litaney, auf Art deroselbigen in eine gewisse Mensur gebracht.*

congregation "with proper reverence." The conductor will use his judgment as to the allotment between two choirs. If one wishes to beat time, one will find the time indicated in the continuo.

Accordingly, here the entire work is for Schütz primarily a problem of rhythm and meter. As a matter of fact, with some very minor melismatic exceptions, he set the music syllable by syllable in such a way that the quarter theses represent the half arses, the latter, however, occurring as seldom as possible, so that a most fluent word declamation ensues, as, for example

♩ ♩ ♩♩   ♩ ♩ ♩ ♩♩♩♩   ♩

Sei uns gnädig, verschon uns, lieber Herre Gott,

♩

sei uns gnädig,   hilf uns, lieber Herre Gott.

The church intonation f g a—g f# g is retained until *am jüngsten Gericht hilf uns, lieber Herre Gott* ("on that final Day help us, dearest Lord and God"); then he reverses the formula to a g f g f# g; on the last page he combines both to a f g a g f# g. The harmonies resulting from the changing bass create still greater variety; but here, too, Schütz endeavored carefully to avoid all unrest. A masterly example of artistic craftsmanship applied to the service of the church!

Finally, we have three pieces for choir boys. They are late examples in a long series of school music. The entire sixteenth century provided compositions for the requirements of grammar-school boys and especially for the use of the choir boys. To be mentioned with especial distinction are Martin Agricola in Magdeburg; Seth Calvisius in Pforta and Leipzig; Math. Le Maistre, *Hofkapellmeister* in Dresden; and Adam Gumpelzhaimer in Augsburg.[14] Schütz himself had added some pieces of this kind to his *Cantiones sacrae* in 1625, the discussion of which we have reserved to the present point. Nos. 36, 37, and 38 represent a three-divisional blessing before meals, with the Lord's Prayer in the middle.[15] Corresponding to this threefold number of 1625 we have No. 10 of the twelve sacred songs of 1657 (p. 171); corresponding to the 1625 *Gratias* after meals — *Cantiones sacrae*, Nos.

---

[14] Cf. Sannemann, *Die Musik in den Lateinschulen des 16. Jhs.* (1904); A. Prüfer, *Über den ausserkirchlichen Kunstgesang in den evang. Schulen des 16. Jhs.* (Diss. Leipzig, 1890); O. Kade, *M. LeMaistre* (1862); K. Benndorf, *S. Calvisius* (Diss. Leipzig, 1894); O. Riemer, *E. Bodenschatz* (Diss. Halle, 1928). DTB X, 2.

[15] Namely, *Prima pars: Oculi omnium / Secunda pars: Pater noster / Tertia pars: Domine Deus.*

39 and 40, constructed similarly to the Blessing[16] — we have, in Chr. Kittel's print, No. 11 of the twelve sacred songs of 1657 (p. 173). What at the beginning of the war was still sung in Latin has now received a German text. This change of text and the changed key (formerly *g* minor for equal voices, now a fourth lower in normal voice setting) have brought about more differences between the two versions than an essentially different stylistic purpose. While, on the one hand, in 1657 some simplification took place, at other places melismatic enrichments are used, always based on suggestions of the text. Only the rhythm has meanwhile been simplified in Schütz, and the will to common textual declamation on the part of all voices is more marked. Thus in place of the antithesis between eighths and halves, characteristic of the earlier period, at *et ne nos inducas in tentationem* ("and lead us not into temptation"), quarters predominate in the German version, though *führen* is painted in eighths and sixteenths; and while at *libera nos a malo* ("deliver us from evil") the *der Verführung Ketten* ("chains of temptation")[17] are indicated by overlappings, the *erlöse uns vom Übel* ("deliver us from evil") is presented in a simple, churchly motet style after the manner of the *Geistliche Chormusik*. The fact that this setting of the Lord's Prayer is eminently useful for church service induced F. Woyrsch to separate it for his collection from its association with music for choir boys.

In the *Domine Deus, Herre Gott, himmlischer Vater (Lord God, Heavenly Father)* (p. 177), it is also very rewarding to observe in the minutest details these connections, so genuinely Schützian, between the form of the words and the construction of the music.

The relation in the case of the thanksgiving compositions is very similar, as is shown clearly by the ending of the first of the three parts: *super misericordia ejus*, with its quiet lines, is developed especially from the point of view of rhythm; on the other hand, *die auf seine Güte warten* ("they that wait upon His goodness") receives richly pictorial melismas on the verb *warten*. Otherwise it remains the same composition, and both times the Lord's Prayer is again placed in the middle.

As the last, the twelfth, composition, the German work of 1657 consists of an *a* minor composition of Latin distichs, a *Hymnus pro vera sapientia ad D(eum) O(ptimum) M(aximum) in Auditoriis et Scholis*. Like the German paraphrase of the *Jubilus S. Bernhardi*, it is performed by two four-voice semichoruses and a

---

[16] Namely, *Prima pars: Confitemini / Secunda pars: Pater noster* (as above) / *Tertia pars: Gratias agimus*.

[17] These still found in the *Hymnorum formulae Portensium alumnorum* (Leipzig, 1777), p. 132: *Pro felici stud. successu*. German by J. Franck & Chr. Peter-Zahn No. 6691.

four-voice *tutti* in nine strophes (I II T, I II T, I II T). The metrical accentuation

Christe, fac, ut sapiam, quia tu sapientia Patris

Solus es, et tecum qui sapit, ille sapit

as always in the case of hexameters and pentameters, Schütz abandoned in favor of the natural word accent.

I surmise that at the corresponding place in the *Cantiones sacrae,* ca. 1625 (or possibly not until 1648?), Schütz's melody to Psalm 150 in the Cornelius Becker collection was sung with the text of a genuinely new Latin school hymn and that, as a result, the *Christe, fac, ut sapiam* even inherited the rather inappropriate designation *hymnus,* as Schütz now wished to present an original composition in the corresponding place.

For so we find Schütz's composition in the Ms. Löbau (entered by Christian Steher 1/4/1670) with the following text — a memorial which throws light on the history of the time:

Grates agamus omnibus   *Qui dira belli vulnera*
Deo parenti seculis,   *Et saeva pestis funera*
Qui liberavit tristibus   *Foedaeque pallorem famis*
Suam malis ecclesiam,   *Ab hac fugavit arcula.*   (7 strophes)

Let us give thanks throughout the ages   Who put to flight from this small sphere
To God the Father,   The cruel wounds of war,
Who freed His church   The terrible death of pestilence
From grievous evils,   And the pallor of horrible famine.
                                                                  (7 strophes)

Those table prayers were not limited to the Dresden Electoral Choir Boy Institute but passed over to the Saxon school choirs. This is proved by a three-voice arrangement in Ms. Pirna 8, of which an excerpt may be appended to prove that one should not, as often happens, underestimate the popular *(volkstümlich)* character of Schütz's music. If one changes the b♭ at *Herre* to *c,* there is a rather beautiful simplification, which gives one a lively insight into the school music used at that time in a small city. (See next page.)

These twelve church and school compositions show us the seventy-two-year-old Schütz humbly devoting his mighty artistic talents to the simple service of the common people. One can say that everything he created after this — and great masterpieces were still to come — was destined for the realization of this one task. We see in reality the world-embracing Faust, who at the end recognizes the simplest goal as the highest, "to drain this stagnant pool" *(den faulen Pfuhl auch abzuziehen)* in order to "stand on free soil among a people free" *(auf freiem Grund mit freiem Volk zu stehn)*.[18]

---

[18] *Faust*, Part II, Act 5. Transl. by Bayard Taylor.

The Christmas Oratorio

At the beginning of the seventh decade of the seventeenth century Schütz composed a large work at the request of the new elector, who, perhaps from his boyhood recollection of the *Resurrection History* of 1623, may now have desired a companion piece. The result was the *Christmas Oratorio*. The work existed in two forms: a first, more primitive one, which A. Schering discovered in 1909 among the Düben manuscripts in Upsala and published as Vol. XVII of the complete works. A second form, dating from 1664, shows considerable development in details. Of this version Schütz at the time had only the voice of the evangelist with the continuo printed. Three identical booklets for singers, thorough-bass player, and violin formed the part of the "Evangelist's Chorus." The complete voices of the "Concert Chorus" *(Concertenchor)*, in manuscript form, he gave out only on occasion. In this we have a significant instance of an author's insistence on his rights both for spiritual and for material reasons. As the "brief memorandum" of Schütz's pupil Alexander Hering,[1] who, with Seb. Knüpfer in Leipzig, had charge of the publication, says: "The author had misgivings about having the parts published, inasmuch as he had observed that, apart from princely, well-established ensembles *(Capellen)*, such 'inventions' of his would scarcely achieve their proper effect. However, anyone desiring to apply for a copy may do so either through Seb. Knüpfer, cantor in Leipzig, or through Alexander Hering, organist of the *Creutz Kirche* in Dresden. With the author's consent these parts may be obtained, in addition to the three printed booklets comprising the 'Chorus of the Evangelist,' for a small compensation." In modern terms (!), Schütz wanted to exercise his personal authorship right with a view to a spiritually and technically worthy performance[2] and also with a view, stressed much less strongly, to personal compensation. The continuation of Hering's comment shows that Schütz had no intention of being self-complacent in his justified reservations: "Moreover, he leaves it free to those who wish to use the parts of the evangelist either to compose for themselves or have others compose ten *concerti* (the texts of which are also to be found on these prints) according to their personal liking and to available performers."

---

[1] Known to us as copublisher of the *Symphoniae sacrae II.*
[2] One will recall from the preface to his collection of 1647 his complaints about the distortion of his works by incompetent performers.

That is to say, it would be better to compose simple pieces of one's own than to bungle with his difficult ones! He also gives permission to change his evangelist's recitatives back to the *choraliter* version, dispensing with bar lines and the continuo. Likewise, he had but a very small edition of this evangelist part printed, "for the sake of avoiding the tedious and extensive copying." He would have preferred to retain even this in manuscript form.

The printing in Vol. I of the Spitta complete edition had to be limited at the time to the presentation of the chorus of the evangelist until Schering could enlarge it with the *intermedia* from the early form in Upsala. To be sure, we still lack the introductory chorus, except for the continuo. It has been shown that this "Introduction to the Birth, *à 9*" once belonged to the old Choir Library of the St. Thomas School at Leipzig.[3] Schütz, however, in 1664 extensively revised the recitatives, enriching them by more plastic nuances of a melodic nature, through more fluent rhythmization, and by the insertion of little continuo interludes at the chief junctures, and the like. This can be clearly seen in Vol. XVII, where the two versions are printed, the one above the other. He also subjected the concert pieces to a careful revision, as shown by the *Particella* belonging to the library of the Berlin *Singakademie*.[4] The instumental parts are sometimes disposed more widely and begin lower in order to develop themselves more effectively; at times the vocal parts are transposed to more brilliant ranges, the angel song in the eighth *intermedium* rising radiantly to the high A. In order to call this charmingly fresh work of the aged Sagittarius completely our own we should have, without interruption, in addition to the opening chorus, the version of the *intermedia* of 1664. With the further progress of the *Denkmäler* editions and the progressive discovery of manuscripts, this would not seem to be a vain wish.[5]

The printed title is as follows:
Historia
of the Joyful and Blessed
Birth of God's and

---

[3] Schering, *Archiv f. MW*, I, 287.

[4] Unfortunately, it, too, is not complete; but it at least gives the first fifteen measures of the hitherto missing second trombone part to *intermedium* five. First report regarding this source by M. Schneider in the *Kroyerfestschrift*, 1934. I owe my acquaintance with the catalog entry by M. Schneider of 1619 to Dr. G. Schumann and Dr. Friedr. Welter. The volumes themselves are apparently in Halle.

[5] Practical edition with piano arrangement, according to Schering's version in Vol. XVII (B & H). Student score by Fritz Stein through Eulenburg. A future edition should not only seek to take into consideration the Berlin versions but should also transpose the entire work from F major to G or A flat.

Mary's Son,
Jesus Christ,
Our Sole Mediator, Redeemer,
and Savior.
As this
on Most Gracious Instruction of His Electoral Highness
of Saxony, etc.,
H. Johann George the Second,
Vocaliter and *Instrumentaliter* into Music
Was Set
by
Heinrico Schützen, Electoral Highness of
Saxony, etc., Senior Capellmeister

Printed in Dresden by Wolfgang Seyffert, 1664,
and to be found there with Alexander Hering, organist,
also in Leipzig to be requested from the Cantor there.

The Prussian State Library possesses a single copy of this edition. On it is written an abbreviated note stating that it is the property of Duke Rudolf August of Brunswick-Lüneburg, dated 1671 from Lüchow, to which place Schütz doubtless sent him this copy before June of that year.[6] It contains a number of corrections indicated in writing.

The structure of the work is as follows:

Introduction for four-voice chorus and five-voice orchestra: *Die Geburt unseres Herren Jesu Christi, wie sie uns von den heiligen Evangelisten beschrieben wird* ("The birth of our Lord Jesus Christ, as it has been described for us by the evangelists"), F major.

1. *Intermedium:* The angel: *Fürchtet euch nicht* — "Be Not Afraid" (soprano, two violettas [violas]); *organo,* F major

2. *Intermedium:* The heavenly hosts: *Ehre sei Gott* — "Glory to God" (six-voice chorus; two violins, viola, bassoon, organ [and *complemento di Viole si placet]),* F major

3. *Intermedium:* Three shepherds: *Lasset uns nun gehen* — "Let Us Now Go" (3 male altos, two flutes, bassoon, organ), F major

4. *Intermedium:* The Magi: *Wo ist der neugeborene König?* — "Where is the Newborn King?" (three tenors, two violins, bassoon, organ), F major

---

[6] Lüchow was ceded to Celle in 1671.

5. *Intermedium:* The high priests: *Zu Bethlehem im jüdischen Lande* — "In Bethlehem in the Land of Judea" (four basses, two trombones, organ), F major

6. *Intermedium:* Herod: *Ziehet hin* — "Go and Search" (bass, two *clarini [Singakademie: "o cornettini"]*)

7. *Intermedium:* The angel: *Stehe auf, Joseph* — "Arise, Joseph" (soprano, two violins, organ), F major

8. *Intermedium:* The angel: *Stehe auf, Joseph* — "Arise, Joseph" (do.), F major

Concluding Chorus: *Dank sagen wir alle Gott* — "Let Us All Give Thanks to God" (four-voice chorus, two violins, viola, two trombones, bassoon, organ), F major.

Thus we have an absolutely uniform tonality in the *tonus lascivus* used as Christmas tone at least since the fourteenth century.[7] Between its pillars only the festoons of the solo recitatives are allowed to sprout forth a little more freely. But even such deviations are kept within the narrowest limits. The artistic center of gravity of the work lies in the eight *intermedia* and the two similarly scored corner pillars, the introduction and the conclusion. During his first Venetian sojourn Schütz had surely run across the concept *intermedium* as a class designation for the festal music pageantry of half-dramatic nature used especially in connection with wedding festivities at the Renaissance courts of upper Italy. About 1620 Daniel Bollius, in Mainz, had interpolated five instrumental movements *(symphoniae) loco intermedii* in his little *John the Baptist Oratorio*. Theo. Selle, for the first time, used such *intermedia* three times as choral interpolations of a contemplative kind in his more extensive Hamburg *St. John Passion* of 1642.[8]

That Schütz (without, of course, aiming at stage presentation) constructed these *intermedia* in a thoroughly dramatic spirit, even approaching the religious folk play, is clearly indicated by the scoring, which is conceived not merely in a musically playful manner but, so to speak, in that of the folk play. This applies to both the vocal and the instrumental scoring: trombones for the high priests (four basses!), recorders for the shepherds (three altos!), trumpets for the king (bass!), strings for the angels (soprano!) and for the Magi (three tenors!). The scoring was just as much in keeping with the respective stations and vocations of the characters as mantles, sheepskins, crown, swan plumage, and golden vessels would have been in connection with dramatic presentations. Such characteristic instrumentation belongs also to the groups of persons in Staden's *Seelewig,* and before this

---

[7] One will recall the *Joseph, lieber Joseph mein,* the *Quempas,* and all the other late medieval Christmas songs.

[8] Cf. my treatise *Aus der Frühgeschichte der deutschen Generalbasspassion (Petersjb.* 1920); reprint of score by R. Gerber in Blume's *Chorwerk* No. 44 (1934).

it was customary in the *intermedia* scenes of the sixteenth century.[9] Schütz had become conversant with corresponding problems through his own ballets, and the Christmas *intermedia* thus give us a kind of compensatory look back at these lost scores.

Besides the uniformity of tonality Schütz used still another spiritual unifying element as contrasted with the wide differences of scoring and the thematic dissimilarities springing from them. It is indicated in the notice which occurs in connection with *intermedia* one, seven, and eight in the "specification for the ten *concerti* with the organ, arranged by the author for this action."

"Under which the Christ Child's cradle is occasionally introduced." This relates to the bass figure which is everywhere met with there:

It also occurs transposed. Again we have a reminder of the folk play which J. S. Bach made over, independently, in his *Christmas Oratorio* in the violoncello passage:

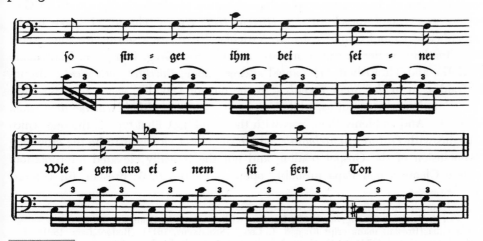

---

[9] In connection with the wedding of Cosimo Medici and Leonora da Toledo (Florence, 1539) Gardane in Venice had sixteen *intermedia* printed, most of which originated with Francesco Corteccia. Here three sea monsters sing to three traverse flutes, three nymphs with three lutes, six shepherds with cromornes, Sileni with *violone;* "Night" is accompanied by four trombones, and "Dawn" opened the *comedia* with a solo song accompanied by *gravicembalo* and *organetti.* The principle remained the same, generally speaking, up to the period of romanticism.

If we search for the predecessors of Schütz's *Christmas History*, we find no full-grown oratorio, at least not on German soil. At best, we have a series of motets on the Gospel narrative, the principal one being the setting *Exiit edictum*[10] by Leonhard Päminger, so rich in delightful *quodlibet* interpolations; also the same composer's Gospel polyphonization for Christmas Matins, *In illo tempore* (!) *pastores loquebantur inter se* ("At that time shepherds said to one another"), which shows a kind of Schützian cradle-rocking:

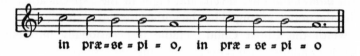

in præ=se=pi = o,   in præ = se = pi = o

Or we have serious motets on the Christmas Day text, such as the six-voice motet in three parts in G. Otto's collection for the year (Kassel, 1604); or M. Vulpius' similarly scored two-part motet (Breslau Manuscript 31), *Ascendit Joseph a Galilaea / Et dixit eis angelus*. Th. Stoltzer, in five four- to five-voice sections (Zwickau manuscript 16), had treated the scene between the angel and the shepherds. The Christmas antiphon *Angelus autem Domini / Et invenietis*,[11] or the text *Angelus Domini descendit*,[12] with second parts differing very widely, then lead with their numerous polyphonization to similar compositions in German: *Der Engel sprach zu den Hirten: Her, Her!* ("The angel spake to the shepherds: Come! Come!"), by M. Agricola;[13] likewise a setting for four voices by Joachim Belitz (Breslau manuscript 13); by Greg. Lange, P. Lütgemann (1597), and Th. Elsbeth. The angel address alone, *Fürchtet euch nicht* ("Be not afraid"), to *in der Stadt Davids* ("in the city of David"), was set by Raselius, M. Franck, and Demantius, while Vulpius has *à 4 Und alsbald war bei dem einen Engel* ("And suddenly there was with the angel"). A final type is the one which begins with *Pastores loquebantur*, where the motet clearly is to be the crowning conclusion of the Gospel reading and not the lyrically elevated interpolation. Here Clemens non Papa probably opens the series *(à 5;* Breslau, 6); Uffereri

---

[10] Examples in my *Evangelienvertonung*, I, 33.

[11] *À 4*, Verdelot *(Evangelia*, 1544); Hassler (with continuo in Donfried, 1622); *à 5*, Clemens non Papa (Breslau manuscript 6); *à 8*, L. Leoni (Schadaeus, 1611), (Bodenschatz, 1621); *à 9*, Hassler (reprinted, *DTD*, XXIV/V, pp. 215 ff.); *à 12*, Gabrieli (Lindner, 1588); for three choruses, R. del Mel (1595).

[12] *A 4*, Cocq (Forster, 1540); Körber (1597); *à 5*, Deis (Joanellus, 1562); Palestrina (Coroll. 1590); *à 6*, Lassus *(Op. mus.*, VII), Erbach (Breslau, 18); Pfendner (ibid., 21, 29); R. del Mel (Coroll. 1590); *à 7*, Gabrieli (Lindner, 1588; cf. *Schütz*, VIII, 171). Massaino (Gruber, 1615); *à 8*, Zuccini (Breslau, 18): *à 2* with continuo, Cifra and Viadana (Donfried, 1624).

[13] Numerous examples in Breslau. Reprint by H. Funck (Bärenreiter).

answers with two voices and continuo (Donfried, 1622); Agazzari increases the solo parts to three (ibid.); Anerio uses eight voices with continuo (Constantini, 1614). That he has the lesson in mind Dulichius indicates by beginning, like Päminger, with *In illo tempore pastores loquebantur*. Then we arrive at outspoken Christmas *concerti*, such as that by Martin Meyer (Breslau, 1678) for S, A, two violins, and organ,[14] on the entire Gospel lesson, while Horn joins in with a quartet cantata.

With regard to this particular work Schütz thus stands alone and as a discoverer, a fact of which he seems to have been somewhat conscious. Despite the role of the evangelist in the *Resurrection History* of 1623, he could say forty years later: "After all, the author will gladly let understanding musicians judge how far he succeeded or failed in this new style *(Aufsatz)*,[15] never, so far as he knows, presented in Germany in print before, a *stylo recitativo* for the evangelist, new both as regards melody and time." The difference between the present work and the *Easter History* of 1623 is that the latter, after all, chiefly retained the recitational formulas *(Accentus-Formeln)* and abandoned them only in the case of definite illustrative considerations, while the *stylus oratorius* of, say, the *Kleine geistliche Konzerte*, though free, to be sure, from ecclesiastical formulae, was nevertheless laden with all the *arioso* pathos of the Florentine and Venetian music drama. The recitative by the present evangelist, moreover, is a fluent *parlando* according to the most natural enunciation of the text, a *secco* recitative, already more in the style of Scarlatti, which Schütz here mastered for himself step by step, as is proved by the number of versions made. The recitatives of the passions again constitute a problem in themselves! What refinement Schütz achieved, primarily by means of rhythm, the following passage will illustrate:

[14] Correlated forms *(Seitenformen)* are, among others, Jak. Reiner, *Facta est cum angelo multitudo* (Breslau, 12 & 31), *à 6;* or L. Leoni, *Ecce annuntio vobis, à 2* with continuo (Victorinus, 1616, and Donfried, 1622). Reprint of the Meyer *concerto* by Fritz Koschinsky (Breslau, 1931).
[15] From *aufsetzen = komponieren*, thus, something like "manner of writing music."

or the melodic light is reserved for the word "Jesus," while at the same time considerable smoothness is achieved in the matter of meter:

In the first *intermedium* a flowing canon between violettas one and two plays above the "child-rocking" bass. Even when there is a free imitational procedure, it recurs again and again; likewise in the later version (Berlin), which is more expanded and begins deeper. The solo song is fitted into the four-beat measure with motives, mostly hemiolic, of very unequal length, which brings great vivacity into the quasi-*aria*. Through free textual repetitions, re-entrances, and points of contact between sectional portions, the words are freely spun out to five divisions with cadences on F, B flat, C, D, F.

In the second little *concerto* the angelic hosts, alternating with, and supported by, strings, develop their full brilliance, in connection with which the *Friede auf Erden* ("Peace on earth") is reserved for the basses alone for a considerable time. The characteristic of the whole lies in the sequences, which rise step by step and nod graciously to one another:

The third *intermedium*, the terzet of the shepherds,[16] discloses its dependence on the text, *Lasset uns nun gehen* ("Let us now go"), its pictorial character in the three-voice *sinfonia* of flutes and bassoon; likewise at *und die Geschichte sehen* ("and see this thing"). Devout, hearty eagerness comes to the fore.

With a drolly serious *fugato* manifestly inspired by the text and beginning in the bassoon, the three holy kings enter:

The glittering

later steps out of their ensemble into the recitative as a reminiscent motive.

In the figure *und sein kommen* ("and are come"), as before in such a passage in Jakob Gallus, we have the whole picture of kneeling before the child.

What pompousness and darkness, on the other hand, in the case of the four black basses of the Talmudists (p. 27), who are anticipated in the Berlin version by the second trombone:

The motive

which is carried through all six parts, has about it something triumphantly grotesque. Schütz apparently developed the trumpet *ritornello* of the Herod *aria* very richly; unfortunately, the second *clarino* voice is missing, but the Schneider note picture gives a satisfactory sketch:

[16] If in the case of the transposition one cannot get falsettos or boy altos for the two upper voices, then, as a matter of necessity, female voices; but even then a tenor should be used for the lowest voice.

The part of Herod, too, has been "extensively and very effectively changed."

Two motives — the excited *und forschet fleißig* ("and search diligently") and the eager *dass ich auch komme* ("that I may come also") — reveal Schütz as one who could describe a man's soul with skill equal to, if not indeed greater than, that of Monteverdi.

While the recitative of the first version before *intermedium* three concluded in the latter's key of F major, in the printed edition Schütz leads it to D in order that the viola symphony, with its cradle-rocking, may enter with more tonal freshness. The huge melisma, *fleuch* ("flee") (p. 36), begins a counter *Bar (Gegenbar)* A B B. At the second occurrence of *umbringen* ("to destroy him") the *f* minor — again above the rocking *ostinato* — should be noted.[17]

The recitative becomes very significant when the words of the prophecy of Jeremiah regarding the weeping Rachel appear[18] (p. 39). In the printed final version Schütz carried out the descending chromaticism at *Viel Klagens, Weinens und Heulens* ("lamentation and weeping and great mourning") in a still more systematic manner by means of simplified notation, in connection with which the fading-away, the aimless breaking-off, in the second version, is especially admirable:

After this the very joyous little *arietta* of the angel is delightfully effective. The concertizing violas are almost wholly occupied with the *Stehe auf!* ("Rise up!") motive. Only a dark reminiscent shadow, *die dem Kinde nach dem Leben stunden* ("they which sought the young Child's life") leads, in passing, to g minor or sobs once in Lombardian rhythm at *Leben* ("life").

---

[17] Cf. on the same text Schütz's *Concerto X*, 58 (*Symph. sacr. III*), p. 518.
[18] Schütz treated it independently, as a *concerto*.

The German *Grates nunc omnes,* which Schütz had set once before as No. 6 of the *Zwölf geistliche Gesänge,* constitutes the concluding chorus — written in a manner characteristic of folk music — which Schütz's pupils — for example, Chr. Bernhard in the peace chorus of the cantata *Wohl dem, der den Herrn fürchtet (Blessed Is He Who Feareth the Lord, DTD,* VI) — were so glad to take as a model.[19] Here and there one will have to beat time equally, since Schütz probably retained the triple time merely to designate a rather rapid tempo:

den follen wir alle mit feinen Engeln loben mit Schalle.

One could not conclude such a captivating work in a more effective and, at the same time, in a clearer way than did the master, who was almost eighty years old. Today it still delights both young and old wherever it is presented — and fortunately this is no longer such a rare occurrence. One can no more compare it to Bach's sisterwork than one can compare the Bach and the Schütz passions. They belong to two different stylistic worlds which can scarcely be compared to each other. We can only say: Blessed that Christmas celebration at which one is permitted to present Schütz's *Christmas Oratorio* — it will become a Christmas matins filled with a heavenly radiance!

---

[19] Schering, in the preface to Vol. XVII and in *Geschichte des Oratoriums,* pp. 147 ff.

(Op. 14.) The Three Passions of 1665-66

In many respects the threefold journey through the Passion history of our Lord according to the evangelists Luke, John, and Matthew became the crown of Schütz's lifework. The sequence given, according to the illuminating discussions of Friedrich Spitta,[1] is doubtless to be regarded as the correct one until proof to the contrary is forthcoming. To be sure, the first volume of the *Gesamt-ausgabe* contains four settings. But the setting according to St. Mark (in F Ionian) was printed in the volume as the result of a caprice on the part of Ph. Spitta similar to that which he displayed when he wanted to rescue the *Passion According to St. Luke* as a youthful work of Bach. Spitta himself had well-grounded misgivings with regard to this work, even though the St. Mark setting appears in the principal manuscript — the high folio choir book of Joh. Zacharias Grundig which C. F. Becker obtained in 1842[2] and left to the Municipal Library of Leipzig. Grundig[3] (1669-1720) came into the Dresden Court Chapel *(Hofkapelle)* in 1692, where he seems to have completed this neat copy of the work from the manuscripts of Schütz which had been left to the choir. In 1697 he came as a sixth-class student *(Sextus)* to the *Kreuzschule*, and in 1715 he advanced to the position of cantor there. Ph. Spitta (preface, pp. xix-xx) has convincingly shown from a single fact that Grundig must have completed the copy as a young man at the instigation of a widely experienced musician. Only the *St. Matthew Passion*, which stands in first place here, bears the authorship designation Schütz together with the year 1666. The genuineness of the *Passio secundum Johannem* is established by the older version in Wolfenbüttel (1665) mentioned before, while the *Passion According to St. Luke*, by its similar style, gives definite assurance of its Schützian authorship. The *Passion According to St. Mark*, however, deviates completely both in the ecclesiastical formulae of the recitatives and in the altogether different style of the choruses. At best it may have been the work — in order to complete the series of four — of a Schütz pupil,[4] such as Chr. Kittel or Al. Hering, but probably

---

[1] *Die Passionen von Heinrich Schütz* (66 pages, B & H).

[2] From a source which I do not know.

[3] B. Engelke, in a letter kindly sent me, is of the opinion, based on Holstein archives in which Grundig is met with as an alto, that his name was Grund(ius). Nevertheless, I cite the article by Held in the *Vjschr. f. MW.*, X, 315 ff., where he and his forbears are always called Grundig.

[4] So, too, with precise analyses, Rud. Gerber, *Das Passionsrezitativ bei Heinr. Schütz und seine stilgeschichtlichen Grundlagen* (Gütersloh, 1929).

not at all of Weckmann, Bernhard, Fabricius, or Dedekind. In addition to this, Geyer's necrology expressly states that Schütz composed three passions. Moreover, the liturgy of the Dresden Court Church provides for only three presentations of the Passion history: for Judica, Matthew; for Palm Sunday, Luke; for Good Friday, John. Ph. Spitta himself shows that the recitatives and the *Gratiarum actio* of the *Passion According to St. Mark* hark back to a point of view which, by 1623, Schütz had abandoned;[5] that the text of the introduction also shows a different word arrangement; moreover, that we do not have before us an early work of the master, since the character of the choruses is not Schützian and cannot be dated before the middle of the century: "This excited manner, bordering on the emotional and even sentimental, and expressing itself in euphonious forms, flourished toward the end of the seventeenth century. It resembles the manner of Kuhnau. With all its tenderness, Schütz's expression of feeling still always has something strong and exalted, also a certain austerity, and, in addition, betrays everywhere its connection with the art of the sixteenth century. All this one seeks in vain in the figural part of the music of the *St. Mark Passion*." Spitta, however, rejects the authorship of both Kuhnau and Grundig. Perhaps a chance circumstance will yet reveal the true author — but he certainly was not Schütz.

With the finest feeling for the intrinsic differences characterizing the personalities of the evangelists, Schütz gave each of the three works[6] its appropriate church tone. Luke he set in F Lydian, at times Ionian;[7] St. John in e Phrygian; St. Matthew in g Dorian. In the case of the two synoptics (Matthew and Luke) he thus produced "friendly simplicity" *(freundliche Schlichtheit)* and "dignified seriousness" *(würdiger Ernst)*, while in the case of the *St. John Passion* the mystical, rhapsodic tone is attained with wonderful effectiveness.[8] However, in order to make clear the extraordinary originality of this triple constellation, it will be necessary to give a brief summary of the history of the figural passion.

I have explained how, in the development of the early polyphonic settings of the Gospels in the fifteenth century, the lessons of Holy Week occupy a central position. About 1480 a passion in the manuscript *Modena Estense lat.* 454/55, with 3-8 (!)-voice choruses of Jews and apostles, shows the arrival at the "dramatic" type with soloists reciting in the usual tone of the lesson. This was to be followed

---

[5] In the *Resurrection History;* see Spitta's introduction to Vol. I, pp. xx-xxi.

[6] Student scores by Fritz Stein (Eulenburg); Bärenreiter editions: *St. Matthew* by Fritz Schmidt, *St. Luke* and *St. John* by W. Kamlah. The concluding choruses of the *St. Matthew* and *St. John Passion* also in Dittberner's *Chorauswahl* (Schwers & Haake).

[7] This, too, speaks against the genuineness of the *St. Mark Passion,* which is likewise in F.

[8] Epstein, in *Petersjb.,* 1929, emphasizes the fact that Ambrosius Beber had given up the recitational tone used in the church.

in the sixteenth century by a Latin offshoot with works by Sermisy, Lassus, J. Reiner, Asola, Vittoria, Guerrero, and Wm. Byrd, while a German Protestant development was to extend by way of Johs. Walter,[9] Scandello,[10] J. Meiland, Gesius,[11] Ambr. Beber, Th. Mancinus, S. Besler, Vulpius,[12] O. S. Harnisch to Chr. Schultze in Delitzsch *(Passion According to Luke, 1653)*.[13] Contrasted with this "dramatic" passion, the "motet" passion subjects the entire story to polyphony, including the narrative of the evangelist and the speeches of the individual persons, although these are not infrequently set off from their surroundings by a semichorus, or, vice versa, by a *tutti*. Of this type we have, from about the year 1500, the four-voice work of Obrecht,[14] which is erroneously met with under the names of LaRue and Longheval and which was expanded ca. 1560 in Silesia to a six-voice composition. Obrecht's work became the point of departure for two genealogical trees: (1) a Latin one, with such names, among others, as Galliculus, Resinarius, C. de Rore, L. Daser, J. Gallus,[15] J. Regnart, B. Gesius; (2) a German one, represented by Joachim a Burgk,[16] J. Steuerlein, J. Machold, L. Lechner,[17] and Chr. Demantius.[18] Schütz's *Seven Last Words* is linked completely to this German motet branch; his *Resurrection History* is extensively connected with it, namely, with respect to solo parts set for several voices. This is not the case, however, with respect to the part of the evangelist. As in the "dramatic" passion, Schütz has him sing chiefly in the recitational (plainsong) church tone *(Choralton, cantus choralis)*, but in a somewhat modernized form, with thorough bass accompaniment. In the passions, on the other hand, he continues the precedent of the "dramatic" branch, which, in the case of Christof Schultze, approaches his date inasmuch as he retains the unaccompanied recitative. From the viewpoint of composition, however, he concludes the motet group which overlaps his day in the six-voice *St. John Passion* of Demantius of 1631, insofar as this Freiberg master is the first to free himself completely from the recitational church tone, the treatment of which was for more than a century the principal problem of the motet passion composition. With Obrecht we still have the liturgical red thread which could be traced through all

---

[9] Reprint by O. Kade, *Die ältere Passionskomposition bis 1631* (1893).
[10] Reprint in Schöberlein & Riegel I, 412 ff.
[11] Reprint in Schöberlein & Riegel and as *Celler Passion* in the Bärenreiter-Verlag.
[12] In the *Denkmäler thüringischer Musik* (Bärenreiter-Verlag).
[13] Reprinted by P. Epstein in the *Veröffentlichungen der Musikbibl. P. Hirsch* (Martin Breslauer, 1930).
[14] Ed. by Daniel de Lange (B&H, 1894) and Joh. Wolf (Obrecht *Ges. Ausgabe*).
[15] Reprint in *DTOe*, XV, 1.
[16] Score in Fr. Jöde's *Chorbuch II*.
[17] Practical ed. by Ameln and Lipphardt (Bärenreiter).
[18] Six-voice, 1631. Ed. by Fritz Blume (Kallmeyer).

these male voices, i. e., cantor, evangelist, and chorus; only the discant of the choir boys was not considered proper for participation in the sacred *cantus choralis.* During the course of the sixteenth century, however, the lesson tone becomes freer and freer in all voices, with many octave transpositions and significant deviations. After Obrecht's composition one may note this vagrant lesson tone in the glorious work of L. Lechner or in the double-chorus *St. John Passion* of Jakob Gallus! Finally, as stated, it makes way for a completely free motet invention in the case of Demantius.

In the domain of the choral passion with mere choral interpolations the originally rigid *accentus* also becomes gradually more tractable. As Gerber has shown, the Silesian Sam. Besler (1612) proceeded most freely before Schütz. Then, as we have just seen, Schütz attempted a radical break with tradition in his *Christmas Oratorio* by constructing the part of the evangelist as a completely free *parlando* recitative over the *basso continuo.* Despite this fact, in one thing in his passion settings he remained conservative. He refused to use, beyond the traditional intro-ductions and the concluding church-hymn setting (which he had introduced in place of the old concluding *Gratiarum actio),* further supplements or additions such as Joachim a Burgk in 1574 had added with his *Passion Prophecy* based on Psalm 22 and Demantius with his *Motet Prophecy* based on Isaiah 53; and he dis-pensed with interpolations such as Th. Selle[19] had ventured to introduce in Ham-burg in 1642 with his chorus-psalm *intermedia,* and Chr. Flor, in Lüneburg in 1667, with his nine solo arias.

Formerly, of course, the further development of the passion settings actually by-passed Schütz's purely vocal passion setting. It passed from Flor's orchestra type by way of J. Sebastiani and J. Theile[20] to Kuhnau and the paraphrase passions on Hunold's, Postel's, and Brockes' versifications. J. S. Bach then placed the second immortal type beside that of Schütz, the further description of which we cannot take up here.[21] What W. Kamlah said in 1934 is well worth remembering:[22]

---

[19] New edition by R. Gerber in Blume's *Chorwerk,* Brochure 44 (1934).

[20] *St. Matthew Passion,* by Sebastiani. Königsberg, 1663, printed 1672, *DTD,* XVII, with Eccard chorale settings rearranged for soprano and choir of gambas. Passion by Theile, Lübeck, 1673, *DTD,* XVII, with four-voice chorus arias or solo numbers in addition to instrumental ritornelles.

[21] Cf. my book, *J. S. Bach,* pp. 198 ff. With regard to the early development, R. Gerber, *Die deutsche Passion von Luther bis Bach (Lutherjahrbuch,*1931); with regard to Chr.Flor, P.Epstein in *Petersjahrb.,* 1929.

[22] In his introduction to the practical edition of Schütz's *Passion Acc. to St. Luke* (Bärenreiter, 1934). Similarly the rewarding article by Walter Blankenburg, *Zu Heinrich Schütz' Passionen* in *Musik und Kirche* (1934).

"The Schütz movement of the last ten years has placed the understanding of Schütz's passions on a new basis. These passions are now no longer included in the field of concert music as antique precursors of the Bach passions but are understood as the completion of the old choral passion and therewith as liturgical music. The step from the concert to the liturgy thus signifies the abandonment of the comparison with Bach."

In addition, it must be emphasized that the historical circumstance that we have come to know Bach's passions primarily as concert pieces does not thereby justify us in identifying them with the world of the concert and thus placing them as much below the Schütz passions as one may evaluate "liturgy" higher than "concert." The Bach passions, too, are truly at home only in the liturgy and should again be won back for it by means of the Vespers of Holy Week. The passion oratorios and cantatas of an altogether different category, such as those of Handel and Graun, were concert pieces. What makes it impossible to compare musically these compositions of Schütz and Bach is their entirely different style of scoring. What keeps them widely separated liturgically is the very different theological spirit of the seventeenth and the eighteenth century. However, what always again unites them as members of a family is the nearness to God of both composers and the fact that both were endowed with genius of the first rank in their understanding of music for the church.

To understand the traditional setting for the different characters according to voices in the case of Schütz and his totally untraditional key and melody disposition in relation to them, one must remember that Luther had chosen the fifth tone for the Gospel, the eighth for the Epistle, based on old church tradition insofar as one could still speak of this.[23] He justified this choice to Johs. Walter (significant of his backward-looking modal aesthetics) by saying "because Christ was so kind a master and because Paul was so stern an apostle." For the Gospel Schütz chose from the very outset the richer type of the passion tone within the following compass:

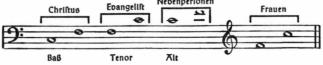

Thus is explained the high position for Peter, Judas, Caiaphas, etc., for which we now must employ tenors, with women instead of boys only where necessary for the maids and the wife of Pilate! Jesus is a bass, while the evangelist may be a

---

[23] Friedr. Gebhardt, *Die musikalischen Grundlagen zu Luther's deutscher Messe* (*Luther Jhrb.*, 1928), especially pp. 98 ff and 141 ff.

light baritone. For the sake of brevity a few typical examples of the old evangelical song formulae may be given, in connection with which we should note that almost the only phrase which has received very rich melismatic expansion is *Eli lama*.[24] This is also the case with Schütz:

---

[24] See particularly Joh. Walter's second setting.

While Schütz retained a certain portion of these formulae in his passions, he not only boldly ventured to transpose them[25] but actually created a new Gregorianism of his own for the three kinds of choral recitations, especially for Jesus. This neo-Gregorianism contains, besides the old ecclesiastical stock formulae, two secular sources of style: the Florentine opera monody and the German song form. For the former we may cite as an example Matthew:

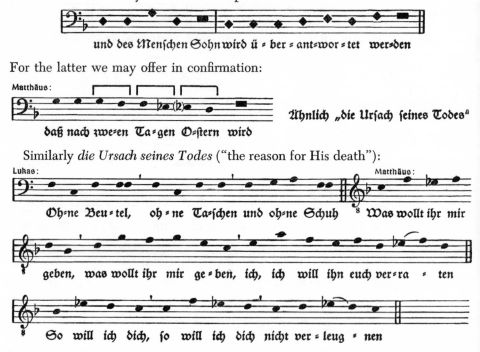

For the latter we may offer in confirmation:

Similarly *die Ursach seines Todes* ("the reason for His death"):

More marked contours *(Bare)* enter the picture as though spontaneously. Since the choruses are set in different keys, deliberately arranged,[26] it is frequently the func-

---

[25] In the *St. Matthew Passion* from F up to g minor, in the *St. John Passion* down to *e* Phrygian. Carl Riedel's *Evangelienharmonie nach Schütz* (1870) adopted 11 of the 15 choruses (Dorian), and only two of the 15 St. Luke *turbae* (Lydian); not a single one of the 16 St. John choruses (Phrygian).

[26] Here also the passions present the previously mentioned climactic sequence: the *St. Luke Passion* stands nearest the apocryphal *St. Mark Passion*, which begins and concludes all choruses in F, inasmuch as it departs from the same F Lydian frame only twice: the first chorus of the multitude begins in C, the *Kreuzige ("Crucify")* chorus concludes in A. The *St. John Passion* shows more change with the structural scheme e—E, e—E, e—E, a—E, e—E, a—E, a—E, e—a, C—E, E—a, (early form A), a—a, e—E, e—A, E—E, e—E, a—E. Most richly varied are the tonalities of the *St. Matthew Passion*: g—G, g—G, g—F, g—D, g—B flat, B flat—B flat, g—A, g—C, F—C, g—D, g—B flat, C—A, C—A, g—G, g—G, g—G, g—G, d—D, F—G, g—C, B flat—G, g—G.

tion of the recitatives by the evangelist to lead to them tonally, which implies not only tonic or dominant transitions to the following sections but also such as are related at the third. Furthermore, as intervening subsidiary cadences are used to present an organization *(distinktionshafte Gliedering)*[27] in speeches of greater length, modulations arise which the old Gregorianism did not know or recognize:

It is these very subsidiary cadences which the Arnold Mendelssohn harmonies took into account. To make them completely understandable to the ear even when the recitation is unaccompanied and not to allow them to become sources of a change in pitch forms one of the chief technical problems in interpretation. However, in many peformances such difficulties have now been completely overcome.

When we review the individual settings of the passions by Schütz, we find that the one according to St. Luke has been strangely neglected.[28] Kamlah is doubtless entirely correct in his surmise as to the reason for this:

> When we shall have learned to stop squinting from Schütz over to Bach, this will undoubtedly be greatly to the advantage of the *Passion According to St. Luke.* The measure of respect in the public evaluation of music is based for the most part on various prejudices, accidents, or indeed on indolence. Thus the public idea of the Bach passions has doubtless evoked its counterpicture in the evaluation of the Schütz passions. In Bach, and hence also in Schütz, the *St. Matthew Passion* is in the first position, with the *St. John* in the second. There is no known *Passion According to St. Luke* by Bach, and hence the public has not been greatly interested in a *Passion According to St. Luke* by Schütz.

Supposedly the question of the setting of this work has the following background.[29] Since a number of the most impressive points, such as the *Eli lama,* are lacking in the Gospel According to St. Luke, and the choruses, too, are far fewer

---

[27] *Distinktionschlüsse* refer to subsidiary cadences which do not as yet lead to the tonic.
[28] Practical ed. by W. Kamlah (Bärenreiter).
[29] According to P. Epstein's introduction to the new edition of Chr. Schultze's *Passion According to St. Luke.*

in number, and the position of this work in Holy Week is not a preferred one, few polyphonists have undertaken its composition. When in 1653 in Delitzsch the *Herr Diaconus* explained the passion story according to this source, the local cantor, Christoph Schultze, wanted to have it sung in passion style and made a setting of it because "according to my knowledge, such has not yet been set forth for musical use." Schultze presented it "for the most part according to the common manner." It is not surprising that Schultze was unfamiliar with the St. Luke setting of Sam. Besler in Breslau. The fact that he does not mention the *St. Luke Passion* by Schütz may indicate that this did not yet exist or at least was not well known, as Schultze was an outspoken admirer of Schütz and a collector of Schütz's works. It is probable that the Schütz setting had not yet been written, but that Schütz had Schultze's work and performed it in Dresden. In comparing the scores of the two compositions it would, therefore, seem likely that in working on the composition himself Schütz utilized echoes of Schultze and wished to develop the latter's work, partly along the same lines. Obviously Schütz's innate boldness and greater power permitted him to outstrip Schultze. Schultze, too, frequently abandons the ecclesiastical choral tone for the purpose of emphasizing happy inspirations. He, too, has a church-hymn setting at the end. His choruses, in part for six voices, are plastic and often surprisingly dramatic. For the most part, however, they are mediocre.

On the other hand, Schütz's very opening chorus immediately shows what a masterpiece he has succeeded in creating in the *St. Luke Passion*. The octave leap which Schütz is fond of giving to one voice in many-voiced cadences here becomes thematic after it has been announced in the third measure at *Leiden* (p. 99).

Wonderful is the voice-leading of the mature master — as from the school of Josquin — which perspicuously restrains its tonal expression by means of pauses, spins the harmony from cadence to cadence with the greatest rhythmic richness, and keeps each voice light and radiant. This transparency can rise to word painting, as in the case of the chorus *Nie keinen* ("Nay, nothing").[30] The F Lydian character of the choruses[31] produces for our ears the effect of being more in the domain of C than in that of F and of barely touching the subdominant. Neverthe-

---

[30] A similar thought pervades the *arioso Mein Jesus schweigt* in Bach's *St. Matthew Passion*. Here the pauses say more than the notes, which merely mark the dripping of the time.

[31] The recitatives proceed in F Ionian.

less, it is amazing how spontaneously the harmony progresses, also in the more
modern sense. Generally Schütz prepares the final cadence on F imperceptibly by
means of several 6/4 chords in the C domain. The "two" swords in the next chorus
suggest a duet beginning *(Duettköpfe)* in accordance with Schütz's number symbolism; *hier, hier, hier* indicates the baroque as well as his own personal fervor.
In the next chorus the *Schwert* ("sword") (p. 106) receives a recurring sixteenth-
note figure; and *Dreinschlagen* ("smite them") also has its pictorial designation.
The question is whether here, as well as in the chorus *Du bist Christus,* some of
the b naturals as the highest notes in the phrase, and also in the descent in the
Lydian, must not obviously be modified to b flat. At *Weissage* (p. 108) the middle
transition to *a* minor forms one of the most beautiful examples of Schütz's subsidiary cadence; likewise at *Diesen finden wir* ("We have found this man pervert-
ing all the nations"), with the Picardized *d* minor modulation on *er sei Christus
der König* ("He is Christ the King"), where the feigned surprise is splendidly
portrayed. The chorus *Er hat das Volk* ("He stirreth up the people"), at the beginning, is manifestly under the sway of *erreget* ("excited"). Nevertheless, the tempo
should not be too fast. What Hermann Finck calls the "common cabbage-chopping
beat"[32] ($\bmJ$ = 60) would be the maximum tempo, preferably $\bmJ$ = 52, with some
acceleration later. At *Hinweg mit diesem* ("Away with Him") the repetition of the
suggestive words, so characteristic of the baroque, indicates a climax. The overlapping motives at *Barrabam* recall the *feritevi* of the neophyte of a half century
before. Such a technique marks a complete triumph in the chorus at *ganze Schar*
("the whole multitude"), where the Monteverdi fourth, f—c# (p. 116), establishes
the atmosphere,[33] and where, despite the beginning in F, the Dorian alone holds
sway:

---

[32] *Der gemeine krauthackerische Schlag.* Herman Finck, *Practica musica* (Wittenberg, 1556).
[33] Also in the case of Bach in similar passages.

One need only observe the last long bass melisma (p. 117) in order to appreciate what fire still glowed in this genius despite his eighty years.

The freely disposed accents in connection with the chorus of the elders (p. 118), *Er hat andern geholfen* ("He Saved Others"), and their, so to say, realistic polyphony bear witness, as do strong metrical changes from eighth notes to whole notes, to almost unbridled savagery. What flippant scorn lies in the dancelike theme of the soldiers! In the curves the Lydian mode actually sounds impertinent:

Here, too, the rhythmic antithesis between outer and inner voices has a madrigalesque effect. The concluding chorus, *Wer Gottes Marter in Ehren hat* ("He Who Will Honor the Woes of God"), uses the last strophe of the old hymn *Da Jesus an dem Kreuze stund* ("As Jesus Hung upon the Cross"). On account of the general Lydian tonality of this passion the Phrygian mode of the old melody could not be used. Nevertheless, the master apparently created for himself a kind of model of his own which one can still detect in the few primary cadences of his song motet.

The treatment of the solo voices, which he has written in F Ionian, is equally fascinating. Even as early as the minnesingers this mode called for triadic formations. Leaps of fourths [34] and fifths join the relation at the third more than is usual in the "gliding" Gregorianism. Characteristic is the line:

This even leads to triadic structures, as in the tone painting (p. 118):

When Schütz builds other church tones into this melodic frame, approaching the folk song, he does so not merely for the sake of a musically appealing change but much rather to do justice to the changing ethos of the text. Note the following combination of pictorial motion and atmospheric modulation:

When Jesus speaks with restrained grief, He usually begins in g Dorian, which then generally relaxes into F Lydian. Note again the following (p. 105):

---

[34] A number of fourths, as at *und fürchten sich vor dem Volk.*

The unnecessarily added accidental, b flat, denotes emphasis. This can be so increased that *arioso* elements become apparent and chromaticism announces itself while changes in meter and tempo occur, as in this speech of Pilate (p. 117):

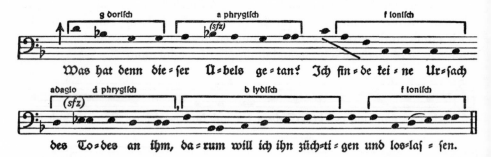

If we add to this some melismatic digressions at *Vater, ich befehle* ("Father, I commend") (p. 121) and *Fürwahr, dieser ist* ("Indeed, this was a righteous man") (p. 121), and some intimated expansions at *Er ist unter die Übeltäter gerechnet* ("And likewise He was reckoned with the transgressors") (p. 104) and *Dies ist der Judenkönig* ("This is the King of the Jews") (p. 120), we have a neo-Gregorianism which, to be sure, still allows the ground types of *initium, tonus currens, mediatio* and *finalis,* and comma-and-question formula to shimmer through but otherwise has retained only the loose unaccompanied recitation and at all decisive points has acknowledged the right of free inspiration. The fact that in spite of all this liberty a firm, uniform harmony binds together the whole is the really grand achievement of Schütz's genius.

Of the *St. John Passion* we have the version which Schütz sent to Duke August to Wolfenbüttel in 1665 (I, 125) and the final form of Grundig's copy. The two versions differ chiefly in the fact that in the second version Schütz added numerous pauses for punctuation *(Interpunktionshalte)* in order to organize or articulate the delivery more effectively — apparently because the first singer of the part of the evangelist had taken it all too hurriedly. A still further text revision followed, since a number of mistakes in memory as well as omissions have occurred. Finally, Schütz here and there formulated the line in a more mobile manner, moving it now more into the light, now more into the shadow, but at the same time again developing more sharply the turns of the church tones, as most extensively at (p. 129):

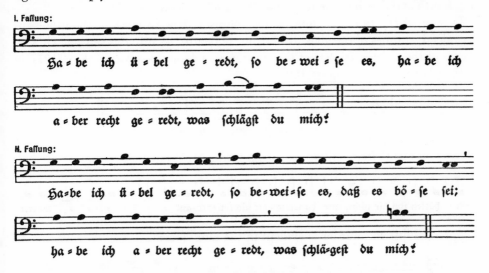

I. Faſſung:

Ha = be ich ü = bel ge = redt, ſo be = wei = ſe es,   ha = be ich

a = ber recht ge = redt, was ſchlägſt du mich?

H. Faſſung:

Ha=be ich ü = bel ge = redt, ſo be=wei=ſe es, daß es bö = ſe ſei;

ha = be ich   a = ber recht ge = redt, was ſchlä=geſt du mich?

Or a melisma is simplified, and thereby at the same time more variety is achieved, as at *Sehet, das ist euer König* ("Behold your King"). The choruses differ only in slight harmonic changes: *Seiner Jünger einer* ("One of His disciples") (p. 130), *Deinen Tod und sein Ursach* ("Thy death and its cause") (p. 144); at *niemand töten* ("no man to death") (p. 132), *zu Gottes Sohn gemacht* ("made Himself the Son of God") (p. 136); a tightening *(Straffung)* at *sondern Barrabam* ("but Barrabas") (p. 133), and the like.

That we are dealing with a Phrygian work is at once established by the tenor in the splendid line (p. 125):

Das Lei = den un = ſers Her=ren Je = ſu Chri = ſti

in which connection one involuntarily hesitates to rationalize this free accentual system through bar lines. The discant, too, is markedly Phrygian, while Glarean would doubtless have designated the bass and the alto as Aeolian with subsiding cadence on the quint *(Confinalschluss)*. The first cadence leads this text to C Ionian; the second part, with the figures at *beschreibet* ("relates") (p. 125) and the lively eighth-note declamation *heilige Evangeliste* ("holy evangelist") (p. 126), moves upward in the circle of fifths by way of subsidiary cadences in G, D, A major to E. Note how the word *Johannes* is enhanced at the end by advancing from the step of a fourth and a fifth to the leap of a sixth and an octave (p. 126).

In none of the three passions do the choruses show so much of the grotesque — indeed, at times of the ghostlike "dance of death" — as in this setting. Thus by means of the wanton triplets at the repetition of *Jesum von Nazareth* (p. 127), or in the insolent octave leap (p. 130):

in the impudent *(frech)* piling-up of the words (p. 131):

Suppressed lust for murder is evident in the alto voice:

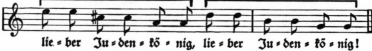

At *nicht diesen, sondern Barrabam* ("not this man but Barrabas") the mosaic in the manipulation of the motives is marvelous. How contempibly abject these soldiers, first with the low genuflection, *Sei gegrüsset* ("Hail to Thee") (with solemn embellishment by the organist), and then the snickering of the disguised triplets in the motive:

Bift du nicht sei = ner Jün = ger ei = ner?

wir hätten ihn dir nicht, wir hätten ihn dir nicht ü = ber = ant = = = = = = wortet

Wir dür = fen nie = mand tö = = ten!

lie = ber Ju = den = tö = nig, lie = ber Ju = den = tö = nig!

In both of the choruses in triple time, *Kreuzige ihn* ("Crucify Him"), the real thirst for blood dances into a prescribed *prestissimo*.

With cynical pleasure the mob[35] trills forth *(trällert):*

Wir ha=ben ein Ge=fet=ze, und nach dem Ge=fet=ze foll er ster = ben!

The high priests fly into an almost hysterical passion. *Wir haben keinen, keinen, keinen, keinen König* ("We have no king but Caesar"). The half notes at *denn den Kaiser* ("but Caesar") show the old double-motive technique of Schütz the madrigalist. The excitement of these scenes is also pictured by the constant wavering between the *e* E and the *a* A region. The whipped-up fury of the high priest(s) leads to the shouted contrast between the groups of eighths, *Schreibe nicht: Der Juden König* ("Write not 'The King of the Jews'") (p. 140), and the drastically broad syncopation at *sondern* ("rather") (p. 142), with the hugely enlarged structure of the passage, *Ich bin — der — Juden König* ("I am the King of the Jews") and its eager eighth notes. In the chorus *Lasset uns ihn nicht zerteilen* ("Let Us Not Rend It") (p. 142), the *wes, wes, wes* ("whose, whose, whose") (p. 142) is apparently also formulated to give a realistic picture of the brawling Hebrews.

Thus this work would present but the delirious dream of an uncanny masquerade, a biting satire on the brutal vulgarity of humanity, were it not for the fact that the individual songs gave us by contrast a most moving portrayal of the noblest suffering.

The very first *accentus* phrase at once delineates the Phrygian tone with b as the recitational tone (p. 127):

Da Je=fus fol=ches ge = re = det hat=te, ging er hin=aus mit fei=nen Jüngern

über den Bach Kidron, da war ein Garten, darein ging Jefus und fei=ne Jünger.

The *über* and *Jesus* receive small characterizations. Here, too, there are hints of "personal tonalities." Jesus often sings in the Mixolydian mode, Peter in the Hypoaeolian, Pilate in the Hypoionian. In view of the very churchly nature of the Phrygian tone, anything songlike is scarcely met with; but at least quasi symmetries frequently occur; compare the threefold *und wärmete(n) sich* ("and warmed them-

---

[35] Here keyed for alto, two tenors and bass, i. e., male chorus alone.

selves") or the words of Jesus, in which connection the accidental again indicates an *espressivo:*

Was fragst du mich darum? Fra = ge die darum, die ge = hö = ret ha = ben ...

(a small *Bar*, A—A—B!)
or the correspondence of the melismas of Pilate to what is released through them:

Se = het, welch ein Mensch! schrie = en sie und sprachen

Similarly, the two sayings of Jesus, *Siehe, das ist dein Sohn* ("Woman, behold thy Son") and *Siehe, das ist deine Mutter* ("Behold, this is Thy mother") (p. 143), obviously correspond to each other. As a matter of fact, all kinds of small forms crystallize in this manner.

These melismas are interpolated in a thoroughly planned manner, and at *kreuzige* (p. 140) they reach a climax with seven notes in the phrase. On *König* (p. 140) there are three; on *dürstet* ("I thirst") (p. 143), there are four notes. How much power of expression may lie even in the slur of but two notes is shown by the last recitative. Note also the different pitches:

sprach er: Es ist   voll=bracht!   Und   nei = get das Haupt und ver = schied.

The concluding chorus, *O hilf, Christe*[36] (p. 153), is a church-hymn setting which adheres strictly to the *cantus firmus,* especially in the soprano. The *Untugend* ("evil ways") and the *arm und schwach* ("poor and weak") are realistically pictured. In spite of this fact, however, the setting is not dissipated in details but once more superbly summarizes the fundamental tone of the work at *Christe, Gottes Sohn* ("Christ, the Son of God") and *bitter Leiden* ("bitter pain"). We feel that no matter with how skillful a blade the master carved his Calvary scenes, nowhere did he wish arbitrarily to put himself forward with "interpretative ingenuity." He always had before him the literal meaning of *liturgia,* "service for the people." On the highest plane his every note speaks with the felicity of true

---

[36] The last strophe of the hymn *Christus, der uns selig macht,* by Michael Weisse.

devotion, as expressed in the last words of his *St. John Passion: Dir Dankopfer schenken* ("to make to Thee an offering of thanks") (p. 144).

Finally, we have the *Passion According to Matthew* (I, 49) in g Dorian.[37] This church tone is for the most part very clearly evident in the individual speeches, such as the one in the strictly diatonic example — which, however, at the same time modulates richly (p. 53):

Nevertheless, Schütz at various times changes over from the F to the B flat (less frequently also into the C) system. The first case can often be recognized in the interval to e flat, as at *Was bekümmert ihr das Weib?* ("Wherefore trouble ye the woman?") (p. 52), *dass man mich begraben wird* ("She did it for My burial") (p. 52), *Ich will ihn euch verraten* ("and I will deliver Him unto you") (p. 52), *in dieser Nacht werdet ihr euch alle ärgern an mir* ("and ye shall be offended because of Me this night") (p. 54), *nimmermehr ärgern* ("never be offended") (p. 54), *eine Finsternis über das ganze Land* ("darkness over all the land") (p. 67). The passage *Meine Seele ist betrübt bis in den Tod* ("My soul is exceeding sorrowful, even unto death") (p. 54) becomes outspokenly *c* minor; *so gehe dieser Kelch von mir* ("Let this cup pass from Me") (p. 55) sinks down to *d* Phrygian; and at

we find the very modern diminished fifth.

Here are collected reminders of song and opera which flowed from Schütz's pen in the *St. Matthew Passion* more freely than in his other settings of the Passion story. We note also that here Schütz treated the text somewhat more independently than elsewhere, partly by small, doubling repetitions, partly by varied treatments which place the well-known words in a surprisingly different light — as we noted

---

[37] Practical ed. by Fritz Schmidt (for the Celle Schütz Festival), Bärenreiter, 1929.

above in his setting of the Lord's Prayer. Thus to the first chorus of the high priests and the scribes we add *Ja nicht auf das Fest!* ("Not on the feast day") (p. 50) to the *auf dass nicht ein Aufruhr werde im Volk* ("lest there be an uproar among the people") (p. 50). Or note *Ich, ich will ihn euch verraten* ("and I will deliver Him unto you") (p. 52); *da, da wird man auch sagen* ("there, there shall also this be told") (p. 52); *so will ich dich, so will ich dich nicht verleugnen* ("Though I should die with Thee, yet will I not deny Thee") (p. 54); *Ich, ich weiss nicht, was du sagest* ("I, I know not what Thou sayest") (p. 58); *Wahrlich, du, du* ("Verily, Thou, Thou"); *Ich, ich bin Gottes Sohn* ("I am the Son of God") (p. 66); *Gegrüsset seist du, du, der Juden König* ("Hail, King of the Jews!") (p. 64). The "balloon power" *(Ballonkraft)* of which we occasionally spoke as applicable to Schütz as well as to Bach makes Schütz fond of having his melodies enter with an "energetic" *(eifrig)* high tone, as, for example, within the space of a few lines (p. 55):

It would be a study by itself to follow up the seeds of form which sprouted everywhere from the imagination of the great master in these superbly formed dialogs, which couple dramatic fluency with the holiest gravity. Note, for example, this short passage:

Or this highly emotional passage, in which the interval of the fifth constitutes the measure of the violent eruption of feeling:

This leads to most impressive spoken melody — at the same time to gestural pictures of movement, as:

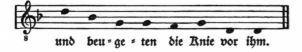

The monodic arch, however, which in the lament of Absalom spread itself so broadly, here at *Eli lama (Mein Gott, mein Gott)* forms a beautiful aureole.

These will serve as but a few examples of similar riches — practically inexhaustible.

The choruses are often extremely short. Therefore they are all the more penetrating *(hämmern sich dadurch desto schärfer ein)*. For example. *Er ist des Todes schuldig* ("He is deserving of death") (p. 57), *Barrabam* (p. 62), *Lass ihn kreuzigen* ("Let Him be crucified") (p. 62), and *Der ruft den Elias* ("This man calleth for Elias") (p. 67). All the others are more richly developed. We have already mentioned the great tonal diversity of the choruses in comparison with the other settings. One notes the *piano* of a malicious conspiracy in the inflammatory rhythm of the *Ja nicht auf das Fest* ("Not on the feast day") (p. 50) (g minor). Very characteristic of Schütz are the sharp metrical antitheses and the repeated words of the group of disciples in the tenor (p. 51)

Note also how this part — in this work the most frequent countervoice *(Konfliktstimme)* — turns about the diminished third e flat—d—c# as if the narrowmindedness of the zealots were to be portrayed as they continually fan their anger by means of their speech. How much more affable is the gentle *fugato, Wo willst du, dass wir dir bereiten* ("Where will Thou that we prepare Thee") (p. 52), with the beautifully swinging cadence! Against such lines the hockets at *Herr, bin ich's?* ("Lord, is it I?") (p. 53), or at *Halt, lasst sehen* ("Let be, let us see") (p. 67), form a contrast all the greater. The canon at the second, assigned to the two false witnesses (first in the upper, then in the lower interval), and the *fugato, Er ist des Todes schuldig* ("He is deserving of death") (p. 57), are technical masterpieces, interesting as such altogether apart from their highly pictorial character.

The calls of the multitude, *Weissage uns, weissage uns, Christe* ("Prophesy unto us, O Christ") (p. 58), break forth wildly and brutally with the closest overlapping. The *Wer ist es, der dich schlug?* ("Who is he that smote Thee?") (p. 58) is molded with a simplicity reminding us of the St. Luke choruses in three-four motives on the four-four framework. The

scarcely suppresses a diabolical laughter. Very significantly this figure returns when the rabbis dismiss Judas with *Was gehet es uns an? Da siehe du zu* ("What is that to us? See thou to that") (p. 60), and when the soldiers deride, *Gegrüsset seist du* ("Hail, Thou") (p. 64) and *der du den Tempel Gottes zerbrichst* ("Thou that destroyest the temple") (p. 65). Observe how these choruses modulate without effort from g minor to B flat, A, C major. What gloomy horror lurks in the b flat of the tenor and the c of the alto after the b natural in the bass at

Mad fanaticism speaks out of the obstinate retention of the rough meter

which we heard almost duplicated in the chorus *Wozu dienet dieser Unrat* ("To
What Purpose Is This Waste?") (p. 51). In *Der du den Tempel Gottes* (p. 65) the
painting, *steig herab* ("come down"), is an old tradition. More important is the
gripping uniformity in which all declaim polyrhythmically: *in dreien Tagen —
hilf dir selber — bist du Gottes Sohn* ("In three days — save Thyself — if Thou
be the Son of God"). For once however, we must, after all, take a look at Bach;
note the following:

In precisely the same way we could compare the chorus *Herr, wir haben gedacht*
("Sir, We Remember"), or we could spiritually confront with each other the two

profoundly emotional passages *Wahrlich, dieser ist Gottes Sohn gewesen* ("Truly, this was the Son of God"). Schütz has more cadences, and yet. . . .

The many correspondences in declamation should, of course, not deceive one into imagining any "influence" of Schütz on Bach. It would be more interesting than important to know whether Bach saw in his youth a Schütz passion while he was with Sam. Drese in Weimar or with J. J. Loewe in Lüneburg. After all, however, perhaps these comparisons show — in spite of the fact that the styles of the times and of the persons are completely dissimilar — how questionable it is to draw too sharp a contrast between the two great masters ("Schütz, the master of the word — Bach, the master of the musical gesture"). While the two giant cantors of Saxon-Thuringian stock — in spite of golden and silver baroque, in spite of granite and marble Dorianism — often come surprisingly near to each other, it is idle to ask who was the greater. Here only one resemblance is beyond question: that which is timeless is on a par with that which is timeless.

In any event, in a passage like *und werde der letzte Betrug ärger denn der erste* ("So the last error shall be worse than the first") (p. 70), with but four voices, with its leap of an octave (or a sixth) upwards and a sixth downwards at the central thought, in closest contrapuntal overlapping, Schütz accomplishes something astounding.

Let us note finally the opening and the conclusion — truly the most precious doors of the noble shrine! One ought really to quote here all the eight large measures of the Introit. Each one of them reveals some miracle: the mystically empty fifths of the beginning, out of which arises, on *Leiden*, the most austere tension between the major ninth and the minor tenth; a Gabrieli tarrying on the C major chord at *unseres Herrn* until the concept *Jesu Christi* stretches out its arms afar to F major and B flat major, and the *Christi*, in pathetic anticipation in the soprano, touchingly fills itself with warmth; now the depicting pen of the apostle becomes alive in all the voices. Does one not see in the painting of Caravaggio[38] how the angel dictates to the heavy man? As new color we now have g minor—d minor for *der heilige Evangeliste*. The tierce relationships, *d—F, c—E* flat, appear in the old Netherlandish manner. And again, after the harsh Monteverdi fourth, e flat—b natural in the bass — the chord of "suffering" resounds on *Matthäus*. (See next page.)

And the conclusion? For its text (p. 70) Schütz selects the last strophe, *Ehre sei dir, Christe* ("Honor be to Christ") of the hymn *Ach, wir armen Sünder* ("Ah, We

---

[38] Kaiser Friedrich-Museum, Berlin.

Poor Sinners"), with which Hermann Bonnus transformed the old folk song *Ach, du armer Judas* into an evangelical church song. Its primarily Ionian-Myxolydian melody was not adaptable to the g Dorian mode of the work as a whole, so the master kept his hands free for his own construction. He used this in various ways. We have striven seriously in this book not to speak in hyperboles. But, confronted by this one number, let us say for once: If everything in this world were properly evaluated, this would be one of the most famous pieces for all people and all times. *Ehre sei dir, Christe:* a g minor cadence, in which the title of the "Anointed," in a gigantic bass arch, tears the lower into the upper dominant and thereby draws first the tenor, then the alto, into its stream, while the soprano, lamenting step by step, withers away out of the c minor into the g minor third. Echolike the soprano begins again, this time all alone, stepping from d to e flat at *der du littest* ("Thou who suffer'dst") — the three male voices follow in the same rhythm; but now the incisive subdominant seventh chord arises: a flat — c—e flat — g, which is mollified chromatically into a dominant of the dominant 6/5 chord: a—c—e flat — f. One expects an E flat major tonic; but this becomes, for the word *Not*, austerely dissonant — e flat — g—b flat — d — and receives its resolution only after the caesura with a chord of the sixth which, as subdominant, sinks back to g minor over renewed chromaticism in both of the lower voices. The second couplet is concluded. A conclusion *(Abgesang)* on the words *An dem Stamm des Kreuzes* ("On the stem of the cross") brightens and simplifies the couplet head to the G major — c minor surface — but surprisingly the one e (entering chromatically in the soprano) urges forward to the sequence C major—F major, then to sink in a painfilled cadence (b flat against c#) to d minor: *für uns den bittern Tod* ("for us Thy bitter death"). This entire period would seem about to repeat itself in abbreviated form; but this time the G major surface (clouded by the minor seventh) leads, not to c minor but, at *Kreuz*, to A flat major, and now, by way of the a flat — b of f minor, to the c minor conclusion. The chain member, *und herrschest mit dem Vater*

dort in Ewigkeit ("and reignest with the Father there to eternity"), forms a new motet section in a serious, vigorous rhythm, with a *c* minor cadence — a sternly looking Christ-King-Judge! This leads a second time to B flat major, the third time to *g* minor. And now humanity — in simple, pitiful thirds, soprano and alto pray *Hilf uns armen Sündern* ("Help us poor sinners"); the bass and the tenor repeat it, and the alto, lying heavily above, only strengthens the representation of our earthly tribulation and guilt, which dies out in empty unison. *Hilf uns armen Sündern zu der Seligkeit* ("Help us poor sinners to blessedness") is the four-voice conclusion of this *g* minor A—B—A *Bar*. What longing lies in the melisma on *Seligkeit*, with its sobbing countermovement!

The final section is the *Kyrie, Christe, Kyrie eleison*. Here Schütz has the courage to present modernisms he never employed before. The dominant seventh and its inversions are used with a sweetness as though the "Neapolitans," on the shoulders of the late Venetians, Lotti and Caldara, were already at work to prepare for Mozart's *Ave verum*. One realizes that Buxtehude, J. W. Franck, and Zachow did not need to derive such means from Italy. The first *Kyrie* (G major) moves in parallel tenths in the outer voices, while the fifth and the octave remain in the inner voices — something not discovered again until romanticism. How mild this 6/5 chord b—f—g—d in c minor! The *Christe*, in which the soprano subsequently shines forth as the "Light in darkness" and devotedly bends and bows itself in the *eleison*, moves first to B flat major, then it recalls the thirds at *armen* and pursues with them the same road back: B flat major and *g* minor cadences move by way of the Phrygian to the D major semicadence, after the discant alone has replied to the *Kyrie* of the lowest voices and the alto has cut in with its torturing ninth. A concluding passage *(Abgesangsregion)*, which rolls along on the D organ point first in parallel tenths, then in still wider-rolling parallel sixths, leads to the Picardian G major as its resting place. It is a movement in which every note written by the eighty-year-old magician discovers new continents.

The unusual thing in these Schütz passions is their twofold character — liturgical subjection and personal experience — and the fact that they do not contradict but rather confirm and strengthen one another. This is because the one who felt and formulated them was a true, enlightened, and noble Christian. "Because in Schütz's passions the subjective and objective sides stand in such complete equilibrium, they have become for us the very epitome of Protestant church music."[39]

---

[39] Walter Blankenburg in *Musik und Kirche* (1935).

Last Works

In his sermon at Schütz's casket Geier relates that finally the composer "continued with great diligence to complete splendid musical compositions on several of the psalms of David, especially the 119th, as well as the passions according to three evangelists." A year before Schütz's death this *opus ultimum* appeared in voice books in Dresden[1] with the title: *The 119th Psalm of the King and Prophet David, in Eleven Compositions. In Addition, the Supplement of the 100th Psalm: Make a Joyful Noise! and a German Magnificat: My Soul Doth Magnify the Lord, with Eight Voices, for Two Choruses. Composed According to the Usual Church Intonations and for the Electoral Saxon Court Chapel. . . . Honored by Heinrich Schütz, Electoral Saxon Senior Kapellmeister.*[2] However, only this title page was printed, together with the last page, in the *Catalogus über H. Schützens 119. Ps.,* etc., while the music was written out carefully throughout by a copyist.

Up to the present time only a single copy of the entire work has been found — in Guben.[3] Unfortunately, it lacks the *cantus et tenor secundi chori* and the thorough-bass voice (see below). Therefore the work is defective, with the exception of the *German Magnificat,* as this is found complete in manuscript in the Grimma Library,[4] with the superscription:

German Magnificat,
for Eight Parts,
for Two Choruses,
Composed
by
Heinrich Schütz,

---

[1] *Gedruckt mit Seyfferts Schrifften,* 1671.

[2] *Königs und Propheten Davids Hundert und Neunzehender Psalm / in Eilf Stükken / Nebenst dem Anhange des 100. Psalms: Jauchzet dem Herrn! und Eines deutschen Magnificats: Meine Seele erhöbt den Herrn. Mit acht Stimmen / auf zweien Köhren / über die gewöhnlichen Kirchen-Intonationen componieret / und zur Churfl. Sächs. Hoff-Capella / . . . verehret von Heinrich Schützen / Churfl. Sächs. ältesten Capell-Meistern.*

[3] Evangelical Church.

[4] Score edition of the *Magnificat,* edited by H. Spitta, in K. Straube's series, *Ausgewählte Gesänge des Thomanerchors zu Leipzig* (B & H); also edited by K. Ameln as *Bärenreiter Ausgabe* 2/55, with title facsimile. See further *MGkK,* 1900, pp. 125 ff.

Electoral Saxon Senior
Kapellmeister,
in His 86th Year.
It Is at the Same Time His Final Work
and His Swan Song.

At the end of the lowest voice in the Guben copy, the second bass, there stands
in the master's unsteady hand the significant word *Finis!* Through the Guben
secondhand bookstore of Kaspar-Buhlmann an organ voice was discovered, which
came into the possession of Stephan Zweig in Salzburg by way of the bookseller
M. Lengfeld in Cologne. Fortunately, it is the copy which Schütz dedicated to his
elector.[5] It shows in autograph on page five some textual additions at the foot of
the page — *[Va-] ter und dem Sohn, Und auch dem Heiligen Geiste* — and
several note improvements, such as the subsequent shortening by half of the note
values in the intonations of the psalm verses. Most important of all, however, on
the prefatory page in a clear handwriting is this dedication:

Wherewith my most humble petition is forwarded to
Your Serene Highness, my most gracious Lord,
that you may show your most gracious favor
to this, to be sure, humble little work,
to have it tried and sung,
at your most gracious opportunity,
in Your Highness' Court Chapel
by eight good voices, with two organs,
by the two beautiful musical choirs
placed opposite each other above the altar.

                                                                    Author.

Here again, then, sixty years after the first Venetian sojourn, the Gabrieli gallery
setting (with the *cori spezzati*) is clearly demanded as the form of execution, and
this probably in the last lines that Schütz wrote.

---

[5] First information by G. Kinsky in *Zs. f. MW*, XII, 597 f. (1930). How may this treasure have
reached Guben? There were a number of points of contact between this Lower Silesian town
and Dresden. Schütz's vice-Kapellmeister, Joh. Georg Hofkuntz (1638-41), had been cantor in
Guben. At the time of Schütz's death the town belonged to Sachsen-Merseburg (!), thus being
subject to Duke Christian, who had been Schütz's last chapel inspector. Perhaps one of the
Guben cantors brought the music along from Dresden? H. Jentsch, *Geschichte des Gymnasiums
zu Guben* (Progr. 86, 1907), mentions as such 1650-69, Christof Peter; 1670-1706, Dietrich Vier-
hoff; 1706-08, Joh. Gottfr. Lehmann; 1708-48, Joh. Keuling.

Schütz remarks autographically on the title page of the *cantus primi chori:*
"N. B. If this work should be published, this (printed) title or the title subjoined herewith in writing may be used." Accordingly, the dedicatory copy was doubtless also accompanied by a manuscript title page, which is missing today.

Since this is the final example of Schütz's will to create, it merits special attention for this reason alone. Schütz loved the 119th Psalm above all others. He selected one of its verses for his funeral sermon. "Composed according to the usual church intonations" shows an acknowledgment of the absolute and the eternal, as does Sebastian Bach's turning, in his later life, to the strict chorale cantata, to the solution of the fugal and canonic problems of his last great works.

The giant 119th Psalm[6] is so divided in the *Antiphonale Romanum* that of the twenty-two subdivisions designated with Hebrew letters two, making eleven larger divisions, are always sung together. Thus: Sundays at prime, parts one and two; at tierce, three, four, and five; at sext, six, seven and eight; at nones, nine to eleven. Schütz divided the psalm in the same way, adding as a twelfth section Psalm 100 and as a thirteenth the German *Magnificat*. To be sure, these divisions are all independent of one another, as is indicated each time by the intonation in the discant and the tenor of the first chorus, and by the doxology, *Ehre sei dir*, which is appended to each section and is also begun each time at the altar. Nevertheless, Schütz viewed the thirteen motets as a great symmetrical unity. This is shown by the arrangement of the tonalities, which begins and concludes with two movements in *a* minor. Each time Schütz changed the psalm tone or the church tone. The first ten tones, with the exception of the seventh, occur, which — as the tonality appears now in the F, now in the G system — gives the following arrangement:

1. Tone: *d* minor	⎫
2. Tone: *g* minor	⎭
3. Tone: *a* minor	⎫
4. Tone: *e* minor	⎭
5. Tone: C major	⎫
6. Tone: F major	⎭
7. Tone: (D major)	⎫
8. Tone: G major	⎭
9. Tone: *d* minor	⎫
10. Tone: *a* minor	⎭

Compare with this our presentation of the psalm tone harmonizations in the chapter titled "The Psalms of David of 1619."

From this the following architecture results, which is also confirmed by the fact that between every subordinate group and its neighbor a perceptible caesura or

---

[6] Through the kindness of Prof. M. Seiffert I was permitted to inspect the photocopy of the *Staatliches Institut für deutsche Musikforschung.* I have added the two hitherto missing voices.

hiatus arises by means of a retrogression at the interval of a second, while within the groups of three's closer relationships exist. One should also note the indicated tonal equivalence not only between 1/2 and 12/13 but also between 3/7, 5/9, and 6/11. In each of the three tryptichs the center of expression lies in the middle number, as if the master had wished once again to direct his special inclination to this; in other words, to 4, 7, 10 (G major, g minor, C major), which produces a broadly swinging arch form in the *a* minor framework:

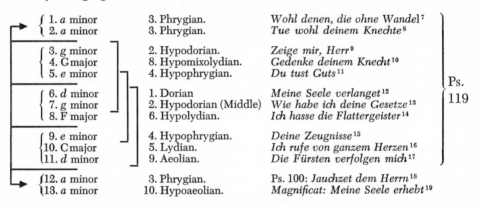

{ 1. *a* minor	3. Phrygian.	*Wohl denen, die ohne Wandel*[7]	
{ 2. *a* minor	3. Phrygian.	*Tue wohl deinem Knechte*[8]	
{ 3. *g* minor	2. Hypodorian.	*Zeige mir, Herr*[9]	
{ 4. Gmajor	8. Hypomixolydian.	*Gedenke deinem Knecht*[10]	
{ 5. *e* minor	4. Hypophrygian.	*Du tust Guts*[11]	Ps.
{ 6. *d* minor	1. Dorian	*Meine Seele verlanget*[12]	119
{ 7. *g* minor	2. Hypodorian (Middle)	*Wie habe ich deine Gesetze*[13]	
{ 8. F major	6. Hypolydian.	*Ich hasse die Flattergeister*[14]	
{ 9. *e* minor	4. Hypophrygian.	*Deine Zeugnisse*[15]	
{10. Cmajor	5. Lydian.	*Ich rufe von ganzem Herzen*[16]	
{11. *d* minor	9. Aeolian.	*Die Fürsten verfolgen mich*[17]	
{12. *a* minor	3. Phrygian.	Ps. 100: *Jauchzet dem Herrn*[18]	
{13. *a* minor	10. Hypoaeolian.	*Magnificat: Meine Seele erhebt*[19]	

The beginning is indicative of the strongly ecclesiastical nature of the work. The intonations stand, doubtless according to choice, in the first discant and in the first tenor. The structural parallelism *(parallelismus membrorum)* is emphasized but seldom by means of antiphonal repetitions, more often by contrast between polyphony and homophony at the semichorus changes:

Intonatio (tertii toni)

8 Wohl de = nen, die oh = ne Wan=del le = ben,

---

[7] *Blessed Are the Undefiled.*
[8] *Deal Bountifully with Thy Servant.*
[9] *Teach Me, O Lord.*
[10] *Remember Thy Word unto Thy Servant.*
[11] *Thou Hast Dealt Well with Thy Servant.*
[12] *My Soul Fainteth for Thy Salvation.*
[13] *Oh, How I Love Thy Law!*
[14] *I Hate Vain Thoughts.*
[15] *Thy Testimonies Are Wonderful.*
[16] *I Cried with My Whole Heart.*
[17] *Princes Have Persecuted Me Without a Cause.*
[18] *Psalm 100: Make a Joyful Noise unto the Lord.*
[19] *Magnificat: My Soul Doth Magnify the Lord.*

However, the antiphonal technique in the case of close overlapping of the semi-choruses is important. The middle part of section four may serve as an example. It has a special fascination, inasmuch as Schütz selected the verse "Thy statutes have been my songs in the house of my pilgrimage"[20] as his funeral text. Manifestly this verse is set off by the densest eight-voice web as the center between the semichorus groups. At *Herr, ich gedenke des Nachts* ("I have remembered Thy name, O Lord, in the night") the master wrote *adagio* with his own hand in the copies. One can observe from the following example how much personal participation, how much warmth of textual exposition, Schütz brought to this very liturgical work. (See pages 690 and 691.)

And so on for two large measures further till, after an eight-voice G major cadence, the second semichorus continues alone (surely also *piano*). (See page 691.) One must mention the many individual characteristics: in section two the chorale-like, simple *Ich bin ein Gast auf Erden* ("I am a stranger in the earth"), in which both choruses follow each other closely; in section five the picturesque *Ehe ich gedemütigt war, irret ich — nun aber halte ich dein Wort* ("Before I was afflicted, I went astray; but now have I kept Thy word"), formed first in figuration, then in

---

[20] *Deine Rechte sind mein Lied in meinem Hause.*

syncopation; very realistically dramatic in the same section is *Ach, ach, ach, daß die Stolzen . . . . ich aber rede, rede, rede von deinem Befehl* ("The proud have forged a lie against me, but I will keep Thy precepts with my whole heart"). The central piece, No. 7, is unusually expressive. It is set off by a doxology spun out with special richness, equaled at best by the one with psalmodic soprano *cantus firmus* in No. 1. Note the almost *arioso*like passage in the middle of the number:

The beginning of *Psalm 100* is full of stormy brilliance. What baroque power and fire are still there despite Schütz's eighty-six years!

The double-chorus German *Magnificat,* which is in *b* minor in H. Spitta's edition, is one tone lower, in *a* minor, in the original. The latter will be the basis of the following remarks. Schütz did not set the verse *Und seine Barmherzigkeit währet immer für und für bei denen, die ihn fürchten* ("And His mercy is on them that fear Him from generation to generation"), just as he did not set *denn er hat grosse Dinge* ("for He that is mighty hath done to me great things") in the *Magnificat* in the *Cantiones sacrae II.* The work, like its sister in the *Zwölf geistliche Gesänge,* is "through-composed" *(durchkomponiert)* without regard for ecclesiastical "tones" and antiphonal usage. One gets the impression that it is a very personal hymn of praise and thanksgiving on the part of the master to his God, a hymn in which he looks back upon his life, blessed and renowned, yet so difficult.

Spitta properly followed the Guben version as far as possible. The Grimma version deviates at a number of places from this; for example, in the first soprano at the very beginning:

A few more passages show that in the Guben version Schütz wanted to treat the word-emphasis *(Wortbetonung)* more simply and more naturally. Toward the close the Grimma version is three measures longer and exchanges the two choruses. The final smoothing-out process in the Guben version aims at condensation.

The tonal disposition is as follows:

Meine Seele	F—A	⎫
Und mein Geist	A—A	⎭
Denn er hat die Niedrigkeit	*a* —A	⎡
Denn er hat grosse Ding	*a* —*d*	
Er übet Gewalt	*d* —A	⎣

Er stösset	a —E
Die Hungrigen	E—G
Er denket der Barmherzigkeit	G—A
Wie er geredt	a —A
Ehre sei	F —A
Wie es war im Anfang	a —A

Hereby an archform presents itself insofar as the first two verses and the two-part doxology correspond to each other tonally, thus forming a framework. The inner territory is again divided, inasmuch as three verses proceed by way of *d* minor, while four progress by way of E and G, always between *a*—A pillars.

In the *Psalms of 1619* we collected numerous examples of such a beginning at a relationship of the third (here F—A major). Here, in more than one sense, the circle between Schütz's first and last great church work closes. The purpose of this modulating beginning may be recognized in the infinitely gentle transition by way of the 6/5 chord c#—a—e—g to *d* minor and its semicadence A major on *meine Seele*. As the entire work shows, there lies herein a deeply felt *(seelenvolle)* emotion in the noblest sense of the word. It is no icily rigid old man who is speaking here; to the very end Schütz remained receptive and kindly to everything human. We feel this especially in the new fondness for warm chords of the seventh and all kinds of liberties which have given Schütz's tonal language that peculiar "romantic" late turn from about the time of the *St. Matthew Passion*, a turn which we can observe also in Chr. Ritter, N. Bruhns, G. Böhm, and S. Ebart. In contrast to this we have stretches of consonances of almost Palestrinian strictness, and archaic conclusions with empty fifths produce a peculiar fantastic mixture. One might speak here, as in the case of Michelangelo, Goethe, and Beethoven, of the "unconcernedness of the style of old age," which has learned to smile mildly, indeed almost a little roguishly, at all the conventional rules of the younger zealots.[21]

It is thus that we see Schütz in the oldest portrait, of 1670, the one which G. Schünemann procured for the Berlin Library, his body bowed by its burdens of eighty-five years, his skin withered and yellow, but his eyes radiating his imperishable spirit! An unknown German artist, developed to virtuosity by Netherlanders, painted the master at the very time he was polishing the German *Magnificat*.

---

[21] With regard to the problem of musical style in old age see E. Bücken, *Geist und Form im musikalischen Kunstwerk,* pp. 105 ff. More general, A. E. Brinkmann, *Spätwerke grosser Meister* (1928).

The beginning of this work gives us, as a fourfold *fecit Sagittarius,* four principal themes characteristic of Schütz, superimposed above one another: in the discant[22] one of his typical monodic themes; in the alto the concluding cadence of an older period; in the tenor the type constructed from steps of a fifth; in the bass the Monteverdi theme:

The antiphonal chorus then cuts across this canonically!

At *erhebt* those "new," exciting, provocative chords *(Reizakkorde)* appear:

This is only the continuation of a melisma

which soon appears augmented, with the text *freuet sich Gottes meines Heilandes* ("hath rejoiced in God, my Savior") — likewise a form of development *(Fortspinnungsgedanke)* which I believe had never before appeared in this manner in Schütz. One is struck later by the free return of the sequence in the doxology at

---

[22] See the preceding example.

Wie es war im Anfang ("As it was in the beginning"). Then note the beautiful passage *er hat die Niedrigkeit* ("He hath regarded the low estate"):

The fact that f is followed, not by E major but by *e* minor, sounds archaic, like Palestrina; then, as in the *Kyrie* of the concluding chorus of the *St. Matthew Passion*, come those "romantically" proceeding parallel tenths in conjunction with the sustained harmony, which leads the answering middle voices to a chord of the sixth, from which they proceed to one of the "new" chords of the seventh on the subdominant of C. Immediately there is, in the *Kleinbar*, a further enjoyment to the full of these IV chords which result from the fall of a third in the bass:

and this sequence, rising in three steps of the circle of fifths, is followed by the corresponding return to G major at *werden mich selig preisen* ("shall call me blessed"). *Alle, alle, alle Kindeskind* ("All generations"), with its baroque repetitions, conducts us back to A major.

The fourth little verse, *Denn er hat grosse Ding an mir getan* ("For He hath done to me great things"), the text of which Schütz must have felt to have been coined especially for him, must be looked at by the reader directly. Here again the fascinating little characteristics of the new harmony accumulate, as this

Phrygian conclusion 7 $\begin{smallmatrix}6\\4\end{smallmatrix}$ 2 $\begin{smallmatrix}\#\\ \end{smallmatrix}$; or in a *d* minor cadence the gripping turn

$\begin{smallmatrix}\#\\a\end{smallmatrix}$ $\begin{smallmatrix}\#\\ \end{smallmatrix}$ $\begin{smallmatrix}6\frown b\\g\end{smallmatrix}$ at *des Name heilig ist* ("and holy is His name") after the dominant

terrace with its spicy harmony

had previously been firmly established — always with the empty fifth conclusions
as a countereffect. Verse five was not set to music. The sixth section, *Er übet Gewalt* ("He hath shewed strength"), has both choruses advance against each other
in the alfresco surface style of 1619. Here alone and at the passage *Abraham und
seinem Samen ewiglich* ("to Abraham and to his seed forever") one looking for
indications of old age might possibly find them. But immediately again in the
seventh verse, *Er stösset die Gewaltigen vom Stuhl* ("He hath put down the
mighty from their seats"), one recognizes the lion (*ex ungue leonem*) by the C
major cadence, which is based on the text and serves as the cornerstone. It gets its
momentum from the f 6/5:

Later there is a similar passage at *und lässet die Reichen leer* ("and the rich He
hath sent empty away").

Here, for once, Schütz pictures *die Niedrigen* ("them of low degree") with the very ancient threnodic parallel fourths:[23]

And again the subdominant seventh, this time II[7], has the function of tone portrayal, as in the following concluding climax, where it paints the idea of "the hungry":

The *Gloria Patri (Ehre sei dem Vater)* then ebbs out in simple chordal changes of the Venetian surface type. Here there was no place for what is "interesting." The fundamental chords simply greet as "harmony" the Holy Trinity whence they have come and whither they ever again return home.

As Schütz's body was soon to return to the elements, so, too, the tone of his life ended in the elemental, dying away at the closing word of every prayer, just as his whole work and being was a manly prayer:

---

[23] In the introduction to F. Woyrsch's selection there is a collection which well illustrates such passages with intervals of the fourth from Palestrina, Lassus, Gallus, and Schütz (for example, *die mit Tränen säen)*; there, too, p. 6, examples of cross relations.

Amen, that is, let it come true!
Our faith do strengthen through and through,
That we may ne'er Thy answer doubt
To what we here have prayed about
Upon Thy Word and in Thy name.
Then firmly we amen proclaim!

Amen, das ist, es werde wahr!
Stärk unsern Glauben immerdar,
Auf dass wir ja nicht zweifeln dran,
Was wir hiermit gebeten han
Auf dein Wort, in den Namen dein.
So sprechen wir das Amen fein.   M. Luther.

Epilog

The Music Situation at the Time of Schütz's Death

"If you will forgive me, gentlemen of the music profession, there now prevails in the church an altogether new kind of song, but one that is prolix, abrupt, fragmentary, dancelike, and not at all reverential. It is better suited to the theater and the dance hall than to the church. We seek art, and as we do, we are losing time-honored devotion to prayer and song."

These words from the sermon which Martin Geier delivered at Schütz's funeral were addressed to the composer's younger colleagues. Perhaps what Geier said was, at that time, somewhat one-sided; perhaps it was an overstatement resulting from the visual angle of an older theologian. Still, like a flash of lightning, the words throw a bright light on the situation existing in those days.

In a manner altogether similar, and as early as 1657, it is stated in the *Kantorei* statutes at Froberg in Saxony that one should use only motets "that are appropriate for the times, have texts taken from, and in harmony with, God's Word, and do not hop about like street ballads, love songs, or the dances of buffoons"[1] *(Rautenstrauch, p. 277).*

In a dedicatory poem addressed to W. C. Printz at the beginning of the second part of the *Phrynis Mytilenaeus* (1696) one J. G. Dieterich describes the deterioration in craftsmanship after Schütz's death:

> The first one blew the horn; the second, the shalmey;
> The third one on his bagpipe made the octave.
> It sounded wonderful. I asked what that might be.
> The one who nearest stood, he promptly said to me:
> These are the latest school, the new composers,

---

[1] A fine collection of further examples in Pirro, *Schütz*, p. 220, note 2: in 1646 Constantin Huygens speaks of the motets of the Italians *wo alles stampft und galoppiert* ("where everything stamps and gallops"). Ismael Boulliau says in a letter that Italian church music was "more suited to induce dancing than to evoke reverence." Jeremias Drexelius (*Rhetorica caelestis*, 1636) speaks of the new kind of song which befits the dance floor rather than the church; J.-B. Casali (*De veteribus sacris Christianorum ritibus*, 1647) inveighs against the custom of clothing sacred texts in worldly melodies and strongly condemns those who allow themselves to be emasculated in order thereby to gain more profit with their voices.

> Those from America, who spread themselves in Germany.
> It sounds full loud and shrill, so that it may be heard....
> Horse-fifths they play and beautiful cow-octaves
> And that which in the stable makes the finest harmony,
> That was the most successful work of art.

At the end of the century, according to a number of witnesses, the new, partly pietistic, partly rationalistic, austerity seems to have won out. Thus Ph. Spener, in a funeral sermon in 1697 for the Berlin cantor Hermann Koch, exclaims that, thank God, the purely instrumental dance music was on the decline in the church; that music should proceed "with Christian gravity and while, to be sure, it should refresh the spirit with joy, this should be of such a nature as to lead to rest and quiet and not to what arouses cavorting and dancing." Similarly, in a funeral sermon by Andr. Schmid (1713): "Worldly sarabandes, buffoonlike minuets, and such things, and whatever else smacks of the comedians and the opera, has long been put aside from our church gatherings, so that we hear little of it in the organ preludes and in the combined instrumental and vocal music."

It is not so easy to present even a partial picture of German music in the year 1672; for as soon as the very aged master Schütz had closed his eyes, an empty space appears before our consciousness, a seething interim, until with the appearance of the two geniuses, Bach and Handel, born thirteen years later, we reach again a new *terra cognita*.

Let us first attempt to enumerate briefly the personnel. Who were the leading musicians of the time? What were the actual works of art? Let us imagine that in 1672, as Charles Burney did a hundred years later, an English music lover had wanted to study the state of music in Germany and that he had landed in Hamburg.[2] At St. Catherine's he would have listened to the unemotional virtuoso organ fantasies of Reinken, the forty-year-old Alsatian; in the refectory of the Dom he would have heard the great *collegium musicum*, where for twelve years the best church-music forces, under the leadership of the Schütz master pupils Weckmann and Bernhard, presented gala performances of oratorios by Caspar Förster and Giacomo Carissimi. Perhaps he might have encountered a splendid duet *concerto* by Weckmann[3] himself, *Wie liegt die Stadt so wüste*, in which Schütz's nobility and a younger tenderness meet in charming equilibrium. From Hamburg our Englishman makes a side trip to Lübeck, where Dietrich Buxtehude (then thirty-five) has presided in a most distinguished manner for seven years at the organ in St. Mary's, formerly played by his father-in-law, Franz Tunder. In his Danish

---

[2] W. C. Printz, in his *Phrynis Mytilenaeus*, gives such a survey on a smaller scale for 1690.
[3] Then thirty-one years old.

accent Buxtehude would tell our traveler of his plan, beginning next year, to unite performances, after the Hamburg manner, more closely with the church by instituting under the name *Abendmusiken* cycles of oratoriolike cantatas. With Buxtehude there is staying a Naumburger, Joh. Theile, aged twenty-six, who had earned his spurs in counterpoint with Schütz in Weissenfels and is now preparing for print, under the eyes of Buxtehude, his new kind of passion music.

Now our "observing traveler" returns to Hamburg, where the music director for the council, Diedrich Becker, plays for him beautiful ensemble sonatas. Becker suggests that in Berlin he visit the eminent Esajas Reusner, who since the preceding year has been court lutenist to the great elector. But the observer turns to Lüneburg, where Christian Flor shows him his settings of songs by Rist, who had died five years previously, and a new passion with solo arias. Then he continues to the lands of the Guelphs: to Brunswick, where the aged Delphin Strungk is still writing jolly songs and between organ solos tells the visitor about Sagittarius, who had just died. He continues to Wolfenbüttel, where Martin Colerus is tormented by the meager support given the court music. He goes to Hanover, where the fiery-headed young violinist Nik. Ad. Strungk exhibits his remarkable virtuosity with modesty that is none too great. Our traveler betakes himself to Halle, where Duke August (who had been baptized with the assistance of Schütz in Dresden) has his young chamber virtuoso, Christian Ritter, perform for him the latter's sweetly romantic chamber cantatas and has his court Kapellmeister, D. Pohle (another Schütz pupil), present his opera *Aspasia*. In the Market Church he is fascinated by a fanciful Communion song, *Miserere, Christe, mei*, by Samuel Ebart, whose successor was to be Handel's teacher, Zachow. Next he visits in Zeitz Schütz's beloved J. J. Loewe. In Weimar the chamber secretary Neumark (who is an able gamba player and a master of song) and court Kapellmeister Adam Drese show him the numerous works of Schütz that are still there. In Erfurt he listens attentively to the sincere motets of Cantor Heinrich Bach, then aged fifty-seven, and in Meiningen he converses with the court Kapellmeister Karl Wolfgang Briegel, aged forty-nine, from Nuremberg, who would like him to be enthusiastic about his spiritual *Gryphius Odes*, which had appeared recently, and his *Musicalisches Tafelconfect*, just off the press. A few miles away, in Eisenach, is Joh. Christof (I) Bach), then thirty years old, in whose cantatas the flame of real genius flares. Joh. Christoph (I) is assisted in the performance on the violin and in singing by his twin cousins, Joh. Ambrosius Bach, the Eisenach town piper, and Joh. Christoph II, from Arnstadt. Joh. Christoph I's brother, Johann Michael, from Gehren, turns the pages and helps with the registration. Our original Burney notes in his diary: "It almost seems to me that I am at the very heart of all music. Here astonishing forces are massing. Here the echoes of Schütz's art appear to be strongest. But much is in the process of transition, and something powerfully new seems to be in preparation." He goes over to Mühlhausen, where the ailing St. Blaise organist and burgomaster, Joh. Georg Ahle, presents to him his *Neues Zehen geistlicher Andachten* and hopes to be able to pass on the famous post of organist to his capable son Johann Rudolf. Now he journeys to Leipzig by way of Weissenfels, where at that very time a faithful pupil is arranging the volumes which Schütz left to the Dresden Chapel. Our traveler notes on all sides that there is much music in the town on the Pleisse (Leipzig). From the tower of the *Rathaus* are heard the fine wind sonatas of the *Hora decima* by Petzel; at the best organ presides Schütz's young friend Werner Fabricius; in the St. Thomas Church the cantatas of Sebastian Knüpfer resound; but it is rumored that their composer will not continue much longer, and as chief candidate for the cantorship at St. Thomas they are considering Knüpfer's fellow countryman from the Erzgebirge, Johann Schelle, now cantor in Eulenburg. In the music shop our Englishman asks to see the latest publications. Johann Rosenmüller's *Chamber Sonatas, Op. 3* have just come in from Venice and are delighting the young musicians. With equal enthusiasm chamber cantatas and clavier pieces in manuscript by Bernardo Pasquini of Rome are examined, while the church musicians are even more fascinated by Joh. Sebastiani's passion, which has just been printed in Königsberg at the expense of the great elector.

Dresden seems no less a center of music. Under the cantor of the *Kreuzkirche*, Jakob Beutel, he hears a gospel *concerto* by the interesting Freiberg physician, Caspar Horn, from Veltkirch, and takes delight in the pure soprano of the twelve-year-old Crucian,[4] Johann Kuhnau, who twenty years later was to originate the clavier sonata and with his *Biblical Histories* was to capture the cantorship of St. Thomas.

In the Dresden Court Opera our traveler attends a rehearsal of Bontempi's and Peranda's *Dafne* as well as of a *Serenade* by the young C. Pallavicino — all very pompous, displaying virtuosity, and completely Italian. He is surprised at how little they now speak here of Schütz. Dedekind, the kindly concertmaster, with a copy of his *Musikalischer Jahrgang für 2 Soprane und Orgel* under his arm, advises him to go to the Saxon provincial towns, where this art is still being intensively cultivated, particularly to Zittau, where the quarrelsome old Andr. Hammer-

---

[4] Member of the Choir of the Holy Cross.

schmidt is still working under the famous Rector Chr. Weise; or to Sorau, to Kaspar Printz — or even to the remote little town of Glashütte, where he might hear reverently performed the *Geistliches Seelenparadies und Lustgärtlein* or the *Suspiria musicalia* of Cantor Samuel Seidel and many compositions by Schütz.

But after the Dresden chamber virtuosi have made his mouth water, the Englishman is drawn to the music center Vienna. Is not the Emperor Leopold I himself considered a first-rate composer? And the world is still full of the grandiose operatic production of Cesti's *Pomo d'oro* five years ago in honor of the imperial wedding. At this time one may attend one of the Venetian gala festival operas by Antonio Draghi, and, in addition, on the same bill one may see a knightly ballet with music by the vice-Kapellmeister, Heinrich Schmelzer. Our traveler visits this artist-composer, then forty years old, to be entertained by his violin-playing — but Schmelzer smilingly refers him to a younger colleague who is then visiting him — still partly in the capacity of pupil — the Olmütz concertmaster Ignaz Franz Biber — who could drive even the young Dresden wonder-fiddler J. J. Walther from the field! Our visitor listens intently to the fine court organist Poglietti as he spins variation chains at the *cembalo*, while in St. Stephen's Cathedral he encounters the astounding improvising of a young assistant organist, Joh. Pachelbel, from Nuremberg. Pachelbel's stories make him eager to journey to South Germany. The reporter goes by way of Salzburg, where he greets Andreas Hofer, the composer of Masses; to Munich, where he visits the modest, aged master of song, Johs. Kuen, is received by the distinguished court Kapellmeister, Caspar Kerll, and meets in his company an eighteen-year-old Italian pupil of whom Kerll expects great things — Agostino Steffani, who at a future time, as abbot-diplomat and friend of Sophie Charlotte, will pass the art of the chamber duet on to the young giant Handel. In Augsburg he meets Scheiffelhut, the assiduous concert artist. An excursion to Stutgart permits the traveler to note that under Ph. F. Böddecker the music in the *Stiftskirche* is poor;[5] here, too, the opera offers nothing. Someone recommends a side trip to Alsace to hear the excellent organist J. G. Rauch in Strassburg and in Molsheim the young master of the organ Georg Muffat. But Briegel and Pachelbel make him eager for a visit to Nuremberg. Here he meets as a fine master of the second rank, from the school of Kindermann, the cantor of St. Sebald, Heinrich Schwemmer, and the organist at St. Giles, Georg Caspar Wecker, as well as the latter's twenty-seven-year-old brother-in-law, Joh. Löhner, who is soon to distinguish himself both in song and in opera. But he is told that the best young

---

[5] Between the death of Capricornus and the call of the elder Kusser to the post it is at a low ebb.

Nuremberg talents had found positions elsewhere — the brothers Krieger in Bayreuth, of whom Philipp, then twenty-three, was to become famous in Weissenfels, and Johann (two years younger), in Zittau; or, in Ansbach, the young Joh. Wolfgang Franck, who later brought the spiritual solo song to new heights in Hamburg. In Regensburg the church music under Kradenthaler might fascinate him, and the seventeen-year-old high-school student Joh. Beer would entertain him with his fantastic musical farces.

But our Englishman is now drawn to Frankfurt on the Main, where devout noblewomen lure him to Pastor Spener's *Collegium pietatis*. Here they sing from Joh. Crüger's Berlin *Praxis pietatis melica*, enlarged with new melodies by the Frankfurt musician Peter Sohr. He converses with the Durlach Kapellmeister Strattner, then visiting there. A cousin of Capricornus, Strattner, in his *Dialoge*, is an ardent worshiper at the shrine of Schütz. In the Villa Frauenstein he listens, in the little music circle, to the devotees as they taste of Briegel's *Tafelconfect;* for this was dedicated to the Frankfurt *Collegium*. And as a conclusion to his German journey he writes in his diary about as follows:

"For one who looks carefully it is remarkable but also completely understandable that in the whole of Protestant musical Germany everything of importance somehow always goes back to Schütz, without, however, his being mentioned much or eagerly performed any longer. This is not really ingratitude; for whatever musician one asks about, Schütz praises him with pride in his own calling and accords him the highest veneration as a man and as an artist. But this generation, after the great war has destroyed immeasurable treasures of the past, attaches itself the more vitally to the eagerly reconstructive, future-seeking present. If one mentions a 'classicist' in the making, such a one is Palestrina in particular, who is rising to legendary heights both as a Roman and as a Tridentine witness. Palestrina is a 'classicist' in the making, largely because of the approbation of Schütz. Throughout the treatise on the art of music written by Christof Bernhard, Sagittarius has recognized the Praenestian as an example to follow. But the hundred-year-old renown of a Lassus and a Gabrieli has long since faded behind the figure of Schütz, and Schütz's own picture is being dissolved imperceptibly in all that he has passed on to his pupils and to their pupils. They all know that the old giant remained to the very end the most modern of them all; but it would appear as though his renown, which began some sixty years ago, had somewhat outlived itself during this period.

"The pygmies breathe more easily when jealously testing their strength against that of their equals than they would if they were to measure it with the colossus, the 'father of the German musicians,' who, so far as age was concerned, could, at the end, rather have been called their grandfather or ancestor. Perhaps, too, he was for them too much the highly cultured patrician's son and the grand seigneur of the Lasso-Tasso period. Since 1648 the German music fraternity has been building itself up anew. There is a 'revolution from below,' instigated by wandering musicians who have been scattered by the war — small town-piper journeymen who scuffle with the beer-fiddlers for their puny new reputations and who, for their part, must first gather gradually again the noble rust of artistic aristocracy."

Those conflicting elements of style which were welded together in Schütz into the richest unity through the power of his personality fell apart among his successors. Schütz understood how to combine all the new boldness of monody with the long-established foundations of counterpoint. Now the cantors, as somewhat helpless reactionaries, grumble against the modernistic insolence of the organists, who scornfully reproach them with their prattling platitudes of outmoded imitations, while they, for their part, experiment with ardor in an endeavor to find how to permeate church music with the operatic luster of a Cavalli and the sweetly austere 6/5 chords of Ziani and Draghi.

Equally ambitious chamber virtuosi try to find a way to break up the instrumental suite (which Froberger had only recently limited to four movements) in the French manner, how to develop it in the *stylo fantastico*, and to add sonata introductions in the Italian manner. Lully's first little Parisian minuets have already come across the Rhine. The student song, which had recently been brought to the highest artistic eminence by Schütz's admirer Adam Krieger in Dresden, is overworked as a constantly orchestrated *aria* or deteriorates into the South German fair-and-festival *quodlibet* of Gletle and Speer.

And so another circle arises in contrast to those artificers *(Artisten)* who, so to speak, exaggerated to a perennial problem the artificiality which Schütz himself had overcome, one which noted and understood the *Kleine geistliche Konzerte* only as "lightly scored utility music," saw in the *Musicalia ad chorum sacrum* merely the renunciation of Italian allurements, and in the last *Sinfoniae sacrae* nothing but the "brilliance." They capitalize on the "Hammerschmidt meter" in a cheap manner; they cater to the indolence of the superficial by means of such statements in the titles of their music as "written in a light style" *(in einem leichten stylo abgefasst)* or "set in a pleasing manner" *(auf eine anmutige Art gesetzt)*. A somewhat cheap, easily written style of parallel thirds moves from Swabia, Franconia, and Bavaria also to Upper and Lower Saxony. The dominant sevenths almost efface the last remainder of linear writing after the manner of the church tones. The popular-song style *(Bergreihenmanier)* is victorious on almost the entire front; new folk songs arise in large quantity, despised at bottom by the artists, although fecund for the future.

And yet a secret Schützian tradition throbs on in a few—in Joh. Christoph Bach, in Buxtehude, and in Mathias Weckmann. They will transmit this to pupils and to their pupils. Therefore at some time the great and the greatest can again sprout forth: the German organ fugue and, behind the "empty nut" of the chordal style *(Akkordwesen)*, the "sweet kernel" of true polyphony. Especially in Eisenach and Halle the "purest concentration" *(reinste Verdichtung)* is coming to the fore.

To these conservers of counterpoint, who really strove to take to heart Schütz's admonition in the preface to the *Geistliche Chormusik*, belongs further J. Jak. Loewe, who says the following in the preface to his two-to-eight-voice canons for voices and instruments on Martin Kempen's *Tugendlieder (Morality Songs)* (1664): [6]

> I am eager to learn what an understanding friend of music will think on seeing these canons of mine. This one thing I can say with due modesty: that after fortune allowed me to visit the renowned land of Italy and to enjoy the instruction of its famous Kapellmeisters and their intimate conversation, it nevertheless cost me much labor to formulate a canon according to their instruction, though one will scarcely believe this before undertaking the work. However, he who is conversant with the subject may judge whether my canons are formed according to the rules of art. At first I was willing to set every canon resolved into its parts, so that anyone who might be frightened away would be relieved of all difficulty. When, however, I counseled more carefully with myself, I hesitated for weighty reasons. Hence I surmise — and my fear will scarcely be in vain — that many whom such work will not please will turn up their noses. But I am persuaded that under the circumstances a weak stomach and one not used to such fare will, at any rate, rebel against it. Furthermore, I am not concerned as to whether a beer-fiddler or quack, who is accustomed only to cans and measures and frequently disgraces true art by clumsy noise, will look askance at these pages; for I do not ask that such journeymen (even though they pose as very great composers and are, in their own imagination, stately smiths of harmony) be the judges of my work or that they approve of it, because I have always enjoyed the favor of the genuinely understanding and thoroughly competent artists who deserve this name with honor. To their judgment I submit these canons.

The other one is Joh. Theile. The learned titles of his Mass compositions are known from J. G. Walther's *Lexikon*. At least the one of 1673 has been preserved in the Paris National Library.[7] In a prefatory dedication Chr. Bernhard says that the Electoral Chapel in Dresden was to be praised, together with the Papal Chapel in Rome, the Imperial Chapel in Vienna, and several other princely chapels, for

---

[6] J. Walther's *Musiklexikon* (1732), p. 368. The work itself, unfortunately, has been lost for the present (Göhler 2, 887 f.).

[7] Vm 896; missing in Eitner, QuL: *Pars prima missarum 4 et 5 vocum pro pleno choro cum et sine basso continuo iuxta veterum contrapuncti stylum.*

the fidelity with which they preserved the *style antico,* with its majestic and pure harmony, as the only dignified church style.[8]

When one recalls how in the preface to the *Musicalia ad chorum sacrum* Schütz reckoned double counterpoint as an indispensable technique for true composers, the chief theoretical writing of Theile, in the BB manuscript, dated "Naumburg 1691," is properly understood.

"*Musical Art Book,* wherein are fifteen altogether unique art pieces and secrets based on double counterpoint...." It is less a textbook than a collection of examples which teach the most remarkable kinds of progressions in the strict composition of canons, suites, and parts of Masses. To these it adds clever German mnemonic rhymes, and with these it frequently calls on the student to develop a missing voice from those given or to formulate a further piece by the exchange of voices and the like. If one considers that the Berlin manuscript goes back by way of Poelchau and Forkel to Joh. Gottfr. Walther, who, in Weimar, with his cousin Joh. Seb. Bach, practiced the same problems in composition, it becomes clear that the Theile *Kunstbuch* represents one of the most important bridges from Schütz to Bach's *Canonic Variations,* the *Musical Offering,* and particularly to his *Art of the Fugue,* which, including, in part, the very notes of the themes, one may call the most grandiose development of what Theile sought to achieve. Theile's second treatise, *Unterricht von einigen gedoppelten Kontrapunkten,* supplements artistic achievements less pretentiously with the appropriate rules and with brief examples.

In the next generation, then, besides J. S. Bach and J. G. Walther, it was the Thuringian Stöltzel who cultivated, though in a more modest way, this Middle German canon problem, as is proved by his canonic Masses and a number of treatises.

---

[8] Pirro, *Schütz,* p. 150. Theile's treatise *Von den Fugen,* manuscript in the *Bibl. der Berliner Singakademie.*

Appendices

Oil Painting of Heinrich Schütz

The directorate of the library of the University of Leipzig kindly provided me with the following information with regard to the oil painting "Heinrich Schütz," which is in their possession: "Besides the inscription Henricus Sagittarius, the Schütz portrait bears still a second one, which had, to be sure, been observed by those who formerly described the painting but apparently had not been read. The inscription is in the upper right hand corner. Since the picture has been severely mutilated along its border, some letters of the inscription are missing. But we may surmise that the correct name of the painter whom the inscription mentions is properly read and supplemented as Christoph Spe(tner). Thus we would be confronted with the Leipzig portrait painter of this name (ca. 1617-99), a number of whose pictures are found in Leipzig collections and in the St. Thomas Church. According to the inscription, he painted the picture in Stedten *(Mannsfelder Seekreis)*. No year is mentioned." However, the local archivist, Prädikant Herm. Etzrodt, remarks that to him there seems to be little probability that this particular Stedten is meant, as he could not imagine who could have enticed the tone master and the portrait painter to that locality. On the other hand, the locality referred to is but a short distance, as the crow flies, from Weissenfels.

Rembrandt's Portrait of a Musician

While up to the present time the picture of Schütz in his sixties was considered the earliest — a fact that contributed to his always being thought of as a man of vigorous old age — a fascinating problem was presented by Bruno Maerker in his article titled *Rembrandts Bildnis eines Musikers — ein Schützportrait,* which appeared in No. 6, Annual 1937-38, pp. 329-345, of *Deutsche Musikkultur* (Bärenreiter-Verlag). The question concerns an early painting by Rembrandt Harmensz van Rijn, which presents a man approximately in the late forties. The music scroll in the hand of the subject of the portrait would indicate that he was a composer or a Kapellmeister. The portrait has been esteemed so highly that it was copied with various techniques by a number of members of the Rembrandt school, though the results were far less satisfactory than the original. If the work in question is a portrait of Schütz, it would have to be assumed — since the great painter never left Holland — that Schütz interrupted his sojourn in Hamburg in 1633, which lasted for several months, with a sailing voyage to Amsterdam and that on this occasion he granted the young genius several sittings. The fact that no allusions to such a journey have been discovered does, of course, make one hesitant; but the absence of evidence would not be without parallels in Schütz's life, since visits to Sweden and Norway are also assumed. Grounds for visiting Holland from the banks of the Alster might be found in the fact that Schütz's friend Jakob Praetorius had been a pupil of Sweelinck in Amsterdam, though, to be sure, Jan Pieterszon had died twelve years previously. His tradition was still alive in northern Holland.

The physiognomical facts speak persuasively for the truth of the supposition, although I rebelled against the hypothesis for a long time. It will be more persuasive if we compare the Rembrandt portrait with the splendid picture of the octogenarian that was discovered by Schünemann than if we compare it with the much more conventional painting by Chr. Spetner. One will then note the striking similarities between the two portraits — the characteristics of the forehead and the eyebrows, the heavy eyelids, the arched nose, the sensitive mouth, and the very unusual chin. Granting the truth of the supposition that we have before us an additional Schütz portrait, then we have not merely some added knowledge regarding the master's physical appearance; but the thought of the meeting of these two, whose natal constellation with Shakespeare we pointed out in the Introduction and whose biographical parallelisms were pointed out in connection with the *Sinfoniae sacrae I*, affords us a new stellar conjunction in the history of art, although, to be sure, neither the master of tone nor the magician of the brush sensed, as is generally the case in such instances, the full significance of the unusual meeting.

Notes on the Publication of Schütz's Works

A documentary find which Othmar Wessely published in the Vienna *Musikerziehung* VII/1 (September 1953), pp. 7 ff., affords a fascinating insight into Schütz's concern for his rights as an author. This document is a letter of the master to Emperor Ferdinand III. It was discovered in the copyright acts *(Impressorialakten)* of the Imperial Court Council, in the House, Court, and State Archives in Vienna and reads as follows:

Most Serene Highness, Most Mighty and Unconquerable Roman Emperor, King also of Hungary and Bohemia, Most Gracious Lord:

All most submissive and ever constant thanks are due Your Imperial Majesty that at my most obedient request you bestowed on me in 1637 your high imperial grace and most graciously granted to me, according to the accompanying true copy, a five-year imperial privilege *(privilegium:* author's copyright) for those musical works which I composed, partly in Latin, partly in German, both sacred and secular, and some also without texts.

Now though I published a portion of these musical works, I purpose to publish others also which I have at hand. But I am concerned lest, now that the five years are drawing to a close, someone will print these works to his own advantage but to my own great disadvantage. Therefore I address to Your Imperial Majesty my most humble petition that you will bestow on me your imperial grace and will renew to me and my heirs the aforementioned *privilegium* for a further period of ten years, and that you will draw it up according to the previous grant.

I shall praise this imperial grace throughout my life, and I shall always remember to pray God for the happy well-being of Your Imperial Majesty and that of your most praiseworthy house, and also for victory over your enemies and over the enemies of the empire.

> Your Imperial Majesty's most submissive, most obedient
> Henricus Sagittarius mp.

Dresden, April 25, 1642

O. Wessely comments on this as follows:

"When Schütz wrote this letter, he was on the point of escaping from the Dresden scene, which had become so unsatisfactory to him, and of seeking a more favorable field at the court of King Christian IV of Denmark, where he received his appointment as chief Kapellmeister on May 3, 1642. Therefore the document dated April 25 was written immediately before his departure for Copenhagen. It is addressed to Emperor Ferdinand III and contains the request for a continuation of an *impressorium*, a copyright privilege, which would protect the owner for a certain time against the pirating of his works in the Holy Roman Empire of the German Nation. The usual period of such *impressoria* was five years, less frequently ten or even fifteen years.

"According to the above, then, it was not the first time that Henricus Sagittarius (Schütz thus Latinized his name) sought this form of imperial protection. It had been granted since the early sixteenth century to such musicians as, for example, Arnold Schlick, the lutenists Hans and Melchior Neusidler, Hans Leo Hassler, Sethus Calvisius, and many others. In the third decade of the seventeenth century Schütz already possessed an Electoral Saxon *privilegium*, as shown on the title page of part one of the *Kleine Geistliche Konzerte* (Leipzig, 1636), where we find the words *Cum privilegio Ser. (enissimi) Electoris Saxoniae*. From this very work, only one year after its appearance, two compositions — No. 10: *Schaffe in mir, Gott, ein reines Herz (Create in Me, God, a Clean Heart)* and No. 12: *Lobet den Herrn, der zu Zion wohnet (Praise the Lord Who Dwelleth in Zion)* — were reprinted in the collection edited by Nikolaus Dunker and titled *Fasciculus primus geistlicher wohlklingender Concerten mit 2 und 3 Stimmen, sampt dem Basso continuo pro organis* (Goslar, 1637). Dunker's own work was protected by an Electoral Saxon *privilegium*. This situation may have aroused in Schütz the desire for a still wider protection of his rights. And thus he turned in the year 1637, as shown in the letter above, with a request (not preserved) to Ferdinand III for an *impressorium* that would be valid throughout the empire. That this was granted him is shown by the title page of the *Ander Theil kleiner eistlicher Konzerten* (Leipzig, 1639), where we find the words 'With the privilege (*Freiheit*) of His Roman Imperial Majesty.' Schütz's observation of the same year (1637) that he expected emoluments not only from the Danish crown prince but from other sources as well might be interpreted as meaning that he was looking forward to increased sales of his works as the result of the safeguard against pirating. Above all, however, two versions of the *impressorium* have been preserved: the copy of the Imperial Court Council and a copy of the original which Schütz enclosed with the letter published here. According to this, the document read as follows:

"'We, Ferdinand III, by the grace of God elected Roman Emperor, at all times increaser (*Mehrer*) of the empire; King of Germania, Hungary, Bohemia, Dalmatia, Croatia, and Slavonia, etc.; Archduke of Austria; Duke of Burgundy, Styria, Carinthia, Crain, Württemberg, Graue in the Tyrol, etc., acknowledge openly with this letter and announce to everyone that our and the empire's dear, faithful Henricus Sagittarius has most submissively made known to us to what extent he planned to publish those *opera musicalia* which he had composed partly in Latin, partly in German, some sacred, some secular, some without words. In order, however, that these might not be pirated by others to their advantage but to his great disadvantage, he approached us with a request for our imperial *privilegium impressorium*.

"'After due consideration we have granted this most submissive request.

"'And we do so through this letter and according to this manner, that he may publicly print, reprint, and offer for sale the aforementioned *musicalia* and may earn the emoluments thereof for himself and his bodily heirs during a period of five years from the time of the appended date; and also that the music not be reprinted by anyone, whosoever he may be, whether in larger or smaller form; not be distributed *(distrahiret)* or placed on sale by anyone unless such person has previously come to proper terms with the aforementioned Henricus Sagittarius and has received permission from him. And we command all our faithful subjects and those of the empire, our inherited kingdoms, principalities, and lands, but especially all printers, bookkeepers, and booksellers, if they violate this *privilegium,* to pay five marks of *löttiges* (pure?) gold, one half to accrue to our treasury (*Cammer*), the other half to the aforementioned Sagittarius. We herewith earnestly command that no one of you print, distribute, or offer for sale the above-referred-to *opera musicalia* within the period of five years, and that you permit no one to do so. In doing this you will incur our own and the empire's serious disfavor and punishment. In addition to the aforementioned punishment, you will forfeit to the frequently mentioned suppliant your printed copies, wherever he or his heirs may find such among you. These are empowered to confiscate the copies without hindrance. They may dispose of them at their discretion, without subjecting themselves to any penalty. But the frequently mentioned Henricus Sagittarius shall transmit at his own expense four copies of each of the above-determined musical works to our imperial chancellery, such copies not to be sold. Furthermore, no copy is to be sold or given away until this obligation has been fulfilled. This document is attested to with the imperial seal, given in the city of Vienna on the third day of the month of April 1637, in the first year of our reign over the Roman Empire, the twelfth over Hungary, and the tenth over Bohemia.

<table>
<tr><td>Ferdinand
(Chancellery notes:)
Ferdinand
v(idi)t
Ferdinand Count Kurz
Ad mandatum
Johann Söldner D(octo)r</td><td>L. S.

v(idi)t
Ph. Strahlendorff.
Ad mandatum sac. (rae) caes: (areae)
rea: (lis) majestatis proprium
Johann Söldner D.(octor)'</td></tr>
</table>

"With this far-reaching assurances were granted Heinrich Schütz. Over against the single obligation to transmit four copies to the imperial chancellery before delivering the publications into the hands of the book trade he acquired for five years the sole disposition of the works published by him. He was protected against pirating, except at his own discretion. In case of violation of his privilege he could confiscate the pirated copies on his own initiative and could dispose of them at his own discretion without himself being subject to litigation. The offending printer or bookseller was subject to a considerable fine, half of which was to accrue to the court treasury, the other half to Schütz.

"However, Schütz's expectations of an increase in the sale of the second part of the *Kleine geistliche Konzerte* did not materialize. At the expiration of the patent period he still had some copies in stock and, therefore, saw himself obliged, in 1642, to seek a prolongation of the *impressorium* for ten years. That Ferdinand III granted this is clear from the copy of the first *privilegium* which Schütz sent in and which served the imperial chancellery as a working copy. The words from *dritten tag des Monats Aprilis* to the conclusion, as well as the signatures and chancellery notices, are crossed out and are replaced with *8. Augusti 1642*. The new chancellery notice is found on the rear of the second page:

Impressorium regarding the *opera musicalia* mentioned within, for Henricus Sagittarius. 8. Au(gusti) 1642.

"In accordance with this, the *Symphoniarum sacrarum secunda pars* (Dresden, 1647) and the *Symphoniarum sacrarum tertia pars* (Dresden, 1650) bear the addition 'With the Privilege (*Freiheit*) of His Roman Imperial Majesty.' On the last page of the *Bassus pro violone* of the first of the two compositions just mentioned Schütz had added — doubtless with a view to increasing the sale of his works — a 'specification of the various musical works hitherto published by the author for the information of the kindly disposed reader.' Two further works, the *Dancklied. Für die hocherwiesene Fürstl. Gnade in Weymar. Vom 7. biss zum 13. Hornungs-Tag 1647* (Gotha, 1647) and the *Musicalia ad Chorum Sacrum (Geistliche Chormusik)*. Part I (Dresden, 1648) bear no copyright notice.

"No other works appeared during the fifteen-year period of the copyright grant. This is the more surprising because Schütz undoubtedly had more extensive plans for publication. He expressly designated his *Kleine geistliche Konzerte* of 1636 as 'messengers' (*Vorboten*) of further publications, and the enumeration in the documents presented above leads one to expect many more publications than are actually at hand for this period. Special notice is to be taken of the music compositions 'without text,' that is, doubtless, instrumental compositions, inasmuch as such have come down to us neither in print nor in manuscript. Certainly, too, a continuation of the *Musicalia ad chorum sacrum* of 1648 was planned, as this publication is expressly designated as Part One; but the continuation never reached publication.

"This striking divergence between the original plans and the actual results seems to have had two reasons. On the one hand, even in early years, after the appearance of his *Op. 1*, the *Primo libro di madrigali* (Venice, 1611), Schütz showed a noteworthy hesitation with regard to the publication of further works. The mature master explained this later in a retrospective biographical letter by saying that he wanted 'to hold back for some years with his now well-laid foundations in music and wished to hold these, as it were, in concealment until he had developed these (*excoliret*) somewhat further, in order that he might then appear with the publication of a worthy work.' On the other hand, the dire economic situation resulting from the Thirty Years' War again and again placed hindrances in his way. Thus he expressly says in 1636 that some of his musical *opera* 'had to remain unpublished for want of publishers.' And even in 1664, in a letter to Duke Augustus of Brandenburg, he still points to the works that remained unpublished for lack of a publisher.

"This may also be the reason why Schütz did not seek an extension of the *impressorium*. At any rate, such requests have not been documented hitherto, and there are no copyright notices on the title pages of his later works."

A Manuscript in Breslau

The *Ms. Stadtbibliothek Breslau CCLV (M 1236)* is a *Historia nativitatis Christi* which, unfortunately, lacks the discant and alto parts. The supporting instrumental voices have been written on slips of school paper of the years 1638 and 1639, primarily by a certain Johs. Kitzingerus. So far as its fragmentary state allows one to judge, the style indicates a position between Schütz's *Resurrection History* and his *Christmas Oratorio*. Indeed, it stands in very close relationship to the former work. In the first place, the notation of the part of the evangelist, in choral notation with transition to mensural notation at the cadences, follows exactly the *Resurrection History* of 1623, e. g., after an introductory *symphonia* with an alleluia chorus recalling the *Seven Last Words*:

Then *capella* and *organo, Ehre, Ehre sei dir, Herr* ("Glory, glory be to Thee, O Lord"); then again the evangelist:

The scene of the annunciation follows, the part of the angel being sung by alto and tenor, that of Mary by two discants. We have the same principle as in the *Resurrection History!* Elisabeth is a solo alto; then follows, for double chorus with a tenor intonation in Latin (despite the introductory *Und Maria sprach* ("And Mary spake"), a German *Magnificat* with the following bass:

The second chorus (*chorus inferior*), *Denn er hat die Nichtigkeit* ("For He hath regarded the low estate"). And *Und Maria stund auf* ("And Mary arose") is, by way of exception, set for four voices, apparently to emphasize the end of the scene.

Then follows the actual Christmas story. The part of Joseph is sung by two sopranos. Though the evangelist remains in F major, he sings the prophecy in A major:

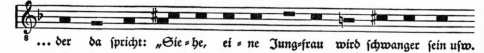

In the scene with the shepherds in the fields the angel sings his *Fürchtet euch nicht* ("Be not afraid") as a soprano solo. The *Ehre sei Gott* ("Glory to God") is set for *Concert & Cantus*, whereupon an "organ-rocking" (*Orgelwiegen*) — doubtless a *pastorale* for organ solo — is interpolated. Two basses sing the *Lasset uns gehen* ("Let us now go") of the shepherds:

When the shepherds had seen the child, they returned to their companions, *preiseten Gott und sprachen* ("praised God and spake"): *Ein Kindelein so löbelich* ("A little Child so worthy of praise"). This is sung by two basses. A genuine Christmas *quodlibet* develops with *Die Hirten auf dem Felde* ("The shepherds in the fields") and *Joseph, lieber Joseph mein* ("Joseph, dearest Joseph mine"), these being introduced with an extensive *symphonia* with the direction *Wiegen zum Chor, pian.* ("Rocking by the chorus, *piano*") — the latter doubtless referring to the bass motive

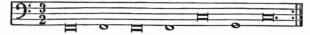

Here we have a relationship with Schütz's work of 1664! Again there follows the "organ-rocking," while the actual chorus, *Joseph, lieber Joseph mein*, with appended *Virgo Deum genuit*, has been subsequently pasted in. The scoring for the Magi ("The wise men from the east") is designated by *4 vocum*. The prophecy, *Und du Bethlehem* ("And thou, Bethlehem"), is sung in *fauxbourdon*, as in the Schütz *Psalms of 1619*. Herod would seem to be a bass. When the Magi had departed, *solus* and *capella* sing antiphonally *Singt und klingt* ("Sing and ring"), with which there is again "rocking in the chorus, *piano*." And now comes the scene in which the angel (two sopranos) sends Joseph to Egypt. Noteworthy here is the animation of the part of the evangelist:

The narrative concludes with *Und er soll Nazarenus heissen* ("He shall be called a Nazarene"). The *capella* with organ repeats the same *Ehre sei dem Herrn* ("Glory to the Lord") of the opening — again a parallel to *The Seven Words!* And now a most unusual *Schützianum*: A chorus follows with the text:

> Lord Christ, on earth below have I succeeded
> In company with Christian folk
> To sing in simpleness Thy saving birth
> In praise and honor of Thy name.
> Grant that I, too, in lasting joy and bliss,
> In heaven's supernal choir,
> With all the angels transfigured,
> May help intone the cry of jubilation:
> All glory be to God on high, etc.

Now this is a development of the verses which Schütz appended to his *Resurrection History* of 1623:

> Lord Christ, below did I succeed
> To sing Thy resurrection.
> Lord Christ, bid me on Judgment Day
> To rise also from my grave;
> Then will I praise eternally
> Thy name in heaven with seraphim.

The music to these words begins, after a *symphonia*, as a solo by the evangelist. Note the correspondence in thought to the *Victoria* of 1623!:

The same *alleluia* that appeared at the beginning forms the conclusion, and this endeavor for unity reminds us of the same principle of symmetry in the *Seven Last Words*. As a setting in score of the *alleluia* and the *Ehre sei* demonstrates, the complete scoring was: *Capella di 4 viole, Chorus superior 4 vocum, Chorus inferior voce et tromboni*. The following is the *alleluia* motive:

The problem involved in this discovery is: Do we have before us a work of a close student of Schütz or indeed a first *Christmas Oratorio* written by Schütz himself ca. 1640? If one recalls that Joh. Ph. Krieger wrote five Christmas oratorios, fourteen passions, and five Easter histories, the latter supposition would not be at all improbable.

In this connection it is most interesting to compare this with the equally little-noticed *Christmas Oratorio* by Tobias Zeutzschner,[1] which is preserved in the *Ms. CCXa of the Stadtbibliothek Breslau*. Since the orchestra, apart from the *cembalo* and the organ continuo, includes two violins, two gambas, two *cornetti* and two *flauti*, two *clarini* (trumpets) and three trombones, the armament *à 18 vocum* is soon attained when we add the vocalists. The little work is in C major, which indicates a departure from tradition. This also takes place when the announcement of the angel to the shepherds is given in full *tutti*. We reproduce here only the soprano parts:

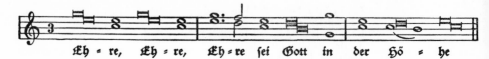

         Eh ⸗ re,   Eh ⸗ re,   Eh ⸗ re sei Gott in der Hö ⸗ he

There is an immediate continuation in D major. The numerous repetitions at *4 pastores mit Schallmeien* (4 shepherds with shawms) as well as by the bass indicate that this is intended to picture the rocking of the child.

Compare with this the Christmas composition by Schütz, *Nun komm der Heiden Heiland.* Relationships to the previously discussed anonymous work in the Breslau manuscript are indicated by the fact that a *symphonia* with an *alleluia* chorus opens the work, while the evangelist's *Höret an die Geburt* is followed by a *tutti, Ehre sei dir.* Both the *symphonia*, with its *alleluia* chorus, and the *tutti, Ehre sei dir,* are repeated at the end of the work, only that now, at the end a

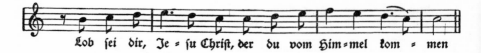

        Lob sei dir, Je ⸗ su Christ, der du vom Him⸗mel kom ⸗ men

and *Ein Kindelein so löbelich,* by the shepherds, are interpolated. Here the whole text is briefer than it is there. It begins, after the manner of T. Elsbeth, with *Die Geburt Jesu Christi war aber also getan, dass Maria, seine Mutter, dem Joseph vertraut war* ("Now the birth of Jesus Christ was on this wise, that His mother Mary was espoused to Joseph"), and concludes with *wie denn zu ihnen gesagt war* ("as was told them"). On the other hand, the narrative song (*Historicus-Gesang*) has now completely freed itself from the recitational (plainsong) tone (*Choralton, cantus choralis*) and has become a genuine continuo recitative except for the fact that it lacks the flexibility of the Schütz *History* of 1664. One might say that here the quasi-Schütz framework of 1640 has been filled with pretty Hammerschmidt utility ware. The following example will suffice:

---

[1] Born 1615 near Glatz; died 1675 in Breslau. Since 1637 he was organist in Oels, since 1649 in Breslau at St. Bernardin, since 1655 at St. Maria Magdalena. He was also a poet and a *notarius publicus*. His *Historie von der Geburt* may be approximately contemporaneous with the work of Schütz.

For the sake of vividness Zeutschner — far more than Schütz — gives some words a rich *coloratura* decoration, as, for example, *und wickelt ihn in Windeln* ("and wrapped Him in swaddling clothes"), *die Klarheit des Herrn leuchtete um sie* ("the glory of the Lord shone round about them"), *und sie kamen eilend* ("and they came with haste"), *und fielen vor ihm nieder* ("and fell down before Him"). The whole work has the compass of a cantata. In place of Schütz's sharply detached *intermedia*, the intention is directed rather to the flowing progress of the narrative, and this intention has been realized in a sympathetic manner.

Individual research should attempt to find additional links between this work and Bach's *Christmas Oratorio*. These links are frequently concealed as cantatas.

Glossary of Periodicals

Acta musicol.: Acta musicologica
A. f. Mw.: Archiv für Musikwissenschaft
Allg. dt. Biogr.: Allgemeine deutsche Biographie
Ambros: Ambros, Geschichte der Musik
Beitr. z. Gesch. d. kgl. sächs. Musik Kapelle: Beiträge zur Geschichte der königlich sächsischen Musik Kapelle
Beitr. z. Gesch. d. landgr. hess. Hofkapelle: Beiträge zur Geschichte der landgräflich hessischen Hofkapelle
Bl. f. d. Musikunter.: Blätter für den Musikunterricht
B & B: Bote und Bock
B & H: Breitkopf und Härtel
D/Z: Deutsche Allgemeine Zeitung
Dt. Lit. Gesch.: Deutsche Literaturgeschichte
Dt. nat. Lit.: Deutsche Nationalliteratur
Dt. Vjschr. f. Litws. u. Geistesgesch.: Deutsche Vierteljahresschrift für Literaturwissenschaft und Geistesgeschichte
DDT: Denkmäler deutscher Tonkunst
DTB: Denkmäler der Tonkunst in Bayern
DTOe: Denkmäler der Tonkunst in Österreich
Eitner QL: Eitner Quellenlexikon
Festschr.: Festschrift
GA: Gesamtausgabe
Ges. Aufs. z. Kgesch.: Gesammelte Aufsätze zur Kirchengeschichte
Gesch. d. dt. Mus.: Geschichte der deutschen Musik
Gesch. d. Mus. in Beisp.: Geschichte der Musik in Beispielen
Gesch. d. prot. Theol.: Geschichte der protestantischen Theologie
Gesch. d. sächs. Oberhofprediger: Geschichte der sächsischen Oberhofprediger
Gesch. d. weltl. Solokant.: Geschichte der weltlichen Solokantate
Gesch. d. dt. Liedes: Geschichte des deutschen Liedes
Gesch. d. neuen dt. Liedes: Geschichte des neuen deutschen Liedes
Hdb. d. MG: Handbuch der Musikgeschichte
IMG: Internationale Musikgesellschaft
Jb. d. staatl. Akad. f. Kirchen- u. Schulmusik: Jahrbuch der staatlichen Akademie für Kirchen- und Schulmusik

Kl. Hdb. d. MFs.: Kleines Handbuch der Musikforschung
KMJb.: Kirchenmusikalisches Jahrbuch
Luther Jb.: Luther Jahrbuch
Mittlgn. d. V. f. d. Gesch. Dresdens: Mitteilungen des Vereins für die Geschichte Dresdens
Monatshefte f. MG: Monatshefte für Musikgeschichte
Monatshefte f. MW: Monatshefte für Musikwissenschaft
Mus. Sion.: Musae Sioniae
MG v. Leipzig: Musikgeschichte von Leipzig
Musikgeschichtl. Aufs.: Musikgeschichtliche Aufsätze
Mus. Jahrb.: Musik Jahrbücher
M & K: Musik und Kirche
Neue Ztschr. f. Mus.: Neue Zeitschrift für Musik
Peters Jb.: Peters Jahrbuch
Phil.-hist. Kl. d. Pr. Akademie d. W.: Philosophisch-historische Klasse der preussischen Akademie
    der Wissenschaften (Philosophical-Historical Division of the Prussian Academy of Sciences)
Profe: Ambrosius Profius, Leipzig printer, Corollarium geistlicher Collectaneorum berühmter
    Autorum. Leipzig, 1649
Sammelbd. IMG.: Sammelbände der internationalen Musikgesellschaft
Schadaeus: Promptuarium
Sch.: Shöberlein-Riegel: Schatz des liturgischen Chor- und Gemeindegesangs
Städt. u. fürstl. Musikpfl. i. Weissenfels: Städtische und fürstliche Musikpflege in Weissenfels
Veröffentl. d. Musikbl. Peters: Veröffentlichungen der Musik Bibliothek Peters
Vjschr. f. Mw.: Vierteljahresschrift für Musikwissenschaft
ZfMW.: Zeitschrift für Musikwissenschaft

Works of Schütz Known to Have Existed, Now Lost[1]

Ach Liebste, lass uns eilen (Ah, Dearest, Let Us Hasten), à 4 ex G (Opitz) Lüneburg
Allelujah, lobet den Herrn (Hallelujah, Praise the Lord), polychoral, 1670 (Dresden)
Allelujah, lobet ihn in seinem Heiligtum (Hallelujah, Praise Him in His Sanctuary), à 16 vel 18,
    Sinfonia:

(Weimar)
Apollo und die neun Musen (Apollo and the Nine Muses), 1617 (Dresden). Beginning: *Caeşar*
    ave: Die unsterblichen Götter (The Immortal Gods)
Audite, coeli (Hear, Ye Heavens), Kassel before 1632
Auf, auf, meine Harfe (Up, Up, My Harp), à 10 (Weimar)
Auf dich, Herr, traue ich (In Thee, Lord, Do I Put My Trust), à 16 & 24, before 1658 (Naumburg)
Benedicite, omnia opera Domini (Bless the Lord, All Ye His Works), à 20 (Leipzig, Thom.)
Canite, psallite, placidite (Sing, Make a Joyful Noise, Serve the Lord with Gladness), à 12 (Kassel)
Christ lag in Todesbanden (Christ Lay in Bonds of Death), Kassel
Confitebor Tibi (In Thee Do I Put My Trust), à 5 & 5 instruments (Weimar)
Dafne, opera, 1627 (Dresden). Beginning: *Ihr sterblich's Volk: Unter diesem Schatten hier (Ye*
    Mortal Folk: Beneath This Shade)

---

[1] Sources: Naumburg, Arno Werner in *Archiv f. MW*, VIII, 413 ff.; Lüneburg, M. Seiffert in
IMG, IX, 593 ff. Kassel, Zulauf, *Gesch. der Casseler Hofkapelle*. Weimar, Ad. Aber, *Pflege der
Musik unter den Wettinern*. Leipzig, A. Schering, *Musikgesch. Leipzigs*. Pirna, W. Nagel in
MfM, XXVIII. Gotha, M. Schneider in *Sb. IMG* VII, 310 f.

Der Herr ist mein Hirt (The Lord Is My Shepherd), à 8 (individual print, Strassburg, 1657; cf.
    Göhler, *Messkatalog)*
Der Herr sprach zu meinem Herrn (The Lord Spake to My Lord), à 17 (Naumburg), in case
    not = II 7, *à 14*
Der Wind beeist das Land (The Wind Doth Frost the Land), 2 T, in D (Lüneburg)
Die ihr den Herren fürchtet (Ye Who Do Fear the Lord), Weimar
Dies ist der Tag des Herrn (This Is the Lord's Own Day), à 6 (Naumburg)
Dies Ort mit Bäumen ganz umgeben (This Spot Encircled All with Trees), S, Bc, in A (Lüneburg)
Domini, exaudi orationem meam (Lord, Hear My Prayer), à 7, 10, 14 (Weimar, Naumburg)
Dorinda, German sec. madr. (Weimar)
Du hast mir mein Herz genommen (Thou from Me My Heart Hast Captured), à 8 (Naumburg)
Ein Kindelein so lobelich (A Little Child Worthy of Praise), Kassel = anon. *à 21* (Leipzig, Thom.)
Ein Kind ist uns geboren (A Child to Us Is Born), à 8 (Naumburg)
Ein wunder Löwe (A Wondrous Lion), Kassel
Einsmals in einem schönen Tal (Once on a Time in Valley Fair), à 2 voices, 6 instruments in D
    (Lüneburg)
Einsmal der Hirte Corydon (At One Time Shepherd Corydon), 2 S, 2 Vls. (Lüneburg)
Entsetzet euch nicht (Be Not Dismayed), Kassel
Erhöre mich, wenn ich rufe (Hear Me, When I Call), à 8 (Naumburg)
Esaia dem Propheten (Isaiah, Mighty Seer, in Days of Old), à 8 (Naumburg, Mattheson)
Es ist erschienen (There Hath Appeared), à 3 (Weimar)
Es ist Zeit, die Stund ist da (The Time Hath Come, the Hour's at Hand), à 4 (Weimar)
Es sei denn eure Gerechtigkeit (Unless Your Righteousness Be), à 8 (Naumburg)
Es stehe Gott auf (Let God Arise), à 13 (Weimar)
Factum est praelium magnum (There Arose a Great Strife), à 9, in C (Lüneburg), probably =
    Es erhub sich, Vol. XVIII
Friede sei mit euch (Peace Be with You), Kassel = portion of the *Resurrection History of 1623*
Geht meine Seufzer hören (Go, to My Sighs Now Listen)
Gelobet sei der Herr (Blessed Be the Lord), à 5, 10, 11, 20 (Weimar)
Glückwünschung des Apollinis u. der neun Musen (Felicitations of Apollo and the Nine Muses),
    1621, *à 12* and 12 Corn. Trp. Text beginning: *Willkomm, willkomm, o schön Auror (Welcome,*
    O Welcome, Beautiful Aurora), Dresden
Gott, man lobet dich in der Stille (Praise Waiteth for Thee, O God, in Zion), à 8 (Naumburg)
Herr, komm herab (Lord, Come Down), Gospel for the 21st Sunday a.Tr., *à 9* (Kassel, Naumburg)
Herr, warum trittst du (Why Standest Thou Afar Off), Ps. 10, *à 8, 12, 18,* in E (Lüneburg)
Himmel und Erde vergehen (Heaven and Earth Shall Pass Away), à 3 (Kassel)
Jauchzet dem Herrn (Rejoice in the Lord), à 6 (Gotha)
Ich trau auf den Herrn (I Trust in the Lord), à 12 (Kassel)
Jesus trat in ein Schiff (Jesus Entered into a Boat), à 8 (Naumburg)
Introduction, *à 9,* to the *Weihnachtshistorie (Christmas Story),* (Leipzig Thom.)
Kyrie eleison (German Litany), à 12 vel 18:

(Weimar)
Kyrie, Gott Vater, à 6 + 6 & 6 instruments in E (Lüneburg, Kassel), *à 6 & 11 ex E* (Weimar)
Kyrie, à 5 (Weimar)
Lobsinget Gott, ihr Männer von Galilaea (Sing unto God, Ye Men of Galilee), à 10, in D (Lüne-
    burg, *à 5 & 10,* Naumburg)
Machet die Tore weit (Lift Up Your Heads, Ye Gates), à 20 (Naumburg)
Magnificat, à 3 & 2 vls. (Weimar)
Magnificat, à 10 (CTB, cap. *à 4,* 2 vls., 3 trombones, bassoon, in D (Lüneburg)
Maria, sei gegrüsset (Hail, Mary), à 5 (Weimar)

Maria (the other setting), Weimar
Mein Freund, ich tu dir nicht unrecht (My Friend, I Do Thee No Evil), à 6 (Weimar)
Mein Freund, komme (My Friend, Come), à 6
Meister, wir haben die ganze Nacht gefischet (Master, We Have Fished the Entire Night), à 8 (Naumburg)
Misericordias Domini, à 6 (Naumburg)
Music to a ballet by Kükelsom and two plays by Johs. Lauremberg, 1634 (Copenhagen)
Orpheus and Eurydice, ballet by Buchner, 1638 (Dresden)
Preise, Jerusalem, den Herrn (Praise, Jerusalem, the Lord), à 6 in *concerto* (Gotha)
Sag, o Sonne meiner Seelen (Tell, O Sunshine of My Soul), à 4, dupl., in G (Lüneburg)
So bist du nun mein Lieb (So Art Thou, Then, My Love), à 6
Täglich geht die Sonne unter (Daily Doth the Sun Set), à 6, Opitz
Tröste uns, Gott (Comfort Us, God), Weimar. Beginning of the thorough bass:

Unser Herr Jesus in der Nacht (Our Lord Jesus in the Night in Which), à 8 (Naumburg)
Unser Leben währet siebzig Jahr (Our Life Endureth Three Score Years and Ten), à 5 (Naumburg)
Venus, du und dein Kind (Venus, Thou and Thy Child), Weimar
Wenn der Herr die Gefangenen Zions (When the Lord Shall Redeem the Prisoners of Zion), à 6 & 6 instruments (Weimar)
Wenn dich, o Sylvia (When Thee, O Sylvia), à 6
Wer ist der so von Eden kömmt (Who Is He That Cometh from Edom), à 10 & 18 per *choros* in d (Lüneburg)
Wer sich dünken lasset (He Who Thinketh), à 4 (Weimar)
Wer unter dem Schirm des Höchsten (Who Sitteth Beneath the Wing of the Almighty), à 5, 2 vls. (Weimar) probably = anon. CCATB *con cap.*, 2 vls., in D (Lüneburg)

Incomplete, etc.

Gutes und Barmherzigkeit (Goodness and Mercy), completed as supplement to this work (Dresden)
Ego autem sum Dominus, à 2, Vol. XVIII (Helmstedt)
Veni, Domini, à 2, Vol. XVIII (Helmstedt)
Wohl denen, die ohne Wandel leben (Blessed Are the Undefiled in the Way), Ps. 119, with Ps. 100 appended (Guben & Salzburg)
O der grossen Wundertaten (O the Great and Wondrous Deeds), 1634, Vol. XVIII (Copenhagen)

Recently Newly Discovered by the Author

Ach Herr, du Sohn Davids (O Lord, Thou Son of David), à 6 (Breslau; *Zf. f. MW*, XVIII)
Ich bin die Auferstehung (I Am the Resurrection) (Breslau, Peters)
Ich weiss, dass mein Erlöser lebet (I Know that My Redeemer Liveth), à 6, Freiberg (Bärenreiter ed.)
Stehe auf, meine Freundin (Arise, My Friend), à 8, questionable (Breslau, *Zf. f. MW*, XVIII)
Machet die Tore weit (Lift Up Your Heads, Ye Gates), à 8, publ. by Peters (Löbau & Camenz)

Recently Newly Discovered by H. Engel

Freuet euch mit mir (Rejoice with Me), publ. by Merseburger
Herr, höre mein Wort (Lord, Hear My Word), publ. by Merseburger

Index of Proper Names

The Works of Schütz Discussed

Becker Psalter XII, 9, 36, 123, 147, 206, 210, 211, 216, 286, 380, 382, 437, 444 ff., 447, 464, 478, 479, 480, 630

Cantiones sacrae (1625) XII, 6, 61, 107, 114, 116, 176, 215, 250, 340, 402 ff., 437, 447, 464, 473, 482, 505, 508, 515, 537, 546, 583, 636, 644

Christmas Oratorio XIII, 97, 184, 216, 219, 512, 552, 649 ff., 714
(Historia nativitatis Christi) 714 ff.

Geistliche Chormusik (1648) XIII, 60, 61, 86, 123, 141, 176, 183, 193, 244, 259, 273, 299, 363, 478, 524, 563, 580 ff., 636, 638, 645, 709

German (Opitz) madrigals 11, 245, 361, 377 ff., 612

Gospel compositions 572 ff.

Italian madrigals (1611-12) 23, 54, 56, 64, 65, 69, 176, 253 ff., 382, 390, 421, 463, 546, 581

Kleine geistliche Konzerte XIII, 132, 159, 160, 161, 215, 232, 251, 282, 478, 505 ff., 529, 544, 546, 603, 626, 655, 708
I (1636) 120, 242, 282, 464, 546
II (1639) 161, 169, 174, 535

Musikalische Exequien XIII, 24, 155 ff., 485 ff., 489, 491, 545, 632

Passions 176, 219, 299, 478, 493, 575, 660 ff.
St. John XIII, 207, 219, 666, 672 ff.
St. Luke XIII, 219, 599, 667 ff., 680
(St. Mark) XIII, 660, 666
St. Matthew 219, 666, 677 ff., 696, 698

Psalms of David (1619) XII, 23, 41, 61, 75, 99, 107, 118, 226, 240, 256, 273, 282, 286 ff., 353, 361, 362, 424, 463, 478, 484, 508, 544, 546, 559, 560, 604, 696, 716

Resurrection History 61, 116, 150, 365 ff., 463, 484, 493, 497, 500, 534, 535, 575, 649, 655, 662, 714

Symphoniae sacrae I (1629) 54, 61, 82, 127, 130, 132, 133, 140, 280, 421, 464 ff., 505, 529, 629
II (1647) 41, 132, 160, 170, 178, 184, 193, 478, 505, 542 ff., 546, 586, 602, 629, 632
III (1650) XII, 109, 111, 132, 160, 185, 192, 194, 232, 478, 544, 546, 560, 575, 602 ff., 708

The Seven Words on the Cross 78, 489, 492 ff., 525, 662

Twelve Religious Songs (1657) 215, 478, 508, 532, 534, 548, 635 ff.

Index of Topics

Plate 1

The house in Köstritz in which Schütz was born *(Gasthaus zum Goldenen Kranich)*

Plate II

Donkey playing a bagpipe.
On the inn *Zum Schützen*
(formerly *Zum Goldenen Esel*)

The Inn *zum Schützen* in Weissenfels.
In the foreground the bay window with the inscription: Christoph Schütz 1616

Plate III

Landgrave Moritz the Learned of Hessen as a young man

Plate IV

The *Collegium Mauritianum* in Kassel, the court school founded by Landgrave Moritz.
Heinrich Schütz attended this school

Plate V

MARPVRG.

Marburg in about the middle of the seventeenth century

Plate VI

The castle in Dresden at Schütz's time

Plate VII

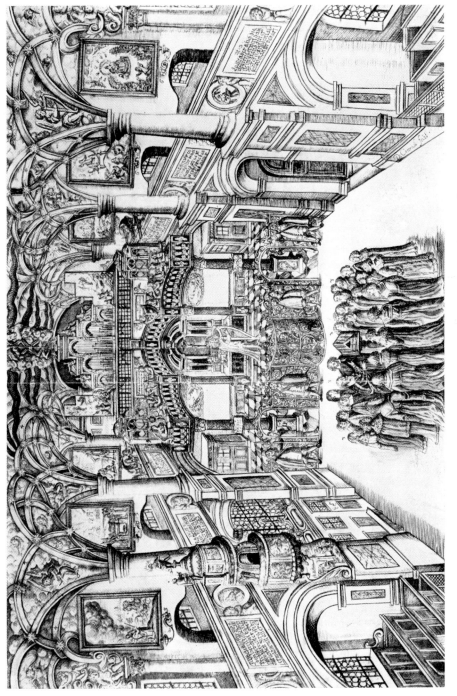

Schütz in the circle of his *Kantorei* in the old Castle Church in Dresden

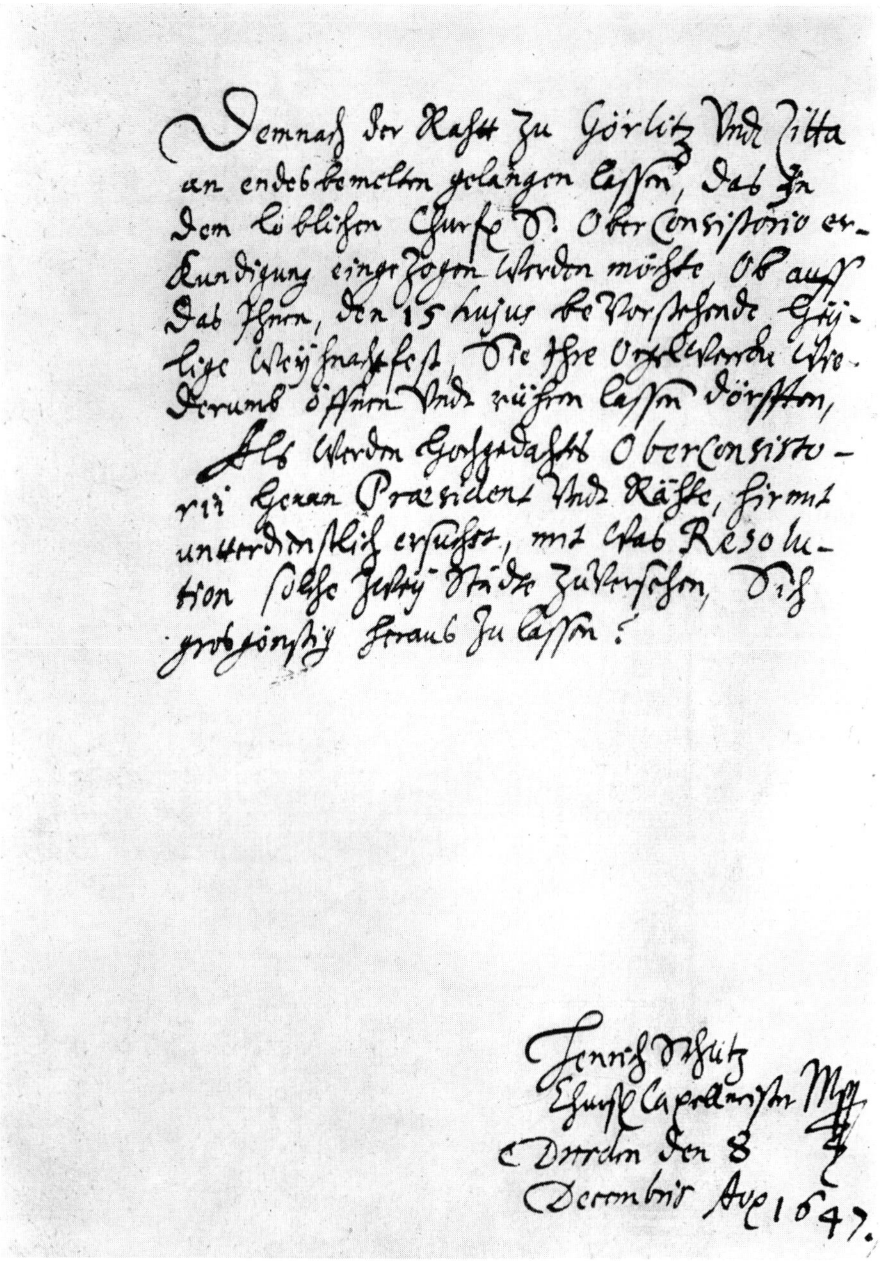

Plate VIII

A letter which Schütz wrote to the *Oberkonsistorium* in Dresden
with regard to matters pertaining to the cities of Görlitz and Zittau (1647).
Original in the possession of Eduard Speyer in Ridgehurst

Plate IX

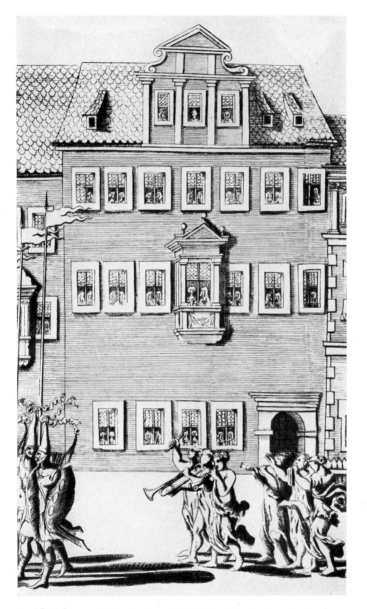

The house in Dresden in which Schütz died. *Moritzstraße 10.*
The *Solmisch-Beyersches Haus*, destroyed by fire in 1670

Plate X

Oil painting of Schütz in Leipzig.
The artist was Christoph Spetner (1617–99)

Plate XI

Hans Leo Haßler (1564–1612)

Plate XII

Michael Praetorius (1571–1621)

Plate XIII

Johann Hermann Schein (1586–1630)

Plate XIV

Claudio Monteverdi (1567–1643)

Vt sol inter planetas, Ita Musica inter Artes liberales in medio radiat.
hinc verè Ouuenius:
Optima Musarum & reliquis idcirco negatur
Artibus à Musis Musica nomen habens

Henricus Sagittarius
Capellæ Magister, ap
Porebam in Hildershin
die 29 Januarii Ao 1690

Album entry by Schütz

Plate XV

Rembrandt Harmensz van Rijn, portrait of a musician of 1633,
probably Heinrich Schütz in his fortieth year

Plate XVI

SERENISS.ᴒ POTENTISS.PRINCIPIS.AC
Dom.DIOHANNIS GEORGII/DucisSAX.
IUL.CLIV.ac MONT.PRINC.ELECTORAL.DIGNIT HERES.
LANDG.THURING.MARCH.MISN.utrIUSᵠ LUSᵠT.CO.
IN MARC.&·RAVENSBERG·DOM.INRAVㄨ
STEIN   EFFIGIES.

Elector Johann Georg of Saxony